Patriotism, Democracy, and Common Sense

ROWMAN & LITTLEFIELD PUBLISHERS, INC.

Published in the United States of America
by Rowman & Littlefield Publishers, Inc.
A wholly owned subsidiary of The Rowman & Littlefield Publishing Group, Inc.
4501 Forbes Boulevard, Suite 200, Lanham, Maryland 20706
www.rowmanlittlefield.com

PO Box 317
Oxford
OX2 9RU, UK

Distributed by National Book Network

Chapter 2 is adapted from a speech delivered by Senator Gary Hart at the Council on Foreign Relations in New York on January 21, 2003.

British Library Cataloguing in Publication Information Available

Library of Congress Cataloging-in-Publication Data

Patriotism, democracy, and common sense : restoring America's promise at home
and abroad / edited by Alan Curtis.
p. cm.
Includes bibliographical references and index.
ISBN 0–7425–4216–5 (hardcover : alk. paper)
1. United Srates—Foreign relations—2001– 2. United States—Politics and
government—2001– I. Curtis, Alan, 1943–
JZ1480.P37 2004
327.73—dc22

2004007565

Printed in the United States of America

∞™ The paper used in this publication meets the minimum requirements of American
National Standard for Information Sciences—Permanence of Paper for Printed Library
Materials, ANSI/NISO Z39.48-1992.

Patriotism, Democracy, and Common Sense

Restoring America's Promise at Home and Abroad

Edited by
Alan Curtis

THE MILTON S. EISENHOWER FOUNDATION

AND

ROWMAN & LITTLEFIELD PUBLISHERS, INC.
Lanham • Boulder • New York • Oxford

To Wang Ying, Miranda Curtis, Florence Curtis, and Fred Harris

Also by Alan Curtis*

The Millennium Breach: Richer, Poorer, and Racially Apart

Locked in the Poorhouse: Cities, Race, and Poverty in the United States

To Establish Justice, To Insure Domestic Tranquility: A Thirty Year Update of the National Commission on the Causes and Prevention of Violence

Lessons from the Street: Capacity Building and Replication

Youth Investment and Police Mentoring

Family, Employment and Reconstruction

Investing in Children and Youth: A Twenty Five Year Update of the National Advisory Commission on Civil Disorders

American Violence and Public Policy

Youth Investment and Community Reconstruction

Violence, Race and Culture

Criminal Violence

*Written, edited, or coedited under the name Lynn A. Curtis.
See EisenhowerFoundation.org for the full text of some of these publications.

ABOUT THE EISENHOWER FOUNDATION

In the late 1960s, after America's big city riots, the bipartisan President's National Advisory Commission on Civil Disorders (the Kerner Riot Commission) concluded, "Our nation is moving toward two societies, one black, one white—separate and unequal."

Shortly thereafter, following the assassinations of the Reverend Martin Luther King Jr. and Senator Robert F. Kennedy, the bipartisan President's National Commission on the Causes and Prevention of Violence (the Eisenhower Violence Commission) concluded, "The greatness and durability of most civilizations has been finally determined by how they have responded to challenges from within. Ours will be no exception."

Since those commissions, the divide between rich and poor has become greater in the United States, the nation has begun to resegregate, voter democracy has diminished, and the challenges from within have become more formidable.

The Eisenhower Foundation replicates scientifically evaluated, multiple-solution successes for children, youth, families, ex-offenders, the truly disadvantaged, and the inner city. The Foundation builds the management, fundraising, and staff capacities of the private, nonprofit organizations that carry out so much of what works in America's inner-city neighborhoods and schools. And it communicates what works to citizens, the media, and decision makers.

Just as the Eisenhower and Kerner commissions proposed national policies based on public-private partnerships, so the Foundation comes together with other institutions to help repair the racial and class breaches in America, extend family into schools and the community, create the inner-city full-employment job training and work-placement strategy that has disappeared from the national debate in the United States, prevent recidivism by the half-million plus who come out of America's prisons each year, facilitate private sector nonprofit initiative at the grassroots, and encourage government to replicate what works.

In its initiatives, the Foundation typically matches resources from public and private funders at the international, national, state, and local levels.

Complementing this programmatic, replication, and evaluation work in a host of locations, the Foundation's foreign, national security, economic, domestic, media, campaign finance reform, and voter democracy reform publications, orchestrated by advisory panels in each area of expertise, seek to articulate a mutually interdependent policy vision for America and the world, based on the lessons of history and the findings of science.

The Eisenhower Foundation is nonpartisan. The views expressed by the contributors to Patriotism, Democracy, and Common Sense *are not necessarily the position of the Board of the Foundation.*

Contents

Foreword

In the new millennium, political common wisdom has begun to dissipate, and old ideologies have begun to blur under new challenges. *Patriotism, Democracy, and Common Sense* will encourage a creative synthesis of new solutions to these challenges.

The Milton S. Eisenhower Foundation is an appropriate facilitator of the synthesis, because the Eisenhower family itself addressed the national conservative-liberal divide in the middle twentieth century. Dwight D. Eisenhower, our thirty-fourth president, was a moderate conservative who gained his fame as the American Supreme Allied Commander in Europe during World War II. His brother, Milton Eisenhower, the president of Johns Hopkins University, was a centrist of moderate liberal persuasion.

More than forty years ago, Milton Eisenhower helped write his brother's single most famous speech, the January 1961 farewell address in which the retiring president warned that "in the councils of government we must guard against the acquisition of unwanted influence, whether sought or unsought, by the military-industrial complex. The potential for the disastrous rise of misplaced power exists and will persist."

Even before September 11, the growth of the national security state had made Eisenhower's warnings prophetic, and the burgeoning of the Department of Homeland Security in response to the terrorist attack has made them even more so—especially given Eisenhower's own long military experience and relatively conservative politics.

It is important for liberals and progressives to understand that many conservative arguments have carved out their own niche and relevance in the growing opposition to the power of radical conservatism. But the flip side of the coin is just as vital. Conservatives and libertarians disenchanted with the falsities and extremes of recent policy must recognize the legitimacy of the emerging critique being offered by liberals and progressives.

The thirty-nine essays in *Patriotism, Democracy, and Common Sense* are a case in point. I would not pretend to agree with all of them. But the volume's five major headings define much of the ongoing political debate and battleground: failure in American foreign and national security policy; failure in American Middle East policy; failure in American economic policy; failure in domestic policy for the middle class, working class, and the poor; and failure in media policy, combined with unprecedented deception and public relations spin.

The practical political effect is simply this: It is going to be very hard for critics of recent policy failures, even conservatives and moderates, not to agree with some of the liberal and progressive analyses and remedies. The United States will indeed have to correct a foreign policy that has antagonized the world and dissipated the good will that existed for the United States after September 11. It will indeed have to deal with a compromised Central Intelligence Agency and court a Europe untrustful of American leadership. Security in the post–September 11 era will have to be fully attentive to democracy. The Palestinians and Israelis will have to accept each other.

The "investor and inheritor" capitalism of recent years is already losing credibility. The financial, political, and moral deficits of the American empire need to be faced and so too the deterioration of middle-class life obvious in some sections of the nation. Honest conservatives must admit that the socialism most prominent in the United States since the 1980s is the socialization of economic risk—the federal bail-out of banks, financial institutions and hedge funds—while almost fifty million Americans are left uninsured against medical and health risk.

In a kindred vein, it is necessary to criticize the failure of "free market–tough state" ideology—the radical conservative notion that the duty of the state is to be tough against international foes but permissive at home, leaving market abuses unrestrained and uncurbed. Markets, too, have excesses that must be controlled.

In the twenty-first century, as part V of this book recognizes, the media have become too concentrated and collaborative with a federal government that regulates and supervises broadcasting. Investigation, truth, and candor have declined. Democratic media reform movements and new independent media must both be part of the solution.

Whether the reader will agree with most or only some of the essays that follow, this volume can only help restore America's promise at home and abroad.

Kevin Phillips
West Goshen, Connecticut
April 2004

Executive Summary

In the late 1960s, the bipartisan Eisenhower Violence Commission, formed by President Johnson and extended by President Nixon, warned that most civilizations have fallen less from external assault than from internal decay.

Over recent years, the internal decay prophesied by the Violence Commission, but also by President Eisenhower in his military-industrial-complex farewell speech, has been reflected in American public policies.

The fault lies on both sides of the political aisle.

The central message of *Patriotism, Democracy, and Common Sense* is that citizens and decision makers need to reverse present policies, which are based on dominating and misinforming people. We need to move forward with new policies based on forging genuine grassroots democracy, understanding the lessons of history, respecting the findings of science, reasserting the old-fashioned common sense of the American people, and restoring the spirit of American optimism and justice that other nations so respected at the end of World War II.

Together, the thirty-nine contributors to *Patriotism, Democracy, and Common Sense* ask citizens and policy makers to actually connect the dots—to move America forward by developing mutually supportive and complementary foreign, national security, Middle East, economic, domestic, inner-city, media, campaign finance, and voting reform policies.

Americans have to ask themselves why our leaders and the media have *not* connected the dots. We are short-sighted, too compartmentalized. We miss the big picture. America and the world suffer as a result.

Accordingly, the first chapter of *Patriotism, Democracy, and Common Sense* is an initial attempt to weave together all of these policies. The remaining sections of the book, each with a grouping of chapters, cover foreign and national security, Middle East, economic, domestic and inner-city, and media policies in more depth. The reader is free to immediately connect all the dots by reading chapter 1 or to skip around, picking and choosing one policy domain at a time in the later sections.

Above all, these are policies by and for average Americans—and average citizens around the world. Whether through inner-city neighborhood meetings, state referendums, national elections, or international deliberations, citizens need to believe again that they can have an impact, creating the kind of peace that President Kennedy said "makes life on earth worth living—not merely peace for Americans but peace for all men and women, not merely peace in our time but peace for all time."

• 1 •

The Big Picture

Alan Curtis

> When in [our] long history other great civilizations fell, it was less often from external assault than from internal decay. . . . The greatness and durability of most civilizations has been finally determined by how they have responded to these challenges from within. Ours will be no exception.
>
> —Final Report, National Commission on the Causes and Prevention of Violence, December 1969

Chaired by Milton Eisenhower, the presidential Violence Commission wisely prophesized the inner decay of America in the new millennium. It is not decay of our vibrant, friendly and innovative people, but of federal policy, conservative ideology and the ruling class.

Many critics, including contributors to *Patriotism, Democracy, and Common Sense* like Ambassador Joseph C. Wilson IV, have been the object of attempts at the highest levels of government to intimidate them, punish them, and label them unpatriotic. These attempts are symptomatic of America's internal decay. Ambassador Wilson was called a "true American hero" by President George H. W. Bush in 1991.

There is nothing unpatriotic or even counterproductive about questioning the government's actions, as Richard C. Leone reminds us in this book. History teaches us that bypassing public deliberation almost inevitably leads to outcomes that nations eventually regret. Looking back, there is a long list of reactions to other threats in which the absence of open debate coincided with the nation's low points. During the twentieth century, the Palmer raids after World War I, the internment of Japanese Americans during World War II, the Bay of Pigs fiasco, Iran-Contra, the secret war in Honduras, and any number of other schemes went badly astray. Public deliberation involves controversy that can be painful and time consuming, but dialogue often prevents bad ideas from taking hold while broadening support for policies that are implemented.

The contributors to this book, then, are supportive of "Mr. Republican," Ohio Senator Robert A. Taft, who said, weeks after Pearl Harbor, "Too many people desire to suppress criticism, [but] "the maintenance of the right of criticism in the long run . . . will prevent mistakes which might otherwise occur."

Patriotism, Democracy, and Common Sense looks at failures and more promising alternatives in American foreign, national security, Middle East, economic, domestic, inner city, and media policies over recent years. As editor, I have forgone a traditional introduction. This opening section is longer, and I beg the reader's indulgence. There is a great deal to cover and a need to pull it together in one place. Few current books try to integrate what is happening, from Baghdad and Jerusalem to Des Moines and the South Bronx.

I have asked three questions: How have present policies failed? What alternatives better fulfill America's promise? And how can the people move the nation from failure to success?

In what follows, I have not tried to compromise out a consensus among all the distinguished authors to the thirty-nine chapters of *Patriotism, Democracy, and Common Sense*. Instead, I have organized the critiques and alternative policies selectively from contributors who have most persuaded me, filled in some gaps, integrated in material from outside sources, and added my own perspectives.

HOW HAVE PRESENT POLICIES FAILED?

In many ways, current federal policy in the United States is based on domination and misinformation.

Domination expresses the arrogance of the richest nation in history, the unchecked will of the only current superpower, the might of our high-tech military force, and the ever-widening income and wealth disparities in America that help define and reinforce our white ruling class.

Misinformation has been generated by skillful and retributive federal government communications offices in concert with a vastly resourced, private-sector, conservative ideology machine. Some American corporate media are part of the machine. Other corporate and mainstream media have not been sufficiently critical and were deferential, in particular, after September 11, when the citizenry sought direction and assurances from its leaders, as the *New York Times* has admitted.

Conservative ideologist Irving Kristol has said, "What's the point of being the greatest, most powerful nation in the world and not having an imperial role?" But policies of domination and misinformation have ill-served the American people and have failed.

What are some illustrations of the domination and misinformation identified in *Patriotism, Democracy, and Common Sense*? In national security and foreign policy, examples include the current doctrine of preemptive, unilateral force and the myth that the September 11 attacks were not preventable. In Middle East policy, illustrations include the invasion of Iraq, the torture and sexual abuse of Iraqi inmates in the prisons we have filled as rapidly as prisons back home, the false claim that Iraq had weapons of mass destruction, and the misinformation that there was a link between Osama bin Laden and Saddam Hussein. In American economic policy, examples include the class warfare declared by the rich against the rest of us, via, for example, tax breaks for the wealthy and welfare for corporations, as well as by the stealth movement of the far right to dramatically reduce, incrementally over time, federal programs that are desired and needed by the middle class, workers, and the poor. In domestic policy, illustrations include America's racially biased, "shock-and-awe," "zero-tolerance" prison building for the poor, giving the United States the highest rate of incarceration in the world—and the deceit that we don't know what works to reverse the despair of the truly disadvantaged and the shame of our inner cities. In the case of the media, domination and misinformation are evident in the consolidation of control by a few corporate media giants, in the myth that America's founders wanted our present undemocratic, corporate, commercial media system and in the smokescreen that there is a left-wing bias to mainstream media.

Consider each of these policy areas:

Failures in American Foreign and National Security Policy

American foreign and national security policy has failed to create a vision current with global realities. With such a vision, the September 11 attacks could have been prevented. The United States has been weakened by a corrupted Central Intelligence Agency, asserted a unilateral and preemptive imperialism that history has shown cannot last, experienced a mismatch between the power of our rulers and the degree to which our population has accurate information about the world, and carried out a misguided and exorbitantly expensive Iraq adventure. It is hard to imagine actions that would generate more hatred and revenge against America for generations to come than the torture and sexual humiliation of Iraqi prisoners. America's invasion of Iraq failed to heed the admonitions of President Eisenhower in his farewell military-industrial-complex speech and squandered resources that should be used for a more sophisticated policy against al Qaeda and a more timely plan for home security.

Lack of Vision. During the Cold War, America's foreign and national security policy was focused on the containment of communism. But there has been little coherent American policy vision since the Cold War ended.

In 2001, the bipartisan U.S. Commission on National Security/21st Century, cochaired by former Senator Gary Hart and former Senator Warren B. Rudman, set out such a vision, predicting terrorist attacks on America and recommending a sweeping overhaul of national security structures and policies. Later, Senators Hart and Rudman cochaired a follow-up panel convened by the Council on Foreign Relations. Little action has been taken by the American government on these recommendations, and now there is another set of crucially important recommendations, from the National Commission on Terrorist Attacks on the United States (the 9/11 Commission), to implement.

Prevention of the September 11 Attacks. Over recent decades, national security policy did not sufficiently focus on the threat of terrorism. Until recently, first priority has been given to Star Wars missile defenses.

The White House, the intelligence agencies of the United States, law enforcement, and the military did not give the terrorist threat top priority immediately prior to September 11. The 9/11 Commission has provided a book-length chronology of failures, as have Bob Woodward of the *Washington Post* and other investigative reporters who have examined dozens of declassified documents. *Together, these failures demonstrate that the terrorist attacks were preventable.*

Here are a few of the failures:

- Al Qaeda and Osama bin Laden did not blindside the United States, but were a threat discussed regularly at the highest levels of government for almost five years before the attacks, in thousands of reports that often were accompanied by urgent warnings to the White House from mid-level experts.
- While the position of national coordinator for counterterrorism originally provided immediate access to the president, the position was downgraded to deputy status by the new national security advisor in 2001, blocking direct access and helping to ensure that the president only heard from his top antiterrorism chief until after September 11.
- In the first eight months of 2001, the administration received far more dire information than it admitted, until the 9/11 Commission forced public disclosures.
- The Associated Press has reported that White House national security leadership met formally nearly 100 times in the months prior to September 11, yet terrorism was on the agenda during only one of those sessions.
- In April and May of 2001, the president, vice president, and national security advisor received memos from the intelligence community titled "Bin Laden Planning Multiple Operations," "Bin Laden's Network Plans Advancing," and "Bin Laden Threats Are Real."
- On August 6, 2001, the president received an intelligence memo titled "Bin Laden Determined to Strike the U.S." Senator John McCain has concluded, "Should [the August 6 memo] have raised more of an alarm bell? I think in hindsight, that's probably true." For example, there is no evidence that the White House put airports on heightened alert as a result of the memo. The White House did not issue a press release and did not hold a press conference with names and descriptions of suspects. The White House did not force re-

calcitrant intelligence agencies to improve the ways they shared all available information about al Qaeda threats.

- Neither President Clinton nor President Bush sought to proactively correct the paralyzing dysfunction that undermined the CIA and the Federal Bureau of Investigation, the two agencies most responsible for protecting the United States from terrorists.
- On September 11, 2001, the White House national security advisor was scheduled to give a speech at Johns Hopkins University addressing "the threats and problems of today and the day after...." According to United States officials who have seen the original text, the address was designed to promote missile defense as the cornerstone of a new national security strategy and contained no mention of al Qaeda, Osama bin Laden, or Islamic extremist groups. (The speech was postponed, and an edited version was given later.)
- The CIA had at least six chances to attack Osama bin Laden prior to September 11, but each time agency higher-ups blocked action.
- The director of the CIA had little contact with the president during much of the summer of 2001, when intelligence agencies, at least at lower- and mid-levels, were warning of a dire terrorist attack.
- The CIA waited until August 2001 to alert the FBI on two of the terrorists, who by then were living in the United States. The FBI was not, of course, able to locate them.
- The FBI failed to follow up on a July 2001 warning from a Phoenix agent that al Qaeda terrorists might be training in American flight schools.
- The FBI failed to understand the significance of Zacarias Moussaoui, the flight school student arrested in August 2001 and later linked to the September 11 hijackers.
- The director of the FBI and his senior deputies in Washington were not informed until after September 11 that the Phoenix and Minneapolis field offices had reported to Washington headquarters in summer 2001 that al Qaeda or other terrorists might be developing a plot involving commercial airlines.
- Prior to September 11, only about 6 percent of the FBI's work force was assigned to counterterrorism. The Bureau has struggled to refocus itself from an interstate crime fighting organization to one that can create a counterterrorism capacity to stop unconventional foreign-based threats to security inside the United States. The reasons have included outmoded bureaucracy, outmoded intelligence collection, an aging computer system that prevented effective communication between agents and headquarters, and a severe undersupply of analysts assessing data and terror threats.
- The FBI's counterterrorism budget was increased before September 11, and it had seventy active leads linked to Osama bin Laden ongoing in summer 2001; but it was unable to piece the leads together.

- A quicker military action by the North American Aerospace Command might have prevented American Airlines Flight 77 from crashing into the Pentagon on September 11. Commanders were in an outward, Cold War mode and not prepared to face the new generation of threats that includes hijacked planes as missiles.

The Corruption of the Central Intelligence Agency. Part of the reason why America has not created a clear and accurate post–Cold War national security policy vision is that, during the last twenty years, the CIA has become so politically corrupted and politicized that it has lost credibility. As director of the CIA in the 1980s, William Casey institutionalized politicalization, which reached its peak in 2002 when George Tenet succumbed to White House pressure to generate a report to justify a prior decision to invade Iraq. That report failed to acknowledge that little proof existed for weapons of mass destruction in Iraq. In 2004, David Kay, the CIA's chief weapons inspector, told Congress shortly before resigning, "I'm personally convinced that there were not large stockpiles of newly produced weapons of mass destruction. . . . We didn't find the people, the documents, or the physical plants that you would expect to find if the production was going on."

As former CIA analyst Ray McGovern points out in chapter 4, the deterioration of the agency in recent years also is illustrated by its loss of imagery-analysis capacity and by dispersal of its public media analysis capacity.

The collection and analysis of satellite and other images had been a CIA operation, but in recent years it was transferred to the Pentagon. Had the CIA possessed independent imagery analysis capacity in 2002, it might have helped show that there were no weapons of mass destruction in Iraq.

In addition, contrary to popular misconceptions, most information about most countries, movements, and groups comes from "open" sources—what is said publicly—and not from intelligence acquired clandestinely. The CIA originally had a strong unit to analyze public information. For example, the unit correctly forecast the reforms of Mikhail Gorbachev in the 1980s. But this stellar, centralized media-analysis capacity was dispersed within the CIA in the 1990s. Had there been a unit of media-analysis practitioners plumbing the statements of Osama bin Laden and his chief lieutenants over the past decade, those analysts might have been able to throw helpful light on his intentions, his tactics, his supporters—and on "why they hate us."

Force and Preemptive Multilateralism. While not a clear vision, a priority on the use of force in foreign policy has evolved among both Democrats and Republicans over the last quarter century, as America has become the world's sole superpower. The use of force has become more unilateral—and now preemptive. The preemptive force has included torture and sexual humiliation by the American military against Iraqi prisoners, just as prisons back in the United States abound in sexual humiliation.

A dangerous imbalance has developed between use of force and use of the other tools of foreign policy—diplomacy, uncorrupted intelligence, economic development assistance, and support for democracy building in countries that genuinely are receptive at the grassroots level. Presently, there is a sixteen-to-one ratio between the budget of the Department of Defense and the budgets for all other foreign operations combined. The United States has the lowest ratio of foreign aid to gross domestic product of any of the twenty-one industrialized nations. Today, we spend $1 billion less per year on foreign aid than during the Cold War. This at a time when one in five of the world's six billion people is living in abject poverty on less than $1 per day in local purchasing parity, with a life expectancy of little more than forty years.

Before September 11, there was a growing list of issues around which the world united, but where America was different. A convention was passed recognizing basic rights for children all over the world; the United States was unable to sign it, whereas virtually every other country has done so. At Kyoto, global warming was recognized as threatening the future of the world; the United States found it impossible to cooperate, even though a new Pentagon report now has issued warnings on global warning. An international criminal court has been created, with the hope that it will help all nations deal with extremism, war, the Milosevics of the world, the Mugabes of this world, and other dictators. Most people in Europe believe this is an advance in civilization, but the United States finds it difficult to support the court.

This unilateralism is part of the American government's attack on "Old Europe." As Lord Wallace reminds us in chapter 7, there has been a rise in anti-Europeanism led by conservatives and the extreme Christian right in America, a right allied with the government (not the people) of Israel against a peaceful Palestinian-Israeli solution. This alliance has set the tone of many American op-ed pages in recent years.

After September 11 and during the buildup to Iraq, America directed much of its anti-Europeanism and preemptive multilateralism at the United Nations. Across most of the world, in the words of Phyllis Bennis in chapter 9, people treasure the United Nations, even while recognizing its imperfections and need for improvement. Contrast this to Richard Perle, the American imperialist conservative who wrote, "Thank God for the death of the United Nations. Its abject failures gave us only anarchy."

In modern democracies, there seldom has been as much of a mismatch as in America today between the power of the rulers and the degree to which their populations have accurate information about the world. In a Pew Research Center poll conducted in twenty-four countries in November and December 2001, substantial majorities in many countries believed that the policies and actions of the United States were a major cause for the September 11 attacks. For example, in non-European countries, 58 percent of the respondents held this view. In the United States, only 18 percent thought

American policies were a major cause of the attacks. Most Americans were unaware of the discontinuity. For a long time, polls actually showed a majority or near majority of the American public believed that there were weapons of mass destruction in Iraq and that there was an absolute connection between Saddam Hussein and al Qaeda. Most of the rest of the world believed something quite different.

Similarly, in 2004, a Pew poll showed that majorities in almost all countries except the United States thought the war in Iraq hurt the battle against terrorism.

The Spectacular, Costly, and Inappropriate Response. Created in part by misinformation by the American government, the inward looking, preemptive, unilateral American policy made it easier for the United States to respond with spectacular, costly action—the invasion of Iraq, which also helped take care of unfinished business from the first Gulf War, based on the unsubstantiated premise that the road to Jerusalem led through Baghdad.

The balance of available evidence from the 9/11 Commission, congressional sources, executive branch officials, and investigative reporting tends to support the conclusion of former White House counterterrorism adviser Richard A. Clarke that, after September 11, 2001, the American government neglected counterterrorism because of an obsession with waging war on Iraq. In his book, *Against All Enemies*, Clarke concludes:

> The administration has squandered the opportunity to eliminate al Qaeda. . . . A new al Qaeda has emerged and is growing stronger, in part because of our own actions and inactions. It is in many ways a tougher opponent than the original threat we faced before September 11, and we are not doing what is necessary to make America safe from that threat.

As if anticipating Clarke, President Eisenhower, in his farewell military-industrial-complex speech during the Cold War, warned, "Crises there may continue to be, and meeting them, whether foreign or domestic, great or small, there is a recurring temptation to feel that some spectacular and costly action could become the miraculous solution to all current difficulties." President Eisenhower asked that we proceed soberly as adults, not go to extremes, not undermine our resilient economy, and not overreact.

But most of President Eisenhower's admonitions were ignored in the spectacular and costly action that is Iraq. In terms of the economic and fiscal balance Eisenhower said was crucial, America is spending about $2 billion a week in Iraq, more than $121 billion the first year, and may continue to do so for the foreseeable future—until, we are told, reconstruction is completed in 2008 or 2009, according to some estimates. But whether reconstruction ever will be completed, in Iraq or Afghanistan, remains an open question. Meanwhile, a projected ten-year American budget surplus of $5.6 trillion estimated at the beginning of the millennium has turned into a budget deficit of $521 billion—far more than triple the $158 billion imbalance of fiscal 2002 and billions higher than the record shortfall of $374 billion of 2003. At the same time, American disapproval of the war in Iraq rose in 2004, according to major public opinion polls.

With considerable justification, one can argue that the $2 billion spent per week in Iraq over recent periods of time could better be spent on a more sophisticated, multilateral policy against al Qaeda; reform of American intelligence agencies; reinvigoration of lagging counterterrorism policies to protect America from more attacks; a new preventive foreign, economic, and democracy development policy; and, perhaps most important of all, a pullback of Israel from the West Bank and the creation of a Palestinian state.

By comparison with present policy, a few years after President Eisenhower's military-industrial-complex warning, President John Kennedy faced the Cuban missile crisis. President Kennedy carried on in a steady way, speaking truth to power and overruling hardliners who wanted to go to war over Cuba. If a similar crisis occurred today, say in a confrontation with a nuclear-armed North Korea or a showdown with China, which may well become the world's next superpower, would American right-wing ideologues similarly be overruled? This is what William Hartung asks in chapter 10.

To help reverse our present course, Congress needs to expand its oversight role in national security policy. As recommended by the Hart-Rudman Commission, a program of ongoing education should provide legislative branch decision makers with more knowledge on national security. Appropriation subcommittees should be merged with their respective authorizing committees. This will reduce the congressional bureaucracy that slows the budget process and will allow more time for oversight of national security policy and of the other priority policies set forth in this volume. Congress also should establish a special body to oversee homeland security, as has been done with intelligence oversight.

To paraphrase President Reagan, are we better off today than on September 11? Worldwide, terrorism increased in 2003, according to the State Department. In 2004, a national poll by the nonpartisan Council for Excellence in Government found fewer than half of all Americans thought the United States was safer than on September 11. Another survey found that two-thirds of Americans believe terror will strike the United States in the near future.

Failures in American Middle East Policy

American failures in the Middle East are in the forefront of overall American foreign and national security policy failures, and so *Patriotism, Democracy, and Common Sense* takes a closer look at Afghanistan, Iraq, Palestine, and Israel.

Afghanistan. After September 11, there was widespread support in the United States and around the world for American military intervention in Afghanistan. Yet today, America's legitimate war in Afghanistan to destroy Osama bin Laden has become little more than a holding action to protect one man in his palace while allowing warlords to reign in the countryside, with little sustained effort to move the process toward either reconstruction or some political accommodation. Deals were cut to enable the United States to operate militarily against the remnants of al Qaeda without reference to what is necessary for future Afghan economic development, political stability, and representative governance.

Iraq. The preemptive unilateral force used in Iraq by America does not build on lessons learned from the history of imperialism. In Vietnam, a poor people's war triumphed over "shock-and-awe" hardware. In the Middle East, Oxford historian Elizabeth Monroe has elegantly recorded how British imperialism was "only a moment in the life of a region with a recorded history of four millennia." Yale historian Paul Kennedy has noted how the rationalizations of World War I–era British imperialists "bear an uncanny resemblance" to the rationalizations of American imperialist conservatives today. Kennedy suggests that America's "moment" in the Middle East may prove to be as brief in the long run as that of England. Jessica Tuchman Mathews, president of the Carnegie Endowment for International Peace, presents a similar view in chapter 3.

Under the pretense of weapons of mass destruction and an unsubstantiated link between Saddam Hussein and Osama bin Laden, America embarked on a war to redraw the political map of the Middle East. The war was designed by the American government to change the dynamics of the Middle East in such a way that a new political order, less hostile to our strategic partner and historic friend Israel, emerges.

As Eric Davis points out in *Patriotism, Democracy, and Common Sense,* the invasion of Iraq was designed to set in motion a ripple effect in which neighboring Iran and Syria, and possibly Saudi Arabia, would feel pressured to institute the types of political and economic reforms commensurate with an American vision of a new Middle East. With the removal of Israel's two most threatening enemies, namely the Ba'athi regimes in Iraq and Syria, this strategy would, it was thought, have a salutary impact on the Israeli-Palestinian peace process. It would send a strong message to Palestinian rejectionists, both Islamists and secularists, that their policies had no future, marginalize Palestine National Authority President Yasir Arafat once and for all, and generate the political forces that would replace him with a pro-American government.

This policy assumed that the populations of Iraq, Iran, Syria, Palestine, and Saudi Arabia all desired democracy—or, at least, the corrupted American version of democracy, with government corporate welfare and tax breaks for the ruling elite, hands-off market economics that increase insecurity for the middle and working classes, and "zero-tolerance," racially biased prison building for the poor. However, these policy assumptions obviously failed to take into account whether the cultures and histories of the Middle Eastern countries make them receptive to democracy, the American version or any other. Eric M. Davis addresses this lack of historical and cultural perspective in chapter 16.

To state American policy in somewhat different words, American leaders have believed that the establishment of American-style democracy in Iraq will pressure other Arab regimes to reform. Reform will promote moderate groups in Arab countries. Those groups will help force Arab countries to withdraw their support for Islamic extremism. According to this view, Palestinian resistance to Israeli occupation then will diminish and clear the way for a new Israeli-Palestinian equilibrium that is favorable to Israel. Of course, this doctrine is frightening to a host of observers in the Middle East and Europe. It could pave the way for more American intervention, say, in Syria. And it would remove from the American government the need to seriously re-engage in solving the central conflict in the Middle East between the Palestinians and Israel.

But Iraq is a country that remembers its history, dating back millennia. The people of Iraq, who remember the Crusaders far better than Americans remember the winner of the last Super Bowl, have experienced humiliation after humiliation at the hands of the West. As the American occupation of Iraq has demonstrated, the people of the Middle East will make American lives difficult there, as, of course Spain and other nations have recognized by pulling their military contingents out of Iraq. The American military's torture and sexual abuse of Iraqui prisoners made the situation immeasurably worse. There is a growth of young people joining terrorist organizations, just as there was a growth of terrorist organizations in Northern Ireland when the United Kingdom unsuccessfully pursued a policy of repression, as Lord Wallace notes in chapter 7. Similarly, Ambassador Joseph Wilson concludes in his chapter, "At the end of it, I think the chances are really good that the consequences will be far graver to our national security than they were going in."

Palestine and Israel. At the same time, compared with the tireless, hands-on involvement and shuttle diplomacy in the Middle East that won President Carter the Nobel Peace Prize, the White House in recent years has demonstrated little leadership to address the heart of Muslim anger in the world: the lack of a two-state solution, which remains the preferred solution of majorities on both sides. Instead, in 2004, the right-wing American government unconditionally endorsed a violence-provoking scheme of the right-wing Israeli government. Initially, the American government gave unprecedented support for Israeli plans to annex large swaths of occupied Palestinian territories in the West Bank and, in effect, declared null and void the rights of Palestinian refugees to return to their homes. This was the first time in the history of the peace process that the U.S. president had preempted negotiations by announcing support for a unilateral initiative by one party. The United States essentially adopted the negotiating stance of the Israeli right: Palestinians can only be dealt with by force and *fait accompli*. The 2004 American preemption was the exact opposite of President Carter's strategy of honest brokering with and mutual respect for both sides.

Unless the United States unconditionally opposes the Israeli government's scheme, the war cries of Hamas and other militants will find a receptive audience. The conservative Israeli government always has been most comfortable fighting Palestinians and Arabs. It knows very well that "disengaging" from Gaza, while retaining the Israeli "right" to bomb or invade the evacuated territory while hunting alleged terrorists, will not bring the conflict closer to resolution. With the American government labeling Palestinians terrorists, the ultra-right Israeli government has more time to pursue an expansionist vision of a Greater Israel—by creating still more "facts on the ground" that the United States is likely to deceptively label "demographic reality."

Failures in Economic Policy

Just as American foreign policy seeks to preemptively impose the American establishment's will on other, poorer countries, so American economic policy is based on class warfare instigated by the rich and ruling class in the United States against the middle class, the working class, and the poor.

As a result, excluding the rich, most Americans are worse off economically today than in 2001. Middle-class baby boomers, who are just beginning to retire, can expect their economic position to further deteriorate. The radical right's long-term objective is to continue tax cuts for the rich and massively increase military spending. This will increase the national debt still more and result in greatly diminished education, employment, and health care investments for the middle class, working class, and poor.

But will the middle class make the sacrifices that conservatives expect of them and their children? The middle class rebelled in the case of Vietnam. The need to reverse course today is all the greater because the United States cannot continue in its role as international debtor, with competitors like the dictatorship in communist China holding large portions of our international debt.

We Are Worse Off. As with foreign policy and national security policy, when we ask whether America is better off today economically than in 2001, the answer to the average American is a decisive no.

Since 2001, the official unemployment rate is higher. But even this higher rate is misleadingly low. As Austan Goolsbee, professor of economics at the University of Chicago Graduate School of Business, has warned, the government in recent years has been "cooking the books" on unemployment. The unemployment rate has been underreported because persons on Social Security disability programs have not been counted as unemployed. If they had been counted, as they had been previously, the unemployment rate would be significantly higher.

In addition, underemployment and middle-class job insecurity are extensive, there are fewer payroll jobs, outsourcing of manufacturing and high-tech jobs to workers in other countries has increased, the rich have gotten richer because of the massive tax cuts given to them, a huge budget surplus has been squandered into a deficit of over $500 billion, and the poverty rate has increased. Child poverty rates are higher in America than in most industrialized countries. Income and wealth inequality remain enormous in America. In 2002, the average pay of chief executive officers in corporations was about 176 times the average pay of workers. Based on *New York Times* accounts, in terms of income and wealth, the United States is the most unequal industrialized country in the world and is growing more unequal faster than any other industrialized country.

The Tax Cuts Are Squeezing Seniors and the Middle Class. The easiest way to frame present American economic policy is by looking at the budget implications of the recent tax cuts of well over $1 trillion, which went disproportionately to the rich.

In chapter 23, Jamie Galbraith makes clear that the beneficiaries of these tax cuts include oil firms, defense contractors, Iraq war profiteers, pharmaceutical companies, mining interests, and big media. These are economic interests whose basic position is maintained by government contracts, rights to natural resources, monopolies, patents, and government-granted protections. Their profits do not depend heavily on strong consumer demand or full employment. Full employment would itself bring other forms of political difficulty for conservatives, like stronger labor unions, pressure for higher wages, higher charitable contributions, and a stronger nonprofit sector.

Especially when considered alongside massive increases in military spending, the recent tax cuts, if continued and made permanent, will take a large toll on the federal budget and affect an array of investments and services important to the middle class, the working class, and the poor.

Where are we heading? Look at Social Security and Medicare. Baby boomers are people born between 1946 and 1964. When this huge baby-boom generation retires soon, costs will go up for Social Security and Medicare. From 2000 to 2030, Social Security and Medicare costs will increase by more than 5 percent of the size of the United States economy. This increase is larger than the United States defense budget.

So there will be more elderly people, and while there will inevitably be some changes in Social Security and Medicare, costs for these programs are going to rise substantially. At the same time, the nation has a variety of serious unmet needs: over 44 million people without health insurance; skyrocketing college tuitions; declines in college scholarships; more and more rich students edging out middle-class, working-class and poor students for slots in the best colleges; decrepit schools for working-class families and the poor; and decaying public infrastructure at a time when September 11 demands world-class public infrastructure.

How are we going to address these unmet needs and still meet the needs of a growing elderly population in future decades? A logical answer would be to raise more revenue, because we will have more expenditures with the aging of the population. *Instead, the American government is reducing taxes on the rich.*

In chapter 22, Robert Greenstein concludes that, if and when the 2001 tax cut is fully in effect, its annual cost will equal: more than three times everything the federal government spends on education at the elementary-, secondary-, and higher-education levels combined; or five times everything the federal government spends on housing and urban development; or twenty-four times the entire Environmental Protection Agency budget. If the tax cut is made permanent, the cost of just the portion of the tax cut going to the top 1 percent of the population will be as large as what the federal government spends on education at all levels.

The Tax Cuts and Increasing Debt Are Part of the Right's Long-Term Ideology. As articulated by Robert Greenstein, the massive tax cuts are part of a long-term agenda by the radical right in America to reduce public programs that benefit the middle class, working class, and poor. For example, a leading strategist of the radical right has argued for reducing by half the size of the domestic part of the federal government over future decades. *As this ideology indicates, the tax cuts and the goal of shrinking the federal government are being pursued as complementary long-terms strategies.* Those pursuing these strategies are patient. They are willing to wait until 2010 to have the estate tax repealed. They are willing to take a long time to squeeze down the federal government, with the squeezing occurring gradually and incrementally but eventually reaching huge proportions.

In 1995, conservative Speaker of the House Newt Gingrich overreached and moved too fast. Today, the extreme right is not repeating that mistake. There is a clear understanding on the part of conservatives that, if one were to publish in the official federal budget today the kind of budget cuts that the recent federal tax cuts ultimately will entail, the tax cuts would have a considerably harder time being passed. *So the deep budget cuts are not being published in the federal budget today alongside the tax cuts.* This is part of the broader strategy to deceive and mislead the American people and an accommodating mainstream media—in economic policy as in foreign, national security, and Middle East policy.

The radical right also is lobbying for still larger tax cuts for the rich. Some want to eliminate all taxes on capital gains, dividends, and other forms of income and move toward a "flat tax." The scheme is to allow deficits to continue to balloon until Wall Street demands larger and larger domestic spending cuts as a condition for holding down long-term interest rates.

The Middle Class and Their Children Don't Have the Financial or Moral Capital to Pursue All Goals. We therefore must confront a fundamental question about what kind of society we want and, in particular, what the role of the federal government should be in helping to bring that society about.

In 1965, when America was ratcheting up its intervention in Vietnam, President Johnson said we had enough resources for both "guns and butter." In response, the great American journalist Walter Lippman wrote a column in which he said that he didn't know whether we had enough *financial* capital for both, but he was sure we didn't have enough *political* and *moral* capital to fight a war in Vietnam and a war on poverty. He turned out to be absolutely right, as Jeff Faux discusses in chapter 21.

The early twenty-first century saw the war and post-war in Iraq diverting more and more money from domestic spending. So the additional economic problem is America's self-appointed burden of sustaining a continued role as the world's police, dedicated to repressing any movement, anywhere in the world, that appears to threaten the imperialism of American conservatives. This policy was set out in the American government's September 2002 National Security Strategy.

Many believe that the United States has neither the financial capital nor the moral capital to pursue such a strategy. Pursuing it would require a substantial sacrifice by the American middle class, which already, for example, is seeing its offspring edged out more and more by rich kids at the nation's top universities. Substantial sacrifice by the middle class is, of course, the political trigger, as it was in Vietnam. Sadly, we have long since learned that what you do to poor people has limited political consequences. However, in Jeff Faux's words, "When you start touching the security of the middle class in a sustained way, then there is trouble."

The Perilous International Position of the American Economy. At the same time, the American economy is in international trouble. We now have a $500 billion annual trade deficit. Under current conditions, if we were to return to full employment in the United States, the trade deficit would be much greater. We have lived decades in a condition of progressive decline in our ability to pay our way in the world through the sale of goods and services, a decline that has been offset for most of that period, and sensationally in the last years of the 1990s, by the willingness of the rest of the world to lend the differences to us, and to do so in dollars—that is to say, in a currency whose issues we control. And therefore the debts were incurred by us on very favorable terms—terms not available, basically, to any other large debtor in the world.

In his chapter, Jamie Galbraith explains how this international monetary order has been in existence for about thirty years—quite a long time for any single international monetary order to persist. The architecture of the present system is not stable, for it depends entirely on the portfolio investment decisions of a small number of major players—notably Japan and communist China—as well as the herd mentality of powerful private speculators. The American media fail to sufficiently remind the public of our vulnerability.

The risk is that, without attending to the decay of our industrial system and the increasing disrepute of America as a world leader because of our policies in Afghanistan, Iraq, Palestine, and Israel, a great part of the international community may stop lending us back our dollars. And oil-rich Middle East countries may increasingly seek to expand their relationships with rising powers like China, which have a pressing need for oil from foreign sources.

Domestic Policy Failures That Mirror Foreign Policy Failures

For conservatives whose long-term goal is to dramatically shrink federal domestic programs, September 11 was a godsend. In spite of its vast resources, America always has neglected the poor. With citizens and a passive media focused on terrorism, the war in Iraq, and the economy, it has been convenient for the American government to practice benign neglect, and more, for the truly disadvantaged and to allow racist practices to flourish.

Presently, there is no coherent American policy for the poor, minorities, the inner city, and depressed rural areas. Instead, we have top-down conservative ideology, unsupported, for the most part, by the scientific evaluation that is necessary to prove that taxpayer dollars are not being wasted, as they have been in Iraq. The ideology is based on free-market rhetoric; public-sector neglect; a racially biased, "zero-tolerance," "tough-state" prison-building war on crime (really a war against the poor); a blind eye to crime by the rich; and an appeal for "faith-based" solutions while we allow communist China, whose official religion is atheism, to hold much of our foreign debt.

The Free Market. As Kevin Phillips remarks in his foreword, the American government is practicing socialism for the rich and laissez-faire for the poor. We are increasingly leaving the fate of most people in America up to the un-tender mercies of what the federal government misleadingly describes as "the market." In fact, that "market" really is a highly concentrated set of powerful corporate players who are quite willing to subvert or corrupt free markets whenever they get in their way, as our experience with Enron, Global Crossing, and other rogue corporations affirms.

The failure of the free-market model to bring anything approaching economic well-being and social stability is apparent not just in the United States itself, of course, but around the world. The virtual disintegration of large parts of what we euphemistically call the "developing" world is one of the great underreported news stories of our time and one of the many failures of corporate-controlled American commercial media.

With the economy booming in the 1990s, many people stuck at the bottom of the economy nonetheless still had jobs. In the new millennium, unemployment for African-American youth was, in 2003, for example, over 30 percent and for Hispanic youth around 20 percent, according to the U.S. Bureau of Labor Statistics. The mainstream media have said little about these numbers.

In the new millennium, the American government has made no attempt to deal with such long term, structural unemployment for minorities, youth, and the poor. Careful evaluations, as well as assessments by *Business Week* and the conservative *Economist*, also have shown that "enterprise zones," with their supply-side ideology, have failed in their attempt to use tax breaks to lure corporations into inner cities to generate jobs for the truly disadvantaged. Earlier, the conservative, supply-side job training program for out-of-school youth, misleadingly called the Job Training Partnership Act, failed, according to the Department of Labor and careful evaluations—in large part because it in fact had little training and mainly followed a scientifically unsubstantiated "work-first" ideology.

Poverty rates, as unemployment rates, declined in the United States during the booming 1990s. But poverty rose in the new millennium. Today, the richest nation in history has 35 million people living in poverty. That is malignant neglect by the federal government. In 2002, the poverty rate for people under eighteen years old in America was over 30 percent among African-Americans and approaching 30 percent for Hispanics, according to the U.S. Census Bureau. Again, mainstream American corporate, commercial media have said little about these numbers.

As originally conceived, "welfare" for the poor (as opposed to today's welfare for the rich) was designed to reduce poverty. Over recent years, "welfare reform" was supposed to be the ticket out of crippling dependency for millions of poor Americans. But the verdict is in. Most of those poor Americans are still poor. A lot of them got off the welfare rolls, but that didn't necessarily get them into economic self-sufficiency—as an increasing body of careful evaluations shows—in spite of the lucky boost that the economic boom of the 1990s provided.

To echo Elliott Currie in chapter 26, if ever the welfare model of the extreme right should have worked it was in the economic boom of the 1990s. For a while, before poverty began to rise in the new millennium, the boom did help produce some statistics that were superficially comforting to the boosters of "welfare reform." But even in the face of the expanded opportunities provided by the boom, most of the people who left welfare did not leave the prison of deprivation.

One way of measuring the failure of "welfare reform" is to look at the "self-sufficiency standard" developed originally by professor Diana Pearce at the University of Washington. This is an attempt to come up with a more adequate measure of poverty than the official one, which everyone except radical conservatives recognizes as much too low.

The self-sufficiency standard tries to calculate how much it would actually cost families, in various places, to pay for all the things they absolutely must have in order to be self-sufficient—like housing, food, child care, and medical care—without having to rob Peter to pay Paul (there are no frills, and no savings, in this budget). In Chicago, for example, the self-sufficiency standard works out to $38,000 for a single parent with one child in school and another of preschool age. How many single parents leaving welfare under the current "reform" rules moved into $38,000 jobs?

Yet it is precisely the failed approach toward attacking "dependency" by forcing single parents into the low-wage labor market—and often depriving them of the job training opportunities that might lead them into those $38,000 (or $48,000) jobs—that is being accelerated by stealth today by the federal government, as the attention of the nation is on national security, the Middle East, and the economy. Elliott Currie reaches this conclusion in *Patriotism, Democracy, and Common Sense.* The kind of serious policy discussion that the self-sufficiency standard should be forcing upon us is not happening. There is no leadership from the White House. Mainstream media appear to be asleep, or not to care.

Public-Sector Disinvestment. To exacerbate the failure of the private "market" for the poor, the federal government has disinvested from or failed to invest in the public sector. An important example is America's failure in education, which is supposed to be a way out of poverty and a ladder to achieve the American dream.

Here are some of the realities of failed education, especially for the truly disadvantaged in America:

- States now spend more per year on prisons than on higher education, while fifteen years ago spending priorities were just the opposite.
- In urban public schools in poor neighborhoods, more than two-thirds of children fail to reach even the "basic" level on national tests.
- There are six million students on the verge of dropping out of high school, and a quarter of high-school students read below the basic level.
- Good teachers are a key to improving student achievement. But 20 percent of teachers retire within three years. In urban communities, 50 percent leave the profession in five years, in part due to low pay and a lack of support from the school system.
- Corporate CEOs make 264 times as much as public school teachers. In the 1960s, corporate CEOs made only a trifling forty times as much.
- On average, America's schools are forty years old and a third of our school buildings need widespread repair or replacement. One in three schools uses trailers or portable classrooms to house students. The National Education Association estimates that more than $53 billion is required to ensure that all schools have adequate infrastructure for Internet access, computers, and technical assistance. $268 billion is needed in repairs simply to bring schools up to basic standards.
- College tuitions are rising rapidly. Currently, about 400,000 qualified high school graduates will not pursue a full-time, four-year degree because of an inability to pay. More than 100,000 students are in danger of dropping out of school due to increased tuition costs. College costs stop nearly half of low-income students from attending a public four-year school. In 1975-76 a Pell grant covered 84 percent tuition at a four-year public school. Now it only covers 39 percent.

What is the federal government doing about these realities in the new millennium? Based on numerous scientific evaluations over decades, one of America's most successful educational programs is preschool—as every middle class and wealthy parent knows. But our preschool program for the *poor*, Head Start, is serving only about half of all eligible children. Early Head Start serves only 5 percent of eligible children. Working-class families find good preschool ever more difficult to secure and to afford. By contrast, many countries in "Old Europe" treat preschool as a human right and provide it for all children. The Committee for Economic Development, formed by major American corporations, reports that $25-$35 billion annually is needed to ensure that all children lacking a pre-kindergarten education receive one. This is less than half of the annual tax cuts pocketed by millionaires in recent federal tax cuts for the rich.

"No Child Left Behind" long has been a term associated with the effective policy advocated by the nonprofit Children's Defense Fund. In recent years, the federal government has misled the public by appropriating the name. But the resulting federal scheme bears no resemblance to the priorities of the Children's Defense Fund. An assessment by the Harvard University School of Education Civil Rights Project of the first year (2002-2003) of implementation has concluded "that federal accountability rules have derailed state reforms and assessment strategies, that the requirements have no common meaning across state lines, and that the sanctions fall especially hard on minority and integrated schools, asking for much less progress from affluent suburban schools. The market-and-choice-oriented policies, which were imposed on schools 'in need of improvement' have consumed resources and local administrative time but have small impacts and are not being seriously evaluated."

The Leave No Child Behind Act focuses on outcomes, without funding the interventions that the best research and evaluations have shown to be necessary to achieve those outcomes. Without quality interventions that sufficiently invest in each child (like better teacher training and smaller classroom sizes) there can, of course, never be quality outcomes. An additional $84-$148 billion annually is required to fulfill the goals of No Child Left Behind and assist disadvantaged students. $84 billion is about what the federal government asked for as one supplemental appropriation for occupation and "nation building" in Iraq and Afghanistan.

Recent conservative federal educational ideology also has asserted that private school vouchers are a viable alternative to public school reform. But there is no scientific evidence that private vouchers are more cost-effective than replications of existing public school reform successes. Opinion polls consistently show that Americans are against vouchers.

Advocates of private vouchers like to say that the issue is choice. That is not so. There are plenty of scientifically proven inner-city public school successes for a school system to choose from, as discussed later. The real issue is accountability. Private schools funded through vouchers are not accountable to the taxpayers whose public sector money finances them.

Inequality in education is, of course, strongly linked to expenditure per pupil. The rich, who tend to support vouchers, often say the issue is not money. But what do the rich do? They send their kids to Andover or Exeter, spending well over

$20,000 a year. If it is good enough for the rich, why isn't it good enough for the poor, the working class, and the middle class? What we need is public financing of education that allows the annual level of investment per child in American inner cities to be the same as the annual level of investment per child in the suburbs.

At the same time, America's neighborhoods and schools are resegregating. As the Harvard Civil Rights Project has documented, the school desegregation advocated by the Reverend Martin Luther King Jr. progressed till the late 1980s, when the courts decided that the goals of the landmark Supreme Court Brown v. Board of Education decision had largely been achieved. Since these short-sighted court decisions of the 1980s, segregation has sharply increased. Today, about two-thirds of African American students and three-fourths of Hispanic students nationally attend predominantly minority schools, one-third of each group in intensely segregated schools.

This, too, is malignant neglect practiced by the American government and leadership. Another example of the lack of public sector leadership on race in America was the forced resignation of the Senate Majority Leader not so long ago for, in effect, praising the segregationist positions of a Senate colleague who had passed away.

Tough-State, Zero-Tolerance Prison Building for the Poor. Tax breaks for the rich, disproportionately white, have been complemented by "zero-tolerance" policing of and prison building for the poor, disproportionately African American, Latino and Native American.

The military strategy in Iraq and some of the most popular policing strategies against the poor in the United States are part of the same conservative ideology. The domestic equivalent of "shock and awe" is zero tolerance in policing. Police undertake "get tough" tactical street crackdowns to increase arrest rates. But there is little evidence that zero-tolerance policing was responsible for much of the decline in crime in the 1990s, as professor Richard Moran has pointed out in the *New York Times*. At the same time, zero tolerance has outraged much of the minority community.

The shortcomings of zero tolerance illustrate deeper, more systematic problems. In particular, a major study funded by the U.S. Department of Justice and six large foundations has documented racial bias across the juvenile justice system. Riots in Cincinnati not long ago were a reminder of African-American perceptions that police racially profile minority youth. Beyond racial profiling, the most basic problem in the criminal justice system is the racial bias in the mandatory minimum sentencing of persons arrested on drug charges. For example, sentences for crack cocaine, used disproportionately by minorities, are much harsher than sentences for powder cocaine, used disproportionately by whites. As one consequence, African Americans constitute 14 percent of drug users nationally but represent 35 percent of drug arrests, 55 percent of drug convictions, and 75 percent of prison admissions.

In the early 1990s, one out of every four young African-American men in America was in prison, on probation, or on parole at any one time, according to the Sentencing Project in Washington, D.C. That is a stunning statistic. Yet today *one out of every three* young African-American men is in prison, on probation, or on parole at any one time in America. In big cities, the number is *one out of every two*. Similarly, we know from Professor Milton Friedman, the conservative economist, that the rate of incarceration of African-American men in America today is four times greater than the rate of incarceration of black men in pre-Mandela, apartheid South Africa. Nonetheless, the fastest-growing group of male prison inmates consists of Latinos.

When it comes to the treatment and degradation of these inmates, there are, not surprisingly, parallels between what was done in Iraq and what takes place every day in American prisons. American policy toward degradation and humiliation in prison is dramatically different from policy in European and other countries. Foreign observers have been shocked by the humiliations in American prisons, as documented by professor James Q. Whitman at Yale Law School. For example, just as an American female soldier was accused of forcing Iraqi prisoners to masturbate in front of others, so American prison guards of the opposite sex can be allowed to view inmates using toilets. These and other American practices are not allowed in Europe.

America now leads the world in incarceration, with over two million people in prison. The United States has 25 percent of the world's prisoners but only 5 percent of the world's population. Especially as a result of the mandatory minimum sentencing policy for drugs, we have more than quadrupled the number of prison cells in America since the 1980s. Over that time, we reduced by over 80 percent appropriations for housing for the disadvantaged. So prison building has become one of America's leading housing policies for the poor, just as it has become one of our leading education policies for the poor. These linkages among housing policy, education policy, prison building, zero tolerance, and racism are big stories, yet corporate-controlled American mainstream media virtually ignore them.

The United States had developed a dual-track system for addressing substance abusers, with the tracks largely defined in racial terms. For minorities, a primary track leads to arrest, conviction, and incarceration. For white Americans, especially those who are more affluent, often there is either no intervention or intervention through the health and treatment system. For people in the South Bronx, drug abuse is treated as a crime. For people in Chevy Chase, it is treated as an illness.

Prison building has become a job-generating, economic development policy for rural white Americans, who send lobbyists with six-figure incomes to Washington to fight for still more prisons. The prison-industrial complex is a perfect domestic parallel to President Eisenhower's military-industrial complex. But mainstream American corporate media have said almost nothing about the parallel.

Having served long sentences, many people now are leaving prison, sometimes at a rate of over 500,000 per year. Some four million do not have the right to vote, by state law. The American government has no effective policy for reintegrating ex-offenders into society and training them to become productive, employed, tax-paying citizens. Even though there are excellent models, like Delancey Street, that achieve such outcomes, there is little incentive for the federal government to replicate them to scale because most ex-offenders, in Florida and elsewhere, would vote against most present federal policies. Why lose an election by giving a fair shake to someone who has paid his debt to society? As a result, recidivism rates are over 70 percent in some places, so offenders are back in their cells and not in voting booths. There is no better example of malignant neglect by the ruling classes in America.

As these recidivism rates imply, we know, based on some of the most prestigious American studies of prison building to date (for example, by a panel of the National Academy of Science), that the criminal justice response to crime is, at most, running in place. However, in spite of a sevenfold increase in the prison population since the late 1960s, the FBI rate of violent crime (based on the aggregation of murders, rapes, robberies, and aggregated assaults reported to police) is significantly higher today (in big, medium, and small cities) than in 1969, when the bipartisan Eisenhower Violence Commission released its final report—and when one of the commission's task forces concluded that "few things are more pervasive, more frightening, more real today than violent crime and the fear of being assaulted, mugged, robbed or raped."

Equally important, rates of violent crime today are much higher in the United States than in almost all industrialized countries. For example, the rate of homicide death for a young man today is about twenty-three times higher in the United States than in the United Kingdom.

When it comes to homicide with firearms, America far outdistances other wealthy nations, most of which have far more restrictions on firearms. The firearms death rate in the United States today is eight times greater than the rates of the twenty-five other wealthy nations combined. In a recent year, handguns were used to murder 2 people in New Zealand, 15 in Japan, 30 in Great Britain, 106 in Canada, 213 in Germany, and over 9,000 in the United States.

But what about the declines in crime in the 1990s? Didn't they occur as prison building surged? What were the reasons, based on the best studies and evaluations available, like the work of professor Alfred Blumstein at Carnegie-Mellon University? Two leading (and interrelated) reasons were the booming economy and the waning of the crack epidemic. Community-based nonprofit organizations appeared to have been successful in some places, like Boston. The Brady Bill, which controlled access to handguns by ex-offenders, appeared to have a national impact. So did community-based, problem-oriented policing. Some of the decline in violent crime was in fact explained by increased imprisonization (estimates are in the range of about 5 percent to about 30 percent). But the impact of prison building was overstated by politicians, the government, the prison-industrial complex, its lobbyists, and naïve media. In addition, prison building has been highly cost-ineffective compared with other options, like diversion of nonviolent offenders into community programs. Nor was the fad of boot camps successful. Its failure was well documented in studies by the University of Maryland that have been published by the United States National Institute of Justice.

In perspective, there is an eerie resemblance between America's preemptive, dominating, nonpreventive, shock-and-awe, high-tech, weapon-intense, community-insensitive, personally humiliating, corporate-profiteering, military-industrial-complex foreign policy aimed at people of different races and cultures and America's zero-tolerance, racially biased, personally humiliating, nonpreventive, prison-building, high-tech, firearm-permissive, corporate-profiteering, prison-industrial-complex policy toward the truly disadvantaged in the United States. Both policy wars have been initiated by the well-off, mostly white, conservative ruling elite. Both are expensive. Both are ineffective. Today, the average American is safe from neither terrorism nor crime. American corporate mainstream media fail to pursue investigative reporting on the resemblance.

Faith-Based Schemes. In recent years, there also has been rhetoric on "volunteerism," "civility," "empowerment" and "faith-based solutions" for the truly disadvantaged. Research has shown that these sometimes can be effective notions at the street level of program implementation. But too often such terms try to mislead the people into conservative double standards. For example, while both Gulf Wars were carried out by large numbers of paid military staff, large numbers of paid support staff, and enormous amounts of high-tech equipment, American inner city programs are encouraged to use unpaid volunteers with totally inadequate equipment, like nonfunctioning computers, in inadequate facilities. This somehow is supposed to "empower" the neighborhood and, presumably, reduce unemployment, poverty, racism, and crime while it improves rotting inner-city schools and does something about nonexistent job training.

Similarly, it presently is fashionable in the private and public sectors to make grants to "faith-based" nonprofit groups. Yet no scientific evidence exists to prove that "faith-based" nonprofit organizations perform better than secular nonprofit organizations. Some nonprofit faith-based groups are successful and some are not; some nonprofit secular organizations are successful and some are not. The key is not faith-based versus secular programming. Research shows the key is whether a nonprofit organization is carrying out interventions that have proven to work and whether the organization has the institutional capacity to cost-effectively implement them.

Communist China offers an example of the hypocrisy of some of the current American "faith-based" rhetoric. America's policy of corporate corruption, hostility to labor unions, market economics, zero tolerance, prison building, and racism is, in some ways, becoming more and more like communist China's. Over the last two decades in China, the evils of "capitalist roadism" have been replaced by the slogan "To get rich is glorious." Corporate corruption abounds. At the same time, the police can arrest and incarcerate a person for three years without a trial. Not long ago, the fifteenth anniversary of the military massacre of democracy-seeking students in Tiananmen Square was celebrated by the government arresting some of the parents of the original demonstrators. The president of China made his reputation in part by overseeing genocide of the minority population in Tibet.

What about democracy? Communist China has a corrupt, nondemocratic, one-party system. Chinese cannot elect their national leaders or form labor unions. Beijing lied on its promise of democracy to Hong Kong and unrelentingly saber-rattles against democracy in Taiwan.

America is the sole superpower, but communist China has superpower ambitions. The American government and American corporations are helping. With Chinese entry-level factory workers earning as little as twenty-five cents an hour, China provides America with cheap goods, including DVD players, televisions, washing machines, textiles, running shoes, furniture, and toys. One estimate is that the United States has lost over 344,000 jobs in recent years because of Chinese imports. The job losses also are helping to force down wages in some American industries. OutsourcingAsia.com predicts that the next big location for offshore outsourcing will be China.

China not only provides the cheap goods. It also lends America the money to buy those goods. From 2001 to 2003, China's holdings of United States debt—U.S. Treasury securities—increased from $109 billion to $194 billion. Today, communist China finances more American consumers and government spending than any foreign lender except democratic Japan.

In recent years, America's annual trade deficit with China has been well over $100 billion. The most effective advocates for maintaining the status quo are not Chinese but American lobbyists on Capitol Hill for American corporations—which profit from trade with China and also often contribute to conservative candidates here. Wal-Mart alone acquires more than $10 billion per year in goods from communist China, which then are sold to American consumers.

In spite of these trends, and in spite of certain similarities between America and China, there is a big difference when it comes to religion. America is the most religious of the industrialized countries, while the Chinese communist leadership has never made any secret of the fact that China is an atheist state. Religious activity is strictly controlled. Chinese policies are based on the premise that religion cannot be allowed to grow unchecked.

This means that the United States is rewarding an atheist superpower competitor-to-be with jobs, dollars, and control of America's future (through the Chinese holdings of our debt). Yet the American government simultaneously tells us that it is giving priority to "faith-based" policy.

Failures of the Media to Serve the People

In pursuing its policies, the American government has been extremely effective in controlling the flow of information to the media about its workings. The government has been helped by a powerful conservative ideological machine linked to media controlled by large corporations.

The Conservative Ideological Machine. Much of the present media environment was shaped by the conservative billionaire Richard Mellon Scaife and his colleagues, as Eric Alterman describes in chapter 35.

In 1964, after the defeat of Barry Goldwater, Scaife and his associates concluded that the conservative message was being framed by what they considered an elite media, unsympathetic to their cause. They understood that, if you don't win the media, you can't win anything else. So Scaife and other conservatives invested hundreds of billions of dollars from 1964 to the present in new institutions to frame conservative ideology.

Strategically, conservatives focused on both media control and media policy. They funded foundations, nonprofit ideology centers, radio and television talk shows, training camps for student journalists, and internship programs. They supported nonprofit institutes that targeted the Federal Communications Commission, Congress, and the courts—to guarantee that they had policies sympathetic to the conservative view of how media should be operated.

As one result, while there were only a few conservative nonprofit organizations and centers for conservative ideology in Washington in 1964, today there are more than 300. Some are small. Other nonprofit conservative centers are huge, with annual budgets in the tens of millions, financed by corporations and conservative foundations.

Eric Alterman shows how the the new conservative institutions created thousands of well-paying jobs as part of a perpetual motion machine for conservative ideology. Prospective employees have been placed in jobs in conservative ideological centers, the *Washington Times, Inside* magazine, the *Wall Street Journal,* and many other institutions of the far right. They have high-salaried careers in this world, and sometimes move over to Fox News or talk radio. Some can speak to millions of people. The ideological machine is enormously useful because it provides conservative activists with a kind of tribal drum to constantly make their voices heard in American politics.

In the 2000 presidential election, the machine was targeted to places that were of paramount importance to the radical right—above all, Florida. Through encouragement by Rush Limbaugh, FreeRepublic.com, and Fox News, thousands of conservatives hopped on planes, flew to Florida, and helped to shut down the vote count in Miami-Dade. Those votes were the votes that would have made the difference, and they were disallowed because the counties did not make the deadline because the vote was shut down.

Well-disciplined, the conservative activist machine can blast e-mail and faxes in the morning and then repeat any given message all day on web sites, Rush Limbaugh, Bill O'Reilly, Sean Hannity, talk radio, cable television, the *Wall Street Journal* editorial page, and the *Weekly Standard.*

Corporate Media. The success of the conservative machine has been facilitated by the corporatization of the media. Competition in the media has declined. Ten corporations now own most of American media.

In chapter 31, Robert McChesney and John Nichols compare corporate media today to the scene in the 1974 film *The Godfather, Part II,* where American gangsters are sitting on a rooftop on Havana in 1958, slicing a birthday cake with the outline of Cuba on it. Each slice represents a casino, given to one of the gangsters to run. That is exactly how media and communication policies have been created in the United States for the last fifty years. Today the media corporations and trade associations have enormous lobbying powers, not because they're concerned about the average citizen but because they're fighting each other for the biggest slice of the American and global cake—they're at war with each other. The one thing they all agree on is that it's their cake, and nobody else should get a slice. It's their private system.

Many of these corporate media, like Clear Channel, General Electric, Fox, and Rupert Murdoch's News Corporation, are big campaign contributors to conservatives. As a result, corporate media often bias their coverage in support of conservative ideology. Together, the conservative propaganda machine and much of the corporate media have helped the American government mislead the American people, convincing large audiences that the government could not have prevented September 11, there was a link between Saddam Hussein and Osama bin Laden, there were weapons of mass destruction in Iraq, the invasion of Iraq would reduce terrorism, tax cuts for the rich would help the rest of us, the budget deficit and high unemployment rates were not a real problem, communist China would not potentially cause problems by holding so much of our debt, there was no long-run conservative plan to shrink programs that benefit the middle class, prison building was effective, "welfare reform" worked, poverty wasn't increasing, segregation wasn't increasing, crime wasn't many times higher here than in most other industrialized countries, and public sector–led reform of the deteriorated public education systems of our inner cities was not possible.

Up to the point where the United States invaded Iraq, a majority of Americans polled were against the war. Yet a study by the nonprofit Fairness and Accuracy in Media found that, in the weeks leading up to the war, there were 393 interviews on the war done on the four major nightly newscasts (NBC, CBS, ABC, and the PBS *NewsHour* with Jim Lehrer). Only three of those interviews were with people opposed to the war. By contrast, media outside the United States had much more negative coverage on and opposition to the war, as Julian Borger of the *Guardian* recalls in chapter 20.

As Robert McChesney and John Nichols remind us, it is not natural for the conservative propaganda machine, corporate media, and the American government to walk in lock-step. This was not the vision of the nation's founders, like Franklin and Jefferson, who understood that, without a diverse, free media, you cannot have democracy.

WHAT ALTERNATIVE POLICIES BETTER FULFILL AMERICA'S PROMISE?

By contrast to the domination and misinformation of present policies, more effective alternative policies can be framed as a priority on common sense and democracy.

"Common sense" is the stuff of Ben Franklin, Thomas Paine, and Thomas Jefferson. The founders of our nation, born in the Age of Enlightenment, believed in reason, not ideology. Reason builds on the lessons of history and the evidence of science. "Democracy" here means policy not based on the "regimentation by a handful of rulers" that President Roosevelt warned against or the control by the "military-industrial complex" that President Eisenhower cautioned against but on "we the people," the opening words of the Constitution. "We the people" means real, one person–one vote power by average citizens and genuine democratic transparency, not stealth decision-making by a small plutocracy in Washington and Wall Street.

What are some examples of common sense and democracy in the alternative policies found in this book? Foreign and national security policy illustrations include a stronger military based on the realities of the twenty-first century, not the policies of the Cold War, and multilateral, preventive foreign aid that empowers nongovernmental organizations in impoverished nations. In the Middle East, common sense and democracy mean remembering the failures of British and French colonial imperialism, recognizing that American torture and sexual humiliation in Iraqi prisons will have a profoundly damaging long term effect, remembering the success of the poor people's war in Vietnam, and creating an equitable peace in Palestine and Israel. In American economic policy, examples of common sense and democracy include the rejection of scientifically unsupported supply-side ideology, including tax breaks for the rich, and creation of a Fair Economic Deal for the middle class, working class, and poor. For the truly disadvantaged, illustrations include replication to scale of successful model programs already proven by scientific evaluations and the facilitation of a "bubble-up" process of grassroots development led by nonprofit inner city organizations, which are much closer to the people than the federal government. The importance of scientific evaluations as the basis for alternative policy has been underscored by a coalition of Nobel laureates and other distinguished scientists, who recently issued a statement that American federal policy often is based not on scientific evidence but on the distortion of facts. Last, common sense and democracy in the media are illustrated by how our founders were against corporate controlled media and by the success of institutions like MoveOn.org in promoting grassroots citizen organizing, advocacy, and fund raising.

Consider a range of alternatives in each of these policy areas:

Alternative American Foreign and National Security Policy

Building on the recommendations of the bipartisan Hart-Rudman Commission, a follow-up independent task force of the Council on Foreign Relations, and the bipartisan 9/11 Commission, new foreign and national security policy needs to evolve from the following principles:

- National security policy must understand the changing nature of conflict.
- America's military response must look dramatically different.
- A reformed military must legitimize preventive diplomacy backed by force and resist preemption.
- Preventive diplomacy requires multilateral action.
- Multilateral action must reassert the legitimacy of the United Nations.
- Preventive diplomacy and multilateralism require increased and more effective foreign aid.
- Counterterrorism policy in America must be implemented with more urgency.
- Counterterrorism policy must balance security and liberty.

National Security Policy Must Understand the Changing Nature of Conflict. With few exceptions, post–Cold War conflict has been characterized by nonarrayed enemies—those representing asymmetrical threats. Asymmetrical threats use ingenuity, not strength, to bypass American military superiority. September 11 was undertaken by nineteen suicidal men at a total cost of about $500,000. They used the Internet and elementary flight instructions. They converted commercial airlines into weapons of mass destruction. Our technology was used against us.

To successfully change the nature of national security policy, America first needs fundamental reform at the CIA. We need to block efforts to politicize the intelligence product and return the CIA to fierce honesty, professionalism, and independence in its analytic product. We need the CIA to be led by professionals like former directors Stansfield Turner or George H. W. Bush, with the character to stand up to White House and Pentagon pressure to usurp the agency's functions and preempt its analysis.

Beyond upgrading the standards by which the United States chooses a director of central intelligence, we need to generate more timely, comprehensive, professional, transparent, and apolitical national intelligence estimates; return imagery analysis, agenda-free, from the Pentagon to the CIA; and reconstitute an independent media analysis capability in the CIA,, as Ray McGovern recommends in chapter 4. With such reforms in place in recent years, America might have been better prepared for the September 11 attacks.

America's Military Response Must Look Dramatically Different. First and foremost, Americans need to be convinced that an alternative to present policy will protect them militarily. America must possess a strong and effective military. The source of that strength lies in the recognition that twenty-first-century military policy must look and perform differently from twentieth century military policy. In the new millennium, American military policy needs to build on technology but also be more human. This is one of Gary Hart's lessons in chapter 2.

Technologically, for example, we need lighter, swifter expeditionary forces to fight terrorism. But military technology swiftly becomes outmoded. Accordingly, instead of building entirely new ships, planes, and tanks, we need to build ships, planes, and tank platforms with long lives. Up-to-date weapons and sensors can be "plugged in" to the platforms and then replaced as technology moves on. The two best current examples of platform technology are the B-52 bomber and the aircraft carrier. The B-52 is over six decades old. Aircraft carriers can be kept in service for fifty years. They are the platforms. We constantly change the weapons and sensors they carry. In the future, more weapons systems need to be so configured.

In terms of the human factor, human resourcefulness is more crucial than ever. The military and our intelligence agencies must recruit and promote with a higher priority on ingenuity. Human intelligence failed us on September 11. All our technology was unable to stop the attacks. Exotic Pentagon communications networks are vulnerable to twenty-one-year-old hackers. On the other hand, American military incursions via precision-guided munitions onboard planes flying from Diego Garcia and aircraft carriers in the Indian Ocean were made possible by very human skills. The incursions were guided by Delta Force personnel wearing civilian clothes and riding mules across the hills of Afghanistan.

A Reformed Military Must Legitimize Preventive Diplomacy Backed by Force and Resist Preemption. In chapter 10, William Hartung concludes that diplomacy backed by force means America in the role of Atticus Finch, as played by Gregory Peck in the film adaptation of Harper Lee's novel *To Kill a Mockingbird*. Peck played a Southern trial lawyer defending the rights of an African-American unjustly accused by whites. Ironically, an America that stood up for justice, defended the underdogs, and felt secure enough to put down the gun instead of automatically picking up the gun at the slightest provocation—an America that was more Gregory Peck and less John Wayne—would be far better suited to fighting a threat like al Qaeda.

Why? Because we are in a propaganda war. The American military policy of talking loudly and arrogantly, carrying many big sticks, torturing prisoners and sexually humiliating them has alienated the majority of the people on the planet. These are the people and governments we need to work with to curb a threat like al Qaeda, a network that functions in perhaps as many as sixty countries. "Regime change" is an irrelevant, costly extravagance in the face of a network like al Qaeda, which can operate with relatively small amounts of money, without government sponsorship, preying on the weaknesses and the complexities of our globalized economic system to sustain itself.

The costs of "regime change" through preemptive war misdirect our resources away from the battle against al Qaeda. In so doing, preemptive war may have increased the ability of terrorists to strike America, not decreased it.

The elimination of nuclear weapons globally also illustrates a policy of preventive diplomacy, rather than preemptive war. An important first step is to better fund and globalize legislation originally passed by Republican Senator Richard Lugar and Democratic Senator Sam Nunn. The Nunn-Lugar legislation created a set of programs designed to neutralize the nuclear capability of the former Soviet Union by helping to pay for destruction of nuclear missiles and warheads and by finding alternative employment for weapons scientists, so they don't sell their skills to the highest bidder on the global market. The United States is worried about Osama bin Laden, a global businessman, obtaining nuclear missiles. So we must ask, where are the nuclear missiles that Osama is most likely to buy? They are in the former Soviet Union.

Of course, the goal should be to get rid of nuclear weapons altogether, just as our domestic goal must be to get rid of handguns. The mere existence of nuclear weapons is dangerous, destabilizing, and demoralizing. Like a loaded gun under your pillow, nuclear weapons are just as dangerous to the folks who have them as they are to folks who don't. Brandishing them and threatening people with them, as the American government has done, is a sure-fire recipe for convincing countries that they need their own nuclear missiles, if for no other reason than to get themselves off the Department of Defense's "regime change" list.

Tyrants around the world surely have noticed the deferential treatment that North Korea, which appears to have some nuclear weapons, got compared with Saddam Hussein, who did not have such weapons. So what the American government seems to be saying by its actions is, in the words of William Hartung in chapter 10, "Get nuclear weapons, and we'll treat you nice, and negotiate. Fail to get nuclear weapons and we'll bomb you into the Stone Age and kill your family." What kind of incentive is that to dissuade dictators from trying to get nuclear weapons?

Preventive Diplomacy Requires Multilateral Action. We need to build and nurture our alliances with other countries. When the State Department recently released a *Patterns of Global Terrorism* report, the spokesperson made a point of saying that the two countries that have given America the most help in dealing with al Qaeda were

in "Old Europe": France and Germany. The State Department made this point to emphasize that, if the American military doesn't stop insulting France and Germany, important ties will be further damaged.

A broad spectrum of people realize that having allies is common sense and that insulting them is a bad thing. If we are to have an effective policy against terrorism, America must follow the money, and that means, for example, leaning on the Saudis and the Pakistanis. We need to have a more responsible approach to the global economy that says, if certain aspects of the financial system must be regulated in order to make sure we don't have another Word Trade Center disaster, and if money therefore has to flow a little more slowly, then so be it.

An alternative foreign policy, then, must take multilateralism seriously. This cannot be just serious rhetorically, as was true under the Clinton administration, which claimed the mantle of multilateralism while it carried out policy after policy that was thoroughly unilateralist in its trajectory. The first steps should include embracing the Kyoto accords, the International Criminal Court, and the Treaty of Rome.

Multilateral Action Must Reassert the Legitimacy of the United Nations. The United Nations must take the lead in Iraq. The first obligation of a military occupying power is to end the occupation. That is true of Israel in Palestine, and it is true of the United States in Iraq. The United Nations has to be the alternative to military occupation.

No one can deny that the United Nations has failed to live up to its 1945 charter in many respects. But attacks on the United Nations by the radical right in the United States fail to realize that, far from being an independent actor, the United Nations was designed as a kind of "holding company"—an enterprise where many members hold a stake but where some shareholders have a proportionately more influential role. The disproportionate stakeholders are the Permanent Five members of the Security Council—the United States, the United Kingdom, France, Russia, and China. Of these, the United States is by far the most powerful stakeholder. As professor Paul Kennedy at Yale has reminded us, failures to act against conflict and improve prospects for world peace are not the fault of the holding company but of the major shareholders, when they cannot agree. The United Nations still has great potential, but only when its major players, beginning with the United States, learn how better to work together.

At the same time, it is crucial to advocate for reforms to make United Nations operations more effective. Perhaps the most important reform is to democratize the Security Council—no permanent members and no vetoes. Of course, such reform is not now politically feasible, but the issue must constantly be put on the table.

More feasible in the short run is advocacy to empower the General Assembly. This is the plan of Phyllis Bennis in chapter 9. Historically, in the first forty years or so of the United Nations, partly because of the Cold War paralysis, partly because of the legacy of colonialism, partly for a host of other reasons, the General Assembly was the engine of motion. It wasn't the Security Council. It was to the General Assembly that newly independent former colonies would send their representatives to claim independence in front of the world. It was the General Assembly that created the United Nations Industrial Development Organization, the United Nations Educational, Scientific and Cultural Organization, and all of the agencies that were designed to help countries of the global South compete on something resembling a more level playing field with the wealthy countries of the North. None of this happened because of Security Council resolutions. It happened because of the General Assembly and its more-or-less democratic approach to things.

Today, in the thinking of Bennis, the best way to empower the General Assembly is for the United States to simply back off—to become a more cooperative major shareholder. Right now, in the General Assembly, fear of antagonizing the United States forms a huge block on the ability of countries to take advantage of the global reach of the United Nations.

We need, then, to transform the United Nations from an institution where only the Security Council matters to a venue for real multinational interaction.

Preventive Diplomacy and Multilateralism Require Increased and More Effective Foreign Aid. In recent years, the American government and the mainstream media have resisted answering the most obvious question: Why was the September 11 attack committed?

In a world where one-quarter of the population lives in abject poverty, there is deep, lasting resentment over how America combines its wealth and power with willful arrogance, self-interest, corporate greed, arbitrary consumption of resources, and hypocrisy. We use a "shock-and-awe" invasion of Iraq to impose "democracy." But what is America's definition of democracy? A corrupt one dollar–one vote system in which the winner lost the popular vote for president in 2000 by over 500,000 votes. People know this around the world. They know how American "democracy" has failed to solve the nation's internal decay—symbolized, for example, by racism, segregation, poverty, inequality, violence, substandard education, job insecurity, inadequate health care, stealth privatization of Social Security, failed campaign financing reform, and failed voter rights reform. Until we reverse our internal decay, America has little "soft power," to use the phrase of Harvard Kennedy School professor Joseph Nye, to change the minds and hearts of people throughout the world.

Corporate-powered globalization is increasing income and wealth inequality, poverty, and despair. The information revolution has created a growing digital divide between the computer literate with future opportunities and the computer illiterate without them. It follows that American foreign policy needs to reduce inequality and close the digital divide.

Terrorists require money, weapons, and people. A national security policy that rejects unilateral preemptive war and focuses more on terrorist organizations must disrupt the flow of money and weapons. But the most vital resource is people. We need to reverse the despair in the impoverished villages of the world by combining economic and diplomatic solutions with military ones. Though the first suicidal attacks did not come from refugee camps, future waves may.

As a first step, as recommended by the Hart-Rudman Commission, the U.S. Agency for International Development should be integrated into a reorganized State Department—so aid can be better coordinated with the goals of economic development, poverty and inequality reduction, democracy building, and protection of human rights.

We then need to significantly change the sixteen-to-one ratio between Pentagon spending and spending for all other foreign operations. In terms of foreign aid, the United States ranks twentieth among the major countries. In terms of fulfilling a commitment made several years ago to fund the basic education of all children in the world by 2015, the Netherlands, Norway, and Sweden have received top marks for coming through with their promises. The United States flunked, coming in third from last among the twenty-two richest countries.

In 2000, the richest countries agreed to increase their foreign aid to a long-term target of seven-tenths of one percent of their gross national products. For the richest countries combined, this amounts to about $175 billion at today's income levels. If used effectively, these resources could substantially reduce, if not eliminate, the worst afflictions of poverty around the world. The money could control the great pandemic diseases of AIDS, tuberculosis, and malaria; increase food productivity of impoverished farmers in the tropics; ensure that children are in school rather than at work; and enable poor households to obtain at least minimally acceptable access to safe drinking water, energy, and markets.

Yet, since 2000, the amount of American foreign aid remains the lowest as a percent of income in the entire donor world—about one-tenth of 1 percent of gross national product. Accordingly, the goal of a newly reorganized American foreign aid program within the Department of State should be to raise the level to the promised seven tenths of 1 percent.

Such a greatly enhanced aid program must structure more professional levels of accountability than at present. The traditional "top-down" economic development process should be overturned. It is more a creator of inequality than an engine of progress. Instead, we need to facilitate economic development that is "bubble up," in part through a greatly expanded role for nongovernmental organizations indigenous to the nations being assisted. As Ralph Nader advocates in chapter 24, we need to facilitate the kind of great contributions of Pablo Freire, or of Hassan Fathy in showing illiterate Egyptian peasants how to build simple, elegant housing from the soil under their feet, or the microcredit successes of the Grameen Bank started by Mohammed Yunis in Bangladesh. A new era of energy renewability and solar energy should be created, as well.

Recent American policy naively has assumed that, over the last two decades, the priorities of the International Monetary Fund and the World Bank have led to prosperity and democracy. Yet, by any reasonable measures, they have not succeeded, argues Nader. They have promoted policies that cause poverty and inequality, harm the environment, and lead to the privatization of basic services, such as water provision. Global growth in the last twenty years has been half of what it was in the previous twenty years. Distribution of income *among* countries has worsened, and the evidence suggests that, by and large, the distribution of income and wealth *within* countries also has worsened. So, in terms of what any sensible evaluation would conclude, our present global development policy of socialism for the rich and free enterprise for the poor has not worked.

Doling out outrageous salaries, benefits, tax breaks, country club privileges, and travel expenses to employees, the IMF and World Bank are corrupt, ineffective, and wasteful—patent failures, condemned as such by more than a few internal critiques. For example, while he was chief economist at the World Bank, Joseph Stiglitz, who was soon to win a Nobel Prize and now is a professor at Columbia University, publicly criticized the IMF for worsening the situation of Indonesia, South Korea, Thailand, and the Philippines. With leadership from the White House and a State Department reorganized as proposed by the Hart-Rudman Commission, the IMF and World Bank should facilitate the same kind of bubble-up rather than top-down economic development process needed by a reformed American aid initiative.

Accompanying reformed economic development should be a program of capacity building in democracy—for countries that want democracy. That democracy should be free of the campaign finance corruption, inequality, and class warfare by the rich against the poor that is central to what the power elite in America call "democracy." Democracy cannot be imposed, a lesson our young country has not yet learned.

Counterterrorism Policy in America Must Be Implemented With More Urgency. The United States today is scarcely more safe than on September 11. The federal government must move more rapidly and effectively to secure America from terrorists and invest its policy at home with the same degree of urgency it used to begin the unnecessary, resource-diverting invasion of Iraq. Short-run, middle-term, and long-run counterterrorism policies can be identified.

Here are just a few examples of short-run policy:

- The federal government needs to immediately implement a system of training and equipping local police, fire department staff, and local public and private health workers to respond to biological, chemical, nuclear, and other terrorist attacks. Federal financing is needed to significantly expand the numbers and quality of such personnel.

- In support of this training, the federal government needs to make federal watch lists and data bases much more available to state and local law enforcement agents—as well as to fire and health officials around the nation. Local responders to terrorist attacks need to be given much more intelligence from federal agencies, so they can better respond.
- The multiple points of American vulnerability to biological, chemical, nuclear, and other attacks must be systematically identified and eliminated. For example, we need to drastically step up inspection of the 21,000 shipping containers that enter our 361 ports every day. The United States now is spending $200 million to $300 million more on airport security, but shipping containers are a greater threat for weapons of mass destruction. The United States needs to do a better job of protecting energy distribution facilities like power plants, pumping stations, and pipeline compressor stations. We need improved protection of our water and food supplies.
- The federal government needs to move more quickly to protect the critical public and private infrastructure of America—the basic industries and systems on which our economy and society are based—including financial structures, communication systems, transportation systems, and energy production and distribution. Minimal progress has been made in protecting these systems.
- The White House and Congress should forcefully require the private sector to create, share, and cofinance vastly improved security to protect critical infrastructure industries. Legal barriers to cooperation among private sector entities should be removed. Corporations have been far too slow in response to the challenges.
- Organized citizens and responsible investigative media should demand accountability from national, state, and local leaders for how governments at all levels are making the population safer from terrorism and for the publication of independent cost-benefit and cost-effectiveness evaluations of progress or lack thereof.
- The FBI needs to better organize for counterterrorism and to ensure that field agent reports on terrorism are taken more seriously at headquarters in Washington. It needs to install state-of-the-art computers and a staff capacity to analyze data on potential terrorism in the United States.

In the middle run, it is important to better assess the Patriot Act, hastily passed after September 11 through an aggressive White House campaign that misleadingly implied that opponents were unpatriotic and aligned with terrorists.

The act does solve an important problem identified by Coleen Rowley in chapter 30 (as well as by the 9/11 Commission): it removes procedural barriers that intelligence and criminal investigators believe prohibited them from sharing information, causing missed opportunities in unraveling plots. But it also permits federal investigators to look at individuals' retail purchases, Internet searches, e-mail, and library usage, all without notification. It allows the U.S. attorney general to detain immigrants based on "suspicion," requires businesses to report "suspicious transactions," allows the government to conduct secret searches without notification, grants the FBI and other agencies greatly expanded access to all sorts of personal and business data with little judicial oversight, and allows for surveillance of any number of domestic organizations and advocacy groups.

Despite the many new powers the Patriot Act grants, a host of experts doubt whether it will actually succeed in reducing terrorist activity. For example, while the act permits the government to collect vast amounts of information, it does not provide the agencies involved the resources required to analyze it. As New York University law professor Stephen Schulhofer has observed, "A large part of what we lack [already] is not raw data but the ability to separate significant intelligence from 'noise.'"

Serious debate over these policies is only now emerging. Many are wary because the government is so secretive and because it has shown such bad judgment in so many policies, like being unable to confront militant Islam with something other than force.

At the same time, even greater powers of search and surveillance may be enacted. There also is talk of legislation that would change the historical prohibition in the United States against the military enforcing the laws of the land. The founders of America understood the threats to democracy posed by stationing full-time soldiers on the streets. Later legislation made clear that Congress understood the difference between protecting the nation from foreign attacks and policing our neighborhoods. Short of martial law, such military policing would be a mistake of enormous proportions. Instead, the National Guard—ordinary citizens on temporary leave—should be trained and equipped for homeland security operations when local and state law enforcement are not enough. This is the recommendation of the Hart-Rudman Commission.

Remember, too, that there are sunset clauses on about half the provisions of the Patriot Act. To determine whether to keep the provisions, we need an independent, nonpartisan commission, created by private sector foundations, to fund an assessment that determines the benefits of the act, asks whether the right people are targeted, inquires whether the American population is being protected, documents whether current provisions have the national and international support needed to succeed, and presents to the American taxpayer the costs of what we are doing compared with the benefits.

In the longer run, America must systematically reform the FBI along the lines recommended by the 9/11 Commission and begin to resolve the decades-long failure of the FBI and the CIA to fully cooperate. The organizational changes being made to American intelligence agencies are only a small part of the solution. The more important task is to make the FBI and the CIA run better. They cannot any longer be dominated by careerists who carefully try to manage their promotions and secure their retirement benefits. Regular infusions of professionals from spheres outside of the CIA and the FBI are needed. The priority at the FBI and CIA should be to secure higher quality managers, analysts, and agents.

Longer-run vision must cast off failed, supply-side privatizing ideology and use public funds to simultaneously improve both our national security and education systems. The world is experiencing an era of dramatic progress in bioscience, materials science, information technology, and scientific instrumentation. Being in the forefront of these and related fields will help fight terrorism abroad and at home—and create millions of new jobs in the process.

However, conservative privatizers have seriously underfunded public-sector-supported basic scientific research in recent years. As a result, the United States has started to lose its worldwide dominance in critical areas of science and innovation, according to federal and private experts who point to evidence like prizes awarded to Americans and the number of papers in major professional journals. Not surprisingly, the American education system has fallen behind other countries. Following the recommendations of the Hart-Rudman Commission, America consequently needs to double the federal research and development budget and to legislate a National Security, Science, and Education Act to generate sufficient numbers of researchers, engineers, scientists, and teachers in math and science. The act also should serve as a major federal response to soaring higher education tuition costs. Grants, not loans, should be provided to students from middle-class, working-class, and impoverished families.

We also need to follow the recommendation of the Hart-Rudman Commission to reinvest in our public infrastructure and, in the process, eliminate our energy dependency on other nations. To meet this goal, the United States will need an increase in conventional energy production (more deep gas wells, for example); adoption of greater transportation efficiency standards; a graduated tax on carbon emissions; increased reliance on renewable energy sources, such as sun, wind, and water; and renewed research in alternatives, including hydrogen fuel cells. If developed wisely, these energy policies will not only help provide physical security but also economic security, through the creation of millions of jobs for the middle class, workers, and the truly disadvantaged.

Alternative American Middle East Policy

The struggle between America and Islam is not an East-West "clash of civilizations," to use the misleading and unconstructive language of the America government. Instead, the struggle that seriously threatens America is an ideological war *within* Islam. A radical Islamist faction is striking out at moderate Muslims and the West.

The United States first must acknowledge and understand the real nature of the struggle. It is more a battle of ideas than bombs. We are losing that war, as our policies in Iraq and Palestine create more and more antipathy in the Islamic world. To win the war of ideas, policy in Iraq and Palestine needs to be significantly altered. We cannot alter that policy without significant help from our moderate Muslim friends. Ideological and religious counterweights must be found to Osama bin Laden and the radical imams. The counterweights must carry on long after the death of bin Laden, because misdirected American policy has strengthened and morphed al Qaeda and related movements into a hydra.

Within this framework, and with an eye to the foreign and national security policy principles in the preceding section, *Patriotism, Democracy, and Common Sense* sets out alternatives to present policy in Iraq, Afghanistan, Iran, Palestine, and Israel.

Iraq and Afghanistan. Progress in Iraq should be based on withdrawal of Americans, multilateralization, provision of security, satisfaction of basic human needs, creation of grassroots democracy at the village level, and reconstruction of the economy, following the proposals of Ambassador Joseph Wilson in this book.

We have multilateralized Afghanistan. We need to multilateralize more, but the progress on multilateralism to date in Afghanistan at least provides a model for the process in Iraq. The imprimatur of the United Nations is needed in both Afghanistan and Iraq.

Beyond these first-priority countries, American policy needs to internationalize throughout the Middle East. Many benefits can accrue. Internationalization would first and foremost create a policy in the region that reflects a wide international consensus. At one level, giving the United Nations, the European Union, and the Arab League, just to name three major institutions, greater voice in the formulation of U.S. policy in the Middle East might complicate American efforts to bring about change in the region. It would increase the number of political actors that need to be consulted in making political decisions in Iraq and elsewhere in the Middle East. However, opening the process to other institutions would greatly simplify the work of the United States. Having to take seriously views to which we may have only given lip service in the past would require a more nuanced American foreign and national security policy sensitive to the people, history, and culture of each Middle East nation.

The United Nations must take over genuine authority in reconstructing Iraq politically and economically. The United Nations should not accept a scheme in which it tries to clean up the mess made by America while the United States still holds ultimate political control over Iraq. The United States should set a date for withdrawal of American troops *and* companies.

Human needs must be satisfied. People need water, food, access to medicine, access to medical treatment, medical insurance, new hospitals, new schools, provision of other public services, and social security when they are seniors. Reconstruction must be based on action, not political rhetoric. Cash must be infused into the economy to allow people to buy goods. Economic reconstruction in manufacturing, oil production, and services must be financed. Iraq must control the means of production and the oil, not American corporations that make generous campaign contributions.

The United States needs to develop a more open and internationally oriented economic policy in the Middle East that does not merely privilege American firms and business interests. The most egregious example of American war profiteering can be found in Iraq, where contracts were awarded, sometimes without competitive bidding, to large firms that already had close ties to the American government, like Halliburton and Bechtel. At least thirty-two top officials in the American government served as executives or paid consultants to top weapons contractors entering government service. President Eisenhower's warning about the military-industrial complex has been ignored.

The populations of Afghanistan and Iraq must feel that they are safe in their own homes, can ride their bicycles, can walk or drive to where they have to go, and can do what they need to do without fear of bodily harm to themselves or their families. That has been accomplished in Kabul. It hasn't been accomplished in the Afghan countryside. To begin to make any progress in Iraq, we need United Nations Chapter 7–authorized peacekeepers and police trainers.

International institutions need to help Iraq reconstruct its defense and security apparatus. Iraq has a long border to protect. It has enemies who wanted to impose their views on Iraq long before America preemptively chose to do so. Those enemies will be there long after we have departed. Iraq needs a policing operation. It's a difficult country to govern, to say the least.

To the extent that any form of democracy is possible in Iraq, given America's success in uniting Shi'i and Sunnis in their common hatred toward us, we need to begin at the village level, as Ambassador Wilson observes. People in the village want to see the same sort of things that people in American communities want to see. They want to see the trash picked up, the kids going to safe schools, the education system functioning well, and the police working effectively to ensure their safety. The initial trainers in democracy building should be European, not American, and Iraqi trainers should take over as quickly as possible.

Iran. As Roger Owen reminds us in this book, the most important thing to observe about Iran is that it is in the middle of a hugely significant process of mutation from a kind of monolithic Islamic government to a pluralistic Islamic one. This is so important to the global history of the twenty-first century that it must be allowed to continue and to work its way through with the real prospect that this mutation will, over time, lead to a more secular pluralism with religion confined to the place where most people believe religion ought to be, in the mosques but not in the offices of government.

Iranians have to be left alone to work things out for themselves. Unfortunately for them, and for the rest of the world, this not going to be an easy passage. There are the repercussions from the American government's talk about regime change. There is the proximity to Iraq, which means that, if things continue to go wrong in Iraq, they could spill over to Iran.

There is also, of course, the question of Iran's nuclear ambitions. Considerable consensus exists among Iranians that they should get themselves into a position where they could produce a bomb if that seemed vital for national self-defense. They live in a region with several nuclear powers already: Israel, Pakistan, and India. And the obvious lesson to be drawn from the different American policies toward Iraq and North Korea is the need to get quickly to a position where you can produce a bomb at short notice to preempt a potential American attack. America needs to be very, very careful and to develop a multilateral strategy that returns to the old notion of a nuclear-free Middle East. That, of course, raises the difficult problem of Israel's weapons of mass destruction. But solutions, however difficult, are possible, and we now turn to them.

Palestine and Israel. The core of Muslim hatred of America is our presidential leadership failure to create an equitable peace between Palestine and Israel. There is a direct link between security on Main Street America and peace in Palestine-Israel, a reality the American government and mainstream American media fail to communicate. Without a new plan that America facilitates but does not preemptively impose, terrorism against America is likely to continue.

In chapter 17, Chris Toensing, executive director of the Middle East Institute in Washington, D.C., articulates such a plan. It proceeds from several premises.

The first premise is that the fundamental obstacle to peace between Israel and the Palestinians is the Israeli occupation of the West Bank, East Jerusalem, and the Gaza Strip, an occupation which has been in place since the conclusion of the 1967 war.

The second premise is that, in the short to medium term, by far the best hope for a mutually satisfactory peace between Israel and the Palestinians remains the two-state solution, as envisioned by U.N. Security Council Resolution 242, whose language the United States helped to draft in 1967. This resolution and its successive follow-up resolutions proposed a state of Israel inside its pre-1967 borders, recognized by the Palestinians and Israel's Arab neighbors, and a state of Palestine in the West Bank and the Gaza Strip. Jerusalem would be the shared capital of both sides, Israel to the west and Palestine to the east. Israeli settlements in the occupied territories would have to be removed or rendered subject to Palestinian sovereignty.

The third premise is that Israeli policy is rendering achievement of the two-state solution increasingly difficult. Not only did the construction of West Bank settlements proceed at a furious pace during the course of the Oslo peace process of the 1990s, but Israel also constructed a series of bypass roads to link the settlements to Israel proper. Together with Israeli military bases, the settlements and bypass roads have established a lattice of Israeli control over the territory of the West Bank and the Gaza Strip that can be exercised even when Israeli troops are not present in every square meter of that territory. The Israeli government is adding to this lattice of control by building a "security fence." In some places, this "fence" is a complex of barbed wire and ditches; in other places, it is a twenty-five-foot-high, concrete, Berlin-like wall. At first, this wall roughly followed the 1967 armistice line, but subsequent phases of construction have made it encroach deep into the West Bank.

The fourth premise is that Israel and the Palestinians are very unlikely to reach a mutually satisfying peace accord on their own without significant external help. Hopelessness on both sides has created an extremely volatile situation, characterized on both sides by disturbing insensitivity to the suffering of the other.

Based on these premises, the United States must sponsor international intervention in the Israeli-Palestinian conflict in the form of an armed peacekeeping force, ideally dispatched by the United Nations, to be inserted into the occupied territories. This form of international intervention offers the best hope of enforcing the two-state solution relatively quickly, with a minimum of further loss of life on both sides. The peacekeepers would replace the Israeli army, which would withdraw from all of the occupied territories inside the pre-1967 borders of Israel. The peacekeepers should be invested with a political mandate as well as a security mandate.

The political mandate must adhere to a strict timetable set by the United Nations. There must be a peace at the end of the peace process. If such a time-delimited political mandate were firmly endorsed by the international community and backed by facilitating diplomacy (not unilateral dictates) by the United States, then public opinion on both sides could very well support final status negotiations aiming at the establishment of the two-state solution and the resolution of other outstanding issues in the Israeli-Palestinian conflict. Despite the lack of hope on both sides for a negotiated peace today, polls continue to show with great regularity that majorities of both Israelis and Palestinians continue to believe that negotiation is the only way to achieve peace and that the two-state solution is the best vision.

Should the negotiations determine that Israeli settlements were to be removed, U.N. peacekeepers might be required to stay and enforce their removal, as such a removal might be politically impossible for any Israeli government. Should the negotiations determine that Jewish settlements would remain as part of the state of Palestine, U.N. peacekeepers might be required to stay and protect both the settlers and Palestinian civilians from the attacks of extremists on both sides. That function, however, should be turned over to the Palestinian police as soon as possible.

U.N. intervention to ensure independence for East Timor makes for an interesting, if imprecise, comparison to the Palestinian situation today. As with the Palestinians, the world overwhelmingly supported East Timorese self-determination, against the wishes of the occupying power, Indonesia, which at the time was heavily backed by Washington. The United States and Australia both resisted deployment of an international force to safeguard East Timorese independence because Indonesia did not accept it, the same reason that is always adduced for the American refusal to back proposals for an international presence in the occupied territories. Finally, though, reports from East Timor became so grim that the United States abruptly informed B. J. Habibie's government that aid was suspended. Three days later Jakarta relented, and today U.N. peacekeepers have successfully overseen East Timor's transition to statehood. The keys to the success of the East Timorese experiment were the very strict timetable and the clearly defined political goals.

American policy should support the rapid deployment of such a peacekeeping force in the occupied territories. The United States should not assume the task of peacekeeping itself. American intervention would have scant credibility among Palestinians, Arabs, and the international community.

However it comes about, any kind of peace settlement has to include a substantial component of economic aid from the United States and the international community. Large-scale economic aid is the most practical way to deal with the refugee issue. Most of the Palestinian refugees in the Arab world, particularly in Jordan, are very well integrated into the economy and even into politics. It is unlikely that they would want to come back. The same goes for the Palestinians living in Europe and America.

The refugees who will need to be resettled are many of those living in the occupied territories and those living in Lebanon. Lebanon has a horrible history of dealing with Palestinian refugees. Lebanese law forbids Palestinians from holding seventy kinds of jobs. This law essentially consigns Palestinians born in Lebanon to lives of menial labor or attempts to get out by any means they can find. Those refugees will need to be resettled in the course of a comprehensive peace settlement. The most logical course of action would be to resettle them in the territory of the future Palestinian state. That will require significant resources.

The economic codependency that once existed between Israelis and Palestinians has now gravely eroded, as Chris Toensing documents. Israel formerly relied upon Palestinian labor, particularly in such fields as construction, and Palestinians relied upon those jobs for their income. Those jobs, by Israeli state policy, have now been filled mostly by immigrants from South Asia, Southeast Asia, and Southeastern Europe. Even after peace breaks out, the new Palestinian areas will need substantial foreign aid and foreign investment to create job opportunities. Some of that will have to come from the Palestinian diaspora. Some of it will have to come from other places in the Arab world and some from the West.

Nowhere is the need for a humane and equitable American foreign aid program based on seven tenths of 1 percent of America's gross domestic product more pressing than in creation and development of the Palestinian state.

America, of course, has a very daunting political environment for the discussion of sane solutions. Conservatives do not want to do anything to jeopardize the Christian-right vote, Christian-right campaign contributions, a share of the Jewish vote, and Jewish campaign contributions. Democrats are equally reluctant to jeopardize the Jewish vote and Jewish campaign contributions.

However, most people in the American Jewish community do not feel represented by the major organizations that claim to represent their interests in Washington. The leaders of those organizations stake out positions considerably to the right of the consensus among the American Jewish community.

Similarly, the Christian right is more extreme in its views toward the Israeli-Palestinian conflict than anything but a small minority of the American Jewish community. What is the basis of the position of American Christian conservatives? Here is one interpretation, by George Monbiot:

> In the United States, several million people have succumbed to an extraordinary delusion. In the 19th century, two immigrant preachers cobbled together a series of unrelated passages from the Bible to create what appears to be a consistent narrative: Jesus will return to Earth when certain preconditions have been met. The first of these was the establishment of a state of Israel. The next involves Israel's occupation of the rest of its "biblical lands" (most of the Middle East), and the rebuilding of the Third Temple on the site now occupied by the Dome of the Rock and al-Aqsa mosques. The legions of the antichrist will then be deployed against Israel, and their war will lead to a final showdown in the valley of Armageddon. The Jews will either burn or convert to Christianity, and the Messiah will return to Earth.

Monbiot claims that perhaps 15 percent of American voters belong to churches or movements that subscribe to these teachings. They are a major political constituency that represents a significant proportion of the conservative core vote. For these people, aggression to secure the Holy Land is a personal, religious issue, not a remote foreign policy.

But the radical right does not have an unbreakable grip on public opinion when it comes to the Israeli-Palestinian conflict, and certainly not on American Jewish opinion, which supports a two-state solution and is mostly antagonistic to the settlements. To better inform American public opinion on alternatives like the plan here, a major campaign is needed to address the typically shallow and deficient reporting of the Middle East in mainstream American media. A reform movement would do well to build on new websites like Electronic Iraq.

Alternative Economic Policy

Following American public opinion in national polls, alternative economic policy needs to rescind the recent tax cuts for the rich and legislate demand-side tax cuts for the middle class, workers, and the truly disadvantaged—all of whom need a Fair Economic Deal. The Deal should provide average Americans economic security against the class warfare of the rich, just as they need physical security against terrorists and criminals. Tax cuts for average Americans should be complemented by increased federal support to students seeking postsecondary education and by demand-side investments in public infrastructure, national security, the reconstruction of the inner city, and new high tech sectors, including alternative energy. As a result, millions of public and private sector jobs will be created. A federal revenue sharing program must stop the financial hemorrhaging of state and local government. The public sector must finance sound Social Security and Medicare systems, while a new National Medical Defense system should ensure that everyone has health insurance. To stabilize America's international financial position, we need to rethink our present commitment to the free-trade system.

What Do the People Say? In recent polls, 88 percent of Americans believed the budget deficit is a "serious" or "very serious" problem. Some 58 percent thought tax cuts should be targeted to middle-income and low-income people, and 40 percent more thought taxes should be distributed equally for all income brackets. That means 98 percent of the people disagreed with tax cuts going mostly to the wealthy. Some 67 percent of the American people in an ABC News-*Washington Post* poll preferred to have more spending on needs like education and health care, rather than on tax cuts for the rich. Three times as many Americans say they want to be in a labor union than are in a union. Some 64 percent said it is the federal government's responsibility to make sure all Americans have health insurance. More than half said the government should create a plan to cover everyone, even if it requires a tax increase on them. Polls also have shown public opinion support for financially sound Social Security and Medicare systems and rejection of privatization.

Rescind Tax Cuts for the Rich. Following these priorities of average citizens instead of the agenda of the ruling class, alternative economic policy needs to rescind tax cuts for the rich and reduce taxes for the middle class, workers, and the poor.

Recession of tax cuts for the rich should be based on precedents from the 1980s, when many such tax cuts were rescinded after average Americans were fully informed of the negative impact on them. After rescission, the longer-run goal should be to reduce welfare for corporations, what Kevin Phillips in his foreword calls the "socialization of economic risk" for the ruling classes. With an eye to Thomas Jefferson's warning against the antidemocratic "aristocracy of our moneyed corporations," the United States needs to return corporate taxes to the levels in force during the Eisenhower administration. We also need to increase the top marginal tax rate for the super-rich to about 50 percent. This would still be far below the top marginal income tax rate of 91 percent during the Eisenhower administration.

Repealing the tax cuts given to the super-rich would return more than $85 billion per year from the richest 5 percent of the population. Returning to corporate tax rates in force during the Eisenhower administration could increase tax revenues by roughly $110 billion more per year. Returning to a 50 percent top marginal income tax rate far below the top rate in the Eisenhower administration could capture as much as $90 billion more per year from the richest 2 percent of the population.

At the same time, we should provide tax cuts to the 150 million hard-working workers who are struggling because they can't afford to buy all they need. Millionaires don't need additional spending money. Workers, middle-class Americans, and the poor do. Their spending will stimulate the economy more effectively, help businesses, and be more fair to the Americans who need fairness the most. There is ample economic evidence that putting money in the pockets of average Americans stimulates the economy much more than further lining the pockets of the rich.

Through these tax costs, the overall economic vision of America needs to return to the demand side and to the robust, full-employment economy that characterized much of the 1990s. A demand-side policy should extend unemployment assistance to the jobless and raise the minimum wage. A living wage is a very important way to assure that lower-income American households have adequate resources. Likewise, the earned income tax credit is a proven, effective model for fighting poverty. It should be protected and expanded. We also need to reverse policies that have made it increasingly difficult for unions to organize in the private sector.

Economic Security: Protection from the Ruling Classes. But demand-side strategies are only part of alternative economic policies. Just as average citizens need physical security to protect them from terrorists and criminals, so they need economic security to protect them from the class warfare launched in America by the rich.

As Jeff Faux observes, it has become a cliché in America that workers must adjust to being churned through many companies, none of which will provide a secure working life. As a result, most workers are in constant anxiety about their economic condition, as companies under pressure from brutally competitive markets abandon responsibility for health care, pensions, and job security.

In addition to unemployment, the American economy contains a great deal of underemployment among wage earners and middle-class citizens. Many wage-earning and middle-class families need two people working to make ends meet. Today, there are almost five million Americans who are working part-time but who need full-time employment. Many are working in low-skilled, dead-end jobs. Many family providers have zero health coverage. The poor always have been worried about decent child care, affordable housing, and enough money to send their kids to college. But today most wage-earning and middle-class families have similar worries.

A Fair Economic Deal. To address the need for economic security, a Fair Economic Deal should be launched that serves a broad middle-class, working-class, and lower-class constituency. The constituency should recapture some of the national mood that existed after World War II, when Americans sought to build a more inclusive, equitable society, one in which everyone had a fair chance of making it.

What story or message might update that post–World War II American feeling and build the new economic alliance for the twenty-first century? Here are some words around which to rally, building on the suggestions of Jeff Faux:

You, the average citizen, are not alone in your search for a safe niche in this I-win-you-lose world. The very rich have profited at the expense of the families of salaried and working people of America. It is not fair for the rich to get richer at the expense of the rest of us. Power has shifted so significantly toward those at the top of the income and wealth pyramid that the majority of Americans who are struggling must mobilize to force the rich and the elites back to the bargaining table. We must close the income, wage, and job gaps.

Americans deserve a higher quality of life. We must invest in the human capital of all of our citizens, so all can deal successfully with technological change and the global economy. The role of the federal government must be to make investments that serve the interests of the salaried and working classes, along with the poor.

The need for a Fair Economic Deal and complementary alternative policies must be better communicated to the American people in practical, commonsense ways. We need more efforts to "personalize" the impact on the daily lives of ordinary Americans of the type of policy choices discussed in this chapter and to bring to life the federal disinvestment that our citizens face if the nation does not change course.

Public Infrastructure Creation and Economic Klondikes. Historically, the public sector has been pivotal for ensuring that economic growth benefits all, services are provided to all who need them, and new jobs are created. Public-sector job stimulation is a countercyclical policy. But the public sector also is the generator of medium- and long-term seed capital that forges the direction the economy takes and creates millions of jobs in the process.

Public infrastructure investment has shaped America's future. Early on, public investment built canals and subsidized the railroads to settle the West. Government financed the first assembly lines. President Eisenhower began building the interstate highway system in the 1950s. Federal investments developed the jet engine, began the exploration of space, and helped develop silicon chips, the computer, and the Internet.

Each of these public sector investment programs created jobs and businesses in the short term. In the long run, they spun off technological advances that became what economist Robert Heilbroner calls economic "Klondikes"—massive veins of private investment opportunities that have been the building blocks of American prosperity.

Other nations have invested hundreds of billions in public-sector infrastructure over recent years, such as the high-speed rail systems in France and parallel investments in Germany and Japan. Yet American public-sector infrastructure investment has declined precipitously under supply-side ideology, beginning in the 1980s under President Reagan. Today, the United States is the only major industrial society not expanding its public infrastructure.

On September 11 and thereafter, America has paid the price—through, for example, a woeful airport security system unprepared for biological, chemical, and nuclear attacks. Here is a starting point for public investments that both create meaningful jobs for unemployed or underemployed Americans and address an urgent national need. A related public-sector, job-creating investment is development of a high-speed train system for the United States. A recent *USA Today* poll found that 47 percent of plane travelers thought flying the most stressful form of transport, but only 2 percent of train passengers found that travel was stressful. Yet our public rail system has been allowed to atrophy by our leaders.

Nowhere is public infrastructure more in need of repair and reinvestment than in America's cities and inner cities. A commitment to redevelop inner cities also represents the best way to bridge the growing racial and digital divides. Schools are in massive need of repairs. We need computer-smart urban mass-transit systems. The National Housing Act of the 1930s, with its commitment to housing as a human right, has been abused by supply-siders. That policy failure can be reversed by new public investment to repair and build housing for the poor, with the work done by nonprofit community development corporations and YouthBuild USA, which can employ thousands.

To complement physical inner-city infrastructure development, the public sector needs to invest in human capital. For example, as Carnegie Corporation reports have shown, a key to inner-city school reform is more and better-trained teachers, assisted by youth-development workers. Hundreds of thousands of additional, well-trained preschool and after-school professionals are needed.

Note, too, that it is difficult to outsource public infrastructure and public service jobs.

A federal seed-capital commitment to forge economic growth in new directions should, as well, create new jobs in a continuously evolving host of high-tech sectors—including enhanced electronic digital imaging (needed by our intelligence agencies, as discussed above), ceramics, advanced composition sensors, photonics, artificial intelligence, robotics (which the Japanese are using to help care for their large senior population), advanced computer-assisted manufacturing, biotechnology, and research and development to find cures for cancer, Parkinson's disease, AIDS, other serious diseases, and the common cold.

The politics of the Middle East could change significantly if the United States became serious about developing electric cars and sources of energy other than petroleum. Even the Pentagon has admitted the threats posed by global warming, and America is in desperate need of a real environmental protection program. With the aging of baby boomers, there is a pressing need for creative advances in institutional and in-home health care. Public seed capital and leadership would address these significant American dilemmas, while creating millions of meaningful jobs for the middle class, working class, and the disadvantaged.

Federal seed capital job creation must be matched by a federal system of job training and human capital investment. It is an epic scandal that America has no such system. The media say nothing. As part of reform, federal aid to higher education must respond to rapidly rising college tuition costs. People who already have graduated and have lost jobs need to be retrained for newly emerging opportunities.

Local Government, Social Security, Medicare, and National Medical Defense. The federal government needs to enact a program of revenue sharing, and perhaps also loan guarantees, to stop the current, destructive hemorrhaging of state and local public services. The hemorrhaging has been made worse by stealth conservative block grant schemes that place greater and greater burdens on localities. We must permit local governments to maintain their services and to avoid regressive tax increases. Reduced services and regressive tax increases both tend to undermine the functioning of the economy as a whole.

The radical right wants eventual privatization of the cash flows associated with both Social Security and Medicare. The plan is a bit like the Cheshire cat, except that it's not smiling. Sometimes you can see it, and sometimes you can't, depending on whether it is politically expedient and when the next election will occur. But it is essential that we stop movement toward privatization of Social Security and Medicare, on the merits of those two programs alone. Our elderly will continue to be with us, of course, and their numbers will continue to increase. So the only real issue here is whether we provide for them in a way that is fair to them.

Universal health coverage needs to be enacted as a human right. Some 44 million Americans don't have health insurance. But health insurance also must be framed as a response to September 11, as the best way to combat biological warfare. After all, people without health insurance tend to delay trips to the doctor or the emergency room. Yet if we want to prevent an outbreak of smallpox, or anything worse, as a result of bioterrorism, we need people to get medical attention right away. Micah Sifry makes this observation in chapter 37. As it is, most hospitals in major American cities go on lockdown on any number of nights a week. They refuse all emergencies because they already are beyond capacity. That is a crisis that no one is talking about, but it could make a huge difference if we try to resolve it now.

Health reform, then, should be packaged not as "universal heath care" or "single payer." We should call it National Medical Defense. For short, we might call it "Star Wards," as Sifry suggests. A National Medical Defense system must crack down on drug prices and health maintenance organization administrative costs.

Stabilizing America's International Financial Position. To stabilize our international financial position, we need a new set of institutions that permit our exports to grow rapidly. That will mean giving up claims to international debt payments in much of Africa and Latin American countries like Argentina and Brazil.

We may even have to rethink our commitment to the free-trade system. If we realistically assess the cost, and if it turns out that we cannot find a way to reconcile a commitment to full employment, America may need to choose full employment over free trade, as a last resort. While other countries eagerly encourage American multinational corporations to relocate, they fiercely protect their own domestic industries, primarily through the use of tariffs—taxes on imported goods—and through the strict regulation of imported labor. America should at least debate the merits of doing the same, especially when our policies help support dictatorships like communist China.

Alternative Domestic Policy

The prime beneficiaries of a Fair Economic Deal that includes greatly improved job security, education security, health care security and Social Security are those other than the rich. The middle class is needed to win elections, and so a Fair Economic Deal must be especially in sync with its priorities. While benefiting mightily from a Fair Economic Deal, working people and the truly disadvantaged, especially those living in inner cities and aging suburbs, have additional needs. *Patriotism, Democracy and Common Sense* looks at those needs.

The key to policy for the poor and workers, virtually unreported in mainstream corporate media, is that we already know a lot about what works, enough to create a domestic policy that is supported by public opinion and that also will help project a more successful American foreign policy.

What Works. Recent public policy and a gullible mainstream media have helped promote the notion that little works for the truly disadvantaged.

That is not true. Since the Kerner Riot Commission and Eisenhower Violence Commission of the 1960s, we have learned a great deal about what doesn't work and what does work, based on scientific studies and careful evaluations. It therefore would make sense to stop doing what doesn't work and start investing in what does work, at "a scale equal to the dimensions of the problem," to quote the Kerner Commission.

Common sense coincides with the conclusions of most experts that we need a continuum of interventions from early childhood through adulthood. Here are just a few examples.

Building on some of the evaluations described earlier, a recent state-by-state study by the RAND Corporation demonstrated that access to preschool increases student achievement, especially in impoverished communities. The benefits that accrue to a child who has preschool include less involvement in crime, less involvement in drugs, less involvement in teen pregnancy, more likelihood to complete school, and more likelihood to become economically independent. So preschool makes economic sense. Head Start and Early Start need to be made available to all eligible poor kids.

For inner city public school children beginning in kindergarten, the *Turning Points* studies of the Carnegie Council and researchers like Joy Dryfoos have shown that, to successfully replicate what works, we need to

- Improve teacher training
- Reduce classroom size
- Restructure academic programs to focus on a core of common knowledge and skills
- Place policy for each inner-city school in the hands of a local management team, led by the principal and including teachers, parents, counselors, and other school staff
- Dramatically increase the involvement of and assistance to inner-city parents
- Provide focused intervention by a mental health team for children with emotional, behavioral, or academic problems
- Create safe environments during the school day
- Create full-service community schools, in which nonprofit organizations are located in the building to provide health, family, community, cultural, and recreational initiatives and to ensure security

In addition, after-school safe havens have proven their worth, based on evaluations by Columbia University, Public-Private Ventures, the Eisenhower Foundation, and several others. Evolving from the formative Carnegie Corporation report, *A Matter of Time* in 1992, safe havens have become known as places where kids can go after school for help with their homework, snacks, social support, and discipline from adult and "near peer" role models.

For high schoolers, a good example of success is the Ford Foundation–initiated Quantum Opportunities program, based on computer learning. Well-trained adult mentors work one-on-one with inner-city high school youth, keeping them on track to good grades and high school completion, working out ways to earn money in the summer, and providing venues for college education, if youth so choose. A key to success is sufficient investment per youth, based on recent evaluations.

When young people do drop out of high school, we know that there are alternatives to the failed, supply-side Job Training Partnership Act that can get them back on track. These are "training first" initiatives, not "work first." Based on decades of evaluations, the Great Society Job Corps program is perhaps the best example of successful job training for youth. Other examples that have had positive evaluations include YouthBuild USA nationally, the Argus Learning for Living Center in the South Bronx, and the Center for Employment and Training in San Jose, California.

Many of the jobs for people who receive training first can be generated by community development corporations in the private nonprofit sector. Community development corporations were the brainchild of Robert Kennedy's Mobilization for Youth in the late 1960s. Initially, there were ten such community development corporations. Now there are thousands.

The capital for community development corporations often can be secured via community-based banking. Here one model is the South Shore Bank in Chicago. Many banks will redline and will not bother with branches in the inner city. When they do, typically a bank will use the savings of inner-city residents to make investments outside of the neighborhood. South Shore does just the opposite. It uses the savings of the poor to reinvest in the inner-city neighborhoods where the poor live. And South Shore still makes a profit. Yet there is no interest by the federal government in replicating this stellar model to scale and no investigative reporting by the media to expose the failure.

Community-based banking investments in inner-city neighborhoods can be secured through community-based, problem-oriented policing—getting officers out of their cruisers and into foot patrols. They work shoulder-to-shoulder with citizen groups to focus on specific neighborhood problems and solve them with sensitive efficiency. In some variations, officers mentor youth. The Police Executive Research Forum and other institutions have undertaken evaluations which have yielded positive outcomes. More community support is generated than with racist, "zero-tolerance" policing methods.

Multiple Solutions. These examples of what works interrelate, or can be made to interrelate, through a wise national policy for the inner city and the truly disadvantaged. For example, community-based, problem-oriented policing can help secure a neighborhood. The security can help encourage community-based banking. Community-based banking can provide capital for community development corporations. Community development corporations can invest that capital in ways that generate good jobs for local residents. Inner-city youth can qualify for those jobs if they have been in job training like Job Corps, YouthBuild USA, Argus, and the Center for Employment and Training. Similarly, inner-city youth can stay in high school if they have been involved in human capital investments like Quantum Opportunities. They can get that far if they have been in full service community schools and after-school safe havens. And they can get that far if they have been in Head Start/Early Start preschool.

In sum, when you ask what works based on scientific studies and careful evaluations, you see what Lisbeth Schorr, at the Harvard University School of Public Health, calls "multiple solutions to multiple problems." The solutions are not single, narrow, and categorical. The solutions are creative, comprehensive, and interdependent. Yet there is almost a total absence of federal government interest in and mainstream media investigative reporting on the potential of such multiple solutions.

National Policy. Elsewhere, the Eisenhower Foundation has estimated that a national policy for the truly disadvantaged that is based on what works, begins to replicate multiple solutions to scale, and has a national impact would have an initial annual cost that is less than the $87 billion supplemental appropriation for Iraq that was approved not long ago. As part of a Fair Economic Deal, such a national policy would, first and foremost, be based on replicating inner-city public school and job training successes—and then on generating jobs through investment in America's public infrastructure, significant enhancement of transportation and health facilities to improve national security, research and development investment in high-tech industries, reconstruction of inner city housing, and reconstruction of inner city schools.

This priority on education and job training means scrapping present "welfare reform." We need to start over. Instead of political misleads that claim to measure success in terms of reduced caseloads, we need to be more honest and measure success in terms of the original goal of welfare: reducing poverty. Poverty should be defined following recent recommendations by the National Research Council and the "self-sufficiency standard" created by Diana Pearce. Local programs that reduce poverty, so defined, should be rewarded. Reformed "welfare reform" needs to combine job training, quality job creation, job placement, job retention, health insurance, high-quality child care, and high-quality transportation services.

To complement a policy of full employment and public education reform to scale, we need racial and criminal justice reform. New policy should begin with

- Replication to scale of positively evaluated models of school integration (as in St. Louis) and housing integration (like the Gatreaux program begun in Chicago)
- Continuation of affirmative action (justified by RAND Corporation and other studies that have measured success)
- Creation of a presidential commission to review the racial-and-gender-biased "concrete ceiling" hiring practices of Wall Street and major corporations, followed by a presidential commitment to break through that ceiling
- Elimination of the racial disparity in drug sentencing
- Reallocation of spending by the failed "war on drugs" from 70 percent law enforcement and 30 percent treatment to a ratio closer to 50-50

Federal and local policy should significantly shift away from prison building and toward cheaper, more effective treatment alternatives in the community, following existing, taxpayer-approved models in, for example, the state of Arizona. Interrelated models of success like the national Delancey Street program for the reintegration of ex-offenders, drug courts, and community courts should be replicated to scale. A National Sentencing and Drug Treatment Commission should be formed to review federal and state sentencing practices, the impact of recent sentencing trends on the fiscal health and public responsibilities of state and federal governments, the impact on serious crime, and the feasibility of a broad range of alternatives. The commission should gather evidence on promising alternatives, including innovations in other nations that have kept their levels of incarceration and crime low by American standards.

Foundations should increase funding to national and local nonprofit organizations and other citizens groups to educate the citizenry on the need for state-based and local-based initiatives against firearms; local alliances between city residents and more conservative "soccer mom" suburbanites in the wake of Columbine-type killings of youth in our schools; litigation against firearms manufacturers; a national handgun licensing system; a federal ban on Saturday night specials; and federal regulation of firearms as consumer products.

Public Opinion. There is considerable public opinion support for this domestic and inner city agenda. For example, the need for new employment policies is high in every poll on the concerns of citizens. A majority of eligible voters favors job training, college student aid, and Head Start. Some 71 percent say educational improvement should focus on reforming existing public school systems, and 75 percent favor improving public schools over providing vouchers. About 70 percent are willing to pay more in taxes if the money went to education, and 84 percent would pay more in taxes if the money went specifically to raising teachers' salaries, reducing class size, fixing run-down schools, improving security, and putting more computers in classrooms. The public is largely supportive of alternative sentencing, particularly for nonviolent criminals, and has a strong commitment to treatment and rehabilitation. Studies show that people appreciate the advantages of offering alternative sentencing options and that they believe it creates a fair, more just system, one which allows judges to evaluate each offender individually.

Domestic Policy as a Tool for Foreign Policy. This domestic policy needs to be framed not just as replicating what works "to a scale equal to the dimension of the problem" as envisioned by the Kerner Riot Commission but also as a way of carrying out the recommendations of the 9/11 Commission, by showing the world that America can fulfill its promise and therefore is a nation to trust, respect, and emulate.

Alternative Media Policy

Until recently, conventional wisdom has been that, while media are important to our democracy, the public cannot be engaged in reform because the issues are too abstract.

However, during the last several years, a movement to democratize the media has emerged. It began with corporate power and media ownership. The chairman of the Federal Communications Commission sought federal rule changes to allow a single network to control more television stations around the country. The rule changes also sought to allow a single media company to control more of a local media market. A coalition of strange bedfellows—from the National Rifle Association and William Safire to MoveOn.org and Noam Chomsky—lobbied against the changes, and a federal appeals court ordered the FCC to reconsider the rules. This was a tremendous victory for media diversity and democracy. The media reform movement is here to stay. We are at a period of time comparable to the early twentieth century, when Republican President Teddy Roosevelt attacked the power, corruption, and greed of huge corporations.

Led by the nonprofit organization Free Press, and its website, MediaReform.org, the emerging movement has recognized, as did the conservatives after the defeat of Barry Goldwater in 1964, that reform must be based on a balance between media control and media policy. Media policy advocacy needs to evolve from high-tech models like MoveOn.org in the United States and *OhMyNews* in South Korea as well as from person-to-person models like Jim Hightower's Rolling Thunder Down-Home Democracy Tour.

Media Control. In terms of control, the need is for new radio networks to counter false claims by the far right. We also need more television programs like *NOW with Bill Moyers* and new journalism that provides democratic alternatives to the right-wing ideology of people like Rush Limbaugh and Gordon Liddy, the conservative ideology of Fox News and Clear Channel radio, and the content of mainstream journalism.

As described in this book, a premiere model for alternative media is the national, daily Pacifica network grassroots news program hosted by Amy Goodman, *Democracy Now.* After September 11, *Democracy Now* became a television radio show, broadcasting on over 150 stations around the country. *Democracy Now* is expanding the number of National Public Radio stations which carry it and broadcasting on public-access television, a much-underutilized resource. Presently, people in a community often don't even know that they have public access. The Pacifica network is proceeding from community to community and reminding people that they have these channels. Media activists lobby their city councils, and council members see the channels written into local agreements. As a result, the councils become energized. This energy needs to be promoted, so that public access becomes a cornerstone for people's media.

Media Policy. In terms of media policy reform, here is a partial list of initiatives, building on the recommendations of Robert McChesney and John Nichols in chapter 31:

- Federal antitrust policy must be reassessed. Because competition and diversity have been under assault for more than two decades, the impact of media mergers on democracy needs to be closely examined. Caps on media ownership, appropriate for a democracy, should continue to be advocated, building on the opposition to the FCC ownership rulings of recent years.

- Congress should roll back the number of radio stations a single corporation can own. Advocacy is needed for Congress to pass legislation prohibiting media cross-ownership and vertical integration. There are tremendous economic benefits to media conglomerations, but they accrue almost entirely to the media owners. The public loses out.
- Citizen advocates must continue to reinvigorate the regulatory process. As FCC commissioner Michael J. Copps has observed, "Most people do not even know that they can challenge the renewal of a local radio or television station if they believe that the station is not living up to its obligation due to a lack of local coverage, a lack of diversity, excessive indecency and violence, or other concerns important to the community."
- Foundations need to greatly expand media training to senior staff of national and local nonprofit organizations, including training for how to be effective on television and funding for communications directors.
- Nonprofit organizations must be given access to low-power FM radio station licenses. Expansion of access was promised several years ago, but a backroom deal in Congress reneged on that promise. Tax incentives should be created to aid in the development of new, community-based, noncommercial broadcasting outlets.
- Foundations must provide much greater support to schools on the cutting edge of media reform, like the Columbia School of Journalism, to produce better trained, more informed journalists and to support more widespread dissemination of leading journals, such as the Columbia Journalism Review.
- A new wave of grassroots advocacy is needed to fight for dramatic expansion of public broadcast funding. Only about 15 percent of funding for public radio and television comes from federal subsidies. What funding does come from Congress is subject to great political pressures. Public broadcasting at the federal and state levels has the potential to provide a model of quality journalism and diversified cultural programming. But that won't happen if cash-starved Public Broadcasting System and National Public Radio outlets are required, as some propose, to rely on the same sort of offensive thirty-second spot advertising that dominates commercial broadcasting.
- Broadcasters must be forced to give candidates free air time. Senators John McCain and Russell Feingold, the authors of the only meaningful campaign-finance reform legislation of the past decade, have proposed such a requirement. The link between campaign-finance reform and media reform must be communicated to the public and acted upon. Media conglomerates now are among the most powerful lobbyists against both campaign-finance reform and media reform. The system works for them, but fails the rest of us.
- Campaigns must be organized to block international trade deals that allow media conglomerates to impose their will on the citizens of the United States

and other countries. Media firms now are lobbying the World Trade Organization and other multilateral organizations to accept a system of trade sanctions against countries that subsidize public broadcasting, limit foreign ownership of media systems, or establish local content standards designed to protect national and regional cultures. They want similar assaults on regulation inserted into the proposed Free Trade Area of the Americas. Congress should not pass trade agreements that undermine its ability to aid public broadcasting, but should protect media diversity and competition.

- Policies that affect the Internet, such as copyright and access, must carefully be scrutinized. Reforms must be enacted that prevent corporate monopoly control. It is important to recognize that already three corporations control about half of the web's traffic patterns.
- The media-reform movement must, on a broader scale, address what ails existing media. Top-heavy with white, middle-class males, television news departments and major newspapers remain beholden to official sources. Their obsessive focus on "if it bleeds, it leads" crime coverage, entertainment "news," and celebrity trials leaves no room to cover the thousands of programs that work at the neighborhood level and the real issues that affect families, communities, and whole classes of people. Coverage of minority communities, women, working people, rural folks, youth, seniors, and just about everyone else who doesn't live in a handful of ZIP codes in New York, Washington, and Los Angeles is badly warped, or almost nonexistent, and reinforces conservative ideology that helps shape public discourse and public policy.
- Thousands of grassroots, community-based, inner-city nonprofit organizations need to become a coordinated force, based on their being trained in communications and media. Grassroots nonprofits need to be funded by foundations to bring on their own communications directors (few have them) and to generate strategic communications plans. Inner-city groups should learn to communicate to the public what their own programs are about and, through this public education, help raise funds and become more self-sufficient.

The MoveOn.org Model. MoveOn.org illustrates the kind of dynamic, courageous, financially self-sufficient organization that can both advocate for these kinds of policy reforms and successfully fight for more control of media by those proposing alternatives to present policy.

MoveOn.org has over two million members. They propose issue priorities and strategies via Action Forum software. The most strongly supported issues rise to the top through democratic voting processes, not unilateral dictates, and these become MoveOn's organizational, action, and advocacy priorities.

Many of MoveOn's experiments are being morphed. Other organizations, such as America Votes, America Coming Together, the Media Fund, and the Thunder

Road Group, are innovating on MoveOn's themes. For example, during the 2004 presidential primaries, there was experimentation with a whole array of online organizing techniques that could change the way campaigns run in the future. Some campaigns had online groups of designers and content producers who essentially were unofficial media teams. They created posters, flyers, and many other things—again in a very decentralized kind of way and in support of alternative policies like those in *Patriotism, Democracy, and Common Sense.*

Similarly, during the 2004 general election, coalitions of advocacy organizations, including MoveOn, raised funds via the Internet for media ads, then created the ads, aired them in targeted states, led get-out-the-vote campaigns, undertook polling research, and organized rapid-response teams on key issues. We need more and more of such coalitions to harness energy and make an impact. We need to refine strategic online advocacy to mobilize people, send petitions, pressure leaders, and organize events.

Whether focused on specific campaigns for political office or on issue advocacy outside political campaigns, MoveOn has pioneered in identifying and sharing with wide audiences the misinformation that is spread by officeholders pursuing failed policies as well as the conservative ideology machine and right-wing media who defend those policies. For example, as Eli Pariser discusses in chapter 32, MoveOn has begun the Daily Mislead (www.mislead.org), which e-mails its members each day, by noon, false information emanating from the executive branch of government.

Similarly, MoveOn is developing a network that allows people to self-organize around media inaccuracies. Using volunteers, MoveOn seeks to keep the extreme right honest by allowing people to report egregious statements that are read and heard in the mainstream media, verify them through a volunteer infrastructure, and then draw on a network of experts who can contact the journalists involved. At the same time, grassroots contingents can complain locally about biased and misleading commentary.

MoveOn also has created Fox Watch (www.AmericanPolitics.com/foxwatch), which utilizes thousands of Americans who monitor the distortions, fabrications, and propaganda of Fox News. Does that mean that Fox News is going to change? No. But what may be possible over the next few years is to make Fox increasingly seen as simply an ideological, knee-jerk network rather than a credible source of mainstream news.

Mobile Phone Technology. In the future, the potential exists for better interfacing MoveOn.org's Internet-based advocacy with mobile phone technology, as explained in these pages by Howard Rheingold. The kinds of alternative foreign policies set forth in *Patriotism, Democracy, and Common Sense* were advocated in demonstrations against the Iraq war using the mobile phones to organize quickly and well. The BBC set up a web site in which people could, from their telephones, take pictures of the huge demonstrations in London and elsewhere. The photos were sent to the BBC, which then posted them. This was, literally, street-level reporting, the beginning of an alternative to CNN.

Mobile phone technology interfaced with the Internet has even more potential in get-out-the-vote strategies and tactics. For example, in the election in Korea not long ago, the man who eventually won, now President Roh, was behind in the polls a few days before the vote. Roh's supporters turned to *OhMyNews*, a kind of citizen news. People submit stories through the Internet and then vote on which stories are placed prominently. It is very popular with the young cyber-generation, who were demonstrating against the American presence in Korea. Using *Ohmynews*, the Internet, and text messaging, they organized a get-out-the-vote surge in the last couple of days that made the difference. The organizers were the first people the new president thanked after he was elected.

The Korean example suggests that, to better communicate alternatives to present policy, we in America need to facilitate a multitude of citizen journalist-activists. Funded by foundations, local and national nonprofit institutions need to train citizens in investigative journalism, fact checking, blogging technology, mobile phone technology linked to the Internet, the *OhMyNews* model, collective action, the organization of peace demonstrations, the organization of election campaigns, and the implementation of get-out-the-vote drives for citizens who support alternative policies. How-to handbooks for best practices need development and electronic distribution. More services are necessary that enable more people to form groups online. Nationwide, face-to-face workshops need to proliferate and systematically teach people how to use the electronic tools available.

Rolling Thunder. To improve communication among advocates for alternatives, and between them and other citizens, we need not just technology but person-to-person organizing for alternatives at the grassroots. One of the best examples is the Rolling Thunder Down-Home Democracy Tour organized by author, radio talk show host, commentator, and activist Jim Hightower, a contributor to this volume.

The Hightower Rolling Thunder Down-Home Democracy Tour gives people a chance to hold "democracy fests" around the country. They last all day long. Speeches are mercifully brief and accompanied by music. Food is provided by local restaurants and community groups. The citizen groups get people to sign petitions. There is a mobilization tent where people can take a dozen different actions right there, that day. Hightower collects everybody's e-mail addresses and feeds them to organizations like MoveOn.org. There are many fun things to do, including a "dunk-a-lobbyist" booth.

The idea is to get people together, let them rub elbows with each other, let them learn that they have a lot in common, and get them to continue on together. Part of the good news is that they do continue. For example, there are potluck dinners on one side of town, then another side, and then another side. The goal is to keep the discussion building, forging action coalitions at the grassroots level.

Rolling Thunders have been held across the nation. They need to be expanded and made a permanent part of the activist landscape and integrated with similar efforts, like the "Wellstone Camps" begun by the late Senator Paul Wellstone to train activists.

HOW CAN THE PEOPLE MOVE AMERICA FROM FAILURE TO SUCCESS?

Democratic power is not given. It has to be taken, aggressively defended, and retaken when it slips from our hands, for the moneyed powers relentlessly press to gain supremacy and assert their private will over the majority.

By leveling the playing field so that elections are based not on money but on what is best for most Americans, clean-money campaign finance reform and voter's rights reform can help facilitate the alternative policies discussed in this volume.

Clean Money Elections

Arizona and Maine are two of the first six states in the country to enact full public financing of elections, what is called "clean-money" campaign reform. "Clean money" inspires hope. Candidates for state office in the reform states do not have to run for office the way everybody does everywhere else. In order to qualify, they have to raise a fairly large number of small contributions. Once they achieve the number they need, based on the size of their district, they qualify for full public funding. They have to agree to raise no private money and to abide by spending limits. If they are opposed by a candidate who is being funded the traditional way, or if they are being targeted by outside groups spending independently, they can obtain additional matching funds so that they have a level playing field upon which to operate.

In recent elections in Arizona and Maine, fully half of the elected officials from both states ran clean. Three-quarters of the Maine state Senate in 2003-2004 was made up of people who ran clean, and more than half the Maine state House. Nearly half the Arizona House; about one-sixth of the Arizona Senate; the Arizona governor, secretary of state, attorney general, and nearly all the statewide offices in Arizona in 2003-2004 were held by people who ran free of dependence on private money. The opportunity to run a viable campaign without dependence on big donors dramatically opened the process to a more diverse array of candidates. More women are running. More Hispanics and Native Americans are running. There is more competition. There are more contested races. There are more third-party and independent candidates. Both Republicans and Democrats have participated.

The candidates elected with clean money say they feel less beholden to financial interests in office. They are independent, as well, of their own party leadership.

They just don't feel like they owe anybody—except the people who elected them. There is no lobbyist who can put an arm around them and say, "Hey, I hear you have a big campaign debt; let me help retire it for you."

Passing clean money initiatives in more states is very important to eventually passisng them nationally. North Carolina has enacted full public financing of judicial elections, operating on the same idea that we shouldn't have our judges corrupted by the need to raise money. New Mexico has adopted full public financing for its Public Regulation Commission, a statewide body that oversees corporations and utilities, whose officeholders are heavily lobbied by moneyed interests. There are about a half dozen other states close to enacting some version of clean-money reform, though with political scandals involving pay-to-play corruption cropping up continually, there are always new opportunities that can't be predicted. Just think of how Enron and WorldCom suddenly lit a fire under Senator Paul Sarbanes's corporate-reform bill in the summer of 2002. To progress, it is important to be prepared to act quickly when the next big scandal emerges, as it eventually will.

In the 2004 presidential campaign, of course, both the Democratic candidate and the Republican candidate rejected spending limits. This rejection should be used as an organizing vehicle in the future—to oppose the buying of the presidency, generate clean-money campaigns in all states, and follow the example of the United Kingdom, with short campaigns and equal amounts of publicly financed television time for all major presidential candidates.

Voter Democracy

Most Americans believe that voting is a universal right, that we elect based on one person–one vote, that all citizens are equal, that we are governed by the rule of law, that the Supreme Court is not political, and that minority views are protected no matter how abhorrent they are to the majority. But these beliefs currently are myths.

Accordingly, the disenfranchisement in recent elections must be used to launch a more powerful voter democracy movement.

After the voting debacle in 2000, the federal government made many promises—for example, to replace unreliable voting machines, train poll workers, and upgrade voter registration lists. Congress passed a Help America Vote Act. Over $800 million was promised for election improvements in 2004. Yet only a small fraction of that sum was made available. Little progress has been made. Continuing abuses have been well documented.

As the Center for Voting and Democracy (fairvote.org) and others have proposed, the nation needs a federal system with federal standards. After September 11 federal workers began monitoring airport security. We need a comparable system for monitoring election security.

The federal government must invest substantial resources in voting technologies that are truly cutting edge and secure, with open-source software, voter-verified paper trails, and the public interest incorporated without resistance. Local election administration should be led by qualified and properly trained officials and poll workers who are not participating in political campaigns or other partisan activity. A national voter registration system needs to assure that we have clean voter lists. New voters should be automatically registered. Felons who have completed their sentences should be allowed to vote. Federal officials should protect voters, especially the poor and minorities, from intimidation. New federal regulations should reverse the partisan gerrymandering that has made competitive elections to the House of Representatives obsolete. All states and counties should be held to high standards by an entity of the federal government that is immune from political pressure. Nonprofit organizations and the media must upgrade their watchdog roles.

More fundamentally, America must reform its presidential election system. We need direct presidential election by popular vote. If the electoral college cannot be abolished for now, instant runoff voting and proportional representation are the next best options. Instant runoff voting means that, rather than just vote for a single candidate, voters have the option to rank the candidates in order of preference: first choice, second choice, third choice. If a candidate receives a majority of first choices, he or she wins. But if not, the candidate with the fewest votes is eliminated—thus failing to advance to the runoff—and a second round of counting occurs. The process continues until there is a winner.

The other option, proportional representation, allocates electoral votes in proportion to the statewide popular vote, not by the present winner-take-all procedure. President Nixon and President Roosevelt both supported proportional representation. It already is used in most presidential primaries and most legislative races in most established democracies worldwide.

Political Alliance

History teaches that lasting reform must build outside of Washington. The American Revolution didn't begin in Philadelphia in 1776 with the signing of the Declaration of Independence but in earlier years of local rebellion. The civil rights movement didn't begin with Martin Luther King Jr.'s 1963 speech at the Lincoln Memorial but in thousands of southern churches. The maverick spirit of the American Revolution and the civil rights movement is still there—in coffee shops, bars, barber shops, working-class churches, and neighborhood block parties. And in conversations with cab drivers, grocery clerks, nurses, janitors, mechanics, restaurant workers, factory workers, and parents upon whom "welfare reform" has been imposed.

The American ruling class will resist campaign finance and voter democracy reform, but step-by-step persistence is needed, persistence that centers on bringing the middle class, working class, and poor together to vote for a Fair Economic Deal and for the policies that polls already show they favor, as documented on these pages. The targets for a new voting alliance should not be just the few who vote but the hundred-million-plus who haven't been voting, at least in congressional elections, because of disillusion with present American democracy, including youthful voters, minority voters, people in aging suburbs, and professionals in the new exurbs.

Focused on elections at the local, state, and federal level, organizing and advocacy for a new alliance needs to be facilitated by organizations and websites like Alternet.org, America Coming Together, Campaign for America's Future, the Center on Budget and Policy Priorities, CommonDreams.org, the Economic Policy Institute, Electronic Iraq, the Harvard Civil Rights Project, the Media Fund, MediaReform.org, MoveOn.org, The Nation.com, Peace Action.org, People for the American Way, Public Campaign, the Sentencing Project, the Rolling Thunder folks, TomPaine.com, and hundreds of others.

Through such organizing, Americans must be convinced that they have a role to play other than paying taxes. Remembering President Kennedy, we must vote in "the kind of peace that makes life on earth worth living . . . not merely peace for Americans but peace for all men and women, not merely peace in our time but peace for all time."

BIBLIOGRAPHY

Mike Allen, "President Campaigns to Make Patriot Act Permanent," *Washington Post*, April 20, 2004.

Eric Alterman, "Lessons from 1964," chapter 35 in Alan Curtis, editor, *Patriotism, Democracy, and Common Sense* (Lanham, Md.: Rowman & Littlefield, 2004).

Phyllis A. Bennis, "Challenging Empire: The United Nations in a New Internationalism," chapter 9 in Alan Curtis, editor, *Patriotism, Democracy, and Common Sense* (Lanham, Md.: Rowman & Littlefield, 2004).

Alfred Blumstein and Joel Wallman, editors, *The Crime Drop in America* (Cambridge: Cambridge University Press, 2000).

Sophie Body-Gendrot, "America Needs Europe," chapter 8 in Alan Curtis, editor, *Patriotism, Democracy, and Common Sense* (Lanham, Md.: Rowman & Littlefield, 2004).

Julian Borger, "We Are Still All Americans," chapter 20 in Alan Curtis, editor, *Patriotism, Democracy, and Common Sense* (Lanham, Md.: Rowman & Littlefield, 2004).

William G. Bowen and Derek Curtis Bok, *The Shape of the River* (Princeton: Princeton University Press, 1998).

Patrick Boyle, "The Best Program You Can't Afford," *Youth Today*, September 2003.

Keith Bradsher, "China Bars Steps by Hong Kong Toward More Democratic Voting," *New York Times*, April 27, 2004.

William Branigin, "Kay: We Were Almost All Wrong," *Washington Post*, January 28, 2004.

Ted Bridis, "Ex-Aide Says Bush Doing Terrible Job," *Milwaukee Journal Sentinel*, March 20, 2004.

William J. Broad, "U.S. is Losing Its Dominance in the Sciences," *New York Times*, May 3, 2004.

Ethan Bronner, "Collateral Damage," *New York Times Book Review*, February 22, 2004.

James Brooke, "Prisons: Growth Industry for Some," *New York Times*, November 2, 1997.

Business Week, "Reinvesting America," January 19, 1993.

Campaign for America's Future, "Bush's Budget Fails Education," at http://www.ourfuture.org/issues_and_campaigns/education/20040202_edu_budget.cfm, February 3, 2004.

Albert H. Cantril and Susan Davis Cantril, *Reading Mixed Signals: Ambivalence in American Public Opinion about Government* (Baltimore: Johns Hopkins University Press, 1999).

Carnegie Corporation, *A Matter of Time: Risk and Opportunity in the Nonschool Hours* (New York: Carnegie Corporation, 1992).

Carnegie Council on Adolescent Development, *Turning Points: Preparing American Youth for the Twenty-First Century* (New York: Carnegie Corporation of New York, 1989).

Carnegie Foundation for the Advancement of Teaching, *An Imperiled Generation: Saving Urban Schools* (Princeton: Carnegie Foundation for the Advancement of Teaching, 1988).

Century Foundation, "Rags to Riches? The American Dream is Less Common in the United States than Elsewhere," Summer 2002.

Sewell Chan and Michael Amon, "Prisoner Abuse Probe Widened," *Washington Post*, May 2, 2004.

Dan Chapman, "We're Trying to Spread a Little Truth," interview with Ray McGovern, *Atlanta Journal Constitution*, December 7, 2003.

Jeff Chapman, Economic Policy Institute, Washington, D.C., personal communication, April 9, 2004.

Jim Chen, "For Good Reasons, China Finances U.S. Deficit," *The World Paper*, March 2004.

Joseph Cirincione, Jessica Tuchman Mathews, Alexis Orton, and George Perkovich, *WMD in Iraq: Evidence and Implications*, Carnegie Endowment for International Peace, Washington, D.C., January, 2004.

Richard A. Clarke, "The Wrong Debate on Terrorism," *New York Times*, April 25, 2004.

Edward Cody and Philip P. Pan, "Beijing Tightens Control of Hong Kong," *Washington Post*, April 7, 2004.

Dalton Conley, "The Black-White Wealth Gap," the *Nation*, March 26, 2001.

David Corn, "Condi's Cover-Up Caves In," CommonDreams.org, at http://www.commondreams.org/views04/0413-14.htm, April 14, 2004.

William J. Cunningham, "Enterprise Zones," Testimony before the Committee on Select Revenue Measures, Committee on Ways and Means, U.S. House of Representatives, July 11, 1991.

Elliott Currie, *Crime and Punishment in America* (New York: Metropolitan Books, 1998).

Elliott Currie, "The Failure of "Free Market–Tough State" Ideology," chapter 26 in Alan Curtis, editor, *Patriotism, Democracy, and Common Sense* (Lanham, Md.: Rowman & Littlefield, 2004).

Lynn A. Curtis, editor, *American Violence and Public Policy: An Update of the National Commission on the Causes and Prevention of Violence* (New Haven: Yale University Press, 1985).

———, *Lessons from the Street: Capacity Building and Replication* (Washington, D.C.: The Milton S. Eisenhower Foundation, 2000), at http://www.eisenhowerfoundation.org/grassroots/fr_CapacityBuilding.html.

———, *To Establish Justice, To Ensure Domestic Tranquility: A Thirty-Year Update of the National Commission on the Causes and Prevention of Violence* (Washington, D.C.: The Milton S. Eisenhower Foundation, 1999), at http://www.eisenhowerfoundation.org/aboutus/fr_publications.html.

———, "What Works: Cost-Effective Investment in African-American Men, Youth and Children," testimony before the Black Congressional Caucus, November 15, 2003.

———, *Youth Investment and Police Mentoring: Final Report* (Washington, D.C.: The Milton S. Eisenhower Foundation, 1998, at http://www.eisenhowerfoundation.org/aboutus/fr_publications.html.

——— and Fred R. Harris, *The Millennium Breach* (Washington, D.C.: The Milton S. Eisenhower Foundation, 1998), at http://www.eisenhowerfoundation.org/aboutus/fr_publications.html.

The Daily Mislead, "Bush Misleads Public About Cause of Deficit, February 3, 2004, at http://www.misleader.org/daily_mislead/read.asp?fn=df02032004.html.

Christian Davenport, "New Prison Images Emerge," *Washington Post,* May 6, 2004.

Eric M. Davis, "Domino Democracy: Challenges to U.S. Foreign Policy in a Post-Saddam Middle East," chapter 16 in Alan Curtis, editor, *Patriotism, Democracy, and Common Sense* (Lanham, Md.: Rowman & Littlefield, 2004).

Gary Delgado, editor, *From Poverty to Punishment: How Welfare Reform Punishes the Poor* (Oakland: Applied Research Center, 2002).

Michael Dobbs, "U.S. Segregation Now at '69 Level," *Washington Post,* January 18, 2004.

Joy G. Dryfoos, *Safe Passage: Making It through Adolescence in a Risky Society* (New York: Oxford University Press, 1998).

John E. Eck and William Spelman, *Problem Solving: Problem-Oriented Policing in Newport News* (Washington, D.C.: U.S. Department of Justice, 1987).

Economic Policy Institute, "Soaring Imports from China Push U.S. Trade Deficit to New Record," February 13, 2004, at http://www.epinet.org/content.cfm/webfeatures_snapshots_archive_11202002.

Economist, "Not So EZ," January 28, 1989.

Peter B. Edelman, *Searching for America's Heart: RFK and the Renewal of Hope* (New York: Houghton Mifflin, 2001).

Dan Eggen and John Mintz, "9/11 Panel Critical of Clinton, Bush," *Washington Post,* March 24, 2004.

Dan Eggen and Walter Pincus, "Ashcroft's Efforts on Terrorism Criticized," *Washington Post,* April 14, 2004.

———, "Ex-Aide Recounts Terror Warnings," *Washington Post,* March 25, 2004.

Harold Evans, "Sorry Seems to Be New(s) Buzzword," the *Guardian Weekly,* June 4-10, 2004.

Douglas Farah, "Al Qaeda's Finances Ample, Say Probers," *Washington Post,* December 14, 2003.

Paul Farhi, "Democratic Spending Is Team Effort," *Washington Post,* March 24, 2004.

Jeff Faux, "The Financial, Political, and Moral Deficits of the American Empire," chapter 21 in Alan Curtis, editor, *Patriotism, Democracy, and Common Sense* (Lanham, Md.: Rowman & Littlefield, 2004).

———, "You Are Not Alone," in Stanley B. Greenberg and Theda Skocpol, *The New Majority: Toward a Popular Progressive Politics* (New Haven: Yale University Press, 1997).

Federal Register, "Job Training Partnership Act: Youth Pilot Projects," vol. 59, no. 71, April 13, 1994.

Robert D. Felner, et al., "The Impact of School Reform for the Middle Years," *Phi Delta Kappan*, March 1997.

Manny Fernandez, "Protest of IMF Planned This Month," *Washington Post*, April 9, 2004.

Milton Friedman, "There's No Justice in the War on Drugs," *New York Times*, January 11, 1998.

Tom Furlong, "Enterprise Zone in L.A. Fraught With Problems," *Los Angeles Times*, May 19, 1992.

Todd Furniss, "China: The Next Big Wave in Offshore Outsourcing," at http://www.outsourcing-asia.com/china.html, June 2003.

James K. Galbraith, "Full Employment and the Perils of Empire," chapter 23 in Alan Curtis, editor, *Patriotism, Democracy, and Common Sense* (Lanham, Md.: Rowman & Littlefield, 2004).

James Glanz, "Scientists Say Administration Distorts Facts," *New York Times*, February 19, 2004.

John M. Glionna, "Making Rehabilitation Into a Serious Business," *Los Angeles Times*, March 22, 2002.

Global Campaign for Education, "Rich Nations Flunk in Educating Poor," at http://www.cnn.com/2003/EDUCATION/11/18/education.aid.reut/cnn.com, November 18, 2003.

Susan Goldberg, "Bush Rips Up the Road Map," CommonDreams.org, at http://www.commondreams.org/headlines04/0415-01.htm, April 20, 2004.

Philip Golub, "U.S.: The World's Deepest Debtor," *Le Monde Diplomatique*, October 2003.

Amy Goodman, "Independent Reporting and the People's Media," chapter 34 in Alan Curtis, editor, *Patriotism, Democracy, and Common Sense* (Lanham, Md.: Rowman & Littlefield, 2004).

Abby Goodnough, "Disenfranchised Florida Felons Struggle to Regain Their Rights," *New York Times*, March 28, 2004.

Austan Goolsbee, "The Unemployment Myth," *New York Times*, November 30, 2003.

Robert Greenstein, "The Coming Budget Crisis and the Rising Threat of Large-Scale Federal Disinvestment," chapter 22 in Alan Curtis, editor, *Patriotism, Democracy, and Common Sense* (Lanham, Md.: Rowman & Littlefield, 2004).

William Greider, *Who Will Tell the People: The Betrayal of American Democracy* (New York: Simon & Schuster, 1992).

Jane Gross, "A Remnant of the War on Poverty, the Job Corps Is a Quiet Success, *New York Times*, February 17, 1993.

Guardian Weekly, "Beijing's Ugly New Offensive Against Democracy," editorial, March 11-17, 2004.

Robert Guskind, "Enterprise Zones: Do They Work?" *Journal of Housing*, January/February 1990.

Fred R. Harris and Lynn A. Curtis, editors, *Locked in the Poorhouse: Cities, Race, and Poverty in the United States* (Lanham, Md.: Rowman & Littlefield, 1998).

Gary Hart, "A Detour from the War on Terrorism," *Washington Post* and http://www.garyhartnews.com/hart/writings/columns/columns_03_09_2003.php, March 9, 2003.

———, "National Security in the Twenty-First Century" chapter 2 in Alan Curtis, editor, *Patriotism, Democracy, and Common Sense* (Lanham, Md.: Rowman & Littlefield, 2004).

———, "The New Security: Economic Growth and Justice in the 21st Century, www.garyhartnews.com, March 4, 2003.

———, "The Other War," *American Prospect*, December 16, 2002.

——— and Warren B. Rudman, *America Still Unprepared—America Still in Danger*, Council on Foreign Relations, Washington, D.C., October 2002, at http://www.cfr.org/pdf/Homeland_Security_TF.pdf

——— and Warren Rudman, "Securing the Homeland," *Newshour with Jim Lehrer*, at http://www.pbs.org/newshour/bb/terrorism/july-dec02/senators_10-31.html, October 31, 2002.

——— and Warren B. Rudman, "We Are Still Unprepared," *Washington Post*, November 5, 2002.

Thom Hartmann, "Exposing the Conservative Straw Man—Productivity," CommonDreams.org, at http://www.commondreams.org/views04/0412-13.htm, April 12, 2004.

William D. Hartung, "Speaking Truth to Power: Preventive Diplomacy Backed by Force," chapter 10 in Alan Curtis, editor, *Patriotism, Democracy, and Common Sense* (Lanham, Md.: Rowman & Littlefield, 2004).

Harvard Civil Rights Project, "No Child Left Behind: A Federal, State and District Level Look at the First Year, HGSE News, February 9, 2004.

Nell Henderson, "Job Growth in March Biggest in Four Years," *Washington Post*, April 3, 2004.

Bob Herbert, "We're More Productive. Who Gets the Money?" *New York Times*, April 5, 2004.

Jim Hightower, "Thieves in High Places," chapter 36 in Alan Curtis, editor, *Patriotism, Democracy, and Common Sense* (Lanham, Md.: Rowman & Littlefield, 2004).

Steven Hill and Rob Richie, "Democracy on the Cheap: The Failure of America's Electoral Infrastructure," CommonDreams.org, http://www.commondreams.org/views03/1212-14.htm, December 12, 2003.

Anne Imse, "Former Senator Hart: America Unprepared for Terrorist Attacks," *Rocky Mountain News*, June 19, 2003.

Douglas Jehl, "Tenet Concedes Gaps in C.I.A. Data on Iraq Weapons," *New York Times*, February 6, 2004.

———, "White House Eyes a Powerful Post for Intelligence," *New York Times*, April 16, 2004.

——— and David E. Sanger, "The Struggle for Iraq: Commission to Decide Itself on Depth of Its Investigation," *New York Times*, February 3, 2004.

Larry C. Johnson, "The War on Clarke," TomPaine.com, March 29, 2004, at http://www.tompaine.com/feature2.cfm/ID/10158.

David Johnston and Jim Dwyer, "Pre-9/11 Files Show Warnings Were More Dire and Persistent," *New York Times*, April 18, 2004.

Richard D. Kahlenberg, "The People's Choice for Schools," *Washington Post*, December 15, 2000.

Joseph Kahn, "A Challenge to China's Leaders From a Witness to Brutality," *New York Times*, March 14, 2004.

Paul Kennedy, "The Perils of Empire," *Washington Post*, April 20, 2003.

———, "U.N. Bashing Misses the Target," Tribune Media Services International, February 10, 2004.

——— and Bruce Russett, "Reforming the United Nations," *Foreign Affairs*, September/ October 1995.

Laurie E. King-Irani, "Awakening the American Political Debate on Palestine and Israel," chapter 18 in Alan Curtis, editor, *Patriotism, Democracy, and Common Sense* (Lanham, Md.: Rowman & Littlefield, 2004).

Jonathan Kozol, "Saving Public Education," the *Nation*, February 17, 1997.

Paul Krugman, "The Health of Nations," *New York Times*, February 17, 2004.

———, "This Isn't America," *New York Times*, March 30, 2004.

Stephen Labaton, "Court Orders Rethinking of Rules Allowing Large Media to Expand," *New York Times*, June 24, 2004.

Steven LaFrance, LaFrance Associates, San Francisco, personal communication, May 4, 2004.

Christopher Lee, "Most Say They Are Less Safe Since 9/11," *Washington Post*, April 1, 2004.

David Leonardhardt, "As Wealthy Fill Top Colleges, Concerns Grow over Fairness," *New York Times*, April 22, 2004.

Richard C. Leone, "The Missing Debate," chapter 28 in Alan Curtis, editor, *Patriotism, Democracy, and Common Sense* (Lanham, Md.: Rowman & Littlefield, 2004).

Eric Lichtblau, "New Details Put FBI's Action Under Scrutiny," *New York Times*, April 12, 2004.

Doris L. MacKenzie and Claire Souryal, *Multiple Evaluation of Shock Incarceration* (Washington, D.C.: National Institute of Justice, 1994).

David MacMichael and Ray McGovern, "Ex-CIA Professionals: Weapons of Mass Distraction: Where? Find? Plant?" CommonDreams.org, June 18, 2003, at http://www.commondreams.org/views03/0425-11.htm.

———, "The Burden of Truth," *Sojourners*, November-December 2003

Christopher Marquis, "New System Begins Rerouting U.S. Aid for Poor Countries, *New York Times*, February 22, 2004.

Jessica Tuchman Mathews, "The Challenge of Managing Dominance," chapter 3 in Alan Curtis, editor, *Patriotism, Democracy, and Common Sense* (Lanham, Md.: Rowman & Littlefield, 2004).

Marc Mauer, "September 11 and the Criminal Justice System," chapter 27 in Alan Curtis, editor, *Patriotism, Democracy, and Common Sense* (Lanham, Md.: Rowman & Littlefield, 2004).

———, *Young Black Men in the Criminal Justice System* (Washington, D.C.: The Sentencing Project, 1990).

Robert W. McChesney and John Nichols, "Creation of the Media Democracy Reform Movement," chapter 31 in Alan Curtis, editor, *Patriotism, Democracy, and Common Sense* (Lanham, Md.: Rowman & Littlefield, 2004).

Ray McGovern, "A Compromised Central Intelligence Agency: What Can Be Done?" chapter 4 in Alan Curtis, editor, *Patriotism, Democracy, and Common Sense* (Lanham, Md.: Rowman & Littlefield, 2004).

Dana Milbank, "Opinion of U.S. Abroad is Falling, Survey Finds," *Washington Post,* March 17, 2004.

George Monbiot, "Their Beliefs Are Bonkers, But They Are at the Heart of Power," the *Guardian* and CommonDreams.org: http://www.commondreams.org/views04/0420-03.htm, April 20, 2004.

Richard Moran, "New York Story: More Luck Than Policing," *New York Times*, February 9, 1997.

Sara Mosle, "The Vanity of Volunteerism," *New York Times Magazine*, July 2, 2000.

Adam Nagourney and Philip Shenon, "Bush Says Brief on Qaeda Threat Was Not Specific, *New York Times*, April 12, 2004.

The Nation, "A New Economic Agenda," editorial, October 6, 2003.

National Advisory Commission on Civil Disorders (the Kerner Riot Commission), *Final Report* (Washington, D.C.: U.S. Government Printing Office, 1968).

National Commission on Terrorist Attacks on the United States (9/11 Commission), *Final Report* (Washington, D.C.: United States Government Printing Office, 2004).

National Commission on the Causes and Prevention of Violence, (the Eisenhower Violence Commission), *Final Report* (Washington, DC: United States Government Printing Office, 1969).

New York Times, "Bad New Days for Voting Rights," editorial, April 18, 2004.

New York Times, "Budgeting for Another Florida," editorial, February 8, 2004.

New York Times, "Dream-Filled Missile Silos," editorial, April 1, 2004.

New York Times, "Fixing Democracy," editorial, January 18, 2004.

New York Times, "How America Doesn't Vote," editorial, February 15, 2004.

New York Times, "A Youth Program that Worked," editorial, March 20, 1995.

Joseph S. Nye Jr., *The Paradox of American Power* (Oxford: Oxford University Press, 2002).

Gary Orfield, Susan E. Eaton, and the Harvard Project on School Desegregation, *Dismantling Desegregation: The Quiet Reversal of Brown vs. Board of Education* (New York: New Press, 1996).

E. Roger Owen, "The Future Political and Economic Architecture of the Middle East," chapter 19 in Alan Curtis, editor, *Patriotism, Democracy, and Common Sense* (Lanham, Md.: Rowman & Littlefield, 2004).

Eli Pariser, "Electronic Advocacy and Fundraising: The State of the Art," chapter 32, in Alan Curtis, editor, *Patriotism, Democracy, and Common Sense* (Lanham, Md.: Rowman & Littlefield, 2004).

Kevin Phillips, *Wealth and Democracy* (New York: Broadway Books, 2002).

Neal R. Pierce and Carol F. Steinbach, *Corrective Capitalism: The Rise of America's Community Development Corporations* (New York: Ford Foundation, 1987).

Walter Pincus and Dana Milbank, "Framework of Clarke's Book is Bolstered," *Washington Post*, April 4, 2004.

Dana Priest, "Congressional Oversight of Intelligence Criticized," *Washington Post*, April 27, 2004.

———, "Panel Says Bush Saw Repeated Warnings," *Washington Post*, April 14, 2004.

Howard Rheingold, "Electronic Counterpower and Collective Action," chapter 33 in Alan Curtis, editor, *Patriotism, Democracy, and Common Sense* (Lanham, Md.: Rowman & Littlefield, 2004).

Julius B. Richmond and Judith Palfrey, "Keeping Head Start Strong and Successful," *Boston Globe* and CommonDreams.org: http://www.commondreams.org/views03/0719-09.htm, July 19, 2003.

James Ridgeway, "Heritage on the Hill," the *Nation*, December 22, 1997.

James Risen, "Ex-Inspector Says CIA Missed Disarray In Iraqi Arms Program," *New York Times,* January 26, 2004.

Corey Robin, "Grand Designs: How 9/11 Unified Conservatives in Pursuit of Empire," *Washington Post*, May 2, 2004.

Ruth Rosen, "Imagine the Unthinkable," *San Francisco Chronicle* and CommonDreams.org: http://www.commondreams.org/views04/0401-02.htm, April 1, 2004.

Coleen M. Rowley, "Civil Liberties and Effective Investigation," chapter 30 in Alan Curtis, editor, *Patriotism, Democracy, and Common Sense* (Lanham, Md.: Rowman & Littlefield, 2004).

Jeffrey D. Sachs and Sakiko Fukuda-Parr, "If We Cared To, We Could Defeat World Poverty," *New York Times*, July 9, 2003.

David E. Sanger, "Calculating the Politics of Catastrophe," *New York Times*, May 2, 2004.

S. Schinke, et al., *The Effects of Boys and Girls Clubs on Alcohol and Drug Use and Related Problems at Public Housing* (New York: Columbia University School of Social Work, 1991).

John Schmid, "American Drive to Buy for Less Has a Price," *Milwaukee Journal Sentinel,* December 30, 2003.

———, "Same Bed, Different Dreams," *Milwaukee Journal Sentinel*, December 28, 2003.

——— and Rick Romell, "China's Economic Boom Hits Home," *Milwaukee Journal Sentinel*, December 27, 2003.

Lisbeth B. Schorr, with Daniel Schorr, *Within Our Reach: Breaking the Cycle of Disadvantage* (New York: Doubleday, 1988).

Clare Short, "Does America Have the Wisdom the Grasp the Opportunity?," chapter 5 in Alan Curtis, editor, *Patriotism, Democracy, and Common Sense*, Lanham, Md.: Rowman & Littlefield, 2004.

Philip Shenon, "9/11 Panel Set to Detail Flaws in Air Defenses," *New York Times*, April 25, 2004.

———, "Panel Plans to Document the Breadth of Lost Opportunities," *New York Times*, April 11, 2004.

——— and Eric Lichtblau, "Sept.11 Panel Cites C.I.A. For Failures in Terror Case," *New York Times*, April 15, 2004.

Micah L. Sifry, "Generating Political Hope in a Time of Fear," chapter 37 in Alan Curtis, editor, *Patriotism, Democracy, and Common Sense* (Lanham, Md.: Rowman & Littlefield, 2004).

Cynthia L. Sipe, *Mentoring* (Philadelphia: Public/Private Ventures, 1996).

Theodore C. Sorensen, *Kennedy* (New York: Harper & Row, 1965).

Sourcebook of Criminal Justice Statistics, 2002, at http://www.albany.edu/sourcebook/1995/pdf/section2.pdf, April 18, 2004.

Mickey Spiegel, "China: Religion in the Service of the State," U.S. Commission on International Religious Freedom, Washington, D.C., March 16, 2000.

Vince Stehle, "Vistas of Endless Possibility: Delancey Street Foundation Helps Felons and Addicts Rehabilitate Themselves into Responsible Citizens," *Chronicle of Philanthropy*, November 2, 1995.

Vivien Stern, "The Courage to Keep on Talking," chapter 6, in Alan Curtis, editor, *Patriotism, Democracy, and Common Sense* (Lanham, Md.: Rowman & Littlefield, 2004).

Richard W. Stevenson and Janet Elder, "Support for War Is Down Sharply, Poll Concludes," *New York Times*, April 29, 2004.

Robert Suro, "More Is Spent on Prisons Than Colleges," *Washington Post*, February 24, 1997.

Ron Suskind, "Can't Win for Losing," *New York Times Book Review*, February 15, 2003.

Nancy Talanian, "License to Criticize the Patriot Act," at http://www.commondreams.org/views04/0402-03.htm, April 2, 2004.

Chris Toensing, "American Leadership to Create a Two-State Solution," chapter 17 in Alan Curtis, editor, *Patriotism, Democracy, and Common Sense* (Lanham, Md.: Rowman & Littlefield, 2004).

Pierre Tristam, "Of Course the Attacks Were Preventable," CommonDreams.org, at http://www.commondreams.org/views04/0420-06.htm, April 21, 2004.

Neely Tucker, "Study Warns of Rising Tide of Released Inmates," *Washington Post*, May 21, 2003.

Uniform Crime Reports, Federal Bureau of Investigation, Washington, D.C., at http://www.fbi.gov/ucr/ucr.htm, April 18, 2004.

"U.S. Trade Deficit with China Surges to a Record High," *Taipei Times*, October 13, 2003.

United States Commission on National Security/21st Century: *Road Map for National Security: Imperative for Change*, Phase III report, February 15, 2001.

United States Department of Treasury, "Foreign Holding of the U.S. Debt," Washington, D.C., April 15, 2004.

David Von Drehle, "Political Split Is Pervasive," *Washington Post*, April 25, 2004.

William Wallace, "The European Mistrust of American Leadership," chapter 7 in Alan Curtis, editor, *Patriotism, Democracy, and Common Sense* (Lanham, Md.: Rowman & Littlefield, 2004).

Washington Post, "The 9/11 Debate," editorial, March 24, 2004.

Mark Weisbrot, "The IMF at 60: Reform Still a Long Way Off," Knight-Ridder/Tribune Information Services and CommonDreams.org, at http://www.commondreams.org/views04/0420-08.htm, April 20, 2004.

Steven R. Weisman, "State Department Report Shows Increase in Terrorism," *New York Times*, June 23, 2004.

James Q. Whitman, "Prisoner Degredation Abroad—and at Home," *Washington Post*, May 10, 2004.

Joseph C. Wilson IV, "Village Democracy and Presidential Leadership," chapter 15 in Alan Curtis, editor, *Patriotism, Democracy, and Common Sense* (Lanham, Md.: Rowman & Littlefield, 2004).

Alan Wolfe, "The New Politics of Inequality," *New York Times*, September 27, 1999.

Christopher Wren, "Arizona Finds Cost Savings in Treating Drug Offenders," *New York Times*, April 21, 1999.

Robin Wright, "Top Focus before 9/11 Wasn't on Terrorism," *Washington Post*, April 1, 2004.

Edward Zigler, "The Wrong Road on Head Start," *Washington Post*, December 23, 2000.

Stephanie Zunes, "Bush Endorsement of Sharon Proposal Undermines Peace and International Law," at http://www.commondreams.org/views04/0415-14.htm , April 15, 2004.

Dave Zweifel, "Stressed Travelers Need Passenger Rail," at http://www.commondreams.org/views04/0331-03.htm, April 2, 2004.

I

FAILURE IN AMERICAN FOREIGN AND NATIONAL SECURITY POLICY—AND STRATEGIC ALTERNATIVES

• 2 •

National Security in the Twenty-First Century

Gary Hart

We are sailing into the new world of the twenty-first century without a compass. Despite the elapse of more than a decade, the vacuum created by the end of the Cold War—and the overnight irrelevance of our central organizing principle, containment of communism—has not been filled by any coherent and compelling new vision. Meanwhile, the interests-versus-values debate grows stale and irrelevant. Along with disgust over corporate corruption and the legalized corruption of politics by money, public apathy today is traceable to a failure of visionary leadership—leadership driven by an understanding of the radically new world we now confront. America is adrift because it has not related its power to its principles. And it will remain adrift until our principles become the foundation of a new grand strategy.

Great powers throughout history have succeeded only when they possessed the genius to imagine, and the will to pursue, a systematic plan to dedicate the means they possessed to the achievement of large national purposes. At the genesis of a new century and a new age, America lacks a grand strategy that has the consensus support of the American people. Instead, too many peoples of the world now see the United States as a great power without purpose—a giant that pronounces rather than listens—and thus as a great danger.

Because we have failed to define our larger purposes, where we want to go, and how we intend to apply our resources to get there, we cannot now define our own national security in this new age. Security is the product of intelligent response to strategic realities. A nation that cannot articulate its strategy is bound to become a victim of confusion in constructing its security. And a state that cannot guarantee its citizens' security soon loses its legitimacy.

FOUR SIMULTANEOUS REVOLUTIONS

Neither strategy nor security can be understood outside our current context. Too few of our policymakers seem fully to appreciate the revolutionary whirlwinds that now shape our destiny. Indeed, we are swept up in at least four historic revolutions. They are, first, globalization, or the internationalization of commerce, finance, and markets; second, the information revolution, now creating a "digital divide" between computer literates and computer illiterates; third, the erosion of the sovereignty or authority of the nation-state; and fourth, a fundamental change in the nature of conflict. Without understanding the impact of these four simultaneous revolutions, a search for national security is futile. To respond to the first two revolutions requires foreign policy initiatives in the Middle East and elsewhere as bold as the Marshall Plan and as encompassing as energy security. To create a national security strategy requires an understanding of the changing nature of conflict in particular, and that requires an understanding of the erosion of the sovereignty of nation-states.

For 350 years, wars have been fought in the field between the uniformed armies of nations with fixed borders to achieve a political result. Rules evolved for these wars: the Geneva conventions spell out the norms for humane treatment of prisoners, the rights of non-combatants, and so forth. But twenty-first-century warfare already looks dramatically different. Nations disintegrate; and when a nation disintegrates, as in the former Yugoslavia, borders disappear. Indeed, part of the process of creating peace among ethnic combatants in a disintegrating nation involves drawing new boundaries and building new nations. And now we have violence being perpetrated by combatants in civilian clothes, representing no nation, attacking civilian targets, with no political agenda and only a fanatical commitment to destruction. Meanwhile, despite belatedly accepting the recommendation of the U.S. Commission on National Security to create a Department of Homeland Security, the Bush administration seems to be preoccupied with national missile defense, which is at best premature, and has one new doctrine, preemption—a beautiful theory murdered by a gang of ugly North Korean facts.

HOW TO DEAL WITH THE NEW VIOLENCE

When the nature of conflict changes, the means of achieving security must also change. The new violence resembles war, but it is not. It resembles crime, but it is not. What is it, and how should we deal with it? For the moment and largely for convenience, we call it terrorism, and labeling every bad actor a terrorist leads us to embrace wretched allies on the always-dubious theory that the enemy of our enemy is our friend. On this same theory, we supported undemocratic and repressive authoritarian oligarchies during the Cold War simply because they were opposed to communism. We set about assassinating foreign leaders we did not like. The bills we accrue from despicable allies and unprincipled policies that undermine the very virtues we claim to defend always come due.

In the past ten years, we have seen a dozen or more low-intensity conflicts between tribes, clans, and gangs. We participated in some, including Somalia, where we experienced the painful consequences of brawling, however well intentioned, in another man's alley—as memorialized in the film *Black Hawk Down*. We passively observed similar bloody conflicts, in Rwanda and elsewhere, where the weapon of choice, a machete, dated to the Bronze Age. We successfully formed ad hoc coalitions of the willing in Bosnia and Kosovo. We earned a quick victory in Kuwait largely due to intensive bombing and maneuver warfare. But, with that exception, post–Cold War conflict has been characterized by "non-arrayed" enemies—those not presented in traditional battle formation—representing "asymmetrical" threats, using ingenuity, not strength, to bypass our military might. Because they did not follow historical conventions, late-twentieth-century wars have seemed to us unfair and somehow more barbaric than conflict has been throughout history.

Yet military breakthroughs have often been achieved by weaker powers. Nowhere was this more evident than on September 11, when nineteen suicidal men in civilian clothes using e-mail, the Internet, elementary flight instructions, and tradesmen's tools converted kerosene-burning commercial aircraft into weapons of mass destruction. There was an evil genius about it. It was a shocking initiation into the twenty-first century, so shocking that it left some with the naive belief that it will never happen again or that, if it does, it will not be in their cities. But does anyone seriously believe that the bin Ladens of the world are done with us?

Our massive military and technological superiority did not protect us from this non-arrayed, asymmetrical, iconoclastic, new form of conflict. Indeed, technology may have seduced us into assuming security. While we poured enormous capital into national missile defense—trying to hit a bullet with a bullet—our enemies turned our own technology against us. Faith in technology can blind us to the necessity of innovation in the age of the transformation of war; faith in technology handcuffed our imagination and lulled us to sleep.

We are now trying to force new forms of conflict into traditional categories so that we can try to understand and respond to them. Our response to the first terrorist attack was to declare "war on terrorism." But that is a two-front war being fought on one front only. So far in Afghanistan, our military has replaced a repressive theocracy with a less repressive but still tribal form of government. But the fate of the most wanted man on earth is still uncertain and our leaders tell us al Qaeda cells still operate in the United States and elsewhere. And we invaded Iraq without adequate preparation—as a recent report by the Council on Foreign Relations has documented—for what experts believe will be inevitable retaliatory attacks on the United States from radical fundamentalist groups. So, it is far too early to declare victory in this war.

Meanwhile, the "warriors" rounded up in this conflict and detained at Guantanamo Bay are denied warrior status. They are also denied criminal status and thus the rights inherent in our criminal justice system. If they are not warriors, and they are not criminals, what are they? The answer is consequential in that it may contain a clue to the broader question of how to define security in the age of this new conflict. We don't know what to call the "detainees" because we don't know exactly what they've done. The Taliban fought for a theocratic regime that harbored an anti-Western, antidemocratic, antiliberal radical fundamentalist terrorist group. Are they warriors or are they criminals? Or are they something else? Are they the wave of the future? Will conflict in the twenty-first century resemble more the high-tech games of Star Wars or the barbaric combat of the twelfth-century Assassins, the medieval Islamic sect widely credited as being the first terrorists?

A RETURN TO THE ASSASSINS

If a return to the Assassins is the wave of the future, and I believe it is, this has dramatic consequences for how we define security and how we seek to achieve it. There are two basic schools of thought about dealing with terrorism. One school believes the threat is inevitable and that we should crush it, including preemptively, in places like Iraq. The other believes that we should try to understand the nature of the threat with considerably more thoughtfulness and eliminate, to the degree possible, its causes. The first school of thought has the virtue of simplicity. The second has the much greater chance of ultimate success.

The preemption approach, moreover, has long-term foreign policy consequences. For example, in Afghanistan, we armed the Mujahadeen to fight the Soviets in the 1980s. Then, when the Soviets left, we rode away and the Taliban took over and eventually provided hospitality to al Qaeda. We mounted a major invasion of Iraq. Now what? If we ride away again, we leave behind a much bigger breeding ground for terrorists that will haunt us in years to come. If we stay, we will be there for a very, very long time and at very great cost.

This new century requires a much clearer understanding of new threats and the causes of those threats than our leaders seem interested in pursuing. Who exactly is our enemy, and why does he hate us? Unlike the clear-cut twentieth-century ideological struggle between democracy and communism, the role of poverty, disease, and despair becomes much more central. The role of cultural difference becomes much more crucial: "Take your filthy movies and go home," cry those who resent us and our popular culture. And the role of resentment—of our wealth, of our power, of our willful consumption of resources, of our arrogance—becomes a much greater factor.

It does not go without notice in the world, especially the impoverished world, that the United States consumes a quarter of the world's energy and produces a quarter of the world's pollution and trash. And to say that this will all be overlooked because multitudes of people would like to live in the United States is to miss the point; we are seen by many to be not only rich but also arrogant, arbitrary, and wholly self-interested.

A NEW DEFINITION OF SECURITY

Let me return to the four revolutions. If globalization opens an even wider gap between haves and have-nots, it will increase poverty and despair, widen cultural clashes, and dramatically increase resentment against us. If the information revolution also adds a digital divide between the computer literate with future opportunities and the computer illiterate without those opportunities, it will swell the swamp of despair, the breeding pool of future terrorists. How short is the time before suicidal young people with nothing to gain and nothing to lose blow themselves up in American shopping malls in a tragic search for martyrdom?

This new age requires, at the very least, a new definition of security and, to achieve it, a toolbox filled with more than weapons. National security in the twenty-first century will require economic and political tools, not simply military ones. Trade and aid programs must become more grassroots and human-scale than top-down and bureaucratic. For example, microloan programs directed at home, land, and small business ownership have proved enormously promising in several countries in Asia and Latin America. And in the political arena, our diplomacy must once again be based on the principles underlying our Constitution and nation: principles of honor, of humanity, of respect for difference. Our diplomacy must be aimed at people, not just governments. We can explain our principles and ideals much better than we have been, but we must then also be prepared to live up to them. The ideals of democracy are not marketed; they are lived.

Of the three resources required by terrorists—money, weapons, and people—the resource most vital is people. Our "war on terrorism" should aim to dry up the swamp of despair found in refugee camps, favelas, and impoverished villages throughout the world. As Robert Kaplan has pointed out, for millions of young people from this swamp, barracks life and terrorist training camps are a step up. Though the first suicidal attackers did not come from refugee camps, it's a safe bet that the next wave will.

THE TWENTY-FIRST-CENTURY MILITARY

But the military component necessarily remains at the core of genuine national security. And that must take into account another policy that we do not usually consider when we're talking about national security. Our government refuses to admit what everyone knows to be true—that our foreign policy and national security priority in the Middle East particularly, are inextricably conditioned by our dependence on oil from that region.

We should either publicly acknowledge that our wasteful lifestyle binds us to a tacit policy of trading American lives for foreign oil or undertake to change our lifestyle. It is a simple choice between selfishness and greed on the one hand and national sacrifice and our national honor on the other.

But we do have to have that military component and we should consider what it should look like. The military of the twenty-first century must look and perform much differently than that of the twentieth. Paradoxically, it will be more technological, but it will also be more human. Technologically, our military will expand into space, but I think that component must be defensive, not offensive.

We are indeed in a "revolution of military affairs" largely driven by technology, but dependent on intelligence collected and analyzed by humans. Our fighting forces are increasingly directed by and through a complex web of command, control, and communications networks all interwoven and interrelated. The first Persian Gulf war was directed from a makeshift headquarters in Saudi Arabia. A decade later the Afghan war was directed from Central Command in Florida. The war in Iraq involves similar refinements. We are relying on UAVs, unmanned air vehicles, and UCAVs, unmanned combat air vehicles, as fast as we can produce them. The commander-in-chief can monitor real-time pictures from these vehicles in the White House.

But high technology can be both extremely vulnerable to and dependent on the human actor. Exotic Pentagon communications networks are vulnerable to twenty-one-year-old hackers. The precision-guided munitions on board planes flying from Diego Garcia or aircraft carriers in the Indian Ocean were guided by Delta Force personnel wearing civilian clothes and riding mules across the hills of Afghanistan.

Even in the age of terrorism and "crime/war," we will need expeditionary forces. But they must be lighter and swifter. Getting there fast is now more important than getting there big. And ultrasophisticated, post–Cold War conventional weapons systems—ships, planes, and tanks—will have to be different. Despite our enormous wealth, we can no longer afford to integrate technology so closely to platforms that the platform must be replaced when technology changes—as it does with lightning speed. We cannot afford ships, planes, and tanks that are outdated the year they come into service. Platforms—once again, ships, planes, and tanks—must be built for durability and long life. The weapons and sensors we place on them must be "plugged in"—that is, readily removable when new ones become available.

The two illustrations are, of course, the venerable B-52 bomber and the aircraft carrier. The B-52, now in its sixth decade of life, is still performing—even though it's older than the fathers of the pilots who fly it. And we keep aircraft carriers in service for over half a century. The platform doesn't change. But the technological sensors and weapons these days change almost overnight. Even then, human ingenuity trumps everything. Delta Force, as I mentioned, used a 3,000-year-old transportation system, the mule, to direct twenty-first century technology.

The roots of current, uneven attempts to transition from twentieth-century weapons and warfare to prepare for what some have called the "fourth generation of warfare" of the twenty-first century can be traced to the military reform movement of the late 1970s. Even then, we reformers were advocating unit cohesion and officer initiative, maneuver strategy and tactics, and lighter, faster, more replicable weapons. Without attention to new people policies and innovative strategy, tactics, and doctrine, cancellation of weapons such as the Crusader artillery piece will by itself not transform the military sufficiently for a new kind of conflict.

Paradoxically, once again, the most technologically superior superpower in human history is now dependent on human ingenuity more than ever. If intelligence fails, as it did on September 11, all the technology in the world cannot save us. (See Ray McGovern's assessment of the Central Intelligence Agency in chapter 4.) To know when, where, and how terrorists intend to strike, and what they intend to use to do so, is almost entirely dependent upon human intelligence collection. Electronic surveillance, intercepts and wiretaps, bugging and pursuing cannot altogether replace the human agent.

IRAQ: AMERICANS DESERVED TO KNOW MORE

We now occupy Iraq. Under these circumstances, and acknowledging the unity of America behind our forces once committed, any attempt to outline a national security policy for the future requires several observations to be made.

The American people deserved to know the costs of this commitment. They deserved to know which members of the international community openly support us, including those with military resources. They deserved to know, most of all, casualty estimates on both sides. We were told none of these things. It cost us 50,000 American lives in Vietnam to learn the lesson that the American people must not be misled, lied to, or treated as incompetent on military engagements.

The U.S. military does not belong to the president; it belongs to the American people. Our support for its commitment to combat is crucial for its success. That support cannot be granted in the dark and without a candid statement by the commander in chief regarding the probable costs in human lives and national treasure of its commitment.

There was yet another assurance the president should have given: that we are prepared for what the Department of Defense, among other institutions, believes will be virtually inevitable retaliatory terrorist attacks on the United States for our invasion of an Islamic country. The Council on Foreign Relations task force that I co-chaired with Warren Rudman reported that we are woefully unprepared for, and still at risk of, future terrorist attacks. It is imprudent in the extreme to attack a nation in a region seething with hostile suicidal forces when we are vulnerable to their retaliation.

A BALANCE BETWEEN SECURITY AND LIBERTY

This leads, of course, right back home to the new age of homeland security. On January 31, 2001, the U.S. Commission on National Security/21st Century strongly recommended to the president that a new national homeland security agency be created to restructure and reorganize federal assets, and well over a year after the first terrorist attack, one finally was established. But the new Department of Homeland Security must not become a domestic Pentagon, a bureaucratic behemoth that crushes initiative and imagination. A very large coordinated agency can succeed only if it integrates functions and at the same time rewards individual creative energy. Presently, the new department is not moving with the sense of urgency it must possess.

Structured from almost two dozen existing federal offices, the new department has, among its many missions, two crucial ones: control of our borders and protection of our critical infrastructure—our communications, finance, energy, and transportation systems.

But an even greater challenge for the nation itself is the search for a balance between security and liberty. Here the role of the standing military in civil society becomes crucial. The Pentagon has created a new Northern Command, headquartered in Colorado Springs, whose duties are as yet unclear. The new command is charged with coordinating the role of the military in homeland security. The easiest and most obvious solution is to put the entire mission in the Department of Defense.

There are, however, important reasons why it is not that easy. A review of the Constitutional debates in 1787 makes clear that the founders understood the danger to a republican form of government from stationing full-time soldiers on the streets of our nation. This was a fear that united the often-divided founders. Indeed, this fear led to the passage of a statute a hundred years later, the Posse Comitatus Act in 1878, prohibiting the military from enforcing the laws of the land. Congress wanted to make it clear that there is a great difference in a democracy between protecting our nation from foreign attack and policing our neighborhoods.

Now some in Washington are saying we should "review" this law with an eye to qualifying or even repealing it. Beware. This would be a mistake of dangerous proportions; the very liberties for which we stand and which we are seeking to protect would be in danger. Short of an emergency of catastrophic proportions and a presidential declaration of martial law, we neither want nor need the 82nd Airborne Division on the streets of Cleveland, Boston, or Denver. And, schooled in constitutional principles and history, the vast majority of professional military officers do not want that mission either.

But who, in addition to our public safety agencies, our police and fire departments and emergency responders, should help respond to an attack and keep the peace and restore order? Might there not be the need for some kind of military capability? Once again, based upon their understanding of classical history, our founders anticipated the future. They created such an army and called it the militia; citizen-soldiers under the immediate command of the various states that can be deployed in times of emergency. Since the late nineteenth century these militia have been known as the National Guard, and they were created and given constitutional status as the first responders and the first line of defense in the case of an attack on our homeland.

Our commission on twenty-first-century national security insisted that the National Guard be given the principal mission of response to homeland attack. These are people like us—teachers, office workers, bankers and business people, nurses and medical personnel—who are or quickly can be trained and equipped for the primary homeland security role. They also do not conjure up the danger of military rule so feared by republicans since the Greek city-state.

A NEW NATIONAL SECURITY FRAMEWORK

So now we can begin to see the outlines of a national security structure and a set of strategies, tactics, and doctrines necessary to protect us in an age of multiple revolutions. First, we must understand the changing nature of conflict and the concurrently changing nature of security. Second, we must appreciate the nature of threats and respond to the causes of those threats not only with military means but also with economic and diplomatic imagination to reduce the despair that fuels terrorism. Third, the military means we use when necessary will look dramatically different from the recent Cold War age. They will capitalize on our technological superiority but recognize its increasing dependence on skillful human direction. And fourth, homeland security must achieve a balance between security and liberty by constant recognition of our peculiar constitutional heritage and the mandate that heritage provides to rely on citizens and citizen-soldiers devoted to civic virtue and civic duty.

For the first time since 1812, our security has become a function of the community. America will prevail in this new age more because of the strength of its citizens than the power of its arsenal. But our citizens must be engaged in this fight, to a much greater degree than they have been, by the president himself.

The new century of paradox dictates that the world's greatest power must look not to its far-flung branches but to its roots; not to its elaborate materialistic systems of production and consumption but to its ideals and principles; not to its greed but to its honor. From 1949 until 1991, we lived under the threat of nuclear war and depended on a policy of containment and a doctrine of deterrence to protect us. That was the basis of our national security. I leave to the reader the task of coining a name for the new national security policy for a new age.

But whatever it is called, we must never forget that those tasked with carrying it out are our neighbors and fellow citizens, men and women with homes and families just like ours. When we take their vigilance and sacrifice for granted, we demean our rich heritage of democratic freedom guaranteed by the bloodshed of generations of Americans who have stood the lonely post far from home to assure our safety and security.

Until we discover ways to eradicate evil from the hearts of those who wish us ill, those who accept the duty of standing that post will risk, and tragically lose, their lives so that we here may enjoy our freedom. Somewhere in the Persian Gulf there is a young sailor who is someone's daughter, a combat pilot who is someone's husband, a young Marine who is someone's son. For the American nation, they are all our sons and daughters.

War is not an instrument of policy; it is a failure of policy. We cannot today discuss the use of military power as an instrument of national policy without the recognition that it is the lives of our sons and daughters that are most immediately at stake. We all must now earn our rights by performance of our duties. And our duty to our sons and daughters requires our policymakers to hold their lives in sacred trust. Only then will our national security be just as well as strong, and only then can we be truly proud of who we are.

BIBLIOGRAPHY

Gary Hart, "In Search of National Security in the 21st Century," speech delivered at the Council on Foreign Relations, New York, January 21, 2003.

———, "Note to Democrats: Get a Defense Policy," New York Times, Op-Ed page A-27, Thursday, October 3, 2002.

———, Restoration of the Republic: The Jeffersonian Ideal in 21st-Century America (Oxford: Oxford University Press, 2002).

——— and Warren B. Rudman, America Still Unprepared—America Still in Danger, Council on Foreign Relations, Washington, D.C., October 2002. At http://www.cfr.org/pdf/Homeland_Security_TF.pdf.

Robert D. Kaplan, The Coming Anarchy (New York: Random House, 2001).

United States Commission on National Security/21st Century: Road Map for National Security: Imperative for Change, Phase III report, February 15, 2001.

• 3 •

The Challenge of Managing Dominance

Jessica Tuchman Mathews

At the beginning of the twenty-first century, the United States finds itself in brand-new territory, which historically is very dangerous terrain, and one which we are very ill-prepared to deal with as a country. This territory is the role of global hegemony, and the new foreign policy challenge can be captured on a bumper sticker: the challenge of managing dominance.

No other power, at least in the last 350 years, as long as we've had nation-states, has ever had a global reach comparable to ours. Britain ruled the seas and its own colonies, but did not ever attempt to dominate the globe. There have been a couple of other attempts at hegemony since the Treaty of Westphalia—the event generally considered to signal the creation of the modern nation-state. The Hapsburgs tried it, Louis XIV tried it, Napoleon tried it, Japan tried, Germany tried it twice, and the record is pretty clear of the result. So the question is, how are we going to do at managing this challenge of dominance?

We had one answer for it, a fantastically successful one, after World War II, when for a brief period we were even more dominant in the world, both in a security sense and economically, than we are today. In those immediate years after the war, the United States represented 50 percent of the world's economy—everybody else was really smashed. Until the Soviets got nuclear weapons, we stood alone militarily as well. Everybody knows what we chose to do then, which was to invest immensely in global public goods, to create a whole raft of institutions. We reached the conclusion that a long-term policy of building the economies of other countries was going to be the most important thing we could do in our own interest, and it was, in fact, an extraordinarily successful policy for decades. Now we are at a moment of making a historic choice again, in very different circumstances, and we seem to be heading down a very different path.

It is remarkable that, just a few years ago, no one used the word "empire" in the same sentence with the name "United States," except for the far left fringe. It was not something the mainstream talked about. Now it has become routine. In fact, the only way to get foreign policy books onto the front table in bookstores right now is to put the word "empire" in the title. There are at least eight such books out there now.

The current American empire is enormously different from those that preceded it. Even those who advocate a very aggressive American stand do not want to conquer and occupy territory. However, the changes in technology, in the size of our economy, and in globalization make it possible to impose our will from a distance—without occupation—and perhaps to an even greater degree than that afforded by direct occupation. Also, today the perception of dominance is much, much greater, much more immediate.

We do not need to occupy a foreign land to have the same degree of influence over its fortunes or to have the same sense of intrusiveness on its future that those who occupied in the past did. And of course we've never had technological levelers like nuclear weapons before.

CAN DOMINANCE LAST?

The first question to ask about managing dominance is whether a moment of dominance like this can last. There are many people who believe it can and will. I am not one of them because the basic driving force of history is human nature. Human nature has its passions, its irrationality, its greed, and its propensity to feel fear, envy, resentment, and misunderstanding across cultures. These aspects of human nature will not change. They are hard-wired.

So no matter how powerful we appear to be at this moment, our moment will be limited, like everyone else's has been. With that transience in mind, we should approach this historical moment with a keen sense of the limits that we confront rather than with a feeling of triumphalism.

WHAT WORLD ORDER AFTER OUR MOMENT ENDS?

How should we then attempt to shape some sort of policy? To me, the best guide is to ask what kind of world order we would like if we were *not* in charge; or put differently, what kind of world order would you like to have the day *after* our moment of dominance ends? If one thinks of it this way, then the questions to ask and attempt to answer arise pretty naturally.

How much international law do you want to have? How much trust among nations? How much cooperation across borders? How strong or weak a set of international institutions do you want to rely on? Or do we rely on ad hoc coalitions shaped for each mission, as Donald Rumsfeld has advocated?

The difficulty with ad hoc coalitions that doesn't get enough attention in the current debate is that they only constitute a crisis-management strategy. They don't leave you anything for dealing with issues between crises. The only way you can do that is with institutions.

AMERICA'S LACK OF KNOWLEDGE

We as a country are poorly prepared for our role of dominance in terms of the knowledge of American citizens about the rest of the world. There probably has seldom been such a mismatch as now between the power of a country and its rulers and the degree to which its population is informed about the world.

Just to give you an example: polls show that a majority of the American public believes there are weapons of mass destruction in Iraq, and a near-majority believes there is an absolute connection between Saddam Hussein and al Qaeda—exactly the reverse of the facts. This long after the war, it's astonishing the percentage of the American people who still believe that there was a connection. Indeed, there are a great many who believe that Saddam Hussein was *responsible* for September 11.

I was in New York during the war one day, taking a taxi in from the airport, and the taxi driver asked me something about the war. I asked if he was in favor of the war, and he said, "Oh, of course I am. . . . I lost a friend on September 11." When I said, "Well, what does that have to do with it?" I thought we were going right off the bridge. But he took it as a given Saddam Hussein was responsible, and he would not hear that Saddam and bin Laden are not the same person. We must improve the knowledge base of our citizenry if we are to effectively and wisely manage our power.

CHRONIC UNDERESTIMATION OF POSTWAR DIFFICULTY

In terms of managing global dominance, we have two options. One is widespread, active cooperation by a large number of nations. The other is unilateral action and particularly—certainly in the security field—use of force.

It is an interesting paradox that it takes bigger armies to manage "post-wars" than it takes to fight the direct hostilities. This is new, and it is a testimony to the power of our war-fighting technology and its sophistication and to the fact that the post-war still has to be managed the old-fashioned way—door to door. This is a lesson that we have learned over and over again and that we keep forgetting.

There is an after-action report about our most recent intervention in Panama and the week of serious rioting that occurred after the intervention. The report concludes that we should have been prepared for the chaos in Panama because of our experience in Haiti. We keep learning this lesson, then forgetting it.

You may remember the fight between Donald Rumsfeld and Paul Wolfowitz on the one hand and General Shinseki on the other about how many soldiers were going to be needed in Iraq. Shinseki in fact was right, but still on the low side. He was right not because of what was needed for the war, but what was needed for the post-war. Think of it in these terms: in Germany after World War II, we had 1,500,000 soldiers, and our sector in Germany covered something like 7,000,000 Germans. We now have about 150,000 people in Iraq, in a country of 24 million. That means the ratio of Americans to persons in the places occupied is roughly about one-fortieth as great in Iraq now as Germany then. We probably had more than we needed in Germany because those people had not yet been sent home or to the Pacific, but it gives an idea of the difference in the ratio.

We need a lot more soldiers to manage the peace. But more American soldiers will only make things worse, and we don't have more soldiers available anyway (with one-third of our active duty force already in Iraq). The only solution is to multilateralize.

Clearly, our technological dominance doesn't help us with post-wars or conflict management. But the more important point is that we as a nation now chronically underestimate the difficulties of the nonmilitary aspects of all our foreign interventions. We wildly inflate our nonmilitary goals in cases like this, without committing the resources that are required to achieve them.

For example, in Iraq our military planning was brilliant and detailed down to the placement of windows on individual buildings in Baghdad, so that weapons could be targeted in such a way as to produce the least collateral damage. This was an extraordinary level of detail, combined with fantastic flexibility. When Turkey refused to let us open the northern front, the plan was changed in a metaphorical minute.

Our planning for the post-war, on the other hand, was a blend of ignorance and wishful thinking. There was an elaborate plan that had absolutely nothing to do with the specific conditions in Iraq.

A DANGEROUS IMBALANCE

Under both major American political parties, we have developed, over the last twenty years, a dangerous imbalance in the priority that we assign to the use of force and that which we assign to the use of the other tools at our disposal for foreign relations—diplomacy, intelligence, economic assistance, and democracy assistance.

We have now reached a sixteen-to-one ratio between the Pentagon budget and the budget for all other foreign operations combined. Sixteen to one in peacetime. We just don't take the nonmilitary side of what we do seriously. It is only on the nonmilitary side that we allow ourselves to indulge in goals, means, and public commitment that bear no resemblance to one another. That's what we did going into Iraq: We had a set of goals which included wildly unrealistic thoughts both about Iraq itself and about the region, we had a set of means, and then we had a set of conversations and public commitment with the American public. The three just don't belong on the same plane. They were completely disjointed.

This imbalance has gotten to a point where it is extremely hard to correct, in part because the State Department has come to be seen as so broken due to its chronic underfunding. And now Congress says "We're not going to put money into it because it's so broken." So then State gets more broken.

At the same time, the Pentagon has experienced a positive, upward spiral. For every dollar you can possibly spend, the technology gets better. So do your people, planning, training, exercises, scenario-building, and mid-career training. All the things that money can buy.

ALTERNATIVE POLICY

In my view, the Democratic Party has abandoned a serious role on security. You cannot run a country on any issue without an opposition, and the Democratic Party feels like it doesn't have credibility on security issues.

Just to give you a sense of what I mean, and I hope I'm not talking out of school, but I was asked to speak at a session on security policy at the House Democratic Caucus. It was a three-hour session, and they had a high turnout. I argued that, until the party could re-establish itself as a serious player on security, it could never again be a majority party. I said that this means more than just being opposed to things. There has to be a coherent set of principles that Democrats are *for,* a coherent strategy, and a carefully articulated budget.

During the discussion, people kept coming up with ideas related to oil conservation, noting if we used less oil then we wouldn't have to be running around invading countries. I said no, that's exactly what I'm *not* talking about. I'm not talking about energy efficiency. You can talk about energy efficiency until you are blue in the face, and nobody's going to think you're a credible player on national security. It's not the same issue.

Somebody else at the meeting talked about the importance of the role of women. Great—it's important that women have a greater role. But that's not a security strategy either. We need a view on core security issues that is visible to the people of this country—a credible and serious alternative to the current one.

This case was laid out in a recent piece that Gary Hart wrote in the *New York Times,* one of the most important articles that has been written in a long time. He wrote that we ought to have a Democratic Defense Policy Board, including the best people from the other side of the aisle and developing these issues in a way that becomes a real resource for people inside. This is the kind of positive, focused action that is needed to bring the Democratic Party into the national spotlight and gain it a voice in the security issues in our country.

CONCLUSION

Many now incorrectly argue that the current aggressive American position on democracy and freedom is a return to Wilsonianism. It is true that Wilson was aggressive on democracy. But Wilson also believed that America ought to be embedded—deeply embedded, to use a current term—in international organizations and rules to which we were not an exception, but an integral part. In other words, Wilson believed that we had to be constrained by the rule of law. The current U.S. administration takes a completely different approach, which is that we should sit on a different plane, above the rest of the international community, and be unconstrained. According to the current fashion, constraints are *ipso facto* dangerous, and a bad idea for America, for the world, and for American security. That is a perversion of Wilson's principles.

What, then, should our goals be as we manage our current global dominance and prepare for a day when that dominance may not be ours?

First, America's foreign policy should be based on alliances, not ad hoc coalitions. Alliances reflect an underlying sharing of values and goals and a common community that does not have to be recreated every single time a problem requires action.

Second, in an era when more and more issues are moving from domestic to international, and from international to global, it stands to reason that problem-solving takes place in international space. So we need strong international institutions.

Third, foreign policy must recognize that issues, resentments, and positive relationships are not contained within a single forum but are spread across forums. We cannot, for example, decide we want to be international on trade policy but unilateral on military policy.

Last, we must create a better balance in spending between diplomacy and force. There was never a secretary of state in a stronger position than Colin Powell to argue that the State Department has been chronically starved of money vis-à-vis the Pentagon. The tax cuts of recent years do not remotely allow America to pursue the kind of foreign policy that is needed.

BIBLIOGRAPHY

Joseph Cirincione, Jessica T. Mathews, George Perkovich, with Alexis Orton, *WMD in Iraq: Evidence and Implications*, Carnegie Endowment for International Peace report, January 2004.

Gary Hart, "Note to Democrats: Get a Defense Policy," *New York Times*, Thursday, October 3, 2002.

Jessica T. Mathews, "Arming the Arms Inspectors," *New York Times,* September 19, 2002.

———, "Iraqis Can Do More," *Washington Post,* September 29, 2003.

———, "Is There a Better Way to Go?" *Washington Post,* February 9, 2003.

———, "War is Not Yet Necessary," *Washington Post,* January 28, 2003.

• *4* •

A Compromised Central Intelligence Agency: What Can Be Done?

Ray McGovern

It is said that truth is the first casualty of war. Truth was the currency of analysis in the Central Intelligence Agency in which I was proud to serve. The agency then was known as a unique place to which one could go and expect a straight answer, unencumbered by political agendas.

Sadly, that has now gone by the board, as the 9/11 commission has documented. Central Intelligence Agency analysis has been corrupted, to the detriment of an America that has no comprehensive national security strategy against terrorism and had no proof of "weapons of mass destruction" before invading Iraq. It is time to acknowledge that the CIA has become so politicized that it has lost its credibility. Even though a remnant of indefatigable analysts in the ranks continues to try to "tell it like it is," the sound they make is akin to that of the proverbial tree falling far out of earshot. They have been sold out, their raison d'etre sacrificed by senior management on the altar of political expediency. The intelligence assessment process is broken, a reality greeted with striking nonchalance by an American government seemingly unconcerned that an essential tool of effective policymaking has been lost.

Compared with the constitutional crisis of fall 2002, when Congress was misled into ceding to the White House its constitutional right to declare war, the corruption of CIA analysis may seem like small potatoes. But the role that senior agency officials played as willing accomplices in the process has made a mockery of the verse chiseled into the marble at the entrance to CIA headquarters: "You will know the truth, and the truth will set you free." Analysts who still take that verse seriously are thoroughly demoralized.

The politicization of the Central Intelligence Agency began to be institutionalized twenty years ago under CIA Director William Casey and his protégé Robert Gates. But it culminated in the fall of 2002, when then-Director George

Tenet succumbed to pressure to conjure up "intelligence" to justify a prior decision to invade Iraq. Had Tenet been tenaciously honest, it is a safe bet that agency analysts would have risen to the occasion. And their input might have helped prevent the launching of our country's first large-scale war of aggression—a war that Tenet and his analysts knew had little to do with the "intelligence" adduced to justify it.

The "high-confidence" judgments of the National Intelligence Estimate "Iraq's Continuing Programs for Weapons of Mass Destruction" of October 2002 are mocked by chief U.S. Inspector David Kay's 2004 report that he could find no such weapons. This constitutes the worst American intelligence debacle in forty years. Not since the National Intelligence Estimate of September 1962 that concluded that the Soviet Union would not risk putting missiles in Cuba (while, in fact, they were already en route) has an intelligence estimate been so wrong on so serious a matter.

The Cuban estimate was wrong—a grave but honest mistake. The estimate on Iraq was dishonest—and no mistake. It provided the cover story for a war launched for a twin purpose: (1) to gain an enduring strategic foothold in the oil-rich Middle East and (2) to eliminate any possible threat to Israeli dominance of the region. While these aims are generally consistent with longstanding American policy objectives, no previous U.S. administration thought it acceptable to use war to achieve them.

That twin purpose leaps out of neoconservative literature and was widely understood from Canada to Europe to Australia. Australian intelligence, for example, boldly told the government in Canberra that the focus on weapons of mass destruction was a red herring to divert attention from the "more important reasons" behind the neoconservatives' determination to launch this war of choice. It strains credulity to suppose that what was clear in Canberra could have escaped the attention of senior CIA officials. They knew it all too well. And, sadly, they proved all too eager to serve up to their masters what was clearly wanted—an ostensible *casus belli*: "weapons of mass destruction" in Iraq. Sycophancy has no place in intelligence work, and certainly not in matters of war and peace. The unforgivable sin is telling the policymaker what he wants to hear—justifying with cooked "intelligence" what he has already decided to do. CIA credibility has taken a major hit, and it is far from certain that the agency can recover. It used to be that, in such circumstances, one would look to Congress to conduct an investigation. But the intelligence committees have given new meaning to the word "oversight."

David Kay's report that "probably eighty-five percent of the significant things" had been found, but no weapons of mass destruction, sent out political shock waves. As a result, another commision was formed, beyond the 9/11 commission. Called the Commission on Intelligence Capabilities of the United States Regarding Weapons of Mass Destruction, this White House–appointed panel will not necessarily convey new insights to the American people.

INITIAL STEPS TOWARD REFORM

Sadly, the CIA I was privileged to serve is no more. Restoration of integrity and credibility will not come until top executive and legislative leaders are able to prescind from politics long enough to understand the serious risks attending the politicization of intelligence. This is not likely to happen soon, but some useful preparatory work has been done.

If any good can come out of the intelligence/policy debacle on Iraq, it would be the clear lesson that intelligence, crafted to dovetail with the perceived predilections of policymakers, spells disaster. This conclusion stands out in bas relief in *WMD in Iraq: Evidence and Implications*, the exhaustive study published in 2004 by the Carnegie Endowment for International Peace.

Carnegie recommended a "nonpartisan independent commission . . . to establish a clear picture of what the intelligence community knew and believed it knew about Iraq's weapons program throughout 1991–2002." This would be an entity independent of the government's own commission on weapons of mass destruction (above). The Carnegie recommendation is eminently sensible. However, my enthusiasm for such panels is dampened by the painful experience of observing presidential and congressional commissions in the past, including the difficulty they encounter in remaining immune to political pressures, the steep learning curve that many commission members typically face, and the fact that such commissions, as often as not, come up with naïve, sometimes mischievous, recommendations.[1] And they often take years to complete their work.

The need to repair American intelligence cannot be left to the dalliance, caprice, and politics that typically taint such commissions. Fortunately, much solid work has already been done by serious scholars. Reading Carnegie's *WMD in Iraq: Evidence and Implications* carefully, a middle-schooler can figure out *what* happened. In this chapter, I will spend some time looking at *how* and *why* it happened. Additional footnotes could be added to the Carnegie study, but the key problems are already clear and the need for repair is urgent. Certain rudimentary steps can be taken even now to inoculate against the further spread of politicization.

This chapter focuses on ways to facilitate the return of fierce honesty and professionalism to the analytic process and to impede efforts to politicize the intelligence product. In an institution like the CIA, significant, enduring improvement requires vision and courage at the top. The nation needs the kind of integrity and courage not seen in a director of central intelligence for a quarter of a century.

It is clear, then, that we need to start right there—with the director. Character counts. Without the right kind of person in that position, the CIA is doomed to be prostituted and marginalized more and more, while strong personalities—in the Pentagon and the office of the vice president, for example—continue to usurp the agency's functions, preempt its analysis, and render it largely irrelevant.

Structural changes in recent years, as well as failings in leadership, have rendered intelligence analysis less complete, less professional, and easier to manipulate. So a good way to start the repair job would be to revert to some of the best practices of the past. Specifically, I recommend below that the United States needs to upgrade the standards upon which we choose a director of central intelligence; generate more timely, comprehensive, professional, transparent, and apolitical national intelligence estimates; return imagery analysis, agenda-free, from the Pentagon to the Central Intelligence Agency; and reconstitute an independent media analysis capability in the Central Intelligence Agency. With such reforms in place in recent years, America might have been better prepared for the September 11 attacks, an understanding of their underlying causes might have been developed, the tenuousness of the evidence on weapons of mass destruction in Iraq could have been injected into the public debate on Iraq, and a new national security agenda more in keeping with Gary Hart's proposals (chapter 2) would have been facilitated.

THE QUALITIES NEEDED IN A DIRECTOR OF CENTRAL INTELLIGENCE

The director of central intelligence (DCI) must be a person whose previous professional performance has been distinguished by unimpeachable integrity and independence. The director must have the courage of his or her own convictions. Without integrity and courage, all virtue is specious, and no amount of structural or organizational reform will make any difference.

Instructive lessons can be drawn from the performance of former director George Tenet and from his predecessors regarding what attributes a director needs to discharge the duties of the office as the National Security Act of 1947 intended.

The director should have already made a mark on the world by excelling in a field unrelated to intelligence work—business, the military, or academia—bringing a well-established record of honesty and competence. If he comes from more humble circumstances than most top administration officials, it is essential that her or his strength of character and self-confidence be such that there is no need to depend on the anointing of Washington *hoi aristoi* for reassurance of self worth.

These qualities are all the more essential because of the mismatch of responsibility and authority in the director of central intelligence's position. As the chief foreign intelligence adviser to the president, the director has broad responsibility for coordinating the intelligence effort of a dozen agencies of government, but has little operational or budgetary control over most of them. As a result, the director's authority is essentially ad referendum to the president. Too many directors of central intelligence, out of a desire to be good team players, have been reluctant to seek and invoke that authority. A notable exception was Admiral Stansfield Turner, whose military background instilled in him an acute appreciation of the need for command authority to match responsibility. Turner knew he had to take determined steps to dispel the ambiguity—and did. Thus, when the parochial interests of, say, the Federal Bureau of Investigation or the National Security Agency got in the way of his intelligence community coordinating responsibilities, Turner would simply meet with President Carter and lay it on the line. "If you want me to be able to discharge my responsibilities as your principal intelligence adviser," he would say, "you need to tell the attorney general to instruct the Federal Bureau of Investigation to be more responsive, and the secretary of defense to tell the National Security Agency to do the same." In other words, there is a way to deal with the anomalies inherent in the director's portfolio, but it takes a DCI who is willing to put noses out of joint in order to assert the necessary authority to do his job. Such directors have been few and far between.

To be concrete, let's take the experience of George Tenet as an example. Here are a few of the things he should have told the president when he was director:

- The FBI is not sharing with my people the information they need. Would you instruct the attorney general to tell the bureau to cooperate?
- The vice president and secretary of defense have each established, in their offices, mini-CIAs to push their own agendas. They are using their privileged access to you to promote intelligence judgments with which my analysts and I do not agree. If you wish me to be able to discharge my statutory duties effectively, please make it clear to them that they are required to vet such analysis with the Central Intelligence Agency so that we can put it into perspective *before* it is given to you.
- The same goes for raw reporting from the field or from liaison intelligence services. I am particularly upset that Israel regularly skirts established procedures and gives raw information to top White House and Pentagon officials before Central Intelligence Agency analysts have time to evaluate it. Quite aside from the fact that by law I am responsible for substantive liaison with foreign services, serious mischief can result when the Central Intelligence Agency is not able to comment on key reports before they are acted upon. Think back to June of 2002, for example, when, on the strength of an Israeli report that the CIA had not had a chance to evaluate properly, you were persuaded to reverse the longstanding American policy of recognizing Yasir Arafat as the duly elected representative of the Palestinian people. Surely, if the crescendo of violence over recent years has proven anything, it is that Arafat simply cannot be left out.

- You need to ensure that the Central Intelligence Agency and other parts of the intelligence community have the opportunity to provide appropriate intelligence input before major decisions are made. Think, for example, of the sudden, arbitrary decision by Ahmed Chalabi, Secretary Donald Rumsfeld, and Ambassador Paul Bremer to disband the Iraqi army. Were my people given the chance, they could have told you that would be a very dumb idea.
- Experience—including mine—has shown that it is counterproductive over the long run for the DCI to have advocated for or become associated with any particular policy. I should have known better than to become so closely associated with the "Tenet Plan" for Israel-Palestine. How, for example, can my analysts retain any credibility for objective assessment of that plan's prospects for success when it bears my name?

The director of central intelligence must *not* need the job, and he must have the self-confidence and courage to resign when the demands of integrity dictate this as the only honorable course. Should the president refuse to honor the kind of requests I have just illustrated, the DCI should give very serious consideration to resigning.

Directors of central intelligence cannot let themselves be used, as the vice president and defense secretary used Tenet, for example. Historically, depending on who was president at the time, several DCIs had the experience of being marginalized by the White House. And some, like William Colby, were fired. But Colby's marginalization and eventual firing came as a result of his standing on principle (and standing up to Henry Kissinger), not for letting himself be used.

It is a myth that the DCI must enjoy a close personal relationship with the president. In fact, doing so is a net minus. The White House is not a fraternity house; mutual respect is far more important than camaraderie. A mature, self-confident president will respect an independent director. The director must avoid being "part of the team" in the way the president's political advisers are part of the team. Overly close identification with "the team" can erode objectivity and cloud intelligence judgments. Former Speaker Newt Gingrich, a frequent visitor to CIA headquarters to "help" with analysis on Iraq, told the press that Director Tenet was "so grateful to the president that he would do anything for him." That attitude is the antithesis of what is needed in a director.

A DCI who has built a relationship of mutual respect with the president does not need to join the briefer who presents the President's Daily Brief. It is far better to encourage those senior analysts to brief, as we did in the past, unencumbered by a boss looking over our shoulder. And in ordinary circumstances, one session with the president per week should be enough face-time to discuss key substantive issues and, when necessary, Central Intelligence Agency operations.

As a general rule, a DCI should not be drawn from the operational ranks of the agency. Major mistakes made by Allen Dulles, Richard Helms, and William Casey provide ample proof that having a spy at the helm is a poor idea. (William Colby, who had an unusually wide grasp of the analytic as well as the operational function of intelligence—and a keen respect for the Constitution—was a notable exception to this guideline.)

A director has to be a wise manager. The director must be able to function effectively while standing astride the structural fault created by the National Security Act of 1947, which allowed for DCI involvement in operational matters in addition to the director's primary role as chief substantive intelligence adviser to the president. This unenviable, schizophrenic portfolio demands uncommon self-confidence, objectivity, balance, and skill—and, again, integrity. Among those who failed the test were Dulles, with the Bay of Pigs disaster; Helms, who, while running large-scale operations in Vietnam, knowingly acquiesced in General William Westmoreland's deceptively low estimates of Vietnamese Communist troop strength; and Casey, with his personal involvement in an array of misadventures in Central America and Iran/Contra, his cooking of intelligence to promote and support those escapades, and his unswerving devotion to the idea that the Soviet Union could never change. The congressional hearings on Iran-Contra and on Robert Gates's nomination to head the agency revealed many examples of how Casey and Gates politicized intelligence analysis.

Although appointed by the president, a director of central intelligence needs to resist pressure to play politics. Some directors of central intelligence have played the political game—most of them ineptly, it turns out. Helms, for example, bent over backwards to accommodate President Nixon—to the point of perjuring himself before Congress. Yet Helms never could overcome Nixon's paranoid suspicion of him as one of that "Georgetown crowd out to get me." Chalk it up to our naiveté as intelligence analysts, but we were shocked when James Schlesinger, upon succeeding Helms as director early in Nixon's first term, announced on arrival, "I am here to see that you guys don't screw Richard Nixon!" The freshly appointed DCI supplemented the news about his main mission by announcing that he would be reporting to Bob Haldeman, not Henry Kissinger. A director must not have a political agenda. Ironically—and to his credit—George H. W. Bush, who had been chair of the Republican National Committee before being named director of central intelligence, was careful to avoid policy advocacy. But even he found it impossible to resist political pressure to appoint "Team B," a group of extreme hardliners, to review intelligence community estimates on Soviet strategic forces.

Neither must a director of central intelligence have a personal agenda. The tenure of John Deutch provided a case study in the disasters that can attend overweening ambition on the part of a director. Deutch made no secret that he was accepting the job only as a way station to replacing his close friend William Perry as secretary of defense. Thus, it should have come as no surprise that Deutch made rather callous, calculated decisions to improve the chances for his candidacy. Deutch gave the Pentagon his full cooperation in covering up the fact for several years that about 101,000 (the Pentagon's current estimate) U.S. troops were exposed to chemical warfare agents, including sarin, cyclosarin, and mustard gases, at the end of the Gulf War. And in 1996 he ceded the Central Intelligence Agency's entire imagery analysis capability to the Pentagon, lock, stock, and barrel (about which more later). Deutch was devastated when President Bill Clinton picked William Cohen to succeed Perry, and he left the Central Intelligence Agency with such a long trail of grave security violations that he needed one of Bill Clinton's last-day pardons to escape prosecution. (Deutch's personal agenda was so transparent that, aside from the people he brought with him to the Central Intelligence Agency to do his bidding, there was hardly a soul sorry to see him go.)

No director of central intelligence should come from Congress, the quintessential example of the kind of politicized ambience that is antithetical to substantive intelligence work. For example, outside intelligence circles, it was deemed a good sign that, as a congressional staffer, George Tenet had been equally popular on both sides of the aisle. But this raised a red flag for seasoned intelligence professionals. As we had all learned early in our careers, if you tell it like it is, you are certain to make enemies. Those enjoying universal popularity are ipso facto suspect of perfecting the political art of compromise—shading this and shaving that. However useful this may be on the Hill, it sounds the death knell for intelligence analysis. In addition to having come from Congress, Tenet had zero prior experience managing a large organization. He played the political game, and he presided over two disasters: September 11 and Iraq.

RESCUING NATIONAL INTELLIGENCE ESTIMATES

There is so much wrong now with the process of creating national intelligence estimates that it is hard to know where to begin the repair work. What follows is some background on the unhappy experience with a highly unfortunate "misoverestimate" and some rudimentary recommendations.

The Weapons of Mass Destruction Estimate

There was no national intelligence estimate on Iraq and its "weapons of mass destruction" before one was ordered and hurriedly prepared in September 2002, several months *after* the administration decided to make war on Iraq. That fact speaks volumes. The last thing the people running American policy from the Pentagon and the Office of the Vice President wanted was a national intelligence estimate from the intelligence community that might complicate their planning. Because it was abundantly clear that none was wanted, none was scheduled. The DCI and his senior managers were happy to acquiesce in this. It got them off the horns of a distasteful dilemma—namely, having to choose between commissioning an honest estimate that would inevitably call into serious question the Pentagon's rationale for war on Iraq (Option A), or ensuring that an estimate was cooked to the recipe of policy—that is, massaged to justify an earlier decision for war (Option B).

Until September 2002, George Tenet was able to avoid this dilemma, in the process abnegating his responsibility as the principal intelligence adviser to the president. Tenet probably calculated (no doubt correctly) that the president would be just as pleased not to have complications introduced after he had already decided for war. And so the director of central intelligence, precisely at a time when he should have been leaning hard on his analysts to prepare an objective estimate, danced away from doing one until it was forced on him.

In mid-September 2002, as the administration began making its case for war, Senator Richard Durbin alerted Senator Bob Graham, then chair of the Senate Select Committee on Intelligence, to the fact that no national intelligence estimate had been written. Graham insisted that an estimate be prepared. To no one's surprise, Tenet immediately chose Option B and picked a trusted aide, Robert Walpole, to chair the estimate. Walpole had just the pedigree. In 1998, he had won Donald Rumsfeld's favor by revising an earlier estimate to exaggerate the strategic threat from countries like North Korea. Key conclusions (since proven mistaken) of that national intelligence estimate met Rumsfeld's immediate need quite nicely and greased the skids for early deployment of a multi-billion-dollar, unproven antiballistic missile system.

Walpole came through again in September 2002, this time on Iraq, and in barely three weeks (such estimates normally take several months). An honest national intelligence estimate on "Iraq's Continuing Programs for Weapons of Mass Destruction" would not have borne that title, but rather would have concluded that there was no persuasive evidence of "continuing programs." But that, of course, was not the answer desired by those who had already decided on war. Thus, a much more ominous prospect was portrayed, including the "high-confidence" (but erroneous) judgments that Iraq had chemical and biological weapons and was reconstituting its program to develop nuclear weapons—judgments at variance with the statements of senior intelligence and policy officials the year before.

In an apologia released by the Central Intelligence Agency in 2003, Stuart Cohen, Walpole's immediate boss as head of the National Intelligence Council, avoided personal endorsement of the judgments of the 2002 estimate but stated his belief that the writers were "on solid ground" in how they reached their judgments. Cohen cautioned that "we do not know" whether physical evidence of Iraq's chemical and biological weapons will ever be found. Cohen added, "If we eventually are proved wrong—that is, that there were no weapons of mass destruction and the WMD programs were dormant or abandoned—the American people will be told the truth." One is left wondering how much longer "eventually" will be.

In 2004, the vice president insisted on "some additional, considerable period of time to look [for weapons of mass destruction] in all the cubbyholes and ammo dumps . . . where you'd expect to find something like that." And, speaking at Georgetown University in 2004, Tenet posed the question himself: "Why haven't we found the weapons? I have told you the search must continue and it will be difficult."

Reform of National Intelligence Estimates

Preventing a repeat of the agency's performance on Iraq will require changes at the most senior level of the Central Intelligence Agency and wholesale decontamination of the National Intelligence Council and the Directorate of Intelligence. Given the current composition and disposition of congressional overseers, that seems highly unlikely anytime soon. What follows, therefore, are some short-run measures to render it more difficult to continue to pollute the analytic process.

The Senate Select Committee on Intelligence and the House Permanent Select Committee on Intelligence need to take an active hand in ensuring that appropriate national intelligence estimates are scheduled, prepared, and completed in a timely way. There can be no excuse for the deliberate absence of a national intelligence estimate on Iraq's weaponry before the administration decided in favor of war. And it is a sad commentary on congressional oversight that no one seemed to notice. When Senator Richard Durbin finally did, the juggernaut for war was halfway there.

Also conspicuous by its absence was a national intelligence estimate on Iraq's alleged ties to al Qaeda and other terrorist groups. General Brent Scowcroft, chair of the president's Foreign Intelligence Advisory Board, felt this issue important enough to put himself on record as saying that evidence of such ties was "scant." But for Secretary Rumsfeld, the evidence was "bulletproof."

These are precisely the kind of polarized conditions in which preparation of an intelligence community–wide national intelligence estimate (NIE) can provide an invaluable service, if it is an objective assessment that is sought. And Congress should have insisted that such an NIE be prepared. George Tenet calculated correctly. The situation in which he found himself, however awkward, was *not* a case of "damned if he did, and damned if he didn't." True, if he "did," Tenet would have been damned—by Rumsfeld, Vice President Cheney, and other members of the "team." This would have been the inevitable result if Tenet had transcended his timidity and directed that an honest estimate be prepared, because Central Intelligence Agency analysts, after painstakingly vetting thousands of reports, continued to find no persuasive evidence of meaningful Iraqi ties to al Qaeda. But "damned if he didn't"?

Hardly. Tenet knew that, given the support he enjoyed among some key members of the intelligence committees for having been a dependable "member of the team" and given the general miasma prevailing among many committee members, there would be little risk to him if he ducked doing an estimate.

Sadly, Iraq is not an exceptional case. For years, George Tenet avoided commissioning an estimate on North Korea, preferring to let the Pentagon and State Department argue endlessly about Pyongyang's nuclear capability and its intentions. North Korea's nuclear capability is a key issue, but so is the more general question of what drives the leaders in Pyongyang. What are their aspirations and objectives? This is the stuff of a traditional NIE. Such estimates are not easy to produce, but in the past there were regularly scheduled NIEs on "Prospects for North Korea" and other critical countries and issues.

It is one thing for North Korea to have the wherewithal to make a nuclear weapon. It is quite another thing to develop a delivery capability that would enable an intercontinental ballistic missile to hit the United States with a nuclear warhead. I alluded above to senior Central Intelligence Agency official Robert Walpole, who in 1998 chaired an estimate that predicted, among other things, that North Korea could have the capability to deliver such a weapon on the United States in five years. This was judged to be of such importance that a congressionally directed action mandated an annual update on the nature and scope of the threat. Three such reports were done, and the date kept slipping for a North Korean intercontinental ballistic missile. But no matter. The 1998 estimate had served its purpose. Its erroneous conclusions had been of immense help in facilitating antiballistic missile funding, the decision to abrogate the ABM treaty of 1972, and initial construction for an ABM system even before it has been adequately tested. As such, the 1998 estimate smacked of what intelligence professionals greet with the deepest distain—what we call "budgetary intelligence."

Beyond appropriate and timely national intelligence estimates, we need a post mortem conducted by an independent body to evaluate the preparation of the 1998 NIE "Foreign Missile Developments and the Ballistic Missile Threat to the United States Through 2015" and a fresh estimate on this same subject, with a new chair to oversee it.

Is there an NIE that addresses the prospects for worldwide terrorism? One should be scheduled and conducted annually, with a sanitized version made widely available.

Then there is Israel, which has more weapons of mass destruction than all the Arab states put together. By what logic do intelligence community managers attempt to exclude estimates on Israel's formidable arsenal when scheduling NIEs on foreign countries with weapons of mass destruction? Do we not have a pressing need for NIEs looking at Israel's intentions vis-à-vis Syria, Iran, and Lebanon? And for estimates of how key Arab states regard Israel's formidable array of weapons of mass destruction?

Perhaps most useful of all, why not a broad-gauge estimate on the entire Middle East region, one that looks ahead to the expected outcome of various scenarios in the next few years? Arguably, there may be a market somewhere for an academic-type look twenty years ahead (like the "2020 Project" recently launched by the National Intelligence Council). But that market is not among policy makers and politicians with maximum horizons of six months, or two to four years. They would be far better served by an NIE titled "Near-Term Prospects for the Middle East," as used to be the custom.

In sum, it is high time that oversight committee members play a more active role in ensuring that the director of central intelligence discharges the statutory responsibility to provide timely national intelligence estimates on key countries and strategic issues, even (indeed, especially) when the administration itself appears just as happy to go without.

The congressional committees also should require more transparency in the process of preparing NIEs. John Adams warned us 240 years ago, "Liberty cannot be preserved without general knowledge among the people." There is good reason for the public to be made aware when an estimate is under way and to receive a summary version of at least the key judgments as soon as possible after the director has signed the estimate and given it to the president. Preparation of an unclassified version is a key step in the process and requires particular care. Consideration should be given to a possible role for committee staff at this editorial end of the process to ensure that what is released to the public is as faithful as possible to the original classified estimate.[2]

The Need for Formal Collegial Review

Last but not least, there should be a formal collegial review of all important NIEs. This used to take place in the National Intelligence Council's predecessor organization, the Board of National Estimates, which was comprised of a dozen or so distinguished men and women, including several from outside the intelligence community. A re-established board of that kind could provide a very valuable service.

Veteran Intelligence Professionals for Sanity, the organization I co-founded, would be willing to devote time and effort to such an important task. Most of us graduated cum laude, so to speak, from our respective intelligence agencies and have the breadth of experience appropriate for such a review function. We are keenly aware of the critical role intelligence can and should play in support of the policy-making process, and we very much care what happens to intelligence.

Stuart Cohen, the National Intelligence Council official I mentioned above, might have avoided an unfortunate inaccuracy had he taken the trouble to read the op-eds and other issuances of Veteran Intelligence Professionals for Sanity members over the past two years. In his 2003 statement, Cohen claimed "No reasonable person could have viewed the totality of the information [on Iraqi weapons of mass destruction] and reached any conclusions or alternative views that were profoundly different from those reached in the NIE." The writings of Veteran Intelligence Professionals for Sanity members consistently contained conclusions and alternative views that were indeed profoundly different. And Cohen never indicated he thought us not "reasonable"—at least back when many of us worked with him at the Central Intelligence Agency.

AGENDA-FREE IMAGERY ANALYSIS

The Central Intelligence Agency has virtually no control over one of the most important sources of intelligence: imagery analysis. Former Director John Deutch ceded responsibility for imagery analysis to the Pentagon. (At the time, Deutch stood atop the short list of candidates to become secretary of defense as soon as his friend William Perry left that post.)

In the heyday of imagery analysis, the Central Intelligence Agency's Office of Imagery Analysis worked very closely with the interagency National Photographic Interpretation Center, proud discoverer of Soviet missiles in Cuba and guarantor of "trust-but-verify" strategic arms control agreements, to constitute a highly professional capability. The National Photographic Interpretation Center was staffed principally by analysts from the Central Intelligence Agency and the Defense Intelligence Agency and was administered by the Central Intelligence Agency's Directorate of Science and Technology. Both the Office of Imagery Analysis (OIA) and the National Photographic Interpretation Center (NPIC) were as thoroughly apolitical as they were professional. John Deutch summarily terminated both.

When Deutch handed over the National Photographic Interpretation Center to the Pentagon in 1996, seasoned imagery analysts—many of whom had spent long years facing down Pentagon attempts to exaggerate the Soviet threat, for example, left imagery analysis in droves. They took other jobs at the Central Intelligence Agency rather than join an outfit in which they knew there would be no career protection for speaking truth to power if the truth in question was unwelcome. The damage from this brain drain could be seen all too plainly in the years that followed: For example, America failed to detect India's preparations to test a nuclear weapon in 1998 and mistakenly bombed the Chinese embassy in Belgrade in 1999. Against this background, Secretary of State Colin Powell's emphasis in a United Nations speech in 2003 on the importance of the "years and years of experience" needed by imagery analysts had an ironically poignant ring to those of us who knew what had happened when the National Photographic Interpretation Center and Office of Imagery Analysis were abolished.

One need not return to the 1990s, however, to see the damage. It is well known that former favorites Ahmed Chalabi and his associates, who now have been disowned by the Pentagon and White House, were paid handsomely for reporting on Saddam Hussein's "weapons of mass destruction" and that this reporting was used to promote the war. Before the NPIC was given to the Pentagon, Central Intelligence Agency all-source analysts could depend on the veteran imagery analysts of the NPIC and OIA to either verify or cast doubt on such reporting. The fierce independence maintained by the NPIC and OIA in resisting command influence and departmental bias in analysis was as important an asset as the experience and professionalism of the imagery analysts. No serious secretary of defense would risk claiming, "We know where they [WMD] are," when he knew that his next telephone call would probably be from the NPIC or OIA saying, "Please tell us where they are. We've checked our own holdings, including the pile of reports from Chalabi's sources, but still cannot find any weapons of mass destruction."

Lack of professionalism showed through in a highly embarrassing way during Secretary Powell's debut as an imagery analyst before the United Nations Security Council in 2003. Just after his appearance, Powell had to sit for a public lecture from then-chief United Nations inspector Hans Blix, who exposed a glaring non sequitur in Powell's argument that two photos demonstrated Iraq's intent to hide chemical warfare–associated activity.

Powell should have known better than to rely on his erstwhile colleagues at Defense; it was not the first time he was burned. In his autobiography, he included a highly instructive vignette from the 1991 Gulf War. U.S. forces were having no luck finding Iraqi Scud surface-to-surface missiles before they could be launched at Israel and other targets. So Powell, then chairman of the Joint Chiefs, was delighted to hear one day that General Norman Schwarzkopf had just told the press that several Scuds had been located and destroyed on their launchers.

Before Powell had time to rejoice, though, his intelligence chief warned that an imagery analyst on Schwarzkopf's own staff had concluded that what had been destroyed were not Scuds, but oil tanker trucks. Powell called Schwarzkopf at once, but Schwarzkopf badmouthed the imagery analyst and delivered such a rich string of expletives that Powell decided to let the story stand—a decision he regretted the next day when CNN showed photos of the destroyed Jordanian oil tankers. The fate of the imagery analyst who identified the tankers is not known; it would be interesting to discover whether his or her accurate call turned out to be career enhancing.

The role played by imagery analysis leading up to the war on Iraq is a major unanswered question. Given the billions invested in the most sophisticated satellite and other imagery systems, it remains a curiosity that imagery could not have at least hinted at what we all now know to be the case—that there have been no weapons of mass destruction in Iraq since the 1990s. (See also David Corn's conclusions in chapter 12 and Joseph Wilson's conclusions in chapter 15.)

The key task of imagery analysis therefore must be returned from the Pentagon to the one agency with a somewhat tarnished but more credible claim to objectivity. The Central Intelligence Agency's Office of Imagery Analysis should be reconstituted. The director of central intelligence should regain control of the imagery analysis capability that was transferred in 1996 from the National Photographic Interpretation Center to the Department of Defense's National Imagery and Mapping Agency (since renamed the National Geospatial-Intelligence Agency).

MEDIA ANALYSIS: A KEY DISCIPLINE OF INTELLIGENCE ASSESSMENT

Media analysis for the American government was instituted in 1941 as a way of gleaning intelligence from German and Japanese open media. After the war, the Central Intelligence Agency received responsibility for media analysis, and its practitioners were housed in the Foreign Broadcast Information Service. Their work quickly distinguished itself by its intellectual vigor and its timeliness. The content analysis techniques and methodology employed in media analysis now represent a key subdiscipline of political science and won Foreign Broadcast Information Service analysts wide respect, both within and outside the intelligence community.

Because the Foreign Broadcast Information Service was devoted principally to collection, it eventually became an office in the Central Intelligence Agency's Directorate of Science and Technology, moving from the Directorate of Intelligence, which is responsible for all-source intelligence analysis. This anomalous perch—an analysis group outside the analysis directorate—had the felicitous, if unintended, consequence of affording media analysts in Foreign Broadcast Information Service an unusual degree of autonomy. This, in turn, made it particularly attractive to serious specialists with low tolerance for layer upon layer of bureaucracy.

As deputy director of Foreign Broadcast Information Service's Analysis Group in the mid-1980s, I was privileged to watch the group's Soviet analysts become the first in the intelligence community to recognize Mikhail Gorbachev for the revolutionary he was. While Central Intelligence Agency Director William Casey and his protégé Robert Gates held fast to the belief that Gorbachev was just a clever commie, Foreign Broadcast Information Service analysts were quick to see—and report—that profound change was in the offing for the Soviet Union.

From the day Gorbachev took power, Foreign Broadcast Information Service media analysts turned in an enviable performance in forecasting and tracking his path-breaking reforms—as is suggested by the titles of some of the early papers: Gorbachev's Arms Control Plan: Breaking With the Past (January 1986) and The 27th Soviet Party Congress: An Agenda for Change (April 1986). There were no early national intelligence estimates or Directorate of Intelligence papers reaching such conclusions, in part because of the well-known bias of Casey and Gates.

Foreign Broadcast Information Service analytic papers on key issues like arms control received particularly high consumer ratings for objectivity and professionalism. (Again, they were the only analytic papers on the street, given the sclerotic effect that the Casey/Gates mindset had on the all-source analysts in the Directorate of Intelligence.) Foreign Broadcast Information Service analysts subjected controversial issues to particularly rigorous scrutiny. Special memoranda analyzing Soviet pronouncements on antiballistic missile research, for example, found eager audiences among key U.S. government consumers on both sides of such highly contentious issues. Though accurate, these studies occasionally ran afoul of Gates, then deputy director for intelligence, who accused the Foreign Broadcast Information Service of poaching on his preserve.

Key players like Secretary of State George Shultz, who had grown openly distrustful of the intelligence coming from Casey and Gates, found Foreign Broadcast Information Service analysis an oasis of professionalism and objectivity. Shultz displayed an unusual openness to new possibilities and urged on President Ronald Reagan the possible merits of reaching out to Gorbachev. We know the rest of the story.

Despite all this—or perhaps because of it—Central Intelligence Agency management abolished the Foreign Broadcast Information Service Analysis Group over ten years ago and dispersed media analysts among three geographically organized units focused on collection. The ability of the analysts to undertake in-depth analysis on increasingly urgent transnational problems like terrorism atrophied. Senior managers from the Directorate of Intelligence who were brought into the Foreign Broadcast Information Service had little appreciation for the power of media analysis, and this contributed further to the decline of the art.

Had there been a unit of media analysis practitioners plumbing the statements of Osama bin Laden and his chief lieutenants over the past decade or so, it is a safe bet that those analysts would have been able to throw helpful light on his intentions, his tactics, his supporters—and, indeed, on "why they hate us." As for the occasional statements attributed to the likes of bin Laden, the present administration is free to dismiss them as propaganda, but it is a pity that no one in the White House realizes that it is possible to squeeze useful intelligence out of such statements. Clandestine collection is by no means necessary to reach confident judgments as to "why they hate us."

This may sound strange coming from an intelligence officer with twenty-seven years of immersion in clandestinely acquired intelligence, but the lion's share of the information about most countries, movements, and groups comes from open sources. The most important data we have about a country's intentions is usually what that country says publicly. All too often the mystique of secret sources can trump more accurate information and common sense. Were any serious media analysts looking critically at what Iraqi media were saying before the war and reporting their findings to those who needed them?

Perhaps a tangible example drawn from recent history will bring further clarity on the merits of media analysis. In 2003, the Australian Senate censured Prime

Minister John Howard for misleading the public with spurious evidence that Iraq had stockpiles of biological and chemical weapons and for suppressing warnings from Australian intelligence that war on Iraq would increase the likelihood of terrorist attacks. Shortly before the censure, Colonel Andrew Wilkie, the only intelligence analyst to resign his post in protest against the war, had given testimony before a parliamentary committee: The Australian government, he said, had received "detailed assessments on the United States in which it was made very clear the United States was intent on invading Iraq for more important reasons than WMD and terrorism. Hence, all this talk about WMD and terrorism was hollow."

Australian intelligence analysts were applying media analysis. From their reading of the documents of the Project for a New American Century and the new, "preemptive" security policy announced by the White House in 2002, they could make confident judgments regarding actual United States motives behind the war. And if further proof were needed, it came in a close reading of what Secretary of State Colin Powell and National Security Advisor Condoleezza Rice had been saying in early 2001, namely that Iraq posed little security threat to its immediate neighbors, much less to the United States, and still less did it have weapons of mass destruction. When Australian journalist John Pilger included the relevant quotations in his documentary, "Breaking the Silence," the laziness and vacuousness that have infected journalism in the United States (as documented, for example, by Robert McChesney, John Nichols, and Amy Goodman in chapters 31 and 34) were held up to ridicule. The American press had not done its homework, as demonstrated by simple media analysis of statements by our own top officials.

For all these reasons, we need to reconstitute a media-analysis capability as an independent entity feeding from Foreign Broadcast Information Service collection and housed in FBIS. It is essential that the analysis group send its analyses directly to the White House and members of the National Security Council with copies to the Central Intelligence Agency and other intelligence agencies and consumers. The person appointed head of this reconstituted analysis group needs to be a fiercely independent, apolitical professional who is fully conversant with the tools and disciplines of media analysis and possessed of the same personal attributes as those needed in a director of central intelligence.

The need for independent media analysis on national security parallels the need for independent alternatives to corporate-controlled media, generally, on all issues, as discussed in part VI of this book.

CONCLUSION

The Central Intelligence Agency and the intelligence community are in shambles. There has not been sufficient discussion of why the departure of George Tenet as director was inevitable. As in the case of Vietnam, an ill-advised war has sucked reason, courage, and integrity out of the system, and there is little prospect of improvement in the short term. At the same time, inaction is not a responsible option. In the years immediately ahead, we are likely to experience crisis after crisis. The United States cannot permit itself the luxury of putting off repair work on intelligence.

Happily, reformers do not face a tabula rasa. Good solid spade-work has been done—by the Carnegie Endowment, for example—in documenting graphically the disconnects between the intelligence estimates and reality. In this chapter I have tried to throw some light on why and how those disconnects exist. We now need to energize what can still be energized and hold the feet of congressional overseers to the fire. At very least we must, as Carnegie suggests, foster a healthy skepticism regarding intelligence claims—particularly in the light of the myriad "misrepresentations" of the past few years—and be alert to alarm bells alerting us to improprieties in intelligence.

Investigative commissions should do their thing, but they should not divert our attention from the problems at hand. We know enough now about what is needed that we can start repairing the process of preparing estimates and creating conditions conducive to truly independent imagery and media analysis.

Regarding Iraq, what is clear is that Ahmed Chalabi and his tailors were able to sell the emperor a new suit of clothes—an invisible suit that could be seen neither by imagery nor media analysis. If in the future the Pentagon and White House are given new alarming reports by new favorite informers—this time regarding, say, Syrian "weapons of mass destruction" and ties with terrorists—imagery and other modes of collection must be enlisted quickly to verify or dismiss such reports. Media analysis, too, must gain a hearing in policymaking circles, if only to show that if the United States continues to be seen as the force behind policies in Israel, we are in for decades more of hate and violence at the hands of millions with literally nothing to lose.

While a good many intelligence analysts have up and left, there are still enough professionals in the Central Intelligence Agency, the Defense Intelligence Agency, the State Department, and elsewhere to meet today's challenges. But they are sorely in need of courageous leadership, honest example, and adult supervision. Sadly, their ranks are dwindling, while those of careerists with a penchant for trimming their sails to the prevailing winds increase. There is little time to lose.

Let the decontamination begin.

NOTES

1. Not every commission is as successful as the Hart-Rudman United States Commission on National Security/21st Century. In 1996, for example, the Aspin-Brown Commission on the

Roles and Capabilities of the United States Intelligence Community recommended transferring to the Defense Department the Director of Central Intelligence's responsibility for processing and disseminating satellite imagery—an egregious mistake, as will be shown later in this chapter. The Senate Intelligence Committee expressed serious misgivings at this evisceration of the Director of Central Intelligence's charter for all-source analysis, but in the end supported the legislation.

2. There have been significant shortcomings in the preparation of sanitized summaries of major estimates. Veteran State Department intelligence official Greg Thielmann notes that it is "enormously important" to stay faithful to the original classified version and believes "there was some damage done to the truth" in preparing the unclassified version of the October 2002 National Intelligence Estimate on Iraq.

BIBLIOGRAPHY

Dan Chapman, "We're Trying to Spread a Little Truth," interview with Ray McGovern, *Atlanta Journal Constitution*, December 7, 2003.

Joseph Cirincione, Jessica Tuchman Mathews, Alexis Orton, and George Perkovich, *WMD in Iraq: Evidence and Implications*, Carnegie Endowment for International Peace, January 2004.

Gary Hart and Warren B. Rudman, *America Still Unprepared—America Still in Danger*, task force report sponsored by the Council on Foreign Relations, 2002.

Douglas Jehl, "Tenet Concedes Gaps in C.I.A. Data on Iraq Weapons," *New York Times,* February 6, 2004.

Douglas Jehl and David E. Sanger, "The Struggle for Iraq: Commission to Decide Itself on Depth of Its Investigation," *New York Times,* February 3, 2004.

David MacMichael and Ray McGovern, "The Burden of Truth," *Sojourners*, November-December 2003

———, "Ex-Central Intelligence Agency Professionals: Weapons of Mass Distraction: Where? Find? Plant?" Common Dreams News Center, June 18, 2003. At http://www.commondreams.org/views03/0425-11.htm.

Ray McGovern, "Case Closed: Tangled Web Unraveling," www.TomPaine.com, February 19, 2004, At http://tompaine.com/feature2.cfm/ID/9991.

———, "Hijacking 'Him' for Empire," Common Dreams News Center, Jan. 9, 2004. At http://www.commondreams.org/views03/1229-02.htm.

———, "Intelligence Shouldn't Exist Just to Serve Policy," *Miami Herald*, August 5, 2003.

———, "Intoxicated with Power," www.TomPaine.com, January 6, 2004. At http://www.tompaine.com/feature2.cfm/ID/9693.

———, "Iraq: Hawks Put WMD Cart Before the Horse," *Miami Herald*, February 15, 2004.

———, "Nothing to Preempt," www.TomPaine.com, January 27, 2004, At http://www.tompaine.com/feature2.cfm/ID/9841.

———, "Still Smoke and Mirrors," www.TomPaine.com, February 6, 2004, At http://www.tompaine.com/feature2.cfm/ID/9917.

———, "War Without Weapons," www.TomPaine.com, February 5, 2004, At http://www.tompaine.com/feature2.cfm/ID/9841.

"Mr. Tenet's Exit," editorial, *New York Times*, June 4, 2004.

National Commission on Terrorist Attacks on the United States (9/11 Commission), Final Report (Washington, DC: U.S. Government Printing Office, 2004).

James Risen, "Ex-Inspector Says CIA Missed Disarray In Iraqi Arms Program," *New York Times,* January 26, 2004.

United States Commission on National Security/21st Century: *Road Map for National Security: Imperative for Change,* Phase III report, February 15, 2001.

• 5 •

Does America Have the Wisdom to Grasp the Opportunity?

Clare Short

We are at a turning point in human history. The Cold War is over, but global integration is speeding up.

Better global communications mean the levels of poverty and inequality in the world are clear to the poor of the world in a way that they haven't been in the past. The poor now see how people in the developed countries live and are more aware of the injustice of it all.

We live, also, at a time of massive availability of knowledge, technology, and capital. We have experienced great success in development. In the last 50 years, more human beings have lifted themselves out of extreme poverty than in the previous 500 years. Many more people are living longer, more children are surviving, more people are literate, and more people have access to clean water.

There has been great progress. But there are also more people in the world than ever before and, therefore, more poor people. So we need to scale up our effort to build on our success. Otherwise, the numbers of poor will continue to grow. If we are wise, we can have an era of enormous reductions in poverty, a great advance across the world, and a growth in a sense of justice and security.

This is all completely possible, based on our own knowledge, experience, and achievements over the last few decades. The real question is, do we have the wisdom to grasp that opportunity? If we don't have that wisdom, we will have a world of growing division, bitterness, polarization, environmental degradation, conflict, failed states, big refugee movements, and terrorism. Since September 11, the likelihood of us taking the unwise route seems greater.

AMERICA'S FAILURE TO COOPERATE

The United States is obviously the world's hyper-power. We don't have the balance of power through which the world has tried to manage itself in the past. We now have one overwhelmingly strong economic and military power in the world. And even before September 11, the United States found it difficult to work with the rest of the world. It seems to be a country that is more inward-looking than most other countries, which is strange, both because it is a country made up of many immigrants and because it is indeed so dominant in world affairs.

There are many examples before September 11 of the United States's failure to cooperate with international agreements. Virtually all the world's countries ratified a convention recognizing basic rights for children all over the world, but the United States felt unable to sign it. The Kyoto treaty recognized that global warming was threatening the future of all of us; again, the United States found it impossible to cooperate. The International Criminal Court was created to try war criminals and dictators, the Milosevics and the Mugabes of this world, but the United States again exempted itself from participation. The United States holds an ambivalent attitude even toward the United Nations, even though most of the world treasures it as a place where we all come together and make rules that apply equally to all.

THE SQUANDERING OF SEPTEMBER 11 SYMPATHY

Although the United States's trend of noncooperation has existed for a long time, the events of September 11 exacerbated it. For many, there is now a feeling that America is like a wounded giant, hurt and lashing out, looking for countries to hit to deal with the sort of pain and anger it feels about the events of September 11. And yet the sympathy across the whole world after September 11 was enormous, and a worldwide process was put in place through the United Nations to require every country to deal more effectively with terrorism, money laundering, and those who provide support for organizations that would do such things as attack the Twin Towers.

Now that atmosphere of sympathy is gone. America is seen as a bully that is not committed to justice for people across the world, that doesn't find it possible to treat other people of different traditions and religions with respect. The anger in the Arab and Muslim world is intense. And I have no doubt that this atmosphere is leading to greater recruitment to terrorist organizations, which is threatening to all of us.

The feelings in Europe are similar to the feelings in the Arab and Muslim world. Europeans often see a parallel between the current U.S. hegemoney and that of the Roman empire. Other empires—the British, Ottoman, and Spanish empires, for example—all had competing centers of power. Like Rome, however, America is the lone hegemonic power in the world. And some feel that the United States, like Rome, will face a decline. The United States spends too much on defense, spreading its soldiers across the world, cutting domestic investments like Social Security and education, and creating growing unhappiness at home. Will the era of American hegemony will come to an end as it over-stretches abroad and fails to address its internal challenges?

A NEW SHARED VISION

What we need are new ideas and a new shared vision for managing this era. The old politics of left and right that divided the world, in most places, after the Second World War are not any longer articulating a clear way forward. Some of the values that we argued over—freedom, the role of the market, social justice—remain the issues that we need to discuss, but many of the remedies of that era are now outdated.

In the old argument about the proper balance between state and markets, the left's tendency was to want to give more power to the states, going, in the extreme, toward the communist system, to state power that was overwhelming, oppressive, and economically inefficient. In the old argument, the right's alternative was excessive market power—letting markets rip, weakening the state, and allowing inequality to grow. Both are old-fashioned and out of date, and we need to agree on the proper role of the states and the proper role of markets to get beneficial economic development, justice, and inclusion. We need to find ways of articulating those values within our own countries and internationally in order to better manage the era we are living in now.

To give an example, in the 1970s, the British Labour Party was very much against the European Common Market, as it was then called, because we had a vision of a just and fair country. We thought that by subjecting the United Kingdom to market competition with the rest of Europe, we would be prevented from creating the paradise of justice to which we were committed.

But we later understood that, as the world integrates and as we all need to trade, one can't insulate one's country from the rest of the world. We needed to be part of the European project and tried to create a Europe that was just for its people and played a constructive role internationally.

Now we have the argument in Europe about "Fortress Europe" and about whether Europe can insulate itself from the rest of the world. There is a growth in extremist right-wing party movement because of antagonism and anger about the large numbers of asylum seekers coming to Europe. We see it in The Netherlands, Austria, Denmark, and other countries. Right-wing racist parties are moving forward very rapidly, arguing against, for example, asylum seekers from Afghanistan, Iraq, and Africa.

Italy and Spain have the experience daily of people coming out of Africa, risking their lives in old fishing boats just for the hope and dream of a better life in a more economically advanced country. Asylum seekers are escaping misgovernment, oppression, and lack of economic opportunities. They are very much like the people who moved to the Americas in the last era of growing globalization, in the early part of the twentieth century.

This influx of asylym seekers makes it clear that we can't make Europe a fortress and have a good life for the people of Europe if people in surrounding countries are suffering the consequences of misgovernment, oppression, and poverty. In order to make our own countries safe and just, we need to spread those values across the international order.

Old assumptions about politics are equally outdated. The old idea was that what is morally right and what is in the self-interest of individuals and countries are in conflict. Whether that was ever true, it is certainly not true now. To protect our self-interest in the wealthy and developed countries, we need to work much more actively for a stronger commitment to justice and equity across the world. Obviously such a shift in emphasis would benefit the poor of the world. But the rich countries need to realize that if we fail to make progress in reducing poverty, we threaten our own self-interest, and the division and damage will come back to haunt us.

One way to do this is to work together for these values through the multilateral institutions we already have in place, like the World Bank, the International Monetary Fund, the United Nations, and the World Trade Organization. Although these institutions are often criticized, they have strengths as well. But they can be made more effective.

For example, the World Bank, as an international public-sector institution supported by taxpayer money, changed in the era of Thatcherism and Reaganomics. Then, its values were to roll back the state and let markets and inequality rip around the world. People were voting for parties that had those kinds of values. But now there has been a big shift, to the Millennium Development Goals (about which more below) and to the measurable and systematic reduction of poverty as the test of economic development. There also is growing recognition that poor people must participate in determining priorities and spending. Top-down doesn't work.

The World Bank must continue to evolve in the direction of measurable poverty reduction and country participation, but the answer is not to abandon the organization. We can't have little projects organized all over the world by every country and nongovernmental organization interested in development. We need a system that is capable of working across the world, in every country in need. We need to use institutions like the World Bank, the Asian Development Bank, and the African Development Bank, to which we all contribute for that purpose.

Similarly, the World Trade Organization is a better route to fair and effective trade than a proliferation of bilateral agreements. This is the only way we will get agreement on rules that give developing countries a better chance to grow their economies and therefore reduce poverty. Some antiglobalization protestors suggest that multinational companies' activities are always harmful. In Europe, though, there is a growing movement that sees these companies as part of the solution. Multinational corporations are increasingly afraid of public opinion, consumer movements, and the growing pension-fund movements. There is widespread agitation in Britain about executives paying themselves a fortune, even when their companies do badly. That has led to all sorts of protests and embarrassment by the leaders of companies. I believe we can have trade rules that ensure that multinationals work within a framework that brings benefits to the countries in which they invest, in which they are not allowed to avoid local taxes or breach environmental rules.

If we have a commitment to use the multilateral public-sector institutions, like the World Bank and the World Trade organization, to generate economic development for the poor and more social justice, we can make the world safer and more stable for all of us.

NEARLY HALF THE WORLD LIVES ON $2 A DAY: THE CHALLENGE OF GLOBAL INEQUITY

We have six billion people in the world now. There were just over one billion of us in 1900. The demographers say that was as many human beings as had ever existed since humanity first evolved. A recent finding of early human activity in Ethiopia is believed to date back approximately 160,000 years. From then to 1900, human population grew to just over a billion in 1900, three billion by 1960, six billion now, and world population is going to rise to eight to nine billion by 2030 to 2050, when, on present trends, it will stabilize.

This is not some peculiar rapid growth of population in developing countries that is different from population growth in industrialized countries. If you look at the history of Britain, for example, in 1710 there were about five million people in Britain, and now there are almost sixty million. When you break the back of poverty and economic development takes place, people live longer, children survive, the population grows, and then it stabilizes. That's the pattern we're getting across the world. But the eight to nine billion people now projected at the level of stabilization will strain the resources of the planet and require us to manage environmental resources more wisely—or we will all face difficulties.

Of the six billion of us, 2.8 billion live on less than $2 a day. That is very nearly half the world's population. This figure of $2 a day represents a purchasing parity equivalent of what $2 would buy in the United States; it is not what $2 would buy in a poor country in Africa. And 1.2 billion live on less than $1 a day, for all needs—less than the local purchasing parity equivalent of what $1 a day would buy in the United States. This is abject poverty. The one in five of us living at that kind of level has a life expectancy of a little more than forty years. They see a lot of their children die before the age of five, they rarely get the chance to be educated, they are mostly illiterate, and they don't have access to clean water. Half of humanity doesn't have access to sanitation. These levels of poverty are like those of Britain during the Industrial Revolution, when child labor, widespread illiteracy, disease, suffering, and early death were commonplace.

On top of all of this, the world is rapidly urbanizing. Half of humanity is now living in cities, and this is speeding up very rapidly. It is projected that in about fifteen years it will be 65 percent. This will lead to all sorts of change, but one of the changes will be a greater likelihood for the poor of the world to protest their condition. The rural poor suffer often in silence, partly because they are widely dispersed. Urban masses of poor or marginalized people are more likely to complain and protest.

In terms of environmental resources, forests continue to be lost across the world, deserts continue to spread, and global warming continues. For example, Bangladesh, which is a very poor country of about 130 million people, is set to increase its population by 50 percent over the next thirty years. At the same time, based on the most likely trends in global warming, Bangladesh will lose a third of its territory because it is on a big river delta. Similarly, the effects of global warming on islands in the Caribbean, the Pacific, and other low-lying parts of the world are going to be enormous if we don't take urgent action.

THE MILLENNIUM DEVELOPMENT GOALS

Thus in our world, at the beginning of the twenty-first century, we have great progress in development but also the enormous challenges of gross inequality. In the face of this and to mark the new millennium, through the United Nations at the General Assembly in 2000 the whole world committed to working together to achieve what are known as the Millennium Development Goals—to halve the proportion of people living in extreme poverty, to get all children in the world into school, to reduce the number of women who die or are left permanently disabled by childbirth, to reduce the levels of infant and child mortality, and so on.

We are, in fact, on track worldwide to achieve the halving of the numbers in poverty. The targets were originally set in 1995, and we are on track for a billion human beings lifting themselves out of abject poverty between 1995 and 2015. After that, there will be another billion because of world population growth. But if we act together now to meet the goals we have set ourselves for 2012, we would build a new world order that is capable of taking responsibility for the whole world together and drive progress forward to systematically reduce this poverty.

On the other targets—like getting all children into schools, increasing child and maternal survival, and accessing clean water and sanitation, we are making progress overall. But we are not on target and we could do better.

Similarly, on trade, in the wealthier countries we all know that access to modern technology and to export and trade has helped grow our economies, generate jobs, and give people the improvements that come from modern technology. But the trade rules of the world are skewed against poorer countries. Africa, for example, relies on exports of unprocessed commodities. The minute Africa starts to process its coffee, cocoa, tea, or cotton, it hits growing tariffs, and therefore current trade rules keep Africa in a state of underdevelopment. At the same time, we in the United States, Europe, and Japan subsidize our agriculture by $350 billion and then it dump on world markets, undercut prices, and undermine the livelihood of poor farmers. It's a very unjust order. We must give developing countries a fairer chance to grow their economies, trade, and get access to modern technology.

ASIA: CONTINENT OF THE FUTURE

Asia is almost certainly the continent of the future. Asia has two massive countries, India and China, each with over a billion in population. Two-thirds of the poor of the world live in Asia, but China has, over the last fifteen years, achieved an enormous improvement in its economic development and its reduction of poverty. There is a fear of China, particularly in America, because of the real prospect that, if China continues to commit itself to economic growth and if it can adjust and open up its political system, it will become a major power in the world in twenty or thirty years. We all need to engage with China. You can't marginalize 1.4 billion people.

India has made less progress than China. A third of the world's poor live in India. India and Pakistan represent the biggest risk of nuclear exchange in the world. Bangladesh is making progress, but it is one of the least developed countries and it faces enormous environmental problems.

Africa is the poorest continent by far. Half its people are a-dollar-a-day poor, 20 percent of them living in conditions of conflict. And if Afghanistan was a threat to the world as a failed *state*, where al Qaeda could hide and organize, then the danger of a failed *continent* is even greater. Yet there has been success in Africa on which, with enough determination, we could build. Conflicts have been ended in Uganda, Mozambique, and Rwanda, and they are reforming, growing their economies, and reducing poverty. Ghana and Tanzania are also making progress, and there is a prospect of peace in massive countries like Sudan and the Democratic Republic of Congo. We need to work with Africa. Otherwise, we are going to have a continent suffering disease, poverty, and conflict refugees. This is an important issue for Europe in particular, because of its promixity to Africa.

A NEW POLITICS

We need a new, post–Cold War politics, one that is guided neither completely by states or completely by markets The private sector has an important part to play in generating growth, particularly in poor countries. But the public sector has an enormously important role in ensuring that economic growth benefits all and that services are provided to all. The state is needed to prevent abuse, monopoly, and corruption and to ensure that there's a decent tax system, basic public services, and inclusion.

In the modern era, you can't have a successful economy if there is a large underclass. That's true in our countries and in developing countries. Education is the commanding height of a modern economy, and there must be quality education that includes all, and provides for all, to develop their talents.

The private sector can and should be ethical. In Europe there is a movement by the pension funds and consumers to boycott or pressure companies that fail to behave ethically in terms of the environment, their behavior in developing countries, and corruption. A growing group of successful companies see ethical behavior as not just good for their reputation but for their businesses as well. They treat their staff with more respect, nurture the talent and commitment of their workforce, and therefore generate high morale. The result is a more effective organization. So the private sector can play a role that is beneficial for all.

We need to defend our best values at home and abroad. We need a deep commitment to social justice and mutual respect, in our own self-interest as well as in the interest of the poor in the world. We could, then, if we can pursue these policies, have a period of enormous uplift, of a reduction in poverty, of a more just world order. If we fail to do so, we are going to have more bitterness and division.

CONCLUSION: TURNING AMERICA AROUND

Across the world, there is a fear that America, the hyper-power, is driving down the wrong road, one leading to more bitterness, division, inequality, and anger. But it is not too late to turn around. Maybe America can learn from Iraq the danger of acting alone or using a few token allies as a fig leaf to conceal that lack of a true coalition. Whatever view any of us take of the road to war in Iraq, the present situation is extremely dangerous. We must be determined to come together to try and help the people of Iraq to rebuild their country and ensure that the coalition doesn't get bogged down in a growing conflict that would simply hurt everyone.

We must solve the Israeli–Palestinian issue and establish two states that can create justice and hope for both peoples. (See, for example, the two-state plan proposed by Chris Toensing in chapter 17.) The absence of a solution to date is the core of the anger in the Muslim world—the feeling that America props up Israel to behave in ways that breach international law and yet is never corrected.

This massive American economic and military power cannot make the United States safe. If America relies on military power and fails to commit to justice, it will make the world more dangerous. The events since September 11, and particularly the war in Iraq, have led to a growth of young people joining terrorist organizations and therefore have strengthened the network of al Qaeda organizations.

The United Kingdom experienced this in Northern Ireland when it first went in, thirty or so years ago, and acted repressively. It led to recruitment to terrorist organizations, and the U.K. learned the hard way that you have to commit to justice for everyone in order to get to peaceful settlement and not encourage terrorism.

Many people across the world find the U.S. government's actions contradictory because anyone who visits America knows its people's generosity, kindness, and helpfulness. There is also a deep religious commitment in the United States. People are more churchgoing in America than people are in Europe. Christianity teaches a very strong commitment to social justice: "blessed are the poor," and "whatsoever thou do to the least of my little ones, you do it to me."

What, then, is going on in the United States? Whatever the causes of this disconnect, the United States must be persuaded, for its own good and for that of the world at large, to work in cooperation with other countries toward justice, development, and mutual respect. These are good human values and will make the world safer for all of us. We need to make a change because the route we are on is dangerous and will lead to more bitterness, division, hatred and suffering.

BIBLIOGRAPHY

Will Hutton, "Third Way for the Third World," Clare Short interview, the *Observer*, December 10, 2003.

Clare Short, "It's official—Saddam was not an immediate threat," the *Guardian* op-ed, August 23, 2003.

———, "The U.S. Needs the World's Help—Now," Salon.com, October 9, 2003.

Patrick E. Tyler, "Ex-Aide to Blair Says the British Spied on Annan," *New York Times*, February 7, 2004.

• *6* •

The Courage to Keep On Talking

Vivien Stern

This chapter discusses how the differences between Europe and the United States have widened and are more openly discussed in recent years. This is not just due to September 11 and the war in Iraq but also to the stand being taken by Washington on a range of other serious international issues.

THE CLIMATE IN EUROPE

To examine how U.S. and European views are diverging, let's first look at what is going on internally in Europe. A close look at the current political situation demonstrates that the balance of virtue does not necessarily lie on one or other side of the Atlantic Ocean. Things are not going so well in Europe. One issue on which we look with admiration to the United States is policy on immigration. In Europe, we are seeing a deeply unpleasant reaction to the arrival in some rather narrow, white, culturally self-satisfied societies of a range of refugees and illegal immigrants from the Middle East, Asia, and the Balkans.

These feelings find fertile ground because of the social anxiety created by the pressure on governments to cut social support and make their economies more "competitive" in the sense the word (which I use with some discomfort) is used by international financial institutions. Thus, right-wing racist politicians are doing well. In Austria there is Joerg Haider and his Freedom Party. Denmark has a far-right party in government. The far right is doing well in Norway, and in France we had the far-right politician Le Pen pushing the Socialist Lionel Jospin out of a race for president. Then there was the Dutch sensation of Pim Fortyn, who was anti-Muslim because they were anti-gay and who was shot. Silvio Berlusconi in Italy has the fascist Northern League in his government. The Portuguese have a far-right party in their coalition.

And of course, as has happened here, September 11 has given the opportunity to the police/security/intelligence (also words I use with some discomfort) agencies to enact repressive policies. European measures on controlling the borders and monitoring citizens and others have been greatly tightened since September 11.

Also, in the United Kingdom a deeply objectionable antiterrorism law went through that allows the United Kingdom to derogate from Article 5 of the European Convention on Human Rights. Article 5 governs the conditions under which people may be deprived of their liberty, and the government needed to seek exemption from it in order to detain some people indefinitely without trial.

THE EUROPEAN RESPONSE TO AMERICAN ACTION

That is the climate in Europe. How are we relating to the United States, and what are our differences?

In the early days after September 11, there seemed to be some hope that the events would shock America and Europe into a new relationship, based on working together to find and deal with those committing atrocities, but also to see the implications. It was hoped that there might be an effort to pay more attention to world poverty; to make the connections between the free-market ideologies of the International Monetary Fund and the World Bank and the increasing impoverishment and hopelessness of much of the world; to enter a little into the perceptions of those who hate the rich world and to try to understand why; and to build a very wide coalition, stretching it to include all those who could be accommodated. Prime Minister Tony Blair expressed some of these hopes in his speeches after September 11, stating for example that "Out of the shadow of this evil should emerge lasting good—above all justice and prosperity for the poor and dispossessed."

It did not happen.

We have a very different scenario. We got the war in Iraq. Instead of a massive increase in aid to the poor, there has been a reduction. At the time of the Cold War, $1 billion more was being spent by America on foreign aid than is being spent now. The United States has the lowest aid level per gross domestic product of the twenty-one industrialized countries and has seen an unprecedented and incomprehensible increase in military spending, an increase equal to the whole defense budget of Italy. The European Union External Affairs Commissioner, Chris Patten, said, "After the smart bombs, we need a smart development policy." There is no sign of that, as Clare Short has discussed in chapter 5.

We have, instead, actions and speeches that make it impossible for really significant players to work with the West. I am thinking in particular of Iran. I was there not long ago. It is indeed a country ripe for pulling into the "civilized" (another discomforting word) fold. The reformers are active and confident. I spoke at a conference and the judges, who were all ayatollahs, listened. At that same conference there was a session on illegal drugs. A university professor said, "In the last few years, 8,000 drug traffickers were executed, but drug trafficking is still going on—worse than ever. Isn't it time to try another way?" Iran is poised to move toward some sort of democracy, as Roger Owen suggests in chapter 19, but it has been alienated by the war in Iraq.

What, then, should we do? Most important, we must prevent the reaction to September 11 and the war in Iraq from undoing the great strides that have been made to create international legality, where the law is used to deal with those who commit terrorist atrocities. Daniele Archibugi of the Italian National Research Council has said that "the principal political task of our present era is to prevent the destruction of the towers from dulling the hope that democracy and legality can assert themselves in states and among states."

David Held, professor of political science at the London School of Economics, has pointed out that "the only defensible, justifiable, and sustainable response to 11 September must be consistent with the aspirations of international society for security, law, and the impartial administration of justice." Aspirations, he says, that were articulated after the Second World War and were embedded in regional law, global law, and global governance institutions.

Another commentator has said that "the world is heading towards disaster if the sole superpower behaves as judge, jury, and executioner when dealing with global terrorism."

The whole area of how far the United Nations is involved, how far the international legal order is involved, is a subject of much discussion in Europe. That question is linked, of course, to the debate in Europe over how we should deal with a world in which America is the great power, the dominant global player militarily, economically, and diplomatically, and takes a line that is not the line Europe would take or thinks is wise.

As the Earl of Sandwich has said in the House of Lords, "The government, by placing themselves so close to the U.S., is entering a dangerous world of black and white solutions." This echoes what Huang Ping from the Beijing Institute of Sociology has said: "Are we keen to prove an old Chinese saying that where there is a war between good and evil there is disaster for the ordinary masses?"

In chapter 7 and elsewhere, another member of the House of Lords, William Wallace, professor of international relations at the London School of Economics, says there are two options:

- To accept the global framework and American hegemony and try to influence at the margins—the Tony Blair idea, or
- To seek to balance American dominance by building up European institutions as an alternative center of power.

CONCLUSION

The foreign policy disconnect between Europe and the United States has critical implications not just for the whole world but for the American domestic agenda as well.

First, the vast increases in military expenditure are at the expense of something else, and that something is American economic and domestic policy, including jobs, education, health care, and Social Security. The result is that what Elliott Currie, in chapter 26, calls the failed "free market-tough state" domestic policy of America gets further entrenched.

Second, the failure to recognize the needs of the poor in the Third World and to take responsibility for their fate is linked to a similar failure in America. If it matters that children in Burkina Faso or Bangladesh do not get adequate health care, it matters in America too. As Immanuel Wallerstein has said, "What we do to the world, we do to ourselves."

Third, the distancing from international law and from international institutions devoted to social justice and equity is also a distancing from social justice and equity in America, as Richard Leone and Yvonne Scruggs-Leftwich make clear in chapters 28 and 29.

The well-being of domestic and international affairs are both at stake in the current clash of policies in the United States and Europe, and we need to fight for both and talk about both. As Peter Meyer of the University of Lille in France has concluded, in these circumstances it is vital that we have the courage to keep on talking.

BIBLIOGRAPHY

Daniele Archibugi, "Terrorism and Cosmopolitanism," Social Science Research Council, *After September 11.* www.ssrc.org/septll.

David Held, "Violence, Law and Justice in a Global Age," Social Science Research Council, *After September 11*, www.ssrc.org/sept11.

House of Lords, Hansard, February 27, 2002, Col. 1500 and 1520.

Imran Khan, "Terrorists Should be Tried in Court," the *Guardian*, October 12, 2001.

Peter Meyer, "Defend Politics Against Terrorism," Social Science Research Council, *After September 11.* www.ssrc.org/septll.

Huang Ping, "September 11th: A Challenge to Whom?" Social Science Research Council, *After September 11.* www.ssrc.org/septll.

Peter Slevin, "United States Urged to Double Overseas Aid," *Washington Post*, February 12, 2002.

William Wallace, "Living with the Hegemon: European Dilemmas," Social Science Research Council, *After September 11*, www.ssrc.org/septll.

Immanuel Wallerstein, "America and the World: The Twin Towers as Metaphor," Social Science Research Council, *After September 11*, www.ssrc.org/septll.

Michael White, "Let us Reorder This World," the *Guardian*, October 3, 2001. Speech to Labour Party Conference, October 2, 2001.

• 7 •

The European Mistrust of American Leadership

William Wallace

September 11 and the war in Iraq have made matters much more difficult for transatlantic relations. However, there has been a longer-term trend, a growing mistrust of American leadership, which predates the American administration that came to power in the new millennium. That trend also includes the weaknesses of the Clinton administration and the obstructionism of Congress.

All of this has led to a rise in what I have to call "shallow anti-Americanism." I mean by this not opposition to the United States as such, but a belief that the American system of government is corrupted by the constant struggle for campaign finance; that American capitalism is self-interested and lobbies in Washington to bend international rules in its favour; and that the American political elite have lost interest in cooperation with the outside world or understanding that such cooperation is also in their own interest. The rejection of the Kyoto environmental treaty and resistance to the International Criminal Court, the landmines treaty, and other aspects of multilateral disarmament have become for Europeans symbolic, even iconic, images of this turning away from international cooperation.

ANTI-EUROPEANISM BY THE AMERICAN RIGHT

The right-wing rhetoric that has flowed since September 11 and the Iraq war was already in evidence well before terrorism became the paramount American issue. European observers are particularly worried about the rhetoric that pours across the op-ed pages and television screens. I keep saying to my right-wing contacts within America that, each time we look at "authoritative" American commentators on television, anti-Americanism in Europe grows further. Richard Perle is one of the most frequent commentators on European television; I often wish that the Defense Policy

Advisory Board could be abolished, because it appears to provide a seat for so many aggressively anti-European hawks.

There seems to have been a rise in anti-Europeanism across the American right, which is also very worrying. That seems to come from several sources. It seems to be associated with the rise of the Christian right, which is a phenomenon that is very hard for Europeans to understand. I was talking about this in Dublin not long ago and decided that the easiest way to explain the phenomenon of the Christian right in the United States was to remind them that the doctorate of Dr. Ian Paisley, leader of the Protestant, hard-line Democratic Unionist Party, comes from Bob Jones University. In other words, the only church in Western Europe that holds the same corpus of views as the Southern Baptists is the Free Presbyterian Church in Northern Ireland, the hardest of the anti-Catholic, anti-European "Unionist" movements. The extraordinary alliance between the Christian right, the conservatives, and the small but influential right-wing Israeli lobby has fueled what I have to say is, sadly, a tone of anti-Europeanism in the op-ed pages of the American press over recent years. One aspect of the op-ed argument is that Europe is a godless society. Another is that Europe, of course, is antisemitic. I was sitting in an evening discussion with Shimon Peres in New York and someone remarked, conversationally, "Well, of course, we all know that structural antisemitism dominates the British media."

There is also the charge that Europe is soaked in welfarism and doesn't spend enough on defense. The opposite side of that, within America, is a conservative right that believes in strong defense but that is otherwise anti-government. Recently Phillip Bobbitt, one of the favorite philosophers of the far right, spoke at the London School of Economics. He was talking about rolling back the legacy of Franklin D. Roosevelt and the growth of the U.S. federal government. We must have minimal government, he argued; we want people to stand on their own feet, to get government off people's backs. But his audience was muttering, "If he's looking to expand Homeland Security to protect and oversee people's lives, and also looking to expand the defense budget, then he is hardly talking about minimal government." That's part of the difference of perspective; Europeans see the civil-liberty aspect of government very differently from the American government.

I worry that the rhetoric about shared and common transatlantic values is, to some extent, now under threat. It is under threat because the dominant group within American politics is deliberately challenging those values. The social democratic compromise between free market capitalism and a social market economy is under attack in America, as Elliott Currie articulates in chapter 26. Also under attack are the notions that citizenship is more than voting and saluting the flag and that people are entitled to a decent safety net. This wider concept of citizenship is still held much more strongly in Europe.

THE SOCIAL AND POLICY DIVERGENCES BETWEEN EUROPE AND AMERICA

Part of this, I think, is because we do now have very different societies. In Western Europe we have very densely populated areas; we have to live in cities, and so we have to make the cities work. We can't move out; there isn't anywhere else to move. The United States, on the other hand, has high geographic mobility. Many people have moved from the cities to the suburbs. There has been tremendous growth to the South and West, at the expense of the North and the East. Pittsburgh now has twenty-five percent of the population it had in 1960. Florida has three times the population it had in 1960. All of this leads to different assumptions about the balance between public and private services; the view from the suburbs is very different than the view from the cities. Assumptions about energy consumption and the balance between public and private transport and assumptions about safe streets and crime all diverge.

What else do we have to worry about? There has been a deep divergence on the Middle East, as a whole. There are fifteen million Muslims living in Europe. They are not all well treated nor well integrated. There are many problems in our Muslim populations, but nonetheless, if you live in a European city, you know Muslims. My children went to a school where 25 percent of the students were Muslim. So my children have grown up knowing a lot about Muslim and Hindu festivals, having friends with whom they discussed the problems of assimilation, and learning about the formalities of a different culture. My generation, before the transformation of our cities by immigration, did not have the same exposure to Muslim culture as my children's generation. In the United States, by contrast, Muslims now form a significant minority but have so far made little cultural impact.

An additional divergence that ought to worry Europeans is that the United States is a self-confident and patriotic society. One of the ways in which it integrates its immigrants is by telling them, "We are Americans." Immigrants are sold by the American ideology and told that they can have the possibilities America offers. In Europe, we are less sure of who we are or of what we should be proud—that's a real problem for all of us. It is no longer quite "the done thing" to be too proud of being right wing or nationalist. A lot of us would say that's a very good thing. We are living in a postnationalist society across Europe, in which nationalist politicians have been pushed to the fringes of political life. But the down side is that it is very difficult to mobilize our populations for any great cause beyond national boundaries. We elect deeply parochial politicians who talk about German interests in terms of stopping at the boundaries of Germany or French interests in terms of defending French agriculture. In Britain, there is a real contradiction in all of this because we have a deeply moral and religious prime minister who makes great speeches about our moral obligations to the rest of the world but who doesn't seem to carry the British public with him.

THE NEED FOR A EUROPEAN ANSWER

The most recent influential American article on this topic was by Robert Kagan in the *Hoover Institution Policy Review* in 2002. It's been influential partly because it has hurt those who read it—it's actually a woundingly accurate analysis. It says that the United States has sufficient self-confidence to project power around the world, to have a concept of global strategy, and to try to pursue it.

By contrast, Europeans have given up on the strategic game and are focused in on themselves. Europeans, says Kagan, are more concerned about maintaining the value of old-age pensions and investing in the education of the young and are not concerned about problems in North Africa or Western Russia, unless they overlap the border in terms of transnational crime. Kagan believes that most Europeans would like the rest of the world, if possible, to go away and, if they won't go away, would like the Americans to deal with them. And then, he concludes, Europeans will complain about what the Americans do.

It's a beautifully written article, and it is horribly accurate in a whole host of ways. And it does require a European answer. Part of what ought to worry us about transatlantic relations at the present moment is the incoherence of the European response. There has been an attempt, within Britain and within France, at some sort of response to this shift in American perception of the outside world, this reassertion of American nationalism.

Tony Blair has taken one approach: to partner with America in Iraq, to say publicly that we are with you 100 percent, and to say privately that we agree with you so far but you have to understand that there are limits and domestic constraints. So far as we can see, Blair has had influence in Washington. I remember a Republican congressman on the radio referring to the Powell-Cheney axis operating in contrast to the Cheney-Rumsfeld axis.

If I were Tony Blair, I'd be quite happy with that description. But I think that in some ways his approach has been mistaken. First, he hasn't actually spoken publicly to the broader American public about the limits of petitioning European support for the United States, which would have helped the position of the American president within a quite divided administration. It would have said something to Congress about the limits of British support.

Second, he hasn't explained what he is doing to the European public, so, for example, his officials could defend his position against charges in the French press that Blair is 100 percent behind everything Americans want to do. The German press has been even worse. Behind the damaging nature of press criticism, the French government has played, actually, a rather constructive game—one which was coordinated with the British within the United Nations. I suspect that we would not have gotten the Security Council resolution that came out without British and French cooperation. And, to some extent, what you have in these two countries is a political elite who recognize that they do want to carry on playing some foreign policy role about international disorder outside Europe.

German foreign policy is struggling to address the problems of the outside world. There are 12,000 German troops outside Germany—a fact that is not much publicized. There has been a revolution in German politics: Germans are there on the ground in Kosovo, Bosnia, Albania, and Kuwait and are about to take over command of the International Security Assistance Force, jointly with the Dutch, in Afghanistan. The Germans are doing more than they are letting on, and that's also true for some other European countries—for example, Denmark, which has Special Forces troops in Afghanistan but which is not terribly proud of it. At the same time, Italian foreign policy is a collection of gestures without content.

Overall, what we have in Europe is ambivalent government and deeply ambivalent populations, with media that represent the United States from a pretty critical angle.

Someone recently observed, "There are too many 1960s liberals still writing for your good newspapers and that constrains what European governments can do." As a 1960s liberal, I am not too sorry about that. If one looks at it from the American point of view, and looks across to Europe, the Europeans do look like a pretty incoherent mess, as Vivien Stern suggests in chapter 6. What Europeans should be doing about that is one of the most difficult and important questions for European policy. The British government is failing to address the central question of how to build greater coherence in European foreign policies. The French government is still hung up on the disadvantages of European Union enlargement to the East and the protection of the common agricultural policy. The German government is extraordinarily hesitant to spell out what is needed—even though it has an excellent foreign minister who has begun to address some of these issues. The European Commission is also extremely weak in this field.

BRINGING EUROPEAN EXPERIENCE TO BEAR

The Europeans perceive the world in a different way from the United States. For example, Europeans do not perceive terrorism as new. We have had different terrorist campaigns for the last thirty years. I found myself on two or three occasions in Washington trying to remind Americans that 3,000 British people have been killed by the Irish Republican Army during the last thirty years and that, much of that time, the Irish Republican Army was funded within the United States. The United States did not see this as something that just had to stop.

My Irish friends tell me, with vigor, that money is still flooding in to support Sinn Fein, which is the best-funded party in Irish politics and is (in the words of the woman who led the Yes-campaign in a recent referendum campaign there) in many ways still a fascist party—willing to wound and beat up its opponents while they play a democratic game.

I have been disheartened by how few Americans are prepared to accept that they have anything to learn from the European experience, from which they ought to recognize that a strategy against terrorism is not taking on the whole of the Muslim world. I was extremely glad to hear the American president saying that Islam is a mission of peace and that he resisted attacks from the religious right, which told him that Islam is a religion of war and that America could take on the whole of Islam. That is *extremely* dangerous, and of course the war in Iraq has created pervasive mistrust and hatred among Muslims of American leaders.

In response, Europeans ought to be seeking to intervene much more actively in the American debate, to bring our experience to bear. And then we should attempt to work better together rather than criticizing each other so destructively.

BIBLIOGRAPHY

Robert Kagan, "Power and Weakness," *Hoover Institution Policy Review*, June 2002.

William Wallace, "Living With the Hegemon: European Dilemmas," from *Critical Views of September 11: Analyses from Around the World* (New York: Social Science Research Council, 2002). http://www.ssrc.org/sept11/essays/wallace.htm.

———, *The Transformation of Western Europe* (New York: Council on Foreign Relations Press, 1990).

———, *Why Vote Liberal Democrat?* (London: Penguin Books Ltd., 1997).

———, with Robin Niblett, *Rethinking European Order* (London: Palgrave MacMillan, 2001).

• 8 •

America Needs Europe

Sophie Body-Gendrot

We have not yet grasped all the implications of September 11 and the Iraq war. We need to abandon our usual ways of thinking because these events made everything interact in new ways: foreign policy, domestic policy, security, religion, politics, solidarity, militarism, and bureaucratic routine. New risks have emerged. We have to give up the old notion that after a war we can return to the same routine.

This time of great uncertainty and increased risk has the effect of producing odd coalitions. Europe is divided on the use of force and the need for international rules. There is a large divide between the United States and numerous non-Anglophone Western societies. The conservative Robert Kagan concludes that Americans come from Mars and Europeans from Venus. The existence of the United Nations and the North Atlantic Treaty Organization is threatened.

Since September 11, American emotions have evolved and nationalism has crystallized, while European attitudes, and French attitudes in particular, changed but in different ways.

There is no doubt that the fear, anger, trauma, nationalism, frustration, and need for security expressed by Americans has been greatly underestimated by Europeans, who have lived with terrorism for a long time.

The first part of this chapter explains why post–September 11 feelings of empathy by Europe toward the United States could not last and why we had a division between those who favored force and preemptive war and those who wanted to follow international law. The second part of the chapter addresses the essence of the transatlantic drift and the present role of the Europeans.

THE DRIFT APART

A feeling of vulnerability and a culture of uncertainty have increased since September 11 and the Iraq war in many parts of the world. During the Cold War, Europe and the United States were united by their common opposition to communism, despite tumultuous tensions when de Gaulle left NATO in 1966. Although the reproaches were as violent as they are now, no American politician at the time called him a coward or called the French "surrender monkeys." No pictures of Normandy cemeteries were produced by the media.

After the fall of the Berlin Wall, there were hints that the East-West conflict had been displaced by North-South antagonisms. With its wealth, power, and technological advances, the North became scapegoated by those who were not part of it or who wanted to compete with it. America was the number-one target. Numerous films and novels portrayed the destruction of American cities by dubious characters, including potential terrorists. Such signals could have alerted American decision-makers, but their degree of self-satisfaction blurred their perceptions.

These attitudes toward America continue in our post–September 11 world. Not everyone wants to immigrate to the United States and become an American, contrary to what some in Washington think. In a Pew Research Center poll conducted in twenty-four countries from November 12 to December 2001, substantial majorities in many countries believed that the policies and actions of the United States were a major cause of the September 11 attacks. For example, in non-European countries, 58 percent of the respondents held this view. In the United States, only 18 percent had this view (table 7.1).

American leaders were not the only ones to be blind. Had Europeans, and Jacques Chirac in particular, read summaries of the books and articles of the conservatives now in power, they could have anticipated what was going to occur. September 11 gave American hawks the opportunity to develop their plans. Not only would they topple Saddam Hussein, but they would develop ambitious pre-

Table 7.1. Question: How Many Ordinary People Do You Think Believe that U.S. Policies and Actions in the World Were a Major Cause of the September 11 Attacks?

	United States Respondents	*Non-United States Respondents*	*Western Europe*
Most people think so	0%	26%	9%
Many people do	18%	32%	27%
Only some people do	48%	29%	37%
Hardly any do	32%	9%	22%
Don't know	2%	4%	5%

Source: Pew Research Center for the People and the Press

emptive strategies, starting with the Middle East and the role Israel should play there.

AMERICA GOING BACKWARD

After September 11, Americans asked, "Why do they hate us?" The question will be asked for years to come. The answer goes beyond an understanding of the frustration of Arab-Muslim countries and their resentment of American hegemony. The answer addresses religious and cultural issues as well as themes like modernity versus resistance to modernity. Little is known in the West about how fragmented and fragile the societies of these Arab-Muslim countries are, at a time when, thanks to globalization and the revolution of information technologies, the world has become more tightly interconnected. So, while it might have been a surprise to the White House, a BBC poll in 2003 revealed that, for 71 percent of Jordanians and 66 percent of Indonesians, the United States was a greater threat to peace than al Qaeda. In eleven countries, 57 percent of the polled had a very unfavorable or an unfavorable opinion of the current American president.

The butterfly effect and the theory of chaos can be interpreted both ways. For American leaders and a majority of Americans, military intervention in Iraq was legitimate if there was the slightest hint that Saddam Hussein could set the rest of the world at risk by selling weapons of mass destruction to potential terrorists. It was difficult to attack terrorist networks, so attacking Iraq was the easiest solution to restore American pride after September 11. But for Europeans, attacking Iraq, located at the heart of a most volatile and explosive region, was suicidal, especially given the European view that there was inadequate preparation for the postwar period and the European belief that the United States had greatly underestimated local nationalism. Most Europeans concluded that the war in Iraq would only encourage Islamist fundamentalists and international terrorism.

Political scientist Stanley Hoffmann has concluded that now "America goes backward." An administration elected by less than half of the voters had "drastically changed the strategic doctrine and the diplomatic position of the United States" by declaring that America had enough power to do pretty much what it pleased. Civil liberties were curbed. The rights of refugees and asylum seekers and the access of foreign students to U.S. schools and universities were reduced. The United States holds in custody an unknown number of aliens and some Americans, treated as "enemy combatants," suspected but not indicted, whose access to hearings and lawyers has been denied. The federal human investment programs that had softened the harshness of capitalism since the New Deal are threatened, observed Hoffmann, by the administration's "relentless war" against them. "Large numbers of old, sick, or very young people, mainly among the poor, will be deprived of financial assistance as the result of administration policies."

SEPTEMBER 11 AND POLITICAL OPPORTUNISM

A French economist has talked about "enlightened catastrophism"—how people and bureaucracies project themselves into the future after a catastrophe in order to minimize or neutralize its reoccurrence. If other attacks are likely to happen, fate should not be challenged and many preventive actions should be pursued.

The American government has taken this perspective. But does the perspective not legitimize and justify actions to control citizen freedoms? Is not government by fear created? Are not preemptive wars then justified? Many other countries have been attacked by terrorists, but most of those countries have not proclaimed themselves to be in a "state of war," and most have not declared all "rogue states" to be the enemy, as the United States has done.

Foreign observers were surprised by the lack of challenge offered in American media to the government's policies. "The political forces that many expected to question policies and express dissent have been remarkably meek and mute," wrote Stanley Hoffmann. In contrast to, for instance, British radio and television, the American media did little to express the complexity of the world to their audience and to illustrate the negative consequences of American isolationism. The concentration of the media in a few hands since the "reform" of the Federal Communications Commission worsened this phenomenon. (See the account by Robert McChesney and John Nichols in chapter 31.) Some editorials were more objective than others, but what is the size of their audience? The number of people who read the *Nation,* watch Bill Moyers, or listen to National Public Radio is relatively small. The absence of debate, disagreement, and negotiated compromise is at the core of the currently ailing American democracy. The right—the duty—of dissent used to be central to the American tradition.

EUROPEAN DISILLUSIONMENT WITH A NARCISSISTIC AMERICA

Great empathy was felt in Europe for America after September 11. Europeans had hoped at the time that their cooperation would be needed. "Planet America is back among us," a British journalist observed. It was expected that "the wound—relative in comparison with European, Russian, Japanese, Chinese, and Palestinian experiences—would bring America closer to the common fate of humankind, would make it more sensitive to the problems of the poor and the weak," a French observer wrote. "Within a few months, the image of a narcissistic, high-strung, and aggressive America replaced that of the wounded, appealing nation, essential for our balance."

After the military intervention in Afghanistan, Europeans concluded that unilateralism was the American word of the day. American leaders seemed to claim the role of gendarmes of the world. The invasion of Iraq greatly reinforced this role of global gendarmerie. Huge demonstrations in many countries opposed the American decision to act alone, without a clear mandate from the United Nations. Polls showed that, in most countries, majorities were convinced that America was acting to defend mainly its own interests, not the common good. (Table 7.2 summarizes these poll findings and makes clear that Americans are more isolated in their views, while Western Europeans fit more in line with the rest of the world.)

Nor should we underestimate the transatlantic divide over Israel. According to a *Wall Street Journal* poll in 2002 and a survey reported in *Foreign Policy* the same year, 38 percent of Europeans supported Israel and 72 percent a Palestinian state, while 58 percent of Americans supported Israel and 40 percent a Palestinian state.

The refusal of the United States to support the Kyoto treaty against global warming had an interrelated impact on the rest of the world. The perspective of the American government was summed up by the president's remark after he refused to sign (emphasis added): "What counts is the well-being of *the people living in this country*" (i.e., the United States). For similar unilateral reasons, the American government did not seem to want the country bound by any international agreement (on land mines, for instance, as well as on steel, the death penalty, antimissile defense, and the International Criminal Court).

It is hardly surprising that the American government's unilateral decision to use force and substitute Saddam Hussein for Osama bin Laden as the number-one enemy to the world's security did not convince America's allies. France, Belgium, Germany, and Russia concluded that the U.N. inspectors were progressing in their effort to detect mass-destructive weapons in Iraq, while the United States claimed that this progress was only made possible because troops were mobilized at Iraqi borders. At the time, the French missed an important opportunity when they did not establish a calendar for inspection reports to the United Nations.

The American government argued that those who did not support its actions were against the United States and in support of the terrorists. France argued that

Table 7.2. Question: Do You Think the United States is Taking into Account the Interests of Its Partners in the Fight Against Terrorism, or Do You Think It Is Acting Mainly On Its Own Interests?

	U. S. Respondents	*Non-U. S. Respondents*	*Western Europe*
Taking into account the interests of its partners	70%	33%	34%
Acting mainly on its own interests	28%	62%	66%
Don't know	2%	5%	0%

even good friends may have disagreements. Had Jacques Chirac given a televised speech at, say, Harvard, talking as a "friend and a loyal ally" and warning a dear friend that he begged to disagree, he might have been better understood by the American public. He missed this opportunity and instead brandished his U.N. veto. That was a very poor move, though it did avoid a "clash of civilizations" scenario.

With 10 percent of the French population being of Arab-Muslim origin and with numerous agreements with Arabic countries, France did not have much leverage. Few in America understood this reality. Today, Islamophobia and Judeophobia are played out at the periphery of French cities, mirroring larger geopolitical tensions. In Washington power-corridor leaks to the press, in conservative magazines, and on the Internet, France often is portrayed as Arab-leaning. For example, writing in the *International Herald Tribune*, William Pfaff observed that France commonly is portrayed "as allied with the radical Arab world out of fear of [its] unassimilated Muslim populations." He quoted the conservative website FrontPageMagazine.com: "France even is 'not a Western country anymore' since in 'many' cities 'no teenage girl can go out in the evening, at least without a full burqa'." Pfaff concluded that "This kind of nonsense sets the tone" for much of the world's varied misunderstandings of France.

The French moves that preceded the rupture between France and America early in 2003 have never been explained to the American public by the American media. It was not a journalist but the dean of the Woodrow Wilson School at Princeton, Anne-Marie Slaughter, who revealed in the *Washington Post* that the French ambassador to Washington had relayed to the administration a French proposal that could have avoided the bitter French-American break. The French proposal was for the United States to forego a second resolution at the United Nations, after which France and the United States would "agree to disagree." This would have made the threat of a veto unnecessary and allowed the United States to proceed to its war. But according to Stanley Hoffmann, the administration preferred a public showdown on a second resolution, something Tony Blair needed at home. The American government preferred helping Blair, a loyal ally, to collaborating with Chirac, "a dissenting, and thus lapsed, ally," in the words of Hoffmann. It was easier to attack France than Russia, China, or Germany. Polls in 2000 and 2002 had shown that between 36 percent and 41 percent of Americans saw France as "an unpredictable ally." Only 7 to 9 percent of Americans said that France was the best ally, compared with the United Kingdom and Germany (25 percent).

Rewriting history is not an easy task. The American decision to intervene in Iraq was taken in the summer of 2002, as Joseph Wilson makes clear in chapter 15. Consequently, all the subsequent manuevering was a smokescreen while the American military got ready. The Europeans were betrayed all along.

THE ESSENCE OF THE TRANSATLANTIC DRIFT

The notion of regeneration is at the foundation of American thought. It implies that the tracks of the past must be obliterated. "Forget about the past and a common history, mythology is over, the world of big blocks is gone," American conservatives seem to say. Now each country has to defend its own national interest and develop its own autonomous policies. The United States will fight for itself in vital parts of the world. The Europeans are to devote themselves to humanitarian concerns in a new division of labor. This is already the case in Afghanistan.

Such views, I think, are at the core of the misunderstanding between the "old" Europe, seen as exiting from history, and the perception of the American government that it is "making history." As early as 1996, Robert Kagan, working with Irving Kristol as an adviser to the White House, asserted that "hegemony must be actively maintained, in the same way that it was actively obtained. . . . Any decrease of this influence would allow the others to play a larger role in molding the world according to *their* needs." In a recent book written with Lawrence Kaplan, Kagan asserts, "United States foreign strategy must be straightforward, idealistic, self-confident, and well financed. Not only must America be the gendarme or sheriff of the world, but its lighthouse and its guide." When interviewed by PBS, Richard Haass, now head of the Council of Foreign Relations, added that America was in a very "creative" moment and that "there is a lot up for grabs." In another speech at a Brookings Institution conference in 2003, Haass stated that "the disaggregation of the European Union" was a goal. Similarly, according to John Hulsman, a specialist on Europe at the Heritage Foundation, the administration's program is indeed to divide Europe selectively, playing individual countries against one another and moving from issue to issue.

It is obvious that Europeans and Americans are engaged in two different debates. But each is only concerned with one of the debates. This does not foster understanding. The French are obsessed by respect for the rules of the international legal system; a country should not go to war without a clear mandate from the international community. This position irritates American leaders. Americans are concerned with the way one manages postdictatorships. On one hand, France has never said clearly that it wanted the fall of Saddam Hussein, and it ignores this type of debate. On the other hand, American leaders have manipulated public opinion to justify their invading Iraq, based on allegations of weapons of mass destruction and on assertions that the end justifies the means.

At the present time, nobody knows if unilateralism comes from the fact that the United States is a "hyperpower" or because it already feels the decline of its empire.

The first interpretation is based on the obvious military victory of America in Iraq, the lack of resistance by Saddam Hussein's regime, and the fall of a tyranny. But the costs of hyperpower action have been the casualties of civilian and military Iraqis, the casualties among American soldiers, the dangerous example given by the concept of preemptive war, the lack of respect for international laws, and the furor and frustrations raised in the Arab world.

The second interpretation, that American unilateralism reflects American decline, is illustrated by the growing national debt of the United States, as discussed by Robert Greenstein in chapter 22. According to a recent report of top monetary strategists, in 2002 the United States consumed 40 percent of the savings of the major industrial countries of the world. At the present rate of debt increase, Americans will consume 100 percent of their savings in three or four decades. Will the external financial dependency of the United States be bearable? In ten years, the American trade deficit has grown from $100 billion to $450 billion. The world has to produce more in order for the United States to spend on and consume imported goods from all over the world.

For Europeans, the alternative may be either to elaborate credible defense and foreign policies or to disaggregate.

For the French, the transatlantic divide is very serious. After forty years, according to polls I have studied, for the first time the stable, friendly attitudes of Americans for France have been shaken. The feuds did not remain confined to the State Department but have spilled over because of the relentless attacks against France by the American administration and American media. A Pew Research poll in 2003 showed that 60 percent of Americans had an unfavorable opinion of France versus a 21 percent unfavorable opinion in 2002. American Republicans were those who most changed their attitudes, by 45 percent, versus a third for Democrats and a third for independents. Propaganda and manipulation by the American administration was effective: 62 percent of Americans supported the use of force in Iraq; 60 percent believed Iraq was responsible for September 11; 44 percent thought weapons of mass destruction had been found, or were not sure; and 75 percent believed the United States exerts a strong leadership in Iraq.

Should these attitudes persist, one can wonder whether we are not moving toward two types of Western societies. The two types appear to differ on perceived security; the role of the state in support of social services; and broad issues like immigration, readiness to go to war, religion, and patriotism.

BUILDING BRIDGES BETWEEN AMERICA AND EUROPE

Current divisions within Europe and the uncertain future of the United Nations and NATO do not necessarily mean Europe will fail to be united in the future. Europe has trump cards. More vigorous decisions are likely to come out of the crisis that political Europe is now experiencing. Depending on individual issues, coalitions will likely be formed with Russia, with China, and with the new European countries. The American government may not be aware that, in the new order of the world, it is better not to be isolated; it is better to have a herd of other friendly elephants nearby (to paraphrase Chris Patten and Pascal Lamy of the European Community). Europe is the only potential friend of the United States. Americans cannot administer any reconstruction, fight AIDS, use intelligence cooperation, or establish commercial rules without Europe. Investment in human resources within the Department of State has constantly declined while military expenditures in the Department of Defense have risen steadily. At the same time, Europe has increased its investments in human resource programs and has no intention of competing with the military spending of the United States.

Many Europeans refuse the choice between a powerful Europe, antagonistic toward the United States, and no Europe at all. A middle way has to be found, based on a dialogue focused on real issues, such as Iran, and our intelligence cooperation. Europe, and France especially, may play a role of passeur, of translator between peoples and cultures. France and other European nations could be catalysts for new networks looking for alternatives.

France needs to ally with the American constituencies that opposed the invasion of Iraq and a policy of preemption. Americans went to war with considerable alarm and reluctance. One third of them opposed the war. The issue of weapons of mass destruction has not gone away, as evidenced by the testimony of David Kay in 2004. The expression of differences need not be interpreted as a weakness in alliances, or as a lack of friendship, but as an opportunity for mutual enrichment.

American foundations, philanthropists, think tanks, and other nongovernmental organizations that disagree with preemptive policy and believe in a policy of "more Europe" must take a much more active role in funding, communicating, and organizing.

More stories need to be written that present the European perspectives left out by mainstream American media. The insights of observers like Paul Krugman, and the specific policies proposed by many of the contributors to this volume, like Gary Hart (chapter 2) and Joseph Wilson (chapter 15), must be much more widely disseminated. New television series by people like Bill Moyers need to be funded. Talk show hosts like Charlie Rose need to feature personalities who bring to life the need for "more Europe." A major round of forums set in and embracing presenters from Europe and America needs to be held. The forums should be covered by C-SPAN and communicated via Internet venues like CommonDreams.org, TomPaine.com, and MoveOn.org. Pressure needs to be exerted on mainstream media like the *New York Times* to better report the views of, for example, the *Guardian* and *Le Monde.*

American nongovernmental organizations should be brought into closer contact with the organizations responsible for the huge antiwar rallies in London, Paris, and the 663 other cities in Europe and around the world. The European organizations did not prevent the war, but their protests were skillfully orchestrated. As Ralph Nader discusses in chapter 24, demonstrations in the United States often are weekend affairs, with little follow-up from Monday through Friday. Many European groups have better planning and better follow-up. Their expertise needs to be shared with their American counterparts through in-person exchanges.

All of these strategies must be converted into political action. The times call for a system in which candidates for public office have a "more Europe" perspective summarized for them in ongoing, common-sense ways that resonate with their constituents.

BIBLIOGRAPHY

Sophie Body-Gendrot, editor, *The Social Control of Cities: A Comparative Perspective* (Oxford: Polity Press, 2000).

———, and Robert A. Beauregard, editors, *The Urban Moment: Cosmopolitan Essays on the Late 20th Century City* (London: Sage, 1999).

———, and Marilyn Gittell, editors, *Social Capital and Social Citizenship* (Lanham: Rowman & Littlefield, 2003).

Stanley Hoffmann, "America Goes Backward," *New York Review of Books*, June 12, 2003.

John C. Hulsman, prepared statement for the House Committee on International Relations, subcommittee on Europe, June 11, 2003.

Robert Kagan, *Of Paradise and Power: America and Europe in the New World Order* (New York: Knopf, 2003).

——— and William Kristol: *Present Dangers: Crisis and Opportunity in America's Foreign and Defense Policy* (San Francisco: Encounter Books, 2000).

Robert D. Kaplan, *The Coming Anarchy: Shattering the Dreams of the Post-Cold War* (New York: Random House, 2000).

The Pew Research Center for the People and the Press, "America Admired, Yet Its New Vulnerability Seen As Good Thing, Say Opinion Leaders," poll, Washington, D.C., December 19, 2001.

William Pfaff, "Seeing Mortal Danger in a Superpower Europe," *International Herald Tribune*, August 3, 2003.

James Risen, "Ex-Inspector Says CIA Missed Disarray In Iraqi Arms Program," *New York Times,* January 26, 2004.

Anne-Marie Slaughter, "A Chance to Reshape the U.N.," *Washington Post,* April 13, 2003.

Wall Street Journal, "Israel's Fence Marks Sharp Change in Attitude About Palestinian State," June 24, 2002.

"We are All Americans Now," headline, *Le Monde* editorial, Paris, France, September 12, 2001.

"What the World Thinks of America," BBC poll, televised June 17, 2003.

• 9 •

Challenging Empire: The United Nations in a New Internationalism

Phyllis A. Bennis

Although many reject the terminology of "empire" with regard to the United States, the truth is that the United States is an empire that is using all of the power that empires have used throughout history.

In the Greek empire, Athens developed democracy narrowly: democracy for some. Athens then realized that it needed to protect its fragile little democracy and so sent troops to the island of Milos and said, "Well, we need your island." The citizens of Milos said, "We don't think so." The Athenians said, "Sorry, but we are bigger and stronger than you. We are taking your island." The people of Milos asked, "What about democracy?" And the Athenians said, "Well, for us, there is democracy. For you, there is the law of the powerful."

I started using that story during the Clinton administration, when there was a great deal of what I considered false commitment to multilateralism. With the Bush administration, no one pretended to be committed to multilateralism, particularly after September 11, when public fear became so palpable. Since then, the American people have been craving leadership, craving an answer, craving some sense that they could be protected from the events of September 11 happening again because, unlike so much of the rest of the world, they haven't had the experience of terrorism over the last hundred years.

This craving for security made it possible for the rising American empire to use power in a way that would never have been acceptable before September 11 except among a minority of people. It was thundered, "We must never have another event like the terrible events of September 11, and we must go to war against Iraq so we never have another event like the terrible events of September 11." In reality, there was no link between Iraq and September 11. But people heard it often enough that it worked. And so the use of unilateral, imperialistic power grew to unprecedented heights.

THE BEGINNINGS OF OPPOSITION

Increasingly, however, people are finding it discomfiting that public opinion means very little to the government. And that, ironically enough, can begin to transform the power of public opinion altogether. Consider this quote: "Thank God for the death of the United Nations. Its abject failure gave us only anarchy. The world needs order. Saddam Hussein's reign of terror is about to end. He will go quickly, but not alone. In a parting irony, he will take the United Nations down with him. Well, not the whole United Nations. The good-works part will survive. The low-risk peacekeeping bureaucracies will remain. The chatterbox on the Hudson will continue to bleat. What will die is the fantasy of the United Nations as the foundation of a new world order. As we sift the debris, it will be important to preserve, the better to understand, the intellectual wreckage of the liberal conceit of safety through international law administered by international institutions."

Guess who said this, and who thinks the United Nations is on the Hudson River, not the East River? This was Richard Perle, resident fellow of the American Enterprise Institute and former chairman of the Defense Policy Board, writing in the *Guardian*, interestingly, in the United Kingdom, not in an American paper, where it might be more easily quoted. What is extraordinary is the openness, the acknowledgment that this is the view of people associated with the American government.

The irony, of course, is that even now, after September 11, there still are moments when the United States looks to the United Nations as the framework for holding other nations accountable to the international law that we violate with impunity—particularly U.N. resolutions and the U.N. charter itself. Our government holds itself outside of accountability to the United Nations, while at the same time it holds other "rogue" states accountable.

The foreign policy that they have brought us since September 11, when the urgent demand of the American people was for safety, has been a foreign policy that is reckless, unsafe, and unfair. And it has shown people around the world that we are unconcerned about safety, fairness, and responsibility.

THE TWO SUPERPOWERS: THE UNITED STATES AND GLOBAL PUBLIC OPINION

In this atmosphere of aggressive American power, the United Nations has emerged as the most important venue for organized resistance to the abuse of unilateralism. Even in the months before September 11, one can see the beginnings of opposition to the rising, uninformed American empire. The United States lost its seat on the

Human Rights Commission the same day it lost its seat on an international drug commission, seats that America had taken for granted would be theirs forever. And for an extraordinary eight-month period in late 2002 and the first half of 2003, the United Nations did exactly what it set out to do in its charter—preventing the scourge of war. The United Nations probably never had a more relevant period than this moment, when it stood defiant against the United States, defiant against an illegal and unjust war. The United Nations helped create the "second superpower." Two days after the extraordinary demonstrations around the world in February 2003, the *New York Times* did something it almost never does: it told the truth on the front page, above the fold. It said that, once again, there are two superpowers in the world—the United States and global public opinion.

The United Nations was part of that second superpower. The United States put enormous pressure on, particularly, the six uncommitted countries within the Security Council, desperately trying to get them to change their votes and say they would endorse an American war. The United States talked about a "coalition of the willing," but others talked about a "coalition of the coerced" and a "coalition of the killing."

In response to the enormous American pressure, it was expected that countries would give in, particularly poor countries like Angola, Cameroon, Pakistan, and Guinea. Chile was expected to fall in line because the United States told the Chilean government that it would not ratify the proposed free trade agreement without Chile's support of the war. And yet Chile stood defiant along with other nations.

The reason for this resistance was that there is a framework within the United Nations that provides political cover and potential for economic support for poor countries to oppose the United States along with more powerful countries like France, Germany, and Russia, who were opposing the war as well. Although many countries eventually acquiesced and voted in favor of the U.S. stand, the potential for the United Nations as a site of opposition was clear.

In February 2003, when that extraordinary Security Council meeting was held, when the two United Nations inspectors gave their report and were expected to provide the last justification for the United States to go to war and didn't do it, the French Foreign Minister said, "The United Nations must be an instrument for peace and not a tool for war." And then there was an amazing response: The Security Council, this staid, formal body where nobody ever blinks, roared with applause. It had never happened before in the history of the United Nations.

The next day there were demonstrations around the world, all saying the same thing: "The world says no to war." Just before the rally began in New York, a small group met with Kofi Annan at the United Nations. The delegation was led by Archbishop Desmond Tutu. The first thing that Bishop Tutu said to Kofi Annan was, "We are here on behalf of all the people that are marching in the 665 cities, that we know of around the world, and all of those millions of people are saying no to war. They are also saying that we claim the United Nations as our own. We claim the United Nations in the name of this global mobilization for peace." It was a moment in which one can see the United Nations' potential as a venue for an extraordinary challenge to the American empire.

THE AMERICAN RESPONSE TO THE UNITED NATIONS

Despite supporting the war in Iraq in significant numbers, the American people have never wavered in their support of the United Nations. According to a Pew Center/University of Maryland poll, when about 75 percent of Americans were supporting the war, about the same percent were saying that America should solve key international problems collaboratively with other nations. One question in the poll gave respondents three choices. The first choice was to solve problems collaboratively with other nations. The second choice was for the United States to solve problems on its own. The third choice was an isolationist choice—withdrawal. Only 12 percent took the second choice and significantly fewer took the isolationist view. Some 76 percent said we should be working with the United Nations, and 88 percent said that the United States should have received permission from the Security Council before going to war.

In that same poll, two-thirds of Americans said that the lesson of the war in Iraq should not be that it's okay for the United States to use its power unilaterally without United Nations approval. Since then, support for multilateralism has remained firm among the American people. All the efforts by the administration to render the United Nations irrelevant have failed.

This support is in stark contrast to the official U.S. presence in the United Nations, which tends to punish nations that have a different opinion. Diplomats remember the letter sent by the United States during the run-up to the Iraq war to almost every member state of the General Assembly, except Israel and the United Kingdom. The operative line in the letter was, "Given the current highly charged atmosphere, the United States would regard a General Assembly session on Iraq as unhelpful and as directed against the United States. Please know that this question, as well as your position on it, is important to the U.S."

REFORM IN THE UNITED NATIONS

How should we go about reforming the United Nations to make it the strong, independent voice of world opinion that it should be? Some want to reform the Security Council by eliminating the veto and the existence of permanent members.

This seems unlikely to happen in the short term, so we need other ideas for democratization and reform of the United Nations.

We need to begin with the General Assembly. Historically, in the first forty years or so of the United Nations, partly because of the Cold War paralysis, partly because of the legacy of colonialism, and partly for a host of other reasons, the General Assembly, rather than the Security Council, was the engine of motion. It was to the General Assembly that newly independent former colonies would send their representatives to claim independence in front of the world. It was the General Assembly that created UNIDO, UNESCO, all of the agencies dealing with the role of international corporations, and all of the economic and social agencies that were designed to help countries of the global South compete on a more level playing field with the wealthy countries of the North.

The best way to empower the General Assembly is for the United States to simply back off because right now we are facing a situation where even in the General Assembly, where there is no veto, fear of antagonizing the United States forms a huge block on the ability of countries to take advantage of the global reach of the United Nations.

One example of this is the issue of protection of Palestinians living under occupation. In 2003, there was a vote in the Security Council, fourteen to one, in favor of providing protection. Kofi Annan had called for Chapter 7 protection, including the force of arms. Others on the council had argued for an unarmed or lightly armed separation force to provide protection. Protection would have been provided not only to Palestinians living under occupation, where there is a clear obligation of the international community that has held that occupation illegal, but to Israeli civilians who face the consequences of occupation, attacks which come as a result of the cruelties and the desperation brought by occupation.

The United States vetoed that resolution, and it was immediately put aside with the reasoning that if the United States would not support it, Israel wouldn't either. But there is another way in which the issue could have been approached. If countries in the General Assembly took their charter mandate to be responsible for assigning funds, they could pass a resolution supporting the creation of a protection force for Palestinians. They could allocate the money to pay for that protection force, and they could recruit troops.

Just imagine a combination of, say, 4,000 United Nations soldiers and police wearing blue helmets, divided up into four groups of a thousand. One group flies to Beirut and drives down to the Israeli border, to the occupied Golan Heights. Another group flies to Cairo and drives to Rafah, at the end of the Gaza strip. The third group flies to Jordan and drives out to the river. The last group is assigned to a ship that sails to the edge of Israeli territorial waters. Israel might refuse it entry, but the U.N. forces would be an important presence—and a visible presence, with the camera crews of Al Jazeera and the BBC and CNN, all watching and waiting for Israel to change its mind.

What would that mean in the context of international diplomacy and public opinion on a global scale? It's hard to know, but it would change something. It would make something possible that isn't possible today.

Another possible area of reform is the fight for the primacy of the United Nations over the Bretton Woods institutions. The International Monetary Fund and the World Bank were supposed to be special agencies of the United Nations. The World Bank is supposed to be accountable to the United Nations Economic and Social Council, not to its highest donors.

CONCLUSION

We now are faced with a scenario in which, as Zbigniew Brzezinski, national security advisor in the Carter administration, said recently, the United States is more isolated in the world diplomatically than it has been since 1945. It also is a moment when diplomats are quitting, when the credibility of the diplomats is being attacked by the right, and when the very notion of diplomacy is being discredited in favor of war. The idea is that we don't need a State Department because we have a Pentagon.

The American government's policy of creating "coalitions of the willing" for each event is very dangerous. We have already seen the tendency during the Clinton administration (e.g., in Kosovo) of sidelining the United Nations and claiming that the approval of NATO is the equivalent of such approval. But NATO is a military alliance, which naturally favors military solutions. That is why NATO should not be the entity making decisions to go to war. That is exactly why we need the United Nations.

How do we craft a new foreign policy that is based on safety, fairness, and responsibility? We begin by recognizing the intersection of domestic and international policy. We can't just talk about a safe America, a secure America. We can only begin that discussion if we talk about a secure America in a secure world. When there is not security for others, we are not secure.

We must return to multilateralism. We must fight for the United States to return to a commitment to international law. We must commit to treaties like the Rome treaty of the International Criminal Court and the Nonproliferation Treaty, particularly Article 6 of the Nonproliferation Treaty, which requires the official nuclear-weapons countries to move towards complete disarmament. We can't expect all other countries, which are not nuclear-weapons states, to accept their nonnuclear status when we are making threats now to get a new generation of "useable" nuclear weapons.

And we must reassert the legitimacy and the centrality of the United Nations. The United Nations must deal with the illegal military occupation of Iraq. The first obligation of a military-occupying power is to end the occupation. That is true of

Israel in Palestine, and it is true of the United States in Iraq. The United Nations has to be the alternative to military occupations.

BIBLIOGRAPHY

Phyllis A. Bennis, *Before & After: U.S. Foreign Policy and the September 11 Crisis* (Northampton: Interlink Press, 2002).

———, *Beyond the Storm: A Gulf Crisis Reader* (Northampton, Interlink Press, 1991).

———, *Calling the Shots: How Washington Dominates Today's U.N.* (Northampton: Interlink Press, 2000).

Richard Perle, "Thank God for the Death of the United Nations," the *Guardian*, March 21, 2003.

Patrick Tyler, "A New Power in the Streets," news analysis, *New York Times*, p. 1, February 17, 2003.

• *10* •

Speaking Truth to Power: Preventive Diplomacy Backed by Force

William D. Hartung

> *The conjunction of an immense military establishment and a huge arms industry is new in the American experience. The total influence—economic, political, and even spiritual—is felt in every city, every state house, and every office of the federal government. . . . In the councils of government, we must guard against the acquisition of unwarranted influence, whether sought or unsought, by the military-industrial complex.*
>
> —President Dwight D. Eisenhower, Farewell Address to the Nation, January 17, 1961

This chapter argues for the return of moderates to the foreign policy arena in the United States. The nation needs to apply to terrorism the kind of balance President Eisenhower advocated in America's Cold War strategy. The United States should pursue a policy of preventive diplomacy backed by force and disregard our present policy of force without sufficient diplomacy. High on the agenda must be a global strategy of eliminating nuclear weapons, building on bipartisan legislation already in place. The downward spiral of foreign aid funding must be dramatically reversed if America ever is to be perceived by the world as a model of democracy, justice, and equality.

American citizens must better educate themselves on what really is happening in the world and build activism into their daily lives. Grassroots activism is the basis for reversing present policy and the deplorable state of American democracy. In terms of action, we are confronted by the "fierce urgency of now," as articulated in the 1967 Riverside Church speech of the Reverend Martin Luther King Jr., who, like Dwight Eisenhower, spoke truth to power.

WHY DO THE AGGRESSIVE UNILATERALISTS ALWAYS WIN?

At its inception, the Bush administration said it wanted strong people with different points of view. The trouble was that those with an aggressive, anti-United Nations, anti-treaty, anti-alliance, unilateral point of view always won out over those few with a more pragmatic point of view, like Secretary of State Colin Powell.

The aggressive unilateralists were willing to use Colin Powell's diplomatic skills when it served a military objective, but they rarely let him finish the job. The Iraq war is a perfect example. Colin Powell secured a 15-0 vote in the U.N. Security Council, indicating that Iraq would face "serious consequences" if it did not cooperate with U.N. inspectors and disarm in a prompt manner. Once they received international support based on one set of assumptions—that there would be inspections, that the inspections would be given a reasonable amount of time to work, and that any military action would be subject to an additional Security Council vote—the aggressive unilateralists decided to upset the apple cart. They tried to undermine the inspections and smear Hans Blix, a perfectly decent and competent diplomat. They made it clear that, if there was no second U.N. resolution authorizing the war, the United States would invade anyway with a "coalition of the willing"—which, as many have pointed out, was really a coalition of the bullied and the bought.

Americans were told that force was going to be only one of the tools in the toolbox when dealing with Iraq. But it did not turn out that way. The Bush administration departed from the way it originally conceptualized the war, through multilateral efforts. It is likely that the aggressive unilateralists had no intention of really pursuing Iraq and terrorism in a more nuanced way and that they only gave lip service to multilateralism to sell war to the public. This was necessary because, when you look at the poll numbers, the American public, especially the vast middle that any candidate needs to get elected president, is not comfortable with the idea of America taking all the risks and paying all the costs without friends and allies to pitch in. Americans don't like high casualties. They don't want to pay a lot of money. They don't want to go it alone. And so in that sense—to keep Middle America on board—Colin Powell was needed.

American voters are not highly informed about foreign policy. That made it easier for the aggressive unilateralists to allege a link between Saddam Hussein and al Qaeda and go to war with Iraq—in part using as its propagandizing tools the conservative think tanks in Washington, the Defense Policy Board, and conservative media such as Fox News and Clear Channel.

From 1989 to 1992, American foreign policy was crafted by moderates like Brent Scowcroft and James Baker, who were able to counter the conservative propaganda machine. But no such counterbalance is present today. The aggressive unilateralists have won out over the pragmatists not only in terms of going to war in Iraq, but also in terms of not involving the president in hands-on, personal diplomacy in Israel-Palestine and not stopping the slaughter in Liberia, among many other examples.

In the public debate on foreign policy, then, it is critically important to ask, again and again, why the aggressive unilateralists always won over the pragmatists and whether these unending victories were healthy for the nation.

HEEDING THE WARNINGS OF PRESIDENT EISENHOWER

Foreign policy can be made healthier for the American people if we heed the warnings of President Eisenhower. Framing policy at the height of the Cold War, President Eisenhower said this "hostile ideology, communism" is "ruthless in purpose, and insidious in method. Unhappily, the danger it poses promises to be of indefinite duration. To meet [the danger] successfully, [we need] not so much the emotional and transitory sacrifices of crisis, but rather those [sacrifices] which enable us to carry forward steadily, surely, and without complaint the burdens of a prolonged and complex struggle with liberty the stake."

In other words, Eisenhower reminded Americans that the struggle against communism needed to be part of our everyday lives. He asked that we not sacrifice our liberties while fighting the struggle. Eisenhower continued: "Only thus shall we remain, despite every provocation, on our charted course to permanent peace and human betterment. Crises there may continue to be, and meeting them, whether foreign or domestic, great or small, there is a recurring temptation to feel that some spectacular and costly action could become the miraculous solution to all current difficulties."

Eisenhower's point here was that there was no silver bullet. Our policy against communism required economic, fiscal, political, and democratic balance. Eisenhower asked that we proceed soberly as adults, not go to extremes, not undermine our resilient economy, and not overreact.

Yet we have done just that since September 11, and so Eisenhower's policy admonitions are as relevant to terrorism in the twenty-first century as to communism in the 1950s.

A few years after the military-industrial-complex warning, President John Kennedy faced the Cuban missile crisis. Kennedy carried on in a steady way, speaking truth to power and overruling hardliners who wanted to go to war. If a similar crisis occurred today, say in a confrontation with a nuclear-armed North Korea or an unexpected showdown with China, would right-wing ideologies similarly be overruled?

Certainly President Eisenhower's admonitions were not followed in Iraq. Iraq was the kind of "spectacular and costly action" Eisenhower warned against. In terms of the economic and fiscal balance Eisenhower said was crucial, America is spending more than $1 billion a week in Iraq and will continue to do so for the foreseeable future—at least until reconstruction is completed (and the current estimate is that it will take until 2008 or 2009). Meanwhile, a projected ten-year budget *surplus* of $5.6 trillion has turned into a budget *deficit* of $521 billion—far more than triple the $158 billion imbalance of fiscal 2002 and billions higher than the record shortfall of $374 billion of 2003.

Similarly, think about the political and democratic balance President Eisenhower sought. There is much rhetoric today about creating democracy in places like Iraq. But there is little reflection on the state of democracy in America. Nor is there much discussion of the link between what is happening abroad and at home. For example, in the name of democracy, a hand-picked regime in Iraq is giving out contracts to corporate friends of the administration in Washington, corporations like Halliburton, Bechtel, and DynCorp. Similarly, back home, the administration was handpicked for office in 2000 by a partisan majority of the Supreme Court, despite the fact that the opposition had received more votes. The power of office and right-wing networks in the media and think tanks then were used to advance the financial interests of corporate supporters and beneficiaries of tax cuts, skewed to the well-off.

What kind of message does that send to the world? Unless America enacts genuine campaign finance reform and genuine voter democracy reform, other nations will continue to correctly point out that the United States has a double standard on democracy. Phyllis Bennis's comparison in chapter 9, of the double standard on democracy of the American and Greek empires is very apropos. And unless we roll back the Patriot Act, other countries will know we are not serious about individual liberties and the right to privacy.

PREVENTIVE DIPLOMACY BACKED BY FORCE

With President Eisenhower's sense of balance as our foundation, the United States needs to build a policy of preventive diplomacy backed by force.

Foreign Policy in Focus, a network coordinated by the Institute for Policy Studies in Washington, D.C., and the Interhemispheric Resource Center in New Mexico, have been developing the theme of "a safer America in a safer world." We need to expand on that theme, spreading hope and opportunity, not fear and loathing. That is a far smarter way to fight global terror than the use of force without sufficient accompanying diplomacy.

We need to use all the tools in the toolbox, not just the military one. President Clinton had the beginnings of a credible policy of diplomacy backed by force, even though he was not able to consistently implement it because of the Monica Lewinsky scandal and efforts by his opposition to undercut him at every turn. To illustrate, over the course of the Clinton administration, progress was made on the North Korean nuclear issue. The North Korean Framework Agreement was a step in the right direction.

Even though Clinton's policy was only partially developed, it was leagues ahead of what we have now, which is a policy outside the mainstream of five decades of bipartisan foreign policy assumptions, Republican and Democratic. Don't forget that many of the treaties that were trashed or criticized in recent years, from the antiballistic missile treaty to the START arms-reduction agreements, were negotiated and signed under President Nixon and President Reagan.

Diplomacy backed by force means America in the role of Atticus Finch, as played by Gregory Peck in the film adaptation of Harper Lee's novel *To Kill a Mockingbird*. Peck played a Southern trial lawyer, defending the rights of an African-American unjustly accused by whites. Ironically, an America that stood up for justice, stood with the underdogs, and felt secure enough to put down the gun instead of automatically picking up the gun at the slightest provocation—an America that was more Gregory Peck and less John Wayne—would be far better suited to fighting a threat like al Qaeda than an America that follows present policy.

Why? Because we are in a propaganda war, and the Department of Defense's policy of talking loudly and arrogantly and carrying many, many big sticks has alienated the majority of the people on the planet. These are the people and governments we need to work with to curb a threat like al Qaeda, a network that functions in perhaps as many as sixty countries. "Regime change" is an irrelevant, costly extravagance in the face of a network like al Qaeda, which can operate with relatively small amounts of money, without government sponsorship, preying on the weaknesses and complexities of our globalized economic system to sustain itself.

The costs of regime change through the doctrine of "preventive war" misdirect our resources away from the battle against al Qaeda. In so doing, "preventive war" may have *increased* the ability of terrorists to strike America, not decreased it.

ELIMINATING NUCLEAR WEAPONS GLOBALLY

The United States is worried about Osama bin Laden, a global businessman, obtaining nuclear missiles. So we must ask, where are the nuclear missiles that Osama is most likely to buy? They are in the former Soviet Union.

There still are places in the former Soviet Union where the security guards are barely paid. They sleep on couches at the worksite because they can't afford a decent place to live. Not only does Russia have thousands of weapons, but enough nuclear material to build tens of thousands more.

What to do? Several years ago, a task force led by a Republican moderate, Howard Baker, and a Democratic moderate, Lloyd Cutler, came up with a very good report, which recommended enhancing "Nunn-Lugar." Nunn-Lugar is the catch-all phrase for a set of programs designed to neutralize the nuclear capability of the former Soviet Union by helping to pay for destruction of nuclear missiles and warheads and by finding alternative employment for weapons scientists, so they don't sell their skills to the highest bidder on the global market. It was conceived by Sam Nunn, the former Democratic senator from Georgia who chaired the Armed Services Committee, and Richard Lugar, the moderate Republican senator from Indiana who chairs the Senate Foreign Relations Committee. The Baker-Cutler report said that the Nunn-Lugar programs were working well, but that their funding should be increased, from about $1 billion per year to $3 billion a year for ten years, a modest figure as measured by Pentagon budgets.

The White House has not shown leadership on this critical issue. Congress has bumped Nunn-Lugar up by about $1 billion, but this level remains far below the recommendations of Baker and Cutler. America's $1 billion outlay for one week in postwar Iraq could have raised funding to the levels needed.

But Senator Lugar, in his own quiet, effective way, has persisted. He has urged that Nunn-Lugar not only be better funded but globalized—not limited just to Russia. He is saying that America needs the funds and the flexibility to buy up bomb-grade materials and destroy them, so they don't fall into the wrong hands.

Of course, the goal should be to get rid of nuclear weapons altogether. There are no "right hands" when it comes to nuclear weapons. Their mere existence is dangerous, destabilizing, and demoralizing. Like a loaded gun under your pillow, nuclear weapons are just as dangerous to the folks who have them as they are to the folks who don't. Brandishing them and threatening people with them, as the American government has done, is a sure-fire recipe for convincing countries that they need their own nuclear missiles, if for no other reason than to get themselves off the Department of Defense's "regime change" list.

Tyrants around the world surely have noticed the deferential treatment that North Korea, which may have a few nuclear weapons, got compared with Saddam Hussein, who did not. So what the American government seems to be saying by its actions is, "Get nuclear weapons and we'll treat you nice, and negotiate. Fail to get nuclear weapons and we'll bomb you into the Stone Age and kill your family." What kind of incentive is that to dissuade dictators from trying to get nuclear weapons? Does the United States even care about nuclear proliferation, or does it think that the Star Wars system is going to save America?

These preventive policies, like expanding and globalizing Nunn-Lugar, are the kinds of strategies the U.S. government should be pursuing, because once you get rid of the nuclear weapons, Osama bin Laden can't buy off some security guard who hasn't had a square meal in three weeks.

America also needs to strengthen the Strategic Offensive Reduction Treaty, or SORT, with Russia. The nonprofit organization Peace Action has said SORT is "sort of a treaty," except for all the loopholes. For example, at the moment, when weapons are taken off deployment, they can be stored, not destroyed. That is absurd. There should be a time line. Now the rules are too vague. We should be working bilaterally and with regional partners, not only in North Korea but also in India and Pakistan, giving them whatever incentives they need to dismantle existing nuclear programs, not build new ones.

In addition, the United States must strengthen the enforcement of the Biological Weapons Convention and the Chemical Weapons Convention. That means America must adhere to the same standards for inspection as everybody else—and there is no reason we shouldn't.

DEVELOPING PEACEKEEPING CAPACITY

Instead of fighting wars against regimes with no known ties to terrorists, or at least the ones we are worried about like Iraq, America should be developing actual peacekeeping capabilities. We barely train our troops to do the kind of policing work we are asking them to do in Iraq. We should be working more closely with countries that know how to train soldiers for policing, like the Canadians, the French, and the Germans, as Joseph Wilson points out in chapter 15.

The Americans trained for peacekeeping in places like Iraq ought to be enlisted military, not National Guard reservists. We need to take pressure off National Guard reservists, who have been deployed in Iraq for too long. A lot of reservists are police, firefighters, nurses, and public-health professionals. We need them in America. We need them on the front lines here if there is another attack at least as much as we need them in Iraq, Afghanistan, Riyadh, Tehran, or wherever the administration next plans to attack.

NURTURING ALLIANCES AND FOLLOWING THE MONEY

We need to build and nurture our alliances with other countries. When the State Department released a recent *Patterns of Global Terrorism* report, the spokesperson made a point of saying that the two countries that have given America the most help in dealing with al Qaeda recently were France and Germany. The State Department made this point to emphasize that, if the Defense Department doesn't stop insulting France and Germany, important ties will be further damaged.

A broad spectrum of people realize that having allies is a good thing and insulting countries is a bad thing. If we are to have an effective policy against terrorism, America must follow the money, and that means leaning on the Saudis, leaning on the Pakistanis. We need to have a more responsible approach to the global economy that says if certain aspects of the financial system must be regulated in order to make sure we don't have another World Trade Center disaster and if money therefore has to flow a little more slowly, then so be it. The ideology of free movement of goods and money should not come at the expense of the safety of our children or of future generations. If we need tighter banking laws to make it harder for terrorists and thugs to use offshore banks and secret accounts to finance their activities, and if that means slowing down the flow of money a bit, that's a small price to pay for a margin of safety for us and those who will come after us.

CHANNELING AID THROUGH MULTILATERAL AGENCIES

As Jessica Tuchman Mathews argues in chapter 3, the downward spiral of foreign aid funding in the State Department must be dramatically reversed if America ever is to be perceived by the world as a model of democracy, justice, and equality.

To help achieve the goal of nurturing alliances, the United States should channel its economic and security aid through multilateral agencies. That way we can secure the benefits of implementing our priorities without a backlash based on the notion that the United States is calling the shots all on its own or buying off key leaders.

For example, instead of having the Saudis building faith-based schools that teach the ideology of jihad, we should be helping build secular schools throughout the Muslim world. But these can't come from the United States. For credibility, they must be funded through the United Nations.

Miriam Pemberton and I have pointed out how America spends between \$6 billion and \$7 billion a year of our scarce foreign aid budget subsidizing weapons exports. That must stop. The money must be converted into economic aid. If we are going to bother to fund programs against HIV/AIDS, the money should pass through the Global AIDS Fund, not be tied to some ridiculous bilateral package that says a nation must teach abstinence before America will provide AIDS drugs.

THE FIERCE URGENCY OF NOW

What can average Americans do about our foreign policy and the deplorable state of American democracy?

They can begin in modest ways. For example, Americans need to better educate themselves about what's going on. Political literacy can be improved by visiting sites on the web that are independent of corporate control, like CommonDreams.org, AlterNet.org, TomPaine.com, and TheNation.com.

Better-informed citizens can then join with others, becoming more powerful through partnerships. One might, for example, join the local chapter of Peace Action (PeaceAction.org), the nation's largest grassroots peace and justice organization, or get on the mailing list at MoveOn.org, the innovative, visionary web-based activist network discussed by Eli Pariser in chapter 32.

The most important thing is for citizens to find a way to build activism into their everyday lives. Some people may get so worked up that they quit their jobs to work for the candidates of their choice—fighting for education all can afford, jobs, job training and retraining, health care, Social Security, and rescission of tax cuts for the rich. Others may take personal risks, like committing civil disobedience at the offices or factories of local war profiteers. Still others may pursue the difficult work of trying to win over friends, colleagues, or professional associates. The main thing to remember is that nothing is too little to matter. Democratic participation needs to become a habit.

We must live every day as if the future of real democracy at home and abroad depends on it—because it does. I began this chapter with Dwight Eisenhower speaking truth to power. I end it with Martin Luther King Jr. speaking truth to power, also at a moment of genuine national emergency. In "A Time to Break Silence," his Riverside Church speech of April 4, 1967, against the war in Vietnam, Dr. King told the people: "We are now faced with the fact that tomorrow is today. We are confronted with the fierce urgency of now."

BIBLIOGRAPHY

Edmund L. Andrews, "Nearsighted Deficit Plan Ignores Problems Down the Road, Skeptics Say," *New York Times*, February 3, 2004.

Howard Baker and Lloyd Cutler, co-chairs, Russia Task Force, "A Report Card on the Department of Energy's Nonproliferation Programs With Russia," final task force report, Secretary of Energy Advisory Board, Washington, D.C, January 10, 2001.

Dwight D. Eisenhower, "Military-Industrial Complex Speech," farewell address to nation, January 17, 1961.

William D. Hartung, *And Weapons for All* (New York: HarperCollins, 1994).

———, *How Much Are You Making on the War, Daddy? A Quick and Dirty Guide to War Profiteering in the Bush Administration* (New York: Nation's Books, 2003).

———, "Making Money on Terrorism," the *Nation*, Feb. 23, 2004.

———, "The Military Industrial Complex Revisited: How Weapons Makers are Shaping U.S. Foreign and Military Policies," *Foreign Policy in Focus* report, February 25, 1999.

The Reverend Martin Luther King Jr., "Beyond Vietnam: A Time to Break Silence," speech at Riverside Church, New York, April 4, 1967.

Harper Lee, *To Kill a Mockingbird* (1960; reprinted New York: HarperCollins, 1999).
Miriam Pemberton and Michael Renner, "A Tale of Two Markets: Trade in Arms and Environmental Technologies," National Commission for Economic Conversion and Disarmament report, Washington, D.C., 1998
United States Department of State, *Patterns of Global Terrorism*, 2002 report, Washington, D.C., April, 2003.
Elmira Woods and William D. Hartung, "Bush's African Agenda," the *Nation,* August 4, 2003.

• *11* •

American Foreign Policy: A Tragic "Success"

Michael Parenti

Many people today believe that American foreign policy is stupid or timid or confused or overextended or bankrupt. The truth is that the current policy is rational. By "rational," I mean it pursues certain goals and maximizes certain interests rather consistently. And, unfortunately, it is strikingly successful in what it does.

THE GOALS OF AMERICAN FOREIGN POLICY

American foreign policy consistently supports those who throw their countries open to Western investment on terms that are completely favorable to the investors, those who open land, labor, markets, and natural resources to be used in service to the market interests of American capital and other big corporate Western investors. The countries that cooperate with this global investment agenda are approvingly labeled by American policymakers and the American corporate media as "pro-West," "friendly to the West," and "pro-American."

At the same time, American policy has consistently opposed those countries, political movements, and leaders who have sought an alternative approach, outside the global corporate free-market system that is now being imposed on the entire world, those who have wanted to be something more than comprador collaborators with American power and Western investors.

These "rogue states" have included a democratic-reformist coalition government, as in Chile under Allende; a Christian Socialist Revolutionary government, as in Nicaragua under the Sandinistas; leftist military governments, as in Panama and under Torrijo and even Noriega, or in Libya under Khaddafi; and Marxist-Leninist governments as in Vietnam or Cuba. Even a conservative, militarist right-wing regime that proves to be an economic nationalist government, as in Iraq under Saddam Hussein, was targeted. These are the kinds of countries that have had their leaders demonized and their populations subjected to massive military assaults by United States forces. During the Cold War, American leaders tolerated and even encouraged some independent and potentially competitive economic development by Third World nations. The poorer countries were supposed to develop their own industrial bases. Aided by western investment, they would come to enjoy prosperity, or specifically a stable, sizable middle class that would keep them from going communist. The fear that they would turn to collective forms of economic development was the motor force behind American policy in the Cold War era (and remains a concern to this day).

Most such Third World development was highly uneven in regard to who benefited and who paid the costs, just as it is highly uneven today in China and a few other places. For instance, the "Brazilian miracle" of the 1960s brought a dramatic increase in Brazil's gross domestic product but also a dramatic increase in poverty. Some industries expanded, especially in the export sector; some people got rich, but millions were left dispossessed, underemployed, and hungrier than ever as land that once grew beans was now used for coffee and beef exports. Western investment in poor countries usually has had a distorting rather than a developing effect because banks and corporations do not invest to help poor people but to help themselves. This explains why the number of poor in the world is growing at a faster rate than the world's population, even while investments increase. Poverty is spreading as wealth is accumulated.

Today, without a competitor like the Soviet Union, American policy has become as nakedly exploitative as its wealth and power allow it to be. Aid programs have been cut. Local industries in the Third World are denied protections and denied markets under "free trade accords" such as the North American Free Trade Agreement, the General Agreement on Tariffs and Trade, the General Agreement on Trade in Services, and the Free Trade Area of the Americas. These agreements really have little to do with trade and certainly are not free. They should be called: "Monopoly Capital Investment Accords."

The goal of American policy today is total domination of a global free-market economy, unchallenged by any competing superpower or even regional power and intolerant of any deviation from the free-market norm. Consider how that policy recently has been applied to Yugoslavia and Iraq.

THE DISMEMBERMENT OF YUGOSLAVIA

During the Cold War, Yugoslavia was tolerated and even encouraged in its independent course as a breakaway from the Eastern Bloc. But after 1990, when there was no Eastern Bloc, there was no reason to have to tolerate Yugoslavia anymore. Here was this rather large-sized country right in the middle of Central Europe, with plenty of problems and imperfections to be sure, yet fairly prosperous, with a decent and roughly equitable standard of living, ruled by a democratically elected coalition government of four parties under the much demonized Slobodan Milosevic, with 80 percent of its economy still publicly owned and showing no interest in opening itself to all-out neoliberal privatization and deregulation, as was being done throughout Eastern Europe. Yugoslavia was resisting free market reforms, it showed no interest in joining the European Union, and it had absolutely no desire to become a part of the North Atlantic Treaty Organization. So something had to be done about Yugoslavia.

It was not long before German and American agencies were supporting every divisive, retrograde, secessionist, nationalist element in Yugoslavia. In Croatia, they backed Franjo Tudjman, a fascist sympathizer and Holocaust denier, who had former Nazi collaborators, that is, former Ustashe, in his party. During World War II, the Ustashe sent hundreds of thousands of Serbs, Jews, and Roma ("gypsies") to their death in the Jasenovac extermination camp. In Bosnia, the Western destabilizers supported Alija Izetbegovic, who himself during World War II had been a member of a fundamentalist Muslim youth unit of the Nazi SS that perpetrated atrocities upon Jews and helped guard the rail lines to Auschwitz. In Kosovo, American interventionists supported the Kosovo Liberation Army, which the American State Department had called a terrorist organization that was deeply involved in the drug trade. Both of those descriptions would still hold for the Kosovo Liberation Army and its newest reincarnation, the Albanian National Army. More recently we heard that the Kosovo Liberation Army has been linked to al Qaeda and other Islamic terrorist organizations. While the Serbs were being demonized by American policymakers and charged with committing all the atrocities, in fact all three of the reactionary secessionist groups (Croatian, Bosnian, and Kosovar Albanian) perpetrated at least as many atrocities against the Serbs and other groups.

So Yugoslavia was broken up into a cluster of little right-wing republics in which everything is privatized and deregulated. Most recently, with the overthrow of Milosevic, this is happening in Serbia, where public services have been shredded to pieces; pension funds have been plundered and disappeared; and unemployment is skyrocketing, as are inflation, poverty, homelessness, crime, prostitution, and all those other good things provided by the free-market paradise.

BATTERING IRAQ

Iraq is another case of a country that no longer has to be tolerated by the American globalists. The Iraqi Revolution of 1958 was only partially undone by the Central Intelligence Agency countercoup of 1968. It is one of the American media's best-kept secrets that Saddam Hussein and his military cohorts were backed and financed by the Central Intelligence Agency. His assignment was to slaughter the Iraqi revolutionaries, the progressives, democrats, communists—all of them, which indeed he did. He even exterminated the left wing of his own Ba'ath party.

But Saddam Hussein then produced a few surprises of his own that made Washington most uncomfortable. He did not turn out to be a perfect comprador leader, totally collaborationist with the West. His government was politically conservative but also economically nationalist. In 1972 the Iraqi rulers nationalized the oil industry and nationalized much of the basic production system. They also pursued economic self-development, setting education programs and health clinics, and were supportive of Palestinian independence.

Some countries in the Middle East have oil but no water. Some have water but no oil. Iraq has quite a bit of both. It has one of the largest oil reserves in the world. Iraq also had the highest standard of living in the Middle East until the Gulf War of 1991, when so much of its infrastructure was shattered. It had a very good agricultural base too, much of which has been destroyed by depleted uranium from the first Gulf War. And a dozen years of cruel sanctions and intermittent air strikes took a further toll. So in 2003 the American administration picked a fight with an already seriously battered country that, despite the sanctions, was trying to rebuild itself.

That policymakers gave us justifications for the war that proved to be misleading and confusing did not necessarily mean they themselves were misled and confused. It may have been that the goal was to mislead and confuse us. Consider the first Gulf War. Many reasons were given to justify the American military onslaught against Iraq. For example, we had to go in there, we were told, because Saddam had invaded Kuwait. Many of us questioned this rationale, noting that Turkey invaded Cyprus, Morocco invaded the Western Sahara, and Israel and Syria invaded Lebanon and were still occupying it in 1990, but the United States doesn't seem bothered by those aggressors. In fact, we continued to give them aid. So why were we supposed to get so upset about Kuwait?

The American government argued that we had to wage the first Gulf War because Saddam was a tyrant. But so are many other leaders. Why the urgency about this one?

Then Secretary of State James Baker said that a war against Iraq would create more jobs and be good for the economy. I thought that was interesting. It was the first time that the administration in power from 1989 to 1992 had shown any interest in creating a jobs program for people. But even auto accidents are good for the economy. They create jobs in towing and wreckage, in health care and rehabilitation, for lawyers, funeral directors, plastic surgeons, state troopers, and for the entire auto industry. The point is, some things may be good for the economy but not good for the human beings who live in that economy.

Despite the monopoly-media bombardment and demonization of Saddam Hussein, American public opinion was not all that enthusiastic for war as late as the autumn of 1990. People were asking, What is this war all about? Why do we have to go fight Iraq? Then in November 1990 a poll was taken that asked, "If Saddam

Hussein develops nuclear weapons, would that be sufficient cause for military intervention?" (The term "weapons of mass destruction" had not yet come into vogue.) In response to that question, the percentage supporting military intervention went up to something like 70 percent. Immediately that became the theme that the administration picked up in 1990. And twelve years later, that was the very same "fright theme" that the administration seized upon in the second war against Iraq.

In regard to weapons of mass destruction, the American government has charged that Iraq has failed to comply for twelve years. In fact, that is not true. In 1998 the United Nations inspection team checked 457 sites. Of these, 452 were in perfect compliance. The 5 other sites consisted of minor, marginal things, like forty-minute delays because the Iraqis raised questions about particulars. Even though inspectors were then allowed to inspect the sites, Iraq was cited for noncompliance because of the relatively minor delays and arguments they raised.

THE REAL REASONS FOR WAR AGAINST IRAQ

Having discovered that the reasons given to justify war are shallow and false, we would be wrong then to conclude that the policy is ill-founded because there may be other reasons that the policymakers are not willing to discuss. I would suggest at least three compelling reasons why America invaded Iraq.

The first reason was the need to maintain a superpower global predominance that imposes the free-market model on the entire world (including within the United States itself), reducing the populations of the world to Third World client-state status and making sure there will arise no competing superpower or even a strong self-directed regional power, such as Iraq could have been.

The second reason for war was the old-fashioned colonialist grab for precious resources. Iraq has 112 billion barrels of crude—some of the best quality in the world; it is the second largest reserve in the Middle East, maybe in the world, except for Saudi Arabia. A lot of this oil has remained untapped. Exploration concessions were made by the Iraqi government to Russia, China, France, Brazil, Italy, and Malaysia. The United States has made it known that, having done away with the Saddam government, it feels no obligation to honor these previous agreements. Some 112 billion barrels of oil at $35.00 a barrel is over $3 trillion. This would be the biggest oil grab in the history of the world. And it is not the first time that American leaders have squeezed out other Western interests and grabbed the oil for American companies. Recall the history of Iran, for instance.

And it was not always oil. British sugar and fruit companies were pushed out of Central America and replaced by American ones. When these globalists no longer have the communists to worry about, they start whacking each other, just as they did through much of the nineteenth and twentieth centuries.

The third reason for war against Iraq was the domestic political advantage it initially brought to its perpetrators. War with Iraq was played the same way that September 11 was played—to further a reactionary, rollback agenda. In 1787 Alexander Hamilton, in Federalist Paper #6, made the point that history is replete with leaders who have pursued foreign adventures in order to distract the people from their domestic grievances. Indeed, the Iraq venture was a perfect example of what Hamilton had in mind. Perpetual war, perpetual crises, and perpetual threat from abroad justify perpetually greater military spending and cutbacks in human services—just as did September 11, 2001. You might recall one of the first things that the government did after September 11 was increase military spending and cut out $15.7 million that was to be allocated to help abused and abandoned children.

In 2002, the administration was reeling because of Enron, WorldCom, and other such scandals. The president and vice president were implicated with Harken (Energy) and Halliburton, insider trading and buying up stock that was being artificially inflated in its price, then dumping the nearly worthless stock at a very high price, with smaller investors holding the bag. Both the president and vice president refused to produce documents and did not cooperate in the investigation. But with the coming of the second Iraq war, that story of corporate scandal and massive thievery has been blown off the front page and out of the evening network telecasts.

That is exactly what the American government did in 1990 with the savings-and-loan conspiracy, the largest theft of the public treasury ever—over $1 trillion of the people's money. We taxpayers will be paying off the bill for generations. In 1990, the federal government just wiped that issue out of the media with a war against the very same Saddam Hussein.

More than a decade later, the American government tried to wipe economic recession from the media and replace it with a focus on patriotism, military leadership, a strong defense, and war. September 11 helped. By late 2002, with war in the air, pleas for patriotism, military leadership, and strong defense again were reinforced, and Republicans (with help from inept Democrats) won a Congressional election they should never have won, given the state of the economy.

War and crises also allowed the reactionaries in the White House to try to suppress domestic dissent. The nation was at war, so everyone had to fall into line. Democracy is a bothersome thing for plutocrats, for those who want to rule primarily in the interests of the top 1 percent of the income bracket.

THE "PROBLEM" OF POPULAR STRUGGLE

To say that policymakers consciously pursue self-serving goals with much success is not to imply that they are infallible. Sometimes unexpected consequences and reactions put them into troublesome situations. In the wake of September 11, the American government was able to invade Afghanistan with relatively little opposition at home and abroad. With the United States much fortified by that now-dubious accomplishment, it expected to enjoy another free victory ride into Baghdad the following year. Instead, the American government was caught by surprise when various members of the U.N. Security Council refused to go along with the American military assault against Iraq. Washington was further discomfited when peoples around the world demonstrated against the anticipated war. Here was an unprecedented development.

First, the antiwar protest movement arose within a matter of weeks and went into action *before* the war began.

Second, the protests were massive in size; for instance, the February 2003 march in London numbered 2 million, the largest public protest in British history. The ones in Madrid numbered close to a million, with demonstrations continuing in almost every Spanish city and town for days on end.

Third, the protests were global in reach, extending into countries as varied as Japan, Lithuania, Indonesia, Russia, Argentina, Finland, Italy, India, Pakistan, Germany, Egypt, Mexico, and numerous others throughout the world; tens of millions of people of different languages, cultures, ethnicity, and political affiliation, all joining in a furious campaign against the American war of aggression that was soon to be. In all, there were protests in 665 cities worldwide.

The protestors were concerned not only about Iraq but also about their own security and sovereignty. They were confronting a renegade superpower whose leaders openly appropriated for themselves a monarchical global control over all others and whose leaders made it clear they would no longer bother with the normal restraints of international law. They would not be held to any past treaties. They openly disregarded the U.N. Charter, the Geneva conventions, and the right of any international court to judge war crimes committed by U.S. military and political personnel. At the same time, they themselves could hold the leaders and combatants of other nations accountable for war crimes.

American leaders even declared that they had a right to pursue "preventive war," attacking anyone, anywhere, anytime as they might choose. And they would not hesitate to be the first to use nuclear weapons if they deemed it necessary, even against countries that had no nuclear arsenal. In all, they made it clear that they were answerable to no one. They had the might, and that made it all right.

But even an overweening superpower possessed with unanswerable military force can sometimes bite off more than it can chew. Along with the global opposition around the world against the invasion of Iraq came an armed people's resistance within Iraq itself. Several thousand American military personnel have suffered disabling injuries and wounds in Iraq; hundreds have died in combat or in war-related operations; and an estimated 10,000 Iraqis have been killed. In both Iraq and

Afghanistan resistance was widespread, violent, resourceful, and unrelenting, while democracy and nation-rebuilding were nowhere in sight.

The federal government warned the American public that it faced "a massive and long-term undertaking in Iraq." Appeals were made in various forms to the United Nations, for example, to assist in policing Iraq. This was the same United Nations that the American government had dismissed back in March 2003 as "another League of Nations" when the United States announced its determination to invade Iraq with or without a U.N. Security Council mandate. Now with a long postwar prospect, the United States wants the United Nations and its member nations to come pick up some of the blood tab. We want other countries to share in the casualties and expenses. A U.N. bailout would lessen the political damage to the administration, which now finds itself trapped in an increasingly fruitless and costly people's resistance.

Despite every threat and subterfuge, despite false proclamations about "weapons of mass destruction" and the like, it seems many millions throughout the world still have minds of their own and refuse to fall into lockstep. This should be an encouragement for further democratic action on our part.

TERRORISM AS A REACTION TO AMERICAN REACTIONISM

Terrorism is a bloody, vicious form of political action often directed against innocent and defenseless people (though usually on a smaller scale than the American state-sponsored terrorism that has resorted to death squads and massive armed operations to claim tens of thousands of victims in scores of countries). While depicted in the corporate media as fueled by a mindless hatred of Western democracy, secularism, and prosperity, the "Islamic terrorists" actually have enunciated a rather explicit opposition to American politico-economic global oppression. Not long ago, William Blum reminded us that terrorists have actually stated their objectives and motives. Here are several of the key instances Blum cites:

The terrorists who bombed the World Trade Center the first time, in 1993, sent a letter to the *New York Times* declaring that the attack "was done in response for the American political, economic, and military support to Israel . . . and the rest of the dictator countries in the region."

A leading suspect behind the October 2002 bombings of nightclubs in Bali, which took more than 200 lives, told police that the attacks were "revenge" for "what Americans have done to Muslims" and because "America oppresses the Muslims."

In November 2001, in his first interview after September 11, Osama bin Laden had this to say: "This is a defensive jihad. We want to defend our people and the territory we control. This is why I said that if we do not get security, the Americans will not be secure either." A year later, a taped message from Osama bin Laden began: "The road to safety begins by ending [American] aggression. Reciprocal treatment is part of justice. The [terrorist] incidents that have taken place . . . are only reactions and reciprocal actions." (I, for one, find it somewhat unsettling when Osama bin Laden sounds more rational than our leaders in Washington.)

That same month, Mir Amal Kansi, on death row for gunning down several people outside Central Intelligence Agency headquarters in 1993, stated: "What I did was a retaliation against the American government" for its policy in the Middle East, including its support of Israel.

Even the Pentagon has lent support to the idea that what American leaders do abroad might have something to do with inciting terrorism. A 1997 Defense Department study concluded: "Historical data show a strong correlation between American involvement in international situations and an increase in terrorist attacks against the United States."

Blum points out that, in a 1989 interview, former president Jimmy Carter told the *New York Times*: "You only have to go to Lebanon, to Syria, or to Jordan to witness first-hand the intense hatred among many people for the United States because we bombed and shelled and unmercifully killed totally innocent villagers—women and children and farmers and housewives—in those villages around Beirut. . . . As a result of that . . . we became kind of a Satan in the minds of those who are deeply resentful. That is what precipitated the taking of our hostages and that is what has precipitated some of the terrorists' attacks."

A number of the right-wing pundits who overpopulate the corporate media maintain that the "Islamic terrorists" attack us because of who we *are*: prosperous, white, free, secular nonbelievers. In fact, if we bother to listen to what the terrorists themselves say, they hate us because of what we *do* to them in the name of peace, stability, and democracy. In Iraq, they also attack us for *where* we are—in their homeland, pumping out their oil, while bringing death, poverty, and destruction to the Iraqi people.

DEMOCRACY AND DISTRUST

Many of our fellow Americans are capable of having a very cynical view of politicians, seeing them as frequent deceivers and manipulators. But unfortunately, when these same politicians claim to be doing battle with some foreign menace, when they claim to be defending the ramparts, then many of our compatriots, with an uncritical trust, rally around the flag.

I once had a student say to me, "This is where you and I differ because I have faith in our leaders." I said, "Excuse me; you have *faith* in our leaders? What are we doing here, religion or politics? I mean, do you light a candle to a picture of our leaders, the way my old Italian grandma did with St. Anthony?" And what does it mean to have "trust" in leaders? Trust is something you extend to loved ones or very close friends and family (and even then, check them out once in a while).

Democracy is not about trust; it is about *distrust*. It is about accountability, exposure, open debate, direct challenge. It is about responsible government, all of which is fortified by a healthy dose of distrust. We have to get our fellow Americans to trust their leaders less and trust themselves a lot more, trust their own questions and suspicions. This is not paranoia; it is responsible oversight. These events do not happen by chance. If they are happening by random chance, why are they always going in the same direction, serving the same interests? No empire and no social structure ever survived without conscious human agency to propagate and defend it. Political and economic leaders act to preserve their interests just as any other people do.

CONCLUSION

American policy has been rational and we should not be deploring its failures but deploring its successes, because these "successes" do not represent the interests of the American people or the people of the world. We should spend less time talking about how stupid and short-sighted the American government has been and more time talking about how relentlessly vicious and resourceful it has been. Then we must attempt to deter it from its current destructive course.

BIBLIOGRAPHY

William Blum, *Killing Hope: U.S. Military and CIA Interventions Since World War II* (Monroe, Maine: Common Courage Press, 2003).

———, *Rogue State: A Guide to the World's Only Superpower* (Monroe, Maine: Common Courage Press, 2000).

Carl Boggs, editor, *Masters of War* (New York: Routledge, 2003).

Thomas L. Friedman, "Why Camp David Turned Bitter: The Carter View," special to the *New York Times*, March 26, 1989.

Edward Herman, *The Real Terror Network* (Boston: South End, 1982).

Michael Parenti, *Against Empire* (San Francisco: City Lights, 1995).

———, *The Terrorism Trap* (San Francisco: City Lights, 2002).

———, *To Kill a Nation: The Attack on Yugoslavia* (London: Verso, 2000).

http://www.AntiWar.com.

• *12* •

Concern and Credibility

David Corn

It has been a cliché that September 11 "changed everything." In fact, if you watch *American Idol* on Fox TV, you see it hasn't changed everything. Large parts of the culture are impermeable.

But September 11 has indeed changed the political and psychological dynamic in this country. The public looks to the president, in a generic sense, in a much different way than it did before September 11. We are looking for a protector-in-chief. All the business about threats before September 11, during the Cold War and the post–Cold War period, were generally abstract to this country.

Outside of the Cuban missile crisis, there were very few moments in time in the last fifty years when Americans actually felt threatened physically, in their homes, and September 11 changed that. The number-one job of the president became protecting American citizens. It became the number-one job of the Federal Bureau of Investigation, the Central Intelligence Agency, the Immigration and Naturalization Service, and a lot of other bureaucracies.

When people look to a protector, they do so with a strong bias in favor of that protector succeeding because they have a direct interest in that person's success. Gore Vidal would call it the "Big Father Figure." But you don't want to look at your Big Father Figure and find fault in him because that means your life is more insecure, and that actually means you have to do some more things for yourself or become further engaged in what are some very, very difficult issues.

Because of this, there now is a tremendous bias in the political system in favor of whoever is sitting in the White House. People don't want to see a failed president, and there is a tremendous amount of deference toward the president when it comes to real threat from terrorism. There is a strong bias in favor of what can be called the conventional approach: be strong, fight back. It is law-of-the-jungle–type stuff. It is what resonates on an emotional level. It is immediate. It may work. It may not work.

One of the most effective political ads in the last twenty years was in the 1984 Reagan campaign: the "bear in the woods" ad. All it showed was the bear—he was a friendly-looking bear—walking through the woods. The message was that some people say there's a bear in the woods, and some people say there's not, but shouldn't we protect ourselves just in case there *is* a bear in the woods?

The bear ad really fed on public fear, and the solution offered was to implement the Republican agenda: to build up the military, create Star Wars, and so on. The Democratic response was to say that Star Wars is destabilizing. It will cause the Chinese to build more weapons, anger our friends in the Soviet Union, and create an arms race between India and Pakistan. All true, but that takes a paragraph to say, and there's no bear to put next to the words.

The lesson is that Democratic policy alternatives must be wrapped in themes with immediacy and resonance. Two central themes we will discuss here are lack of concern for and lack of credibility with the rest of the world.

LACK OF CONCERN

America is indeed the last superpower and does, indeed, have real security concerns. We talk about Islamic terrorism, nonproliferation, and instability in other parts of the world. But the issue is whether these are things the United States can handle alone or, even if we can, whether we might do a better job if we had some friends and partners working with us. The notion of working with the rest of the world for our own interest is something that can be made politically acceptable. But if America wants countries to be concerned with our security, we have to be concerned with theirs.

It is stunning that the United States was able to get away with the anti-French campaign and forget about the Germans, Russians, Chinese, Mexicans, and Canadians—all were opposed to the war. The United States ignored international opinion on the Kyoto treaty, the International Criminal Court, twelve different conventions on chemical and biological weapons, and the racism conference in South Africa. We told the rest of the world, "we're not playing with you. We're taking our ball and going elsewhere."

Democrats did get the Bush administration to go to the United Nations regarding Iraq. The administration sought permission for war. It tried to finesse the request, to look like America was doing the right thing. In fact, we didn't get permission, but Democrats still applauded the administration for going to the United Nations.

Real concern, of course, means going far beyond applause. We need to form partnerships. That means agreeing with some of the priority agenda items of the other parts of the globe. The Middle East obviously is one.

LACK OF CREDIBILITY

Concern for the rest of the world ought to be one theme through which Democrats present their policy alternatives. Another should be the theme of credibility.

The absence of weapons of mass destruction in Iraq lost the United States a great deal of credibility in the world. Not only did the administration fail to find weapons of mass destruction, but it didn't even move quickly to secure nuclear facilities. The International Atomic Energy Agency did know what nuclear materials existed—materials that could be used in dirty bombs and uranium that could conceivably be processed into weapons-grade material. But when we invaded Iraq, no American was assigned to go to these sites and secure those areas. So we had the sorry spectacle of locals going into the al Tuwaitha nuclear facility, which is only eleven miles south of Baghdad, and taking barrels holding uranium, dumping them out, bringing them back to their homes, filling them up with water and bathing and drinking from them for weeks before they were bought back by international inspectors for $3 a barrel.

The Patriot Act is equally illustrative. If the American government could demonstrate an honest need for all the provisions in the act, it might be acceptable. But honest need has not been demonstrated.

Weapons of mass destruction and the Patriot Act are just two of the more obvious areas where America has lost its credibility. We fight for freedom in Iraq at the same time that we cut deals with Uzbekistan, which has about 7,000 political prisoners. We fail to effectively deal with nuclear proliferation and disarmament. We pass on the Kyoto treaty and do little to encourage alternative energy sources to prevent global warming. We fail to address poverty and inequality in any meaningful new way and give no priority to reforming the World Bank and International Monetary Fund into institutions responsive to local development needs and human-rights policy. We champion free trade but don't create cost-effective and humane policies for the workers who are affected. We sign trade accords that preserve the free flow of capital and ignore the rights of workers. We sit back as NAFTA decimates local farmers in Mexico who then join the ranks of the impoverished in Mexico City. We don't implement policies like Dick Gephardt's proposal to create a global minimum wage, adjusted to the cost of living in every country.

The loss of credibility is a serious security issue for the United States. When credibility is lost, the American government becomes less effective in terms of doing what actually might be needed, if not today, then a month or a year from today. What if there is a legitimate security issue that arises in North Korea involving weapons of mass destruction? The United States now has a harder time making the case. What if there is a new civil-liberties-threatening device that the Justice Department thinks would really help against a new threat? The Department now is hindered from action.

THE MEDIA

Mainstream media will not do much to develop these themes of concern and credibility. They did a fairly good job on weapons of mass destruction, but the story will fade unless there is a continuing political element to it.

As Eric Alterman, Amy Goodman, Robert McChesney, and John Nichols discuss in part V of this volume, most media today, owned by huge corporations, exist primarily to make a profit. The owners no longer are families with public-affairs missions.

The newspapers present a great amount of the material on how America has been misled in Iraq. The problem is that it doesn't get covered as a meta-story, as an overarching story, because no one is making that case. The media are geared toward covering drama and tension—that is what kept the Clinton impeachment and Whitewater alive. With the impeachment and Whitewater, the Republicans ran with the ball. They held hearings. They kept accusing the president of doing this, that, and the other thing. The political press takes its cues from political players, so it kept the stories alive. Accordingly, today, if there were Democrats stressing overriding issues of concern and credibility, there would be press coverage. That could still happen if more information leaks out and Democrats make bolder statements that political media can run with. Short of that, we cannot expect corporate media to generate an issue-oriented frame.

SENSITIZING THE CITIZENRY

With Americans looking for a Big Father, the government can ride the conventional approach very far, as long as nothing catastrophic happens. The only chance we have is to set forth bold alternative policy made appealing to the Americans who have been sensitized—and angered—by our lack of concern for and credibility with the rest of the world. Luckily, there are new ways of organizing, and groups such as MoveOn.org are paving the way, as Eli Pariser discusses in chapter 32. These grassroots efforts are the best hope for creating an alternative to the current destructive policy.

BIBLIOGRAPHY

David Corn, *Blond Ghost: Ted Shackley and the CIA's Crusades* (New York: Simon & Schuster, 1994).

———, *Deep Background* (New York: St. Martin's Press, 1999).

———, *The Lies of George W. Bush: Mastering the Politics of Deception* (New York: Crown Publishing, 2003).

• *13* •

The Necessity of Persuasion: Keeping Congress Engaged

Alton Frye

This chapter discusses the need for new foreign policies and how to achieve them. The search for enlightened policy has to take account of science and of history because any rational policy has to build upon evidence, analysis, and judgment. Judgment can take account of factors beyond the evidence—values and considerations that lie outside the frame of reference for the particular subject—but it is obviously pernicious to have the evidence or the analysis infected by *a priori* judgment insensitive to the findings of the investigation and study. That is a recipe for self-deception and for collapse of public confidence in the integrity of decision making. I make this preface because we have some reason to be concerned about it in the current state of affairs, and we need to be open-minded in awaiting further study and examination, which I hope will proceed in the Congress in due course.

There is another test for determining what a rational and enlightened policy can be and should be. In a pluralistic nation, we must always meet the test of persuasion. We have to be able to demonstrate a respect for those who differ with us, and we have to be able to persuade them that our course is wiser and sounder than the one to which they may initially be attracted.

CURRENT FOREIGN POLICY

Not all of America's recent foreign policies have been misguided. I would include among the praiseworthy initiatives the fact that the government has put forward a Millennium Challenge account concept that has real promise for enhancing and making more effective America's foreign-assistance programs. If it is funded as promised, there will be more money. But, equally important, it has a structural design that is winning high respect among people in the development field. We also have to list the powerful initiative that was mounted with regard to HIV/AIDS, the recognition that we have a global problem that must draw resources and multilateral effort. That owed a lot not only to President Bush and the internal dynamics of his administration—Secretary Powell was concerned about this from the first day he arrived—but obviously it drew on the specific interests and concerns of Senator Bill Frist, the Senate leader.

We also need to note, on the plus side of the ledger, that the Bush administration crossed the threshold to endorsing a two-state solution of the Israeli-Palestinian chronic conflict. That was a big change, and it bore on the process that now has been resumed.

Likewise there has been an important dynamic in the trade field. The Doha round of negotiations, with European Trade commissioner Pascal Lamy and Robert Zoellick working together, has a good deal of promise and importance and is getting some high-level attention.

Clearly, there was justified military action against al Qaeda in Afghanistan, and that deserved a great deal of praise, just as postwar operations in Afghanistan have invited questions because of their inadequacy and insufficiency. We cannot be satisfied if the outcome is to perpetuate "warlordism," even if we are gratified that al Qaeda has been substantially damaged.

I would note that, although he later shifted course, President Bush did respond to the counsel of the Congress expressed in specific resolutions and to the advice of Prime Minister Blair and other allies when he went to the United Nations Security Council in the fall of 2002. It wasn't the first impulse of the administration, but the American government did seek and win a unanimous Security Council resolution that returned the inspectors to Iraq to try to enforce prior Security Council resolutions.

Even the controversial national security strategy has emphasized the necessity of multilateral solutions across a broad range of international problems. That is why, in fact, at the United Nations the inside circle around the secretary general had a lot of praise for the national security strategy. Even though the policy has been sensible in the main, its more problematic features are, of course, the dubious emphasis on preemptive doctrine, which, as it evolved, was hard to distinguish from preventive war.

FOREIGN POLICY ALTERNATIVES

Despite these foreign policy successes, the balance sheet of recent American foreign policy shows a lot of heavy liabilities. The preemptive doctrine attracted critique, as did the notion of a permanent American dominance in world affairs. There are many things to be said about all of this. I will only make one point, because we already are into a situation where there is an obvious impediment to effective implementation of the notion of preemption. Preemption, without sound intelligence, is Sampson without eyes. It can bring down the temple. And we have seen real cause to worry that intelligence was flawed, perhaps manipulated, or misread. This cautions against any repetition of a resort to the kind of preemption we have now seen.

As discussed by Jessica Tuchman Mathews (chapter 3) and Joseph Wilson (chapter 15), among others in this volume, a central problem has been the erosion of traditional alliance relations and the rising animosity toward the United States—perhaps centered on the government but more broadly directed against America and Americans—in many parts of the world. There are doubts across the globe that American power is guided by sufficient wisdom and restraint.

World attitudes are very complex. The structure of opinion in much of the world still shows a striving for things associated with America. There remains a desire to prosper and to acquire many of the material benefits associated with the American economy. But that is not the only element. We are in danger, not of meeting the classical goal of statecraft—"it is better to be respected than to be loved"—but of being more *feared* than respected, and we need to take account of that as we contemplate options for our policy in the future.

Conceiving constructive alternatives to current policy requires that we first eliminate some of the unwise or implausible options for policy. The beginning of un-wisdom in the last few years, in my opinion, was to allow the rhetoric of the "axis of evil" to distort policy. It was a rhetorical flourish that has not served the country well. But it does define three subjects that need to be addressed: Iraq, North Korea, and Iran.

IRAQ: THE NEED FOR INTERNATIONAL PARTICIPATION AND LEADERSHIP

Those of us who doubted the wisdom of war in Iraq, based on the evidence presented, nevertheless had to pray for its quick success. Who could have wanted it to be prolonged once we had committed force? Even before force was employed, the problem has always been what would come next, and what would follow even a quick military victory.

There is a marvelous passage in a letter that Winston Churchill wrote to David Lloyd George in the 1920s. It was a time when Churchill shared responsibility for British oversight of Iraq. He lamented, and this is a close paraphrase, that Britain found itself spending, at that time, eight million pounds a year for "the privilege of living on an ungrateful volcano."

Those who are trying to make a go of it in Iraq have reason to think of those words. There are increasing doubts now that this transition can be managed effectively by a narrow coalition of occupying powers. The legal specification that the United States and Great Britain have accepted the obligations and responsibilities of occupying powers seems, to a number of people, a promising development. But it is not going to be sufficient, in my view, for two countries to assume that they can carry this off as agents in total control.

The notion that "we broke it, so we bought it" is widespread among allies and critics. But the reality is that we are not likely to be able to fix Iraq by ourselves. The time is already upon us when we need to be rethinking how to engage other participants in the reconstruction effort, and that means sharing authority.

This is neither Germany nor Japan after World War II. It is not Vietnam, though you can find elements of it that might bear some similarity. It is much like the Philippines after the Spanish-American War of 1898, where for several years we found Americans bogged down in a small-scale guerilla operation. We were fighting Aguinaldo and others in the Philippines for years, and that is likely to be the pattern that could emerge in Iraq. We are not likely to suffer massive casualties, on the order of Korea or Vietnam, but the steady drip of small numbers of casualties and fatalities may be so amplified that there will be a dramatic decline in the capacity and willingness of Americans to stay the course.

At this stage, we need help, but we do need to stay the course. We cannot simply pick up and leave and run the risk of, say, fundamentalist Islamists seizing power, perhaps fracturing the country. The reconstruction and legitimacy that we need in Iraq demand much wider international participation and international leadership. We need to yield guidance over the entire process to a U.N. authority.

NORTH KOREA: A NUCLEAR MOBILIZATION BASE

North Korea is another part of the "axis of evil." "Axis," of course, is the term originally applied to the German/Italian/Japanese relationship in World War II, and our European friends will know the name Theo Sommer. Sommer wrote his doctoral dissertation on Germany and Japan in the war, and there's a wonderful phrase in his German that just describes how decrepit that relationship was. He described Germany-Japan as "komplizen ohne komplizitat"—accomplices with no complicity.

Now we are in roughly the same situation. This is not an axis, and if they are complicit in any way that we might be worried about, it is hard to find. Even the reported trade in weapons and technology between Pyongyang and Tehran is a selective, occasional transaction, not a comprehensive bargain that would qualify as an "axis."

In North Korea, we face stark and unforgiving truths. There is no acceptable military option on the peninsula. We are deterred—as North Korea should be. We are deterred by the reality that if war came, there would be, in all likelihood, thousands of artillery rounds on the city of Seoul, with a population of millions of people, within twenty-four hours. It is not merely a threatening claim made by Pyongyang that they could turn Seoul into a "valley of fire." It is, in fact, within their capability to do so.

So we are deterred. And the only hope we can have for turning North Korea back from the path toward weapons of mass destruction, specifically nuclear capabilities, and toward a missile program that is troublesome to us in the extreme is the path of negotiation. There is a lot to be said for what has been tried in recent years—engaging China, South Korea, Japan, and Russia. But time is not a free good, and we can't spend endless amounts of time attempting to get North Korea to sit down with all of us in response to their demand that they meet with the United States as the principal interlocutor. If we have to yield to their demand for bilateral negotiation, as I think we should, we need to face that quickly. We will always be able to consult with the others outside the negotiating room.

Under the best of circumstances, North Korea is very likely to retain what is often called a "nuclear mobilization base." They have the knowledge, they have some of the capabilities, and they are very likely to be able to move in that direction again, whatever they promise, on day one. At this stage, the urgency is to re-engage the International Atomic Energy Agency to monitor what is going on in the North, ideally to reconnect North Korea to the obligations it originally accepted under the nonproliferation treaty.

We may be headed toward a need to interdict North Korean ships at sea. That is safer than the notion of attacking them on land, but who knows what that might trigger? They can't fight us at sea, but they can inflict a lot of harm on land, and we will need to approach that issue, if it becomes necessary, with great caution.

IRAN

Iran is the third element in the "axis of evil," and we need to understand there that the options for interfering in Iran are generally counterproductive. Embracing the reformers and the students in the streets is not likely to help them gain power. Even if we only applaud them, as some public statements have done, we run some risk of undermining those we favor as political forces within Iran.

In some quarters one is hearing about the Osirak precedent, the precedent in which the Israelis attacked the Iraqi nuclear reactor from which they feared nuclear weapons would soon emerge. And some are referring to that in discussions about Iran. That is a very flawed idea. The notion of military strikes to destroy or retard the Iranian nuclear program looks less and less plausible because of the structure of that program. It is very dispersed, and it is multitracked. Clearly it has clandestine features. We discovered some of those clandestine features, and indeed the International Atomic

Energy Agency has been on Iran's case because its nuclear program has been outside the agreed game plan to some degree. And that's the way Pakistan succeeded, after all, in gaining its nuclear-weapons capability.

These activities are very problematic but do not invite effective military response. The only plausible option is to elicit Iranian restraint through political engagement, for which there are two requirements, given our distance from Tehran ever since the hostage crisis: We have to encourage and exploit the ties between our Western European friends and the Russians with Iran, rather than constantly berating them. Somewhere back in the mind of many Americans, there is the fear, not entirely unjustified, that our friends are seeking commercial advantage, and we must discourage that, as we did with the so-called Iran-Libya Sanctions Act.

At this stage, in addition to encouraging our friends to engage actively with the Iranian government to moderate any interest they might have in breaking out of their nuclear-restraint obligations, we have to put ourselves in the situation of those in Iran. American forces now flank the country. We are in Afghanistan, we are in Iraq, and American forces are populating the southern reaches of the Persian Gulf, actively operating there in a variety of aerial and naval modes. We have to figure out a way to communicate with Tehran and to conduct our own security operations in a manner that will reassure them that they are not the next on the target list.

It is very hard for Americans to appreciate the radically different perceptions that have taken hold in the Islamic world—not just Iran, not just Iraq, but throughout the Middle East and throughout Islam, more broadly.

A very sophisticated Arab diplomat pointed out something recently that would never occur to an American. While the administration wisely moderated some of the original rhetoric, after President Bush inadvertently used the term "crusade" at one point, deep historical suspicions persist. From the Islamic perspective, consider a couple of the aspects of the 2003 Iraq war. In Islam, many of the crusaders centuries ago came from France. They were known as "Franks"—the very name of the general who commanded the force that attacked Iraq. This was totally accidental, but the Arab diplomat says it compounded the psychological reactions in the region. And who was the senior British advisor to Franks? *Cross*. General Cross. We laugh about this, but put it in the mind of a totally different culture; even though they will rationally recognize it has no bearing on what transpired, it registers. It connects to a history that is very different for them than for us.

THE NECESSITY OF PERSUASION

If persuasion is essential to a sustainable policy, Congress is the institution that forces leaders to bear the burden of persuasion. The election of 2000 was the closest thing to a mandate for coalition government that our system is capable of producing. It did not yield the kind of coalition, the cooperative environment, one might have hoped for—mainly because of the impact of September 11. After September 11, there was such a powerful rallying to the president that questions were submerged and the path of cooperation was not necessarily viewed as essential. Yet the basic balance in the Congress has remained extremely close, infighting has been intense, and it is not likely to end.

But beyond the partisan contest that continues, there are two larger challenges crucial to Congress's capacity to function in an age of terrorism. First, Congress needs to make sure that it can operate if Congress itself becomes a target of terrorist attack. Many think that the plane that went down in Pennsylvania on September 11 could well have been headed to the Capitol. So the danger of an attack on the Congress, killing or incapacitating a sizeable fraction of the membership, is real. It requires some action.

The second challenge that is indispensable, institutionally, is to define a path that guarantees Congress will remain engaged and effective in the stream of decisions about the use of force in this open-ended war against terrorism. A decision at one point in time may not fit the circumstances and facts as they emerge. Just as wars sometimes go sour and presidents have to change policy en route, and generals have to shift strategies, Congress has to be able to adjust its policy guidance from time to time.

Ensuring Congressional Continuity

A commission chaired by Lloyd Cutler and Alan Simpson recently issued a report urging for a constitutional amendment to deal with the problem of potential discontinuity in Congress's operations. This problem is unique to the House of Representatives. If the Senate loses a member, a governor can appoint a replacement—that is the standard procedure. But the Constitution only provides one way to replace a member of the House of Representatives: by special election. That special election, in recent years, has taken an average of about four months across the country.

That is too long. Particularly in an emergency, you don't want gaps in congressional membership. To begin with, if it were a really large gap, you might have quorum problems. Furthermore, in the case of the House in particular, you could have entire states denied representation. Seven states have only single members. You could lose major representation with even a fraction of the House of Representatives killed or incapacitated.

We must have some provision for temporary, gap-filling representation in the House. My view is that such temporary representation is best determined by each representative. I favor having each representative designate, in advance, an agent to act for him or her in the event that he or she is not able to function for a period. This would be an agent chosen by the elected member on the basis of his or her legitimacy as the representative of that constituency. This is *not a successor* but someone who would temporarily carry on the duties of office until a special election of a successor can take place. One reason to favor a comprehensive arrangement for such temporary designees is that, in the case of temporary incapacitation, the arrangement would permit a member to resume his duties and a special election would not be needed. Representatives would also be more confident in a procedure that empowered them to choose their own agent, in the expectation that the designee would yield the office if the representative were able to resume his duties. This would be very akin to what the French do in their National Assembly. The French choose alternates as a part of elections to the Assemblée Nationale. So there are precedents and other experiences that we need to have in mind for this.

The argument over this has been very intense, because some members of the House are profoundly committed to the view that only a person elected can vote in the House. There are some tangential precedents in the House and Senate, although none in the House in recent years. People have used proxies as a sort of way of conveying intent, through committees mainly, rarely in other cases. They use paired voting in the Senate as a way of permitting members to act in absentia. So there are variations that are not directly on point, but close enough to establish some precedence.

Some members do not wish to have a constitutional amendment, which would in any case require a long process for approval. But I believe there is scope for the House to address this problem. I read the relevant court cases as justifying the House to authorize a member to designate a temporary agent under its Article I rulemaking authority. That's an arcane legal argument, but we must solve this problem, and we must have prompt action on it.

KEEPING CONGRESS ENGAGED

We also must make sure that we keep Congress engaged in the stream of decisions likely to arise with regard to the use of force in the war on terrorism. We have had a running disagreement between the Congress and the executive branch about the so-called war powers. Part of that disagreement has been based on a substantial misunderstanding of what the War Powers Act is, what its intent is, and what it does. So we first have to get the premise right if we're going to shape a constructive congressional role in this realm.

Contrary to many interpretations, the war powers resolution was designed primarily to force Congress to reach decisions, after years of incapacity to do so during the Vietnam War. Senator Javits and the other primary authors had a great regard for the necessity for vigor in the chief executive, but they recognized that there had to be a mechanism to guarantee that the Congress would face the issue and vote on the policy involved in the use of force. That is the premise that commends itself as we think about how to craft the current process.

My recommendation is that we play a variation on the War Powers Act, separating policy judgment from the consequences of that judgment. The War Powers Act is one that ties a judgment on the merits of the military operation to a timetable for disengagement. My argument now, since we have not been able to make that statute work effectively, is that we should separate any consequence—any timetable for disengagement, any termination of funding—from the basic policy decision. We should set that verdict aside as a decision to be reached separately, and the policy issue should be presented to the Congress in pristine form. Is this a use of force that should be initiated, sustained, or terminated? The objective should be to reach the policy judgment in pure form. Is it wise for the country to enter or continue on this military path?

To accomplish this, we have a device already in place. Presidents, complaining all the while, have nevertheless filed the reports required under the War Powers Act, beginning with President Ford in the Mayaguez case in 1975. Reports were sent forth by President Bush, for example, in the early months of the Afghanistan operation. Those reports could be the occasion to trigger a congressional debate and vote expressing the policy verdict, and that is a device that I think we should encourage Congress to exercise.

THE ROLE OF CONGRESS IN NATIONAL COHESION AND INTERNATIONAL STANDING

For America to be effective in the world, we must maintain national cohesion. We will not do that if we find ourselves drowning in legislative-executive disputation, protractedly and repeatedly. Cohesion is a hard thing to come by. It is a precious national asset, and not just inside our own body politic.

During the Kosovo intervention, Congressman Thomas Campbell and some two dozen other legislators sued President Clinton in connection with the War Powers Act. When the bombing stopped after sixty days, the issue was treated as moot and did not reach a Supreme Court decision, as the congressmen hoped. In the course of that case, General Edward Meyer, one of our most distinguished military officers, wrote a letter to Congressman Campbell, saying, "I believe it is essential that when American servicemen are sent into combat, they have the support of their fellow Americans. The War Powers Act causes the people's representatives, the Congress, to take a position, and not leave the troops dangling on threads of definition and interpretation." That is a compelling argument to keep Congress in the act.

There is the additional consideration that how Congress stands on the ways we use the nation's mighty arsenal bears crucially on America's standing in the world. Even among our closest allies, American power elicits mixed reactions—awe and fear, respect and anxiety. That should surprise none of us. Military and economic capabilities of the magnitude America possesses cannot fail to cause alarm in other countries, however benign our intentions. That alarm is heightened to the degree that American force appears to be too easily employed. In the eyes of others, no less than of American citizens, American military action may be seen as most legitimate when it is demonstrably subject to democratic governance. Marshaling international coalitions to wage the war on terrorism will depend, importantly, on giving our allies confidence that American power is guided and restrained by a disciplined relationship between Congress and the president.

BIBLIOGRAPHY

Alton Frye, *Humanitarian Intervention: Crafting a Workable Doctrine* (Boulder: Lightning Source, 2000).

———, *A Responsible Congress: The Politics of National Security* (New York: McGraw-Hill, 1975).

———, project director and editor, *Toward an International Criminal Court?* (New York: Council on Foreign Relations Press, 1999).

Theo Sommer, "Europe and the American Connection," from *America and the World* (New York: Council on Foreign Affairs Press, 1979).

• 14 •

Security and Democracy in the Post–September 11 Era

Raymond Shonholtz

In 1989, an empire that wasn't—fell. A new era of democracy rushed into the gap created by the fall of the Soviet Union and the breakup of the empire into discrete states. A new term was born, "nation building," and applied during the twelve years that elapsed between 1989 and 2001.

Americans knew about projects and programs, development and reconstruction, and we had an idea about the critical elements that were required for a democratic nation. Putting all of this together, we ushered in an era of nation building, committing substantial resources, technical knowledge, and expertise to the project.

We vaguely recognized that democratic nation-building related to the security of the United States, its allies, and the West generally. At the same time, as Americans began to believe that "democracies do not go to war with one another," we developed a more intense interest in creating stable governments to foster trade, economic development, privatization, and global exchange through new markets.

THE NEED TO REGULATE MARKETS

It might be fair to say that between 1989 and 2001, American policymakers gave relatively higher priority to democracy as a primary vehicle for supporting market economies—and relatively lower priority to market economies as a primary vehicle for supporting democracy.

What is the basis for this assertion? To function in an equitable manner, market economies require rigorous regulation. Yet the democracies that began developing after the fall of the Soviet Union rarely, if ever, had the institutional capacity, professional management, or systems in place to regulate capitalism. The result was "crony capitalism"—private corruption and state corruption. Those in power came to benefit more from an unregulated economy than they could realize by providing their constituencies with equitable economic opportunity, health and educational benefits, or open-society institutions and services.

With market-economy policies trumping democratic institution building, economic and social inequities rapidly became apparent in Eastern Europe and the former Soviet republics. In the transition from authoritarian rule to democratic governance, a new set of conflicts emerged. These conflicts appeared simultaneously with all the conflicts and issues long suppressed by authoritarian regimes. Ethnic and national minority issues, environmental degradation, and social repression became common subjects of newspaper articles, intellectual discussions, and minority focus within the activist, political, and intellectual communities of the new democracies.

In addition, the simultaneous process of democracy building and market-economy generation has created conflicts.

As figure 14.1 summarizes, the fall of authoritarian regimes released long-repressed issues, creating conflicts in the transition to democratic society and conflicts between democracy building and unregulated market economies. Democratic theory, practice, and institution building generate tensions and issues by their nature. Even when regulated, market economies generate competition, monopolistic tendencies, and aggregation of wealth and other resources. To reduce the tension generated by the democratization of the market economy requires well-managed state regulatory systems. For example, corporations seeking protection of intellectual property rights can achieve their goal only through a professionally managed state regulatory enforcement system. This is difficult to achieve in a market managed by crony capitalism supporting a corrupt political structure.

DEMOCRACY AS A SECURITY ISSUE

Before September 11, 2001, we saw these issues and conflicts as complex dimensions of nation building and conflict management. After September 11, many now appre-

Conflict Management in the Context of Nation Building: Three Domains of Conflict
• Conflicts suppressed by authoritarian regimes • Conflicts created in the transition to democratic society • Conflicts that persist under democracy, where a managed regulatory market economy is absent

Figure 14.1.

ciate that democratic nation building really is a security requirement and that democracy is the best response to terrorism by America and the west.

Democracy is America's best security against global terrorism. Policymakers can no longer acquiesce to state policies that disproportionately impact the well-being, health, educational opportunities, and livelihood of citizens in developing democracies. These fundamental issues are the *sine qua non* of democracy. They are the foundation of the security of the democratic state. They serve as a bulwark against terrorism at home and abroad.

The era of nation building that opened in 1989 was closed by terror on September 11, 2001. In the new era, as an instrument of state and global security, democracy building is a minimal requirement of security and should be a primary focus of foreign policy. Recognizing that the "marriage" between developing democracies and emerging market economies cannot be severed, we need to closely examine what is required in the new democracy era of post–September 11 security. Figure 14.2 highlights the requirements.

Even a passing review of these daunting requirements signals both the degree of their complexity and the need for their integration. In developing these requirements in transitioning societies, democracy builders have come to learn that two

What Is Required to Build a Democratic Nation with a Market Economy?
Democracy Requires: • Constitutional governance • Elected and accountable representatives • Rule-of-law-based institutions • Credible systems for dispute management • Civilian control over security and military forces • Open and free press • Open and engaged civil society • Institutions of learning, education, and health • Religious freedom and tolerance
Market Economy Requires: • Macroeconomic stability • Property rights and a legal regulatory infrastructure • Regulated competitive markets • Transparency and lack of corruption • Access to fair and open international, cross border, and regional markets

Figure 14.2.

primary preconditions govern the likelihood of success: time and consistency of effort. While resources are essential, none of the requirements in figure 14.2 can be accomplished in a few years. They require consistent, patient, and persistent effort to achieve success.

When, as I believe now is necessary, democracy is framed as a security issue, democracy builders can look at other long-term security strategies and draw comparisons. Because security is most often expressed in military terms, it is fair to draw on military examples to express what now is needed for democracy building perceived as a security requirement. Several military examples come immediately to mind. They include the Demilitarized Zone in Korea (fifty years), NATO (fifty years) and United Nations peacekeeping forces on the border between Israel and Syria (forty years).

For example, we were prepared to commit resources, personnel, and political will over a fifty-year period to ensure the security of the Korean Peninsula and like territories. This is the type of commitment required to make democracy a bulwark of security in the post–September 11 era of democracy building. Maintenance of effort and sustained resources have secured the military peace. Similar requirements now are needed to secure the peace that democracy offers in developing societies. Nothing short of such security will keep America and the west safe from terror in the short and long term.

As in 1989, we live in a new period requiring new thinking, concepts, resource allocation and commitment. In the post–September 11 era, we need to rethink all that we learned and apply it anew to achieve new goals.

Democracy must trump market inequities for our security at home and abroad. Developing democracies need equitable systems of justice, market opportunities, social services, and safety nets. They need access to the benefits that have made Western democracies strong in today's terms. The benefits include access to education, gender equality, human rights, good health, medicines, and social advancement. Such benefits must be developed as practical, well-financed policies, not as vague, lofty goals. Goals do not provide security; only results, achieved through accomplished tasks, now can protect us.

Democracy promotion has to be our foreign policy. It is the only policy that secures our common interests at home and abroad.

BIBLIOGRAPHY

Raymond Shonholtz, "A General Theory of Conflicts and Disputes," Partners for Democratic Change, December 1, 2003. http://www.partnersglobal.org/resources/Shonholtz-120103.pdf.

———, "Community Mediation Centers: Renewing the Civic Mission for the Twenty-First Century," *Mediation Quarterly*, Volume 17, No. 4, 1999.

———, "Conflict Resolution Moves East: How the Emerging Democracies of Central and Eastern Europe are Facing Interethnic Conflict," *The Handbook of Interethnic Coexistence*, ed. Eugene Weiner, pp. 359–368 (New York: Continuum Publishing, 1998). http://conflict.colorado.edu/files/crc/schonholz.htm.

———, "Constructive Responses to Conflict in Emerging Democracies," paper presented at the United Nations Development Program Conference, Inter-Regional Forum on Coping with Crisis and Conflicts, Bucharest, Romania, April 2–4, 2001. http://www.partners-global.org/resources/article8.html.

———, "Neighborhood Justice Systems: Work, Structure, and Guiding Principles," *Mediation Quarterly,* Volume 5, 1984.

II

FAILURE IN AMERICAN MIDDLE EAST POLICY—AND STRATEGIC ALTERNATIVES

• 15 •

Village Democracy and Presidential Leadership

Joseph C. Wilson IV

Iraq is a country that remembers its history, dating back millennia. They will outlive this occupation. They will make our lives difficult there. At the end of it, I think the chances are really very good that the consequences will be far graver to our national security than they were going in.

—Joseph C. Wilson IV

Some recently have written nostalgically about an era to be resurrected, when Americans will walk across their empire, as the British did in jodhpurs and pith helmets. I call what is happening today the "jodhpur and pith helmet revolution." It is an image of Jessica Tuchman Mathews's evocative concerns in chapter 3 about "creating and managing dominance."

WEAPONS OF MASS DESTRUCTION

Iraq was not a pre-emptive war. There was not an imminent threat to our national security, as we know now. Iraq was a war of choice, and it was not a war for the reasons that were provided by the American government in the run-up to the war, particularly when the White House went to Congress.

This was not a war about weapons of mass destruction. It had nothing to do with whether you believe or don't believe the intelligence reports. For example, the alleged sale of uranium from Niger to Iraq never happened. The administration knew that from February 2002.

On the eve of sending troops into battle in Iraq, President Bush stated that "intelligence gathered by this and other governments leaves no doubt that the Iraq regime continues to possess and conceal some of the most lethal weapons ever devised." But in 2004 David Kay, the Central Intelligence Agency's chief weapons inspector, told Congress shortly before resigning, "I'm personally convinced that there were not large stockpiles of newly produced weapons of mass destruction. . . . We didn't find the people, the documents, or the physical plants that you would expect to find if the production was going on." Similarly, in a report issued in 2004, the Carnegie Endowment for International Peace found that the government "systematically misrepresented the threat" from Iraq.

Beyond the false "weapons of mass destruction" argument, a second rationale for Iraq was the alleged link to terrorism. But the United States itself acknowledged the weakness of this argument. The U.N. charter would have permitted the United States to act, had there been links to terrorism. In addition, the Patriot Act gave President Bush full authority to act on behalf of the United States when he thought there was an operational link between a foreign government and al Qaeda. But in fact the U.S. government did not go to war based on the Patriot Act or the U.N. authority.

A third rationale for the war was that Saddam was a brute. But there are many brutes out there. Are we going to take them all down? Saddam may have been a special case because his use of chemical weapons and brutal murder of citizens constituted genocide. But there is a convention in the United Nations accepted by the world—the Genocide Convention. We could have gone to the United Nations and debated Iraq on those terms, and we could have done it decades earlier. But we didn't.

IRAQ: A WAR TO REDRAW THE POLITICAL MAP

In reality, this was a war to redraw the political map of the Middle East. It was a war that was put together by American zealots, the goal of which was to change the dynamics of the Middle East in such a way that a new political order, less hostile to our strategic partner and historic friend Israel, emerges. Such a new political order is desirable but is unlikely as an outcome of military invasion, conquest, and occupation.

The United States has gleefully attacked the international institutions that have served this country well for the past forty-five years. The American government has undone many of the foreign policy successes that we have had and that we have undertaken in the thirty years during which I have been in Washington. For that I am profoundly disturbed. I say this as a person whose proudest moment in his diplomatic career was serving as George H. W. Bush's charge to Baghdad and subsequently as ambassador to Gabon.

As a result of recent foreign policy, a schism could develop between traditional Republicans, the Brent Scowcrofts of the world, and conservative Republicans. I have been approached by any number of people who are George H. W. Bush–traditional Republicans and who are willing to take nonpartisan stands, but nonpartisanship stands directly in conflict with conservative ideology.

THE SKILLFUL USE OF POWER

The issue of power and foreign policy has never really been between hard and soft power, though that is an interesting distinction. Rather the issue always has been the use or abuse of force, confused with the legitimate exercise of power. I define force as the brute imposition of our will without regard to the legitimate concerns of the other party. Power, on the other hand, is the legitimate use of all the tools of statecraft, hard and soft, military when necessary, as well as a panoply of other options when possible. These options include intelligence, economic sanctions, economic assistance, public diplomacy, and strategies that are subversive or seductive.

As we go about exercising leadership and our will in foreign policy, the choice always has been between imposition of force and skillful use of power.

THE THREAT OF TERRORISM AND WEAPONS PROLIFERATION

America faces two threats over the next generation that I think are central to our national security: terrorism and weapons of mass destruction. And we face the nexus between the two threats.

Concern about terrorism and the proliferation of weapons of mass destruction was out there well before September 11. It was in the Clinton national security statement and in the Nunn-Lugar legislation, passed before September 11, to get the weapons of mass destruction off the streets of the Soviet Union. (See William Hartung's discussion of Nunn-Lugar in chapter 10.) The U.S. Commission on National Security/21st Century, chaired by Warren Rudman and Gary Hart, predicted the terrorist attacks on America and laid out a sweeping overhaul of national security structures and policies.

Unfortunately, the potential for these threats being realized in a way that again victimizes the American population in dramatic fashion is increased exponentially by the worldwide resentment to the militaristic actions that we have taken, to our willingness to run roughshod over international institutions and agreements. Remember, for a vast majority of the countries, the United Nations is the only forum in which they can make their complaints known to the world.

AFGHANISTAN, IRAQ, ISRAEL, AND PALESTINE

Many argue that the winds of change are blowing through the Arab world because of the American invasion of Iraq. These arguments are correct. Unfortunately, these are not the winds of liberal Western democracy that we would like to see. These are the winds of resentment—as yet another humiliation is inflicted upon a population that remembers the Crusades far better than we remember the winner of the Super Bowl.

Where, then, do we stand at present in the places of greatest recent concern to America—Afghanistan, Iraq, Israel, and Palestine?

In Afghanistan, the legitimate war to destroy an enemy who had inflicted grievous harm on a population has become little more than a holding action to protect one man in his palace while allowing warlords to reign in the countryside, with little sustained effort to move the process toward either reconstruction or some political accommodation. Deals were cut to enable the United States to operate militarily against the remnants of al Qaeda without reference to what is necessary for future Afghan stability and representative governance.

In Iraq, we pursued the highest-risk, lowest-possible-reward strategy of invasion, conquest, and occupation. The occupation left us exposed to a growing insurgency and an increasing hatred that runs the risk of spilling over from the rest of the Arab world. I get notes every day from military officers, journalists, and nongovernmental organizations in Iraq. They talk about the problems associated with just living in downtown Baghdad—stories that they can't get into their own newspapers, including the *New York Times*.

People in the Middle East understand when Osama bin Laden talks about the expulsion of Arabs from Granada in the fifteenth and sixteenth centuries. It was the same in Bosnia. Before we could get through to people, we had to patiently listen to history dating back to the thirteenth and fourteenth centuries. Yet when you come into any office of the National Security Council in Washington, the fifteen minutes allocated for a meeting doesn't really allow time to discuss anything other than the immediate subject at hand.

In Israel, the United States has been AWOL for many years, while more than 600 Israelis and 2,000 Palestinians have been killed in a vicious and particularly traumatizing cycle of violence. The tentative and fragile cease-fire will hold only if the American government is prepared to remain engaged for a sustained period of time and is ready to assert pressure at the highest level on both sides to make necessary compromises.

The future does not bode well. Seventy-five percent of the Palestinian capacity has been destroyed in recent years. Our former interlocutor, Abu Mazen, had a popularity rating among Palestinians that is below the statistical error rate of the polls. The Hamas, which we are calling upon to be dismantled, is seen by many Palestinians as a viable symbol of resistance in the occupied territories and also is a supplier of goods and services in the absence of other government services being provided.

The dismantling of two towers and the withdrawal from a couple of towns and a couple of roads does not an Israeli concession make. Equally, continued Palestinian attacks on Israeli civilians only further traumatize Israeli and, by extension, the American Jewish community.

I have argued for years to Arab audiences that there has been nothing worse for Arab and Palestinian interests than this second intifada, that Palestinian suicide bombers are a shame on the Palestinians generally, and that the trauma that they have inflicted upon Israeli society is perfectly understandable. It traumatizes Israeli society when Palestinian kids blow themselves up in restaurants and kill thirty Israelis. A reaction is provoked—not just in Israel but also among Israel's staunchest supporters. The process of finding peace is made much more complicated.

Some say that we can't want peace more than the Israelis and the Palestinians do. The argument probably is accurate, but it is an abrogation of diplomatic responsibility to walk away from the process.

One of the roles that diplomacy fills in a time of conflict is to occupy space and time among belligerents while the facts on the ground change in a way that will lead to a more favorable negotiated solution. But to walk away and allow the cycle of violence to further deepen has been a dereliction on the part of this administration. It has been very difficult to get that point heard over the past several years.

WHAT TO DO?

What to do, realistically speaking? My answers are consistent with the suggestions of Jessica Tuchman Mathews in chapter 3. Let me concentrate on Iraq, Afghanistan, Israel, and Palestine.

Iraq and Afghanistan

It is not a bad idea to encourage democracy in the Middle East. But those of us who have done democracy a long time know how difficult it is, in the best of circumstances. It is much more difficult when the democratizing power also is the occupying power, and one that doesn't necessarily have in mind the best for the citizens of the country it's attempting to democratize. Not that we shouldn't try to democratize—but the use of the military ought to be judicious at best and ought not to hinder the tools of democratization.

Of course, you never get a second chance to make a first impression, and the first impression we made was not the first impression that most of us would have wanted us to make. But we can try to make a second impression. Reform in Iraq must be based on multilateralization, provision of security, satisfaction of basic human needs, creation of grassroots democracy at the village level, and reconstruction of the economy.

Multilateralize. We must internationalize as quickly as possible in Iraq.

One trick here is not to forget Afghanistan. We have to stay the course in Afghanistan because there is still work to be done against terrorism there. But we also have to stay the course to ensure that this particular failed state, taken on by America, is not allowed to lapse back into more failure.

We have multilateralized Afghanistan. We need to multilateralize more in Afghanistan. But the progress on multilateralism to date in Afghanistan at least provides a model for the process in Iraq. The imprimatur of the United Nations is needed in both Afghanistan and Iraq.

Multilateralization in Iraq is just like a high-risk oil exploration venture in the old days, before the science of drilling was better. The issue is spreading the risk, not taking all the rewards for yourself. If you succeed, there will be enough rewards for everybody. If you fail, you don't want to be left holding the baby alone.

Authorize Peacekeepers. The United States is asking the population of both Afghanistan and Iraq to take a leap of faith—away from traditional societies where there is protection by clans, tribal warlords, village chiefs, clerics, or dictators.

To move away from their traditional societies, the populations of Afghanistan and Iraq must feel that they are safe in their own homes, can ride their bicycles, can walk to where they have to go, can drive their cars, if they have cars, and can do what they need to do without fear of bodily harm to them or their families.

That has been accomplished in Kabul. It has been accomplished somewhat in some places, like Kurdistan and Northern Iraq. It hasn't been accomplished in the Afghan countryside, and certainly hasn't been accomplished in Baghdad.

We need to flood Iraq with United Nations Chapter 7–authorized peacekeepers if necessary, and flood it with police trainers. The United States does not have a national police force. We have a national investigatory agency, the Federal Bureau of Investigation, but we don't do policing the same way some of the Europeans do. For example, the Italians and the Spanish, who were allies of ours in the Iraq invasion, have the *carabinieri* and the *guardia civile*. The French have the *gendarmerie*. They train to military doctrine. They do policing activities. We need their help.

We need to reconstruct the defense and security apparatus of Iraq. Iraq has a long border to protect. It has enemies who wanted to impose their views on Iraq long before we got there, and who will be there long after we have departed. Iraq needs a policing operation. It's a difficult country to govern, to say the least.

Satisfy Basic Human Needs. People's human needs must be satisfied. Among other things, they need water, food, access to medicine, and access to medical treatment. It was really significant to me when I saw the first trucks arriving in Iraq with humanitarian assistance. We saw one or two trucks. Then the camera panned out into the group of consumers of that humanitarian assistance, and you saw a demand for at least six trucks.

When you have demand that exceeds supply by such a margin, there will be fighting for the limited supplies. So the answer is equally obvious. If you have demand for six truckloads worth of supplies, bring nine trucks in. When you want to change the hearts and minds of people to make them receptive to reform, satisfy their basic human needs.

Create Grassroots Democracy at the Village Level. Political revitalization and democracy building is tough work. The best adage on democracy that I have heard is that it's a bit like an English lawn. You have to seed it, water it, and then roll it every day for 600 years. Then it will look really good.

As we know from the American experience, democracy is something that is built brick by brick. America wants Iraq to be friendly with its neighbors, provide a national system of representative governance, espouse human rights, and provide foreign policy that is consistent with American values—but these priorities are not necessarily the issues with which someone in an Iraqi village is concerned.

People in the village want to see the same sort of things that people wanted to see in my town in California when I was growing up—and the same kinds of things people living in Washington, D.C., would like to see. They want to see the trash picked up, the kids go to a safe school, the education system functioning well, and the police working effectively to ensure their safety.

So democracy building cannot begin top down in Baghdad. We need to begin in the villages and work up. That will mean a huge investment. The investment cannot be just American. As I have said, other western nations and the nongovernmental organizations need to be in Iraq—to serve as trainers, mediators, and sounding boards, as just people there to listen to the gripes that you get at the village level. So it is a matter of positioning yourself at every level in such a way that you're there, occupying space and time, as the people around you deal with the issues most important to them.

Democracy cannot be built without economic reconstruction. Before it can solve the longer run issues of manufacturing, production, and oil exports, economic reconstruction must infuse cash. We need to flood Iraq with $20 bills. People need to be able to buy goods, to stave off some of the complete desperation that is gripping the population.

Israel and Palestine: Constant Presidential Involvement

The thorn must be pulled from the side of the region. The road to peace in the Middle East still goes through Jerusalem.

Policy on Israel requires constant presidential involvement. As Brent Scowcroft has proposed, the United States needs to apply the same level of energy in reinvigorating the Arab-Israeli peace process as it used in lobbying for war in Iraq. America needs a big on-the-ground presence in the region of the Israeli-Palestinian conflict, again to occupy space and time.

Israel never will do anything without America, its guardian. So Americans are needed. But what is the other presence that helps spread the risk to Americans a little bit more? The one I keep coming up with is an American presence that makes it more difficult for Palestinians, Hamas, and Islamic Jihad to go after Arab soldiers. The Arab presence might be in the form of Egyptian or North African soldiers.

On settlements in the occupied territories, Yitzhak Rabin understood that Israeli policy should not be thickening of the borders but rather an agreement with the Palestinians to police their own territories in a way that was credible and that allowed Israelis to feel secure within their borders. Thickening of the borders is an artificial security anyway, given technology and given the ability to move asymmetrical weaponry in and out of the cities, as we see with suicide bombing. Yet today Israel continues to thicken its borders.

Today a majority of Israelis do not want to continue the settlements. This provides an opportunity for the Israeli government. But for the government to reverse the policy of thickening borders would be an act of great political courage—because it also could be political suicide. Still, it is important to make some movement on settlements.

My own judgment about Hamas is that the key to diminishing its influence is to build from the center out. If you build a moderate center, then you put the fringe back where the fringe belongs—on the fringe and not in the center, where it currently holds too much power.

That really means empowerment of the Palestinian Authority. We need to be prepared to underwrite public social services to the community. We need to develop public-sector capacity in Palestine. The argument is analogous to the need in America to save our public schools with sufficient investment in them and not to abrogate responsibility and accountability through private-school voucher schemes.

The trouble with military counterattacks is that there is a lot of collateral damage. It seems to me that, even though in the short term you are going to probably get a greater level of Israeli casualties, because the attacks aren't going to stop, you must start treating those attacks as criminal acts. What happens within such a criminal justice framework? For one thing, you don't have these horrible roadblocks and lockdowns of these entire cities for all but two or three or four hours per day. In this way, life is made better for the average citizen. So framing the issue in criminal-justice terms can help build moderation from the center out. And by making life better for the average Palestinian, Hamas will become isolated.

Terrorism and Africa

As we look at terrorism and the phenomenon of weapons of mass destruction, we must touch on Africa. The American government has no new original ideas from what was put forward in 1998. It hasn't come to grips with conflict resolution in places like Liberia and Congo. To a certain extent, America has farmed out responsibility for conflict resolution–type activities largely to former colonial powers. In my judgment, this farming-out policy perpetuates hegemony and relationships that have not been terribly healthy. Look at Cote d'Ivoire and Sierra Leone.

We need to get more involved in conflict resolution, and we need to get more involved in the other tools of statecraft, including foreign aid, economic assistance, debt relief, assistance to militaries, and training of police forces. We also need to focus on the phenomenon of failed and failing states as breeding grounds for terrorism and other transnational activities that impact our national security—whether they are health-related matters like the viruses of ebola and HIV/AIDS or narco-terrorism, money laundering, and other international criminal activities.

THE POLITICS OF TRUTH

The United States needs to use power instead of force. We need to finance nation building, work with the United Nations, and build a multilateral strategy.

Disdain for these policies by the government ill serves the American people. Prominent conservatives speak openly of the destruction of the United Nations as one of the benefits in our occupation of Iraq.

But the truth is that we have spent almost fifty years developing international relationships that have served our broader national interests well. We should never forget that since their creation, the United Nations and its companion institutions have far more often served our interests than blocked them.

BIBLIOGRAPHY

George W. Bush, State of the Union speech, White House transcript, January 28, 2003.

Joseph Cirincione, Jessica T. Mathews, George Perkovich, with Alexis Orton, *WMD in Iraq: Evidence and Implications*, Carnegie Endowment for International Peace report, January 2004.

Gary Hart and Warren B. Rudman, *America Still Unprepared—America Still in Danger*, Council on Foreign Relations, October 2002. http://www.cfr.org/pdf/Homeland_Security_TF.pdf.

Dana Milbank and Walter Pincus, "Bush Aides Disclose Warnings from CIA," *Washington Post*, July 23, 2003.

"NOW with Bill Moyers," Joseph C. Wilson interview conducted Feb. 18, 2003, PBS. http://www.pbs.org/now/transcript/transcript_wilson.html.

Joseph S. Nye, *The Paradox of American Power* (Oxford: Oxford University Press, 2003).

James Risen, "Ex-Inspector Says CIA Missed Disarray In Iraqi Arms Program," *New York Times*, January 26, 2004.

"Truth, War, and Consequences," interview with Joseph C. Wilson IV, PBS *Frontline*, conducted August 12, 2003. http://www.pbs.org/wgbh/pages/frontline/shows/truth/interviews/wilson.html.

United States Commission on National Security/21st Century: *Road Map for National Security: Imperative for Change,* Phase III report, February 15, 2001.

Vicky Ward, "Double Exposure," *Vanity Fair* profile on Joseph Wilson and Valerie Plame (Wilson), January 2004.

White House transcript, March 17, 2003.

Joseph C. Wilson IV, *The Politics of Truth* (New York: Carroll & Graf, 2004).

———, "Seeking Honesty in U.S. Policy," *San Jose Mercury News*, September 14, 2003.

———, "What I Didn't Find in Africa," *New York Times* op-ed, July 6, 2003.

• *16* •

Domino Democracy: Challenges to U.S. Foreign Policy in a Post-Saddam Middle East

Eric M. Davis

More than a year after the invasion of Iraq by the United States, it is still unclear exactly why the United States decided to invade in March 2003 to overthrow the Ba'athist regime of Saddam Hussein. In retrospect, it is obvious that many of the reasons that the United States gave were not, in fact, the main motivations for attacking Iraq. From a policy perspective, analyzing motivations may appear to represent water under the bridge. However, the motivations behind the U.S. attack were, and continue to be, closely linked not only to thinking about American policy in Iraq but to its broader policy in the Middle East as a whole. A better understanding of the thinking that shaped American policy in Iraq not only provides insights into why the U.S. government is experiencing such difficulties in achieving its policy objectives in Iraq but also whether American policy in the region is based on sound assumptions. What were the reasons why the United States invaded Iraq, and what do they tell us about the strengths and weaknesses of American foreign policy in the Middle East?

WHAT DOES THE UNITED STATES REALLY MEAN BY "DEMOCRATIZATION"?

My thesis is that the invasion of Iraq constituted the first step in a larger and audacious process of reshaping the political and economic terrain of the Middle East. I refer to this process as "domino democracy" because it envisions the transformation of Iraq into a democratic polity with open markets and a technocratically and non-ideologically oriented government—a model that the United States would like to see replicated in other Middle Eastern states, particularly Iraq's neighbors. While no one can dispute a foreign policy objective that aims to encourage democratic governance, the real question is what the United States means by democratization of the region and how the policy of domino democracy will affect the citizenry of countries in question. For many Middle Easterners, the stated American goal of promoting democracy in the region is viewed with deep suspicion. They point to past American support for many authoritarian regimes, including that of Saddam Hussein during the 1980s, failure to support Palestinian reformists in their efforts to create a Palestinian state based on norms of political participation and transparency, and failure to bring pressure on autocratic monarchies such as Saudi Arabia to implement democratic reforms. Many Arab and non-Arab analysts also view domino democracy as a cover for extending U.S. economic influence in the region, particularly in oil-rich states such as Iraq. In addition, large contracts were awarded in Iraq, often without a bidding process, to firms such as Halliburton, Bechtel, Parsons E&C, and WorldCom. These corporations were closely linked to Vice President Cheney and other members of the Bush administration. The contracts reinforced the view that our foreign policy was seeking to enhance American economic power in the region.

The influence of economic interests is a particularly important question because domino democracy is intimately linked to a second component of recent U.S. policy, namely the spread of market economies. While opening new markets can have many positive repercussions for the Middle East, it can also, as has been evident elsewhere, such as in Russia, Eastern Europe and China, lead to great discrepancies of wealth between economic and political elites and the populace at large. The adverse effects caused by market reforms and structural adjustments may alienate large segments of the populace, including intellectuals and the nationalistically minded middle classes, thereby providing an opening for supporters of authoritarian rule to mobilize coalitions against political and economic change.

WHY DID THE UNITED STATES INVADE IRAQ?

Before examining the inner workings of domino democracy, it is useful to examine the arguments that have been offered to explain why the United States invaded Iraq. The stated reason for the invasion was that it constituted part of a larger global war on terrorism, especially because Iraq was said to possess weapons of mass destruction that could be used in military combat. Indeed, arguments were made that Iraq could mobilize and introduce its weapons of mass destruction into combat in a very short period of time.

In retrospect, the concern that Saddam's regime had a significant military capability to use weapons of mass destruction appears to have been far-fetched. While the Iraqi regime may have possessed plans or even the capacity to produce such weapons, it did not have the stockpiles or delivery systems that would have made these weapons systems a meaningful threat. To date, no weapons of mass destruction have been discovered despite vigorous efforts by the United States to locate these weapons systems after occupying Iraq. With the extensive debate that developed after the war in Iraq was officially declared to have ended in May 2003, and especially in light of the escalating American casualties, the continued problem of establishing political and economic stability in Iraq, and the ongoing debates of whether the Bush administration manipulated intelligence about Iraq's possession of weapons of mass destruction to justify invading the country, an answer to this question has gained significance. If the stated reason for the invasion was to remove the Ba'athist regime's weapons of mass destruction capacity, and this turned out not to be the real motivating factor, then many Americans can raise the question of whether the continuing human and material losses in Iraq serve the national interest.

Another argument that was offered to explain the invasion was that the United States coveted Iraqi oil. Many Iraqis came to this conclusion after realizing that, in addition to Saddam Hussein's Republican Palace, the United States only stationed troops outside Iraq's Ministry of Oil after having entered Baghdad in April 2003. Those who have claimed that the March-April 2003 war was influenced by concerns for Iraqi oil have focused on Iraq's position as one of the world's largest oil producers, possessing the second largest proven reserves after Saudi Arabia, and on the close ties between Vice President Cheney and other Bush administration figures and the American oil and natural gas industries.

Despite its intuitive attraction as an explanation, the desire to control Iraq's oil industry does not seem to have been the main impetus for the American invasion. It will take at least three years and probably closer to five years for Iraqi oil production to reach pre-1991 Gulf War levels. Further, much of the money that will be generated from future oil sales will need to be dedicated to reparation payments that Iraq still owes Kuwait as well as to outstanding debts owed Russia and other countries from the Iran-Iraq war of 1980–1988. Given the sensitivity of the United States to accusations, even before the invasion, that it was trying to appropriate Iraqi oil, it does not seem likely that the American government will attempt to control Iraq's oil industry. Despite the extensive advantages that they give to foreign investors, investment laws that were promulgated by the Iraqi Governing Council, the transitional government with limited powers under the United States occupation authority, specifically exempted the oil sector from privatization and foreign ownership.

Finally, the failure of the United States to cite the extensive human rights abuses of Saddam Hussein and his Ba'athist regime as factors leading to the invasion rules this out as well as a major motivation for the invasion. Despite the fact that human rights organizations such as Human Rights Watch, the United Nations, the Iraqi National Congress, and INDICT have been documenting the widespread use of torture, execution, and imprisonment without trial for an extensive period of time, no U.S. administration had made this issue a core component of American foreign policy in the Middle East. Clearly, the Ba'ath Party's abysmal human rights record, which some would argue verged on genocide, did not play a significant role in the United States' motivations for invading Iraq.

If none of these three reasons—weapons of mass destruction, oil, or human rights—were critical in leading the United States to depose the Iraqi Ba'athist regime, what did the United States hope to accomplish by toppling Saddam Hussein? The main motivation for the United States invasion of Iraq, I would argue, was the centerpiece of a bold vision to remake the political map of the Middle East. In this vision, the destruction of the Iraqi Ba'athist regime represented the first step in a process of creating democratic governments where authoritarian regimes formerly held sway and replacing inefficient and corrupt state-run public sectors with market economies.

DOMINO DEMOCRACY: THE UNDERLYING AMERICAN POLICY

I call this "domino democracy" because the United States' actions in Iraq were viewed as setting in motion a ripple effect in which neighboring Iran and Syria and possibly Saudi Arabia would feel pressured to institute the types of political and economic reforms commensurate with an American vision of the new Middle East. With the removal of Israel's two most threatening enemies, namely the Ba'athist regimes in Iraq and Syria, domino democracy would likewise have a salutary impact on the Israeli-Palestinian peace process. It would send a strong message to Palestinian rejectionists, both Islamists and secularists, that their policies have no future, marginalize Palestine National Authority President Yasir Arafat once and for all, and set in motion the political forces that would replace him with a pro-Western government that was democratic and transparent.

The vision of a democratic Middle East with polities devoted to strengthening the institutions of civil society and expanding opportunities for economic growth appears attractive on its face. Few could oppose the goal of an arc of governments stretching from Palestine to Iran that functioned according to the norms of political participation, transparency, and public accountability.

Nevertheless, there are at least two questions that need to be raised in assessing the process of implementing domino democracy. First, what is the United States' vision of this new political configuration of the Middle East, and how realistic was it to assume that this goal could be achieved? Second, to what extent does the United States understand how to implement this process? Finally, depending on how this process was implemented, what could we expect the impact to be on the countries that are the target of this policy? Put differently, to what extent is the United States *genuinely committed* to the stated goal of this policy in Iraq and neighboring countries, which was to help promote democratic transitions that would provide genuine autonomy and widespread political participation to citizens who had been freed from rule by authoritarian regimes?

As has often been argued since the overthrow of Saddam Hussein and the Ba'athist regime, it was clearly more difficult to win the peace than it has been to win the combat phase of the war. In other words, domino democracy cannot be implemented through a military strategy alone. Indeed, the very idea of establishing democratic polities grounded in strong civil societies is based on the assumption that the populace of the respective countries in question need to be actively involved in creating the transition to democracy. The problems that plagued the ostensibly democratic constitutional monarchies that Great Britain and France imposed during their colonial rule in Iraq and elsewhere in the Middle East following the Ottoman Empire's collapse at the end of World War I decisively demonstrated that democracy is only as strong as the participation of citizens in its daily functioning.

What, then, were the assumptions underlying the notion of domino democracy? How viable were these assumptions, and what hypotheses about the future of Iraq and its neighbors logically flowed from these assumptions? If the assumptions were flawed, what could be done to rectify these flaws so that a democratic Middle East might still become a reality? If the United States was not truly committed to the policy that it publicly espoused, or was unwilling to significantly adjust its strategic and economic interests in the region should they run counter to the American policy of democratic change, what could be done to pressure the American government to live up to its commitments?

To think through these issues, I have chosen five case studies: Iraq, Iran, Syria, Palestine, and Saudi Arabia, through which to examine the assumptions underlying the concept of domino democracy.

Before proceeding to an analysis of the individual cases, I would argue that American foreign policy in the Middle East has suffered from a number of conceptual fallacies that make the prospect of domino democracy's success highly doubtful. The first I would call the *fallacy of homologous structure*. By this, I mean that all the countries that the United States hoped to see turn toward democracy were viewed as emerging from the same historical and structural configurations and as responding to the same imperatives in their projected transition to democracy. That is, it was assumed that the populations of Iraq, Iran, Syria, Palestine, and Saudi Arabia all desired the same outcomes—namely, a transition to a democratic polity that was structured along lines much like that of the United States, with limited state interference in the economy and a dominant role for the private sector in economic growth. This fallacy, which ignored the different historical, cultural, and hence structural configurations of the respective polities in question, was related to two derivative fallacies. One was the *presentist fallacy*, by which I mean the lack of attention to the specific histories of the individual nation-states of the Middle East, while the other was the *fallacy of lack of sensitivity to cultural specificity*, by which I mean ignoring the importance of incorporating the impact of local cultural heritages in the future political development of those countries the United States would like to see turn to democracy.

Iran

To elucidate these two concepts, we can examine the case for democracy in Iran. Two decisive victories in sequential presidential elections by Mohammed Khatami, himself a cleric, the capturing of 75 percent of the seats in the Iranian *majlis*, or parliament, by reformers, the rejection of the Khomeini legacy by the overwhelming majority of Iranians under age twenty-five, and the ongoing student demonstrations calling for democratic reforms that have occurred in Iran all point to a country with a strong civil society and democratic leanings. The existence of a vibrant and internationally acclaimed film industry is another indicator of a strong civil society, understood here in associational terms, that undergirds democratic politics in Iran, despite the efforts of institutions created under the Khomeini regime, especially the repressive and unelected Council of Guardians, to suppress it.

However, while large numbers of Iranians reject Khomeini's stamp on the 1978–1979 Islamic Revolution, they are equally adamant about not accepting a return to the type of polity that existed under the Western-oriented regime of the former Shah, Mohammed Reza Pahlavi. Interestingly, many of the young Islamist radicals who participated in the seizure of the American Embassy in Teheran in 1979, holding Americans hostage for 440 days, are now in the vanguard of demanding democratic reforms. Apart from the highly unfortunate characterization by the Bush administration of Iran as part of the "axis of evil," the majority of the country desires a transition to democracy. Unfortunately, U.S. policymakers have shown little or no sensitivity to the desire of many Iranians to retain a political system in which Islamic values play an important societal role alongside a robust and pluralist democracy, a flourishing press, and creativity in intellectual and artistic expression. That the United States has made little effort to understand the role of political culture in the possible transition of specific Middle Eastern countries to democracy is yet another indicator of a "one-size-fits-all" approach to political change in the Middle East. That conservatives in the Bush administration such as Richard Perle, Paul Wolfowitz, and Douglas Feith, who articulated the policy of domino democracy, said so little about the paradox of Iran—the quintessential example of an Islamic revolution that produced strong democratic tendencies, only kept in check by the Council of Guardians, the secret police, and the Khomeinist militia, the *Basij*—is indicative of the lack of comprehension of the larger sociopolitical forces shaping the contemporary politics of the Middle East.

Iraq

In neighboring Iraq, the role of religion in politics has differed substantially from that in Iran, despite the fact that the Shi'a constitute the majority of the population in both Iraq and Iran. The Iraqi marja'iya, or Shi'i clergy, lost much of its political power after World War I during which it assumed an important if not central role in opposing Great Britain's occupation of Iraq after it invaded the country in 1914. The marja'iya played a central and largely ecumenical role during the June through October 1920 Revolution by mobilizing opposition to Great Britain's refusal to create a democratic government and calling for unity among all Iraq's ethnic and confessional groups including the Jews, Christians, and Muslims. After many members of the politically minded clergy were arrested or expelled by the British during the 1920s, its role in politics was greatly diminished.

With Shi'a largely excluded from the state bureaucracy and the military by the majority Sunni-Arab–dominated Hashemite monarchy, which the British imposed through a rigged referendum in August 1921, many Shi'is became teachers, intellectuals, and political activists who turned to secular parties such as the Iraqi Communist Party, the Ahali Group, and its successor, the National Democratic Party, and even the Ba'ath Party after it was founded in Iraq in 1952.

Among the Shi'i marja'iya, cleavages developed in which older and more traditional leaders rejected mixing religion and politics. The rationalist tradition of Iraqi Shi'i scholarship, which characterized much of the Iraqi marja'iya's writings, often was not commensurate with an activist role in politics. Further, many members of the clergy stood in competition with their Iranian colleagues who resented the greater prominence of the Iraqi Shi'i shrine cities of Karbala', al-Najaf, and al-Kathimayn.

For many members of the Shi'i marja'iya, mixing religion and politics signified greater influence of Iranian Shi'is in Iraq's internal affairs. On the other hand, because many Sunni Arabs identified the mixing of religion and politics with increased Shi'i influence in public life, Sunni Arabs also refrained from supporting religious-based political movements. Among the Kurds, tribal politics has always trumped religio-political movements. Thus, unlike Iran, the outcome in Iraq was the playing down of the role of religion in politics, and the lack of development of any serious religio-political movements in Iraqi politics.

While both Iran and Iraq are predominantly Shi'i countries, Shi'a in Iraq means something very different from Shi'a in Iran where the clergy have maintained a much stronger corporate sense of political identity since the late 1800s. Having played a major role in the 1905–1911 Constitutional Revolution, the Shi'i clergy became the main focal point of opposition to the regimes of Reza Shah after 1923 and then his son, Mohammed Reza Shah, after World War II, until the latter was overthrown in 1979. Nevertheless, when faced with a secular nationalist regime led by Mohammed Mossadegh, the clergy helped the CIA and the Iranian army overthrow him in 1953 and return Mohammed Reza Shah to power.

In 1963, the Iranian clergy led a major uprising against the Shah's regime and his efforts to implement the so-called White Revolution, which had been promoted by the Kennedy administration. The weaker role of Iraq's Shi'i clergy in nationalist politics compared with the much stronger one in Iran helps explain in part the inclination of many Iranians toward incorporating Islamic norms in modern political life and discourse. In other words, in Iran the clergy has been viewed as a more vigorous political actor in protecting the national interest against foreign intrusion, compared with a more apolitical clergy in Iraq that has not played such an activist role.

The Shah's excessive cultural affinity with the West, and his lack of sensitivity to the traditions of his subjects, likewise created a strong suspicion of the motives of Western countries, especially the United States, which backed the Shah and his repressive policies and free market orientation. Although Saddam Hussein and the Ba'ath Party were also extremely repressive, they always maintained much closer ties to popular and tribal culture in Iraq. While many Iraqis opposed Saddam's policies, there was never the view of the Ba'ath in Iraq that it was culturally alien in the way in which the Pahlavi monarchy was viewed in Iran.

Thus, the United States' lack of historical perspective fails to realize that the different pathways that have led various Middle Eastern countries to potentially engage in a transition to democracy have different roots and thus require different forms of analysis. The fact that the United States has often been responsible for thwarting democracy in the past behooves American foreign policy makers to be especially sensitive to these historical determinants when trying to promote political change. This historical backdrop requires such policymakers to realize that they need to offer concrete policies that detail the ways in which they expect to implement democracy rather than limiting themselves to broad statements in support of democratic transitions. Otherwise, United States policy runs the risk of simply being seen as replicating what are viewed as the disingenuous policies of the past—calling for democratic reforms while simultaneously supporting dictatorial regimes.

Another example of the American lack of historical perspective was the position the U.S. government took toward the reconstruction of the Iraqi economy. L. Paul Bremer, the United States interim administrator of Iraq, unequivocally called for privatization of the Iraqi economy, including the oil industry. Bremer and most American policymakers seemed unaware of the political significance to Iraqis of state control over their oil resources.

The fact that the Iraqi oil sector was under foreign control from the inception of oil production shortly before World War I, and that foreign concessionaires paid Iraq minimal royalties until the Hashimite monarchy was forced, through national pressures, to renegotiate these royalties in 1952, seemed lost on the Bush administration. As far as I know, no prominent member of the Bush administration ever acknowledged in public the symbolic significance of the oil industry to Iraqi nationalist sensitivities. After the leader of the 1958 Revolution, General Abd al-Karim Qasim, began the process of nationalizing the oil industry in 1961, the process was finally completed by the Ba'athist regime in 1972.

Countless foreign oil experts have commented on the incredible effort that Iraq's state or public-sector oil engineers, technicians, and workers made during the period between the 1991 Gulf War and the March 2003 U.S. invasion to keep Iraqi oil flowing in relatively large quantities, despite the lack of spare parts and pressures placed upon them by the Ba'athist regime to increase output. To automatically assume that private firms will be able to produce oil more efficiently than the current state-controlled industry fails to consider the political history behind national control of Iraq's oil resources, the high level of efficiency that public employees demonstrated in keeping Iraq's oil flowing during an extremely difficult period, and the ability of public-sector managers to maintain labor peace through establishing bonds of trust with the oil workers that would not necessarily be in place should private—that is, American and other Western—firms assume control of production.

Syria

In neighboring Syria, large numbers of the educated classes are increasingly cognizant of the degree to which their own Ba'athist regime's authoritarianism and nepotism are preventing the country from reaching its economic potential, thereby causing the country to fall farther and farther behind other countries in the region in technological development and economic output. This is particularly true in relation to Syria's arch-enemy, Israel, with which it has been engaged in a protracted struggle for more than fifty years. However, Syria's neighbor to the north, Turkey, which is also pressing forward with economic reforms, might become a regional economic powerhouse, especially if it is accepted into the European Union. If neighboring Iraq is able to complete a transition to democracy and reestablish its oil industry, Syria would face neighbors with powerful economies whose citizens would enjoy much higher standards of living and greater political freedoms, highlighting still further Syria's stagnant economy and political repression. That Bashar al-Asad, the current president of Syria, headed a national organization for computer literacy before becoming president is an indicator of the extent to which the younger generation of Syrians is aware of the country's underdevelopment.

The United States does not seem to have an established plan for bringing about political change in Syria, having publicly ruled out a military invasion along the Iraqi model. American policy pronouncements indicate that the United States will continue to put pressure on Syria, especially economic pressure, in an effort to have it soften its opposition to the Israeli-Palestinian peace process, to cease hosting organizations within its borders that the United States considers to be terrorist, and to allow Syrians greater openings for free expression and criticism of the government. The American government has also given tacit blessing to congressional efforts to pass the Syria Accountability Act as another means of pressuring the Asad regime to loosen its political and economic hold on the country. This bill would monitor whether the Syrian government is making efforts to rid the country of organizations that the United States characterizes as terrorist.[1]

Here again, U.S. foreign policy is wanting. U.S. policy toward Syria is indicative of another fallacy, namely the failure to recognize the structural interdependence of the countries in which the United States hopes to promote democratic change. This fallacy fails to recognize the extent to which change in one country is dependent on events occurring in one or more of the other countries of the region. Hence, domino democracy, while itself reflective of a goal for the region as a whole, does not situate the major players in the process in any type of integrated model of political change. Instead, the United States seems to be applying a generalized model to all the countries without realizing that the path to reaching democratic governance differs radically in each case.

In Syria, it seems clear that Hafiz al-Asad's younger son, Bashar—not his father's original choice to lead the nation—seeks to bring about meaningful political and economic change, perhaps along the lines of what Mikhail Gorbachev attempted to implement in the Soviet Union in its waning days.[2] However, Bashar is still surrounded by many of his father's former aides, such as Vice President Abd al-Halim Khaddam, who strongly oppose any reforms that might threaten their political and economic positions within Syria's state apparatus.

Ba'ath Party apparatchiks who oppose reforms possess an effective tool to stymie any change by constantly pointing to Israel's refusal to alter its settlement policies in the West Bank and the Gaza Strip or to enter into serious negotiations about returning the Golan Heights to Syria. The United States' failure to realize the extent to which change in Syria is directly linked to changes in Israeli policy toward settlements, the Palestinians, and the Golan Heights make its pronouncements about bringing political and economic change in Syria almost meaningless. Indeed, bringing more pressure to bear on Syria within the context of little or no change on the part of Israel and its policies toward the peace process only strengthens the Ba'athist hardliners who argue that Syria is being asked to make major concessions while the Israelis are making none. The implications of the notion of structural interdependence in relation to domino democracy is clear. Unless the United States goes beyond bland statements opposing continued Israeli settlement in the West Bank and Gaza, not only does it strengthen the hands of Ba'athist hardliners, but it potentially undermines the reformers such as Bashar al-Asad, who can be accused of being tools of the United States in working to bring about change but receiving no benefits that serve Syrian national interests in return.

Palestine

Palestinian society represents another possible example of a move toward democratic governance. During extensive interviewing in the summer of 1999, just before the recent al-Aqsa *intifada,* or uprising, I was struck by the fact that virtually every conversation with Palestinians began with a litany of complaints about Yasir Arafat. These complaints centered on the extensive corruption that pervaded the Palestine National Authority and its use by Arafat to repress dissent and as his privy purse. Only later in these conversations did the conflict with Israel enter into the discussion, indicating that Palestinians viewed internal issues of democracy and transparency as of greater importance than the struggle with Israel.

Nevertheless, the virtually complete subordination of the Palestinian economy to Israel after 1993, and the carte blanche given by the United States and Israel to Arafat's Palestine Liberation Organization in suppressing all institutions of civil society that were established by the United National Leadership after the onset of the first intifada in 1987, seriously undermined the possibilities for a transition to democracy. The decision by Israel to subordinate the Palestinian economy to its own financial interests helped Arafat and his PLO supporters tighten their hold on power because, in an economy that was weak and characterized by high unemployment, their control over the distribution of jobs and benefits became critical to Palestinians seeking to sustain themselves and their families.

The widespread corruption in the newly created Palestine National Authority after 1993 under Arafat's leadership, and the suppression of largely secular organizations that might challenge Arafat, namely those that were formed during the 1987–1993 intifada, provided a space for expanded influence of radical Islamist organizations such as Hamas. The failure of the United States to place meaningful constraints on continued Israeli settlement of the West Bank and Gaza served to increase the influence of Hamas, Islamic Jihad, and other smaller Islamist organizations such as the Muslim Brotherhood.

As terror attacks on Israel began to mount during the mid and late 1990s, Israel responded by destroying much of the Palestine National Authority's police and security infrastructure, making it even harder for the PNA to control Islamist organizations. The current American administration's decision to sever ties with Arafat was ironic, because the United States had overseen his installation in power in 1993 and supported his dismantling of those secular institutions of civil society created after the 1987 intifada that might have facilitated transition to democracy. In retrospect, this was a deeply flawed policy, the consequences of which were only realized later.

Saudi Arabia

The Saudi case differs dramatically from the other four cases. The most powerful monarchy in the Middle East, the Saudi regime has created great resentment by excluding from all political and economic decisionmaking the highly educated Saudis who are not members of the royal family. Often having spent considerable effort acquiring education abroad or within Saudi Arabia itself, this group resents its exclusion from participation in public life despite having made major contributions to the country's economic development. This resentment is fueled by the fact that many members of the Saudi royal family enjoy political and economic power merely due to their lineage and contribute little to the development of the country.

Given Saudi Arabia's position as the world's largest source of proven oil reserves (although that may be surpassed by Iraq in the future), its central position within the Organization of Petroleum Exporting Countries, its strategic significance, and the large number of lucrative contracts it provides American firms, it is not difficult to understand why the United States has been reluctant to exert significant pressure on the Saudi monarchy. Indeed, of all the countries in which the United States would like to see a democratic transition, Saudi Arabia has received the least pressure to enact major political and social reforms. This is true despite the Saudi regime's policy of providing funds to radical Islamist organizations in Pakistan, Egypt, and elsewhere that adhere to Saudi Arabia's very puritanical Wahhabi interpretation of Islam, in an effort to divert attention away from the monarchy's close ties to the United States and the West. Until serious pressure is brought to bear on Saudi Arabia, the one case in which the United States has significant influence, there will be little hope for reforms and the heightened probability that radical Islamist organizations will acquire greater strength in reaction to the regime's continued corruption and repression.

INTERNAL TRAJECTORIES AND EXTERNAL EVENTS

Because the structural and historical imperatives of Iran, Iraq, Syria, Palestine, and Saudi Arabia are very different, I am suggesting that a transition to democratic politics in each country will not necessarily follow the same trajectory. At the same time, none of these countries can be viewed in isolation from the others, as events in one shape events in the other. We need to underline, then, that each country needs to be viewed in terms of its own internal political trajectory while realizing that its policies are simultaneously constrained by events in the region external to it. Unless United States policy in the Middle East region can grasp these two principles, it cannot expect to be successful, much less bring about significant democratic change in the region.

PREREQUISITES FOR DEMOCRATIC TRANSITIONS

I would like to suggest further five principles that the United States should follow as prerequisites to the implementation of democratic transitions in Iraq and the broader Middle East.

Admission of American Mistakes

First, the American government should initiate a "political cultural offensive" that seeks to win the hearts and minds of politically influential actors in the Middle East, especially the educated middle classes, the lower middle classes, and working classes that aspire to upward mobility. Key to this process is building trust among these groups, through confronting a history of very costly policy decisions by post–World War II American administrations toward Middle Eastern governments and their peoples. Specifically, the United States needs to publicly admit that many of the policies that it followed in the past in the Middle East were flawed. In 2003, President Bush acknowledged that our past policies have not brought about democratic change in the Middle East. That acknowledgment was a step in the right direction. However, we also need to recognize that many in the region view such statements with suspicion as long as they are not accompanied by a parallel recognition that United States support for authoritarian regimes was a mistake and one that it will avoid in the future.

The United States needs to especially focus on the history of American foreign policy in the countries in which it seeks to encourage development of democratic governance. Whether Nuri al-Sa'id and the Hashimite monarchy in Iraq prior to 1958 or the Takriti Ba'athist regime of Saddam Hussein during the 1980s, the Shah in Iran or the monarchy in Saudi Arabia, the United States needs to realize that the educated middle classes, those most amenable to supporting democratic transitions, have a historical memory that needs to be taken seriously. The educated middle classes are justifiably skeptical about the intentions and commitments of the United States. They need to be given not only verbal assurances but the specifics of *how* the United States expects to encourage authoritarian rulers to move to democratic rule and, once a democratic transition has been made, how democratic governance will be sustained.

One example of admitting past mistakes would be our support for the Shah of Iran, whose highly repressive regime engaged in serious human-rights abuses and attempted to create an excessively Western cultural orientation for Iran that excluded most Iranians from their national Islamic heritage. The United States' calls for democracy in the Middle East will only ring true if we acknowledge the extent to which we followed flawed policies in the past. While acknowledging flawed policies in the past might initially provide anti-American grist for the mill, the long-term impact will be to engender greater respect for the United States in the Middle East as citizens of the region realize that we are not an arrogant superpower but rather one willing to acknowledge past mistakes and make a significant break with them.

Removal of Israeli Settlements

Second, the United States needs to act immediately to demonstrate that it is serious about finding a solution to the Israeli-Palestinian dispute. For many Middle Easterners, United States policy toward the Israeli-Palestinian dispute has heavily favored Israel, despite more recent statements supporting the creation of a Palestinian state. Unlike Middle Easterners, who possess a long historical memory, American policymakers still do not seem to have grasped the extent to which the European colonial regnum in the Middle East is still part of the region's collective memory. While it is true, as Western analysts sometimes point out, that references to colonialism reflect a "politics of victimization," European colonial rule had a very real and traumatic impact on large parts of the Middle East. Whether American policymakers are willing to admit it or not, many Middle Easterners view the creation of Israel as an extension of British and French colonial rule, only now under U.S. auspices.

Despite the hostility to Israel and the Israeli-American alliance, under the right circumstances I believe that a large percentage of Middle Easterners would be willing to live in peace with Israel. Among Israelis, a large percentage, sometimes a majority, have indicated in numerous public opinion polls that they would be willing to remove most if not all settlements if that would lead to a lasting peace with the Palestinians.[3] To achieve this end, the United States should begin by calling for an immediate end to Israeli settlements in the West Bank and the Gaza Strip. These settlements are not in the military, economic, or political interests of either the United States or Israel. They also cause the Palestinian people great hardships, whether through the confiscation of Palestinian land to build settlements, through building so-called bypass roads around settlements that disrupt Palestinian economic and social life, or by Israel's erecting the so-called "security fence" that ostensibly is meant to prevent further suicide bombings but which seems more designed to physically separate settlements from surrounding Palestinian towns and villages, often to the economic detriment of the latter.

An unequivocal condemnation of increased settlement activity and an articulation of consequences should it continue, such as the withdrawal of loan guarantees to the Israeli government, is central to the type of structural approach that demonstrates an understanding of the interdependence of the many impediments to creating democratic rule in the Middle East. Not only would the condemnation of settlements in the West Bank and Gaza conform to international law under which they are illegal, but it would send a message to Israel's neighbors, whose support we seek for democratic transitions, that we have become more even-handed in our approach to the region. Once this perception is achieved, the United States would find that groups with which it hopes to create alliances would be more sympathetic to its goals. Conversely, this policy would undermine and undercut the ability of hard-liners in Iran, Syria, Palestine, and Saudi Arabia to use a hypocritical anti-Zionism as an excuse not to enact political and economic reforms.

Creation of International Political Consensus

Third, we need to internationalize our foreign policy in the Middle East. Following this strategy would have many benefits. It would first and foremost create a policy in the region that reflects a wide international consensus. At one level, giving the United Nations, the European Union, and the Arab League, just to name three major institutions, greater voice in the formulation of United States policy in the Middle East might complicate American efforts to bring about change in the region because it would increase the number of political actors that would need to be consulted in making political decisions in Iraq and elsewhere in the Middle East. However, at another level, it would greatly simplify the United States' tasks. Having to take seriously views to which we may have only given lip service in the past would require a more nuanced and sophisticated foreign policy. Making the necessary concessions to internationalize American efforts in Iraq and elsewhere in the Middle East might yield the type of international consensus that, in the end, would make the achievement of a democratic Middle East easier by reducing the hostility that exists in many elite and educated circles toward any initiative that originates with the United States. Militarily, an internationalized foreign policy would reduce the pressures on United States forces in the region through the manpower and financial contributions made by other nations to peacekeeping missions in the region.

Development of International Economic Policy

Fourth, the United States needs to develop a more open and internationally oriented economic policy in the Middle East that does not merely privilege American firms and business interests. The most egregious example of this policy can be found in Iraq, where contracts were awarded, sometimes without competitive bidding, to large firms that had close ties to the Bush administration. As with the argument that an internationalization of our diplomatic and military efforts in the Middle East might weaken our influence in the Middle East, it could also be argued that opening economic opportunities to non-American firms might negatively affect our ability to expand our trade and economic influence in the region. However, creating a more stable political environment in the Middle East, one that could be expected to emerge with a reduced United States political, military, and economic profile in the region, would actually benefit American firms due to the dramatic increase in business activity that would result from such stability.

As the *Arab Human Development Report* recently indicated, the Middle East, especially the Arab world, suffers from a serious lack of integration into the global information technology revolution.[4] Only eighteen persons per 1,000 in the Arab world own or have access to a computer, while only 1.6 percent of the Arab world's population has Internet access. The publication of books in the Arab world is only 1.1 percent of the world average while the number of translated books is only 4.4 per million. These statistics compare unfavorably with most other regions of the world. While the argument that an expansion of trade necessarily brings democratic politics in its wake is often facile, there is no question that expanded commercial activity among the Arab world, the larger Middle East, and the West will foster liberalization in the region. If the level of hostility toward the United States in the Middle East—a level that many observers say is unprecedented at present—does not decrease in the coming decade, this could severely hamper the ability of American firms to benefit from trade and investment in the region.

Initiate People-to-People Exchanges

As a final principle, the United States needs to engage in a major public relations effort to convince the peoples of the Middle East that it does not oppose their aspirations for development and that it does not conform to many of the stereotypes in the region as a "godless" and morally lax country. While an attempt to engage in a major public-relations campaign, the "Shared Values" initiative, was begun by the State Department's Office of Public Diplomacy and Public Affairs in the wake of the September 11 terrorist attacks, this effort was not successful and the director, the undersecretary for public diplomacy and a former advertising executive, Charlotte Beers, resigned in 2003. This project sought to produce television spots for Arab television, many of which were subsequently banned by local governments.

What I am suggesting is a more dynamic program in which intellectuals and political, religious, and business leaders would actually be brought to the United States from the Middle East to tour a wide variety of American public and private institutions. Similarly, large numbers of American counterparts would visit Arab and other countries of the region to participate in "town meetings" where intercultural contact could be facilitated. A dramatic initiative such as this, one that would go well beyond the electronic media, would provide the type of direct, face-to-face contact between Americans and Middle Easterners that speaks to Middle Eastern cultural norms and that would work to undermine mistrust and stereotypes.

RECOGNIZING AMERICA'S NEED TO CHANGE

In sum, the United States needs to transcend the implicit arrogance in a foreign policy that calls on others, namely those in the Middle East, to change but does not recognize this country's need to change as well. This is not a call for national self-flagellation or mea culpa, but rather an admission that our foreign policy in the Middle East has had its beneficial side but has also been based on flawed principles and assumptions. Just as the Iraqis, who watched American forces defeat Saddam's army, were reluctant to nail their flag to the U.S. mast, given our failure to support their 1991 intifada against Saddam Hussein's regime, so many Middle Easterners are going to be reluctant to become actively involved in processes of democratic transitions if they are not first convinced that the United States is committed to such transitions. If the concept of domino democracy has any meaning at all, it starts at home with the fundamental restructuring of United States foreign policy in the Middle East. The United States' own example can provide the best stimulus for positive change in the region.

NOTES

1. Legislation has been introduced in the House and in the Senate called the Syrian Accountability Act, by Senators Barbara Boxer (D-California) and Rick Santorum (R-Pennsylvania) as S. 2215, and in the House by former Representative Dick Armey (R-Texas) and Representative Eliot Engel (D-New York), H.R. 4483. This legislation would impose sanctions on Syria until the president certifies that Syria has ceased its support for terrorist groups, has withdrawn its forces from Lebanon, has halted its development of missiles and biological and chemical weapons, and is in compliance with the United Nations resolutions concerning Iraq. The proposed legislation would impose the following sanctions: (1) a ban on military and dual-use technology exports to Syria; (2) a ban on any financial assistance to United States businesses for their investments or other activities in Syria; and (3) two additional sanctions that the president must impose from a menu of six, including a ban on United States exports to Syria, a ban on United States business investment in Syria, downgrading the U.S. diplomatic representation to Syria (at present, there is an American ambassador), travel restrictions on Syrian diplomats in the United States, and others.

2. Actually, Hafiz al-Asad wanted his eldest son, Basil, who was killed in an automobile accident in 1994, to assume the presidency. Like his father, Basil had a reputation for authoritarianism and corruption.

3. See, most recently, the poll sponsored by the James A. Baker II Institute for Public Policy at Rice University, and the International Crisis Group in Washington, D.C.: "Survey: Majority of Israelis and Palestinians Support Peace Proposal," www.crisisweb.org, November 24, 2003.

4. See "Executive Summary," *Arab Human Development Report*, www.undp.org/rbas/ahdr, 3–4.

BIBLIOGRAPHY

Eric M. Davis, *Challenging Colonialism: Bank Misr and Egyptian Industrialization: 1920–1941* (Princeton: Princeton University Press, 1983).

———, *Memories of State: Politics, History, and Collective Identity in Modern Iraq* (Berkeley: University of California Press, 2004).

———, "Saddam's Sons," interview with Margaret Warner, PBS *NewsHour with Jim Lehrer*, July 22, 2003.

——— and Nicolas Gavrielides, editors, *Statecraft in the Middle East: Oil, Historical Memory and Popular Culture* (Gainesville: University Presses of Florida, 1991).

David E. Sanger, "Bush Asks Lands in Mideast to Try Democratic Ways," *New York Times*, November 7, 2003.

"Survey: Majority of Israelis and Palestinians Support Peace Proposal," James A. Baker II Institute for Public Policy, Rice University; International Crisis Group, Washington, D.C., November 24, 2003. www.crisisweb.org.

United Nations Human Development Programme, *2002 Arab Human Development Report*, Executive Summary (New York: United Nations, 2003). www.undp.org/rbas/ahdr.

• 17 •

American Leadership to Create a Two-State Solution

Chris Toensing

Every contemporary American president has tried and failed to broker a comprehensive solution to the Israeli-Palestinian conflict. But because of the changes that have occurred over recent years, the stakes for the American administration's grudging and very belated effort—the much-discussed "road map"—are much higher than they have been in the past.

Certainly, the stakes are very high for Israelis and Palestinians. The cease-fires in the recent years of low-intensity war cannot bring a permanent end to the conflict. The two-state solution, which remains the preferred solution of majorities on both sides, is in grave danger because of Israel's settlement policy and the rapidly lengthening wall that Israel is building in the West Bank. As much of the very negative image of the United States in the Arab and Muslim worlds stems from American policy toward the Israeli-Palestinian conflict, the stakes are higher for the United States as well.

American failure to broker a two-state solution before facts on the ground render it obsolete will fuel anti-American sentiment in the region, particularly if the United States occupation of Iraq continues to go badly. It is time for the United States to throw its weight behind the kind of drastic solution that is called for by these drastic times.

PREMISES FOR A NEW PEACE PLAN

The proposal presented here proceeds from four basic premises. The first premise is that the fundamental obstacle to peace between Israel and the Palestinians is the Israeli occupation of the West Bank, East Jerusalem, and the Gaza Strip, an occupation which has been in place since the conclusion of the 1967 war. The occupation is an obstacle in all of its manifestations: the settlements, the Israeli military presence and, crucially, the severe limitations on Palestinian freedom of movement and commerce that have been tightened steadily since the outbreak of the second intifada in 2000. Israel's lack of security stems primarily from the persistence of the occupation. The right of return for Palestinians made refugees in 1948, on the other hand, is a much less intractable point of contention than many think.

The second premise is that, in the short to medium term, by far the best hope for a mutually satisfactory peace between Israel and the Palestinians remains the two-state solution as envisioned, if not very precisely articulated, by United Nations Security Council Resolution 242, whose language the United States helped to draft in 1967. This resolution and its successive follow-up resolutions envisioned a state of Israel inside its pre-1967 borders, recognized by the Palestinians and Israel's Arab neighbors, and a state of Palestine in the West Bank and the Gaza Strip. Jerusalem would be the shared capital of both sides, Israel to the west and Palestine to the east. Israeli settlements in the occupied territories would have to be removed, or rendered subject to Palestinian sovereignty.

The third premise is that, unfortunately, the facts on the ground are rendering achievement of the two-state solution increasingly difficult. Not only did the construction of settlements proceed at a furious pace during the course of the Oslo peace process of the 1990s, but Israel also constructed a series of bypass roads to link the settlements to Israel proper. Together with Israeli military bases, the settlements and bypass roads have established a lattice of Israeli control over the territory of the West Bank and the Gaza Strip that can be exercised even when Israeli troops are not present in every square meter of that territory. This lattice of Israeli control covers the entirety of the territory that is envisioned as making up a future Palestinian state. The Israeli government is adding to this lattice of control by building a "security fence." In places, this "fence" is a complex of barbed wire and ditches; in other places, it is a twenty-five-foot high concrete wall. At first, this wall roughly followed the 1967 armistice line, but subsequent phases of construction have made it encroach deep into the West Bank. The wall creates a concrete noose around the town of Qalqilya, for instance. There is only one exit from Qalqilya, leading east toward the other Palestinian population centers. A substantial number of villages and agricultural lands are being cut off from the rest of the West Bank by the wall. In a classic understatement typical of American diplomacy vis-à-vis the Israeli-Palestinian conflict, Bush administration National Security Adviser Condoleezza Rice called this wall "problematic." But the wall is considerably more than problematic. It violates the spirit of every vision that not only the United Nations but also American administrations have espoused for the resolution of the conflict.

The fourth premise is that Israel and the Palestinians are very unlikely to reach a mutually satisfactory peace accord on their own without significant external help. Despite recent unofficial initiatives, the prospect of such an accord is bleaker now than it has been at any point in the past thirty years. Although it may evacuate a few hilltop settler outposts here and there, Israel's current government represents the territorial ambitions of the settler movement. The present Israeli government will not compromise those ambitions unless it is forced to do so. The Israeli peace camp, in both its moderate and radical incarnations, is still a marginal force in Israeli politics, though recent unofficial peace initiatives may change that. On the other side, the Palestinian Authority has lost its former capacity to force controversial accords with Israel upon the population and upon the various armed factions in the Palestinian polity. The Palestinian Authority has lost substantial political ground to Hamas, and militant elements in the secular parties, which are not going to negotiate on matters of substance until the occupation has ended. Hamas, in particular, is making a bid to replace the Palestinian Authority as the de facto steward of the Palestinian cause. Palestinian violence against Israeli civilians has gravely decreased Israeli hope for peace through negotiations. On the other side, Israeli violence against Palestinian civilians, particularly in the course of the major tank invasions of the West Bank in 2002, has greatly decreased Palestinian hope for the two-state solution. Hopelessness on both sides has created an extremely volatile situation, characterized on both sides by disturbing insensitivity to the suffering of the other.

A PEACEKEEPING FORCE

Based on these premises, the United States should act soon to sponsor international intervention in the Israeli-Palestinian conflict, in the form of an armed peacekeeping force, ideally dispatched by the United Nations, to be inserted into the occupied territories. This form of international intervention offers the best hope of enforcing the two-state solution relatively quickly, with a minimum of further loss of life on both sides.

The peacekeepers would replace the Israeli army, which would withdraw from all of the occupied territories inside the pre-1967 borders of Israel. The peacekeepers must be empowered to stop, with force if necessary, Israeli military or Israeli settler attacks on Palestinians, as well as Palestinian attacks upon settlers and Palestinian attempts at infiltration into Israel proper to attack Israeli civilians with suicide bombings or other armed attacks. That power will be necessary to convince Israelis that the United Nations presence aims to protect them from outside attack, and to convince Palestinians that the United Nations presence is not just a new foreign occupation. In line with the latter objective, the peacekeepers would remove all of the internal checkpoints and roadblocks that currently constrain Palestinian travel and commerce between towns and villages and lift the current system of curfews that keeps many Palestinians trapped in their homes.

Most important, the peacekeepers need to be invested with a political mandate as well as a security mandate. They must not be a proxy Israeli army with a mandate only to dismantle Hamas and the other militant groups. They must not be a simple buffer between hostile combatants, as the United Nations force known as the United Nations Interim Force in Lebanon has been in the past. They must not be there merely to police a ceasefire between combatant forces that remain in place, as that would constitute a de facto legitimization of the Israeli occupation and place the peacekeepers in the crossfire. They must be empowered to do more than observe and report, so as not to repeat the unhappy experiment of the toothless Temporary International Presence in Hebron, which has been in place since 1997.

Effective peacekeepers need to go to the occupied territories with the explicit political purpose of ending the Israeli occupation and establishing favorable conditions for the two-state solution. That kind of deployment would enforce the spirit of successive U.N. resolutions.

The political mandate must adhere to a strict timetable set by the U.N. Security Council. There must be a peace at the end of the peace process. It cannot be a process for the sake of process, open to political manipulation by the negotiating parties and open to sabotage by external actors like Hamas, who no doubt will seek to sabotage it. If such a time-delimited political mandate were firmly endorsed by the international community and backed by the diplomacy of the United States, then public opinion on both sides could very well support final status negotiations aiming at the establishment of the two-state solution and the resolution of other outstanding issues in the Israeli-Palestinian conflict. Despite the lack of hope on both sides for a negotiated peace today, polls continue to show with great regularity that majorities of both Israelis and Palestinians continue to believe that negotiation is the only way to achieve peace, and that the two-state solution is the best vision. Physical insecurity is the worst enemy of the basic core realism about the conflict among both Israelis and Palestinians.

Should the negotiations determine that Israeli settlements were to be removed, then United Nations peacekeepers might be required to stay and enforce their removal, as such a removal might be politically impossible for any Israeli government. Should the negotiations determine that Jewish settlements would remain as part of the state of Palestine, then United Nations peacekeepers might be required to stay and protect both the settlers and Palestinian civilians from the attacks of extremists in both the settlers' and the Palestinians' ranks. That function, however, should be turned over to the Palestinian police as soon as possible.

There is a risk that more ideological Israeli settlers in the West Bank would resort to violence to derail the mission of the peacekeeping force. Deployment of a peacekeeping force would probably not be cost-free, regardless of the identity of the peacekeepers. However, the majority of the settlers are living in the West Bank because the housing is cheaper, again made so by Israeli state policy. In the context of a comprehensive settlement which relocated them to comparable housing in Israel proper, they would have absolutely no motivation to take up arms against peacekeepers. To preempt the risk of attacks from both Israelis and Palestinians, the paramount aspect of the peacekeeping mission must be its political mandate to enforce the two-state solution. There must be a strict timetable—when this settlement is evacuated, when that section of the border is set—and clearly defined political goals, so that any party attacking the peacekeepers is seen by both sides, and by world opinion, as a would-be saboteur of the political mandate. Again, this proposal is risky, but much less risky for Israelis, Palestinians, and regional stability than continuation of the status quo or, worse, the disappearance of the two-state solution as a realistic prospect. The further the international community allows the two-state solution to fade, the greater the likelihood of increased Israeli-Palestinian violence.

EAST TIMOR AS A PARTIAL MODEL FOR PALESTINE

U.N. intervention to ensure independence for East Timor makes for an interesting, if rather imprecise, comparison to the Palestinian case. As with the Palestinians, the world overwhelmingly supported East Timorese self-determination against the wishes of the occupying power, Indonesia, which also at the time was heavily backed by Washington. The United States and Australia both resisted deployment of an international force to safeguard East Timorese independence, because Indonesia did not accept it, the same reason that is always adduced for the American refusal to back proposals for an international presence in the occupied territories. Finally, though, reports from East Timor became so grim that the United States abruptly informed B. J. Habibie's government that aid was suspended. Three days later Jakarta relented, and today United Nations peacekeepers have successfully overseen East Timor's transition to statehood. The keys to the success of the East Timorese experiment were the very strict timetable and the clearly defined political goals.

One major difference between the two cases is Palestinian violence against Israeli civilians, particularly the gruesome suicide bombings. This is something that the East Timorese never did to the Indonesians. That is why U.N. peacekeepers in the occupied territories would need the power to disarm and, if necessary, arrest those Palestinian militants who probably would continue to target Israeli civilians during a genuine time-delimited peace process in order to derail it. The loyalty of radical elements within Hamas to an ideology which does not include a state of Israel would pose genuine political problems during a United Nations peacekeeping mission. But over time, the popular appeal of Hamas would diminish for the very simple reason that the occupation would be over. The source of the appeal of Hamas at present is that Palestinians see Hamas resisting occupation, while the

Palestinian Authority does nothing. With a peace process with peace at its end in place, Palestinians would rapidly come to see Hamas violence as an obstacle to peace. More moderate voices in Hamas might begin urging the group to participate in the process so as not to lose their political base and so as to be able to compete in future elections as a "normal" political actor. The risk of Hamas attacks against peacekeepers and/or their political mission is considerable but exponentially smaller than continuation of the status quo, which is making the stance of rejectionists within Hamas seem more and more appealing.

AMERICAN SUPPORT FOR THE PEACEKEEPERS

American policy should support the rapid deployment of such a peacekeeping force in the occupied territories. Ideally, the United States should not assume the task of peacekeeping itself, either unilaterally or in the guise of NATO. Unilateral intervention would have scant credibility among Palestinians, Arabs, and internationally—given the American history of opposing much less robust versions of international intervention, the level of American military and financial aid to Israel (despite its failure to comply with U.N. resolutions), and particularly the American administration's intervention on Israel's side during the three West Bank offensives of 2002. For the sake of the force's credibility and its chances of success, the United States needs to support the United Nations in enforcing its own resolutions. Even if the peacekeepers had to be Americans exclusively, their mandate should come from the United Nations. The force should not be a unilateral political venture.

In any event, close American identification with the peacekeeping force is vital because of the leverage that the United States can bring to bear upon the Israeli government, which naturally will bitterly oppose suggestions of international intervention in the conflict. Israel's resistance to the United Nations investigative commission for Jenin in April of 2002 will be many times magnified in the event of a serious proposal to introduce peacekeepers. Therefore, the Israeli government should not be allowed veto power over discussion of the idea, and should be given strong inducements to cooperate. American aid packages to Israel should be conditioned upon its acceptance of the framework outlined above, and the United States should vigorously promote international intervention in its diplomacy, explicitly as a way of saving the two-state solution for the mutual security of both Israelis and Palestinians.

A time-delimited process with clear political goals and security guarantees would garner significant support from the Jewish and Arab communities in the United States. American leadership in this area would also reawaken the Israeli peace camp, and give dovish elements of the Israeli Labor Party a concrete political platform from which to regain their electoral strength and a voice in the Israeli media. The settlements are deeply unpopular in Israel. If the Israeli government continued to oppose this kind of peace deal, its opposition would increasingly look to Israelis in the moderate center as nothing but emotional attachment to settlements, which have very little to do with Israel's security.

ECONOMIC DEVELOPMENT

However it comes about, any kind of peace settlement has to include a substantial component of economic aid from the United States and the international community writ large. One big reason why is that this is the most practical way to deal with the refugee issue. Most people who have studied the refugee issue know that when Palestinians talk about the right of return, they do not envision that four million Palestinian refugees are going to come knocking on the doors of their old homes in Haifa. It is politically unfeasible for any Palestinian negotiator to sign away the right of return, which is guaranteed by United Nations Resolution 194, but Israeli recognition of the right would not mean that the right would be exercised. Most of the Palestinian refugees in the Arab world, particularly in Jordan, are very well integrated into the economy and even into politics. It is unlikely that they would want to come back. The same goes for the Palestinians living in the West.

The refugees who will need to be resettled are many of those living in the occupied territories and those living in Lebanon. Lebanon has a horrid history of dealing with Palestinian refugees. Lebanese law forbids Palestinians from holding seventy kinds of jobs. This law essentially consigns Palestinians born in Lebanon to lives of menial labor or attempts to get out by any means they can find. Those refugees will need to be resettled in the course of a comprehensive peace settlement. The most logical thing is that they would be resettled in the territory of the future Palestinian state. That is going to require lots of money. Also, under the resolution passed way back in 1948, refugees have a right to compensation for loss of their homes and property. That compensation will have to be paid. Israel should foot some of the bill, but it is very likely that the United States will need to pay a large chunk of it.

In the long term, for economic development in a future Palestinian state, one thing not sufficiently appreciated is that the economic codependency that once existed between Israelis and Palestinians has now gravely eroded. Israel formerly relied upon Palestinian labor, particularly in such fields as construction, and Palestinians relied upon those jobs for their income.

Those jobs, by Israeli state policy, have now been filled mostly with immigrants from South Asia, Southeast Asia, and Southeastern Europe. Even after peace breaks out, the new Palestinian areas will need substantial foreign aid and foreign investment to create job opportunities. Some of that will have to come from the Palestinian diaspora. Some of it will have to come from other places in the Arab world and some from the West.

DOMESTIC POLITICS IN THE UNITED STATES

America, of course, has a very daunting political environment for the discussion of sane solutions. Conservatives do not want to do anything to jeopardize the Christian right vote or a share of the Jewish vote.

Most people in the American Jewish community do not feel represented by the major organizations that claim to represent their interests in Washington. The leaders of those organizations stake out positions considerably to the right of the consensus among the American Jewish community.

But the Christian right is far more extreme in its views toward the Israeli-Palestinian conflict than anything but a small minority of the American Jewish community. For example, even before the announcement of the "road map," there was a conference in Washington which brought together leaders from the Likud-supporting minority of the American Jewish community with the Christian right—specifically to lobby against the "road map."

The solution is to advance bold ideas that can compete with the bold ideas of the right, as Gary Hart has articulated in chapter 2. The right does not have an unbreakable grip on public opinion when it comes to the Israeli-Palestinian conflict, and certainly not on American Jewish opinion, which supports a two-state solution and is mostly antagonistic to the settlements. What is missing from the political arena is a way forward that holds out hope of achieving a lasting peace with security guarantees for both Israelis and Palestinians. The road map, though it has positive elements, is not such a way forward. Both sides see it as something to be manipulated or endured until it collapses of its own weight, largely because the American government is so palpably uninterested in it.

CONCLUSION

The two-state solution is on life support. It is a dubious proposition that the road map, or any comparable initiative, can save it. The road map certainly cannot save the two-state solution without high-level American involvement in every stage of the process and substantial investment of the political capital of the presidency. This is very unlikely. Those of us who support peace in Israel-Palestine and a responsible role for the United States in the Middle East must advocate forcefully for a reversal of the traditional American unwillingness to internationalize the diplomacy of this conflict. Internationalization and meaningful intervention are the best hope for bringing peace to Israel-Palestine. The alternative could be much, much worse than the already unacceptable status quo.

BIBLIOGRAPHY

Bilal Elamine and Chris Toensing, "Groundswell," *Middle East Report*, No. 226, Spring, 2003.

Micah L. Sifry and Christopher Cerf, editors, *The Iraq War Reader: History, Documents, Opinions* (New York: Touchstone, 2003).

Chris Toensing, "Dilemmas of the Left-Liberals," Beirut *Daily Star*, August 6, 2003.

———, "Holding Syria Accountable, Though Selectively," Beirut *Daily Star*, September 13, 2003.

———, "The Answer is in the Force," *Boston Globe*, May 5, 2002.

———, "The Harm Done to Innocents," *Boston Globe*, September 16, 2001.

———, radio interview, *This is Hell*, WNUR 89.3-FM, Chicago, January 24, 2004.

———, "To Deny Iran Atomic Weapons, Create a Nuclear-Free Region," Beirut *Daily Star*, December 16, 2003.

———, "U.S. Support for the Iraqi Opposition," *Foreign Policy in Focus*, January, 2003. http://www.fpif.org/papers/iraqoppsupp.html.

• 18 •

Awakening the American Political Debate on Palestine and Israel

Laurie E. King-Irani

To the average American, much of what this volume covers on the Middle East may seem new, strange, or unusual. That is because what we learn from the mainstream media about this part of the world, and America's involvement therein, is usually quite deficient and shallow. Insufficient reporting on the Middle East is a key issue for Americans to address because democratic debate, discussion, and decision making must be anchored in accurate and objective knowledge of reality. This belief was the motivating force behind the launching of Electronic Intifada and Electronic Iraq, websites I cofounded with my colleagues Ali Abunimah, Nigel Parry, and Arjan El Fassed.

These websites focus on the human and the humanitarian dimensions of conflicts in the Middle East. In so doing, they aim to encourage people to see current political developments in this region through the frameworks of international law, the universal declaration of human rights, and the underpinnings of a just and democratic international order.

The key criteria for such a democratic order are equality, justice, and respect for the rule of law, notions that comprise the foundation of this chapter.

FOREIGN AND DOMESTIC POLICY

This volume embraces foreign, economic, domestic, inner city, and media policy alternatives, a breadth of coverage that is important not only for America but also for the world. It is increasingly difficult to separate the "foreign" from the "domestic," whether we are talking about events, markets, policies, or sentiments. We are living at a time when the global and the local, the national and the international, intersect dramatically and constantly, in surprising, sometimes wonderful, sometimes frightening ways. If nothing else, the events of September 11 should have taught us that.

Of the many possible lessons that could have been learned from September 11, the American government has only considered—and deftly marketed—a very few, all of them packaged under the general rubric of the global war on terror. Along with the Patriot Act, the war on terror has led to the surveillance of Arab- and Muslim-Americans and initiated all sorts of "total information awareness" schemes. American government policy applies, then, as much at home as it does in Kabul or Baghdad.

Recent policy has been very comfortable with the word "global"—as long as it is used in the context of the "global projection of American military might" or the "expansion of global markets," on terms that benefit the United States much more than its economic trading partners. But the American government has not been comfortable with the concept, let alone the practice, of global justice. In fact, during recent years the American government has been actively hostile to the progressive evolution of international humanitarian law and international criminal prosecution. Indeed, a Human Rights Watch staff member recently referred to the American government as "launching a global jihad against international justice."

Among the collateral damage of the last several years has been the cessation of American support for and participation in the emerging, multilateral framework of international justice and accountability. The United States has withdrawn support for the global campaign against impunity for war crimes and crimes against humanity. The government's withdrawal from the International Criminal Court (ICC) and attempts to undercut the court by signing coercive non-extradition (Article 98) treaties with numerous countries in the developing world, the adoption of the principle of preemption, the launching of the war in Iraq in contravention of Chapter 7 of the United Nations charter, and the erosion and reversal of tort law domestically will have longer-lasting and much more deleterious effects on the American population, and perhaps on the entire world, than anything that al Qaeda could have dreamed up.

As the great twentieth-century political philosopher Hannah Arendt noted in her monumental work *The Origins of Totalitarianism,* "All that is needed to achieve total domination is to kill the juridical in humankind." Recent American government policy seems to have grasped this early on; American antipathy to the United Nations and multilateral frameworks of international law and treaties predated the events of September 11. The United States has pursued unilateralist policies in recent years, demonstrating hostility toward global justice and the deliberative processes of international bodies that gave us the Geneva Conventions and the Conventions on the Prevention of Torture and Genocide.

ELECTRONIC INTIFADA

Recent American government policy has been not only conservative but in fact medieval, positioning itself as global liege lord, demanding tribute, obedience, and subservience from its vassals—all other states—as crusades are pursued, accompanied by the rhetoric of divine guidance in the holy struggle against evildoers. There is no place in such a neomedieval world view for deliberation, debate, or dissent. There is little role, if any, for the rule of law. We have entered a postmodern Dark Age, and it will take a lot of hard work and cooperation, at home and abroad, to reverse our slide toward totalitarianism, obscurantism, and coercive force, all of which require that we revitalize the principles and practices of a true democracy.

Countering this new Dark Age will take, in fact, an intifada, to use a word that has been much maligned and seldom understood in the United States.

Commonly translated in the media as "an uprising," "intifada" has come to have connotations of violence, terror, and hatred, implying a total breakdown of the social order. In fact, a more precise translation from the Arabic is "a shaking off, an awakening." And the word means to shake *oneself* off, so it has a reflexive, contemplative element to it and thus denotes the personal beginnings of wider political transformations. An intifada is about questioning the status quo in order to attain justice and to assert human dignity and human rights in the face of powerful, unjust, and crushing forces. An intifada, given this definition, is indeed a proper response to injustice and impunity. (It is interesting, and timely, to note in this regard that the first use of the term "intifada" in reporting on the Middle East came decades earlier, in characterizing grassroots social movements for justice and political representation in Iraq in the pre-Saddam period of that long-suffering country's history.)

In response to mainstream media and American official misrepresentations of the Israeli-Palestinian conflict and of the nature and goals of the Palestinian intifada, my colleagues and I launched the Electronic Intifada website in 2001 to challenge and critique conventional assumptions about the Israeli-Palestinian conflict, its underpinnings, and the requirements for its successful resolution. Billed as "a weapon of mass instruction," the site attempts to cut through spin and to question generally unchallenged opinions with analyses, on-the-ground reporting, and occasional humor. It is a fresh approach and apparently much appreciated. Along with our other site, Electronic Iraq, we currently receive between 300,000 and one million visits, not hits, a month, and we also receive quite a lot of mail, which falls into two categories. One is, "We will kill you," and the other category, which is very interesting and instructive for those working to build progressive links among various groups, is fan mail from former and current Central Intelligence Agency members, foreign policy officials, journalists, schoolteachers, housewives, college students, and all sorts of people in the United States who very much like what we are doing. Many people in Europe also are interested. The European visitors to the site are probably better informed than Americans about the situation in the Middle East and are more comfortable with our style and content.

Electronic Intifada cannot be characterized simplistically as either a pro-Palestinian or an anti-Israeli site. It certainly is not an antisemitic endeavor either but rather an attempt to preserve and advance the frameworks of global justice by encouraging people to view the Israeli-Palestinian conflict through the lens of international humanitarian law rather than seeing it as an ancient, biblically based battle or as an ethnic conflict far too complex to understand, let alone resolve. One of its most basic messages is "One yardstick for human rights."

We started Electronic Intifada and Electronic Iraq because there is so much that the mainstream media are not presenting. After the Israeli incursions into the West Bank in 2002, we saw a huge increase in the numbers of people visiting the site and a lot of interesting inquiries come from journalists. Our site was featured in *Foreign Policy,* the *Washington Post,* the *Financial Times,* the *Nation*, and other places, so that brought more people to us. The first thing we hear is, "I'm glad that you exist, because I would never have known this just from watching the TV or reading the newspaper. How come we don't know this?"

That is what a lot of people say: "Why don't we know this?" A good question. These are important things for Americans to know. Living in Canada since August 2001, and watching the September 11 aftermath develop from Canada, I was depressed that, after 4,000 people died horrific and unjust deaths, few Americans tried to learn the lessons needed to avoid such scenarios in the future.

Electronic Intifada and Electronic Iraq try to find the intersection among technology, information, and politics. The sites are interactive, incorporating blogging software, thus allowing people to upload stories, photos, and videos directly to the two sites.

The sites have reference departments about, for example, the Geneva Conventions, the Oslo Accords, and the American State Department's *Annual Report on Human Rights*. So we have all the documentation anyone would need. But we also try to bring in people from the grassroots—Israelis and Palestinians who are living through this daily freak show of political insanity—to give us their viewpoints. We have diaries on the site where people can upload their daily experiences. And we have satire as well, on our "al-bassaleh" page, which means "The Onion" in Arabic.

All of this helps to draw people into the realities of Middle Eastern life. As a result, more questions and critical thinking often are initiated than might evolve from more academic presentations.

ENDING THE ISRAELI OCCUPATION

The Israeli-Palestinian conflict, plainly and simply, is about a longstanding and chronic failure to apply U.N. resolutions and international law. Its driving force is continued impunity for a clear pattern of grave violations of international law in which the United States is quite complicit. If concerned Americans want to support the rule of law at home and abroad and advance the cause of disseminating democracy and a just sociopolitical order throughout the world, particularly in the Middle East, they could find few better starting points than joining an international campaign to end the Israeli occupation of the West Bank and Gaza.

As Americans, we have a greater chance to achieve this worthy end than we do of influencing events elsewhere in the Middle East. That is because we are so complicit in an Israeli occupation that has become increasingly brutal, an occupation that angers not only the Arab and Islamic world but also Europeans, Asians, and Canadians. All of this stirs resentments and mistrust of the United States throughout the world. This is a lot of unpleasant baggage that everyone could do without.

Ending the occupation would benefit not only Palestinians but also Israelis and Americans. It is no secret that Israel has violated international law with impunity for decades in the West Bank and Gaza Strip. As an occupying power, Israel has gravely breached the Geneva Conventions by building settlements, diverting water, and undertaking extrajudicial killings, including use of very imprecise Apache attack helicopters, which usually take out several civilians along with the intended targets. Such acts also violate the United States Foreign Assistance Act of 1961, which stipulates that the United States is not to disburse foreign or military aid to countries evidencing a clear pattern of grave human rights abuses. A cursory review of Israeli actions in the Occupied Territories provides more than enough evidence for Israel's violation of this American law.

Israel has used torture, arbitrary detention, collective punishment, and the imposition of sieges on a largely unarmed civilian population. Violations of international humanitarian law, and disregard for a whole raft of United Nations resolutions, have become part and parcel of Israeli practices in the West Bank and Gaza. Indeed, infractions of international law and resolutions are woven into the very sinews of the institutionalized system of inequality and oppression that is the occupation.

From the perspective of Israel's key ally, the United States, future stability in the Middle East hinges upon maintaining the status quo in the Israeli-Palestinian conflict by wringing maximum concessions from the Palestinians while demanding minimal sacrifices or behavioral changes from Israel. The current road map to peace, though nominally a slight improvement on the Oslo accords of a decade ago, implicitly grants Israel permission to continue violating international laws and U.N. resolutions. Just like the Oslo accords before it, the road map sidelines those laws and resolutions in a rush to hammer together a dubious peace based on pressure tactics and expediency rather than an enduring peace built on the sturdier foundations of global justice.

As international legal scholar Kathleen Cavanaugh has noted, "Alarmingly, these flawed political agreements [the Oslo accords and the Dayton agreement] have assumed de facto legal status, and have replaced international law in practice.

As a result, compliance with international human rights law and humanitarian law has been rendered negotiable. The deftly woven ambiguity of the Oslo accords may have secured the initial Israeli-Palestinian agreement, but this ambiguity has also enabled Israel to claim compliance with the accords while clearly seriously violating international law."

Continued Israeli violation of international humanitarian law is not just a problem for Palestinians suffering under a cruel occupation, the full extent and dimensions of which are rarely presented to an American television audience. Israeli impunity is also the primary catalyst for the criminal Palestinian suicide bombings that have brought violence, death, and destruction to the very heart of Israel's cities. When victims of longstanding and serious rights violations do not have recourse to proper channels, when they cannot obtain restitution and closure through the courts, the state, the international community, the media, the United Nations, or The Hague, they may well take matters into their own hands, as some Palestinian factions unfortunately have done. Terrorists are not born but made. It stands to reason, then, that they can be unmade and that terror can be halted. This is another key message of our websites.

Before us is a choice. Behind us are searing landscapes of impunity. Americans are in close touch with the slaughter in Manhattan in September 2001 but less in touch with the continuing atrocities committed by all sides in Israel-Palestine. In these scenes of mass destruction and death, the cries of the bereaved and the odors of death erase local particularities. They remind us of humanity's infinite capacity for cruelty and violence, but we must never forget that human beings are also capable of creating and dwelling in landscapes of social and political justice.

The foundations of this alternative landscape are not hidden, unattainable, or imaginary but clearly encoded in the universal declaration of human rights and international human rights law, particularly the Fourth Geneva Convention, adopted after World War II to help prevent grave violations of civilians' rights during times of armed hostility.

The establishment of the International Criminal Court brings us one step closer to realizing these landscapes of hope, despite the alarming American decision to withdraw from this important attempt at ensuring global justice and its further attempts to defang the court with the aforementioned nonextradition treaties. The United States, like its close ally, Israel, has sent the world a disturbing message: "We are above the law." This message poses dangers for Americans, Israelis, and others. American and Israeli hostility to international law will only lead to more deaths of Israelis and Palestinians and possibly Americans as well. Because we do have a choice between crime or justice, violence or peace, murder or life, we need to put teeth into international law and build landscapes of hope upon the charred landscapes of impunity spreading so rapidly in the Middle East, which can even reach here, again, to our own shores.

THE DOUBLE STANDARD

United Nations Security Council Resolution 687, which required Iraq to disarm, was not just about Iraq.[1] The resolution states that the whole region should be disarmed from weapons of mass destruction, so the onus is on everyone—including Israel. But Israel never has been pressured. (An excellent recent book by an Israeli scholar, Avner Cohen, discusses the Israeli nuclear project. He couldn't go back to Israel for several years because he was afraid that he would end up like Mordechi Vanunu, a technician at the Dimona plant who revealed that there were something on the order of 250 warheads in Israel.)

So double standards pervade the Middle East. Not enough people in the United States realize how those double standards work on the intersubjective level—to poison attitudes toward America throughout this troubled region.

Israeli noncompliance does place a great bludgeon in the hands of the undemocratic, brutal regimes of the Middle East who feel that they don't have to play by the rules since Israel doesn't. If Israel is made to comply, then the Arab regimes won't have any excuse. They won't have what is known in Arabic as *mismar juha*—a folk term that means something like "a red herring," or an excuse. The red herring is used very deftly in the rhetorical discourses of the Syrian, Saudi, and previously the Iraqi political elite to avoid complying with international law and disarmament.

It is good that Saddam has gone. He was a massive human rights abuser. But we need to apply the same yardstick to everyone. All nations need to abide by the Geneva Conventions and the Universal Declaration of Human Rights. We have to put teeth into these international institutions and laws so that nobody will say, "Oh well, that country doesn't have oil, so if they want to kill five million people, who cares?" We have to care. We can't let that happen, because impunity anywhere encourages impunity elsewhere. If you see you can get away with it in Liberia, then something will happen in Congo, or something will happen in Indonesia. Those issues don't really make it into the media. We just brush them aside, "Oh, tribal people, primitives, they kill each other, how horrible. Next story."

DEBATING ISRAELI LOBBYISTS AND CHRISTIAN FUNDAMENTALISTS

An intifada against impunity can inform the political debate in America. Americans need to openly discuss the Israeli-Palestinian conflict and ongoing Israeli infractions of international law through its occupation of Palestinian lands.

By examining this conflict seriously, and critically interrogating the real problems of continuing with the occupation, one can also accomplish a lot of other things. Analyzing this issue can lead to a serious analysis and critique of issues such as the need for accurate and fair media in a democracy, which of course leads to a deeper inquiry into open, inquiring, and democratic debate on this and other foreign policy issues that for too long have been the domain of so-called "experts." No American citizen should uncritically abandon such weighty matters to a special class of professional pundits.

A close examination and critique of the Israeli occupation also would likely lead to a deeper engagement with the pressing question of campaign finance reform. Having worked in Washington for two years as editor of *Middle East Report*, I know from talking to people on the Hill and at various think tanks of all political stripes that one of if not *the* biggest obstacle to an honest accounting of American complicity in the brutalities of Israeli occupation is the fear among elected officials of a negative and well-organized response by the pro-Israeli lobby. It is no secret that this powerful lobby will handsomely finance anyone opposing an elected official who dares to raise such questions publicly. This leads to elections and representation that are not reflective of the actual opinions, feelings, hopes, and analyses of the vast majority of the American voting public. This is a major impediment to a truly democratic order in the United States and ought to be confronted by concerned Americans in a fearless manner.

A close look at American support for the Israeli occupation would imply, as well, a closer and more critical look at the American arms trade. Israel is probably the largest recipient of arms and military aid packages, and indeed, the Middle East as a whole is the largest recipient of American military assistance of all types—hardly a sensible policy decision given the volatility of this region, not to mention a history of American armaments ending up in the hands of the Taliban as a result of the Byzantine aid policies of the Reagan years. And as noted in a BBC presentation that aired not long ago—causing a lot of problems between the BBC and Israel—Israel does, indeed, have quite an arsenal of nuclear and chemical weapons, though it has usually issued denials of this fact.

Addressing these and other issues associated with the ongoing Israeli occupation and American complicity therein would also encourage the American public to consider the relative benefits and costs of compliance with international humanitarian law by both the United States and its allies. There may be short-term gains to be reaped from being "above the law," but in the long run it can only set dangerous and destabilizing precedents, particularly in this region of multiple and growing conflicts over borders, rights, and resources. It is probable that water wars will figure prominently in the future of the Middle East, and without an international legal framework these will be very dangerous conflicts indeed.

Last but not least, a serious engagement with the Israeli-Palestinian conflict and the Israeli occupation might enable us to comprehend the dangers of demagoguery and manipulative rhetoric, which nowadays is combined in Washington with disconcerting Christian fundamentalist discourse and bigoted viewpoints. Christian fundamentalists are a key conservative constituency. They believe that the war in Iraq was inevitable because, in their reading of events, Saddam Hussein and the government of Iraq represented the whore of Babylon in the Book of Revelation. It behooves all of us, regardless of party, to expose this ideology, because it is profoundly dangerous and crazier than anything that Osama bin Laden can come up with.

REDEFINING THE CONCEPT OF TERROR

An honest and critical engagement with the multiple issues underlying the continuing Israeli occupation—biased media coverage, lack of campaign finance reform, the presence of weapons of mass destruction in Israel, and the stake that Christian fundamentalists have in opposing a two-state solution—would help Americans redefine the concept of terror. Terror in America is now a key symbol and a buzzword that has become so diffuse and so large that we are no longer using terror and terrorism constructively in public discussions and policy debates. Rather, terror and terrorism are using *us*—by stirring up thought-blocking feelings of fear, impending doom, helplessness, rage, and revenge. These are not the bases of decision making in a great democracy. America must not be allowed to become a demagogic nation.

If we were to define terror more closely and to study the definitions of terror and terrorism provided under international law, we might begin to see that terror is nearly always the fruit of impunity. Terror is the harvest sown by institutionalized systems of inequality, humiliation, and despair, and these problems can be healed only through building and strengthening the institutions of justice, not by launching preemptive wars abroad while also building up military and intelligence capacities at home that threaten the freedoms we all cherish as Americans.

In the face of these growing foreign and domestic dangers, we indeed need an *intifada*. Now.

NOTE

1. United Nations Security Council Resolution 687, passed on April 3, 1991, established the formal cease-fire between coalition forces and Iraq. Key among the cease-fire terms was the prohibition against Iraq's retaining, acquiring, or developing weapons of mass destruction and long-range missiles. In addition, there was a demand that Iraq unconditionally accept the destruction, removal, or rendering harmless of its weapons of mass destruction under international supervision.

BIBLIOGRAPHY

Hannah Arendt, *The Origins of Totalitarianism* (New York: Harcourt, 1948).
Kathleen Cavenaugh, "The Cost of Peace: Assessing Oslo," *Middle East Report*, No. 211, Summer 1999.
Avner Cohen, *Israel and the Bomb* (New York: Columbia University Press, 1999).
Peter Ford, "Belgium Makes Justice Less Global," *Christian Science Monitor*, June 24, 2003.
Laurie E. King-Irani, "Fellini in Palestine," opinion page, *Bint Jbeil*, April 2, 2002. At http://www.bintjbeil.com/A/araa/020402_irani.html.
———, "Rituals of Reconciliation and Processes of Empowerment in Post-War Lebanon," in *Traditional Cures for Modern Conflicts: African Conflict Medicine*, edited by I. William Zartman (Boulder: Lynne Rienner, 1999).
United States Department of State, Bureau of Democracy, Human Rights and Labor, "Country Reports on Human Rights," 2003 report, February 25, 2004.
www.ElectronicIntifada.net.
www.ElectronicIraq.net.

• 19 •

The Future Political and Economic Architecture of the Middle East

E. Roger Owen

This chapter first addresses the war on terrorism and the decision to use Iraq as a kind of showcase for the American government's policy of preemptive intervention. It then discusses the pressing issues of Iraq and democracy, Iran, and the future economic architecture of the Middle East.

THE WAR ON TERRORISM

The way the war on terrorism was presented by the American government was very disturbing to many people. The U.S. government could have petitioned the nations of the world to help confront what was essentially a criminal act. The call would have been for an intensified campaign of police and intelligence activity—building on what most nations had been heavily engaged in before September 11. Such a request would have been readily understood. (For example, Usama El-Baz, the Egyptian presidential adviser, at a meeting in Washington said clearly, "You have to know that these terrorists are, in fact, criminals.") It would have activated the very real sense of sympathy which existed for the people of the United States at this time. It would have created alliances based not on arm-twisting but on a strong perception of mutual interest. And it could not have been interpreted in the Muslim world as a very thinly disguised attack on Islam.

You cannot really orchestrate a sensible policy when you are engaged in these large and spurious questions about conflicts between civilizations, or what's wrong with Islam, or the alleged economic underperformance of the Muslim world. It is a good stick with which to beat your enemies, if that is what you want to do. But for many reasons, such a perspective will not tell you very much about modern Iraq.

In fact, to frame policy in terms of "conflicts of civilizations" makes a proper appreciation of what is going on in Iraq—or indeed Iran or anywhere else in the Middle East—more difficult because it attaches the wrong weight to religion. Such a framework causes people to homogenize groups like the Shi'a as though they were one single entity professing one kind of view. Shi'i communities are extraordinarily faction-ridden, and the history of Shi'ism in Iraq is one of constant disputes about religious leadership, about how to engage with the government in Baghdad, and about relations with Iran. The implications of all this are fairly obvious. Perhaps most important of all in present circumstances, it becomes impossible for any single leader to deliver something you might want to call the "Shi'i vote."

The declaration of such a war on terrorism provided a wonderful cover for all kinds of other questionable activities. This is certainly true of the attack on civil liberties in the United States. As far as the Middle East is concerned, the war gave license to the Israelis to carry out policies in the occupied territories which they might not have contemplated in other circumstances. And the war on terrorism also meant that, for all the American government's talk of encouraging greater democracy in countries like Tunisia and Egypt, such countries, if they cooperated with America, would be exempt from serious criticism of their own human rights abuses. Such countries also could proceed with preparing for a "republican succession," so that, for example, President Mubarak could be succeeded by his son, Gamal. Hence more green lights for America's allies to do things which are clearly contrary to America's longer-term interests.

Lastly, for all the often very sincere talk of the need for dialogue and discussion between Arabs and Muslims, on the one hand, and Westerners, on the other, the polarization produced by the declaration of the war on terrorism has been such that real dialogue continues to be almost impossible. Even with the best will in the world, the Arabs and Muslims feel so threatened by American policy that they cannot help but dig themselves into defensive positions from which few are clever enough, or wise enough, to extricate themselves. For their part, their Western interlocutors are caught somewhere between explaining and condemning their own governments' policies in ways which encourage further obfuscation and misunderstanding. Meanwhile, the cherished goal of mutual tolerance and understanding becomes ever more elusive, ever more distant.

THE INVASION OF IRAQ

The war against Iraq was at best premature and misguided. The means for dealing with the particular problems posed by Iraq's alleged weapons regime had not been exhausted, and there was no U.N. legitimacy for the course that was taken unilaterally by the United States and Great Britain. Given the extraordinary polarization of opinion during the lead-up to the war, critics of the American government's policy were more or less automatically debarred from any discussion about how to deal with the Saddam Hussein regime or any eventual successor. As the critics of the war included most of the people who actually knew what was going on in Iraq and who might have been used to check some of the wilder claims of the pro-war members of the Iraq opposition in exile, the American government deprived itself of a vital policy-making tool. But this, of course, was exactly what its more hawkish members wanted anyway. The early nineteenth-century English wit Sidney Smith told of seeing two East London fishwives shouting at each other from their doorways on two sides of a street. He is said to have observed, "You know why they will never reach agreement? They are arguing from different premises." Such is the case now.

We are now in an interesting period in which people are examining the efficacy of postwar policies pursued in Iraq. It is an issue of the greatest importance. But it is also vital to continue to question whether the war should have been carried out at all. Whether or not the whole thing turns out to be a disaster—and the balance of advantage for the Iraqi people as whole is likely to be a negative one—the general question of the pros and cons of forcible nation building by military intervention is one that is unlikely to go away.

America's invasion of Iraq contained a very high degree of political risk. The continuing risk, postwar, is forcing the administration to ever more expensive measures to manage the situation in Baghdad. At what stage might America come to understand that the game is not worth the candle, as President Nixon was forced to do in the case of Vietnam?

AMERICAN ADMINISTRATION IN IRAQ

However the U.S. administration is able to improve the immediate chaos in Iraq, the situation could still blow up as a result of one of those apparently trivial incidents that regularly took place in Europe's colonial past, to trigger a national or seminational uprising that, though contained, produces a sea change in local political attitudes. For example, the way in which Kurdistan can be fitted into a new united Iraq without Turkish interference must be handled with great delicacy. In such situations, you have to think very seriously about the speed and urgency needed to attend to the most vital questions without getting bogged down in the kind of endless detail that requires more and more foreign experts to fix things. In other words, time is not on our side in postwar Iraq.

Americans can learn from Britain. The way colonial administrations imagine colonial societies very much affects the kinds of measures they take and the kinds of institutional approaches they create to facilitate local representation. In Iraq, American policy is committed to individual rights and one person/one vote.

Some American policy makers are proceeding toward one person/one vote by recognizing that Iraq is a country of communities. As a consequence, representation must come through communities, and therefore by extension political parties must be agents of communities. A good example of this line of thinking is provided by the American-sponsored Mosul Municipal Council, consisting of representatives not of districts or economic interests but of the local ethnic and religious communities. So you have a Christian and you have a Yazedi, and you have various types of Muslims. It also is true that many American policy makers assume that Iraq is a bellicose, anarchic place that can only be run by strong men. That has led to local administrations being based on a combination of communal representation and representation by ex-military officers. Such a combination makes it more difficult to create an environment in which ideological parties can flourish, in which the Iraqi people feel that there is some point to voting for parties that are other than the ones that represent them in a communal, ethnic, or religious way.

Another lesson from British colonial history is the use of empire as a kind of laboratory for experimenting with ideas which you believe have either been imperfectly implemented in your own country or not implemented at all. There is a recent book about the way in which the technique of fingerprinting was developed by police officers in Calcutta based on the widespread indigenous use of fingerprints to sign documents. But you could only do this in an Indian context where the necessary, tedious work of comparing prints could be carried out with large numbers of Indians who spoke English and who had just enough education to allow them to be trained for this type of work.

By the same token, there are many policy makers in the United States who want to use the Iraqi economy as a laboratory for free enterprise. For example, Iraq is a rentier state—that is, one where all the oil revenues pass straight into the coffers of the regime, which then uses them to maintain its own hold on power. One recent, lunatic idea to get around this problem is to simply hand over individual shares of the revenues to individual Iraqis—as if this could be done with any precision and fairness in a country with so few banks, so little trust of government, so few mechanisms for transmitting central policies from Baghdad to the provinces. Proponents of the individual handout scheme sound as though they are talking about quite a different country.

One way of trying to prevent such schemes from being implemented unilaterally in postwar Iraq is to insist on more congressional oversight, more trips to the region by congressmen, and particularly by those with staffers who know something about Iraq and about colonial situations of this type. It is also important to listen to what the World Bank has to say to the Europeans and to the representatives of the nongovernmental organizations. It may well be a frustrating process, but it should proceed with as much openness and democratic decision making as possible.

DEMOCRACY IN IRAQ AND ELSEWHERE

But there are many obstacles against democracy for Iraq, just as there are for the rest of the Arab Middle East. Let me just mention three.

One which Egyptian officials like Usama al-Baz are very conscious of is that even with the best will in the world, any Middle Eastern regime that says it wishes to democratize faces the accusation that it is only bending to the pressure of the United States. This is, at once, the kiss of death. The obstacle can be overcome but not easily. A Middle Eastern regime that truly wants to democratize must reach back into its history. It must identify moments when democracy began to be practiced and to learn appropriate lessons as to why some of these initiatives failed and which others might have borne better fruit in slightly difficult circumstances. In the case of Iraq, for instance, there was, perhaps surprisingly to many, a reasonably open and properly contested election in 1954. (Actually, there were two elections in that year; the second was managed by the government to produce the results it wanted.)

So local traditions do exist which you can go back to and, it would seem to me, use to bypass the endless and completely futile discussion about whether Islam is compatible with democracy. At the very least, by going back in history, you can demonstrate that, by and large, the failure of the system of contested elections in Egypt, Syria, and Iraq in the 1930s and 1940s had little if anything to do with religion and much more to do with the problems of managing a one person/one vote system in what were then predominantly peasant societies dominated by a small rural elite. It would be nice to imagine—although still impossible to prove—that the huge increase in Middle Eastern urbanization in the past few decades has made this particular problem easier to address.

A second potential obstacle to democracy will be the way in which America manages Iraq. Management of Iraq is supposed to be a shining beacon, of course, at least as far as the American government is concerned. But if it isn't, what kinds of lessons will the other peoples of the Middle East draw about this experience, its possibilities, and its limitations?

A third potential obstacle is illustrated by the debate in Washington, Baghdad, and many other places about the uses and abuses of the electoral process. As Fareed Zakaria has correctly asserted in his recent book, *The Future of Freedom: Illiberal Democracy at Home and Abroad*, the fact that, say, the ruling regimes in Russia or Venezuela hold regular elections does not mean that they need to pay more than rhetorical respect to human rights or the rule of law. Such a claim might be used as an argument for going slowly, for saying that you first need to establish all kinds of other institutions, like efficient police and courts, before democracy can proceed. This occurred in the former British Empire, where the prescribed conditions for electoral democracy never actually materialized, often because the stresses and strains of a period of enforced waiting for new institutions undermined the very conditions needed for success. Listening to American officials talking from Baghdad, one sometimes gets the impression that there will never be a moment in which the United States believes the Iraqis ready for such a test.

Clearly, the practice of regular elections is very easy to abuse. It can be subject to endless manipulation, as in Egypt, Tunisia, Algeria, and Morocco, and still be used to maintain the impression in Washington or the European Union that things are moving in the right direction. Nevertheless, elections have several very important characteristics which make them indispensable as part of any process of regime change. They are the only way of establishing regime legitimacy. They encourage a vital sense of participation among the citizens. And they provide the best way for competing political parties to bring their programs and policies to the attention of a national audience.

In the Middle East, as in many other regions of the non-European world, elections are the only way of sending certain kinds of signals about the sincerity of an administration's wish to encourage greater popular participation, to allow some kind of accountability, to permit pro-government parties to be overthrown and opposition parties to come to power. Elections also produce a sense of popular empowerment. Witness the excitement produced by the first election after the overthrow of a dictatorial regime, as in, say, South Africa, with the people willing to line up for hours and hours to vote. It matters. It is part of the process of making people feel that what they say and do is of some political significance.

The obvious conclusion to be drawn from all this is that all timetables must be carefully followed and there should be a movement toward freely contested elections in Iraq as quickly as possible. The more that this can be done under international auspices and in cooperation with the Europeans, the better.

RELATIONS WITH IRAN

The most important thing to observe about Iran is that it is in the middle of a hugely significant process of mutation from a kind of monolithic Islamic government to a pluralistic Islamic one. This is so important to the global history of the twenty-first century that it must be allowed to continue and to work its way through with the real prospect that this mutation will, over time, lead to a more secular pluralism with religion confined to the place where most people believe religion ought to be—in the mosques but not in the offices of government.

But the Iranians have to be left alone to work this out for themselves. Unfortunately for them, and for the rest of the world, this is not going to be an easy passage. There are the repercussions from the American administration's wilder talk about regime change. There is the proximity to Iraq, which means that if things go wrong there they will spill over to Iran, the more so as the Tehran regime is inevitably held responsible for a large part of it.

There also is the question of Iran's nuclear ambitions. It seems to me from talking to the Iranians that there is a considerable consensus among them that they should get themselves into a position where they could produce a bomb if that seemed vital for national self-defense. For one thing, they live in a region with several nuclear powers already: Israel, Pakistan, and India. For another, the obvious lesson to be drawn from the different American policies toward Iraq and North Korea is the need to get quickly to a position where you can produce a bomb at short notice to preempt a potential American attack. This is a complicated equation. You may bring on the very thing you want to avoid. The nuclear issue is enormous and too dangerous to tackle on a unilateral or piecemeal basis.

So there are three messages which should be sent to American policy makers. First: Be very, very careful. Let the indigenous Iranian process take its time. Second: It will take much longer than you imagine. Don't be beguiled by Thomas Friedman's notion that the Iranian young people who listen to pop music and access American pornographic sites are the shock troops of revolutionary change in Iran. The demand for change will not be organized in that kind of way. Third: There needs to be an international approach best achieved by returning to the old notion of a nuclear-free Middle East. That of course raises the difficult problem of Israel, but solutions, however difficult, are possible, as Chris Toensing has articulated in chapter 17. If you try and pick off countries one by one, then you simply store up more trouble for the future by encouraging the idea that the only way to defend yourself is to go the North Korean route.

ECONOMIC INTEGRATION AND DEVELOPMENT

One of the consequences of the first Gulf War was the prominence given to the notion of Middle East North Africa as a way of establishing a new economic architecture for the region. The idea was to encourage better economic relations between Israel and its Arab neighbors as a vital underpinning for the ongoing Israeli-Palestinian peace process. The whole project was developed through four Middle Eastern economic summits in which representatives of the national private sectors played a prominent role. There was much stress on the establishment of new pan–Middle Eastern institutions, like a development bank tentatively promised to Cairo. The initiative then came to an untimely end with the sharp deterioration of Arab-Israeli relations, which marked the period of the Netanyahu government, elected in 1996.

Now it seems that the American government wants to create a new architecture of the Middle East based not on regional institution building but on bilateral arrangements focused on the offer of specific free trade agreements between the United States and certain favored Middle Eastern countries like Bahrain and Morocco.

Paradoxically, this reproduces one of the worst features of the European agreements with the Middle East, in which efforts to encourage greater economic integration are also based on the promotion of bilateral relationships between the European Union and its regional partners. But the European Union process does at least have the great advantage of providing aid targeted to some of those specific industries most likely to suffer once the free trade provisions of the new treaties kick in after ten years. As the Europeans said to the Tunisians and the Egyptians: In ten years' time, you are going to have to reduce your tariffs on textile imports, so give us a list of your textile factories and let us help you update them so that they have some chance of competing with us down the road.

This seems to me a sensible way of going about things, and one which it would be good for the United States to copy. But it isn't the whole answer if the aim really is to promote greater regional economic integration, as the United States apparently desires. A better way forward would certainly be to revive the Middle East North Africa strategy via a new series of multinational conferences.

Nevertheless, we also have to ask ourselves if there aren't even better methods of encouraging the larger goal of more rapid Middle Eastern development. One method would be not only to get as many of the region's states into the World Trade Organization as we can but also to make sure that the World Trade Organization itself monitors the whole process effectively enough to ensure that the promises to open up, to lower tariffs, to pursue best global economic practice are properly implemented. This should probably involve giving the World Trade Organization secretariat sufficient power to go around and say to governments, if necessary, that they are not living up to their obligations. Meanwhile, let the global community take heart from the findings of a new international survey by the Pew Research Center that a larger proportion of people in the non-European world than was previously supposed do believe in the importance of greater openness and more trade, so long as the whole process does not affect their own core values.

It will be a hard battle. The fear of American intentions and American anger is so great at the moment that officials in the World Bank, in the European Community, and elsewhere are crippled in their efforts to develop new ways to promote Middle Eastern economic progress. Yet there is also some hope that, as a result of Washington's need for international assistance in Iraq, it will be forced to become more flexible in its approach.

THE FUTURE OF THE MIDDLE EAST

In sum, America needs to hand over responsibility in Iraq to an international coalition led by the United Nations, including the United States. This coalition should then organize elections for a provisional government responsible for creating a constituent assembly to draw up a permanent constitution. Then, after a nationwide general election, a legitimate Iraqi government should be allowed to negotiate the terms under which foreign companies (including oil companies) are allowed to operate in the country, foreign aid is provided, and those foreign troops necessary to provide internal security (until a new Iraqi army and police force are able to perform these duties by themselves) operate.

In Iran, the United States needs to join with the European community to maintain a creative engagement with the Iranian government designed to encourage a transition toward a parliamentary democracy based on the rule of law. In the Middle East at large, the United States needs to abandon its present policy of bilateral economic negotiations with favored individual states and work with all to try to create a regionwide free trade area.

BIBLIOGRAPHY

Anthony H. Cordesman, *The Iraq War: Strategy, Tactics and Military Lessons* (Westport, Conn.: Praeger, 2003).

Mark Danner, "Iraq: The New War," *New York Review of Books*, pp. 88–91, September 25, 2003.

Thomas L. Friedman, "The View from Tehran," *New York Times*, June 26, 2002.

E. Roger Owen, *A History of Middle East Economies in the Twentieth Century* (Cambridge: Harvard University Press, 1999).

———, *State, Power, and Politics in the Making of the Modern Middle East*, 2nd ed. (London: Routledge, 2000).

George Packer, "Letter from Baghdad: War After the War," *The New Yorker*, pp. 58–85, November 24, 2003.

The Pew Global Attitudes Project, "Views of a Changing World 2003," Pew Research Center for the People and the Press, Washington, D.C., June 3, 2003.

Thomas Powers, "The Vanishing Case for War," *New York Review of Books*, pp. 12–17, December 4, 2003.

Fareed Zakaria, *The Future of Freedom: Illiberal Democracy at Home and Abroad* (New York: Norton, 2003).

• 20 •

We Are Still All Americans

Julian Borger

To cite *Le Monde* from September 2001, "We are all Americans now." This time, however, we are so, not out of sympathy but because we all feel dragged along in the wake of American domestic and foreign policy.

We could never have foretold quite how important a turning point the Florida fiasco was in the 2000 presidential election. I believe that an American government, led by the candidate who won the popular vote nationally, would have acted differently. It would have gone to war in Afghanistan after September 11. It would not have gone to war in Iraq, it would not have opted out of so many international treaties and obligations, and it would not have lurched toward unilateralism.

Some see this turn toward unilateralism and military intervention as part of a continuous trajectory starting with the Korean War and running through Vietnam, Central America, the first Gulf War, the Balkans, and finally the invasion of Iraq. They call it the "American empire in the making." But to bandy words around like "empire" suggests a sort of fatalism, and it clouds the varying nature of each juncture.

THE NATURE OF U.S. MILITARY INVOLVEMENT

The importance of not lumping together all military interventions is perhaps best illustrated by the Balkans. My point of view is very heavily influenced by spending time as a reporter in Croatia, Bosnia, and then Kosovo. I believe quite strongly that the American-led NATO intervention there was a rare instance of a just war, a war driven by morality, a morality that filtered through the public opinions in Britain and America to their respective political leaderships, which made the decisions.

Nonintervention before 1995 in Bosnia was the obscenity, as was nonintervention in Rwanda. To a certain extent we have to step aside from the post-war in Iraq to make independent and sensible decisions about what ought to be done in places like Congo and Liberia, where there are very pressing cases for American leadership. The military intervention in these circumstances does not represent neocolonialism. It represents, at best, some sort of international attempt at decency.

The Bosnia and Kosovo conflict showed that the murderous dictators who people said couldn't be stopped, and the intractable civil wars people said couldn't be stopped by external intervention, could in fact be stopped with a relatively light show of force.

In the case of Bosnia, the conflict was stopped, despite what we were told about how the Serbs kept German divisions pinned down in the Balkans for years and would have done the same to NATO. I believe one of the more promising developments of the 1990s was the reevaluation of the U.N. doctrine of nonintervention in the internal affairs of other countries, to begin to make exceptions for genocide and for other atrocities of a sufficiently high brutality.

But the just nature of the Bosnian intervention makes the Iraq war all the more depressing. In the absence of finding weapons of mass destruction, the promising and the useful principle of humanitarian intervention was exploited as a sort of stopgap, as the most cynical of fig leaves for this particular foreign adventure, which has been motivated by a mixture of oil and American domestic political paranoia.

From a humanitarian point of view, the time to intervene in Iraq would have been more than a decade ago, when Saddam Hussein embarked on genocidal campaigns against the Kurds and the Shi'a. By the time the United States and Britain went to war in Iraq, the effective deterrents against genocide were basically in place. It was a brutal dictatorship, but not necessarily worse than a score of others around the world. And if saving lives was an issue, then Congo should clearly have been at the top of the list.

The war in Iraq hasn't stopped the killing but has added to it. The war undermined the case for the future use of force, in conditions under which force might genuinely prevent another genocide or might genuinely avoid a real threat of catastrophic proliferation.

We should not turn away from foreign military involvement. Instead, we should be exerting as much energy in serious debate about intervention to stem the bloodshed in Congo and Liberia as pushing for the restoration of self-rule in Iraq. But such military intervention has to be within a broader legal and institutional framework, and this is a framework that the American administration is intent on destroying.

With the administration's backing, Congress cut off aid, in theory, to every country that failed to sign a specific exemption for American soldiers from prosecution under the International Criminal Court. The administration has not just unsigned its own treaty that established the court; it has committed itself to bullying other countries into falling into line, to try to destroy the institution.

As the world's sole superpower, the American government believes that it doesn't have to be subjected to the same rules as other countries. But unless Washington makes an effort to build some kind of new moral and legal infrastructure for the post–Cold War world under which the issues of human rights transcend borders, the military interventions it undertakes, even those with humanitarian motives (as Bosnia and Kosovo) ultimately will be doomed. American actions overseas will continue to be perceived as the self-interested whims of a global bully.

COMMUNICATING THE FAILURE IN IRAQ

In Iraq, American and British troops are stuck with the consequences of an entire litany of bad decisions. There is no choice but to pursue the current counterinsurgency against the Saddamists and the many guerrilla groups that are appearing. There is no other way now than for the Americans to fight their way out and at the same time flood the country with cash in an attempt to buy their way out.

You can't destroy a country's government and then withdraw before a genuine replacement has been built. You can't leave chaos in your wake. There is no excuse for the American failure to plan for and have a constabulary standing by. America ignored the reports about the need for a force to restore public order after the main fighting had ended. Disbanding the Iraqi army was a criminal mistake, and it cost the United States a great deal of credibility. One would have thought that the United States would have learned that lesson in Panama and the Balkans, where the lack of postcombat policing produced well-documented problems.

The flow of aid in Iraq has to be turned on properly, and the failure to pay civil servants and soldiers and show progress toward rebuilding civilian infrastructure is also a lapse of mind-boggling ineptitude. The lapse is all the more inexcusable because it was made first in Afghanistan before it was repeated in Iraq. That sort of ineptitude is inevitably going to cost the lives of American and British soldiers, not to mention Iraqi and Afghan civilians.

This point certainly has been made in Britain, but less so in America. The British stereotype is that Americans have a short, MTV attention span. But the lapses in American policy can and should be spelled out to the American citizenry and debated publicly. Americans must be made to grasp the consequences of the ineptitude in Iraq.

The daily choices made by American editors have a lot to do with the citizenry grasping the truth. In the British journalistic tradition, the newspapers do decide that we are going to have a crusade about this now, and we are going to keep on hammering about it, and it will become the news. If the *Daily Telegraph* or the *Guardian* decides to have a sustained rant about a certain subject, then it is picked up in the electronic media as well. The politicians follow. There is a different power structure between journalism and the politicians in Britain than there is in America, which is probably just a function of Britain being a much smaller country. But the potential still exists for American nongovernmental organizations to pressure mainstream media and use alternative media to point out the way American lapses have repeated themselves.

The worst outcome from the point of view of the media would be for the general public to believe that somehow Iraq had become a problem solved. This is what the American general public obviously believes about Afghanistan.

Amid the confusion and turmoil in Iraq, the important lessons of September 11 are beginning to fade, and one of those lessons was that the United States can't be insulated from the very deep ingrained anger and hopelessness that exist in the Middle East and the Arab world.

America and Western Europe can't be made safe without the investment of serious amounts of political and financial capital in the Arab world. Iraq must be stabilized and rebuilt, and demonstrably not at the expense of the Iraqi natural resources doled out to corporations that have all contributed to conservative interests and conservative election campaigns.

Iraq does have a sizeable industrial infrastructure. It has civil engineering expertise and construction companies. To continue to ignore that capacity would obviously be another in a long list of very devastating mistakes in the war and post-war.

THE ULTIMATE ISSUE: DISMANTLING THE WEST BANK SETTLEMENTS

Many American conservatives believe that the road to Jerusalem runs through Baghdad. If democracy can be established in Iraq, they reason, other Arab regimes will feel pressure to reform. Reform will promote moderate groups in Arab countries. Those groups will help force Arab countries to withdraw their support for Islamic extremism. According to this logic, Palestinian resistance to Israeli occupation then will diminish—and clear the way for a new Israeli-Palestinian equilibrium that is favorable to Israel.

This doctrine is frightening to a host of observers in the Middle East and Europe. It could pave the way for more American intervention, say in Syria. It would remove from the American government the need to seriously reengage in solving the Israeli-Palestinian conflict. Without resolution, runs the counterlogic, any move toward true democracy in the Arab world will bring Islamic extremists to power.

What really is needed is investment of White House time and political capital—to acknowledge that this Baghdad-to-Jerusalem scenario is unrealistic and to give momentum back to the Middle East peace initiative. When you talk to the staff of

Prime Minister Blair, they say the American government promised breakthroughs in the Middle East. The prime minister helped the Americans, so now the Americans must return the favor. But putting overt pressure on the Israelis now is taboo in America.

The Palestinians have reformed their administration and the military pullbacks have begun, but the ultimate ground-level issue in the Middle East is dismantling the settlements. Palestinians have to be seen on Al-Jazeera going back to their olive groves. They must be seen as going back to their family land for there to be any sense of momentum.

The importance of this single issue is hard to overstate. Given political realities, it is impossible to imagine dismantling of the settlements. On the one hand, we would be seeing Palestinians going back to the olive groves, but on the other we would be seeing Israeli settlers being ripped out of the West Bank, and that's going to be difficult. That is the bitter pill that any Israeli leader would have to swallow, and any American president standing behind that Israeli leader would have to take a whole lot of flak from his base in order to push Israel into it. As difficult as this would be, it obviously has been done before, in the Sinai, and reasonable new solutions have been proposed (see Chris Toensing's plan in chapter 17).

Without movement on the issue of settlements, Arab hatred of America will deepen and metastasize. In a way, all of this is extraordinary, because the Arab world is the most instinctively pro-American place I have ever lived. They all play basketball in Ramallah. They dream of the National Basketball Association, and they dream about American scholarships. The amount of goodwill that has been lost there is quite striking. It has to become an issue at some point because it is so directly tied to what America is facing now in the war against terrorism.

I am not saying al Qaeda is at its heart a ward of the Palestinian Liberation Organization. But it is able to live in the Middle East and the Islamic world because of the U.S. failure to do anything about Israel-Palestine over the decades. Only by going to the source of that problem are you going to begin to take al Qaeda apart.

In the long run, the only place where the tide of the American war on terror can be turned is on the hilltops of the West Bank.

These connections emerged very clearly in the public debate in Britain and in Europe. Yet they really don't figure in the public debate in America, nor are they prominent in the American media. Arguably it is not the media's job to make these connections, but the American media were happy enough to allege a connection between Saddam and al Qaeda, as well as to allege a connection between Saddam and weapons of mass destruction.

The West Bank settlements are part of the solution, and for them not to be part of the American public debate, for reasons of long-held taboos, verges on the absurd. Many politicians admit the connection but feel unable to raise the issue. At some point, the line has to be crossed. For how long can this kind of dissonance go on?

The right-of-return issue is the Palestinian equivalent of the settlement issue. But if the settlements are seriously addressed, then the mood may change and the difficult may become easier.

THE FUTURE OF TERRORISM

As David Corn observes in chapter 12, a key question is whether the Democrats will put these issues on the map. They are the underlying issues that make it more likely that at some point down the road in the next few years there will be a terrorist attack using a weapon of mass destruction.

The absence of American debate on the core Israeli-Palestinian issue represents a very serious dysfunction in American political life which could literally have catastrophic consequences for Americans and Brits and Europeans and Iraqis and Afghans.

At the end of the day, *Le Monde* was right. We are still all Americans.

BIBLIOGRAPHY

Julian Borger, "Bush Keeps Faith with the Hawks," the *Guardian Weekly*, January 29–February 4, 2004.

———, "It's the Intelligence Deficit, Stupid," the *Guardian Weekly*, February 5–11, 2004.

———, "The Spies Who Pushed for War," *Guardian Unlimited*, July 17, 2003.

———, "U.S. Puts New Bad Guys in the Picture," *Guardian Unlimited*, February 12, 2003.

———, "U.S. Turns Ally into Enemy," the *Guardian*, August 28, 2003.

———, "We are All Americans Now," headline, *Le Monde*, September 12, 2003.

III

FAILURE IN AMERICAN ECONOMIC POLICY—AND STRATEGIC ALTERNATIVES

• 21 •

The Financial, Political, and Moral Deficits of the American Empire

Jeff Faux

In 1965, when we were ratcheting up our intervention in Vietnam, Lyndon Johnson said we had enough resources for both "guns and butter." In response, the great American journalist Walter Lippmann wrote a column in which he said that he didn't know whether we had enough *financial* capital for both, but he was sure we didn't have enough *political* and *moral* capital to fight a war in Vietnam and a war on poverty. He turned out to be absolutely right.

Economic historians still debate Johnson's decision not to raise taxes to pay for the war in Vietnam and thus to continue the illusion that the war could be paid for without any inconvenience. But clearly we did not have enough political capital to fight both a foreign and a domestic war at the same time.

In the early twenty-first century, the war and post-war in Iraq have diverted money from domestic spending. But we should all be clear and remember that this "diversion" didn't start with September 11 or when we decided to go to war against Iraq. The erosion of domestic spending in public investment for such things as jobs, public health, public education, and physical infrastructure started a long time ago. The process has been led by Republicans but abetted by many Democrats. Indeed, I would date the beginning of this trend to the second half of Jimmy Carter's term.

When Bill Clinton said the "era of big government is over," he was *not* telling the truth; certainly, our defense apparatus is as "big government" as you can possibly get. Of course, we all know that he wasn't talking about the big *military* being over but rather any big effort to deal with our domestic problems. The effect was to take the heart out of a serious domestic agenda. So the erosion of the domestic public sector is not something that just started; we face a long-term crisis in the funding of public-investment programs that make the economy stronger, distribute the wealth more equitably, and provide opportunities for people at the bottom.

The present economic problem is the burden of sustaining a continued role as the world's policeman, dedicated to repressing any movement, anywhere in the world that appears to threaten the hegemonic authority of American business and political elites. This policy was set out in the American government's September 2002 National Security Strategy.

It is true that we reconstructed Germany and Japan after World War II. But they were both first-world nations to begin with. Since then, the U.S. record has been dismal. Just look at conditions in our backyard—Central America and the Caribbean. A half-century after the Eisenhower government overthrew the democratically elected government in Guatemala, that country is an economic and social basket case.

Look also at our experience in Iran in the 1970s. The Central Intelligence Agency engineered a coup against the previous government and then championed the new Shah as a great modernizer. First on the agenda was modernizing agriculture, turning over small farms to agribusiness. This resulted in uprooting masses of people from their villages and sending them to the cities, where they became bitter, impoverished supporters of radical Islam. We don't seem to have learned anything from that experience. As a matter of fact, the discussions about how to rebuild Iraq and what to do in Afghanistan seem to me more simplistic today than the discussion was in 1978.

The United States has neither the financial capital nor the moral capital to pursue the National Security Strategy of September 2002. Pursuing that strategy would eventually require a substantial sacrifice by the American middle class. And that, of course, is the political trigger. Sadly, we have long since learned that what you do to poor people has limited political consequences. However, when you start touching the security of the middle class in a sustained way, then there is trouble.

MORTGAGING THE FUTURE

It is, in part, a matter of simple arithmetic. The government's tax cuts of recent years are already mortgaging the future. If the tax cuts were to remain, by 2011 they would require an 80 percent cut in all domestic programs of the federal government, most of which affect the middle class. That is politically impossible. Our political system is headed for a crash just on the budgetary track alone.

The tax-cut burdens would come on top of problems that this economy already has. Currently the American economy is floating on a consumer-spending bubble. As the government admonished us to do, we went to the malls after September 11, and we are still shopping. We are still shopping because we are still borrowing. Consumer credit is at an all-time high, and it continues to grow. It is a matter of simple arithmetic that people cannot forever continue to buy at a rate that rises faster than their income.

Unfortunately, the stock market bubble of the 1990s will not come back for a long time. It takes decades before investors forget the pain of seeing some $10 trillion in assets disappear. It also takes a long, long time before the overinvestment in excess capacity that was created by the stock market boom gets absorbed. Moreover, the conditions that created the corporate scandals associated with the deflated stock market have not been cleaned up. Some fines have been levied and promises to behave better have been made, but very little has been done to change the basic regulations that govern corporate finance in America. The problems remain, and investors know that. Whatever happens to the stock market, it is not going to go back to the levels that we saw in the late 1990s for a long time.

For a while, the unsustainable boom of the last half of the 1990s hid the general job and financial insecurity that has been spreading throughout the United States over many years. Economic mobility in America has been declining, not just for people in poverty but for average working people whose jobs are insecure, whose health care is insecure, whose education for their children is insecure. Access to education tells us a lot about the kind of society we are building. The price of a college education is going up very rapidly. As a result, we are beginning to see the creation, or the re-creation, of class divisions as children become more trapped in the conditions of their parents. A recent study showed that 65 percent of the difference in income among people of the same generation is now explained by the income of their parents. That is, if you grow up poor, you have a 65 percent chance of remaining poor. The same study compared mobility in the United States with European countries that the media tell us have societies flooded with welfare that undercuts economic mobility. Yet welfare states like Finland and Sweden have greater economic mobility than the United States.

Another economic issue that is emerging is the chronic balance-of-payments problem. U.S. trade deficits are growing every year. The U.S. savings rate is very low, so we are not able to finance our own deficits. We are financing the deficits by borrowing and selling assets overseas. You don't have to be a Ph.D. in economics to understand that you cannot keep borrowing forever in order to consume.

Before the mid-1980s, we were paying for the trade deficits with income and wealth derived from foreign investments abroad. But as the deficits continued, our national liabilities have outpaced our assets. The United States' foreign debt now covers about 22 percent of our gross domestic product. Goldman Sachs thinks it is going to be 40 percent in another three or four years. This, too, is unsustainable.

Just as there has been little reform of domestic financial markets, there has been little reform of global financial markets. After the global financial crisis of 1997, many assertions were made about international rules to prevent the flow of short-term "hot money" from destabilizing, vulnerable economies. Little of significance has been changed, but the Bush administration's security agenda simply assumes away these vulnerabilities.

Recent American policy also has assumed that the economic policies pursued with such vigor by the International Monetary Fund, the World Bank, and the U.S. Treasury over the last two decades are paths to prosperity and democracy. Yet by any reasonable measures they have failed. Global growth in the last twenty years has been half of what it was in the previous twenty years. Distribution of income *among* countries has worsened, and the evidence suggests that by and large the distribution of income and wealth *within* countries has also worsened. So in terms of what was promised, in terms of what would be a sensible evaluation of any kind of program, our present global development policy of socialism for the rich and free enterprise for the poor has not worked.

So we have underlying economic problems that will make us—in the long term—unable to afford the kind of empire that the administration wants to impose. We can't afford both empire and democracy.

SENSIBLE ECONOMIC POLICIES

Economics is not as complicated as economists would like us to think it is, and a sensible set of economic policies is not a great mystery. We pretty much know what we need to do to make the American economy work better. We need to repeal the tax cuts of recent years; we need to have national health care; we need to have a long-term energy plan; and we especially need to help state and local governments. A list of common-sense policies wouldn't take three minutes to compile.

Globally, we need a grand bargain between nations of the North and South, in which the South accepts enforceable human rights and labor standards appropriate to different levels of development and the North accepts an obligation for sustained capital investment in these countries.

We also need coordinated economic policies among the major economies—especially Europe, Japan, and the United States—in order to expand and sustain global demand.

Putting policies on paper is not difficult; the *politics* are the problem. In the United States we have a two-party system, but one party, the Democratic Party, is not working. It is a dysfunctional institution.

One of the measures of a dysfunctional institution is that it does not act on what it knows.

For example, the leadership of the Democratic Party knew early in 2001 that the Republicans were going to try to co-opt their economic issues with a tax cut, which was called a "job stimulus." The Democrats were passive, and the Republicans got credit for sending a $300 rebate to every taxpayer.

The experience taught the Democrats that they needed an economic program for the November 2002 election. But they couldn't come up with anything meaningful. As one congressional staffer said, "Yes, we had a lot of these meetings, but every time somebody came up with a good idea, it was turned down—because it was either going to cost money or offend some political contributor." If these are the criteria the Democrats use to guide alternative economic policy, all the meetings and task forces in the world will not help them.

THE DOMESTIC CONSEQUENCES OF THE QUEST FOR EMPIRE

Building on these economic and political assessments, let us turn to the American quest for empire and its domestic consequences. Specifically, in this section I want to suggest that viable alternatives to the empire's domestic policy have not been offered; an alternative plan to address fear has not been articulated; domestic support in America for imperialism is not new; the domestic benefits of empire accrue to the ruling class and corporations; and there is a domestic limit to the empire's resources.

Viable Alternatives to the Empire's Domestic Policy Have Not Been Offered

Some Democrats are hoping that the postwar occupation of Iraq goes away and that the issue of the United States in the world goes away—so that they can get back to talking about the economy.

But this will not be so easy; for one thing, the Republicans are systematically taking domestic issues away from the Democrats. Take education, for example. The polls still show that people think the Democrats are a little better on this issue. But the Democrats have to be a *lot* better.

Along similar lines, Republicans got credit for the recent Medicare bill. I think this Medicare bill was a mistake on many counts. It was ineffective, and whatever benefits were provided will not appear until 2006. Moreover, it was designed to open the door to privatization. Yet there is an impression in the mind of much of the public that the Medicare legislation was a step forward. So some of the issues which many people thought would help the Democrats may be off the table or at least neutralized.

What we learned in 2002 was that fear trumped the economy. The Democrats repeated to themselves, "It's the economy, stupid." That was true in 1992 and 1996, and it should have been true in 2000. Unfortunately, it was not.

But remember, in the election of 2002, the United States had lost two million jobs in two years. There was a huge corporate scandal that involved crooked CEOs, which voters tend to identify more with Republicans than with Democrats; yet the Democrats lost the Senate, did not win back the House, and generally had a poor day.

An Alternative Plan to Address Fear Has Not Been Articulated

Part of the problem is that Democrats have no real story that deals with the fear that has permeated the electorate since September 11. Their domestic story about security is "spend more money." It is probably true that we should spend more money. Certainly we shouldn't be spending *less* money to help the states and localities deal with issues of homeland security. But it is hardly a dramatic and winning program to propose simply increasing the budget. The average voter doesn't have the time or information to sort out the exact budgetary needs.

The international story the Democrats had recently was also problematic. In effect, most had agreed it was a good idea to invade Iraq. Their criticism was that the American government's attempts at diplomacy failed to get enough international support. Actually, however, when you think of the circumstances, the American government did pretty well at diplomacy. The majority of the British people were against the war, yet we got Tony Blair to come out and support it. The majority of the Spanish people were against the war, yet the United States got President Aznar to agree to come out and support it. The proposition that the problem was diplomacy, rather than policy, has not been very convincing for the average American citizen.

If you believe that Saddam Hussein was a direct threat to the United States, what difference did it make in the end if the United Nations supported the war or not, or if anybody else supported it or not? If it was justified for the United States to make this unprovoked and preemptive strike on another country, violating international law, then what difference did it make what kind of coalition we put together? The typical American citizen doesn't believe that the United Nations is going to protect him or her from al Qaeda. So, if you agree with conservatives that the war has made Americans safer, whether America had a coalition or not is quibbling around the edges for most voters.

In part, that's why a majority of Americans still support what we did in Iraq. You don't have a fundamental debate among the elites on this issue. Many American elites—Democrats as well as Republicans—agree with the notion that the United States is responsible for the world and have convinced Americans that the only way that you can be protected against another September 11 is to have the U.S. military crush everything suspicious that moves. In the absence of any other framework, like the one Gary Hart proposes in chapter 2, why not? The present framework also obviously happens to be a road to wealth and power for the ruling class.

For other Western elites, there are advantages to the United States being responsible for the world. Europeans, for example, don't have to spend so much money on defense. For the developing world elites, it's an opportunity for access to American wealth and power, just as during the Cold War, the U.S. government was willing to spend money in order to get their support. The United States is now doing the same in its demand to be exempt from the authority of the international court.

There is no reason for any other government in the world to support this demand except money—in the form of military and economic aid.

Domestic Support in America for Imperialism Is Not New

The American imperialism of recent years is built on the past. It didn't arrive in 2001. For a long time the Cold War motivated the United States to take an aggressive posture in the world. It overthrew governments in Iran, Guatemala, Chile, Indonesia, and other countries. Morally right or wrong, effective or not, these actions were supported by most Americans as essential in the war against communism. The Cold War has been over for more than ten years, but the imperial habits of the American policy class did not disappear. During the 1990s, its imperial habits continued in an economic forum. The use of the International Monetary Fund and the World Bank, the creation of the World Trade Organization, and the passage of the North American Free Trade Agreement were all efforts of the U.S. government to impose certain social, political, and economic forms on other countries.

The kind of imperialism that Bob Rubin and Bill Clinton pursued is much different from the more recent kind of imperialism we have seen; it is less violent, gets us into less trouble, didn't get us into quagmires, and we could get out. We could pull the money, write off the loan. But this form of imperialism is not necessarily morally superior to the other. For example, when Clinton's Secretary of State, Madeleine Albright, was asked on public television about the 500,000 children who were estimated to have died in Iraq during the sanctions, she replied, without hesitating, "We think it's worth it."

Much poverty, massive suffering, and social dislocation arise from our self-declared right as a superpower to impose our will on the rest of the world, even before 2001. It helps answer the question of why the Democrats are so ambivalent on Iraq and the issue of empire. It's because much of their policy establishment agrees with it. They might not like the tactics, the crudeness at the United Nations, and the boycotts of French wine, but basically they agree.

The Benefits of Empire Accrue to the Ruling Class and Corporations

It is important to distinguish political interests and class interests in politics. Politics, as a famous American political scientist once said, is a question of "who gets what," and you can't understand that unless you have an understanding of who is who.

We understand this issue a lot better in the domestic realm. Any observer of American politics can see, at least in broad strokes, the interests of labor, capital, poor people, and the middle class. They can understand the interests of coal companies and agriculture, the interests of California and Maine. But when it comes to foreign affairs we don't have the information and language that allows us to identify class issues. Open up any newspaper or magazine and you will read the phrase "United States interests" or "national interests" over and over. When it comes to thinking about the globe, there is just one unit of analysis, and that's the country. Yet our experience of domestic politics is that there are important agendas that cross subnational state and city borders. They used to say, "Politics stops at the water's edge," and when you're at war, that certainly makes sense. But in a globalized economy, where capital and ownership and economic and financial interests are transnational, does it make sense for us to still assume that there is a rock-bottom thing called "American interests" that covers all or most Americans?

Several years ago, American public television aired *Commanding Heights*, a program based on Daniel Yergin's book. One segment was about the expansion of trade, and Laura Tyson, Bill Clinton's chair of the Council of Economic Advisors, was interviewed. She said the reason the Clinton administration wanted to expand trade was to give "our" corporations access to other markets.

If you are the typical American viewer, that might sound pretty good. You might assume that helping our corporations would also help you. Yet look at how our corporations think of themselves. As long ago as 1959, a Ford Motor Company executive said in a Senate hearing, "Well, Senator, we're not exactly a United States corporation. When we're in the United States, we're a United States corporation. When we're in Germany, we're a German corporation. When we're in Brazil, we're a Brazilian corporation."

The disconnect between economic institutions that have seemingly American names and the way that they operate in the world is not a secret. You can read *Business Week*, read the *Wall Street Journal*, and talk to businesspeople. They see the world as their market. They see the world as the place where they produce, and they may or may not be headquartered in the United States. If they are located here, they may or may not be in another ten years. Their words, their own speeches, clearly indicate that they think of themselves as world corporations.

So what does it mean that the U.S. government is protecting "our" corporations? This language creates an illusion of a linkage between the interests of American citizens and multinational corporations that has been broken for years. It obscures the class issues attendant on a globalizing economy. Here in North America, for example, we have one common market covering the United States, Canada, and Mexico. In this common market, is it so clear that the interests of the average Mexican worker are closer to the interests of the average Mexican billionaire than they are to the average American or Canadian worker?

In our domestic political discourse, we recognize class interests, but this sort of analysis stops at the borders. Yet the *Economist*, *Business Week*, and the *Financial Times* tell us we are increasingly living in a borderless society. If that is true, then we must start thinking about class interests in a way that is different.

The assumption that global politics is just a function of nation-state interests has obscured the influence of the oil business in our invasion of Iraq. This may not be the only reason we went to war in Iraq, but I will assert that it was one reason. When you ask the typical American voter about this, they are a little embarrassed that we've gone to war to secure this oil and make sure that we can run our sport-utility vehicles and air conditioners and other wasteful uses of energy. But the conclusion usually is that we may be wasteful, but that is just who we are. From this selfish perspective, it appears that there was a national interest in securing Iraqi oil.

In fact, there is a world market for oil. After the 1970s, the Organization of Petroleum Exporting Countries understood that the oil in Saudi Arabia, Venezuela, Iraq, and everywhere else had no value unless it could be sold to consumers in the United States, Western Europe, and elsewhere. The companies that end up expanding Iraqi oil production are not going to earmark it for American customers. They will sell it to whoever will pay the price. Thus, to the extent that oil was a motivating factor for the invasion of Iraq, it was about securing oil and the opportunity to sell oil for people who are in the oil business—those whom Laura Tyson would include as "our" corporations. Any benefit for the average American voter or consumer is purely coincidental.

The decision to invade Iraq was not just motivated by economics. Power itself is a motivator. But again—power for whom? It makes some Americans excited to watch American power demonstrated on television. But who actually gets to exercise that power? Typically, it's the people who are part of the policy establishment. The secretary of defense dominates any room in the world when he walks in because he represents American power, the American Army, and the American Treasury. At a conference in Germany during the Cold War a German businessman said to me, "Don't ever forget that when General Electric walks into the room, the Sixth Fleet walks in with it." Economic and military power are connected.

But what power does the average American citizen get from all this? The benefits of the game of empire for the average American in whose "interests" all this is being pursued are slender, but the costs are great: job opportunities lost, taxes to pay now or later. The American government may retain the recent tax cuts, but the average American, of this and the following generation, will pay through the nose for those cuts. Already, older people are stretched because of the high price of prescription drugs and the lack of national health care. It has been four decades since the Head Start program began, and less than half of all eligible poor children are funded. And now the typical American is earning the world's hatred to boot.

A decent American society would be one in which everyone has access to affordable health care and everyone has access to a decent house. A society that could deliver those simple things is really incompatible with the notion of American empire, both the Republican version and the Democratic version.

The United States is not going to change from the outside. It's really up to everybody who is an American to change it or it will not be changed. Iraq is a wakeup call for how dangerous it can be when elites are allowed to pursue their own interests and cover up their agendas with rhetoric about natural interests and the myth of American exceptionalism.

There Is a Domestic Limit to the Empire's Resources

A while back *Harper's* published an article titled "The Romance of Empire." It is worth reading. The author, Thomas de Zengotita, started off with a quote from an American general saying to the effect that "Of course we can take over this country. We are Americans."

I know what it feels like to think that we Americans are different from everyone else—to think that we are more competent, honest, and moral. And to think that therefore only America can secure the world. This is arrogant and dangerous, both for us and for the world. It's dangerous for us because we do not have the resources or the will to do what we boast that we will do.

After the invasion of Iraq, an American general said it was going to take hundreds of thousands of troops to pacify Iraq. The reaction from the American government was "that's nonsense." Years ago I spoke to a military man about an invasion of Cuba. He said we would need 500,000 troops just to occupy that relatively small island that is only about ninety miles from Key West. I don't know what our resource needs eventually will amount to in Iraq, but this is a huge undertaking; and it was undertaken under the obscurity and the fog of this notion of American exceptionalism.

It is also dangerous for the world because we don't have the knowledge and ability to absorb other cultures and other situations in the world. After the North American Free Trade Agreement was passed, Jorge Castaneda, who later became the foreign minister of Mexico, wrote a book about it. He's a very smart guy and very pro-American. He said Americans never understood Mexican history, Mexican culture, and Mexican economics. If we don't understand Mexico, what do we know about Afghanistan? What do we know about Iraq? We're full of observations about what it's going to take, what's good for other people, how they'll absorb democracy, how we're going to teach people in the Middle East to buy and sell—people who have been buying and selling for thousands of years. But there's a limit to our resources, there's a limit to the will of our people, and there's a limit to our own capacity.

HOW THE HELL DID THIS HAPPEN?

How do we start weaning America's politics away from this imperial mindset? We need a counter-story of how America lives in the world that addresses the September 11 fears. We need to start the debate we never had after September 11, which was, "How the hell did this happen?"

It is impressive, the way the conservative propaganda machine shut down that conversation right after September 11. "We don't want to talk about *why* this happened," we were told by the talking heads from one end of the country to the other. All we had to know is that the people who did this were evil. If you take the word "evil" seriously, it has no historical context. It is just there. It has no past, it has no future, it's just evil. This view precluded any kind of a serious discussion, and in fact those who did question it were accused of being unpatriotic and undermining the troops. The unresolved question of why September 11 happened is poisoning our body politic. We need to ask ourselves why that happened.

One theme of this book is the need for communicating better with average citizens. Robert McChesney, John Nichols, Amy Goodman, and Eric Alterman propose new media policy in part V. That policy must include an honest discussion about government.

One telling anecdote that illustrates this issue. During the television debates in the 2000 election between Gore and Bush, George Bush turned to the audience several times, pointed at Al Gore, and said something like, "This man thinks that the government can spend your money better than you can. I'm for giving *you* the money, putting it in your pocket." What was instructive about this was not what Bush said, but what Gore *didn't* say. Gore did not respond by framing what the public sector does but rather attempted to change the subject. Gore could have said, "So, Mr. Bush, do you want us to take back the money we spend on the military? Social Security? Medicare?" Or he could have said, "How many of you want to take an elevator to the thirty-fifth floor that hasn't been inspected by the government? How many of you want to go to the supermarket and buy meat that hasn't been inspected by the government?" But he said none of these things and let Bush take the upper hand on the issue.

Another lesson is from the health care debate in the 1990s. The conservatives accused the Clinton administration of involving the government in health care, and typically the Clinton spokesperson would deny this, pointing instead to the proposed special corporations that would be set up to administer the health plan. The spokesperson then proceed to describe a scheme that became unbelievably complicated and incredible in detail—all to hide the truth that the government would indeed have run the health care system. By trying to conceal the government's role, they made the public suspicious. The public sensed their lack of conviction.

A NEW STORY ABOUT HOW AMERICA CAN LIVE IN THE WORLD

If we ever want to provide an alternative to the current policies on foreign and domestic issues, we must go back to showing how alternatives to present policy will mean a better, more secure life for the average American. We must communicate how the recent tax cuts are redistributing income to the benefit of the rich. And we must communicate how that shift to the rich will limit the good life for the middle class. Most of all, we need to have a new story about how America can live in this world, how we can deal with the fear from September 11.

We have to start imagining the United States *not* responsible for the world. We have to start imagining the United States pulling back from this arrogant notion that we can make the world safe for democracy and free enterprise. A more inward-looking America would be a good thing for the world. There are some common-sense questions that we ought to start to ask. Why are we still in NATO, years after the end of the Cold War? We have some 80,000 troops in Germany. What are they doing there? Who is it that we are protecting Europe from? Already the productivity of five European countries is higher than that of the United States. Does Europe now, with an economic community that is going to be larger than the United States, need our protection? What are we doing with 40,000 troops in Korea? Don't China and Japan have an interest in keeping North Korea from invading South Korea? Why are we fighting a civil war in Colombia? Certainly not to keep drugs from coming here; some of the people we are helping are themselves in the illegal drug business.

This is not isolationism. We live in a big world. We are now in a common market with Canada and Mexico. The problem is we have no social contract. We have become responsible for doing something about the condition of our neighbor, Mexico, where 45 percent of the people live on less than $2 a day. Why isn't the development of our own neighborhood our international project? Certainly what goes on in Mexico has a greater impact on the average American citizen than what goes on in many, many other places.

A less assertive America in the world would be a better citizen. We would pay our dues to the United Nations without demanding that all its agencies do exactly what we want them to do. We should join the international court and give it the authority that an international court needs to have.

There are lots of ways we can be in the world that do not involve chasing the imperial will-o'-the-wisp. For all of our establishment's bravado about being responsible for the world, the United States ranks twentieth among the major countries in terms of foreign aid.

Is a more inward America politically viable? It is said that people love war and that they love to wave the flag. Yet Richard Nixon won the election of 1968 promising to end the war in Vietnam, and Dwight Eisenhower won the election of 1952 promising to end the war in Korea. We shouldn't assume that war is always popular.

If the goal of America in the next twenty years is to change the world, the average American citizen has virtually no role to play except to pay taxes, support the troops, and shut up. You can join the army or maybe join the Peace Corps, which is a lot more dangerous today than it was ten years ago, but that's just about it.

We need to start building another conversation in this country. We need a national dialogue about what America ought to be twenty years from now, a conversation that includes what cities and neighborhoods ought to be like. And once you start asking what we should be like, you bring "we" back into the conversation in a healthy way.

Right now, most Americans think about the future in a very personal way. They don't ask, "How can I change it?" They ask, "How can I survive it?" People want forecasts so that they can make the right investments, or so they can live in the right cities, or so they can make the right career choices. It's all important, but we need to bring back a notion of the future as something that *we* can create.

During the 200th anniversary of the Declaration of Independence, in 1976, there were a series of efforts around the United States to ask the question, "What will our town, what will our state, what will our city be like in the year 2000?" There were projects called California 2000, Atlanta 2000, and Chicago 2000. They had different names, but they got people together and asked this very, very important question about what they thought about the future.

Some of the activities were no more than Chamber of Commerce boosterism. Some of them were about land-use planning. Some got into questions of race, gender, poverty, access to services, and so on. The Carter administration funded some of this. It wasn't very costly, and I think it's time to revive the meetings. We don't have to do it exactly the same way, but the spirit, the notion of having a national discussion of where this country ought to be would reveal the incompatibility between the direction this country is now headed in the world and what it is that Americans want.

Let's do a thought experiment for a moment. Imagine Al Gore as president of the United States. Imagine hundreds of Americans dead in the period after the administration declared the war in Iraq over. Imagine two million jobs lost since Gore was elected president. Imagine a trillion-dollar surplus evaporating into a $500 billion deficit. Imagine that he obviously misled the American people about the reasons for going to war. Imagine that his friends were getting huge war-profiteering contracts. Imagine that his CEO pals were guilty of ripping off pension funds, and he systematically refused to reform the financial markets.

Al Gore's impeachment would be a daily topic of conversation. He would be ripped to shreds in America with this record. Against Clinton's peccadillo—that in the end, the American people clearly didn't care about—we are talking about first-class reasons here for an impeachment process. Yet Congress will not act.

Nor is Congress likely to act on a constitutional amendment that limits campaign contributions. But we need to continue to press the issue as a long-run strategy. Clearly, public financing is not working. What we need is a mindset that asserts our rights as citizens, our right to be in this debate, our right to take umbrage, and our right to be outrageous, just the way the ruling class does. Until we do that, it will be very, very hard for us to get a real alternative before the American people.

The time has come, I think, for a real opposition to empire. We don't need to do empire better, to get more allies better, to be smoother politically and diplomatically. We need a better idea than empire of how America ought to be in the world.

BIBLIOGRAPHY

Madeleine Albright, "We Think the Price is Worth It," *60 Minutes* interview, May 12, 1996.

Jorge Castaneda, *The Mexican Shock: Its Meaning for the United States* (New York: New Press, 1995).

Jeff Faux, "Fast Track to Trade Deficits: Mushrooming Foreign Debt Begs For Strategic Pause Before Approving New Agreements," Economic Policy Institute Issue Brief No. 170, Washington, D.C., November, 2001.

———, *The Party's Not Over: A New Vision for the Democrats* (New York: Basic Books, 1996).

———, coeditor, *Reclaiming Prosperity: A Blueprint for Progressive Economic Reform* (Washington: Economic Policy Institute, 1996).

——— and Marjorie Allen, "American Labor's Stake in Cuba's Future," *Working USA*, January-February 1999.

United States Department of State, "The National Security Strategy of the United States of America," International Information Programs, Washington, D.C., September, 2002. http://usinfo.state.gov/topical/pol/terror/secstrat.htm.

Daniel Yergin and Joseph Stanislaw, *The Commanding Heights: The Battle for the World Economy* (New York: Free Press, 2002).

Thomas de Zengotita, "The Romance of Empire and the Politics of Self-Love," *Harper's*, July 1, 2003.

• *22* •

The Coming Budget Crisis and the Rising Threat of Large-Scale Federal Disinvestment

Robert Greenstein

If the recent tax cuts are continued and made permanent, they ultimately will take a large toll on the federal budget and affect an array of services important to both the middle class and the poor.

The purpose of the present chapter is to spell out the unprecedented challenges the federal budget faces and to call for a common-sense debate on federal budget priorities as they affect average Americans and those who are less fortunate.

WHERE ARE WE HEADING?

Where is the federal budget headed? A starting point in answering this question is the well-known fact that when the baby-boom generation retires, costs will go up for Social Security and Medicare. Baby-boomers are people born between 1946 and 1964. They are numerous. When they retire, Social Security and Medicare will cost more. The cost of Medicaid long-term care also will rise.

From 2000 to 2030, Social Security and Medicare costs will increase by more than 5 percent of gross domestic product—that is, by more than 5 percent of the size of the U.S. economy (see fig. 22.1). This increase is larger than the U.S. defense budget.

So the nation faces a challenge: How do we navigate our way through the period of the boomers' retirement, meeting our promises to the elderly, without severely squeezing the rest of the budget as the cost of the programs for the elderly rises?

At the start of 2001, it was projected that over the next ten years we would be spending about $700 billion in interest payments on the national debt. Estimates from early 2004 suggest we are more likely to spend about $2.5 trillion on interest

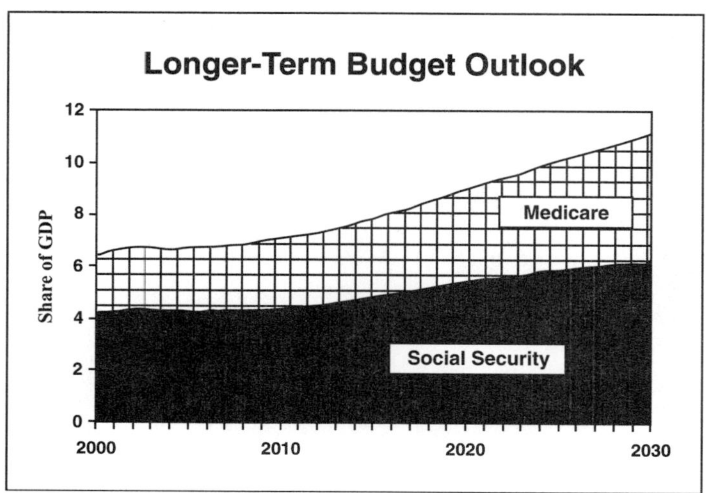

Source: Congressional Budget Office
Figure 22.1.

payments over the 2002–2011 period, or $1.8 trillion *more* than was projected three years earlier (see fig. 22.2). We are now on a course under which interest payments on the debt will rise to and then surpass $300 billion a year and will exceed $450 billion a year by 2014. Combined with the increases in Social Security and Medicare costs, this threatens to leave less room in the budget for everything else.

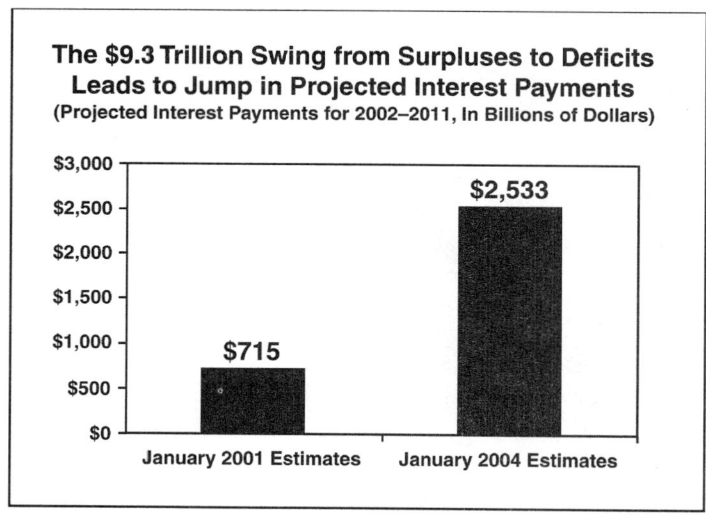

Source: Congressional Budget Office
Figure 22.2.

In short, there will be more elderly people, and while there will inevitably be some changes in Social Security and Medicare, costs for these programs are going to rise substantially. At the same time, the nation has a variety of serious unmet needs—44 million people without health insurance, environmental problems, educational inadequacies, and decaying infrastructure, among other issues. How are we going to address these unmet needs and still meet the needs of a growing elderly population in future decades?

A logical answer would seem to include the basic point that, among other things, we are going to need to raise more revenue because we will have more expenditures with the aging of the population. Instead, fiscal policy is moving in the opposite direction.

THE 2001 TAX CUT

If you listen to popular descriptions of the 2001 tax cut, you often hear that tax cut described by its proponents as "moderate and prudent" in size, and you hear the figure that it cost $1.35 trillion over ten years. But the "official" cost estimate of the tax cut enacted in 2001 is $1.35 trillion only because of a series of slow phase-ins and artificial expiration dates that camouflage part of the law's ultimate cost.

What we want to look at is the cost of the 2001 tax cut *when it is fully in effect.* It has been proposed that the tax cut be made permanent. What would that cost?

As figure 22.3 indicates, when the 2001 tax cut is fully in effect, its annual cost will equal more than three times everything the federal government spends on education at

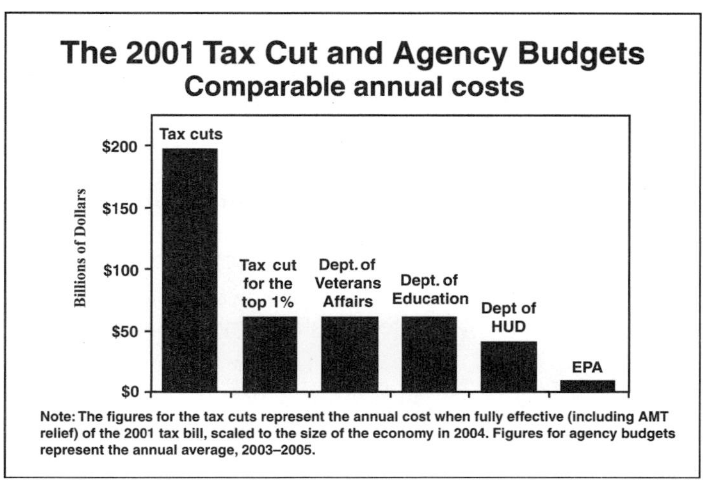

Source: Center on Budget and Policy Priorities
Figure 22.3.

Annual Cost of Tax Cut Compared to Agency Budgets

When fully in effect, the annual cost of the tax cut will be:

- Five times as large as the budget of the Department of Housing and Urban Development
- Three times as large as the budget of the Department of Education
- More than three times the Department of Veterans Affairs and Department of Transportation budgets
- Twenty-four times larger than the EPA budget

Source: Center on Budget and Policy Priorities
Figure 22.4.

the elementary, secondary, and higher education levels combined, or five times everything the federal government spends on housing and urban development, or twenty-four times the entire Environmental Protection Agency budget. If you look at the second bar in figure 22.3, you also see that when the tax cut is fully in effect the cost of just the portion of the tax cut going to the top 1 percent of the population will be as large as what the federal government spends on education at all levels.

So this is not a small tax cut; it is a very large one. Figures 22.4 and 22.5 can help provide some perspectives.

Here is another way to get one's mind around the size of the 2001 tax cut. Within the Washington Beltway, some of the same people who describe the 2001

Annual Cost of Tax Cuts for the Top 1 Percent Compared to Agency Budgets

When fully in effect, the annual cost of the tax cut for the top 1 percent of filers will be:

- Twice the budget of the Department of Housing and Urban Development
- Larger than the department of Veterans Affairs and Department of Transportation budgets
- As large as the Department of Education budget
- Nearly nine times as large as the EPA budget

Source: Center on Budget and Policy Priorities
Figure 22.5.

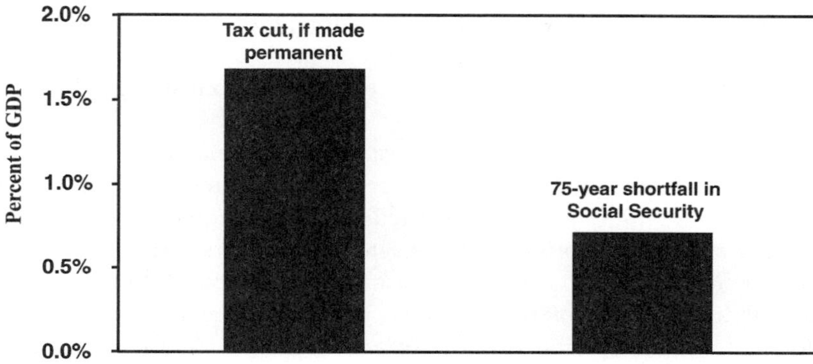

All figures are "net present values" of cost from 2002–2076. Estimates of the tax cut assume all provisions are permanent (including ATM relief) and grow only with the economy after 2011.

Source: Center on Budget and Policy Priorities
Figure 22.6.

tax cut as "moderate and prudent" tell us that we have a massive shortfall ahead of us in Social Security.

The Social Security shortfall is typically measured over a seventy-five-year period. By contrast, the cost of the tax cut is usually given over a ten-year period. So let us compare apples to apples. Take the cost of the tax cut and ask how its cost over seventy-five years, if it is made permanent, compares with the Social Security shortfall over the same seventy-five year period. The cost of the 2001 tax cut over the next seventy-five years is more than twice the seventy-five-year Social Security shortfall, as figure 22.6 illustrates.

POLICY RESPONSES TO A WORSENING FISCAL OUTLOOK

Faced with these developments, what might policymakers do? Consider a historical analogy. Twenty years apart, two conservative Republican present or former governors ran for president with the centerpiece of their platforms being a large tax cut: Ronald Reagan in 1980 and George W. Bush in 2000. Both won. Both pursued their tax cuts. Both delivered. Their tax cuts were both passed by the middle of their first year in office.

For other reasons, by their second year in office in both cases, the nation was in a recession, and a combination of factors, including the tax cuts, had led to a dramatically changed fiscal situation, with large deficits looming for years.

We sometimes forget that Bob Dole and Howard Baker, in their leadership roles in a Republican Senate, responded in 1982 by crafting the Tax Equity and Fiscal Responsibility Act of 1982, which Ronald Reagan signed and which had the effect of canceling out the equivalent of about 30 percent of the tax cut Reagan had secured the previous year.[1]

We sometimes also forget that, in Ronald Reagan's final seven years in office, he did not pursue large additional tax cuts that were not paid for. His big tax-reform initiative in the mid-1980s included large reductions in income tax rates, especially in the higher rates. But he proposed those rate reductions as part of a tax-overhaul proposal that closed enough tax breaks so that the Tax Reform Act of 1986 was revenue neutral. It did not shrink the federal government's revenue base.

Now fast-forward twenty years. In 2000, George W. Bush also campaigned on a big tax cut. He was elected and got his tax cut enacted. In fairly short order, for a variety of reasons, the fiscal picture worsened dramatically. Was his prescription like the one that Republican leaders pursued twenty years ago? It was not. In fact, it was the reverse. Essentially, it was to pass more tax cuts without paying for them.

New tax-cut legislation was signed into law in May 2003 with an official cost of $350 billion. Many newspapers have reported that the ultimate cost of the legislation is likely to be at least $660 billion. Figure 22.7 shows where that figure

Cost of Bill Through 2013 If Tax Cuts Are Extended

(In billions of dollars)

Dividend and capital gains [expires 2008]	$325
Top bracket rate reductions	74
Child tax credit [expires 2004]	90
10% bracket [expires 2004]	45
Tax breaks for married couples [expires 2004]	55
Expand Sec 179 business expensing [expires 2005]	35
Increase AMT exemption [expires 2004]	18
State fiscal relief	20
TOTAL	$662

Source: Center on Budget and Policy Priorities
Figure 22.7.

comes from. All of the provisions except one in the 2003 tax-cut law had artificial expiration dates (many being December 31, 2004). What appeared to be envisioned is that anyone who ran for election in 2004 saying that he or she did not want to extend these tax cuts beyond December 2004 would be met with attack ads labeling him or her as a tax increaser. If, as many expect, all of these tax cuts are extended, the cost of the new tax-cut law would turn out to be $660 billion over the ten-year period.

THE IMPLICATIONS OF THE TAX CUTS

What are these tax cuts likely to mean for the role of the federal government in American life? Three numbers help us answer this question.

The first number is 1950. Federal revenue in fiscal year 2004 will be at its lowest level, measured as a share of the economy, since 1950. Federal *income*-tax revenue will be at its lowest level as a share of the economy since 1943, as seen in figure 22.8. What did the federal government do and not do in 1950? There was no Medicare or Medicaid. There was not much federal aid to education and nothing like food stamps or Head Start. We had a very different federal government, particularly for people who were less fortunate. We did have Social Security and unemployment insurance. But many of the basic things the federal government does today were not done then. Another example is that the federal government did much less environmental protection then. This was before the Clean Water Act and the Clean Air Act.

Here is a second striking number. When the Bush administration began, extending all provisions of the tax code that were scheduled to expire and that would come up for renewal carried a cost of $22 billion in the tenth year. Today, following enactment of the 2001 and 2003 tax-cut laws, we have so many tax cuts with artificial expiration dates that the cost in the tenth year of extending all tax cuts that are officially scheduled to expire is $430 billion (see fig. 22.9).

Federal Revenues in 2004 As a Share of the Economy—A Historical Comparison

All Federal Revenues	**Lowest since 1950**
Federal Income Tax Revenues	**Lowest since 1942**

Source: Center on Budget and Policy Priorities
Figure 22.8.

Cost in Tenth Year of Extending All Expiring Tax Provisions

Before President Bush
As of January 2001, the cost in 2011 of extending all expiring provisions was $22 billion
Today
The cost in 2014 of extending all expiring provisions is $430 billion

Source: Bill Gale and Peter Orszag, The Brookings Institution: "Sunsets in the Tax Code," May 26, 2003.
Figure 22.9.

The Medicare bill passed in 2003 costs at least $400 billion over its first decade and more than $1 trillion over the next decade. By 2014, simply extending all of the expiring tax cuts will cost $430 billion in a single year.

Figure 22.10 is a reproduction from a technical volume that was part of the Bush administration's fiscal year 2004 budget. (The title for fig. 22.10 differs from the more technical title that appeared in the budget, but the material in the graph is the same.) This graph was both revealing and disturbing. It shows that under "2004 Budget Policy Extended"—that is, under the policies proposed in President Bush's fiscal year 2004 budget, extended into the future—the expectation was for deficits every year for the next fifty years, with the deficits eventually exceeding 10 percent of gross domestic product.

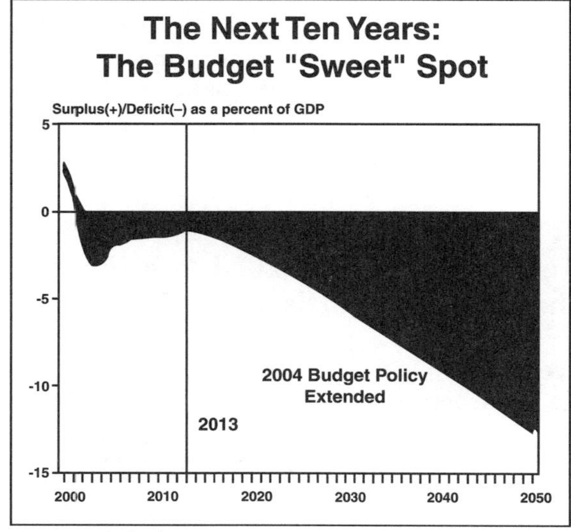

Source: Federal Fiscal Year 2004 Budget
Figure 22.10.

The budget accompanied this graph with a discussion about how we need to get *spending* under control to avert serious long-term fiscal problems, as though losses of tax revenue had nothing to do with this problem.

Here we begin to see the connection between the tax cuts and a larger agenda. Grover Norquist, head of the Americans for Tax Reform and a leading conservative strategist, has articulated a goal of cutting the size of the domestic part of the federal government in half over a period of a few decades. As Norquist's vision may indicate, the tax cuts and the goal of shrinking the federal government are being pursued as complementary long-term strategies. Those pursuing these strategies are patient. They are willing to wait until 2010 to have the estate tax repealed. They are willing to take a long time to squeeze down the federal government, with the squeezing occurring gradually and incrementally but eventually reaching quite large proportions.

The mistake of Newt Gingrich in 1995—of overreaching and moving too fast—is not being repeated here. I believe there is a clear understanding on the part of proponents of this agenda that, if one were to publish in the budget today the kind of budget cuts that the recent federal tax cuts ultimately will entail, the tax cuts would have a considerably harder time being passed. So the deep budget cuts are *not* being published in the budget today alongside the tax cuts.

THE BLOCK GRANT STRATEGY

But such budget cuts are coming. Indeed, we can see some initial signs of them in the Bush administration's budget proposals. When one looks across the Bush budget, one of its noteworthy features is the degree to which it proposes converting various social programs into block grants. People often debate block grants by discussing how much flexibility state agencies have—and should have—in operating various federally funded programs. But I believe the principal reason for the inclusion of these block-grant proposals in the budget is a fiscal one.

Funding for block-grant programs tends to erode over time. For example, the welfare-reform block grant—which provides funds for basic cash assistance to poor families with children as well as for welfare-to-work programs and child care for working-poor families—is on track to decline 22 percent in purchasing power from 1998 (the block grant's first full year) to 2009. Similarly, funding for the State Children's Health Insurance Program, which insures low-income children, is nearly 20 percent lower in 2005 than when the block grant was established in 1997. And funding for the Social Services Block Grant, which funds an array of social services for low-income, vulnerable children, seniors, and people with disabilities, has lost 84 percent of its purchasing power since the block grant's inception in 1973.

The Bush administration plan would convert about two-thirds of the Medicaid program into a block grant. Today, the federal government pays 50 to 80 percent of a state's Medicaid costs, depending on the state. (The national average is 57 percent.)

If people lose their jobs and their employer-based health care coverage in an economic downturn and apply for Medicaid, and Medicaid costs consequently go up, the federal government pays its share. If an epidemic comes along and health care costs increase, the federal government pays its share. If there is a breakthrough in medical technology that saves lives, improves health, but costs a lot of money (like a new set of AIDS treatments that are extremely expensive), the federal government would pay its share for people who are eligible for Medicaid.

Under a block grant, however, all this ends. The federal government sets in advance a fixed dollar amount that each state gets in a given year. If health care costs are more than that, the states have to foot 100 percent of the difference. In return, states are freed from various federal rules and standards. But that primarily means states could cut the Medicaid program more heavily to deal with the loss of federal funding.

Moreover, Medicaid is now an entitlement. Any eligible family or individual who goes to the Medicaid office and applies must be given coverage. Under a block grant, a state can tell an eligible family, "We're sorry, but we have run out of money for the year. Get on the waiting list. Come back next year."

This is especially significant because, with the coming retirement of the baby-boom generation, there will be more low-income elderly people and individuals with disabilities. (The older the population, the larger the percentage of the population that consists of people with disabilities.) As a result, every budget projection shows large increases in Medicaid costs in future years and decades. It is unclear how states are going to meet these mounting costs unless they get more federal help in covering them.

In my view, the federal government needs to take on a larger share, not a smaller share, of the cost of insuring a group we call "the dual eligibles." These are low-income elderly people and persons with disabilities who are eligible for both Medicare and Medicaid. Instead, the proposed Medicaid block grant moves in the other direction. Over time, the federal government would likely bear less of the cost, and states would be faced with choices between covering escalating Medicaid costs (which many states likely would have difficulty affording) and cutting their Medicaid programs by scaling back health insurance for low-income people.

STATE BUDGET CRISES

Many states continue to face substantial budget deficits. Numerous states have responded by instituting deep budget cuts (for example in child care and aid to local governments and in the form of tuition increases). In some states, there have been sizable cuts in health care. Some states also have raised taxes.

Why are states facing such large budget problems? A standard conservative cable-TV sound bite is, "They've spent irresponsibly and gotten themselves into trouble." In fact, state spending grew slightly *more slowly* in the 1990s, on average, than in previous decades. The major reason for the current state budget crises is that state revenues have eroded significantly.

State revenues have declined in substantial part as a result of the economy and the bursting of the stock-market bubble. In addition, in the late 1990s a number of states made the same mistake the federal government has made in the last two years: they cut taxes too much. There also are serious structural problems in many state tax systems. Let me look briefly at these structural problems, particularly with an eye on corporate taxes.

Normally, when we hear about corporate tax avoidance, we think of it at the federal level. We hear stories about corporations relocating overseas or having a mailing address in the Grand Cayman Islands to escape federal taxation. We do not often recognize that the same thing goes on at the state level. For example, corporations can set up shells in Delaware. They effectively transfer their profits to the shells so that they don't show profits in the states where they are doing business. Delaware doesn't tax these transferred profits. As a result, corporations can avoid significant amounts of state corporate income taxes. Figure 22.11 shows that, fifteen years ago, corporations were paying 6 to 7 percent of their profits, in the aggregate, in state taxes. They are now paying about 5 percent.

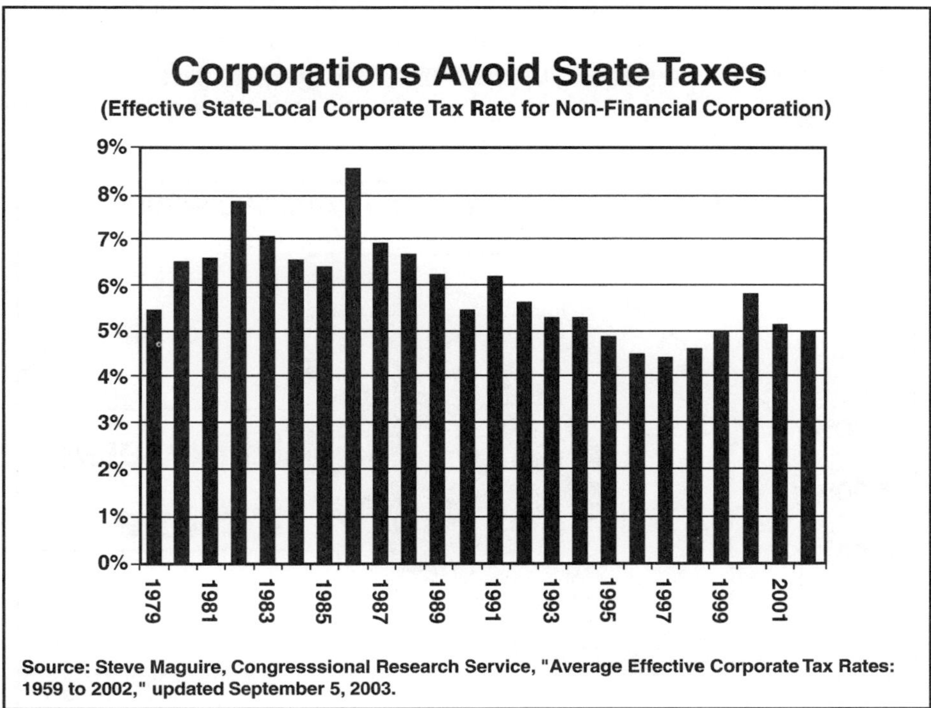

Figure 22.11.

Figure 22.12 is also of interest. It suggests that corporate tax avoidance has been growing more rapidly at the state level than at the federal level. This chart covers the economic boom years of 1995 to 2000. During this boom period, the amount of federal income taxes that corporations paid rose at an average rate of about 6 percent per year, reflecting the strong growth of corporate profits. But during this same period, the amount of *state* income taxes that corporations paid grew at an average rate of only 3 percent per year, or only half as much. The fact that state corporate tax revenues grew only half as much as federal corporate tax revenues during this period suggests that corporate tax avoidance may have been growing more rapidly at the state level than at the federal level.

Another problem is that state tax codes are regressive in many states. In recent decades, income growth has been greatest at the top of the income scale. If a state tax system is regressive and has a lower effective tax rate for high-income people than for others, the state does not capture in revenue a sufficient share of the growth in the economy when income growth is concentrated at the top of the scale.

In short, there are serious structural problems with state finances. In the past few years, we have witnessed cuts in basic services at the state level of a magnitude that few of us would previously have thought possible.

These developments in the states also are related to the change in policy direction by the federal government. The federal government, which can run deficits in downturns, should be doing much more now to ease the state budget crises. The federal government could have instituted a sizable countercyclical revenue-sharing

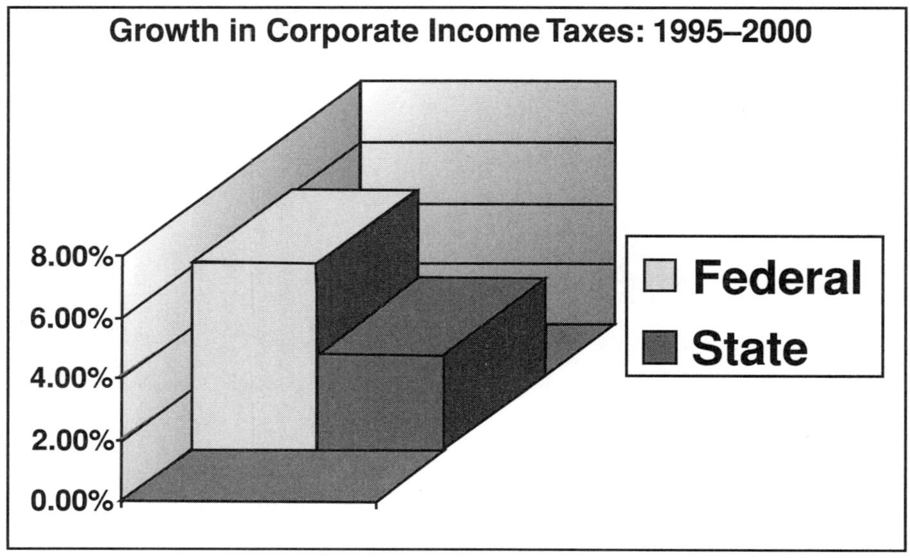

Figure 22.12.

program. It has not. It took eighteen months of effort just to secure $20 billion in fiscal relief to states in the tax-cut legislation enacted in May 2003, when what was needed was about double that amount. The long-term state budget outlook is even more disturbing. Two thirds of Medicaid expenditures today are for the elderly and disabled. That fraction will increase as the population ages and will cause severe fiscal distress for states, badly squeezing the funding available for education and other basic services that states deliver, including aid to local governments. A remedy is apparent and available—to have the federal government take on a larger role, in partnership with the states, and to bear a larger percentage of the health care costs of low-income seniors and people with disabilities. Whether this will actually occur is another story.

WHAT KIND OF SOCIETY?

As I noted earlier, federal revenue collections are now at their lowest level, as a share of gross domestic product, since 1950. Federal revenues will rise somewhat as the economy recovers but will remain low by historical standards. If the 2001 and 2003 tax cuts are extended and relief from the Alternative Minimum Tax is extended, as most observers expect, average federal revenues over the coming decade will be lower as a share of gross domestic product than average federal revenues were in the 1960s, 1970s, 1980s, or 1990s. Yet we are only a few years away from when the first boomers begin to collect Social Security and enroll in Medicare.

We must confront a fundamental question about what kind of society we want, and, in particular, what the role of the federal government should be in helping to bring that society about. We now are heading down a track where we may eventually be confronted with an unpalatable choice between running persistent deficits that eventually become so large they damage the economy and radically scaling back the domestic role of the federal government. If radical budgetary contraction occurs, it is likely to be not the "weak claims" that are hit hardest but the "weak clients," to use David Stockman's apt terminology.

There is, however, one bright note. There does not seem to be an overpowering national constituency to shrink the role of the federal government radically or to pass all of these tax cuts or make them all permanent. We sorely need public debate on these overarching fiscal policy issues—that is, on national budget priorities. If we simply allow the federal revenue base to continue shrinking, there eventually will be adverse effects on many public-policy issues that we care deeply about. We also will need to make changes in Social Security and Medicare so that the large growth in these programs in the decades ahead does not result in large, persistent deficits or leave insufficient room in the budget for other important priorities.

Now, I would caution that a plan that proposes to take *most or all* of the dollars slated to go for tax cuts and to use these funds for social-program improvements instead is not likely to succeed with the public. And it should not. That would likely still leave us with crippling long-term deficits. The recent tax cuts are sufficiently large, however, that it should be possible to design a broad program that scales them back substantially and uses a significant portion—but not most or all—of the saved revenues to address critical unmet priorities.

Restoration of fiscal responsibility is an essential ingredient of such a program. A healthy portion of the savings from more responsible fiscal policies will need to be used to restore the nation's long-term fiscal health so that we do not pass excessive burdens on to future generations.

In early 2001, the federal government said it would improve education, provide a drug benefit, improve government programs and services in other ways, and have plenty left over to fund the large tax cut and still pay down the debt. As Jeff Faux has articulated in chapter 21, Americans increasingly understand that there is *not* enough money to do all of these things. We have to make choices among them.

But organizations and individuals with views consistent with those expressed in this volume have not done a good enough job in making the choices and tradeoffs clear to the public. More needs to be done, for example, to educate the public about linkages between recent federal policies and the depth of the budget crises in the states. We could be providing more temporary fiscal relief to states, but the money is going instead to extremely large tax cuts for the nation's wealthiest individuals, despite the fact that large tax cuts for the well-to-do are likely to be less effective in stimulating the current weak economy than increased fiscal relief to the states would be.

When a library or a public-health facility is closing in a community due to state or local budget cuts, there ought to be discussion of whether the federal government could have eased such problems if it were pursuing different fiscal priorities and not conferring such large tax cuts on the very affluent. We need more efforts to "personalize" the impact on the daily lives of ordinary Americans of the type of policy choices discussed in this chapter and to bring to life the federal disinvestment that our citizens face if the nation does not change course.

NOTE

1. The revenue raised by the 1982 Act equaled about 30 percent of the revenue lost under the 1981 law, not counting the revenue lost as a result of provisions of the 1981 law that automatically adjusted (or "indexed") various provisions of the tax code for inflation. The indexing provisions are not counted here because prior to the enactment of the 1981 law, Congress made adjustments in the tax code every few years that had the rough effect of adjusting various parts of the code for inflation.

BIBLIOGRAPHY

Center on Budget and Policy Priorities, Center for Economic Development, and the Concord Coalition, "The Developing Crisis—Deficits Matter," and "Mid-Term and Long-Term Deficit Projections," Washington, D.C., September 29, 2003.

Peter A. Diamond and Peter R. Orszag, *Saving Social Security: A Balanced Approach*, The Brookings Institution, 2004.

Joel Friedman and Robert Greenstein, "The President's Proposal to Make Tax Cuts Permanent," Center on Budget and Policy Priorities, Washington, D.C., January 20, 2004.

William G. Gale and Samara R. Potter, "An Economic Evaluation of the Economic Growth and Tax Relief and Reconciliation Act of 2001," *National Tax Journal*, March 2002.

Robert Greenstein and Richard Kogan, "Analysis of the President's Budget," Center on Budget and Policy Priorities, Washington, D.C., February 5, 2004.

Robert Greenstein and Isaac Shapiro, "The New, Definitive CBO Data on Income and Tax Trends," Center on Budget and Policy Priorities, September 23, 2003.

John Holahan and Alan Weil, "Block Grants are the Wrong Prescription for Medicaid," The Urban Institute, May 27, 2003.

International Monetary Fund, "U.S. Fiscal Policies and Priorities for Long-Run Sustainability," January 7, 2004.

Iris Lav, "Federal Policies Contribute to the Severity of the State Fiscal Crisis," Center on Budget and Policy Priorities, Washington, D.C., December 3, 2003.

Cindy Mann, Melanie Nathanson, and Edwin Park, "Administration's Medicaid Proposal Would Shift Fiscal Risks to States," Center on Budget and Policy Priorities, April 22, 2003.

Peter Orszag, Richard Kogan, and Robert Greenstein, "The Administration's Tax Cuts and the Long-Term Budget Outlook," Center on Budget and Policy Priorities, March 19, 2003.

Alice M. Rivlin and Isabel Sawhill, *Restoring Fiscal Sanity: How to Balance the Budget*, The Brookings Institution, 2004.

Robert E. Rubin, Peter R. Orszag, and Allen Sinai, "Sustained Budget Deficits: Longer-Run U.S. Economic Performance and the Risk of Financial and Fiscal Disarray," presented at the AEA-NAEFA Joint Session, January 4, 2004. http://www.cbpp.org/1-13-04confpaper.pdf.

• 23 •

Full Employment and the Perils of Empire

James K. Galbraith

In this chapter, I assess current American economic conditions, suggest that stagnation in the medium term is not necessarily inconsistent with the American government's strategic vision, note the perilous international position of the American economy, review the vast expense of maintaining empire, question our short-sighted energy policy, and suggest economic policy alternatives that can complement the foreign, domestic, and media policies presented in other parts of this book.

CURRENT ECONOMIC POLICY

We are passing through a period of economic stagnation, and this remains true in spite of good economic news that began to flow in mid-2003. But underlying difficulties remain, and recent federal responses to them have been superficial. Stagnation is therefore likely to reassert itself *as such* after an interlude of better news.

Business investment has not recovered from the information bubble, a speculative mania which peaked and collapsed in 2000. Capacity utilization is low, and investment is unlikely to recover soon. This is especially the case for sectors like telecommunications where excess capacity does not quickly become obsolete.

At the same time, the prosperity of the late 1990s was fueled by an unprecedented willingness of American households to borrow and to spend ahead of their incomes. Through the entire postwar period, American households had tended to spend a couple of percent of gross domestic product less than they earned. After the middle 1990s, they started spending more. Spending went up by 3 to 5 percent of gross domestic product, actually ahead of incomes. That could not and did not continue. The adjustment of spending toward income began in 2000, slowing down the economy. Unfortunately for the future, it is not yet complete. Because of the climate of very low interest rates that has been created for American households, families have continued to add to their mortgage debt and to spend the proceeds of the loans. This, too, cannot go on forever. It is especially unlikely to form the basis of an enduring new expansion. Rather, it is more likely that household spending will slow, rather than accelerate, in the medium-term future.

We also have an enormous and continuing crisis in state and local government financing. Unlike the federal government, state and local government cannot borrow, except clandestinely, to cover current deficits. As they either cut their services or in some cases raise taxes, state and local governments are adding to the downward pressure on the economy as a whole.

In the very short run, this bleak picture is being obscured by two developments. First, there is the enormous increase in federal budget deficits, far larger than almost anyone anticipated, and which proved sufficient to jump-start economic growth last year. Some parts of the tax cuts recently enacted did flow to the middle class, and so accounted for some recent growth. As the military continues to restock its equipment following what is being used up or worn out in the course of the post-war in Iraq, that expenditure will have further effects on current economic activity.

The second development is a continuing (and also unprecedented in recent times) policy of very low interest rates. As each cut in interest rates goes through, households refinance and there is a little more spending. This is good for the economy, but not so good for financial institutions. Monetary policy will contribute to good economic news in the immediate future; the Federal Reserve has all but promised low and stable interest rates. But they will not be enough to generate a new, sustained, and strong expansion on the basis of rapidly rising household consumption spending in later years.

So while there will be good news in the short run, it is unlikely to endure. Over a strategic time horizon of a few years, it is much more likely that stagnation will continue. Conceivably, recession will return. Absent a mobilizing event like another large war, either of those outcomes is, in my judgment, more likely than the possibility that we will see another sustained expansion, carried on for four or five years, strong enough to create a return to the full employment of the 1990s.

It is quite illusory to say, as some who stand on the Democratic side of the spectrum have been saying, that the problem is one of budget deficits per se—whether the current deficit or those expected in the future. By this reasoning, if we were only to return to Clinton-era policies of balancing the budget, we would be back to Clinton-era prosperity. Such a view simply reflects a failure to understand the larger financial balances and underlying realities in America and the world today.

It is also illusory, or at least strategically ill-advised, to frame the long-term policy needed in terms of stimulus packages. Such a frame implies that imparting a single, brief, powerful impetus to the economy can bring us an enduring return to expansion. That assumption also is incorrect. I am not arguing against the usefulness of stimulus packages, but to conceive of them as comprising a recovery program is to ask more than they can deliver.

DOES THE ADMINISTRATION WANT FULL EMPLOYMENT?

The architects of recent economic policy are not entirely unhappy with this state of economic affairs. Stagnation is in line with a larger political agenda of continuing tax cuts on financial wealth. Those cuts are an extremely inefficient way to generate new spending, and to the extent that they force offsetting cuts in public investment and services, they will prove counterproductive. But they can always be justified as yet another impetus for the economy on supply-side grounds, or some other such mumbo-jumbo.

The recent tax cuts were actually something quite different. They were part of a longer-term strategy to assure that financial wealth is essentially free of tax. The purpose of this, in part, was to compensate some of the wealthy for the losses they incurred in the sluggish economy.

The economic coalition that benefited included oil firms, defense contractors, pharmaceutical companies, mining interests, and big media. These are economic interests whose basic position is maintained by government contracts, rights to natural resources, monopolies, patents, government-granted protections, and privileges of one kind or another. Their profits do not depend heavily on strong consumer demand or full employment. Full employment would itself bring other forms of political difficulty for conservatives—like stronger labor unions, pressure for higher wages, higher charitable contributions, and a stronger nonprofit sector.

THE CHESHIRE CAT: ARE SOCIAL SECURITY AND MEDICARE VIABLE?

Stagnation and the tax cuts also have returned America to budget deficits, totaling roughly $400 billion per year. By themselves, these deficits have been large enough to start up economic growth, overcoming the drag from state and local cuts and excess capacity. But they are still not large enough to bring about a strong and enduring expansion. In relation to gross domestic product, they are not historically unprecedented. But they are large enough, in dollar terms, to make a strong political impression. If continued into the future, they could be used to justify further attacks on the basic social services that underpin the quality of American life, particularly for our older population. I am particularly thinking of Social Security and Medicare.

Conservatives plan eventual privatization of the cash flows associated with both Social Security and Medicare. The plan is a bit like the Cheshire cat, except that it's not smiling. Sometimes you can see it, and sometimes you can't, depending on whether it is politically expedient and when the next election will occur. We therefore face the possibility of a return to a rhetoric of fiscal responsibility and deficit hysteria, which will make it very difficult to sustain Social Security and Medicare as viable programs.

THE PERILOUS INTERNATIONAL POSITION OF THE AMERICAN ECONOMY

At the same time, the American economy is in international trouble. Under current conditions, if we were to return to full employment in the United States, the trade deficit would be enormous. We have lived for thirty years in a condition of progressive decline in our ability to pay our way in the world through the sale of goods and services, a decline which has been offset for most of that period, and sensationally in the last years of the 1990s, by the willingness of the rest of the world to lend the difference to us, and to do so in dollars—that is to say, in a currency whose issue we control. And therefore the debts were incurred by us on very favorable terms—terms not available, basically, to any other large debtor country in the world.

This international monetary order has also been in existence for about thirty years, which is quite a long time for any single international monetary order to persist, if you look over the last century or more. And the architecture of the present system is not stable, for it depends entirely on the portfolio investment decisions of a small number of major players—Japan and China, notably—as well as the herd mentality of powerful private speculators.

The risk is that, should we try to return to full employment without attending to the decay of our industrial system and the increasing disrepute of the country as a world leader, a great part of the international community may stop lending us back our dollars and be unwilling to hold them until they are much cheaper to acquire. Indeed, the recent dramatic gains of the Euro against the dollar are a sign that this may be happening already. While the falling dollar has some benefits for exports and is very good for the dollar-reported earnings of U.S. multinational companies, it may engender the eventual opposition of the American financial community. A defense of the dollar, effectuated by raising interest rates, would then be highly damaging to the expansion.

It is also true that to get to full employment, given the current account deficit that would then prevail and the likely reticence of households to greatly raise their debt burdens, America would need to run budget deficits that really would be enormous by the standards of American political imagination. As noted, with our large budget deficits, we are growing but not making serious progress toward full employment; we are perhaps five to seven million jobs short of what we would need. Imagine needing a budget deficit of $800 billion, twice as large as what we have, in order to receive enough traction to move down the path toward, let's say, 4 percent unemployment once again. That is a very large number. One would have a very difficult time selling it as a positive program in Washington.

These numbers are not made up by me out of things that I would like to see happen. They are simply calculations of what the public deficit would have to be if the international situation remains as bad as it is and if the household sector continues to want, as the household sector characteristically does want, to have its income at least in even balance.

Maintaining Empire: Vastly More Expensive Than Acquiring It

The economics of empire are pertinent here. Let me stop short of saying that we went into Iraq for the oil. We don't actually know whether that's true. What we do know is that, when we got there, we found that oil actually was there. And weapons of mass destruction were not.

However, there may have been people who believed, for reasons that have always been a little bit mysterious to me, that physical control over the oil fields and the supply mechanisms for oil would somehow help us with the larger instability of our international economic position. I have never been entirely clear what exactly that mechanism would be, beyond simple stabilization of the price of crude oil. Whatever the mechanism, the thinking behind it radically underestimated both the moral and the material cost of maintaining control in the region.

This is something which is quite apparent about the economics of empire, in general. Empires are acquired, and historically have been acquired quite cheaply by small expeditionary forces. The American government did not invent the idea of sending a small force to acquire a large territory in a militarily inferior part of the world. The British and the French did that in Africa a century ago. Not to mention the Spaniards, in Mexico. With very few men, Spain conquered a territory much richer than Spain itself at the time.

The problem is that maintaining empire is vastly more expensive than conquering it in the first place. India, which did not have an organized military resistance movement at all, absorbed one third of the British army at the peak of empire and proved much of the cause of the decline of the British empire. I exaggerate; of course the world wars played an important role. But India was a creditor of the United Kingdom at the end.

The situation we are facing in the Middle East is one where we put very light forces in, without calculating what a reasonable person would have estimated to be necessary to control the environment once we got there. We do not, of course, control that environment now. The initial occupation was disastrous, clearly, from the standpoint of establishing confidence that we could control the environment in the long run. That disaster gave rise to a much greater resistance than we expected, and we are now in an environment where we are suffering losses because of our initial failures. Those losses are likely to continue over time.

We all hope that the situation can be mastered and an Iraqi government established with sufficient power and confidence and support from the population to provide the security that Iraqi economic construction will require. But we should face the realistic possibility that this may not happen. America may need to choose between renewing our commitment to force and violence in a way that will horrify opinion everywhere, or abandoning the exercise and leaving behind a state which we no more control, in economic terms, than we did before. Certainly, reports are that the grand plans to build a "free market" economy in Iraq have fallen victim to the realities of guerrilla war.

Meanwhile, it is probably not correct to say that the resource drain of the imperial venture is so enormous that we simply, in some sense, can't afford it. I don't think that is true. I think that, if we wanted to keep 250,000 or 400,000 soldiers in the Persian Gulf for five years, we could do it. But such a policy would have a crippling effect on the ability of our political and social system to mobilize the resources that are necessary to deal with any other problems in a serious and sustained way, as Jeff Faux has discussed in chapter 21.

AMERICAN ENERGY FAILURE

Let us suppose, then, that one way or another we come to acknowledge failure of the scheme to exercise complete and effective control over oil supplies from the Persian Gulf. This will not mean ending our economic or our security relationship with that region. Rather, it will mean accepting that we cannot entirely control developments there, and that we ought to be better prepared for adverse events from time to time. One of the key questions that we must deal with is the energy future of the economy in which we live.

Recent American policy has not seen past the very large reserves of crude oil that exist in the Middle East. The American government wants to maintain the current basis of our economy, which is an automobile and petroleum-based system with a much dispersed pattern of housing. But at the same time, if you look over the horizon of a half a century or more, it's likely that worldwide production rates for petroleum will decline, for geophysical reasons if not also for political ones. (Oilfield production rates already started declining in this country thirty-three years ago, and we're now seeing declines in the rate of natural gas production.) It follows that even if we want to control those remaining pools of oil, it will take an increasing effort to do so against more competition from the rest of the world.

At some point, for a brighter future, it simply becomes economically sensible and even cheaper to invest in new energy policy. We need alternative patterns of American life which better conserve fossil fuels, make alternative sources of energy available, and bring about a whole spectrum of energy adjustment to create a more balanced economy.

If we *don't* develop energy alternatives, then, down the road, we are going to find ourselves in an inferior position compared with countries that face this reality sooner and invest the capital required to make life easy, tolerable, and efficient in ways that also are profitable for private business enterprise.

Here is a very basic fact about empires. However many resources you put into maintaining an empire, when you eventually leave those resources are gone. So far as you are concerned, the resources are wasted. They are no longer part of your national patrimony. They don't yield a return that can support future standards of living that an empire has come to expect. But if you invest at home, build on what you have, and make economical uses of the resources you expect to have, then those capital investments last for centuries, sometimes even for millennia.

In discussing recent federal economic policies, one is often tempted to play the game of class warfare. This game has its uses. For example, the recent policies certainly did not appeal to the working class, as the Reagan administration did. Yet class warfare is not necessarily a prudent political strategy. Specifically, not all the wealthy are opposed to the rest of us, and certainly not in terms of their objective economic interests. There is a tradeoff between having the wealth and being taxed on it. One can make a very strong case to *some* of the wealthy that they would be better off with an economic policy that generates strong economic activity and profits—and that permits those profits to be taxed to support a higher level of social activity. Not everybody will buy into this argument. But you don't need to have everybody in order to build a majority for a new policy. All successful progressive movements in America have sought alliances with the far-sighted and public-spirited among the rich.

POLICY ALTERNATIVES

Now is the time for significant alternatives. It is not the time for small or incremental changes. You can either be for imperial strategy, or opposed to it. You can either be for a strategy that relieves financial wealth of taxation, or opposed to it. If we don't have a serious alternative, it would be better not to have one at all.

But we do have serious alternatives. The first is a re-commitment to a strategy of collective rather than unilateral security, as Jessica Tuchman Mathews, Gary Hart, and others have articulated in their chapters. Collective security is more just. Collective security is more likely to be successful, but it is also wise for economic reasons. Collective security is simply cheaper. Everybody has to police themselves, and police for others, reciprocally. If a country tries to police the world, the incentive for everybody else to cooperate goes down dramatically. And the cost goes up even more dramatically. One can make a powerful argument that the strategy of unilateral assertion of American power is simply not viable on economic grounds. It is not going to work. The American military is, I believe, fully aware of this.

Empire is mainly a matter of garrisons. And, at the end of the day, if you want to maintain a garrison, you have to be prepared to sacrifice soldiers on a daily basis over a very, very long period of time.

If we don't want that, then we must revisit the early post–World War II vision, a historical high point in world history in which we attempted to build not only security institutions but also economic institutions that provided for a mutual process of development and financing on equitable terms. It cannot be done on commercial terms, on the terms that commercial bankers usually require their commercial customers to accept. It has to be done with very long-term financing, at low interest rates, and under a controlled environment. That was the Bretton Woods vision. It worked for twenty-five years. We kicked it to pieces in the 1970s. In truth, we Americans benefited from that action for a period of time. But nobody benefits if the current system collapses and no viable set of institutional frameworks is put together to replace it.

At home, we need to commit ourselves to a policy of full employment. Given that the private sector is probably not going to take the lead, as it did, very happily, in the late 1990s for quite some time, the public sector must step forward. One just has to recognize that there is a time when the public sector's intervention in these matters becomes necessary.

A great many of the things that most need doing, particularly the reconstruction of our urban fabric—transportation networks, environmental protections, education reform, and health care reform—are substantially, if not wholly, public functions. Here is where we ought to be investing high levels of energy and resources. Much can be done at the state and local levels, with the federal government assuring the stability of financing.

That brings me to a very important short-term proposal. America needs to enact a program of revenue sharing, and perhaps also loan guarantees, to stop the current, destructive hemorrhaging of state and local public services. We must permit those governments to maintain their services and to avoid regressive tax increases. Reduced services and regressive tax increases both tend to undermine the functioning of the economy as a whole.

It is essential that we stop the movement toward privatization of Social Security and Medicare, on the merits of those two programs alone. The fact is that our elderly are going to continue to be with us, and their numbers are going to continue to increase. So the only real issue here is whether we provide for them in a way that is fair to the poorest or change the systems that provide for them in a way which enriches certain constituencies and makes life much more unstable and insecure for most of the elderly population of the United States.

We need health insurance to cover all Americans. That is obviously long overdue.

We need to compress the structure of pay. While many people emphasize the problem of CEO fraud and theft, it seems to me that we should not omit the issue of the minimum wage. The minimum wage is a very important way to assure that lower-income American households have adequate resources. Likewise, we need measures which promote collective bargaining and restore an environment in which unions can work effectively.

The earned-income tax credit is a proven, effective model for fighting poverty. It is something which ought to be protected and expanded.

We ought to tip our hats to those who have tried very hard to keep the bankruptcy laws functional for individuals, because in a situation in which debts are getting more and more problematic for larger and larger numbers of American households, the last thing America needs is for millions of people to be thrown into a situation where they essentially can't escape from the debt crisis for the rest of their working lives.

Finally, we need to think in a serious way about how to stabilize our international financial position. We need a new set of institutions that permit our exports to grow rapidly. That will mean giving up claims to international debt payments—in much of Africa, in Argentina, and I believe fairly soon in Brazil as well—that are in any event counterproductive.

We may even have to think about whether our commitment to the free trade system, which I am very reluctant to give up, is worth the cost. If we realistically assess the cost, and if it turns out that we cannot find a way to reconcile the commitment to free trade, in principle, with the commitment to full employment in practice, I would choose full employment over free trade. I say that with reluctance because it seems to me that so long as there is an alternative which permits us to continue to be good neighbors particularly to countries like Mexico, we should pursue that alternative. The question is: can we make it work?

Obviously, to pay for this over the long run, it is implicit in everything I have said that the recent federal tax cuts should be virtually and completely repealed. Not immediately, because the issue is not revenue in the short run. And perhaps not entirely, because there was merit to some of the middle-class components of the cuts now in effect. But our economy will need a revenue system to support the level of public activity that we will need to pursue in the years and decades ahead. And for that, America's wealthier taxpayers will need to contribute more than they are doing under the Bush tax law. I believe and hope that many of them will appreciate the necessity of this.

THE MATRIX

In sum, America's long-run goal should be full employment. But our task is not merely to return to the very happy environment of the late 1990s. Even Republicans can keep the economy growing at 2 or 3 percent. But I don't believe the Republicans will get the economy growing more rapidly than that for years on end, beyond the sprint we will probably continue to see as a result of war spending and one-time tax measures and easy credit timed for the election year.

Our more basic task is to think very seriously about the strategic horizon. We need to look very hard at how the world is unfolding in front of us, about the way the United States is fitting, and ought to fit, into that world. That, I believe, is the project the Eisenhower Foundation is engaged in. We must put together the full matrix of foreign, economic, domestic, and media policies necessary to make a true alternative work.

BIBLIOGRAPHY

Maureen Berner and James K. Galbraith, *Inequality and Industrial Change: A Global View* (Cambridge: Cambridge University Press, 2001).

Kenneth S. Deffeyes, *Hubbert's Peak* (Princeton: Princeton University Press, 2001).

James K. Galbraith, *Balancing Acts: Technology, Finance and the American Future* (New York: Basic Books, 1989).

———, *Created Unequal: The Crisis in American Pay* (New York: Free Press, 1998).

———, "The Bush Tax Cuts Will Do a Number on Us," *Newsday*, May 23, 2003.

———, "The Unbearable Costs of Empire," the *American Prospect*, November 18, 2002.

Robert Skidelsky and John Maynard Keynes, *Fighting For Freedom, 1937-1946*, (New York: Viking, 2000).

• 24 •

Concentrated Power without Responsibility

Ralph Nader

In this chapter, I want to review the decline of American democracy; propose that the American power elite is more interested in control than domination; suggest that September 11 further unleashed three virulent forces—commercial materialism, corporate welfarism, and diminution of civil liberties; warn that, as a result, public resources have been misallocated; set out an alternative foreign policy, based on assertive and anticipatory peace strategies, not war and belligerent provocations; and propose better-organized forms of strong resistance and advocacy for alternative policies.

THE CLOSING DOWN OF AMERICAN DEMOCRACY

Relentlessly, American democracy is being closed down.

What was done in 1965 with my book *Unsafe At Any Speed*—with the hearings before the Ribicoff Committee, bringing the executives of General Motors to the hearing, swearing them under oath to tell the truth and resulting in the enactment of the Motor Vehicle and Highway Safety Laws which, irregularly enforced, have saved over a million lives in the United States, and more abroad, by manufacturers having to meet our standards—could not be done today. The follow-through from Rachel Carson's *Silent Spring* could not happen today.

None of the institutional changes made by people who started out anonymously—with nothing but a credible case to make against an injustice or hazard—could happen today. We don't have the congressional committees to do the job; and we don't have the media to follow the issue on a regular reporting beat, as was the case with *Unsafe at Any Speed*. Nor has recent policy shown an interest in "homeland security" on the nation's highways, workplaces, and the environment.

This is a sobering observation—because we are very good at establishing indicators that tell us what is happening in the economy by weekly increments or decrements. But we are poor in developing standards by which we measure the rise or decline of our democracy and its democratic processes, both procedurally and through the substantive output that comes from an open society. Yet on many fronts, the signs are unmistakably clear. The economy is growing while poverty is increasing. The economy is being concentrated in fewer and fewer hands, thus leading to masses of capital being unproductively invested and instead redirected into the casino capitalism we have seen in financial and other markets.

Access to our courts—whether it is legal services for the poor, their class actions, or other systemic litigation—is now prohibited. The rights of wrongfully injured people against their perpetrators, under tort law, are being relentlessly squeezed.

As Robert McChesney and John Nichols discuss in chapter 31, the media are in the hands of fewer and fewer conglomerates; we are down to seven giant conglomerates controlling most of the circulation and most of the viewership and listenership. One radio conglomerate owns 1,300 radio stations. Ten years ago, no company could own more than a dozen or two radio stations. So what we are hearing and seeing is syndicated pap indentured to corporate advertising interests and a reduction in local coverage, local reporting staffs, and local stations generating their own material. Amy Goodman has much more to say about radio in chapter 34.

We have seen a decline in our democracy in terms of the commercialization of elections, where money now speaks much more strongly than it did twenty, thirty, or forty years ago. Basically, candidates, elections, and governments have been corporatized. We are seeing a decline in our democracy in the relentless propaganda that devalues public enterprise and public investment and that thinks that privatization, or more accurately corporatization, should swarm over the entire political-economic system.

Yet it is public enterprise and public investment that made our transportation system possible, our communication system possible, our health care science system possible—and that made possible the burgeoning industries like aerospace, semiconductors, biotech, and much of the pharmaceutical industry. Without government research and development, little of this would have happened. That is why the present situation is so out of control. Because we don't have a major-party opposition pattern in place that speaks truth to propaganda.

We don't have fearless chairpersons of congressional committees, as was the case in the 1960s and early 1970s, overseeing and investigating—like Senator Fred Harris, Senator Gaylord Nelson, Senator Frank Church, Senator Abe Ribicoff, Senator Wayne Morse, Senator William Fulbright, and congressmen John Moss and Benjamin Rosenthal—there are few replacements here. So what we have seen is the Federalist concept of separation of power and countervailing powers in our government being converged into a one-party state in most congressional and senatorial jurisdictions, and heavy power located in the executive branch. The Patriot Act, which only had one dissenter in the Senate, Senator Russ Feingold, was followed by the stampeding assent of the Democrats. In recent years, one piece of legislation after another, serving large corporate interests, passed the Democratically controlled Senate and the Republican-controlled Senate.

AMERICA IS INTERESTED IN CONTROL, NOT DOMINATION

What has happened is, I think, a new version of concentration of power worldwide. Until the occupation of Iraq, the United States was not interested in domination. It was interested in control. Domination, British and French and Portuguese empire-style, involves constantly having to visibly justify the domination and involves some responsibility for the natives because the troops are there—in India and Africa. Control achieves the same objective without any responsibility and with minimum visibility. This pattern of splitting ownership from control also has been the evolution of our property system in the United States.

Corporate interests like Michael Milken weren't really interested in owning the billions of dollars reposited in savings and loans by millions of workers. Milken was interested in just controlling the investment of that money. And so throughout our political economy, the people legally own the public airways, but the broadcast industry controls them. The people legally own the public lands that run through America, but the mining interests, timber, and energy interests and others control their disposition. Public revenues are turned into corporate assets and profits via vast varieties of direct and indirect corporate welfare from stadiums to bailouts, from giveaways to tax shelters and subsidies.

The people, through their labor pension funds, own one-third of the stock on the New York Stock Exchange, but the Board of Directors, the insurance companies, the banks, and the corporations like IBM control the workers' $5 trillion or so of pension money. This pattern makes the controlling process much more difficult to challenge because it's not domination, it's not ownership, it's control. And such control is the exercise of concentrated power without responsibility.

In foreign policy, this pattern has been perfected under both Democratic and Republican regimes. It involves moving in, achieving military objectives, and then leaving the country in wreckage. It involves destabilizing countries like Cambodia and Zaire and leaving the internecine slaughter behind for the natives to suffer. Cutting and running—striking and running—has been the pattern, right through Afghanistan, which is now 99 percent controlled by violent warlords whose forces are engaged in predatory activity, pillage, rape, and looting. Cutting and running—even the first road-building project took two years to get underway, the first road-building project between Kabul and Kandahar. Of the money that was promised the Kabul government only a portion has been extended, and certainly not for what has been called rebuilding or reconstruction—as the financial minister of the Karzai government, Ashraf Ghani, has pointed out time and time again.

The massive failure of intelligence agencies, whose annual budgets now total more than $30 billion, to uncover the tracks of the attackers who left their tracks all over the country for four years prior to September 11, has not resulted in a serious review of the performance of these intelligence agencies, as Ray McGovern carefully documents in chapter 4. The budgets of intelligence agencies have been expanded. That was the reward for what prudent commentators are calling one of the greatest intelligence failures in our history. They failed to listen to their field office reports to Washington, from people like FBI agent Coleen Rowley (see chapter 30).

SEPTEMBER 11 UNLEASHED THREE VIRULENT FORCES

September 11 came, and the aftermath of that massacre unleashed three virulent forces in American society, which had already been underway but are now in the process of running amok. The first is commercial militarism. This is an opportunity pointed out in the notorious *Wall Street Journal* editorial, shortly after September 11, while rescuers were still trying to enter the wreckage of the World Trade Center. The *Wall Street Journal* wrote an editorial to American business saying, in effect, go for it: this is a great opportunity—you can get your taxes reduced, you can get regulation reduced, you can get law enforcement reduced, you can get immunity.

The commercial militarists were one arm of that exhortation, and they saw an opportunity to push faster through Congress military weapons systems designed for the Soviet Union era of hostility—weapon systems that are distinctly not tailored to the new threat Mr. Bush was describing. And so we saw hundreds of billions of dollars in the pipeline for weapons like the F-22 and other weapon systems, which were either unnecessary, redundant, or wouldn't work—even by standard military strategy yardsticks, weapon systems condemned both inside the Pentagon and by retired admirals and generals—some of them part of the Center for Defense Information. The critical supply and logistical shortcomings in Iraq for United States infantry further raised questions about the way the American government spent taxpayer dollars over recent years.

The second virulent force was represented by the corporate welfarists, who began blaming everything on September 11 in order to demand all kinds of privileges—subsidies, handouts, giveaways, immunities, and tax benefits. The insurance industry moved in this direction—and the airline industry immediately succeeded in this direction for billions of tax dollars as they laid off 80,000 workers.

The insurance industry illustrates my father's answer to the question, "Why will capitalism always prevail?" He asked us that question when we were children. And his answer was, "Because socialism will always be around to save it." That's what terrorism insurance is all about and that is what the national subsidy state is all about—with their guarantees of loans, with their cash subsidies, with their tax expenditures—an indirect way that Washington writes a check to big business. These are giveaways of natural resources and public research and development—to the drug, oil, gas, timber, and hard rock/mining industries. So there is a vast expansion of this corporate welfare demand, with thousands of lobbyists swarming over Capitol Hill.

The third virulent force was symbolized by John Ashcroft. These are people who are damaging civil liberties and due process for trials in the name of what they conceive to be national security. The major expression of the autocratic ideologues was October, 2001, when the notorious Patriot Act was passed, an act that remarkably shifted authority away from the judiciary, our final review branch of government, to the executive branch; shifted additional authority from the Congress to the executive branch; and allowed unbridled discretion in defining the term "terrorism" and in defining material aid to terrorists. The act allowed such broad discretion that it is hoped that even the Rehnquist court will declare part of the statute unconstitutional. Its provisions perfunctorily allowed search warrants of homes and businesses without telling the owners or occupants, breaching the confidentiality of grand jury proceedings, and a massive indiscriminate invasion of personal information. On the ground, there were arrests without charges, imprisonment without attorneys, indefinite detentions of material witnesses, and prosecutorial misconduct in trials.

The act strengthened the 1996 violation of civil liberties, passed under the Clinton administration, and took it to new depths of autocratic control. It also provided the basis for the emergence of a new operation in the Pentagon called the Total Information Awareness Program, temporarily suspended by an alarmed Congress. This dragnet program, of course, does not apply to the administration, in terms of total information awareness. It applies to 290 million Americans and people in residence here. (For more on the Patriot Act, see Richard Leone, Yvonne Scruggs-Leftwich, and Coleen Rowley in chapters 28, 29, and 30.)

These three virulent forces show no signs of abating, no signs of significant other-party challenge, and in the due-process area only signs of judicial rejection—still subject to final appeal.

RESOURCES CONSEQUENTLY HAVE BEEN MISALLOCATED

The corporate welfarists and the commercial militarists are devastating the allocation of public budgets—away from economic and health necessities, environmental programs, public-works repairs, educational programs, and marketplace and other safety programs.

In the two years since September 11, 2001, about 500,000 Americans have died from preventable causes in just four areas: highway crashes, air pollution, medical malpractice, and occupational safety. Every year, 58,000 people die from occupational safety hazards, according to the Occupational Safety and Health Administration; 65,000 people die from air pollution, according to the Environmental Protection Agency; 80,000 people die from medical malpractice, the grossest form, just in hospitals, not in emergency rooms, or clinics, or doctor's offices, according to the Harvard School of Public Health. And some 42,000 people die on the highway, according to the Department of Transportation.

Now, this is not the end of it. About 200,000 children a year are damaged—brain damaged or otherwise, by the ingestion of lead-contaminated paint coming off their crumbling apartment walls, or lead-contaminated drinking water. Asthma has taken an awesome toll of children. By any definition, these are weapons of mass destruction. By any definition, these are preventable forms of violence. By any definition, they should have commanded the attention of the President of the United States. Instead, they commanded the diminishment of their budgets, their visibility, and White House support. And so now the word "terrorist" is not only monopolizing the concept of demonstrative violence that is preventable in our country—not to mention abroad—but is being applied to any insurgency and any resistance to any autocratic or dictatorial regime not supported by the U.S. government and its multinational corporate patrons.

It is difficult to exaggerate the impact of these forces on our society. But let me try to put them in historical perspective. Watergate was a picnic compared to what's going on today. McCarthyism was minimalist compared with what's going on today. McCarthy had no law enforcement power, although he launched a mass-hysteria witch hunt. He was not attorney general. He could not unleash the police—no matter how many supporters he may have had with his red-baiting. The first step, here, is to recognize the gravity and the relentless institutionalization of these assaults on our democracy and of these assaults on our constitutional separation of powers.

It is hard to remember a time when the executive branch was more dominant—more unjustifiably dominant, I might add—than it is today. It was dominant in World War II, but there was a broad consensus and, one might add, a fairly elaborate justification. What is the justification today, other than the political polls and rewards, the political distractions from addressing domestic necessities, and the personal, psychological profile of the president?

THE PUBLIC NEEDS TO DEBATE PRIORITIES AND SYMPTOMS

This brings me to the next area of commentary—a very sensitive one. There are very elaborate standards for mental illness in our country. They are being evaluated, revised, and changed. But they apply exclusively to individuals. They do not apply to institutions. Yet institutions should be subjected to standards of mental health and mental illness. When corporations refuse to have their deadly pollutants curtailed, decade after decade, knowing the death and injury and property damage they cause, those are mentally ill corporations. When drug companies like Bristol-Myers Squibb are subsidized by tax dollars and given the results of the research at the National Cancer Institute free, and when they then charge patients $14,000 for six treatments for ovarian cancer, that is a form of corporate mental illness. Perhaps a form of kleptomania.

People react to anthropomorphic evaluations. The reason why they are much more scared of street crime than they are of a city, daily being smogged with larger and broader devastation to health and safety, is because they can envision a street criminal—it's anthropomorphic. And we need to apply anthropomorphic standards to our impersonal governmental institutions, as well.

A while back on *60 Minutes*, Mike Wallace was interviewing Bob Woodward. The interview was unique in the sense that it was interspersed with recorded segments of the interview that Mr. Woodward had with President Bush. President Bush was heard on that program saying the following: "I don't have to explain or make explanations for what I say; others who say things to me have to explain what they say." He said it himself. He said he makes decisions based on his gut instinct. Now that is a personality who needed to be clinically examined, because of the power of the presidency. Those were his own words, not the projection of some two-dollar psychiatrist. He said it again and again.

Those were serious symptoms of messianic militarism and corporatist mania being observed in the White House. And, as often reported in the media, those symptoms were so monomaniacal in terms of single-minded focus that they produced conditions and misallocations of priorities that endangered and depleted our country from within and without. The public assessment of the Bush White House and the default of the Democratic Party must be made not simply in a defensive posture of our civil liberties being eroded, our privacies being invaded, and our priorities for people in dire need being disregarded. They must be made in an affirmative manner, namely recent American foreign policy and its domestic blowback against this country—seriously, relentlessly—as well as the rest of the world.

WHAT IF FOREIGN POLICY WAS BASED ON PEACE, NOT WAR?

A few comments on the nature of our foreign policy. We have blown the nineties. The nineties were a spectacular opportunity to do it right—economically, politically, and internationally. We had no major enemy. More than that, our major enemies were on their knees. The Soviet Union had been broken up and was totally introverted with its own problems—begging for disarmament in return for some economic aid. The communist regime in China was busily transforming criminal communism into criminal capitalism. There were some elements in the military-industrial complex that were looking for a major enemy but couldn't find one until it became apparent that it was a terrorist gang known as al Qaeda, whose power has been widely exaggerated to date.

General Douglas MacArthur warned us in 1957 about a government exaggerating foreign threats in order to expand military budgets. Under the greatest manhunt in history, a widely dispersed, decentralized, suicidal, fanatical, and organized international terrorist organization had not struck back in the United States, as of the writing of this book. Was this because its ability was exaggerated? That's an important question that is never asked on the media. But we know every year roughly how many people are going to die on the highways, in the hospitals from medical malpractice, from the environment, in the workplace, and from malnutrition. We have no way of actually predicting the terrorist attacks, but vastly more funds are expended than on the routine annual casualties noted above.

And yet what has happened is that the concentration of power in the nineties made it impossible for our democracy to flower and for our foreign policy to extend the best from our country. There is no country in the history of the world that has had such an opportunity to help the world and itself and blown it on a more grand scale than the United States government has done. Recent foreign policy has been almost entirely militaristic and unilateralistic. It was conducted in an offensively rhetorical manner that doesn't play around the world. From worldwide support right after September 11, much of the world has turned against our government.

A foreign policy that will spend more on the wheels of another B-2 bomber than it will spend on malaria research has priority problems. Leaving aside Social Security and Medicare, about one half of the American government's discretionary budget is now military expenditures, with no major enemy. What would the U.S. foreign policy be if it was based on the ultimate national security, which is global justice?

The attackers on September 11 did not come from Scandinavia. They came from societies that have been brutalized—societies run by dictators, too often supported and armed by the United States. They came from conditions that even conservatives have commented on as breeding grounds for this kind of terrorism. Still, as Ray McGovern discusses in chapter 4 and Jeff Faux in chapter 21, the taboo in this country was never ask why they did it because that was twisted into an interpretation of rationalizing what they did. If you don't ask why these people are doing these things, you will *not* understand how to prevent a recurrence.

And so our foreign policy does not spend resources on waging peace, which is an elaborately thoughtful and strategic challenge. It spends huge resources preparing for or engaging in war. It spends very little on global infectious diseases that are killing millions and heading toward this country in drug-resistant strains, such as tuberculosis and virulent flu strains. It spends very little money on leading the world in energy renewability and solar energy—which would have enormous beneficial consequences, not only for the preservation of land resources and water and air resources but also for the ability of solar energy to reach territories for economically productive activity.

We do little to expand and illuminate the genius of the Third World other than to give out HB1 visas and promote a massive brain drain to this country. And, therefore, we cannot and do not elaborate the great contributions of Paulo Freire in literacy education, or of Hassan Fathy in showing illiterate Egyptian peasants how to build simple, elegant housing from the soil under their feet, or the micro-credit successes of the Grameen Bank started by Mohammed Yunis in Bangladesh. Recent American policy has seen tens of millions spent on dubious propaganda to build democratic attitudes in the Middle East—at the same time that donations to the venerable American universities of Beirut and Cairo have been starved.

Instead, it's the World Bank and the International Monetary Fund that are the fountainhead models of economic development. They are patent failures, often condemned as such by more than a few internal World Bank critiques. Instead, we have the World Trade Organization and the North American Free Trade Agreement, which subordinate health, safety, and environmental standards to the imperatives of international commerce within secretive autocratic procedures in Geneva. Harmonization communities and closed-door tribunals further undermine domestic sovereignty in a race to the lowest common denominator. These institutions are shaped, nurtured, and supported by multinational corporate strategies of international trade and investment.

RESISTANCE: THE NEED FOR ORGANIZATION AND AGGREGATION

When people ask us why there isn't more resistance in this country, I have three observations, very quickly. One, there are very few organizers. No social movement can ever advance without full-time, paid organizers—whether it's the civil-rights movement, the labor movement, the women's suffrage movement, or the Farmer-Populist Progressive chapter of our history. You ask yourself—there were many rallies around the country against the war in Iraq. But how many organizers were around on Monday morning?

The second is that people who are resisting are not putting enough of their resources to support these organizations long-term. Rallies of 100,000 to 200,000 people should not just leave crushed Coke cans and other debris on the area where they rallied and marched. They should lead to the hiring of more full-time organizers in permanent offices. Major resistance movements are based on very mundane things, like sign-up sheets, passing the bucket, remembering that there are weekdays following weekend rallies.

Third is the lack of aggregation. Aggregation is a little-known tool of social change. When physicians put full-page ads against the war in Iraq and when labor people, military people, and clergy sign petitions and put notices in newspapers, there is a need for all of these groups to coordinate and follow up. Usually that doesn't happen. Protests are here today, gone tomorrow, with few ripples (see www.EssentialAction.org). There is no aggregation; there is no synergy which keeps the galvanizing momentum visible.

It is aggregation, then, that is so important in terms of any strategy to redirect American foreign policy, to wage peace everywhere and to make the peoples of the world the top priority, not corporate greed or bureaucratic indifference.

Organizations such as MoveOn.org and MediaReform.net have integrated electronic organizing with grassroots organizing, online advocacy with online fundraising, and follow up with some early aggregation. There are prospects and precedents, then, for resistance to build on in the future.

BIBLIOGRAPHY

"After the Attacks, Will the IRS Offer a Break on Tax Payments?" *Wall Street Journal*, September 15, 2001.

Rachel Carson, *Silent Spring* (Boston: Houghton Mifflin, 1962).

Ralph Nader, *Crashing the Party: Taking on the Corporate Government in an Age of Surrender* (New York: St. Martin's Press, 2002).

———, *The Ralph Nader Reader* (New York: Seven Stories Press, 2000).

———, "The Ultimate Oligarch," *In the Public Interest*, syndicated column, February 27, 2004.

———, *Unsafe at Any Speed: The Designed-in Dangers of the American Automobile* (New York: Grossman Publishing, 1965).

Mike Wallace, interview with Bob Woodward, *60 Minutes*, November 17, 2002.

• *25* •

Resequencing the DNA of Capitalism

William Greider

I am optimistic, and have always been, about the American condition, its prospects, and its possibilities. If you look to the middle distance and squint a bit, you can see an era of internal reform and discovery in this society, which is quite promising. The reason I can believe is because the book includes a lot of smart citizens, mostly not connected with government in any way, who are working on such reform.

ECONOMIC REMEDIES

While I'm optimistic about the middle and long-run future, I'm pretty grim about the present and the immediate future. The American empire is founded on quicksand, and it will fall. It will probably fall sooner because of recent foreign policy, based on the grand illusion which both parties have promoted for the last twenty or thirty years about American economic and military power. Many lies about our condition have been promoted by both parties. Those lies are going to come unglued in the next five or ten years, with wrenching adjustments.

When I wrote my book *One World, Ready or Not* about the global economy, the net indebtedness of the United States to the rest of the world was about 8 percent of our GDP. It is now 25 percent. It is rising at a rate that in a decade or less it will be 50 percent of our GDP. As Jeff Faux says in chapter 21, this is unsustainable.

Is anybody in American politics, except a few revolutionaries on the sidelines, talking about this? The answer is no, because both parties are deeply implicated in the deceptive construct of the global system. For thirty years, we propped the global system up for our own pleasure by buying more than we produced. The rate of that imbalance has accelerated even as, in the 1990s, we celebrated a new economy that the world so admired.

This really is old economics. There isn't anything modern about it. Sooner or later, the creditors get nervous. They don't renew the loans or expand the credit line. That is the moment this country is approaching.

Along with some others, I have been the bag lady on the street corner, waving the banner about America's net indebtedness for twenty years. The establishment, the media, and all right-thinking economists have found one reason after another not to talk about our indebtedness in honest terms, and that's built deep into the ruling class, or the "governing elite" if you prefer, in and out of government. This posture will not change until we get smacked in the head.

The change could occur when the euro becomes the trading currency for oil, which is logical and not unreasonable for the world or for Europe. Or it could happen when Germany or France, whom we've enjoyed belittling in the last few years, decides just not to renew the rollover investments.

In its own way, Europe's economy is dysfunctional at the moment, and Europeans need to get their heads straight, too. But there will be investment opportunities in Europe that look better than America, and when that day comes, there will be a little accompanying political pique, because they will say, "You're the folks who told us we were Old Europe, right?"

More immediately, the question remains whether America's economy can recover its normal energies for sustained expansion. If the economy stays down long enough, the global trading system will be severely damaged, and might even unwind.

The remedies for the economy are kept at a distance for good reason. They're old liberal heresies, and neither the Democrats nor the Republicans want to touch them, nor do they really understand them. One of the mysteries of history is that what people learn through struggle or pain may be forgotten in a generation or two, and that's essentially what's happened to economic policy. The Federal Reserve needs to re-inflate the currency. The federal government needs to embark upon a major stimulus program, with concrete spending and projects that really do generate business activity. And the government needs to liquidate some of its debts, both corporate and household.

The political system may not respond to these ideas. The people in power are clinging to their old orthodoxy, their old ideas, what got them to where they are, and they don't want to give up on it. They especially don't want to admit that supply-side economics, which tilted toward wealth and against wages, is over and that our economic system needs fundamental restructuring. We can say that to Japan, but saying it about our own system is threatening. It opens the book to all sorts of questions which have been suppressed for many years about economic imbalances, forms of enterprise, directions of public investment, and governing arrangements that led us to this point in history.

THE PIONEERS OF OUR AGE

My book *The Soul of Capitalism* is an attempt to get people to focus their minds and energies on how American capitalism functions. One of my premises is that we are at a point in history, with the Cold War over, when we can question how the American economic system deals with scarcity and production so that everybody, not just the ruling class, has at least a minimal level of housing, food, and wherewithal. From the 1950s on, with the exception of the very poor, virtually all Americans have lived as consumers beyond the necessities.

About eighty years ago, John Maynard Keynes prophesied this day. When it came, he said, human beings would be up against a real human problem. For the first time in the history of mankind, they would face the question of how to live wisely, agreeably, and well in the midst of this abundance, and I would add, despite the abundance, because this society today is peculiarly torn by the pressures of our wealth.

The problem raised by Keynes permeates American society today, and not just among the working class and among the poor. You can sit in the most affluent neighborhoods and living rooms and hear a very similar discussion about their lives. People describe themselves as confined by the economy, confined in their choices, and confined by demands to keep following those same choices. They feel trapped, injured. Around them they see their society and community deteriorating, bowled over by the forces of enterprise and government in ways they have utterly no control over, much less a voice in decision making.

Yes, we are fabulously wealthy as a country, but are we truly free? We must put that question back on the table again, because in their guts, if not in their articulations, a majority of Americans probably have this feeling.

Unless society wants to simply surrender its deeper values to enterprise, and we know society would perish if it did, then we have to change capitalism—really change it and not just enact a few more regulatory laws to hold down the fraud and greed. I mean going into the bowels of the system and reordering the structure command and control in this society where it really exists—in enterprise and finance, not in government—and altering the operating values, the narrow premises by which enterprise and finance make choices. I want to tinker with the DNA of American capitalism. I want organic, fundamental reordering.

This probably sounds rather far-fetched, but there are lots of Americans already working on this issue. To be sure, most are working in localized and somewhat limited ways, but I introduce a lot of these people in *The Soul of Capitalism*. I call them the pioneers of our age because indeed they are.

From various starting points these pioneers have figured out that people do have power, much more power than they imagine, if they figure out how to apply the leverage of that power as investors, workers, consumers, and voters. *The Soul of Capitalism* describes the mechanics of what are now really scattered fragments. People are learning slowly that there is somebody on the other side of the mountain doing the same thing in a very different realm, and that some things can be done together to give us more power.

Many such people gave up on politics a while ago. Without anybody telling them, they figured out that neither political party had any intention of addressing the fundamental problems of capitalism and so they decided to do the best they could in their own circumstances.

Such decisions are totally consistent with the story of our country. If you go back through American history, yes, there were important legislative victories and presidents who were real leaders. But the really profound changes always began with people on the ground, creating new ways to improve their social reality, their circumstances, like the people at MoveOn.org today (see chapter 32). Then others would see they could do the same. This is slow, tortuous change, but it's deep, because it has real people experiencing it; and if people can change the social reality, sooner or later, even politics will follow.

It takes patience, but given the decayed state of our democracy, I would rather hang out with those people than, say, go to a Democratic convention. Here I disagree with Jeff Faux. In chapter 21, he says it's not about new ideas, it's about doing the politics. I think politics begins when one party or the other begins dealing with new ideas, ideas which are now off the table.

EMPLOYEE-OWNED COMPANIES

Let's look at some of the concrete ideas that are in motion. In *The Soul of Capitalism* I take a look at consumption, work, capital, production, and the power of what I call imperious finance. I look at the strange results, particularly the ecological destruction we get from our system, the command and control of the corporation and how it might be altered. I look at politics, government, and public works. The original understanding of public works, which built capitalism and this society for 200 years, is now deranged, corrupted. Why don't we talk about it in politics? We all know why we don't talk about it: because people in politics are deeply complicit.

In the last twenty or thirty years, the terms, conditions, and quality of work have all been severely degraded in this country. This power imbalance, we were told, was due to "market forces."

If you read Barbara Ehrenreich's book, *Nickel and Dimed*, you got a glimpse of what happens at the working-class level. But you can see the same process underway way up the line, among professional and middle managers and technicians, people who we used to think were above the shop floor and free of the routines of working-class, unionized laborers. One would think the Democratic Party would be talking about this. But the Democratic Party hasn't talked about these issues in thirty years—not just about the corrupted regulation of labor organizing, which has been turned into a useful tool for management to control unions, but about the much broader experience.

The New Deal was one of the great moments in our history, but the New Deal and the progressive era before it did not resolve the deeper questions of capitalism. They certainly ameliorated conditions, improved relationships, and helped a lot of people. But one of the things the New Deal never quite confronted was the feudal master-servant relationship in workplaces. If that sounds harsh, think about it. I have yet to encounter anyone—workers, middle managers, owners, CEOs, young people—who, after reflection, fails to acknowledge the master-servant relationship.

The people in charge get to command the behavior of the people below. If they are in the factory, the boss tells them what they can say, what they think, what they do, and in most cases—not all, fortunately, but in most workplaces in America—they have no right to participate in the decisions or even talk back when they think the boss has got it wrong.

Elaine Bernard, who teaches labor studies at Harvard, has said that the workplaces in this country are factories of authoritarianism polluting our democracy. How can you expect people to be citizens when they spend their work days taking orders and turning off their brains? I've heard that phrase so many times from working people: "I just do the shift. I turn my brain off; the inspectors will catch the mistakes. They don't want me to raise complaints, and if I do make suggestions, they will use them against me." That's a reality for millions and millions of Americans.

So the road to reviving our democracy and restoring authenticity may start in the workplace rather than in electoral politics. For many years, I have been an advocate for what I think is the most direct and reliable solution to the problem. It's an old word of capitalism: ownership. People have to own their own work.

How do they do that? They can do it through a cooperative. They can do it through a partnership, like lawyers. And they can do it through employee-owned companies. Such companies have grown in the last twenty years, thanks partly to some tax advantages that Russell Long and Louis Kelso got into law.

The corporation and the employment system are the central engines of inequality in our society. The inequality isn't just about outrageous CEO salaries, which we know ballooned in the last twenty or thirty years (although if the employees had some advisory voice in how rewards are structured in a firm, who would imagine they would produce the system that we have now?). It has to do with the distribution of returns, the profits that go back into internal reinvestment, but that also are distributed to "the owners." One hundred years ago, during the rise of the great industrial corporations and the progressive reform era, the fiction was allowed to flourish, and we cling to it still, that the shareholders are "the owners." In the last few years, we have had a fairly dramatic demonstration of the fraudulence of this fiction. In the name of shareholder value, a bunch of corporate titans not only committed great frauds to their own benefit, but also wrecked their companies in the process, all ostensibly to serve the shareholders, who of course were meanwhile left in tatters, their savings wiped out.

If ownership means who's in charge here, who controls this property, the real owners are a relatively small group of insiders—top management, maybe a few block-share stockholders who own big percentages, and some key financial firms that collaborate in the decision-making of the firm. In most cases, everybody else who participates in this company is shut out, especially people who thought that they were in some vague way owners too, because that was the rhetoric they heard. They owned shares, and they also devoted their lives to these companies, and it was quite embittering.

I've heard this story literally hundreds of times from people who, in their middle years, at age forty or forty-five or fifty-five, discover that the company has just thrown them over the side, that they were, after all, expendable.

Employee-owned companies in fact leveled off in their growth in the second half of the nineties—precisely because of this deception called stock options, this funny money floating through the upper reaches of our society. To resume the growth, we need real, structured ownership. I have spent a lot of time with pioneering labor leaders, managers, and even some owners who have made the transformation to employee-owned companies. It is very hard to do, because you really have to transform human relationships within the firm. You need to create some degree of democratic ethos within the firm, ideally a formal system for participation. You still have a CEO—somebody still has to take the heat and give the orders. So it's not a democracy, exactly. But it's a firm in which everybody knows they're both worker and owner.

COLLECTIVIZED WEALTH

Structural reform is also deeply relevant to finance capital and how it behaves. One development that hasn't gotten much attention is "collectivized wealth" and is potent with possibilities. It also drives right-wingers crazy.

I am talking about the fiduciary institutions—from pension funds to mutual funds to all the other pools of other people's money where capitalism relies upon fiduciaries. Those fiduciaries own something like 60 percent of the thousand largest companies in America. They are overwhelmingly the biggest players in the stock market but in many other financial assets as well. There has been a struggling campaign for some years to get more social responsibility from those fiduciaries. The campaign has been led by religious leaders, buyers, and labor leaders, among others.

There is an acceleration of those different perspectives coming together and understanding that they're all playing in the same game. Together, they may have some leverage—not just through shareholder petitions or amendments but through real leverage—active investors who are willing to punish companies for their behavior.

The process starts, or ought to start, with pension funds, particularly the public pension funds, which often are managed by elected boards, or labor-managed pension funds, which are smaller but still have over $400 billion.

People must become more aware of a new theory of this collectivized wealth in our capitalism. Potentially, the new theory is revolutionary—and we must figure out how to make it come alive. The theory is presented in a book called *The Rise of Fiduciary Capitalism* by James Hawley and Andrew T. Williams. Hawley and Williams have developed a concept of "universal owners." A pension fund that invests across the whole market has an interest different from the companies owned by the pension fund. And, of course, the workers who put their money in the pension fund have a different interest from the companies they own. The practice of American corporations is to throw off their costs on others. These thrown-off costs are called "externalities." Examples of externalities are dumping toxins into a river or betraying a community that helped finance a new factory.

Hawley and Williams point out that externalities are costs to the pension funds, because pension funds are invested across the economy. A pension fund is as close to a universal investor as any institution can be, and it will pay the burden. Whether through higher public spending, slower economic growth, or lost innovation, all of the costs out of which these companies make profits will become losses to the broad portfolio of the pension funds.

That's an explosive concept, because it does bring deep social objectives into the belly of the beast. As pension funds learn how to judge companies on externalities and other behavioral indicators, withdraw their capital, and say "Sorry, we don't want to play your game," there's enormous power.

GOVERNMENT

Where is government in this story? Government often is a maligned force, and it would be nice to change that. But we can't trust government to make wise and broad public-spirited choices on the subject of reforming capitalism—not yet, anyway. That's unlikely to happen until a new politics arises that shows politicians they can escape from their relationships with money patrons and with the particular sectors that they've always supported and begin to make other choices.

I'll give you some examples. A while back, the *New York Times*, and only the *Times*, as far as I could tell, had an amazing front-page story on the recognition by McDonald's of what the ranks of consumers, farmers, social agitators, environmentalists have been saying for years—that growth hormones in animals and other antibiotics are bad for people, animals, and the environment.

McDonald's told its suppliers it would be good if they didn't use these growth hormones. That's enormous market power, and it sent a deep tremor through the American meat industry. Government has dodged this issue for twenty years. Democrats and Republicans have dodged it. McDonald's is going to change that industry.

Where did this come from? It came from People for the Ethical Treatment of Animals, the Sierra Club, Friends of the Earth, and local agitators. This is food. Food, like work, is one of those great, bubbling issues in this society. But neither the Republicans nor the Democrats will touch it. (Dennis Kucinich is an exception—he has an advanced position on all of these issues.) But it would be a lot easier if we had politics that led to government leadership, if not regulation, on subjects like food. In the meantime, people will do the best they can, and they're making some headway in areas the politicians are afraid to face.

The federal government, particularly, but also state and local governments, now routinely subsidize the very behavior they are supposedly trying to stop with their regulatory systems. Meanwhile, the regulatory systems are either captured by the regulated industries or degraded in ways that we're all familiar with.

We need to take on the question of what is public investment, and why are we investing in companies that offend our values and don't lead us anywhere in the future except to repeat the old injuries. We need to take a deep breath and rethink, in fundamental ways, the model regulatory system that was developed during the New Deal.

We need to rethink, as many environmentalists are doing, how a regulatory system might work that doesn't always turn into a kind of game of cops and robbers and political influence, but that leads an enterprise toward higher standards of behavior in a more or less continuous way. This is not beyond the imagination of human beings. But right now we are playing in a regulatory system that the present administration can so easily degrade, without us doing much about it. The fact is that there's a fundamental problem underneath that we need to address.

SOCIAL TRUST

Then there is scale. This country spent most of its first 150 years with deep suspicions of bigness inherited from experience and from a European past. Now we have a system that hardly stops to ask questions when conglomerates, consolidations, and takeovers build institutions that are bigger and bigger, and when businesses become more and more narrow and pointy-headed at the top.

Antitrust doctrine has almost nothing to say about these corruptions of scale. Lawyers who are young and able to think free of recent history need to redevelop an antitrust doctrine—what I would call "social trust." Antitrust is kind of an archaic phrase, and you would begin with a presumption that when the big boys come together, the burden of proof is on them. They have to really demonstrate in concrete, convincing ways that the society will benefit, not just their particular bottom lines.

We've had so many failures of the present system in recent years. The AOL Time Warner merger is an epic catastrophe, not just for the stockholders who lost approximately $200 billion, but for the employees and for communications. Yet it's not on the political agenda. The creation of megabanks—Citigroup, Morgan Chase, J. P. Morgan Chase and the others—has already demonstrated this failure of scale. These institutions have been in the crosshairs of criminal investigation. They won't be indicted, of course. We know that, following Enron and the other disasters.

There is a huge disconnect between what mostly ordinary folks are trying to contend with on the ground across the country and what politicians accept as "issues." We must try to reconnect with the broad countryside, to have honest discussions with real people about how they see the world. That's the predicate for reviving our democracy—and, in the process, the Democratic Party.

ACTION

How do we begin converting these long-range ideas into action?

It wouldn't hurt if some Democrats started to articulate them. These ideas are not ready for prime time, so you can say quite a lot without fear of being contradicted on the roll call. You're not even going to have a roll call, much less win. But what the right has learned over thirty to forty years is that losing is not bad for advancing an idea. And Eli Pariser has had the same experience with MoveOn.org in recent years (see chapter 32). Losing gets you to the table. You sketch out perhaps grandiose visions of what these ideas will accomplish, you get your head beat in, and you go and meet some more. Then you come back the second time and it sounds a little more plausible, and you go ahead with it.

There are a lot of things that the federal government could do to help. A few state and local governments already are helping in modest ways to take the ownership idea. In the mid-nineteenth century, the federal government created agents for every farming district in America and an elected board locally. We are not ready for that today, but the idea is appealing. At some point, I can imagine revising the tax code to make sure everybody in America becomes an owner of their own work, one way or another, and an owner of that equity that produces a nest egg. We can change the regulatory system. The federal government can enforce a "three strikes, you're out" policy for polluters, for example.

Two models can help the process. One is based on the home-ownership reforms of the 1930s. Up until 1940, something like one-third of the families in America owned their own homes. Then we changed the rules of credit, extended the life of home mortgages, and created agencies that supervise the housing market. Now nearly 70 percent of the families in America own their homes. That is a deep reform that profoundly changed this country. It gave people of ordinary means a whole new understanding of their lives, what their stake was, what their future was, and what they might pass on to their children. (Home ownership reform has been degraded in the last twenty years because people are literally spending down their equity in homes to stay afloat.)

The other model is homesteading in the nineteenth century. Again, the federal government essentially provided capital to families who were willing to develop their version of sweat equity.

I have become rather conservative about a timetable for action because I've seen so many really good, strong ideas ruined and destroyed because they were brought to the legislative process before they were ripe for legislation, before the advocates had the political strength to pass them intact. It is better to lose and better not to push for ultimate victory until you really know what the idea involves for people on the ground, they understand it, and they have absorbed it as part of their reality. Then we can begin the kind of ground-up action that provides hope for our long-term future.

BIBLIOGRAPHY

Barbara Ehrenreich, *Nickel and Dimed: On (Not) Getting By in America* (New York: Henry Holt/Owl Books, 2002).

William Greider, "Deflation," the *Nation,* June 30, 2003.

———, *Fortress America: The American Military and the Consequences of Peace* (New York: Public Affairs Press, 1999).

———, *One World, Ready or Not: The Manic Logic of Global Capitalism* (New York, Simon & Schuster, 1998).

———, *Secrets of the Temple: How the Federal Reserve Runs the Country* (New York: Simon & Schuster, 1989).

———, *The Soul of Capitalism: Opening Paths to a Moral Economy* (New York: Simon & Schuster, 2003).

———, *Who Will Tell the People? The Betrayal of American Democracy* (New York: Touchstone Books, 1993).

James Hawley and Andrew T. Williams, *The Rise of Fiduciary Capitalism* (Philadelphia: University of Pennsylvania Press, 2000).

Paul Krugman, *The Great Unraveling: Losing Our Way in the New Century* (New York: Norton, 2003).

IV

FAILURE IN AMERICAN DOMESTIC AND HUMAN RIGHTS POLICY—AND STRATEGIC ALTERNATIVES

• 26 •

The Failure of "Free Market–Tough State" Ideology

Elliott Currie

In the long run, the most important impact on domestic policy of September 11 and the subsequent mobilization for the war on terrorism may be that those events have served to obscure developments in American society that are both very troubling and very revealing of the limits of our present social and economic policies.

It's not so much that September 11 has had a large and *direct* impact on our domestic situation. To be sure, we have shifted considerable money very quickly to "homeland security" and to boosting the military budget in the name of carrying out the war on terrorism and the war and its aftermath in Iraq. This is not small change. But what is probably more important in terms of domestic policy is that the events since September 11 have focused our national attention away from the home front, especially from such critical domestic problems as poverty, job flight, inadequate education, and persistent violence and from the increasingly evident failure of our current social policies to make real or enduring progress against those problems. As a result, that failure has been largely off the radar screen (at least until very recently) and almost entirely absent from the policy agenda, even as the structural crisis of American society becomes more and more apparent.

THE FAILURE OF "FREE MARKET–TOUGH STATE" POLICIES

Let me put it as strongly as I can: I think that the collapse of what we might call the "free market–tough state" model that has driven American social policy for at least the last twenty years is the biggest but least reported political news story of our time.

By "free market–tough state" I mean this: On the one hand, we are increasingly leaving the fate of most people in America (and the world) largely up to the untender mercies of the market—or rather what we misleadingly describe as "the market" but what is really a highly concentrated set of powerful economic actors who are quite willing to subvert or corrupt the market whenever it gets in their way (as the experience with Enron, Global Crossing, and other rogue corporations affirms). This has been coupled with the systematic strengthening of the mechanisms of government control over the people who represent the casualties of the social dislocations and deprivations that the so-called market model predictably brings.

The failure of this model to bring anything approaching economic well-being and social stability is apparent not just in the United States but around the world—as Clare Short (chapter 5), Vivien Stern (chapter 6), Jeff Faux (chapter 21), and others have eloquently noted. The virtual disintegration of large parts of what we euphemistically call the "developing" world under the long-term impact of this model is itself one of the great underreported news stories of our time. There are some troubling signs of that larger failure here at home as well. Those signs include the increase in poverty and the increase in crime.

THE INCREASE IN POVERTY

The "free market–tough state" has failed to reliably reduce economic deprivation in America. As we all know, welfare "reform" was supposed to be the ticket out of crippling dependency for millions of poor Americans. But the verdict is in. Most of those poor Americans are still poor. A lot of them got off the welfare rolls, but that didn't necessarily get them into self-sufficiency—as an increasing body of careful research shows—in spite of the lucky boost that years of sustained economic boom provided.

If ever the conservative welfare model should have worked, in short, it was in the economic boom of the 1990s. And that boom did help produce some statistics that were superficially comforting to the boosters of welfare reform as we practiced it. Most of the people who left welfare did not leave the prison of deprivation. One way of looking at this issue is to consider the implications of the "self-sufficiency standard" calculations developed by the sociologist Diana Pearce, a long-time antipoverty advocate. This is a new attempt—along the lines of the earlier "lower budget" developed some years ago by the Labor Department—to come up with a more adequate measure of poverty than the official one, which everyone recognizes as much too low.

The self-sufficiency standard tries to calculate how much it would actually cost families, in various places, to pay for all the things they absolutely must have in order to be self-sufficient—housing, food, child care, medical care, and so on—without having to rob Peter to pay Paul (there are no frills, and no savings, in this budget). For the city of Chicago, for example, the self-sufficiency standard works out to $38,000 for a single parent with one child in school and another of preschool age. How many single parents leaving welfare under the current "reform" rules moved into $38,000 jobs?

Yet it is precisely the failed approach of attacking "dependency" by forcing single parents into the low-wage labor market—and often depriving them of the realistic chance to gain higher-level skills so they could make $38,000 (or $48,000)—that is being accelerated today by Congress and the administration. The kind of serious policy discussion that the self-sufficiency standard should be forcing upon us is not happening, even though the most recent census data show an increase in family poverty in America, the unsurprising result of a continuing and massive loss of stable jobs across the country.

THE INCREASE IN CRIME

Then there is the persistence of violence. One part of the "free market–tough state" ideology has been the use of an ever-harder fist to crack down on crime and drugs, or at least the crime and drugs that *poor* people do. In chapter 27, Marc Mauer makes clear how massively we have done that, what it has done to our prison system, and how it has affected racial inequality in America.

Yet major crime as reported by the FBI has been rising in many places around the country, including in Oakland, California, near where I live. As in the rest of the nation, much of the increase in homicide in Oakland involves young minority men. This in California, where not long ago we passed Proposition 21, which made it easier to crack down on gang violence by sending juveniles more easily to adult court and toughening sentences for gang-related offenses; where we've had a "three strikes" law for nearly a decade that could put a lot of these young men away for life; where we increased the prison population almost eightfold since the end of the 1970s and stuffed it to the rafters with precisely the kinds of young inner-city men who are now increasingly shooting each other on our streets.

The number of homicides in Oakland is roughly in the same league as London—a city twenty times its size. But even more revealing is a recent news article on Oakland's tragedy of youth homicide. The article quoted a staff person at a funeral home, who is described as their "director of homicide events." Can there be a more telling indication of the state of American violence in our time than the idea that, in an American urban neighborhood, the local funeral home needs a special staff person whose job it is to deal with homicides?

So the persistence—and increase—in violence is another clue that the reigning model of social policy in America isn't working the way legions of commentators, pundits, and politicians of both parties assured us it would. The reality is that, after more than twenty years of implementation, this model hasn't delivered; and, again, that includes almost a decade of economic boom which gave this model the best chance it could possibly have had to deliver the goods.

WILL THERE CONTINUE TO BE A VACUUM OF SERIOUS POLICY?

Instead, the country is in a state of deepening internal crisis. The economic boom of the 1990s masked, to some extent, the dimensions of that crisis. As soon as the boom ended, the veil was lifted. But we are not looking hard as a nation at what lies under that veil—and that is in part because since September 11 we've been mostly looking in another direction.

Deflection of our vision cannot last for long, especially if the current economic uncertainties continue and their effects on the quality of life in the United States deepen. There is already evidence of considerable anger and anxiety, especially over the relentless erosion of jobs and the continuing crisis in affordable health care. The question is whether that anger and anxiety can be channeled toward a constructive attack on their structural sources.

There is no guarantee that it will. Indeed, we face a rather frightening possibility at the start of the twenty-first century that life here at home will get a lot worse for many people as the inability of our failed model of social and economic development to address the root contradictions of our society becomes more and more evident. But at the same time, no political force will emerge that is capable of putting those issues on the agenda in an honest and progressive way. Instead, both major parties will vie with each other over which one will win the allegiance of the affluent and rather conservative voters that make up what we somewhat euphemistically describe as the political "center."

As a result, there will be a vacuum of serious policy. There will be no serious efforts to confront the causes of our deepening social crisis, and there will be a consequent slide into what could be extremely grim conditions as poverty continues to increase, jobs continue to flee the country, everyday violence rises, schools deteriorate further, and adequate health care slides out of the reach of more and more ordinary Americans.

In that situation, we could easily imagine a deepening shift in America, in which a confident and focused right steps in to fill the vacuum by offering solutions that are at least straightforward, even if they are reprehensible. If we then had more terrorist attacks as well, raising the level of fear and endemic anxiety even further, it is not far-fetched to say that we could see a very frightening political response indeed, one that would surely involve tightening the social controls of the "tough state" even further, with all the threats to our civil liberties that will involve. That has been the usual response to the growing national and international instability brought on by the "market" model, and I believe we could expect more of the same.

HOW TO RECRUIT AMERICANS AWAY FROM THE "ARMIES OF THE SILENT"?

Will that really happen? I don't know, but I do know that the only certain way to avoid it will be to build a political constituency that is bold enough and tough-minded enough to challenge this whole failed model of social development, not just tinker with it. The constituency must be willing to put issues like the need for much greater public investment, the need for human-resource investment in our schools, the need for a universal health care system, and the crying need to establish a living wage firmly on the political agenda. A political movement, in short, that can honestly and forthrightly address people's real concerns about how they will pay their bills, secure decent health care for themselves and their kids, keep their sons and daughters safe on the streets, and get them a decent education.

How do we now broaden our base, mobilize more troops? How do we recruit more Americans away from what the Chilean writer Ariel Dorfman has called the "armies of the silent"?

ENCOURAGING DEVELOPMENTS

Today I see at least two encouraging developments in our political culture. One is the new and enormously refreshing burst of progressive political energy that was represented in some of the 2004 Democratic presidential primary campaigns and has been illustrated by creative and effective use of the mobilizing capacities of the Internet, as with MoveOn.org and MediaReform.net (see chapters 31 and 32). This has significantly altered the political landscape and catalyzed a long-dormant enthusiasm among many people—perhaps, especially, the young.

A second potentially positive shift is more subtle but even more important. It's often been remarked that Americans' view of government has changed somewhat in the aftermath of September 11. After decades of being taught to believe that government was always the problem and never the solution, Americans woke up to understand, in the most bitter way, what happens when government falls asleep at the wheel and fails to provide elementary protection from violence. And they also saw government acting heroically—government in the form of firefighters and cops who lost their lives saving others. We saw another example of this appreciation of government services—and perhaps even of the taxes that pay for them—in the devastating Southern California wildfires of 2003. Cutting taxes and slimming state and local government seemed like less compelling goals while Californians watched public-sector workers saving their homes and neighborhoods from catastrophe.

From this newfound awareness of what government can do in these crisis situations, it is not a big jump to understanding that there are other kinds of jobs that government needs to do, and could do—including things like providing health care for kids, replicating what works in our schools, creating a system for financing higher education, and tackling poverty. How long that new understanding will last is anybody's guess. Reason enough to seize the political moment while we can.

BIBLIOGRAPHY

Michael K. Brown, Martin Carnoy, Elliott Currie, Troy Duster, David B. Oppenheimer, Marjorie M. Shultz, David Wellerman, *Whitewashing Race: The Myth of a Color-Blind Society* (Berkeley: University of California Press, 2003).

Elliott Currie, *Crime and Punishment in America* (New York: Holt, 1998).

Peter Edelman, *Searching for America's Heart: RFK and the Renewal of Hope* (New York: Houghton Mifflin, 2001).

Fred R. Harris and Lynn A. Curtis, editors, *Locked in the Poorhouse* (Lanham: Rowman & Littlefield, 1998).

Policy Research Action Group, *Newsletter*, November 2001.

• 27 •

September 11 and the Criminal Justice System

Marc Mauer

Not long ago, I was talking with a friend who works for a national women's organization. We were bemoaning the state of the world these days, and she was saying that her organization has now started to shift its thinking in the wake of recent federal policy. Her organization now is looking at the political scene to try to prevent things from getting worse rather than making any advances. I reassured her that we had been doing that for twenty-five years now in criminal justice.

From the political context in which we work, the United States has in recent years become the world leader in rates of incarceration. We have some two million people behind bars in this country. This is about six times the number of people locked up as there were just thirty years ago. If you look at international comparisons, we lock up our citizens at about five to eight times the rate of other industrialized nations and use our prison system, certainly the death penalty, to a degree that is really unimaginable among other democratic nations. They look at our policies with a great deal of horror. We know also that, at current rates, an African-American male born today in the United States stands a 29 percent chance of doing time in prison at some point in his life. So, essentially, three of every ten African-American males born today can expect to go prison for at least a year, if current trends continue. We also know that the prison expansion has been fueled by the "get tough" movement—and more recently by the war on drugs—to the point where today nearly a quarter of the two million people behind bars are locked up for drug offenses. This is about ten times the figure of just twenty years ago—a remarkable change in a relatively short period of time.

That's the bad news, but there has been some recent good news. Over the last several years, many of us have noticed some openings in the debate, discussion, and understanding of these issues. Certainly we've seen it in the area of the death penalty. For example, governors in two states, Illinois and Maryland, have declared a moratorium on the use of the death penalty. Much more media and legislative attention has been given to the issue. There is much greater skepticism about the wisdom of mandatory sentencing and much greater receptivity to alternative ways of sentencing people, particularly drug offenders. We have seen an expansion of drug courts to divert people into treatment. In California and other states, voters have approved ballot proposals aimed at diverting drug offenders into treatment rather than prison. There are some very encouraging signs, or at least a moderation of what some of those trends have been like for three decades.

THE IMPACT OF INTERNATIONAL AND DOMESTIC TERRORISM

How have September 11 (and other incidents, such as the sniper experience in Washington, D.C.) affected these modest openings for reform? In broad terms, there have been three possible effects. In some areas, the effects of September 11 were not as bad as we had feared they might be, in others progress has halted, and in still others unanticipated opportunities have emerged.

First, there are areas of impact that are not as bad as they might have been. If we look at what goes on in the courtrooms—in day-to-day sentencing and processing of people charged with crimes—some of us had feared, in the first months after September 11, that further assaults would be made on the Constitution in the name of fighting terrorism. We had been concerned that new and harmful policies and practices would filter down to so-called ordinary defendants in the courtrooms, not just those suspected of terrorism.

By and large, that fear has not been borne out. If you are an average burglary defendant in the courtroom, you may or may not get an adequate defense. You may or may not get a reasonable sentence. But we haven't seen the sort of stripping away of basic constitutional rights in the way that we have in the so-called war against terrorism. Some defense attorneys will say that this may be true for most burglars, but if your client happens to be a burglar of Middle Eastern descent, he may want to look for a quick plea bargain rather than taking the case to a jury.

There are exceptions: The seventeen-year-old sniper suspect Lee Boyd Malvo was snatched away from federal authorities and taken to Virginia, where he temporarily was not allowed an attorney to represent him. This enabled the police to question him for seven hours without an attorney. When Malvo's guardian showed up at the jail to counsel him, he was told, "Please leave your business card and we'll get back to you." So all of these protections are very fragile and can be attacked or thrown out pretty quickly in certain circumstances.

The second area is framed by issues where we have collectively made progress for some time but where the momentum has slowed down dramatically. The most obvious example is racial profiling. Over recent years, we have documentation, originally on the New Jersey Turnpike and then elsewhere, of police activity consciously designed to profile African-Americans and other groups. These practices have been struck down in many cases by courts or legislative actions. In some of the more thoughtful police departments, there have been internal changes designed to control racial profiling.

Now, after September 11, racial profiling is often justified in the name of fighting terrorism. But the sniper case shows all the harmful results of racial profiling—not just necessarily what it does to the individuals who are unjustly stopped or accused but to public safety in general. In the sniper case, all of us were looking out for a middle-aged white guy. We don't know how much this distorted direction that was given to us by the so-called profile experts on television led people to dismiss other information, other evidence that might have helped the police do something more quickly. Right now we certainly don't see a lot of activity on Capitol Hill or in many state legislatures—even though there had been quite a bit of momentum until recently.

Another area where momentum has slowed is progress on challenging the death penalty. There had been a very significant opening or questioning of death penalty attitudes for nearly the first time in a generation. We had seen public support declining a fairly good extent in opinion polls and the moratorium movement gaining some momentum. There was a slowing down of the machinery of death in many places around the country. Now, in many cases, certainly since September 11 and as illustrated in the Washington sniper case, there has been a rush to kill. There was the spectacle of Lee Boyd Malvo with prosecutors jockeying about where he was going to be tried, with the main rationale for each state being efficiency in how quickly a death penalty could be produced. Maryland does not execute juveniles and, therefore, that was given as a primary reason why the case should be turned over to Virginia, to see if they could execute Malvo as quickly as possible. Disturbingly, there was no discussion of why Maryland, and indeed a majority of the states, do not have a death penalty for juveniles. The reason is that most of the civilized world believes that this is an uncivilized thing to do. The United States is in the company of about a half-dozen nations in allowing execution of juveniles. Those nations include Syria, Iran, and Nigeria. They hardly are models of respect for human rights. Yet the assumption in the Malvo case was that the goal should be to execute and that we should welcome the most efficient way to do this—before we know anything whatsoever about who this seventeen-year-old is, not to mention questions of guilt and innocence.

The third area is that of unexpected opportunities. One example of this is the prison system. September 11 contributed to exacerbating the fiscal crisis in many states, and many states are dealing with very difficult issues as they try to balance their budgets and assess their priorities. Some governors' offices and state legislatures are beginning a real reconsideration of the wisdom of continuing to expand prison building forever. Prisons are very expensive budget items in the states. But the last thirty years of unprecedented prison expansion has taken place in both good economic times and bad. The bad economic times have never slowed construction. This is really the first time in a generation that we are seeing a debate about the wisdom of building more prisons.

This debate has come about for a couple of reasons. First, there is the fiscal crisis. It is a very real dollars-and-cents issue. Second, we saw declining crime rates for much of the past decade, and along with that came a little less emotion and politicizing of the issue (though this may change, because crime has risen in recent years). We haven't seen quite as many candidates running on a "get tough" platform as we might have seen ten or fifteen years ago. There has been a little less political hay to be made of these issues. Third, there is a greater understanding and acceptance of alternative measures for dealing with crime, starting with community policing and going through drug treatment for convicted offenders, with many things in between.

Many of the kinds of options, other than prison, that we have been talking about are beginning to take hold in many communities. So this gives policymakers something constructive that they can point to, rather than continued prison expansion. It is also true that, for every state that is reconsidering prison expansion, there is another state that is cutting funds for drug treatment, drug courts, alternative sentencing, and similar programs. We haven't won that battle, but at least there is a battle to be fought and there is potential for progress.

REACTIVE RESPONSES AND OVERKILL

A comparison of September 11 to the sniper case tells us something about how we address social problems. In both cases, the response was incredibly reactive; it was overkill. It refused to deal with what, in a former time, we used to think of as root causes, a concept that is now out of fashion. Following September 11, the response was more bombs and more wars and whatever it took to make all of that happen. There is certainly no discussion about national priorities. There was certainly no discussion about national energy policy and the demand for oil and whether that might or might not have some connection. Just a zeal to engage in war and retaliation as our primary and sole response.

When it came to the sniper case, there were very similar kinds of thinking. We had a race to execute as the sole goal of what needed to happen in the case. The snipers needed to be punished; there needed to be consequences. But nothing we do is going to bring back the lives of the ten people who were killed. This rush to execute was about prosecutors jockeying for political attention.

Much of what is not being discussed is the problem of guns. There are lunatics in all sorts of civilized countries, but when lunatics don't have access to high-powered weapons, they don't end up killing lots of people. This remains the only industrialized country with enormous numbers of guns in the population.

Every time we have one of these events—whether it's Columbine or snipers—we have a discussion about gun control for about twenty minutes, which then fades as we quickly move into the punishment phase. There is no forward thinking, nothing about trying to prevent the next incidents. As long as there are this many guns around, we know we can almost predict that there will be more incidents. We don't know exactly what they will look like, but they happen with great regularity.

WHAT STRATEGY DO WE PURSUE?

So, where do we take all of this? What does it mean in terms of our strategy? These are difficult times; there are no easy answers. In two broad areas we need to be thinking about our message and our messengers.

In terms of our message, what do we want to try to communicate? We need to broaden our message and broaden the critique of the policies. My recent book, *Invisible Punishment*, is an edited collection of essays in which various scholars consider the collateral consequences of imprisonment: how a prison and jail system of two million affects not only people locked up, but their families and communities—in particular, the low-income communities that are most affected by these policies. Increasingly, we are seeing enormous ripple effects of our imprisonment policies.

We have had an enormous increase in the number of women incarcerated in the last two decades—at a far greater rate of increase than for men. As a result, on any given day about a quarter million children have a mother behind bars. If we look at the race of children who have a parent in prison, one of every fourteen African-American children today has a parent who is locked up. We can only begin to project some of the resulting impacts over the next generation. In some communities, enormous numbers of people are cycling in and out of the prison system, back in the community. The recycling affects the whole fabric and stability of those communities—in terms, for example, of marriage and family formation, community leadership, and the role models we see in these neighborhoods.

These ripple effects are very significant. Some of them we can quantify. We can measure how many people are going through these systems. In other ways, we can only speculate about the impact because we have never had a situation like this before, where the prison-state has become such an integral part of our public policy and affected this many people. We need to examine these consequences. We need to examine the impact of the drug war and ask whether it is helping or hurting policy on general substance abuse.

We know that some four million Americans were not able to vote in the November 2002 election, as a result of losing their voting rights because of a felony conviction. So we are talking about questions of democracy as well. We need to broaden the prison discussion so that the issue is not just how much time John Smith, convicted of burglary, should spend in prison. We need a broader discussion about how John Smith became a burglar. What are our sentencing options? And how do we prevent the next John Smith from ending up in the courtroom next week?

We also need to question policymakers who argue that the public is demanding present policy. The public is concerned, legitimately, about crime. The public wants to do something about crime. But I am not convinced that the public *only* wants to build prisons as a means of dealing with that problem. There is a great deal of public opinion data and other experiences that show us the public is much more receptive to broader analysis and critique.

When we turn from the message to the messengers, we need to think beyond the sort of traditional reformers—in two ways. One is toward people working in the system every day—the police, the prison wardens, the prosecutors, the judges—many of whom, if only privately, are very concerned about the direction policy is going. Many prison wardens will tell you that half the people in prison wouldn't need to be there if we had some other options available for them. And many police chiefs recognize that just arresting people from now until forever is not the solution to our crime problem.

We need different approaches and we need to open opportunities for those voices to get out there. It is a very different kind of message when it is coming from a police chief than when it is from the director of the American Civil Liberties Union.

We also need to mobilize the people most affected by present policies—people living in low-income minority communities. I speak of offenders, former offenders, and their families. They have very little political power and influence in this society. Their numbers are increasing very substantially, and they have voices, roles, and messages that need to be communicated. We need to figure out who those messengers are and what their messages should be. For example, when it comes to mandatory sentencing, there are horror stories but also heartwarming stories. There are people who have been sent away for many years as a result of harsh drug policies, but families and communities have been organizing to try to get them out to call their cases to public attention. A modest number of cases have had some success.

MORE CONSTRUCTIVE WAYS OF PROMOTING PUBLIC SAFETY

To conclude, the issues are challenging. The case for more incarceration is much thinner all the time, and there is a growing body of research and growing public receptivity to doing things in different ways. What we need to do now is coordinate the various issues. How do economic changes, social structures, family formation, and crime all fit together? With an understanding of the interrelatedness of the issue, we can collectively begin to develop solutions and policies that look to much more constructive ways of promoting public safety and building strong families and communities.

BIBLIOGRAPHY

P. M. Harrison and J. C. Karberg. *Prison and Jail Inmates at Midyear 2002,* Bureau of Justice Statistics, Washington, D.C., 2003.

Marc Mauer, "Comparative International Rates of Incarceration: An Examination of Causes and Trends," presented to the U.S. Commission on Civil Rights, The Sentencing Project, Washington, D.C., June 20, 2003.

———, *Race to Incarcerate* (New York: New Press, 1999).

———, with Meda Chesney-Lind, *Invisible Punishment: The Collateral Consequences of Mass Imprisonment* (New York: New Press, 2002).

Josh White and Susan Schmidt, "Ashcroft May Hear Sniper Evidence Today; Decision on Venue for First Prosecution Nears; Alabama May Have Edge," *Washington Post*, November 5, 2002.

• 28 •

The Missing Debate

Richard C. Leone

The response of any administration to the devastating attacks that took place on September 11, 2001, would have been swift and sweeping—and unconditionally supported by virtually every citizen. The attacks also could have served as a trigger for the creation of an unprecedented international response, a grand global coalition encompassing most of the civilized world in a battle against terrorism.

Yet looking back, we can see that the federal government has squandered much of this potential for broad international support and for domestic bipartisanship. Instead, there is ample evidence that September 11 became a springboard for an ideologically driven unilateralism in global affairs and for an aggressive radical domestic agenda. This policy revolution occurred despite the fact that Americans strongly prefer a less divisive approach to international affairs and national security, as embodied in the familiar phrase "politics stops at the water's edge."

Despite the significance of recent policies, debate about the nation's course has been slow to develop. While the quantity of discussion has increased sharply, it continues to fall far short of what would be expected and justified by the scope of recent foreign policy.

THE PATRIOTISM OF QUESTIONING THE GOVERNMENT'S ACTIONS

The problem is evident if we consider just one category of recent policies, those that could have significant and lasting impacts on the civil liberties of American citizens. Perhaps this issue has remained below the media's radar screen because so much attention has been centered upon the continuing consequences and costs of the war and post-war in Iraq. Perhaps another factor is the federal government's overt efforts to discourage and even intimidate those who wish to debate its policies.

There is nothing unpatriotic or even counterproductive about questioning a government's actions. History teaches us that bypassing public deliberation almost inevitably leads to outcomes that the nation ends up regretting. Looking back, there is long list of reactions to other threats in which the absence of open debate coincided with many of the nation's low points. During the twentieth century, the Palmer raids after World War I, the internment of Japanese Americans during World War II, the Bay of Pigs fiasco, Iran-Contra, the secret war in Honduras, and any number of other ventures went badly astray. Public deliberation entails controversy that can be painful and time consuming, but it often prevents bad ideas from taking hold while broadening support for policies that are implemented.

For months following the September 11 attacks, however, politicians, the press, and citizens remained off balance, unable to resume the normal rough and tumble of democracy. Still today, we as a nation continue to digest the dramatic alteration of the world. We were sure before September 11 that the United States was the unchallenged global economic leader—the preeminent nation, without conventional military rivals, that was culturally and politically admired and imitated.

Perhaps the specific actions taken by the federal government should have come as no surprise. Key officials were quick to put forward their own longstanding beliefs about greater government secrecy, less fettered law enforcement, military activism, and unilateral aggressiveness in international affairs as exactly the right remedies for the new threat. Indeed, the Patriot Act that the executive branch authored, and that Congress passed almost entirely intact, was among the most far-reaching and invasive legislation since the Espionage Act of 1917 and the Sedition Act of 1918. Other measures that the federal government put forward—sometimes only as trial balloons—went even farther.

The Patriot Act permits federal investigators to look at individuals' retail purchases, Internet searches, e-mail, and library usage, all without notification. It allows the U.S. attorney general to detain immigrants based on "suspicion," requires businesses to report "suspicious transactions," allows the government to conduct secret searches without notification, grants the Federal Bureau of Investigation and other agencies greatly expanded access to all sorts of personal and business data with little judicial oversight, and allows for surveillance of any number of domestic organizations and advocacy groups.

Despite the many new powers the Patriot Act grants, many experts doubt whether it will actually succeed in reducing terrorist activity. While the act permits the government to collect vast amounts of information, it does not provide the agencies involved the resources required to analyze it. As New York University law professor Stephen Schulhofer has observed, "a large part of what we lack [already] is not raw data but the ability to separate significant intelligence from 'noise'."

While the American Civil Liberties Union, the American Library Association, the Electronic Privacy Information Center, and other privacy and civil liberties groups tried to prevent the historic changes in civil liberties embodied in the Patriot Act from becoming law in the heat of the moment, their efforts went virtually unnoticed. Even those members of Congress traditionally known as strong voices in favor of civil liberties said little about the legislation. The executive branch launched an aggressive campaign on behalf of enactment, implying that anyone opposing the Patriot Act could be considered soft on terrorists, the message of which echoed President Bush's comment after September 11: "You are either with us or with the terrorists."

Substantial debate of federal government policies did not take place for nearly two years following the terrorist attacks. Perhaps the simple passage of time since the attacks greatly contributed to the opposition's newly found voice. However, the effect of an increasing number of reports about the adverse impacts of recent policies combined with the determination of the executive branch to pass additional legislation that would infringe on Americans' civil liberties should not be overlooked.

The Department of Justice, for example, has announced that it might monitor conversations between attorneys and detainees. The attorney general rewrote FBI guidelines to allow agents to monitor all political, religious, and advocacy groups without any evidence of wrongdoing and to make it easier to monitor Internet activity. He reversed the policy underlying the Freedom of Information Act that required agencies to begin with the presumption that information should be publicly available. In addition, male immigrants already legally in the United States from twenty different countries, mostly Arab and Southeast Asian, now are required to register with the INS, regardless of their status. Those who fail to register are subject to fines, entry in the National Crime Information Center database, and possible deportation. In the process, the federal government detained almost 1,200 men, the vast majority for immigration violations, and refused to release their names or any other information about them. Some have been deported, others have been released, but several are still incarcerated.

In June 2003, the Justice Department Office of the Inspector General released a comprehensive 198-page report detailing the treatment of hundreds of additional Muslim men who were detained in the days immediately following September 11, and exposing a number of abuses committed by the department and the FBI in the wake of the terrorist attacks. The report's findings raised concern not only among immigrants' rights activists and civil libertarians but also among members of Congress and the media, something not even the passage of the Patriot Act was able to accomplish.

Of the 762 detainees, only Zacarias Moussaoui (who was already in custody before September 11) ultimately was charged with terrorism. The detainees were held in prison for long periods without being charged. Many were held secretly, unable to contact family members or seek counsel. There was evidence of mistreatment and, in Brooklyn, cases of physical abuse. Even upon release, it took the FBI on average eighty days to clear the names of the detainees, making it virtually impossible for the men to live in their communities without suspicion. Yet the federal government has maintained it had done nothing wrong. The Justice Department argued that its actions were necessary in the war against terrorism and announced that the Justice Department "makes no apologies" for the treatment of the detainees.

A similar pattern of detention without prosecution has emerged regarding the detainees in Guantanamo Bay, Cuba. While the U.S. government has said that the detainees have connections to terrorist organizations, none of them has been charged with terrorism. In fact, the only people at the camps who have been charged are an American government translator and a chaplain.

THE THREAT OF A SECOND PATRIOT ACT

The growing doubt surrounding federal antiterrorism policies has not slowed a push for increased power to pursue terrorism suspects. There is support in many circles for an expansion of the Patriot Act, an endorsement for a Patriot Act II. Patriot Act II would grant the Department of Justice and law enforcement officials even greater powers of search and surveillance than those offered by the original Patriot Act. If passed, this legislation would:

- Severely restrict public access to information about those who have been detained, making it prohibitively difficult, if not impossible, for family members, the media, and even attorneys to determine detainees' status or location.
- Increase the FBI's ability to obtain a search warrant as well as expand its wiretapping privileges, both with little court supervision. In many cases, an FBI agent would be able to obtain a search warrant by simply telling a secret court that he suspects an individual of planning terrorism. The agent would not have to provide any supporting evidence of this claim, and the individual likely would never know that a search warrant had been filed against him, that his phones had been tapped, his e-mail read, or his house and belongings searched.
- Amend the Freedom of Information Act to prevent any information about aliens who are being investigated for terrorism from being released. Such measures would cripple further immigrants' rights in the United States and threaten journalists' ability to provide detailed and accurate reporting.

While conservatives claim that such efforts are necessary to prevent future terrorist attacks, scholars such as Schulhofer question whether this level of secrecy actually would improve national security.

These actions have caused a stir among members of Congress. In contrast to their prior silence, members of both parties have reacted vocally and negatively to news of a possible second, even more far-reaching piece of legislation. Ironically, it was the discovery of the secretly drafted Patriot Act II, in large part, that facilitated the only serious, sustained debates in Congress about provisions in the *original* Patriot Act.

The number of members of Congress questioning the recent antiterrorism policies has grown. Some have introduced legislation that would limit executive branch authority. Among the issues debated is the longevity of the Patriot Act itself. As established in the original act, approximately half of the provisions will expire in December 2005 if Congress does not renew them. Among the laws scheduled to sunset are the FBI's expanded wiretapping authority and an increased ability to acquire business records in intelligence investigations.

Perhaps more important than the individual provisions, the sunset clause represents a limit on government's power. By requiring that these measures be reenacted after a defined period, Americans are offered some form of assurance that key provisions will last only as long as the emergency—or at least be automatically reconsidered after enough time elapsed to review their costs and benefits.

Yet even this effort to ensure basic checks and balances has not taken place without a battle. Some conservatives do not see the Patriot Act as a wartime provision and have proposed making permanent all laws included under the Patriot Act. Unlike the first time around, bipartisan opposition by key members of Congress to such a measure has ensured that, at least for now, the existing sunset provisions will stand.

OUTRAGE OVER THE POINDEXTER TERRORISM FUTURES MARKET

In 2003, a new debate arose, this time a result of the discovery of Admiral John Poindexter's plans for a terrorism futures market. Poindexter, then director of the Pentagon's Defense Advanced Research Projects Agency, had begun developing a system that would enable anonymous investors to place bets on when and where future acts of terrorism would take place. Not only was the executive branch aware of the project, but it even had requested $8 million toward its development. In addition to a poorly thought-out idea that was doomed to fail, the concept was unethical at best and considered morbid and deeply disturbing by many. While some government officials, including Admiral Poindexter, defended the idea as an innovative use of futures markets and market forces, the majority of Congress and the American public were outraged and disgusted. Within days of the news leak about the program, the White House officially put an end to further work in the area and Poindexter resigned.

THE WISDOM OF "MR. REPUBLICAN"

These events have somewhat strengthened the position of civil liberties advocates. Unfortunately, the American public remains remarkably quiet. While 62 percent of Americans feel that the FBI's policies may be intrusive, an overwhelming majority (79 percent) think that investigating threats, even if it results in a loss of privacy, is more important right now than respect for privacy (18 percent). Americans also trust government more today than just a few months before the September 11 attacks. According to a Gallup poll, in May 2001 52 percent of Americans thought that the U.S. government had so much power as to pose an immediate threat to Americans' rights and freedoms. Yet on the two-year anniversary of the September 11 attacks, only 39 percent thought government had become too large and powerful.

The American public, in large part, is still unsettled. The avalanche of events dominating the media and private conversation—the anthrax attacks, Afghanistan, the "shoe bomber," the Washington area sniper attacks, North Korea, frequent color-coded changes in the nation's security level, the war and post-war in Iraq, and suicidal terrorist attacks in many nations—have caused fear and confusion to linger. The nature and complexity of current threats, both real and imagined, inevitably strengthen the argument for continuation of the policies of recent years.

In the current circumstances, however, we might all learn something from the man who was known as "Mr. Republican." Speaking less than two weeks after Pearl Harbor, Ohio Senator Robert A. Taft said, "As a matter of general principle, I believe there can be no doubt that criticism in time of war is essential to the maintenance of any kind of democratic government. Too many people desire to suppress criticism simply because they think it will give some comfort to the enemy. If that comfort makes the enemy feel better for a few moments, they are welcome to it as far as I am concerned, because the maintenance of the right of criticism in the long run will do the country maintaining it a great deal more good than it will do the enemy, and it will prevent mistakes which might otherwise occur."

Those words ring true today. Clearly, we have much to talk about: a difficult conflict in Iraq, ongoing instability in Afghanistan, continued failure to locate our most dangerous foes, constraints on liberty and legal due process at home, and even a new readiness to condemn as disloyal those who raise questions. Americans often seek entertainment as much as enlightenment in their consumption of political information, but that appetite can be hazardous to the national health. We need to know more; we need to subject our policies to the most rigorous tests of debate and investigation; and we need to seek to reconstitute the all-too-fleeting unity of purpose at home and abroad that existed in the immediate aftermath of September 11. It will be an enormous undertaking—and it is one that depends upon the engagement of all of us if it is to succeed.

BIBLIOGRAPHY

ABC News, September 10, 2002, surveyed 1,001 adults, margin of error +/− 3%.

ABC News/*Washington Post* poll, December 17, 2002, surveyed 1,209 adults, margin of error +/− 3%.

Robert J. Blendon and John M. Benson, "Polling Indicators about Civil Liberties in a Time of War," *Indicators*, Fall 2002.

Darren W. Davis and Brian D. Silver, "Civil Liberties vs. Security in the Context of the Terrorist Attacks on America," American Political Science Association Report, August 2002.

Joan Didion, "Fixed Opinions, or the Hinge of History," *New York Review of Books*, January 16, 2003.

Paula DiPerna, Media, Charity and Philanthropy in the Aftermath of September 11, 2001 (New York: The Century Foundation, 2003).

Thad Hall, Homeland Security Watch (New York: The Century Foundation, February 2003–October 2003).

Thad Hall and Anthony Sutton, Visa Tracking (New York: The Century Foundation, July 2002).

Richard C. Leone and Greg Anrig Jr., eds., *The War on Our Freedoms: Civil Liberties in an Age of Terrorism* (New York: Public Affairs, 2003).

Anthony Lewis, Security and Liberty (New York: The Century Foundation, 2003).

Stephen J. Schulhofer, "At War With Liberty: Post-9/11, Due Process and Security Have Taken a Beating," *American Prospect*, March 1, 2003.

———, *The Enemy Within: Intelligence Gathering, Law Enforcement and Civil Liberties in the Wake of September 11* (New York: The Century Foundation Press, 2002).

John F. Stacks, *Scotty: James B. Reston and the Rise and Fall of American Journalism* (New York: Little, Brown, 2002).

Senator Robert A. Taft, Chicago speech, December 19, 1941.

Patricia Thomas, The Anthrax Attacks (New York: The Century Foundation, 2003).

Gregory C. Treverton, Intelligence, Law Enforcement and Homeland Security (New York: The Century Foundation, 2002).

Tova Andrea Wang, Civil Liberties and the Presidential Candidates (New York: The Century Foundation, November 2003).

———, The Debate Over a National ID Card (New York: The Century Foundation, May 2002).

———, The Devil's in the Details: Overlooked Highlights of the Report on 9/11 Detainees (New York: The Century Foundation, June 2003).

———, The Military Tribunals Debate (New York: The Century Foundation, October 2003).

• 29 •

It Is Time to Break the Silence

Yvonne Scruggs-Leftwich

Even when pressed by the demands of inner truth, men do not easily assume the task of opposing their government's policy, especially in time of war. Nor does the human spirit move without great difficulty against all the apathy of conformist thought within one's own bosom and in the surrounding world. Moreover, when the issues at hand seem as perplexed as they often do in the case of this dreadful conflict, we are always on the verge of being mesmerized by uncertainty.

But we must move on. Some of us who have already begun to break the silence of the night have found that the calling to speak is often a vocation of agony, but we must speak. We must speak with all the humility that is appropriate to our limited vision, but we must speak.

Perhaps a new spirit is rising among us. If it is, let us trace its movement well and pray that our own inner being may be sensitive to its guidance, for we are deeply in need of a new way beyond the darkness that seems to close around us.

—The Reverend Martin Luther King Jr.

In this critical period in our nation's history, those of us who search for alternative national policy would do well to remember Dr. King's words. These words suggest ways of framing more productive post–September 11 alternatives as new ways beyond the darkness that seems to close around us—ways that reflect the emerging opinion among African-American leaders.

DO NOT SEND SMART BOMBS ON DUMB MISSIONS

Dr. Joseph E. Lowery, president of the Georgia Coalition for a People's Agenda and chairman of the Black Leadership Forum, has asked the federal government not to continue sending "smart bombs on dumb missions," referring to trigger-happy posturing toward new, yet-unknown, and illusive locations. He cautioned that, "We have affirmed violence as an acceptable means of solving problems. We have led the way in the United States and, like Libya and China, we still use the death penalty. We fill up our prisons (with people of color) and we don't seem to learn that violence begets violence. . . . We have sown the wind and now we are reaping the whirlwind."

Eddie N. Williams, president of the Joint Center for Political and Economic Studies, also has expressed concerns about priorities and balance in America's security responses. In the Joint Center's *FOCUS* magazine, Williams wrote that the federal government urged us to return to business as usual: "Believing this to be our patriotic duty, we heed [the] call. And while we must accept that life will never return to 'normal' as we knew it prior to September 11, we still must commit as a nation to rebuilding businesses, the financial markets, consumer confidence, *and building new coalitions"* (italics mine).

Also writing in *FOCUS*, Eisenhower Foundation board member Roger W. Wilkins, professor of American Studies at George Mason University, has addressed patriotism and the need to defend the nation against terrorism, but has pointedly questioned the impact of policies which have been implemented or considered since September 11: "I'm much more patriotic than I thought I was. My patriotism has a lot of dissent in it, but it's patriotic nonetheless."

REVERSE THE ASSAULT ON CIVIL LIBERTIES

Some of the federal government's recent policies are eroding our constitutional protections and summarily taking away our civil liberties. For example:

- Military tribunals for civilians and their unilateral description as "enemy combatants" violate our habeas corpus and other established protections.
- Eight thousand racially profiled "Muslim" detainees, including established, prominent American-born black Muslims, well known to African-American leadership, have been covered in secrecy.
- Incommunicado retentions can, by their very anonymity, involve almost any person of color: maybe an immigrant, maybe not.
- Carte blanche powers given the Justice Department also grant, by inference, arbitrary powers to law enforcement officials in general, and this cannot be good news for black and Hispanic males across the country.
- The abrogation of attorney-client protections cuts to the core of American democratic guarantees.

These assaults on civil liberties are a call to action to avert a headlong drive toward totalitarianism. We need to revisit Hannah Arendt's landmark book, *The Ori-*

gins of Totalitarianism, to remind ourselves that the outer reaches of repression, when allowed to flourish unchecked, abridge everyone's rights, not just the rights of those targeted.

SEPTEMBER 11 HAS ALLOWED PUNITIVE, INTOLERANT POLICY TO CONTINUE

According to the operations research tools of "branch and bound analysis," the tragedy of September 11 inadvertently provided an additional set of optional approaches for accomplishing some preexisting objectives. September 11 and the consequent homeland security responses raised considerably the possibility of success of policy actions that have their genesis in prior punitive, intolerant policy intentions. This outcome is more nonpartisan than is comfortable for many of us, given an apparent lack of opposition from either side of the congressional aisle. Such an outcome is further strengthened by the reluctance of a majority of lawmakers to take a strong stand against excessive and extreme measures that are moving forward without responsible checks and balances.

The federal government's failed "free market–tough state" agenda, as discussed by Elliott Currie in chapter 26, defines punitive, intolerant policies. A good example is control by the states of welfare administration through the vehicle of the 1996–1997 "welfare reform" legislation, Temporary Assistance for Needy Families (TANF). A cursory look at emerging statistics reveals that the rolls have been reduced, but with draconian, cynical and—unfortunately—correctly predicted results. Those results include:

- Short-term jobs, often lasting no longer than three months, followed by more short-term jobs or serial unemployment
- No benefits, because of the temporary nature of the jobs
- Low-paying jobs, requiring that workers hold two and three simultaneously
- Reduced or curtailed housing subsidies
- No affordable child care, if any at all, especially needed by workers having two and three jobs
- No or few food stamps, or reduced food stamp allowances
- Lack of transportation money to get from one job to another

Now there is emerging a poorer, more marginal, less secure, "former welfare-recipient" class, whose children are poorer, hungrier, less supervised, and much more at risk. These children were left behind by a "Leave No Child Behind" policy. Welfare began as a program to reduce poverty, yet poverty has increased in the new millennium during "welfare reform."

Other previously failed policies now finding fertile ground for stealth implementation include the shift in resources from social programs to the war machine and to upper-income tax brackets. These ideas originally also were proposed through former Speaker Newt Gingrich's "Contract with America."

In addition, post–September 11 responses have given fresh meaning to racial profiling, the new mechanism for neutralizing and suppressing the power and impact of racial and ethnic difference. Added to so-called antiterrorism profiling of "colored" people, as mentioned above, are recent studies by the Justice Policy Institute that show a growing, inverse, and destructive statistic. There are fully one-third more black men in prison than there are in colleges and universities. Given this equation, racial profiling emerges as the primary tool which is central to maintaining this inverse racial imbalance. Lock them up and keep them uneducated. In chapter 27, Marc Mauer provides more perspective on the negative racial impacts of incarceration.

We need to set forth alternative post–September 11 policies—solutions to persistent problems facing our society. The problem is not one of ignorance about sound remedies or about things that work but of failed moral resolve, a lack of old-fashioned intestinal fortitude, and the reality of the cynicism and the protective self-interest that drive American politics.

THE NATION NEEDS TERRORISM MANAGEMENT

The United States is undertaking an impossible and irrational task by defining "terrorism destruction" rather than "terrorism management" as an objective. Tough talk about capturing the terrorists "dead or alive" projects a "Gunfight at the OK Corral" mentality, more suited to the taming of the tumbleweed and tortilla flats of the nineteenth-century, wild American West than to the building of collaborations with other nations on whom the search for terrorists—through twenty-first-century, land-mined mountain passes and sand bunkers of the Middle East and Northern Africa—must depend. Hyperbole must be sacrificed to the higher imperative of world survival.

Stubborn ignorance of the complex ethnicity and culture of the non–Anglo Saxon world does not stand the United States in good stead. Just as we have matured as a nation to understand that a child is not an underdeveloped adult, so our government must realize that the developing world is not just a group of sun-drenched distant relatives who speak a foreign language.

For example, the arrogant rejection by the United States of any responsible official role as participants in the World Conference Against Racism, held in Durban, South Africa, during the month immediately preceding September 11, 2001, is well documented. America's bad behavior at the conference demonstrated how naive American foreign policy is about the symbolism that undergirds our expressed interest in international collaboration and global coexistence. Very junior administration representatives, without authority to do anything absent instructions from Washington, hung around the corridors of deliberations at the Durban conference prior to September 11. Immediately after the terrorism of September 11, top-level American diplomats seeking support for an antiterrorist initiative importuned the same Third World leaders who personally had navigated the conference corridors and had been snubbed by American officials the week before. The symbolic retribution was obvious and emphasized the need for global collaboration.

The preemptive invasion of Iraq and the pursuit of postwar policy against internal Iraqi resistance have captured the headlines of mainstream media and pushed aside calls for global collaboration, criticism of stealth policy that further disadvantages minorities within America, and discussion of voter and campaign-finance reform in response to the 2000 election.

One of our responses must be a laser focus on Congress, both the Senate and the House of Representatives, where most members are nearer the average American's economic and social profile. It is this body of individually elected, legitimately inaugurated, and constituent-accountable public officials that offers a truth-telling and fact-seeking venue. Both houses of Congress must ask, as a matter of conscience and of national security: Who knew what? When? How much?

Pronouncements questioning the loyalty and patriotism of anyone who deigns to challenge present policy should not be permitted to prevail. It is the proper province of members of Congress to enforce and protect the Constitution and the constitutional rights of all of their constituents. Those who seek alternative policies must demand that members of Congress carry out their sworn duties to investigate.

MEDIA ALLIES MUST UNITE

As we break the silence, we should not discount African-American media. There are 205 weekly publications that reflect the black voice. They reach a lot of people. They would reach more people if they had better funding, if people ran more ads in the paper, and if they could afford to hire and keep more reporters.

But people still read them, and we have not really incorporated them into the conscious litany of resources that can be used to communicate the alternative policies in this book. The African-American media already are on the same page as this volume. They are already talking about human-rights abuses, with good reason. It is a cliche but it is still true: When general America sneezes, African Americans get pneumonia. African Americans are especially sensitive to the abuses of the Patriot Act.

Three good examples of African-American media that need to be better utilized are the *Chicago Defender*, published by Vernon Jarrett, the distinguished journalist; the Baltimore and Washington *Afro-American* newspapers, published by a family that is now in its fourth generation in the publication; and the *Jackson Advocate*, which has been bombed so many times that they have a new location every year, because they speak truth to power and they threaten people who do bad things. (Similarly, see Amy Goodman's account in chapter 34 of how the Ku Klux Klan bombed Pacifica Radio.)

Of course, regional media are not just African American. There are Latino media, Asian-American media, gay media, labor-affiliated media, and the media of organized religion. There are other media outlets that are secondary in the perception of most Americans. These other media outlets reach people whose voices are not now being heard, people who are not in the decision loop. All have well-developed communications networks. Local radio sometimes offers more liberal voices, operating without the corporate weight that burdens so many big-city newspapers. The progressive movement has a great many allies, and these allies have the ability to listen and to speak.

All of these allies need to be part of a coalition for alternatives to recent federal policy. They need to be among those organized for grassroots forums that continue to develop the alternatives to domestic, foreign, economic, and media policy as articulated on these pages.

Mainstream media need to be critiqued more aggressively following the recommendation of Robert McChesney, John Nichols, Amy Goodman, and Eli Pariser in chapters 31, 32, and 34. Reformers should meet with the editorial boards of mainstream media to press for alternatives. Advertising needs to be purchased in mainstream media, following the examples of MoveOn.org and TomPaine.org.

THE GOVERNMENT MUST RECOGNIZE OTHER CULTURES AND PEOPLES

In their work in the field of public administration, James March and Herbert Simon wrote about satisfactory versus optimal standards. Finding the optimal alternative is a radically different problem from finding a satisfactory alternative. An alternative is optimal if (1) there exists a set of criteria that permits all alternatives to be compared and (2) the alternative in question is preferred by these criteria to all other alternatives. But an alternative is satisfactory, or satisfies, if (1) there exists a set of criteria that describes minimally satisfactory alternatives and (2) the alternative in question meets or exceeds all of these criteria.

Most human decision making, whether individual or organizational, is concerned with the discovery and selection of satisfactory alternatives. Only in exceptional cases is it concerned with the discovery and selection of optimal alternatives. Since September 11, America has been satisfying when it should be optimizing. Unless the nation seeks optimizing alternatives, unless we are willing, actively willing, to think outside of the box, we will fail to stem the tide of pre-emptive imperialism. If that occurs, our lives will be profoundly different beyond the most morbid fantasies which we entertain after September 11.

Many Americans suffer from what the psychologists call "cognitive dissonance." It permits the understanding only of occurrences which we have experienced previously. It encourages us to interpret new, unfamiliar experiences through the prism of things we already know about. Cognitive dissonance can prevent our recognition of and respect for other cultures and people and cause us seriously to miscalculate how other people and other cultures interpret us and what we do.

The consequences of cognitive dissonance will literally kill us all if we do not intervene and carry out alternatives to present policy. We have the tools. What we need to do now is marshal our will.

The Bible says, "Without vision, the people will perish." In "Where Do We Go From Here" Dr. Martin Luther King Jr. encouraged vision: "The whole structure must be changed. A nation that will keep people in slavery for 244 years will "thingify" things—make them into things. Therefore, they will exploit them and poor people generally. And a nation that will exploit economically will have to have foreign investments and everything else and will have to use its military might to protect them."

All of these problems are tied together. Let us therefore be dissatisfied, and then we'll recognize that out of one blood God made all men to dwell on the face of the Earth. Let us be dissatisfied.

BIBLIOGRAPHY

Hannah Arendt, *The Origins of Totalitarianism* (New York: Harcourt, 1948).

Fred R. Harris and Lynn A. Curtis, eds., *Locked in the Poorhouse: Cities, Race, and Poverty in the United States* (Lanham: Rowman & Littlefield, 1998).

Justice Policy Institute, *Cellblocks or Classrooms? The Funding of Higher Education and Corrections and Its Impact on African-American Men* (Washington, D.C.: Justice Policy Institute, August 2002).

Rev. Martin Luther King Jr., "Beyond Vietnam: A Time to Break Silence," speech at Riverside Church, New York, April 4, 1967.

———, "Where Do We Go from Here?" Southern Christian Leadership Conference speech, August 16, 1967.

Joseph E. Lowery, "Civil Rights Legends" (Atlanta: ABC Television production, 2002).

James G. March and Herbert A. Simon, *Decision-Making Theory* (Stanford: Stanford University, 1958).

Roger W. Wilkins, "Perspectives," *FOCUS* magazine, Joint Center for Political and Economic Studies, January 2002.

Eddie N. Williams, "Business as Usual?" *FOCUS* magazine, Joint Center for Political and Economic Studies, October 2001.

• 30 •

Civil Liberties and Effective Investigation

Coleen M. Rowley

The balance between individuals' civil liberties and the need for effective investigation is hard to maintain even during so-called normal times, let alone times of increased terrorist threat or war. It is, admittedly, a difficult balancing act.

—Coleen M. Rowley, *New York Times*, March 6, 2003

Civil libertarians warn that privacy and liberty are at risk in America, that a combination of lightning-fast technological innovation and the erosion of privacy protections threatens to transform George Orwell's Big Brother into a very real part of American life, turning the nation into a "Surveillance Society."

At the same time, law enforcement and other government authorities tell us that they need additional powers and new technological tools to effectively investigate in order to bring criminals to justice and prevent acts of terrorism.

What is the truth? The debate has been monopolized by the people who are the most passionate on the issue—the partisans on both extremes. Many have observed and complained about the unwise, needless, and in some cases bizarre restrictions placed on law enforcement at the expense of victims and the public. But a review of old FBI files from the communist "Red Scare" era and the protests and civil disobedience of the 1960s and 1970s shows how real or perceived threats can easily result in overreaction by authorities that threaten citizens' rights. (FBI Director Robert Mueller III has himself chronicled the various abuses that have occurred in the United States during times of crisis: the "Palmer Raids" of 1919, the Japanese internment during World War II, and the FBI's COINTELPRO program of the 1960s and 1970s.)

Accordingly, in this chapter I want to eliminate some of the misinformation and hyperbole in the debate on civil liberties and effective investigation since September

This chapter represents Coleen M. Rowley's personal views, and not those of the FBI.

11 and the Patriot Act. I want to highlight valid points on both sides of the issue in order to achieve a better understanding of the problems facing America today.

The debate needs to proceed in an informed but dispassionate way. Only by debating the true problems facing law enforcement and national security, and the true costs of law enforcement action, can we dispel public paranoia, obtain public cooperation, and thereby maximize Americans' security without too high a price on personal freedoms.

THE PATRIOT ACT

The Patriot Act is 342 pages long and contains about 160 provisions. Very few people are conversant with every change made by the legislation. It is safe to say, however, that at least some of the provisions in the Act are noncontroversial. For instance, Section 102 of the Act contains the "sense of Congress" condemning discrimination against Arab and Muslim Americans. In addition, many provisions were on the drawing boards long before September 11—for example, to remedy gaps in the law as it dealt with emerging computer technology and electronic communications.

Other provisions were added specifically in response to September 11 because of the new threat of terrorism. The most controversial provisions of the Act are those which have been repeatedly cited in news articles and discussed on civil-libertarian websites. These provisions include requests for business records, use of "sneak and peek" search warrants, provisions for e-mail surveillance, permission to share intelligence-driven information with criminal investigations and prosecutors, and definitions of terrorism that raise questions about the First Amendment right to dissent. Consider the following provisions.

REQUESTS FOR BUSINESS RECORDS

Section 215 of the Patriot Act allows the FBI to request Foreign Intelligence Surveillance Act (FISA) orders for business records and other "tangible things." The main criticisms of this provision by civil libertarians are that the FBI need not show probable cause or even reasonable suspicion; persons served with such orders are prohibited from disclosing the fact to anyone else; and there is no notification to the person whose records are obtained.

These criticisms can easily be countered. Criminal subpoenas and court orders for business records and other materials held by third parties have never required any showing of probable cause or even reasonable suspicion—because they are not "searches." They are not considered searches because, in the legal sense, one does not have a reasonable expectation of privacy in matters that one has openly entrusted to someone else.

For example, the bank records of someone suspected of committing bank fraud are usually obtained by the FBI through a subpoena requiring only relevance, not any level of suspicion (in fact, there is a federal privacy protection law that *prohibits* search warrants from being used to obtain records from certain third-party holders of records, those intending to publish; in those cases, the law specifies that subpoenas *must* be used). It can be argued, and government officials have done so successfully, that it should not be harder to investigate terrorist suspects than ordinary criminal suspects.

This section of the Act does not allow for investigation of Americans *solely* based on exercise of First Amendment rights. For example, the FBI would *not* be able to seek records about someone who merely wrote a letter to the editor criticizing government policy. However, this First Amendment protection only extends to citizens and permanent residents. Many if not most criminal subpoenas and court orders contain provisions prohibiting the third party from notifying the subject and, with only a few exceptions, law enforcement need not inform criminal subjects that their records have been obtained. Court orders for nondisclosure are usually available to delay any required notice until the conclusion of the investigative phase. (Otherwise, preliminary investigative steps would tip off the subject.) It is true that a criminal subject, if and when charged, will eventually learn of the evidence that the government has obtained, including any records. But if a terrorist is charged criminally, he or she would also probably learn of the fact that the federal government had obtained his or her records from a third party through the FISA method.

There is much concern over the potential for infringement of First Amendment protection by use of Section 215 authority with libraries and bookstores to ascertain the books a person has read or purchased. This concern has even resulted in internal policies or local resolutions being adopted to mandate noncompliance with relevant provisions of the Act. However well-intentioned such concern may be, it is misplaced. As a practical matter, it is easier to obtain an ordinary grand jury subpoena than to obtain a FISA court order under Section 215 to seek library or bookstore records. It also should be recognized that such limited use of subpoenas has on occasion been justified. For example, when the Unabomber's "manifesto" cited four obscure books, the FBI promptly served subpoenas on certain libraries to ascertain who had checked out those books.

We know that the September 11 hijackers relied on public-access computers, including those available in libraries and stores like Kinko's, to communicate with each other via the Internet. There is a legitimate need for speedy access to records of such computer usage. (This would, of course, not include the content of any stored communications in computers, which must normally be obtained through a criminal or FISA search warrant demonstrating probable cause.) In fact, since September 11, FBI contact with libraries has been minimal and sporadic. In 2003, the attorney general announced that, thus far, no Section 215 order had been served upon any library. In any case, long before the Act, access to computer usage and other library records was possible via the subpoena route, requiring nothing more than a showing of relevance.

Thus, although this section of the Act creates an additional avenue through the FISA court to potentially obtain records, it does nothing to widen the government's power to acquire them and thus poses no additional risk to First Amendment protection in this area.

On the other hand, a little-noticed section of the Act, Section 505, allows FBI special agents to issue national-security letters to obtain three common types of records: an individual's telephone and Internet service provider toll and transaction records, bank records, and credit records. This delegation of authority down to special agents-in-charge has greatly streamlined and speeded up the process of issuing national security letters. The Department of Justice also expanded the authority to issue national security letters in preliminary investigations. It is also only fair to note that long-term secrecy accompanies the use of national security letters and the information obtained by the FBI. A further provision, tucked inside an intelligence-spending bill which was signed into law in 2003, expands the ability of the FBI to obtain a host of third-party records from a wide range of entities such as casinos, realtors, and the U.S. Post Office. (This legislative expansion was, however, far from a cakewalk. More than one third of the House, including fifteen conservative Republicans, voted against what some dubbed "Patriot Act II," stating that "expanding the use of administrative subpoenas [national security letters] and threatening our system of checks and balances is a step in the wrong direction.")

USE OF "SNEAK AND PEEK" SEARCH WARRANTS

Section 213 of the Act creates a uniform standard for courts to authorize delayed notice in execution of certain search warrants, as long as no items are actually seized.

So-called "sneak and peek" search warrants predate the Act. Section 213 merely made existing court practices uniform. Despite the temporary secrecy associated with this authority, there is strict judicial review of the justifications given and the length of delayed notice necessary (the standard is "reasonable cause," which is defined to include endangering the life or physical safety of an individual, flight from prosecution, evidence tampering, witness intimidation, or otherwise jeopardizing an investigation). Along with a subject's right to pursue appropriate remedies after the fact, this judicial review should provide sufficient protection against abuse.

In 2003, the House of Representatives voted to prohibit the use of "sneak and peek" warrants. However, even if this measure were to pass the Senate and be enacted into law, it is not clear what effect it would have because many courts had previously found inherent judicial authority to order such delayed notice in appropriate cases.

PROVISIONS FOR E-MAIL SURVEILLANCE

Section 216 of the Act deals with "pen/trap" information. On a telephone, "pen/trap" data are the numbers dialed into or from a target number. No search warrant establishing probable cause is necessary because courts and Congress have long determined that one does not have an expectation of privacy in the numbers alone. This type of information can therefore be obtained with a pen register court order approved by a magistrate judge.

Section 216 broadens coverage to Internet communications. The Internet communications equivalent to "pen/trap" data consists of the "to" and "from" headers of e-mail letters. It only makes sense that a pen register–type court order be available to obtain the limited to/from information in the e-mail context. The subject line is, however, considered to be content and can only be obtained with a search warrant.

The American Civil Liberties Union (ACLU) objects to the nationwide aspect of such orders. The issue here is that a judge cannot monitor the extent to which his or her order is being used. This objection, too, misses the mark. No such monitoring really ever occurred for regular telephone "pen/trap" orders. Before the availability of nationwide effectiveness, court orders had to list every conceivable communication carrier, which became more and more difficult with constant additions and changes in telecommunication carriers.

PERMISSION TO SHARE INTELLIGENCE-DRIVEN INFORMATION WITH CRIMINAL INVESTIGATORS AND PROSECUTORS

Section 218 of the Act allows law enforcement to conduct surveillance or searches under the FISA if a "significant purpose" is foreign intelligence. Debates on this part of the Act center on the phrase "significant purpose."

A criminal search warrant requires probable cause that a crime has occurred and that evidence of the crime is likely to be found at a particular place. However, searches on possible attempts by foreign countries to spy on the United States don't always have criminal searches as their objectives. A foreign intelligence officer—a spy—operating in the United States may not be breaking any criminal laws. In addition, American authorities may wish to neutralize such an officer's activities without prosecuting him.

For these reasons, a separate avenue to conducting foreign intelligence surveillance and searches was created in 1978 through FISA. In order to get authority to search or monitor wire or electronic communications under FISA, FBI agents must show probable cause that the target is a foreign power or is acting on behalf of a foreign power. Over time, in my opinion, it had become harder and harder, in a practical sense, to obtain a FISA warrant. Practically speaking, there is no litmus test to scientifically quantify any given legal standard. So meeting any of the given standards will always be somewhat subjective.

Then international terrorism hit the United States. An international terrorist group is a "foreign power" under FISA. The FBI therefore was free to obtain orders to search and conduct surveillance of suspected terrorists under FISA authority. But terrorist acts are inherently almost always criminal as well. This reality caused problems because there was supposed to be a "wall" between the criminal and the intelligence investigation of specific terrorists.

As a result, both criminal and intelligence cases would be opened. But the FBI intelligence agent could not share any information with the FBI criminal agent working on the same matter—for fear that it would be seen as an end run around the criminal process. The criminal standard appeared to be stricter and harder to satisfy than the secret intelligence process. Consequently, the FISA Court demanded strict database checking, reporting, and other procedures to ensure that the primary purpose of any FISA order was for intelligence gathering and not for evidence gathering that could be used to prosecute the terrorist criminally.

For the most part, this regimen had worked fine when dealing with foreign country–sponsored spying. So few questioned how absolutely insane the "wall" was when applied to international terrorism. That is, no one questioned it until after September 11. Then there were plenty of questions—including those raised by the dramatic testimony of an FBI agent in the New York office. Prior to the attacks, he had been thwarted from launching a criminal fugitive investigation of two of the September 11 hijackers for exactly this reason.

After September 11, then, there was plenty of reason for the Department of Justice to seek to bring the wall down. This was accomplished in the Act—with the change of essentially one word. Instead of intelligence having to be "the" purpose of a FISA order, Section 218 said it only need be a "significant" purpose. The wall was brought down, allowing sharing of intelligence-derived information with criminal investigators and criminal prosecutors.

This practice was subsequently approved in a 2002 decision by the FISA court of review. The decision opened the door to conducting both types of investigations, criminal and intelligence, on the same terrorist subjects. An investigator can select the type of criminal or intelligence method that may be the most effective. Then the information can be shared fully with every federal investigator or intelligence officer having an interest. This ability to combine the best of the criminal and intelligence worlds has become perhaps the main rationale for the current argument by the FBI that it ought not to be split up, or have its intelligence function severed, as some legislators have proposed.

But with the throttle now set at full-speed ahead when it comes to FISA initiatives in the war on terrorism, we must ask about the potential for their abuse. The judges appointed to the FISA court are the first line of defense to prevent abuse of the process. But subjectivity is inherent in this judicial process. It may be that FISA judges are even more susceptible to subjectivity than regular federal district judges because of the cloak of secrecy that surrounds their decisions and the fact that there is no appeal except in the event of any decision that adversely affects the government. (There has only been one appeal ever taken in the history of the FISA court.)

Above all, the FISA process should not become an end run around the normal criminal process. Foresight and oversight must be exercised so this doesn't happen—now or somewhere down the road. It can even be argued that the perception of an "end run" occurring is enough reason to consider instituting an independent oversight review process.

DEFINITIONS OF TERRORISM AND THE RIGHT TO DISSENT

The Patriot Act defines domestic terrorism as "acts dangerous to human life that are a violation of the criminal laws of the United States or of any state" and that "appear to be intended . . . to influence the policy of a government by intimidation or coercion" (see Section 802). Civil libertarians believe this "overbroad definition" creates a new crime, which may be used against activists exercising their rights to assemble and to dissent. However, the phrase "acts dangerous to human life" consists of strongly limiting language. This limiting language should exclude all lawful activism. For someone to be defined as a domestic terrorist, he or she must first commit a crime that is an act dangerous to human life. Property damage, even damage of great magnitude, is not enough.

On the other hand, some types of severe property damage, such as the setting of arson fires or the spraying of gunfire into what may be believed to be an unoccupied building (as, for example, occurs repeatedly at Planned Parenthood clinics around the country) could be seen as so reckless in endangering human life as to fall under this definition. The rights of all American citizens to engage in lawful protest by speaking, writing, marching, and other nonviolent acts must, however, be protected.

Close attention also should be paid to the use of large-scale interviewing initiatives; police monitoring of public events, including marches and other lawful protest events; the use of tipsters and other informants; and other privacy-defeating database mining initiatives. Such initiatives must not limit the exercise of our First Amendment rights.

Unfortunately, there are indications that the FBI failed to pay close attention when, in anticipation of large protests in Washington, D.C., and San Francisco against the war in Iraq, it issued an intelligence bulletin in 2003 to law enforcement officers around the country that seemingly blurred the distinction between First

Amendment–protected speech and acts of terrorism. The bulletin has since been posted on the FBI's website. The purpose of the bulletin is to "provide law enforcement with current, relevant terrorism information developed from counterterrorism investigation and analysis." The bulletin discusses how protestors sometimes have used training camps to rehearse for demonstrations, the Internet to raise money, and gas masks to defend against tear gas.

Whether due to overzealousness or simple carelessness, this bulletin blended lawful protest activities, civil disobedience, and terrorism together, providing little in the way of constructive guidance and perhaps unnecessarily confusing the nation's law enforcement officers who are responsible for policing such events. For example, shortly after the bulletin was issued, Miami police are reported to have unjustifiably fired rubber bullets and used batons, pepper spray, tear gas canisters, and concussion grenades on people demonstrating against Free Trade Area of the Americas meetings in Miami.

However, when certain lines are crossed, like commission of acts dangerous to human life, then First Amendment rights should not be used to shield perpetrators. For instance, because Kathleen Soliah (who later named herself Sara Jane Olson) spoke at protest rallies in the early 1970s, her exercise of First Amendment rights should not serve to obscure what else she did or to protect her from being brought to justice for her participation in a Symbionese Liberation Army pipe-bomb murder attempt, bank robbery, and other crimes.

Unfortunately, there are always a few persons who, at some point, lose patience with nonviolent, lawful methods of advocating on behalf of their cause or are otherwise driven to cross the line to domestic terrorism. Sometimes such persons seek to employ their First Amendment and other civil rights as covers for their behind-the-scenes criminal acts. This does make it more difficult, but not impossible, for law enforcement to protect the public.

THE INCREASE IN SURVEILLANCE

Let me turn now from specific sections of the Patriot Act to related policies and problems, including the increase in surveillance, mass-detention initiatives, and the need for the Freedom of Information Act.

The Dangers of an Orwellian Future

Department of Justice interrogations of large numbers of young Arab men fitting certain criteria have received harsh criticism from civil-liberties organizations. So have the announced-but-never-implemented Operation TIPS (Terrorist Information and

Prevention System) and the Pentagon-proposed Total Information Awareness project (recently renamed the "Terrorist Information Awareness" program). The loosening of guidelines allowing FBI agents to enter public places (including churches and mosques) and to surf the Internet have also met with criticism from civil libertarians.

In *1984*, George Orwell wrote, "How often, or on what system, the Thought Police plugged in any individual wire was guesswork. It was even conceivable that they watched everybody all the time. But at any rate, they could plug in your wire whenever they wanted to."

In terms of heightened surveillance potential and consequent loss of privacy, the dangers of a *1984* future for America cannot be overstated. One does not need to be an alarmist to agree with Steven Aftergood, director of the Project on Government Secrecy at the Federation of American Scientists, that "there is an enormous temptation to expand surveillance and information gathering. And unless there is an effective system of checks and balances, sooner or later this kind of surveillance is going to get out of control."

The Dangers of Corporate Surveillance

The ACLU is right in pointing out that the increase in surveillance is as much due to the private sector as it is due to the government. The danger stems not from a single government program but from a number of parallel developments in the worlds of technology, law, and politics.

Let me relate some of my own experience. Despite having an unlisted telephone number, not registering my driver's license and cars to my home address, and attempting to remove my name from a major commercial database, the national news reporters were on my doorstep within an hour of my May 21, 2002, letter to FBI Director Robert Mueller, published May 28, 2002, in *Time* magazine. I joked that they seemed more effective in tracking persons down than the FBI. They told me it only took a couple of keystrokes on the computer to find me.

During a LexisNexis training session a few months later, I had the instructor input my name, and despite my earlier attempts to be unlisted, my name, address, telephone number, and children's names popped up immediately—along with how much we had paid for our house.

So an enormous amount of information has been gathered on almost every American by private businesses as well as government entities. It is now just a question of mining the information to exploit its value. The cameras that capture one's presence in all types of public venues are not usually those of any law enforcement or government officer but of security-conscious private entities. For example, Minneapolis police have installed many "crime-fighting surveillance cameras" downtown, with $250,000 of the cost paid by the Target Corporation.

The Exercise of Discretion

Consequently, fear exists that such cameras, if misused by public officials, could chill public protest activity protected by the First Amendment or otherwise invade persons' privacy. But the key to whether these initiatives ultimately will be a good or bad thing lies in discreet use of the stored data. For example, it turned out to be a good thing recently that a Californian had a surveillance camera fixed on his neighbor's property. The camera recorded a portion of the kidnapping of his neighbor's child. It also proved beneficial that a surveillance camera apparently recorded a bit of Timothy McVeigh's vehicle during his bombing of the Alfred P. Murrah Federal Building in Oklahoma City. In addition, the banking industry and the FBI have long and good experience in the use of footage from bank surveillance cameras to identify bank robbers.

Exercise of discretion similarly should be required in terms of follow-up to all information obtained from citizen tipsters. Even without a formal program of registering citizens who furnish tips, the (at times panic-struck) public has been more than willing to call in information and tips to the FBI and other law-enforcement agencies. In calling for greater vigilance, citizens and noncitizens alike have been repeatedly encouraged to report what they see or know. Only a small percentage of this information may turn out to be valuable in actually uncovering a terrorist or terrorist plot. But even that small percentage may justify law enforcement's continued encouragement of citizen reporting and a certain amount of time invested by law enforcement in tracking down such tips. Discretion must be exercised by law enforcement not only in determining which tips or leads to follow up but also in deciding the amount of documentation to retain.

Some in the FBI have criticized the Bureau for not showing sufficient discretion—because all leads are being followed. The *U.S. News & World Report* quotes unnamed supervisors saying, "You used to look at threats; you knew what had validity; you'd get to them after you got all these other things out of the way. Now no matter how bizarre or how routine, you go after them." Similarly, FBI spokesman Bill Carter was quoted as saying, "At one time, when information came to us, a lot of times based on experience, the investigator would say, 'Nah, this is not something we will follow through on,' but after the September 11 attacks, the director has stated that no counterterrorism lead will go uncovered."

This strategy, however, ignores the mounting number of documented instances of federal agents, facing intense pressure to avoid another terrorist attack, who have acted on information from tipsters with questionable backgrounds and motives, touching off needless scares and upending the lives of innocent suspects. Federal officials defend their strategy of running most such terrorist tips to ground, calling it critical to thwarting another attack. But we must be careful that we do not abdicate our responsibilities in evaluating citizen tips and informant information before acting in a way that negatively impacts innocent persons.

Coupled with this broad no-tip-will-go-uncovered policy was the Department of Justice's announcement in 2003 of new national security guidelines that allow the FBI to conduct a threat assessment of potential terrorists or terrorist activity without initial evidence of a crime or national security threat. Although this policy is justified by Department of Justice officials as necessary to prevent acts of terrorism before they occur, the ACLU and others have criticized "the notion that the government can put your life under a microscope without any evidence that you're doing anything wrong." A study released in 2002 by Syracuse University, using Justice Department statistics, appears to confirm the position of the ACLU. Of the thousands of people referred by the FBI and other federal investigators to prosecutors in connection with terrorism since September 11, 2001, only a handful have been convicted and sentenced to long prison terms.

DETENTION AND DEPORTATION

In the same vein, new initiatives undertaken by law-enforcement agencies must be closely scrutinized to ensure they truly serve the needs of public safety. An example of such an initiative that should be scrutinized consists of the "special registration" rules for immigrants that, according to news reports, have required nationals from twenty-two countries to sign up with immigration authorities. As a result, there are reports that more than 13,000 Arab and Muslim immigrants are in deportation proceedings, mostly for routine immigration violations, like not registering a change of address.

At the same time, Supreme Court decisions have recognized that a "right to not be talked to" has never existed in our country and that "it is an act of responsible citizenship for individuals to give whatever information they may have to aid in law enforcement" (see the *Washington v. Glucksberg*, *Miranda v. Arizona*, and *Chavez v. Martinez* decisions cited in the bibliography).

Mass-detention initiatives are of great concern. As I noted in my February 26, 2003, letter to FBI Director Mueller, "The vast majority of the one thousand-plus persons detained in the wake of September 11 did not turn out to be terrorists. They were mostly illegal aliens. We have every right, of course, to deport those identified as illegal aliens during the course of any investigation. But after September 11, headquarters encouraged more and more detentions for what seem to be essentially public-relations purposes. Field offices were required to report daily the number of detentions in order to supply grist for statements on our progress in fighting terrorism . . . from what I have observed, particular vigilance may be required to head off undue pressure (including subtle encouragement) to detain round up suspects—particularly those of Arabic origin." (My figure of "one thousand–plus" detainees was based on the FBI's daily press statements issued after September 11. The Department of Justice's Office of Inspector General report, cited in the bibliography, actually counted 762 illegal aliens detained after September 11.)

The temptation exists to fall into an "us-versus-them" attitude, reserving the most aggressive initiatives for Middle Eastern males. The most common citizen tip received by the FBI sounds something like: "I don't want you to think I'm prejudiced because I'm not, but I just have to report this because one never knows. I'm worried and I thought the FBI should check it out." The tipster then provides general information about an Arab or Middle Eastern man who is a neighbor or coworker. Typically, the information includes nothing specific to potential terrorism. Should such a tip be followed up? Or is it little more than racial profiling? These are perhaps the most important questions today and in the future.

The Department of Justice has exempted its anti–racial profiling policy from application to the "war on terrorism." This is a troublesome decision. On right-wing talk shows, we hear people say, "All Muslims aren't terrorists, but all the terrorists were Muslims." The Justice argument here is that we must do everything in our power to learn of the next attack before it happens—and then prevent it. This means many false leads must be pursued.

However, before September 11, the single most dangerous terrorist groups in the United States consisted of radical Christians, the kind of groups with which Timothy McVeigh had ties. Not all Christians were terrorists, but all the terrorists were Christians. Did we post FBI agents at every Sunday church service? Of course not. The FBI targeted the radical factions that perverted Christianity for their own evil purposes.

Today, then, we need to concentrate law-enforcement efforts on the extremist groups and violent individuals who are suspect based on specific, reasonable evidence. We need to follow this process for suspects who are radical Muslims, radical Christians, radical animal/environmental rights believers, or whomever the evidence suggests should be investigated.

THE PENDULUM HAS SWUNG TOO FAR

It was clear to some experts ahead of time, and to almost all experts and nonexperts alike in hindsight, that our country was complacent in a variety of ways prior to September 11. Very few people believed that foreign terrorists would strike on American soil to the extent they did. This mindset made most "emergency" law enforcement actions and court orders for national security almost nonexistent. Prior to September 11 and other terrorist-type incidents (including the anthrax letters and the D.C.-area sniper shootings), we would probably not have tolerated the myriad intrusions and restrictions on our personal lives and affronts to our dignity that we now all seem quite willing to put up with (including airport inspections of removed shoes and use of scanners to examine one's body cavities).

What's happened since September 11? The pendulum has really swung, at least with respect to terrorism. Without adequate oversight, the pendulum risks swinging too far, violating the rights of citizens and immigrants without appreciable gains in security.

What are we actually talking about in terms of possibly giving up "civil liberties"? All people may be created equal, but it's pretty obvious that our rights to "life, liberty and the pursuit of happiness" are not equal. Life is a lot more important than liberty, which in turn is more important than one's pursuit of happiness. The oft-recited quote that "the Constitution is not a suicide pact" reflects this ordering. Because our right to life, and thus to security, is itself a liberty, and the most precious and important one at that, the weighing of civil liberties versus security is, in essence, a false debate.

Despite Patrick Henry's lofty words "Give me liberty or give me death" which urged Americans to war against the British, it turns out that few incarcerated individuals who have lost their civil liberties and personal freedoms commit suicide. In fact, it turns out that most people who have been placed in concentration camp–type existences even worse than prison, and who have lost every shred of their humanity, still seem to want to cling to life.

Of course, most people who are not in prison and who commit suicide are unhappy—and we can debate endlessly about which rights are paramount. But if the reader agrees with me that life is very high on the list, then consideration of the tradeoffs between life and the other liberties often is necessary when it comes to practical ways of preventing acts of terrorism. These tradeoffs can only be avoided by improving the ability of law enforcement to "home in" on the real criminals and terrorists. But law enforcement does not presently have the ability to divine criminal intent by reading minds. So our ability to accurately identify the real culprits is always limited by fixed factors—most importantly by the state of forensic science and by the amount of existing inside information furnished by informants and confidential sources. In an ideal world, this means there would be efficient methods for narrowing a given pool of suspects without having to interview them, surveil them, ask others about their activities, and in some cases subject them or their possessions to interception, seizure, or forensic testing. Unfortunately, the ideal world does not presently exist and identifying criminals and terrorists still requires use of these methods.

How these investigative actions are undertaken is of great importance. For example, given the present reality that homing in still requires the use of many of these standard law-enforcement activities (like citizen tips, physical surveillance, electronic surveillance, searches, seizures, and forensic testing), the intrusion can be greatly alleviated and minimized if done in a professional, respectful manner (and after September 11, FBI agents were afforded training in just this area). In some instances, how an investigative action is undertaken may actually prevent a potential risk to civil liberties from being realized. Even the impact of true liberty deprivations such as detaining or arresting individuals can be greatly alleviated by professional conduct appropriate to the circumstances. Efforts by the FBI director and other management to reach out to the most affected groups in the Muslim community have gone a long way toward improving how such law enforcement actions are perceived.

By contrast, it has been demonstrated, for example in Northern Ireland, that draconian restriction of civil liberties in combating terrorism has led to more terrorism.

THE FREEDOM OF INFORMATION ACT AND PROTECTION FOR WHISTLEBLOWERS

Issues of national security require considerable secrecy. But terrorist threats uninvolved with foreign-country sponsorship may not require as much secrecy because they are more like criminal than traditional intelligence matters. Sufficient generic data can be provided to key congressional oversight committee members—information like the number of times each particular investigative technique is used, within a set of agreed-upon categories.

The Freedom of Information Act (FOIA) fulfills a necessary watchdog function. The act often is viewed as a nuisance, or worse, by law enforcement and intelligence officials charged with protecting national security. But litigation involving FOIA requests usually is decided by a small cadre of experienced judges who are adept at balancing the watchdog function of the act with the government's need for secrecy.

Better legal protection for government whistleblowers should be enacted. At present, federal laws are either inapplicable or ineffective for many government employees such as FBI agents. As I said in a recent letter to selected senators in support of proposed legislation designed to remedy this problem: "Prior to my personal involvement last year in a specific matter, I did not fully appreciate the strong disincentives that sometimes keep government employees from exposing waste, fraud, abuse, or other failures they witness on the job. Nor did I appreciate the strong incentives that do exist for government agencies to avoid institutional embarrassment. . . . Unfortunately, the cloak of secrecy which is necessary for the effective operation of government agencies involved with national security and criminal investigations fosters an environment where the incentives to avoid embarrassment and the disincentives to step forward combine. When this happens, the public loses. We need laws that strike a better balance, that are able to protect effective government operation without sacrificing the agencies' accountability to the public."

THE IMPORTANCE OF INTEGRITY

The generally accepted goal of preventing acts of terrorism is accompanied by the potential for intrusions into the lives of ordinary, innocent American citizens and especially into the lives of immigrants and travelers in America. I emphasize the word "potential" to describe the intrusions. Care must be taken so the potential is not realized. Successful future terrorist attacks on American soil will greatly magnify the likelihood of intrusions and abuses.

To avoid this outcome, we need more than mere lip service and assurances from on high; we need concrete proposals for employing additional safeguards. To address the difficult questions, we need free, open, and informed debate with an eye to enhancing, rather than eroding, mutual trust. In 2002, I testified before the Senate Judiciary Committee about problems I saw with the FBI's bureaucracy and intelligence gathering. I concluded then, as now, on the importance of integrity.

The final reason I can think of for the FBI to adhere to the highest standards of integrity is another self-serving one. Since joining the FBI, I can't tell you how many debates, both public and private, I've engaged in about where the line should be drawn between the needs of effective criminal investigation and preserving the rights of innocent citizens. The trick is to be as surgical as possible in identifying the criminals and those dangerous to our country's security without needlessly interfering with everyone else's rights. From what I've seen in recent years, I can safely assure you that the FBI usually does a pretty darn good job of this. Although such debates always begin with addressing specific provisions of the policy or law in question, they almost always boil down, in the final analysis, to one thing: Trust. It's hard to win the debate if the person on the other side simply refuses to trust what you're saying about how the law or policy is applied in practice. In fighting the current war on terrorism, the federal government has already asked for and received further investigative powers. Although it can be argued that many of the new powers are simply measures to apply prior law to new computer technology or things that any private citizen can do, some members of the public remain apprehensive that the FBI will go too far and will end up violating the rights of innocent citizens. It may be necessary to ask for certain other revisions of policy, or even law. The only way the public's distrust can be alleviated, to enable us to do our job, is for the FBI, from the highest levels on down, to adhere to the highest standards of integrity.

BIBLIOGRAPHY

American Civil Liberties Union report, "Federal Court in Detroit Hears Arguments Today in ACLU Challenge to Patriot Act," December 3, 2003.

Bill Carter, quoted by Michael Moss, "False Terrorism Tips to F.B.I. Uproot the Lives of Suspects" *New York Times*, June 19, 2003.

Chavez v. Martinez, 2003 U.S. LEXIS 4274.

Department of Justice, Office of the Inspector General, "The September 11 Detainees: A Review of the Treatment of Aliens Held on Immigration Charges in Connection with the Investigation of the September 11 Attacks" (Detainee Report), June 2, 2003.

Amy Driscoll, "Judge: I Saw Police Commit Felonies," *Miami Herald*, December 20, 2003.

Miranda v. Arizona, 384 U.S. 436 at 477-478 (1966).

Michael Moss, "False Terrorism Tips to F.B.I. Uproot the Lives of Suspects" *New York Times*, June 19, 2003.

Robert Mueller III, speech to American Civil Liberties Union, June 12, 2003.

———, speech to Stanford Law School, October 18, 2002.

George Orwell, *1984* (New York: Random House, 1992).

"Protecting the Nation: The FBI in War and Peace," Transactional Records Access Clearinghouse study, 2002. http://trac.syr.edu/tracfbi/findings/aboutFBI/keyFindings.html.

Solana Pyne, "Making Enemies," *Village Voice*, July 9-15, 2003. http://www.villagevoice.com.

Coleen Rowley, February 26, 2003 memo to Federal Bureau of Investigation Director Robert Mueller III, published in the *New York Times*, March 6, 2003.

———, memo to Federal Bureau of Investigation Director Robert Mueller III, dated May 21, 2002; *Time* magazine, May 28, 2002. http://www.time.com/time/covers/1101020603/memo.html.

———, statement to Senate Committee on the Judiciary, oversight hearing on counterterrorism, June 6, 2002.

Celia Rumann and Michael P. O'Connor, "Into the Fire: How to Avoid Getting Burned by the Same Mistakes Made Fighting Terrorism in Northern Ireland," *Cardozo Law Review*, Vol. 24, No. 4, April, 2003.

Jay Stanley and Barry Steinhardt, *Bigger Monster, Weaker Chains: The Growth of an American Surveillance Society*, American Civil Liberties Union Technology and Liberty Program, January, 2003.

Rachel L. Swarns, "More Than 13,000 May Face Deportation," *New York Times*, June 7, 2003.

Nancy Talanian, "Guide to Provisions of the USA Patriot Act and Federal Executive Orders That Threaten Civil Liberties," Bill of Rights Defense Committee. http://www.bordc.org/index.html.

U.S. News & World Report, "Special Report: Inside the FBI," May 26, 2003.

Washington v. Glucksberg, 521 U.S. 702 at 721 (1997).

Shaun Waterman, "Figures Show 'Hype' of Terror War," United Press International, December 8, 2003.

V

FAILURE IN AMERICAN MEDIA POLICY—AND STRATEGIC ALTERNATIVES

• 31 •

Creation of the Media Democracy Reform Movement

Robert W. McChesney and John Nichols

I think it is absolutely essential in a democracy to have competition in the media, a lot of competition, and we seem to be moving away from that. . . . Preventive war . . . could lead to eternal war around the world.

—*Walter Cronkite*

The quote above, by the most trusted name in American news, reflects a growing concern about the need to create more competition in American media in the wake of post–September 11 policies. Media are key to a democracy, to our society. And it is becoming more and more clear to a lot of people that our media system is not natural. Moses didn't hand a tablet to Thomas Jefferson, who handed it to Rupert Murdoch, who read that "Ten companies shall own most of our media and make piles of money selling advertising to middle class and affluent consumers." The American media system is completely the result of government laws, policies, subsidies, and regulations. It is a created system.

If you look at our largest media companies today, each of them without exception is built on a government-granted monopoly right or subsidy—usually both. The companies have television stations and networks. Those networks are government-granted monopoly franchises given by the government to companies, for which they are not charged, to use scarce public resources. Or they have cable monopolies in their communities. Or, most important of all, they have copyrights, in which the government protects their monopoly rights over any period of time longer than one year. This vast government system of monopoly policies, subsidies, laws, and regulations has a value that runs into hundreds of billions if not trillions of dollars.

The debate on media in the United States is not about regulation versus deregulation, government bureaucrats versus free markets and entrepreneurs. Regulation is unavoidable, even in a purely competitive market. The debate is about whether we are going to have regulation in the public interest serving informed, debated public values or whether we are going to have regulation purely in the service of private corporate interests, transacted behind closed doors.

THE MEDIA DEBATES OF THE FOUNDING FATHERS

The regulation of media has always been part of U.S. law. That is why copyright is in the Constitution of the United States. We have had profound and important debates in policies over how to set up the media system from the very beginning of the republic. Jefferson and Madison were not perfect people by any means, but they were two of our most visionary founders. And they were the two founders who put the most thought into what sort of policies would create a free press for a viable democracy. They understood, as did everyone in the founding generations of the republic, that you cannot just let commercial interests do whatever they want. That does not create a free press. The founders understood that you needed to put in place core policies to foster a diverse, free press, or else you wouldn't get one and you couldn't have a democracy. It was a source of government and public policymaking that was crucial to the survival of the republic.

A good example is how the Constitution called for Congress to establish a national post office, an institution of fundamental importance in the era before the telegraph and railroad. It was to be the institution that united the country. One of the great debates of the founders was over how much the post office would charge magazines and newspapers to be mailed. In the eighteenth century, almost all publications were distributed by mail. The distribution cost was almost as high as that of printing. The vast majority of items mailed in this period consisted of magazines and newspapers.

In 1792, one extreme position in the debate over how much to charge newspapers and magazines was taken by Benjamin Bates, the grandson of Ben Franklin. Bates was publisher of the great Republican Jeffersonian newspaper *The Aurora* in Philadelphia. He argued that all publications should be charged for mailing. The other extreme position was taken by James Madison, who argued that all publications should always be sent for free by the government, that there should be a total subsidy of every publication. Any form of charge for mailing, Madison argued, would be a form of censorship, which would cut into the diversity of a free press that was so necessary for the republic to survive. Madison lost the debate, but to this day we still heavily subsidize the mailing of commercial publications.

MEDIA POLICYMAKING TODAY: CUTTING THE CAKE IN HAVANA

If our media system is based on structure (who owns and operates the media, and what motives explain their actions), and if this structure is, to no small extent, based on policies set by the government, then one must look at the nature of the debate that creates those policies. That debate really is the nucleus of the atom. What sort of debate creates the policies that set up the structure that produces the content and quality of the media? What is included in the debate? What is not included?

Since the founding of the United States, the nature of the debate has changed dramatically. If, in the first generation or two, the debate was actually a fairly open public process, by the twentieth century it became a debate largely off limits to public participation, done behind closed doors by powerful special interests. Today, the public is fed the line that the system we have is "natural," while private commercial interests use their power to divvy up the goods among themselves. As a result, we have a media system that reflects the needs and interests of those who made the deal behind closed doors.

The way to understand media policymaking in the United States today is to watch the great film *The Godfather, Part II* from 1974. There is a wonderful scene in the middle of the film when the American gangsters are in a Havana hotel room in 1958, when Batista and the mob were running Cuba. Hyman Roth and Michael Corleone are celebrating Hyman Roth's birthday party. A cake is brought in with the outline of Cuba on it. Hyman Roth slices up the cake gives a slice to each American gangster. And as he does, he is saying, "Okay, Louie, you run this casino; Frankie, you run that casino." He divided up the island among the gangsters. While he's doing this, Hyman Roth is saying, "Isn't it great to be in a country where the government respects private enterprise?"

That is exactly how media and communication policies have been created in the United States for the last fifty years. Today the media corporations and trade associations have enormous lobbying powers, not because they're concerned about us but because, like Michael Corleone and Hyman Roth, they're fighting each other for the biggest slice of the American and global cake—they're at war with each other.

But the one thing they all agree on is that it's their cake, and nobody else should get a slice. It's their private system. And that's really what the whole struggle is about today. The public needs to sit at the table on that hotel roof and engage in debate. The public needs to throw these guys off the roof.

The more grassroots Americans know about these issues, the more they weigh in and the more likely we are to get policies that will be dramatically different from what we now have. We *can* make our commercial media markets more competitive and less concentrated. And we *can* open up significant space for nonprofit and noncommercial voices, not only to survive, but to prosper.

THE FEDERAL COMMUNICATIONS COMMISSION AND THE INVASION OF IRAQ

Until quite recently, the conventional wisdom has been that, while the media are important in our democracy, the public can't be engaged in reform because the issues are too abstract. It also has been assumed that, if we win all the other foreign, economic, and domestic policy-reform fights, media reform will follow. The analogy here is to the New Deal, where conservative media were hostile to President Roosevelt but warmed up to his policies once it became clear that there was popular support for them.

Over the last several years, there has in fact been dramatic change. The key has been the Federal Communications Commission rule-making on media ownership. In 2003 Michael Powell, chairman of the FCC, sought several rule changes. One would allow a single network to control television stations reaching 45 percent of all American households. Another would allow a media company to buy up a local daily newspaper, as many as three television stations, eight radio stations, and the cable system in a single market. The White House supported these changes—presumably because the beneficiaries would be big campaign contributors, like Clear Channel, General Electric, and Rupert Murdoch's News Corporation.

But, in a very public debate, the FCC did not vote unanimously for these and other rules. The vote was in favor, but the vote was split three to two among the five commissioners.

Michael Copps, one of the dissident commissioners, is a historian of the Progressive and New Deal eras and a former Senate staffer. Copps immediately recognized what was wrong with the proposed rule changes and fought to publicize the problems. We cannot emphasize enough how important it is to have a reform player on these regulatory commissions, someone who is willing to challenge the slow-motion coups that often occur on them.

Through the publicity created by Michael Copps, and the efforts of a host of media-reform advocates, as many as three million Americans contacted the FCC and Congress to demand that controls against media monopoly be kept in place. Knowledgeable observers on Capitol Hill say that, in 2003, media ownership was the most-discussed issue among constituents, trailing only the war in Iraq, the biased American coverage of which illustrated media monopoly.

Some of the most intense opposition to the rule changes was triggered by the failure of American media to cover the invasion of Iraq and its impact on terrorism with any kind of critical objectivity. As Copley News Service Washington correspondent George Condon concluded, "Look at this White House press corps. It's just abdicated all responsibility."

Millions of Americans questioned media coverage of the Iraq invasion, but their questions were unfocused. Americans didn't know where to turn their energies. Congress and the White House wouldn't listen. So the public looked around, and a few very visionary groups like MoveOn.org and Code Pink (the women-for-peace group) were there to help channel popular energy and concern over media war coverage. As suggested by Walter Cronkite in our opening quote, here was a key link between September 11 and corporate media reform. In turn, this focus on media and the war helped to build energy to oppose the FCC rules, because the rules were another media issue already in play.

Soon an extraordinary coalition of strange bedfellows had turned against the Federal Communications Commission changes, ranging from MoveOn.org and Noam Chomsky to the National Rifle Association and William Safire.

As a result, the Senate voted overwhelmingly to block the implementation of the changes. More than two hundred Republican and Democratic members of the House signed a letter to overturn the FCC rules.

A federal appeals court then ordered the FCC back to the drawing board to reconsider the controversial rules. This was a tremendous victory for media diversity and democracy. The old days are over. The rooftop of Hyman Roth and Michael Corleone will never be again.

The media-reform movement is here to stay. We are at a period of time comparable to 1886, when the eight-hour day came into place; to 1896, when William Jennings Bryan began to put the power and corruption of corporations on the agenda; or to 1970, with Earth Day, when the environment became established as a permanent issue.

We have created a new, nonprofit organization, Free Press, and a new website, MediaReform.net, to help that movement and they attracted more than two thousand participants to the first National Conference on Media Reform in 2003.

THE NEW MEDIA-REFORM AGENDA

What long-term, permanent media-reform agenda now is being developed that helps us move beyond what otherwise are gloomy, post–September 11 times?

Reforms in foreign, economic, and domestic policy need to be pursued, but we should learn from the far right that a great deal of energy must be invested in media. Starting with the defeat of Barry Goldwater in 1964, conservatives have understood that, if you don't win the media, you can't win anything else, as Eric Alterman describes in chapter 35.

Strategically, conservatives took two basic routes—media control and media policy. The conservatives funded foundations and think tanks, radio and television talk shows, training camps for student journalists, and internship programs. At the same time, they funded nonprofit institutes that targeted the FCC, Congress, and the courts to guarantee they had policies very sympathetic to the conservative view of how media should be operated.

The same mix is necessary for media reform today. We need to push for new radio shows, new television shows, and new journalism that provide democratic alternatives to the horrendous content of Rush Limbaugh, Gordon Liddy, the Fox News Channel, and mainstream journalism generally. We need new watchdogs, like "Fox Watch" at the American Politics Journal (AmericanPolitics.com).

We also need broader-based media-policy reform. Some of the most important components of that reform are as follows:

- Antitrust policy must be reassessed. Competition and diversity have been under assault for more than two decades. The impact of media mergers on democracy needs to be closely examined. Caps on media ownership appropriate for a democracy should be debated and agreed upon.
- Congress should roll back the number of radio stations a single firm can own. Advocacy is needed for Congress to pass legislation prohibiting media cross-ownership and vertical integration. There are tremendous economic benefits to media conglomeration, but they accrue almost entirely to the media owners. The public loses out.
- Citizen advocates need to reinvigorate the regulatory process. As FCC commissioner Copps has observed, "Most people do not even know that they can challenge the renewal of a local radio or television station if they believe that the station is not living up to its obligation due to a lack of local coverage, a lack of diversity, excessive indecency and violence, or for other concerns important to the community."
- Nonprofit groups must be given access to low-power FM radio station licenses. Expansion of access was promised several years ago. But a backroom deal in Congress reneged on that promise. Tax incentives should be created to aid in the development of new, community-based, noncommercial broadcasting outlets.
- Foundations must provide much greater support to schools on the cutting edge of media reform, like the Columbia School of Journalism, to produce better trained, more informed journalists and to support more widespread dissemination of leading journals, such as the *Columbia Journalism Review.*
- A new wave of grassroots advocacy is needed to fight for dramatic expansion of public broadcasting funding. Only about 15 percent of funding for public radio and television comes from federal subsidies. What funding does come from Congress is subject to great political pressures. Public broadcasting at the federal and state levels has the potential to provide a model of quality journalism and diversified cultural programming. But that won't happen if cash-starved PBS and NPR outlets are required, as some propose, to rely on the same sort of offensive thirty-second spot advertising that dominates commercial broadcasting.
- Broadcasters must be forced to give candidates free air time. Senators John McCain and Russell Feingold, the authors of the only meaningful

campaign-finance-reform legislation of the past decade, are now proposing such a requirement. The link between campaign finance reform and media reform must be communicated to the public and acted upon. Media conglomerates now are among the most powerful lobbyists against both campaign finance reform and media reform. The system works for them but fails the rest of us.

- Campaigns must be organized to block international trade deals that allow media conglomerates to impose their will on the citizens of the United States and other countries. Media firms now are lobbying the World Trade Organization and other multilateral organizations to accept a system of trade sanctions against countries that subsidize public broadcasting, that limit foreign ownership of media systems, or that establish local content standards designed to protect national and regional cultures. They want similar assaults on regulation inserted into the proposed Free Trade Area of the Americas. Congress should not pass trade agreements that undermine its ability to aid public broadcasting; it should protect media diversity and competition.
- Policies that affect the Internet, such as copyright and access, must carefully be scrutinized. Reforms must be enacted that prevent corporate monopoly control. It is important to recognize that, already, three corporations control about half of the web's traffic patterns.
- More broadly, the media-reform movement must address what ails existing media. Top-heavy with white middle-class men, television news departments and major newspapers remain beholden to official sources. Their obsessive focus on "if it bleeds, it leads" crime coverage and celebrity trials leaves no room for covering the real issues that affect families, neighborhoods, communities, and whole classes of people. Coverage of minority communities, women, working people, rural folks, youth, seniors, and just about everyone else who doesn't live in a handful of ZIP codes in New York and Los Angeles is badly warped, and it creates badly warped attitudes in society. Those attitudes shape public discourse and public policy. Media reformers must support the struggle to expand access to the airwaves and to assure that independent and innovative journalists, writers, and filmmakers have the resources to create media that reflect all of America.

A core group in Congress now has signed on to media-reform policy development. The group includes people like Tammy Baldwin of Wisconsin, Sherrod Brown of Ohio, John Conyers of Michigan, Russ Feingold of Wisconsin, Dennis Kucinich of Ohio, Jim McDermott of Washington, and Bernie Sanders of Vermont.

For example, during the 2004 presidential primary campaign Dennis Kucinich criticized ABC's Ted Koppel on the air for failing to focus on serious issues important to the American people. The criticism was during a debate in New Hampshire. The audience erupted into sustained applause when Kucinich criticized the networks, and later responses from around the nation were equally intense. Kucinich then turned the controversy into what the late Senator Paul Wellstone used to refer to as a "teaching moment" by issuing this statement:

> The response of the American people to the exchange between Ted Koppel and me demonstrates that there is great concern about the proper role of the media in a democratic society. The American people clearly do not want the media to be in a position where they're determining which candidates ought to be considered for the presidency and which ought not to be considered for the presidency. Such practice by the media represents a tampering with the political process itself. The role of the media in this process has now become a national issue central to the question of who's running our country, and I intend to keep this issue before the American people, and I look forward to engaging America's news organizations as to what they might be able to do to be more responsive to the public concerns that are reflected in the powerful response to the issues I raised in the exchange with Ted Koppel.

REFORM: BALANCING CONTENT AND POLICY

In terms of media-reform content and media-reform policy, it is important to understand a couple of things. If you want to produce, on your own, high-quality television news or print journalism and do really good work, it costs quite a bit of money. Compared with such investment in media-reform content, media-reform policy is much less expensive. And policy work ultimately has a much bigger payoff. The problem, though, is that policy work is fairly abstract, and there is not an immediate payoff. If you are someone who has $100 million to spend, and you put it into policy work, you can fund the entire media-reform movement for a decade easily, and then some. But you might not win anything. If you take the same money, you can produce a pretty amazing output of journalism for a year or two or three, and you will be able to see something tangible. But, at the end of three years, you are out $100 million, and you might be back to square one.

Given these pros and cons, a balanced reform strategy is needed—embracing both content and policy. As we press for reform on both fronts, we need to remember the words of Bill Moyers in his keynote address at the 2003 National Conference on Media Reform: "We have to get our fellow citizens to understand that what they see, hear, and read is not only the taste of programmers and producers, but also a set of policy decisions made by the people we vote for."

BIBLIOGRAPHY

Stephen Labaton, "Court Orders Rethinking of Rules Allowing Large Media to Expand," *New York Times*, June 25, 2004.

Robert W. McChesney, *Rich Media, Poor Democracy* (New York: New Press, 2000).

——— and John Nichols, "Up in Flames," *The Nation*, October 31, 2003.

http://www.MediaReform.net.

Bill Moyers, *Keynote Address to the National Conference on Media Reform*, published by CommonDreams.org, November 8, 2003.

John Nichols, "Cronkite Fears Media Mergers Threaten Democracy," *Capital Times*, Madison, Wisconsin, November 8, 2003.

———, "Kucinich Makes Media an Issue," *The Nation*, December 16, 2003.

——— and Robert W. McChesney, "Turning the Tide: It's Time to Stop the Enronization of the Media," *In These Times*, March 1, 2002. http://www.InTheseTimes.com.

———, "Only One Source for News Hurts All," the *Capital Times*, Madison, Wisconsin, February 26, 2002.

• 32 •

Electronic Advocacy and Fundraising: The State of the Art

Eli Pariser

In this chapter, I want to suggest MoveOn as one model for organizing, advocating, and fundraising around the kinds of issues articulated in this book. The goal of MoveOn is to bring ordinary people back into politics. Because today's political system revolves around big money and big media, most citizens are left out. The lockout has accelerated since September 11. MoveOn is an electronic organizing catalyst for grassroots political involvement of busy but concerned citizens.

The MoveOn family of organizations consists of three entities. MoveOn.org, a 501(c)(4) organization, primarily focuses on education and advocacy on important national issues. MoveOn.org PAC, a federal political action committee, primarily helps members elect candidates who reflect MoveOn values. The MoveOn.org Voter Fund, an organization covered by section 527 of the tax law, primarily runs ads exposing failed policies in key battleground states.

Begun by Joan Blades and Wes Boyd, two Silicon Valley entrepreneurs in the late 1990s, MoveOn asks its members, now numbering more than two million, to propose issue priorities and strategies via Action Forum software. The most strongly supported issues rise to the top, and these become MoveOn's organizational, action, and advocacy priorities.

GETTING INVOLVED

Just out of college, I got into MoveOn almost by accident. In the days after September 11, I was thinking about the tragedy and becoming increasingly worried that it might lead to a very serious change in policy direction for this country and other countries.

I was a web designer at the time. I thought, okay, I'll put a web page up and post some thoughts on how you might address the issue of terrorism, and specifically the attacks on September 11, without launching a never-ending war.

After I put my web page up, I sent it out to about twenty of my friends, just to see what they thought. A friend of mine sent along a petition, which had language very similar to what I posted, so I put the petition on the web site, too, and figured my job was done.

After a couple of days, I checked my e-mail and I had 300 messages from people from all over the world, writing about my website. Soon I got a call from the server administrator, who said, "Your web site's going down. There are too many people visiting it." I realized that 40,000 people had signed the petition. Then the BBC called and said, "So what's this all about?" At that point I realized that this was out of my hands.

Over the next two weeks, about half a million people not only came to the web site but actually signed the petition. I was getting calls from journalists all over the world. I remember one particular journalist in Romania. Five different people had forwarded him e-mail that I had originally sent to my friends. The Romanian asked, "Who are you? What are you doing?" And I said, "Well, I'm just this guy. I've got a web site that I started in my living room. And apparently it's hit a chord."

Then I started getting e-mail from the half-million people who had signed the petition, saying, "Okay. This is great. What are we going to do? Let's do something." I realized that it wasn't enough just to set up my web site. I really had to organize it.

At that point I got in touch with MoveOn, and we essentially merged the two entities. That's the way I embarked on this amazing trip. Since then, the group of people who spontaneously came together over concern for the direction the country was going after September 11 formed the base for our Iraq work and allowed us to mobilize very early on to start talking about the war and then post-war policy.

That group of people reached out to their friends and acquaintances, and the size tripled. MoveOn now consists of 1.4 million people here in the United States and another 700,000 abroad. I still can't fully comprehend that when I hit the "send" button on my e-mail, I'm talking to more than two million people.

Part of my story illustrates why online organizing and advocacy can be so effective. One reason is that it's cheap. I spent $35 on a website, and a half a million people were able to use it. It can be personal, so the message to my friends was actually from me. It wasn't a slick, organized appeal. There is a way that this medium can touch people directly. It hasn't been fully co-opted yet by businesses or corporate entities—and we need to organize against such co-option. It's still mostly a person-to-person medium, and that can be very powerful.

Another important aspect of the online organizing world is that you can simply reach people in the moment they are available with an opportunity to take action or to be involved immediately. In some ways it's unparalleled. In a moment, as events unfold, you can get something to them that's quick, easy, and allows them to do what they want to do.

It is very important that, at heart, MoveOn is a two-way medium. My involvement with MoveOn's foreign-policy work didn't come about simply because I put up a website. It happened because I put up the website, people responded by e-mail, and I responded to their e-mail. There is a two-way stream of communication.

BUILDING LONG-RUN CONSTITUENCIES

MoveOn has been exploring how online organizing can help build broad constituencies and broad consensus around important issues. There are many significant opportunities on issues. One of the most powerful and intriguing developments is the aggregation and cross-pollination that has occurred. As Robert McChesney and John Nichols suggested in chapter 31, we got 1.4 million Americans into MoveOn on the basis of opposing the invasion of Iraq, and then many of these people wrote in, saying "We're also concerned about the media environment. We heard Jonathan Adelstein and Michael Copps, the commissioners who voted against the Federal Communications Commission ruling. Let's support them." The ability to bring people together on an issue like the war, and then to address an issue like media consolidation, seems to be very powerful. The power is to address a wide variety of issues and help people make the connections among them, in ways that mainstream media, conservatives, the executive branch, and Congress do not.

Another exciting dimension to online organizing is the simple idea that you can fight and get stronger, even if you lose. By taking a stand and connecting with people emotionally as you organize, you can begin to build a constituency that doesn't go away. So, unlike a traditional rally or march, where you never capture that information, when you're doing this kind of online organizing, you're able to take the energy that comes in and use it to organize a constituency that then takes action. For example, in the fight against the FCC, when its chairman, Michael Powell, decided that he wasn't interested in what grassroots folks had to say, we began to work with those same grassroots people, who had communicated to us their energy to fight. We now have a powerful constituent base for fighting broader media-consolidation issues in the long run.

The underlying idea here is that, if you take on the big, important political fights, you'll bring people in, mobilize them for the immediate fight, and then get them excited for the next fight. That is very powerful organizing. And it's possible, in part, because capturing the people who come in, and keeping them connected, is so much easier in this web-based medium than in most other media.

PROVIDING THE OPPORTUNITY TO SELF-ORGANIZE

The MoveOn strategy also offers unparalleled opportunities for people to self-organize. Our idea is that you actually can trust most of the people out there. Traditionally, there's a sense that the activists in the field need to be led, instructed, and directed to a degree which, in our experience, simply isn't the case.

My favorite example is when we decided it would be important for members of Congress to meet with people, in their home districts, who were concerned about the war in Iraq. We had about two weeks to organize, and no preexisting arrangements with any members of Congress. Because we had only four staff members and no standing volunteer corps, we decided that the only way we could meet our goal was to provide an infrastructure that would allow people to self-organize in their own communities and run the meetings themselves. The results were pretty remarkable. Meetings took place across the country. Almost every senator and a great majority of the congressional districts had meetings. We received calls from congressional staff essentially saying, "Who are these people? We're used to seeing the same old people talking about the same old issues. But these were new people. They came in, they didn't have a staff person with them, they didn't hold any official organizational title, they were eloquent, and they were organized. What's going on?" By providing people with an infrastructure, with a few simple tools, and a few simple guidelines, we were able to excite and motivate people to organize themselves. That is an extremely exciting piece of the work.

FINDING CONSENSUS AND MOTIVATING OTHERS

In addition, the two-way nature of this medium allows you to listen to a group of half a million people in a way that may not have been possible before. For example, MoveOn undertook an online primary. To prepare for the primary, we wanted to ask each of the candidates some questions about their campaigns. Rather than submit these questions ourselves, we essentially allowed our members to come up with the questions. People submitted questions, and other members rated them. The questions that floated to the top were the questions that we submitted to the candidates. Our members sent MoveOn about 1,700 questions, and over 30,000 people rated them. What came to the top and were submitted to the candidates were extremely eloquent and thought-provoking questions. They evoked some great responses from the campaigns.

So there's a way in which you can aggregate and help people sort through their own responses. MoveOn uses this process to determine our direction. We'll say, "What are some important issues to be working on right now?" We look at what floats to the top. You can find a consensus among a very large group of people in a very un-laborious way, compared with what's possible in the offline world.

As we look to the future, MoveOn is experimenting with a lot of things. But what really is exciting is seeing many of these practices become much more common. Other organizations—such as America Votes, America Coming Together, the Media Fund, and the Thunder Road Group—are innovating. In the end, that will lead to even more exciting opportunities. For example, during the 2004 presidential primaries, there was experimentation with a whole array of online organizing techniques that really could change the way campaigns are run in the future. Some campaigns had online groups of designers and content producers who essentially were unofficial media teams. They created posters, flyers, and many other things—again, in a very decentralized kind of way.

Similarly, during the 2004 general election, coalitions of advocacy organizations, including MoveOn and covered under section 527 of the tax law, raised funds via the Internet for media ads, created the ads, aired them in targeted states, led get-out-the-vote campaigns, undertook polling research, and organized rapid-response teams on key issues.

We need more and more of such coalitions to harness our energy and really make an impact. We need to further build on the idea of online organizing of strategies around which people mobilize—to send petitions, contact leaders, and attend events.

MoveOn's organizing certainly reaches the Internet-connected demographic, which tends to be white, middle class, and educated. But we are looking to expand our reach, and I think there are ways we can connect with low-income communities. For example, our political action committee is a get-out-the-vote-type effort that tries to mobilize people who need to be mobilized. Can we get volunteers who are coordinated online to start working in neighborhoods and in areas that don't have a heavy online infrastructure in place? We will try to answer that question and may need help from the kind of inner-city nonprofit organizations. In so doing, perhaps we can begin to help address the digital divide.

FRAMING IDEAS IN MAINSTREAM MEDIA

Our priority has been on using the Internet and online organizing to democratize media and communication, getting around the establishment-centered mainstream media and elite media system. But we also have been thinking about ways to get the kind of recommendations in this volume into the mainstream and elite media, and about ways of critiquing these media systematically.

As Eric Alterman suggests in chapter 35, we need to learn from conservatives and develop a powerful think tank infrastructure to develop ideas, frame them in mainstream and elite media, identify credible people who can communicate the messages, pitch stories to reporters, and train a new generation of communicators through media schools.

Such infrastructure development has not been the primary domain of MoveOn, although we are considering a venture-capital fund raised from our members to begin building new institutions. We also have had an impact with the paid ads that have appeared in mainstream media. For example, our large "Mis-state of the Union" ad in elite newspapers said "Sixteen untrue words in the State of the Union message helped push America into war with Iraq. It's now clear that the remaining 5,397 words were just as misleading." Another ad was the television spot in targeted states that highlighted the net loss of jobs during recent years, something unprecedented since the Hoover administration.

Building in part on the success of these ads, MoveOn has carried out a grassroots fundraising campaign to raise $10 million for producing and purchasing television "issue advertising" on policy misleads and failures. The MoveOn.org Voter Fund has produced powerful public education television spots and aired them in targeted states. MoveOn members were asked to propose thirty-second television ads for our "Bush in 30 Seconds" contest. A panel of judges, including Michael Moore, selected the best. Illustrating the corrupted state of corporate media, CBS refused to air the winning commercial during the 2004 Super Bowl, on the false grounds that the winning ad did not meet its broadcasting standards. Yet CBS did air a federal antidrug ad that showed a young woman on drugs watching someone drown.

So CBS helped MoveOn raise the real issue—corporate media double standards. At the same time, the best ads in our contest have been extensively shown on CNN and broadcast media outside of the Internet.

LAUNCHING THE DAILY MISLEAD

MoveOn also is developing a network that allows people to self-organize around media inaccuracy and media bias. I am talking about news stories that essentially are not true, but that quickly assume the status of fact. One such story during the 2000 election campaign was that Al Gore was a liar and said he made up the Internet. While untrue, this story quickly assumed the status of fact because there simply wasn't an organized infrastructure to respond to the journalistic outlets that were carrying the story, shame them, and push them into more balanced reporting. At the same time, there was a very aggressive right-wing media machine working to get the story out there and well placed.

Using volunteers, we can one-up the extreme right wing by allowing people to report egregious incidents that occur in the mainstream media, verify them through a volunteer infrastructure, and then draw on a network of experts who can contact the journalists involved and play an inside game. At the same time, a grassroots contingent can beat down their doors with concerns about their biased and misleading commentary. We have begun to implement this idea with MoveOn's "Daily Mislead" (www.Misleader.org), a day-to-day chronicle of the federal government's distortions, assembled by MoveOn members and staff and then e-mailed by noon Eastern Time. Similarly, we have created Fox Watch (www.AmericanPolitics.com/foxwatch), which utilizes thousands of Americans who monitor the distortions, fabrications and propaganda of Fox News.

Ideally, we want to start to create an environment in which it simply is more trouble than it's worth for some of these news agencies to get their misleads out there. Does that mean that Fox News, for example, is going to change overnight? No. But I think what is possible over the next few years is that Fox becomes increasingly seen as simply a knee-jerk conservative network rather than a credible source of mainstream news. By highlighting the examples of extreme prejudice and extreme ideological dogma, it's possible to turn the tide, in many respects, in terms of media content.

FUNDING VIA MEMBERSHIP

MoveOn not long ago received a $5 million matching pledge from billionaire George Soros. In response, Fox's Bill O'Reilly claimed that MoveOn was "an extremist organization." We are putting the Soros funds to good use, and O'Reilly's words helped us raise more money. But the real key to our funding is that it is based on our membership.

Membership financing is a great model because it takes traditional fundraising and turns it on its head. You can be a member for free, and if you appreciate the service that we offer, then we ask for contributions. We find that more than pays for our operating overhead.

But even more excitingly, when we have a special project with great immediacy, we can count on our base to rapidly provide funding. For example, with our advertising against the FCC regulations, we went out to our base and said, "Look, we need to raise about a quarter of a million dollars to make this advertising campaign go." Within eighteen hours, that money came in, and it came in from donors whose donations averaged $35 apiece. The idea that you can harness lots of small donors is exciting.

MAKING AMERICAN DEMOCRACY WORK AGAIN

The future won't necessarily be to the benefit of democracy. There are two paths we can follow, and one could be potentially very dangerous. You develop these small islands of people who agree with each other entirely and who are able to filter out the rest of society, so they all visit the same websites. They get their news from these very specialized sources, they talk only to each other, and they reinforce their existing prejudices. They aren't challenged by data from outside of the system. All of the techniques that MoveOn has helped develop could be used very successfully in a way that would not serve the country well and would not increase civic discourse.

The other, preferred path is the opportunity to develop broad appeals that bring people together, introduce them to each other, expose them to different arguments, engage them in the political system, and empower them to become active citizens. For example, MoveOn has paired its members at random across the country and had them interview each other. You had people like a high-school student in New Jersey interviewing a septuagenarian in Alabama about his political beliefs. There is a way in which this technology can be used as a tool to bring people together—people who would never have been in the same room under other circumstances. The process can build new coalitions.

In terms of which path we take, it really depends on who does the organizing. It's our choice.

Perhaps the most promising development we can look forward to is a reversion from one-way communication as a primary communication mode to not just bilateral but multilateral communication. The idea is that, as we move into a networked world where less and less of the news and the information we receive comes from a single authoritative source, we build networks and communication media that allow lots of people to talk to lots of people. Ultimately, that process will create a society very conducive to democracy.

The Internet and online organizing are powerful tools that help people undertake work in democracy—with economy and efficiency. They allow people to connect with each other, listen to each other, converse, debate, trust, collaborate, and organize. By joining together and fighting together, we really can make American democracy work again.

BIBLIOGRAPHY

Frank Ahrens, "FCC Plan to Alter Media Rules Spurs Growing Debate," *Washington Post*, May 23, 2004.

http://www.AmericanPolitics.com/foxwatch.html.

Dan Balz, "Democrats Forming Parallel Campaign," *Washington Post*, March 10, 2004.

http://www.BushIn30Seconds.org.

Joe Garofoli, "MoveOn, a Political Force Online, Receives $5 Million Matching Gift," *San Francisco Chronicle*, November 23, 2003.

Glen Justice, "Advocacy Groups Permitted to Use Unlimited Funds," *New York Times*, page A-1, February 19, 2004.

http://www.Misleader.org.

http://www.MoveOn.org.

Chris Taylor and Karen Tumulty, "MoveOn's Big Moment," *Time*, November 24, 2003.

http://www.TruthUncovered.com.

• 33 •

Electronic Counterpower and Collective Action

Howard Rheingold

The founders of America knew well about factions and structured the Constitution to balance them, so that none would have unfair control over the political process. But we now have a conservative political faction that has colluded with the owners of mass media to influence the beliefs of voters. Some of the owners are part of the political faction. As one result, for example, polls show that a majority, or close to it, of Americans still believe that weapons of mass destruction were discovered in Iraq and that Iraqis were the hijackers on September 11. At the same time, media ownership has consolidated, financially contributing immensely to the conservative faction, and is given preferential economic treatment by that faction (chapter 31). As a result, we have a vicious circle of corruption and influence that subverts the right of American citizens to be informed. The process is extremely dangerous to democracy.

One way to begin to reverse this dangerous process is to fulfill the potential of what Eli Pariser (chapter 32) calls "multilateral communications." My phrase is "many-to-many media." Such media can be utilized to advocate for and organize around the foreign, economic, domestic, and media policy alternatives set out in this book.

Because the potential of Internet-based media to offer a significant counterpower to corporate mass media has only recently begun to be demonstrated, it is not yet clear whether Internet media will pose a significant challenge. But I think it can. Technically, every desktop and now every pocket that has an Internet-enabled device is potentially a globally reachable printing press, broadcasting station, place of assembly, and organizing tool. That has enormous potential power.

However, knowledge about how to use this potential effectively has been slow to catch on. The potential has been there for quite awhile. It is only recently that we have begun to see movements like MoveOn.org, and Mediareform.net organize and mobilize counterpower and collective action with skill and demonstrable impact. We are beginning to see acceleration in the evolution of the technologies, the power they possess, and the methodologies for using that power.

I see three arenas for potential leverage: alternative news media, the public sphere, and collective action. I want to concentrate on collective action, so I'm going to move quickly through the first two areas. But I think, in the long term, the first two also are very important.

ALTERNATIVE NEWS MEDIA

Alternative news sources to the mass media, to what people see on television and hear on the radio and read in the newspapers, have been touted for quite awhile. But now we are seeing millions of people circulating stories personally via e-mail, broadcasting stories via weblogs, and even reporting from the streets via mobile blogging. In some parts of the world, we're seeing a kind of citizen journalism emerging. There is something called *Ohmynews* in Korea that's a little bit like citizen journalism.

A weblog, of course, is simply a web page that a person can easily update and publish to the world. Weblogs (or "blogs") lower the barrier to publishing on the web. There are over a million blogs now. That number probably will reach into the tens of millions soon, through mass efforts by AOL and Google to expand the phenomenon.

The simplicity of weblogging technology is important. When you make a particular medium or technology a little simpler to use, sometimes you can have a dramatic effect. For example, the Internet was around for a while before the web came along, with the web giving it a visual interface. You could do everything that you can now do on the web, more or less, with the Internet, but you had to kind of be a computer geek and enter arcane commands. Now you can point and click. The mass media still reach most people most of the time and are the most effective way of getting a message across. Yet for a long time mass media were the only source, and now this is no longer the case.

In corporate mainstream media, the priority is on stories that maximize profits and returns to stockholders. Bloggers are not motivated by profits. In no small part, they are motivated by their political beliefs.

Bloggers also have the potential to become a movement of fact checkers, millions of people who can go out, do the research and legwork on mass media stories, and expose lies and propaganda. A good example of how this could work is Ambassador Joseph Wilson's disclosure that there were no African uranium sales to Iraq (chapter 15). There were many people in the intelligence community who knew that stories of such sales were lies. Had the blogging community been better organized on such an issue, as might be possible in the future, Ambassador Wilson could have been assisted in his disclosures, in response to which his wife was revealed by conservatives as a Central Intelligence Agency agent, thereby compromising American intelligence operations against terrorism.

The constant barrage of propaganda on talk radio, talk television, and the mass media can be countered, to some degree, by the formulation of "rapid-reaction weblogging teams." If effectively mobilized to detect and fight back against propaganda, weblogging could affect national media and national policy.

As alternative, more democratized, web-based media begin to compete with corporate mass media, there are problems to face. An obvious dilemma is quality control. How to sort out misinformation and disinformation? This is a problem consumers of mass media (including the *New York Times*) also face. Can alternative media create quality controls that would better solve the problem and so generate an advantage compared to mass media?

Another problem is literacy in how to consume and create alternative news. The level of literacy presently is low and unevenly distributed. But this can be remedied, as I will discuss below.

Potentially the greatest problem is monopoly ownership and government surveillance. The same power and corporate elite who control mainstream media could try to neutralize the democratizing effect of blogging. Control and censorship of the Internet is possible—one can imagine new provisions in a new Patriot Act. Here is where the advocacy spearheaded by Robert McChesney and John Nichols (chapter 31) is essential. The heat must be kept on the Federal Communications Commission, for example, and the scope of citizen regulatory concern must be ever-widened and enhanced.

THE PUBLIC SPHERE

The second arena for potential leverage is the public sphere. By the public sphere, I mean public debate on the issues. As Robert McChesney and John Nichols have described, public discourse has been eroded severely by the mass media. Very few people have the power to dictate what very many people see, hear, and believe is happening in the world. But the public sphere is very much alive in chat rooms, listservs, message boards, and weblogs—particularly in weblogs where people of different political stripes link to those with whom they disagree. We are seeing at least some kind of two-way traffic between people or factions who hold very different views. Although the discussions online about political issues are extremely lively, they are very undisciplined and subject to disruption, particularly because the nature of the medium masks the kind of intentionality that is conveyed by body language, tone of voice, and facial expressions. Incivility can often swamp these discussions.

The art of political debate among citizens has been debased, but it certainly is not dead. Online media are a place where political debate can happen now and in the future. But, again, literacy about the way to argue online and the importance of civility in the public sphere is not widespread or evenly distributed.

COLLECTIVE ACTION: DEMONSTRATIONS

I wrote *Smart Mobs* because I noticed, worldwide, that we are reaching a kind of threshold. That threshold has been reached before—with the printing press, telephone, television, and other technologies that have enabled people to organize collective action in ways and on scales not previously possible. I see this as a convergence of the availability of computation. Today's threshold is based on the availability of mobile telephones. There are many more mobile telephones than personal computers in the world, and there will be more still in the future. Increasingly, those mobile phones are linked to the Internet. So we're seeing a convergence of mobile media, computation, and the Internet. In the long run, this is a significant hybrid, and collective action is one of its unique characteristics.

In terms of alternatives to policy since September 11, the best examples of mobile communications occurred as part of the worldwide demonstrations against the invasion of Iraq. As with the mobile communication swarming tactics during the Seattle anti–World Trade Organization demonstrations in 1999, the self-organizing capabilities of the Internet and the mobile phone allowed demonstrators against the war in Iraq to assemble quickly and well. We saw an advance in the literacy of the users. For example, the BBC set up a web site in which people could, from their telephones, take pictures of the huge demonstrations in London and elsewhere. The photos were sent to the BBC, which then posted them. This was, literally, street-level reporting, the beginning of an alternative to CNN. With the price of high-quality digital video dropping, I think we have the possibility of anti-American demonstration videos and Rodney King–type beating videos made everywhere and then streamed to the Internet.

Earlier, in Manila, the presidency of Joseph Estrada was accused of corruption. There were hearings in the Philippine legislature. Everyone in the Philippines watched on television, much as the Watergate hearings were watched in America. When some legislators associated with Estrada shut down the hearings, tens of thousands of people hit the streets, all of them wearing black. Within a couple of days, millions of people demonstrated in the same place that the demonstrations against the Marcos regime had happened. All of this was organized by text messaging. People sent text messages to friends, who then forwarded the text message to everyone in their telephone address books. The message went out, "Go to Esda [the name of the square where people gathered] and wear black." Tens of millions of messages circulated. There is potential, of course, again, for misinformation and disinformation in this sphere and for demonstrations that are not peaceful and not democratic. But this one was peaceful, it was democratic, and it did strongly contribute to the fall of the Estrada regime.

In Venezuela, during the coup against Hugo Chavez and the countercoup, the organizers of the first coup had the mass media on their side. According to my informants, every twenty minutes television and radio would announce: "Go demonstrate." The counterdemonstrators, the pro-Chavez demonstrators, had only their mobile telephones, text messages, and e-mail to organize, and they did so effectively.

In terms of demonstrations, we are seeing a classic arms race between authorities and demonstrators. News is being transmitted that you can't find in mainstream media. That news may come from primary sources on the street. It may come from media outside the United States, which may well have a different point of view than American media, as Julian Borger reminds us in chapter 20. The point is that a real alternative now exists.

Right now, this is very uncontrolled, emergent behavior, the result of many millions of people using these tools in terms of photos, videos, and words.

COLLECTIVE ACTION: ELECTIONS

Demonstrations are the most dramatic form of collective action, but the use of these technologies in the electoral process is more important. Campaign aides already can be seen with a Blackberry two-way e-mail device in one hand and a cell phone in the other hand. To me, that begins to signify a sophisticated use of the technology to coordinate get-out-the-vote strategies and tactics. Certainly, in the days and hours before an election, the ability to effectively mobilize and deploy get-out-the-vote forces in the streets is very important. Up-to-date information that you can broadcast and update via the Internet is important, as is the availability of that information, at the right time and in the right place, through mobile telephones.

In the election in Korea not long ago, the man who eventually won, now President Roh, was behind in the polls a few days before the vote. Roh's supporters turned to *Ohmynews*, a kind of citizen news. People submit stories through the Internet and then vote on which stories are placed prominently. It is very popular with the young cyber generation, who were demonstrating against the American presence in Korea. Using *Ohmynews*, the Internet, and text messaging, they organized a get-out-the-vote surge in the last couple of days that made the difference. The organizers were the first people the new president thanked after he was elected.

In America, MoveOn.org also has organized major breakthroughs, as Eli Pariser has discussed in chapter 32, and I would hope that MoveOn.org can build on mobile communications for collective, elective action in the future.

In addition, we also have seen the political campaigns demonstrate the use of MeetUp.com. That is a classic example of collective action. MeetUp.com is a web site where people who want to can meet face to face around a particular interest or issue. Even if they don't know each other or know who each other are, they can meet. Some candidates have used MeetUp.com to self-organize face-to-face meetings of their supporters. Campaigns also have used the web to collect donations from individuals—small donations from many people used in support of grassroots insurgency. When this fundraising proved successful, the mass media picked it up.

As they now exist, the two major political parties in America already have centralized organizing, plus a kind of hierarchical, decentralized organizing. But a self-organized, decentralized organizing is something new, and it has a lot of potential for giving voices to people who are not necessarily represented by the voices of the orthodoxy.

In addition, there are sites that I have not seen used as much as, say, MeetUp.com. There's Upoc.com. You can use Upoc.com to get people to sign up for the equivalent of a listserv, or a mailing list for mobile phones. I predict that somebody—I think Jerry Falwell is a good candidate for the first person—is going to organize his constituency so that he can get them into an Upoc.com-type list. He then will send out volumes of text messages organizing people to call and fax Congress around a particular issue on the eve of votes. I haven't really seen lobbying on a mass scale using mobile telephones yet. Americans are just beginning to take up texting the way they have elsewhere in the world. But I think we will soon see much more widespread use of text messages on mobile phones.

Spamming millions of people is not as effective, by far, as getting every one of your constituents to send a message on an issue to every one of the people in their address books—that is, to everyone in their social network. It's something that can't be used too often, but it is a potential untapped power.

I think the critical uncertainty in using these media for collective action is education. How can you trust the messages that you've received? How can you know whether to trust a group that wants you to join?

A MULTITUDE OF CITIZEN JOURNALISTS AND ACTIVISTS

We need to facilitate a multitude of citizen journalist-activists. Local and national nonprofit institutions need to train citizens in investigative journalism, fact checking, blogging technology, mobile phone technology linked to the Internet, the *Ohmynews* model in Korea, collective action, the organization of peaceful demonstrations, the organization of election campaigns, and the implementation of get-out-the-vote drives for citizens who support the kinds of alternative policies in this book. How-to handbooks for best practices need development and electronic distribution. More services are necessary that enable more people to form groups on-line. Nationwide, face-to-face workshops need to proliferate and systematically teach people how to use the electronic tools available. Those tools should be integrated into ongoing, populist face-to-face meetings, like Jim Hightower's Rolling Thunder Tour (chapter 36) and the Wellstone forums discussed by Jeff Faux (chapter 21).

Hybrid technology and enlightened policy, based on the lessons of science and history, must synthesize. Existing successful venues of protest and action like MoveOn.org and Mediareform.net must spearhead a drive to prevent corporate media and the American conservative power elite from blocking such a synthesis of technology, democracy, policy, and grassroots action. All of these strategies can be implemented inexpensively to create change.

BIBLIOGRAPHY

Dan Gillmor, "A New Brand of Journalism is Taking Root in South Korea," www.siliconvalley.com, posted May 18, 2003.

Leander Kahney, "Citizen Reporters Make the News," wired.com, posted May 17, 2003.

MoveOn.org meetup tool: action.moveon.org/meet.

http://www.Ohmynews.com.

Howard Rheingold, "From the Screen to the Streets," *In These Times*, October 28, 2003.

———, *SmartMobs: The Next Social Revolution* (New York: Perseus Publishing, 2002). http://www.smartmobs.com.

———, *Tools for Thought: The History and Future of Mind-Expanding Technology* (Cambridge: MIT Press, 1984, 2000). http://www.rheingold.com/texts/tft/vc/book.

———, *The Virtual Community: Homesteading on the Electronic Frontier* (Cambridge: MIT Press, 1993, 2000). http://www.rheingold.com/texts/tft/.

http://www.inthesetimes.com/comments.php?id=414_0_1_0_C%20.

• 34 •

Independent Reporting and the People's Media

Amy Goodman

In this chapter, I want to show how independent media are essential to revive American democracy. The failure of the mainstream media to speak out on the invasion of Iraq heightened the need. "Terrorism" is being defined by establishment "experts" in ways destructive to long-term solutions. That is why dissent of mainstream media needs to become commonplace and why we need to better alternative venues of communication, like public-access television. There is hope: The media-reform movement is here to stay.

THE PACIFICA TRADITION

Founded in 1949, Pacifica Radio is the only independent media network in this country. It gives voice to the marginalized, to those who are not usually heard—people who are actually a majority in this country. When the marginalized speak for themselves, the caricatures and stereotypes that fuel hate groups can be broken down.

When it went on the air in 1970, Pacifica's Houston station was blown up by the Ku Klux Klan. When the Grand Dragon went on trial, he said the Houston bombing was his proudest act—he understood how dangerous Pacifica Radio can be.

When Paul Robeson was whitelisted, or blacklisted, from almost everywhere in this country except a few black churches, he knew he could come to Pacifica Radio. He could go to KPFA and his voice would be broadcast.

When James Baldwin debated Malcolm X over the effectiveness of nonviolent civil disobedience and the effectiveness of sit-ins, the debates were broadcast on WBAI Radio in New York.

In the early 1950s, Pacifica pioneered the idea of listener support that we all know now from PBS and NPR. But the idea was not to turn to the corporations. Similar to how MoveOn appeals to its members (chapter 32), Pacifica turns to listeners and asks: If you appreciate what you hear, can you contribute something? It has stayed with that tradition for fifty-four years. PBS and NPR started with it, but while they have gone to "enhanced corporate underwriting," Pacifica hasn't. It is why we say we're the only independent media network in this country.

INDEPENDENT REPORTING AND THE GULF WAR

Look at who owned the media during the first Gulf War. CBS then was owned by Westinghouse and NBC owned by General Electric. Westinghouse and General Electric are major nuclear weapons manufacturers. They made most of the parts for most of the weapons in the war. So was it any accident that what we saw on television was a military hardware show?

We so often saw reporters who were in those high-tech helicopters or tanks, talking about what it felt like and interviewing the soldiers who were operating them. But what did it feel like to be the civilian *target* of these weapons? That's where the reporters should be as well.

The 2003 invasion of Iraq melded the military and the media more perfectly. We were introduced to the very appropriate phrase of "embedding" reporters in the military. We had reporters embedded on the front lines. Their lives depended on the soldiers who they were reporting on. But where were the reporters embedded in the Iraqi families in Baghdad? Where were the reporters embedded in the peace movement—to give us a picture everywhere of the responses to and the repercussions of the war?

Consider the playing cards with Iraqi officials on them that were given out by the American military in 2003. If you think the cards were given to American soldiers so that they could find and take in the Iraqi officials, think again. The playing cards were given out to reporters as part of a media ploy. When it reported that an Iraqi official had been caught, CNN would hold up his picture embedded in the playing card. So between the grainy images with the targets on them that we saw of the war—which looked like a video game—and the deck of cards, what was the American government conveying, especially to the young people in this country? That war is a game, that it is bloodless?

But what about the thousands of Iraqis who were killed? We heard and saw little of them, even though the role of the media is to convey the whole story. On "Democracy Now!" the program that I host, we did an interview for an hour with CNN anchor Aaron Brown. We asked him about CNN's approach to the war. For example, we asked why CNN didn't show pictures of casualties in Iraq. He said they're "tasteless." War is tasteless. But if we go to war, I believe it is the responsibility of the media to show what is on the ground—the facts, the brutality of war.

Al-Jazeera was thrown off of the floor of the New York Stock Exchange and NASDAQ after it showed American soldiers who were prisoners of war. There was a discussion about not showing pictures of prisoners of war because doing so violated the Geneva Conventions. At the same time, there were big color pictures in the *Washington Post* and the *New York Times* of Iraqis, butt-up, face in the ground, in their underwear. These, too, were prisoners of war. They wouldn't show the Americans, but they would show the Iraqis. We need a single standard, especially as journalists. It will reduce a lot of the anger against Americans around the world.

SPEAKING OUT ON SEPTEMBER 11

This brings us back to September 11, 2001. Ironically enough, just a few blocks from ground zero in New York, "Democracy Now!" was programming on the significance of September 11, 1973, when Salvador Allende, the democratically elected leader of Chile, died in the palace as the U.S.-backed Pinochet regime rose to power. We were doing the show on September 11 because more declassified documents had come out further implicating Henry Kissinger and Richard Nixon in the coup and in the rise to power of a man, Pinochet, who ended up killing thousands of Chileans and who ruled for seventeen years, to the benefit of corporations like ITT that had supported the coup.

President Bush came to ground zero a few days later. There was a chant that went up around him: "U-S-A! U-S-A!" Although I understood the sentiment, I thought, this was not the answer to what had taken place. The answer was, and is, a global community united against terror. In so many other cases that we cover day after day, people are terrorized by military regimes that have been supported by the United States. Americans need to learn that history in order to change in the future.

Over and over, the media repeated that this was the first time terror has come to American shores. What about Native Americans? What about slavery? September 11 was horrible, the killing of people from 100 nations around the world. But we have to understand that September 11 fits into a continuum that cannot continue. We have to unite with people all over the world in changing American foreign policy.

PEOPLE OF SEPTEMBER 11 WHO CRITICIZED AMERICA'S FOREIGN POLICY

To illustrate the need to change our foreign policy, let me give you some September 11 stories that were not accurately or fully reported.

Right after September 11, people who lost loved ones at the World Trade Center started to speak out, people like Rita Lasar. She's a seventy-year-old woman who lost her brother, Abe Zelmanowitz, on the twenty-seventh floor of the World Trade Center. Abe wouldn't leave until the emergency workers came up for his best friend, Ed, who worked next to him and was a paraplegic. And so he waited, and he went down with so many others.

A few days later, President Bush invoked Abe Zelmanowitz's name at the National Cathedral speech in Washington, and Rita Lasar quickly understood what was happening. She wrote a letter to the *New York Times*, and it was published. She wrote: "Even as I know the worst pain of my life, it will not ameliorate it; it will not ease my suffering, to know that a sister in Afghanistan will lose her brother soon. Not in my brother's name, not in my name."

Phyllis and Orlando Rodriguez also were grieving. They lost their son, Greg, above the 100th floor of the World Trade Center. They too wrote a letter. It didn't get published anywhere, but it swirled around the Internet and said the same thing as Rita Lasar's letter: "It will only increase our pain to know that a mother and father in Afghanistan will experience the same kind of suffering that we feel today. Not in our son's name."

Then there's Jim Creedon. I met him the day the bombs started to fall in Afghanistan. In New York City, people marched from Union Square up to Times Square, to the armed forces recruiting station, holding signs in protest. James Creedon stood on a pickup truck and described his experience as an emergency worker. He had been injured on September 11, but went back to try to help other people. He spoke so eloquently against war, saying that he was trained to save lives and he didn't want to know that an emergency worker in Afghanistan would be digging through the rubble like he was. I thought there would be a long line of reporters who would interview him. So I raced over. And he was right outside the *New York Times*. But no, there was no one there. So I asked him if he would come on the show to talk about his experiences.

In its coverage of September 11, America's corporate media let some people like Rita Lasar, Phyllis and Orlando Rodriguez, and Jim Creedon talk of their pain and loved ones. But corporate media cut away when description changed to proscription and to their opposition to war. American media cut away to experts on terrorism, the Henry Kissingers and the Oliver Norths.

THE TERRORISM OF EXPERTS

Henry Kissinger said: "We not only have to go after the terrorists, we have to bomb the countries that harbor them." I started to get nervous, because I live in the same city as Henry Kissinger. Look at what happened in Chile and how deeply Kissinger was involved with the subversion of that democratic government. And what resulted? Thousands of people were terrorized and killed. Americans now know the pain: We have our September 11, and so do they.

Look at Vietnam, Laos, and Cambodia. Millions of people were terrorized and killed. Look at Indonesia; it was Henry Kissinger who, as secretary of state with then-President Ford, went to Indonesia and met face to face with Suharto the day before Indonesia invaded East Timor, December 7, 1975, and gave the go-ahead for that invasion.

Ninety percent of the weapons used by the Indonesian military against the people of East Timor were from the United States. The State Department clearly understood that it was in trouble, that the weapons were sold on the condition that they would not be used offensively. So the State Department sent Henry Kissinger a cable saying: We've got to deal with this or Congress is going to cut off military aid to Indonesia. Kissinger held a high-level meeting with his State Department officials and castigated them for leaving a paper trail by sending him the cables. He said: "We will not kick our ally in the teeth."

Kissinger knew exactly what was happening, and what ensued from 1975 until recently was one of the worst genocides of the twentieth century. The Indonesian military, armed to the teeth by the United States, trained and financed by America, killed off a third of the Timorese, 200,000 people. Proportionately, it was larger than what Pol Pot did in Cambodia.

The reason we know about Pol Pot's atrocities is that he was an official enemy of the United States. The president and the secretary of state continually spoke out against him, as they should have, and the papers dutifully reported. In the case of Indonesia invading East Timor, the United States sided with Suharto, the long-reigning dictator who killed so many of his own people in Indonesia, not to mention the Timorese.

From Ford to Carter to Reagan to Bush, right through the Clinton years, they continued to arm the Indonesian military until 1999 when the United Nations finally brokered an agreement that would allow the Timorese to do what they'd always asked for—simply to hold a referendum so they could decide their own future, a referendum for self-determination. They voted for their freedom.

In all of this, the role of the American media unfortunately followed a pattern. From the day after the invasion to 1991, not one word was mentioned about one of the great genocides of the twentieth century. For seventeen years, NBC, ABC, and CBS never mentioned the words "East Timor."

WHAT IS TERRORISM?

So my question is: What is terror, who represents terrorism, and how seriously can we take the media, given the media's decisions on who gets to be seen and heard?

Leading up to the war in Iraq, most Americans were opposed to invasion. And yet media personalities (I won't call them journalists) continually intoned that 90 percent of Americans were for war.

During that lead-up to invasion, a lot of people started to feel a bit crazy: Who is for this? And who was asked? Who was called and asked these questions? What were the questions that were asked, if in fact these polls were done?

"Do you believe the killing of innocent civilians should be avenged by the killing of innocent civilians?" I believe that, if asked this question, more than 90 percent of people in this country would say no. Americans are a compassionate people.

By beating the drums for war, the media "manufactures consent," as Noam Chomsky calls it. So it's quite amazing that, leading up to the invasion now of Iraq, most people still were opposed. Of course, that changed when the invasion actually happened, because people equate supporting the troops with somehow supporting the war and not wanting to threaten any American's life.

But until the point where the United States invaded, the majority of people were opposed. How was that reflected on television? Fairness and Accuracy in Reporting did a study. In the week leading up to the secretary of state making his case for war at the Security Council, and in the week afterwards, there were 393 interviews on the war done on the nightly news shows of NBC, CBS, ABC, and the PBS NewsHour with Jim Lehrer, the four major nightly newscasts. Only three interviews were with people opposed to the war.

It's not just Pacifica, NPR, and PBS that are using the public airwaves. It doesn't matter whether you were for the invasion of Iraq or not. The media have the responsibility to bring us the views of people all over the country and world. The people who were excluded were not the silent majority. They were a silenced majority, silenced by the mainstream media.

AMERICAN CENSORSHIP IN IRAQ

During the invasion of Iraq, al-Jazeera, the Mideast equivalent of CNN, showed nonstop casualties, dead children on the ground. I would bet that if the American media had shown those pictures for a week and if there had not been censorship, Americans would have said, "There has got to be a better way." It is up to the media to tell the truth. Instead, we had Fox, MSNBC, and NBC name their coverage of the invasion the same name that the Pentagon gave it, Operation Iraqi Freedom. It's too bad the Pentagon didn't stick with its original name. Originally the Pentagon put forward: "Operation Iraqi Liberation." The problem was the acronym: O-I-L. So the Pentagon changed to: "Operation Iraqi Freedom."

During the war, Michael Moore gave a speech in which he called for the withdrawal of American troops from CBS, NBC, ABC, and CNN. We had situations where people like Wesley Clark, on the payroll of CNN, were questioning an embedded reporter in the field who was dressed in the same kind of camouflage. You could not figure out whether he was a soldier or whether he was a reporter. General Clark was questioning the reporter, and the reporter was saying: "Yes, sir; no, sir; yes, sir."

As Julian Borger of the *Guardian* discusses in chapter 20, the response of the media outside this country was vastly different from the media inside this country. Outside, in Spain for example, the elite press went on strike for a day. Two Spanish reporters were killed. And they said no to the prime minister, we're not going to mark down your words. They said "shame" and they walked out to the American embassy, stopped traffic in the intersections, and shouted "murderer, murderer!"

COMMONPLACE DISSENT

Similar to the way Eli Pariser and MoveOn.org define reform in chapter 32, we need to challenge mainstream media to use the airwaves responsibly, but we also must build another kind of media.

That is what we are doing at Pacifica Radio and at "Democracy Now!" the national, daily, grassroots, human-rights news hour that I host. Two years ago, we were on about twenty radio stations. After September 11, we expanded to television. We are the only televised radio show in this country, and we are broadcasting now on more than 150 stations around the United States. We are broadcasting in a number of cities in Canada as well. Our radio broadcasts are based on low-cost, high-tech appropriate technology.

In television, we are bringing together the largest public media collaboration in this country, and it is absolutely essential we break the sound barrier. We are broadcasting on our original Pacifica radio stations, in five of the largest so-called markets in this country—Houston, Los Angeles, New York, Washington, and San Francisco. But we also are broadcasting on Pacifica affiliates around the country. For example, we are increasingly on NPR stations, because people who were originally with NPR started to question the dearth of alternative voices there. And in fact, NPR stations are raising more money in their fundraising drives on "Democracy Now!" than on "All Things Considered" and "Morning Edition."

As we have seen in the coalition against the FCC media-consolidation rules, lines are breaking down now between Democrats and Republicans, conservatives and liberals. The labels are not so easily attached. Conservatives, like progressives, deeply care about privacy, about corporate control of their lives, about people losing their pensions, and managers running away with the loot of these large corporations.

Pacifica's goal is to make dissent commonplace in this country, because that protects us all. That's what the media are for.

ALTERNATIVE VENUES

The public media collaboration we are involved with is broadcasting not only on radio stations, but also broadcasting on shortwave radio internationally, and through video and audio streaming at www.DemocracyNow.org. More than 20,000 people, inside and outside the United States, are hitting our site every day now.

Pacifica is broadcasting on public-access television as well. This is a much-underutilized resource. Public-access television is very important in this country. How has public-access television developed? As the media monopolies moved in, and as cable moved from community to community, the company, let's say Comcast or AOL Time Warner, got a monopoly in a town. The town didn't want the roads ripped up every five minutes, so they granted the monopoly. But in exchange, the municipality or the city negotiated an agreement and said: "We want to make sure you assure there are some public-interest channels." And so they set those channels aside.

Many times, people in a community don't even know that they have public-access television, and certainly the company isn't going to tell them. So we go from community to community and tell people: "You know, you have these channels." Media activists go to their city council, and they see it written into the agreement, and the city council gets excited. They can broadcast their council hearings.

We need a people's media in this country. Public-access television is a cornerstone for that. And now, as the cable industry is getting older, the monopolies are in place, the cables are laid, and the communities renegotiate their contracts, the people often don't have the power to demand that these large companies keep the public-interest channels. So the companies take them away. A community might have four channels and might then get cut down to one.

But if people are informed, they can fight back and maintain those channels, and people can make their own media. When you make your own media, you are much more media-literate and you can even take on the mainstream media. You can say: I understand what they did here; where is that diversity of guests that we need? You start at the community level.

Pacifica is on public-access television on eighty stations. We now broadcast live, because we're also on satellite television. There's DirecTV and Dish Network. On Dish Network, we are on one nonprofit channel, called Free Speech TV, Channel 9415. Public-access television stations can get the dish, just like you can at home, put it on the station, and broadcast the show live.

So we can take on the major network morning shows. Before it was impossible because they spent millions in satellite technology that none of us could ever afford. But now we have simple, appropriate technology that allows us to broadcast live around the country. Every single community can model its own human rights, grassroots news hours, bringing together the local and the global, and see it as very doable, and then take on the networks and say, where are these other voices? It's all part of a continuum.

That continuum must include low-power FM. It's where people start. It's something that was defeated by the last Congress. Unfortunately, the charge against lower-power FM was led by the National Association of Broadcasters, lobbying Republican senators, and National Public Radio, lobbying Democratic senators. It was a stealth campaign, and they won. I went to the NPR national board meetings and saw some of the dissident general managers, saying: "Why are we opposing low-power FM? This is how we got our start, this is where we get our people, and now we are squelching it so that those people can't grow up and have local community control."

THE GOOD NEWS

But the good news is that there is hope. We can be successful in lobbying Congress and fighting back on a wide variety of issues—based on the success of the campaign against FCC media consolidation. Pacifica Radio played its part, broadcasting the alternative hearings that were held by the two dissident commissioners, Adelstein and Copps, who refused to go along with Michael Powell and the other two commissioners. The dissidents said: "We're not just going to have one public hearing; we don't care if you make this official or not, we'll go from community to community."

In the Pacifica broadcasts of these hearings, thousands of people were heard from, around the country and across the political spectrum. As one consequence, Michael Powell was raked over the coals by the Senate Commerce Committee—by Trent Lott and Barbara Boxer—because, when people found out what was happening, they protested the kind of absolute corporate gift that was being given to these companies.

The mainstream television networks didn't cover the story, but did file a brief with the FCC in support of media consolidation. Still, the people learned through alternate media, like MoveOn.org and MediaReform.net, and through lobbying across the political spectrum, from Code Pink to the National Rifle Association.

The media-reform movement is here to stay, and that movement has the potential to lobby on a wide variety of issues, from low-power FM and public access to broader antitrust policies. I'm hopeful, too, when I see how the death row of Illinois is empty now. That's because of grassroots activists, starting with mothers of men on death row, who have now, one by one, been exonerated, and many others. Their work led to crusading reports in the *Chicago Tribune* about the disparity, particularly the racial disparity, in the death penalty, which affected the conservative Republican Governor, George Ryan, who had to sign those death warrants. Ryan called for a moratorium, and now he's ended death row in Illinois.

I'm hopeful because on May 20, 2002, the people of Timor, after twenty-five years, celebrated their freedom. It was Independence Day. "Democracy Now!" on Pacifica was the only American network there for the week, sending daily, broadcast-quality reports over the Internet, which then aired on television around the country. On May 20, 2002, we joined with 100,000 Timorese as they watched the flag of the Democratic Republic of East Timor raised, and this nation of survivors celebrated its freedom.

And I'm hopeful because of books like this, looking at the future. Where do we go from here in this post-invasion America, in this post–September 11 America? I think we've learned a tremendous lesson—that a global community can unify against terrorism.

BIBLIOGRAPHY

Noam Chomsky, *Manufacturing Consent: The Political Economy of the Mass Media* (New York: Pantheon Books, 2002).

———, with David Goodman: *The Exception to the Rulers: Exposing Oily Politicians, War Profiteers, and the Media That Love Them* (New York: Hyperion Books, 2004).

Amy Goodman and Jeremy Scahill, "Drilling and Killing: Chevron and Nigeria's Oil Dictatorship," 1998 George Polk Award–winning documentary for radio reporting.

———, "Killing for Oil in Nigeria," *The Nation*, March 15, 1999.

Hudson Mohawk Independent Media Center, with Amy Goodman, "Independent Media in a Time of War," documentary, 2004. www.hm.indymedia.org.

Henry Kissinger, "Phase II and Iraq," *Washington Post*, January 13, 2002.

Rita Lasar, "One Week Later: How to Answer the Horror?" Letter to the editor, *New York Times*, September 18, 2001.

Steve Rendall and Tara Broughel, "Amplifying Officials and Squelching Dissent: FAIR Study Finds Democracy Poorly Served by War Coverage," Fairness and Accuracy in Reporting, *Extra!* Magazine, May 6, 2003.

• 35 •

Lessons from 1964

Eric Alterman

Building on my book *What Liberal Media?* this chapter focuses on the rise of conservative media over the last forty years. It concludes with lessons for advocacy and media in support of the foreign, economic, and domestic policy alternatives set forth in this book. Primarily, I want to consider the "elite" media, located largely in New York and Washington. The elite media are composed mostly of the top political reporters for the *New York Times,* the *Washington Post,* the *Los Angeles Times,* the *Wall Street Journal*, the top networks, the top opinion magazines, and the cable news shows.

When we discuss the media today, there are many issues on the table. They include the phony charge of "liberal bias," the terrible problem of media ownership concentration, the focus on profits that is killing so many media companies, and the collapse of journalistic standards. But even if these issues didn't exist, and even if there were a perfect candidate who ran on the kinds of positions staked out in this book, that candidate still would have difficulty communicating the value of those positions to the American public.

Why? To answer that question, it is necessary to go back to the 1964 election. That election was key to how the media have changed in our lifetimes. In 1964, the media were conservative in many ways. But the elite media were more liberal than the rest of the nation on most issues. They were certainly more liberal on civil rights. They were more liberal on economic policy. They were committed Keynesians. They didn't have any use for Milton Friedman or monetarism. While they were "cold warriors," the elite media didn't support a unilateral showdown with the Soviet Union, as did much of the conservative right.

The Republican candidate in 1964, Barry Goldwater, ran an honest campaign, and he had lots of movement conservatives behind him. Those movement conservatives were rather unsophisticated about national politics. The most prominent and important movement conservative in terms of the media was the billionaire Richard Mellon Scaife. Because Goldwater was speaking the honest truth to the American people, as he understood it, the movement conservatives expected that the country would respond, that Goldwater would be elected president, and that everything would be transformed, as Goldwater promised.

Instead, not only was Goldwater beaten in a landslide, he had become the national laughing stock. All the influential pundits—like Walter Lippmann, James Reston, Joseph Alsop, and Joseph Kraft—were writing columns after election day suggesting that the Republican Party was headed for oblivion, that it was going to disappear unless it amputated its conservative wing and moved to the left of the Democrats on some of these issues, particularly civil rights.

Richard Mellon Scaife realized that the values he and his friends believed in would never amount to much if the candidates who espoused them could not get their message through this liberal-elite media prism, which was twisting them and distorting them so that they sounded ridiculous by the time they reached the American people. He was right, basically. So Scaife decided to build himself a better media, so that he could have voices heard without what he understood to be distortion and perversion of the message. He and other wealthy conservatives invested heavily in new institutions that could frame the conservative message. Corporations joined in, through the influence of people like Robert Bartley, Irving Kristol, and William Simon.

Hundreds of billions of dollars have been invested in these new institutions since 1964. As a result, while there were only a few conservative nonprofit and other organizations in Washington in 1964, today there are more than 300. Some are small. Others are large, like the Heritage Foundation, with an annual budget of more than $30 million.

THE IDEOLOGICAL MACHINE OF THE FAR RIGHT

Scaife and his colleagues created a parallel media world, an entire world view, a kind of cocoon in which hundreds of thousands or perhaps even millions of people could live comfortably. I was graduated from college in 1982. I was a columnist for my college newspaper and then went to Washington to make my fortune for two years before returning to graduate school. During those two years writing for the *Nation* and other small liberal publications, I think I made a grand total of $500.

By comparison, David Brock was graduated from college the same year. He was a columnist for his college newspaper, the *Daily Californian*. He went to Washington at the same time I did. He ended up with a million-dollar advance from the Free Press for a book on Hillary Clinton without even a book proposal. The only question he was asked by his publishers was "Is she a lesbian?" And he had the good sense not to answer, because if he had given the correct answer and said no, then he probably only would have gotten half a million dollars.

There are thousands of young conservatives who have gone to Washington in recent decades and been placed in jobs in conservative think tanks, the *Washington Times*, *Inside* magazine, the *Wall Street Journal,* and many other conservative institutions. They have made entire, incredibly well-funded careers in this world, and now they can work for Fox News or on talk radio. Some can speak to millions of people who hear nothing but the conservative message. So a kind of ever-replenishing, perpetual-motion machine has been created for conservative ideology. The machine is enormously useful, because it provides conservative activists with a kind of tribal drum to constantly make their voices heard in American politics.

In its most pristine form, the impact of this ideological machine was felt in places like Florida in 2000. Through encouragement by Rush Limbaugh, FreeRepublic.com, and Fox News, thousands of conservatives hopped on planes, flew to Florida, and helped to shut down the vote count in Miami-Dade. Those votes were the votes that would have made the difference, and they were disallowed because the counties did not make the deadline because the vote was shut down.

Incredibly well-disciplined, the activist machine of the Republican Party can blast e-mail and faxes in the morning and then repeat any given message all day on FreeRepublic.com, Rush Limbaugh, O'Reilly, Hannity, talk radio, cable television, the *Wall Street Journal* editorial page, and the *Weekly Standard.* It is a very impressive accomplishment. And because so many Americans have become alienated from politics, those who are part of the machine have political value well beyond their numbers. The political left has nothing like that.

In terms of its activist base, the left is incredibly dispirited. The difference between Ralph Nader and Ralph Reed is instructive. Ralph Reed built institutions within the Republican Party and ended up controlling many of those institutions. By comparison, Ralph Nader seems to be destroying the Democratic Party and opening up avenues for Republican takeover.

The creation of the new conservative media landscape also has redefined discourse in the mainstream media. I have given hundreds of talks on the media power of the far right, and at least half of the time someone will stand up and say, "I wish you would stop whining, Dr. Alterman, because, yeah, sure, we admit it, we have Fox News, but you've got CNN."

That is the way the world is framed by conservatives today. Their line is that there is a conservative view and a liberal view, and the liberal view is whatever is not the conservative view. So if the conservative view is defined as "the best way to get the economy going is to give billionaires a tax break and give nothing to the working people," and "the best way to maintain the peace is to invade countries preemptively and unilaterally," then what used to be the right becomes the center. What used to be the center becomes the left, and what used to be the liberal view is outside of the room entirely, banging on the doorway, trying to be heard. This is the frame, over and over in political discourse today. Those who try to discuss liberal alternatives face an onslaught by the right and are forced to fight a rear-guard action on conservative turf. Liberalism has become so conservative these days that it's really just a definition for "not nuts."

LESSONS FOR ADVOCACY TODAY

Those who advocate many of the policies in this volume therefore are roughly where the conservatives were in 1964. But we don't have the luxury of wasting enormous amounts of money, as did the conservatives. So we need to be smart and strategic.

The encouraging thing I would say about our moment today is that people understand the extent of the problem. Although I had some problems with the leadership of the movement against the war in Iraq at some of the rallies, I was enormously excited by how quickly mainstream people got the message, came out, and protested. They wanted to be felt and heard, around the world, as a voice for a sane foreign policy. Similarly, grassroots organizing against the FCC rule changes was incredible, especially given the complexity of the issue.

A while back, I gave a talk in Brooklyn cosponsored by twenty-one separate groups. The groups illustrated how progressive advocacy and media now are being done more intelligently. People are dividing up the work that has to be done. You've got leaders talking about a progressive cable network, and a liberal talk-radio network has been established, as well as a brand-new think tank that will take on the Heritage Foundation. You've got MoveOn.org, which is a magnificently sophisticated organization harnessing the power of the Internet. And you've got new troops, motivated by the antiwar battle and the FCC battle. No one was prepared for the extremism of recent federal policy, and that extremism has helped create more organization and cooperation on alternative policy.

We have learned the price of speaking too closely to our principles at the cost of our effectiveness. I am not saying that we throw out our principles. But let's fight about it after we have won. Let's worry about what divides us once we are in power. Let's not fight about who's to blame for having lost. That can be more satisfying emotionally, but we don't have the luxury of such feelings anymore, especially when you see the cost in terms of people's lives. The stakes in foreign, economic, and domestic policy are too high.

We are at an incredibly propitious moment in American history, and there are some very encouraging signs. But we are so far behind and the landscape is so large that we have no choice but to be extremely focused and strategic. We need to make thoughtful choices before we expend our resources.

BIBLIOGRAPHY

Eric Alterman, "Liberal Signs of Life," *Stop the Presses* column, *The Nation*, July 14, 2003.

———, "Sorry Seems to be the Hardest Word," *Stop the Presses* column, the *Nation*, January 29, 2004. http://www.thenation.com/doc.mhtml?i=20040216&s=alterman.

———, *The Book on Bush: How George W. (Mis)Leads America* (New York: Viking Press, 2004).

———, *What Liberal Media? The Truth About Bias and the News* (New York: Basic Books, 2003).

———, with Mark J. Green, of *When Presidents Lie: Deception and Its Consequences* (New York: Viking Press, 2004).

Jeffrey Toobin, *Too Close to Call* (New York: Random House, 2001).

VI

ACTION, ORGANIZING, AND POWER

• 36 •

Thieves in High Places

Jim Hightower

About a year ago, I saw a bumper sticker on a pickup truck in Austin, Texas, that said: "Where are we going, and what am I doing in this handbasket?"

Most people in the country, I find, have a strong sense that something fundamental is happening here, something that is bad for them and bad for our country. I think we're in another of those "when in the course of human events" moments that Jefferson wrote about, a moment in which it's not King George III in England, it's not royalty, but global corporate power that is usurping our democracy and usurping decision-making over every aspect of our lives.

The founding ethic of the common good is the idea that we're all in this together. But the conservatives are supplanting the ethic with a new ethic of greed that says: I've got mine; you get yours; never give a sucker an even break; caveat emptor; I'm rich and you're not; adios, chump. That's pretty much what it comes down to.

They're separating the good fortune of the few from the needed fortune of the many. We see it in plutocratic actions that they take: There is the tax giveaway, more than a trillion dollars now to the top one percent of wealth-earners in our country; at the same time they provide zero to the twelve million children of working families who do indeed pay income tax. Meanwhile, while they're shoveling money up to the very top, there was a net loss of more than two million jobs from 2001 to the end of 2003. Ten million people are presently unemployed, and there was a 184 percent increase in long-term unemployment from 2001 to the end of 2003. I mean, imagine what they would have been doing if they had actually won the 2000 election.

Then of course there is the growing autocracy: The Homeland Security Act, Patriot I, and now Patriot II. It's not a very pretty sight at all.

We see it in a lot of other ways: The new imperial presidency, the executive authority that's being asserted and, I'm ashamed to say, that the Congress is going along with, allowing it to happen. Those are the edicts and directives that are coming out of the White House, many of them late in the evening on Friday, when the media doesn't get hold of them and there's no chance for other people to react.

In my book *Thieves in High Places,* I wrote a little section in which I took the sum of the environmental edicts that occurred from March of 2001 when they came into office to March 2003, just a two-year period of time. It's not the individual items that are significant here. It's the impact of the whole volume. The edicts coming out of the White House are fundamentally changing the rules of the game, which are being bent more and more in favor of the plunderers and the spoilers and the speculators out there.

THE WOBBLYCRATS AND AUNT EULAH

The rich need representation too, and they have it in the White House. But where's my party? Where's the Democratic Party? I was elected to two terms in the state of Texas on the Democratic ticket, much to the amusement of the people down there, but nonetheless there I was, and proud to have been so, and proud to be a Democrat in the old Democratic tradition.

But now it's become the Wobblycrat Party, too willing to go along with the corporate interests. I'll tell you a personal story. My old Aunt Eulah used to farm up in northeast Texas in Bonham, on the Red River. The congressional districts of Carl Albert, Sam Rayburn, and Wright Patman were adjacent there, back in the old populist days, right along that river.

So we do have a history that we can look back at with some pride. My Aunt Eulah's husband, Ernest, died early, about fifty years of age, and Eulah had to leave the farm. She moved in with her daughter, Velma, down at Maud, Texas, and worked as a waitress in the Maud Cafe there. Well suddenly, much to our amazement, Eulah disappeared. She just up and poof, she was gone. We didn't know what had happened. But we finally learned that a Mr. Green (we never did learn his first name), a traveling salesman and an apparently dazzling figure, came through to the Maud Cafe, swept Eulah right off her feet, and just hauled off with her.

We finally got a postcard from Cheyenne, Wyoming. Mr. Green had taken Eulah to the Cheyenne Rodeo and Eulah was just giddy beyond belief. She had never seen such a thing, and she was just filled with romance and said that they were next going to Oregon. Just a few days later we got a mournful telephone call from Eulah, late at night. In Oregon, Mr. Green had come to understand that Eulah did not inherit any money from husband Ernest and the farm. They were tenant farmers. So Mr. Green took off and we had to send bus money to bring Eulah home with us.

I think of my Democratic Party in terms of Eulah and Mr. Green. Mr. Green has run off with the Democratic Party and I'm wondering, if we sent bus money would they come home? They have been swept off by lobbyists and corporate money, the same money that the Republicans take. And they've taken off their old Sears Roebuck work boots and strapped on the same Guccis and Puccis that the Republicans are strutting around in.

LET'S BLOW THE FOAM OFF THAT BEER

Not too long ago, Tom Daschle was asked on one of the Sunday morning yackety-yak shows why the Democrats didn't offer some sort of bold alternative to President Bush's latest tax cut for the wealthy, and Daschle said: "Well, you have to take one step at a time." And you think: Really? I mean, is this an AA program? In recent years, the White House didn't take one step at a time. It took great kangaroo leaps out there, changing our country. If the meek ever inherit the Earth, Daschle and gang are going to be land barons.

Then we heard from the Democratic Leadership Council types: Oh well, Bush was so strong, we couldn't fight him; we had to be more like him, in fact. He had all the money. He had the popularity. The media were behind him. He was the War President. And he had a mandate. All right, he didn't win the presidency actually in 2000, but in 2002, with the congressional off-year elections, he got a mandate. He won both houses of Congress.

Well, let's blow the foam off that beer about that 2002 "mandate." This is really important. I'm not big on numbers, but follow this briefly with me. These are numbers that Curtis Gans assembled in his great electoral research on the congressional elections of 2002. Some 33 percent of eligible voters voted in congressional elections in 2002—33 percent. Of those, 17 percent of the eligible voters chose Republican candidates, 15 percent chose Democrats, and 1 percent chose "other." So there's the Republican mandate. That's it—17 percent of the eligible voters in America represent the Republican mandate, with which they now are trying to undo our democracy.

That is not a political juggernaut, 17 percent of the eligible voters. They can't get any more than that. In fact, that's the same 17 percent that the Republicans got in 1982, in the first off-year election under Reagan. Newt got a little better than that. He got 19 percent of eligible voters in 1994, when he swept to power and imploded under the force of his own ego. And that's as much as they're going to get, because they have a policy that Americans do not agree with. They're not going to increase their total above 19 percent of eligible voters.

Yet they won in 2002 essentially because the Democrats didn't run. George Washington Plunkett, a Tammany Hall boss at the turn of the last century, said: "The Democratic Party of the nation ain't dead, though it has been giving a lifelike imitation of a corpse for several years." That's where I think we are right now.

What was the bumper sticker for Democratic congressional candidates in 2002? It was: "Well, we support the tax cut for the rich too; and, yeah, we're behind the homeland-security thing; and by the way, we're for the Iraq war, too, but we're not quite as enthusiastic as the White House is about it all. So vote for us." That didn't work. It's hard for the donkeys to win the race if they're going to carry the elephants on their backs. We have to have our own policies and appeal to our own folks.

GETTING WORKING STIFFS BACK INTO THE POLITICAL GAME

When I first came to Washington, just about the time the crust of the Earth was cooling some years ago, I worked at the Library of Congress Congressional Research Service, and subsequently left and was in Texas. There I got a call from somebody up there who said the new senator, Lloyd Bentsen of Texas, had sent an interesting request to the Congressional Research Service. The question was: "What is a populist? The senator thinks he might be one."

I might be the king of France, you know. I mean, it's one of those things—if you have to ask, you're not.

But this is both the crisis and the challenge that we face today, that we face for our democracy. There's no populist party unabashedly and unequivocally offering to battle on behalf of the workaday majority of this country, on behalf of the two-thirds of Americans who are politically homeless right now. That's 121 million people who did not vote in the congressional elections.

Bob Dylan had that song: "The pump don't work 'cause the vandals took the handles." They've taken the handle from our electoral process. Workaday people don't have a lever to pull that has credibility, that says, "Your life is going to be different if you'll choose this party; we're going to stand with you."

So here's my wacky idea for you. Instead of the Democratic Leadership Council strategy of trying to weasel into office by siphoning off 1 or 2 percent of that 17 percent of those wishy-washy soccer moms and office park dads that the Republicans get, what if we began to talk like Democrats again and go after the 67 percent of the people who aren't voting? We don't have to get them all. What if we get 10 percent of them? Every election would be won if we won 10 percent of the people who presently are not voting. Those are our people.

My message is simple. We can't change America's policies until we change America's politics, and that means putting the working stiffs back in the political game. Now, how you going to get them in the game? Well, here's another wacky idea: Let's appeal to their self-interest. I know the media jumps on any Democrat who goes to an African-American group or a Mexican-American group or a labor union or anything else and says, "Ah! They're pandering to their base." Well, the Republicans don't mind pandering to their base. I mean, damn right; political parties exist to pander to their bases. And we've got a bigger base than they do, by God.

NO MORE FIDDLE-FADDLE

So why don't Democrats appeal to their base again? They can do it by offering things that are good for America: health care for everybody, based on a single-payer system, not this fiddle-faddle where we've got this formula where certain seniors will be able to get some prescription benefits under this program or that program, but only at a certain level of income. I mean, the eyes glaze over. You don't understand what they're even talking about because they're not talking about you. Health care for everybody, that's our program.

Free education for everybody, from preschool through higher education, and higher education is defined as however you want to define it. That might be a mechanic's degree; it might be a chef's degree. You can be whatever you want to be; it's free. The GI Bill did that and it paid off enormously to our economy, it paid off enormously to the taxpayers, it paid off enormously to our country, and indeed to the world. Let's have a GI Bill again, but a bill for everybody.

What about tax reform based on eliminating the payroll burden on the working stiffs and putting that burden on the wealthy people who ought to be paying for it? Now that would excite the taxpayers out there who are now not voting.

Public financing of elections, not the McCain-Feingold bill and then all the loopholes are built around that. We're going to publicly finance all elections. Put a program out there that people can see.

HOLY THOMAS PAINE

Well, I'm told, "Hightower, you can't talk like that any more, because since September 11, everything changed. You've got to set all those agendas aside, we've got to be united against the evildoers around the world, march in step, don't ask questions, be quiet." They actually say "be quiet." Some of our own progressive leaders have said "Well, hunker down, stay low, beneath the radar, and be quiet."

Well, holy Thomas Paine. I mean, since when do patriotic, freedom-loving Americans cower in quietude? If you don't speak out when it matters, when would it matter that you would ever speak out? This is the time.

Mark Twain said: "Loyalty to the country, always; loyalty to the government when it deserves it." Very different things. Now is the time to be speaking out, not just about the Iraqi situation and the endless war on terror in whatever country we're going to be assaulting next, but about this full agenda, about real national security.

Plus, we have no right to be quiet. Too many democracy fighters before you and me fought, bled, and died to make it possible for us to be noisy, to be agitators, to organize, and to protest. If we stay quiet, the autocrats and plutocrats win; democracy, freedom, and justice lose. The opposite of courage is not cowardice; it's conformity. Even a dead fish can go with the flow, right? So what are we going to be?

Besides—and here's my happiest message for you—the American people don't want us to be quiet. They're roiling for engagement.

THE AMERICAN PEOPLE BELIEVE THIS STUFF

I come to you as a rare bird: a progressive optimist. I'm lucky because I get to travel a lot, and with my radio show and newsletter and other work that I do I don't just have to take information off of the television or out of the newspapers or just watch what's going on in Washington. If you look outward rather than inward, you would be a progressive optimist as well, because people want exactly what you and I want. We want our country back. We want it back from the greedheads and boneheads, the spoilers and speculators, the big shots and bastards who have stolen our country from us.

We also want the America that we thought we were born into, the America of egalitarian ideals based on the founding principles that I think include at least three things: economic fairness, social justice, and equal opportunity for all people. The American people believe in those things, deeply believe in them, and have them in their heart and in their gut. They don't always act on them because they're rarely appealed to by the political process.

But that's what all of our issues come down to. You can take any issue that you're dealing with, but it comes down to those principles of fairness and justice and equal opportunity for all people, and that's the program we ought to be taking to the American people.

Benjamin Franklin wrote, "America's destiny is not power, but light." And the light he was talking about was the light of justice, fairness, and opportunity for all people. That's what the world's people are looking to America for, yet they're seeing quite a different thing.

The people of the world are not mad at Americans. They're mad at American corporations and American government. They discern the difference, and we've got to begin to discern the difference here too and recognize the difference and go to the people themselves with those values of justice, fairness, and opportunity for all people. This is not just soft stuff. It's not just a feel-good sentiment. It's core to who we are as a people. In *Thieves in High Places*, I look at polling data in a section called "America the Possible." We hear, for example, that America has turned conservative. Well, on budget priorities, 67 percent of the American people prefer to have more spending on needs such as education and health care than to have the administration's latest tax cut. That's from an ABC News–*Washington Post* poll.

If there is to be a tax cut, 58 percent think it should be targeted to middle-income and low-income folks. Some 40 percent more think taxes should be cut equally for all income brackets. Now, I'm not great at math, but that's 98 percent of the people who disagree with the tax cuts going to the wealthy.

On health care, 64 percent say it's the federal government's responsibility to make sure all Americans are covered. More than half say the government should create a plan to cover everyone, even if it requires a tax increase on them.

On public education, 71 percent say educational improvement should focus on reforming the existing public school system rather than finding an alternative. And 75 percent favor improving public schools over providing vouchers; 70 percent are willing to pay more in taxes if the money went to education; 84 percent would pay more in taxes if the money went specifically to raising teachers' salaries, reducing class size, fixing run-down schools, improving security, and putting more computers in classrooms.

On the environment, six out of ten say the government is doing too little to protect the environment from corporate plunderers. Only 10 percent say it's doing too much. And 67 percent feel strongly that our country should do whatever it takes to protect the environment.

This is not the conventional wisdom that we are getting from the establishment media. This is what the American people believe.

CHARLENE NELSON BEAT THE BANKERS

The American people basically agree with us, and we ought to be appealing to that deeply held belief. I've got better news in *Thieves in High Places*, in another section called "America the Beautiful." The news is that we don't have to create a progressive movement in America. It's already out there, and it's moving. It's fighting, and more often than not, it's winning.

I write a lot about this in my newsletter, *The Hightower Lowdown*, which I put out monthly, about things that are happening out in the country that the establishment media is missing. Take, for example, the living-wage campaign. While Congress won't even address the minimum wage, more than 100 cities have passed living-wage ordinances, not $6.15 an hour, but $7.50, $8.50, $10.50, $11.50, with health care and retirement benefits, indexed to inflation in some cases.

Washington state did it through an initiative on the statewide ballot and got 84 percent of the people to support a living wage indexed to inflation in that state.

Wal-Mart, you know, oh well, Wal-Mart's a beast of a corporation; you can't beat Wal-Mart. Well, that's hogwash. Wal-Mart is being defeated almost daily in this country. I was in Arizona recently, not a bastion of liberal thought. Food and commercial workers, teaming up with all kinds of other folks, including a lot of Republican neighborhood associations, defeated ten Wal-Marts in the last three years in the state of Arizona. It's happening all across the country, people standing up for their own communities, for the kind of businesses they want to have.

In recent years, Congress did nothing except exacerbate the privacy invasion by corporations and governments. In North Dakota, a woman named Charlene Nelson, thinking herself to be a conservative Republican, learned that they have a law there that a bank can't sell your credit information or your banking information without getting your written approval. So the bankers changed the law. They went to the legislature and got the law changed to where they could sell the information without consulting with you.

Charlene was outraged. She organized a petition drive and got an initiative on the ballot in six weeks, which is unheard-of in that state. The bankers pooh-poohed it and said, "Oh well, just this crazy lady out there," and in fact began to attack her personally. But suddenly the petition drive picked up steam. Charlene got phone calls from all across the country. She phoned the networks. They got her on talk radio. Her campaign began to expand. Bankers knew they had a problem. They put $100,000 into the initiative. They did all kinds of crazy stuff.

But 73 percent of the people of North Dakota voted with Charlene Nelson against the banking establishment, and they got privacy put back. It can happen at a grassroots level, just one person standing up and rallying people and saying "No, we're not going to let you change who we are as a people. We're not going to let you just negate the Fourth Amendment and invade our privacy."

Four states already have public financing of elections: Maine, Arizona, Vermont, and Massachusetts (though Massachusetts won't finance it). In Maine they went through their first cycle of elections using public financing. The result was that one-third of their House and one-half of their state Senate were elected without taking any corporate money. That is going to change politics in that state. (Micah Sifry has more on Clean Money campaigns in chapter 37).

North Carolina has passed public financing for its judicial elections and New Mexico passed it for public-utility elections. The list of examples goes on and on, from sweatshop reform to food-system reform.

ROLLING THUNDER AND CAMP WELLSTONE

Enormous changes are taking place out at the grassroots level. Our job is to connect the parts to each other. People on one side of town who are fighting for a living wage don't know the folks on the other side of town who are battling a toxic waste dump, and they don't know the folks outside of town who are fighting against a hog factory.

So our job is to first go to the grassroots, and decamp from Washington, D.C. We need to put money into genuine grassroots efforts, and to put what we call "patient capital" out there, and to give groups time, because it takes time to build. My friend Fred Harris once said you can't have a mass movement without the masses. And that has been our problem as a progressive movement. We've been trying to have a mass movement by talking to it from Washington, rather than by getting out with it at the grassroots level. That's our strength, that's where we have power. Those are our folks.

We've got to build coalitions at the grassroots level. I have made such connections with my Rolling Thunder Down-Home Democracy Tour. The tour gives folks a chance to put on democracy fests around the country. We provide speakers, musicians, and a sort of "how-to" template.

Rolling Thunder has been enormously successful because people want to get together. Not just high-tech politics but high touch. So these are like county fairs of democracy. They're day-long things. We intersperse speeches. We make the speeches short, by the way. You've got to do twenty-minute speeches, with music. We've got food from local restaurants and community groups. The community groups do the tabling and get people to sign up on petitions.

We have an action tent where people can take a dozen different actions right there that day. We collect everybody's e-mail addresses and feed them into the progressive cause. Some of MoveOn's e-mail comes from our organization and our efforts. Ben and Jerry come with their stuff and their toys. They have a "dunk-a-lobbyist" booth. There are all sorts of fun things that we do.

The slogan of the Rolling Thunder Tour is, "Let's put the party back in politics." It ought to be fun. Politics shouldn't be just a boring thing we do in the last month of an election. It ought to be something we do all the time, get people together, let them rub elbows with each other, and know that they've got a lot in common, and get them to continue on together. Part of the good news is that they do continue. They have conversation cafes. They have potluck dinners on one side of town, then another side, and then another side. They just keep it moving and keep the discussion building, and try to forge action coalitions at the grassroots level.

Molly Ivins, Barbara Ehrenreich, Michael Moore, Jesse Jackson Jr., Cornel West and all sorts of great people have teamed with us on Rolling Thunder. We've been to places like Austin, Seattle, St. Paul, Tucson, and Pittsburgh. This kind of thing needs to be kept going, to be made a permanent part of the political landscape because we need to get folks together. It's not enough just to talk to them as data in our computers. We physically need to talk to them and give them a chance to talk back and then to organize and train and keep it going.

Camp Wellstones are another example. They are a phenomenal and wonderful effort. Paul had 5,000 people who had been through his training—volunteers who were ready to hit the streets for his reelection. That was power. That was why he was going to win, particularly by reaching out to young people. Others, like Joel Rogers in Madison, Wisconsin, and Dan Carroll in Eugene, Oregon, are doing terrific work, approaching foundations and other funders to build training, outreach, and organizing strategies.

We need to have a message, messengers, and media outlets. We must find ways to talk to more and more people. That's a lot of what I do with my speechifying, newsletter, and radio show. I'm on about 125 radio stations now, which is good, and we're in major markets like San Francisco and through the Pacifica Network, Washington, D.C. We need to put more radio networks together. But it won't be easy, I can tell you. Clear Channel owns a third of all radio stations. It is not going to take my kind of programming. My radio commentaries have been kicked off stations that were bought by Clear Channel.

So we need to fight the FCC and the mainstream corporate media, working through the movement created by Robert McChesney and John Nichols (chapter 31). As part of the fight, I appear on the establishment media, like *Hardball with Chris Matthews* and do battle, as do Michael Moore, Molly Ivins, Al Franken, and many others.

But we can't fool ourselves that establishment media are going to be our venues. We need to create strong alternative venues and support those venues. We must find those radio stations that do have a license and a wattage to reach some people—and support those stations. We need to develop more grassroots speakers bureaus and newsletters to reach folks. It is guerrilla, almost door-to-door kind of work.

We need to model ourselves on the populist movement of the late nineteenth century, the last great grassroots political movement in the country. The movement created its own party, created its own financing system, was an advocate for labor, and backed women's suffrage. At the time, the populist movement also was shut out by the media. The establishment newspapers ridiculed the movement—so the movement created its own newspapers. A newspaper syndicate was created.

The populists also created a speakers bureau of 40,000 people. They had national speakers, regional speakers, state speakers, local speakers. On any given night, 40,000 people could hit the streets and give the message. We don't have forty people who are doing that today. Yet there are thousands of people who could do it. For example, we have speech teachers in high schools and community colleges and universities, all fully capable of teaching folks to make presentations. We could indeed have 100,000 people on the street, in the schools, in the Kiwanis Clubs, out there every day, talking about these issues and principles, reaching out to a still-broader constituency.

The other thing we need to have is money, through small donor contributions. MoveOn has had wonderful success in building small-donor lists. My newsletter has brought on 100,000 subscribers in three years' time. That's happened because, one, people want that kind of information. Two, it's a short publication, four pages. It doesn't just burden you, torture you, lying there on your coffee table. And three, it's cheap. You can get an initial subscription for ten dollars. We have found that people will give you ten dollars for anything, and it's more than $9.95. You'll get more response for $10.00 than $9.95, and a lot more than $10.95. $10.00 is a magical number. I think $20.00 is another level. People will give you that level of money.

We need a lot of people out there, and we must give them a reason to give that money. If we do, then we'll put a little "progress" back in "progressive."

Let me conclude with this thought. There's a moving company in my town of Austin that has an advertising slogan that I've usurped: "If we can get it loose, we can move it." That's fundamentally what our challenge is, I think. Just get it loose at the grassroots level, and the people will move it for themselves.

BIBLIOGRAPHY

Richard S. Dunham, "The Big Impact of Small Voting Shifts," *Business Week*, November 19, 2002.

Jim Hightower, *If the Gods Meant Us To Vote, They Would Have Given Us Candidates* (New York: HarperCollins, 2000).

———, *There's Nothing in the Middle of the Road But Yellow Lines and Dead Armadillos* (New York: HarperCollins, 1997).

———, *Thieves in High Places: They've Stolen Our Country and Its Time to Take It Back* (New York: Viking Press, 2003).

Molly Ivins, *Bushwacked* (New York: Random House, 2003).

Michael Moore, *Dude, Where's My Country?* (New York: Warner Books, 2003).

Edward Walsh, "Election Turnout Rose Slightly, to 39.3%; GOP Mobilization Credited" *Washington Post*, November 8, 2002.

• 37 •

Generating Political Hope in a Time of Fear

Micah L. Sifry

We are in a colossal conflict between hope and fear. Hope is our friend. Fear is our enemy. In his book *Indispensible Enemies: The Politics of Misrule in America*, political essayist Walter Karp wrote:

> There is, in this republic, one great wellspring animating citizens to act in their own behalf. Their own understanding that, by means of politics and government, what is wrong can be righted and what is ill can be cured. In a word: Hope.
>
> The opposite condition, the condition safest for party power is public apathy, gratitude for small favors, and a deep general sense of the futility of politics. Yet there is nothing natural about political apathy, futility, and mean gratitude. What lies behind them is not "human nature" but the citizens' belief that politics and government can do little to better the conditions of life; the belief that they are ruled not by the men whom they've entrusted with their power, but by circumstances and historical "forces"—by anything and everything that is out of human control; the belief that public abuses and inequities are somehow inevitable and must be endured because they cannot be cured.
>
> The condition of public apathy and futility, however, is swiftly undone by reform and even by the convincing promise of reform. Every beneficial law reminds the citizenry anew that the government, which is their government, can help them remove evils and better the conditions of life. Every law which remedies an abuse reminds the citizenry that other abuses can be remedied, as well. Every beneficial law rips the cover of inevitability from public inequities and rouses the people from apathy. Reform in America does not bring passive contentment to the citizenry—it inspires active hope.

THE GOOD NEWS: CLEAN-MONEY ELECTIONS

With these words in mind, let me start with some good news from the states of Arizona and Maine. Public Campaign, where I work, collaborates with these states very closely. Arizona and Maine are two of the first six states in the country to enact full public financing of elections, what we call "Clean Money/Clean Elections" campaign reform. "Clean Money" inspires hope. Candidates for state office in the reform states do not have to run for office the way everybody does everywhere else. In order to qualify, they have to raise a fairly large number of small contributions. Once they hit the number they need, based on the size of their district, they qualify for full public funding. They have to agree to raise no private money and to abide by spending limits. In addition, if they are opposed by a candidate who is being funded the traditional way or, if they are being targeted by outside groups spending independently, they can get some additional matching funds so that they have a level playing field upon which to operate.

This is now the second cycle where these laws have been in effect, though this was really the first full test. The result from Arizona and Maine is that fully half of the elected officials from both states ran clean. Three-quarters of the Maine state Senate in 2003-2004 are made up of people who ran clean, as are more than half the House. Nearly half the Arizona House; about one-sixth of the Arizona Senate; the Arizona governor, secretary of state, attorney general, and nearly all the statewide offices in Arizona are held by people who ran free of dependence on private money. Not only that, but the opportunity to run a viable campaign without dependence on big donors has dramatically opened the process to a more diverse array of candidates. More women are running. More Hispanics and Native Americans are running. It is hard to quantify, but we think more working-class people are choosing to run for office. There is more competition. There are more contested races. There are more third-party candidates and independent candidates. These are not just Democrats; there is a fairly high level of participation from Republicans, too. There even is a Green elected in Maine to the state legislature.

These people tell us that they feel less beholden to moneyed interests in office. They are more independent, in general. They are independent, as well, of their own party leadership. They just don't feel like they owe somebody. There is no lobbyist who can put her arm around them and say, "Hey, I hear you have a big campaign debt, let me help retire it for you," and before you know it another good person has been trapped by our corrupted system.

This is like living in America when Wyoming and Idaho had just given women the right to vote. It was a radical idea then. But here we now have some states that are already making it possible for candidates to run free of any dependence on private contributions and the results are very encouraging. We need to defend these victories. We need to expand them.

How are we going to proceed? Winning "Clean Money" in more states is very important to eventually winning it nationally. North Carolina has enacted full public financing of judicial elections, operating on the same idea that we shouldn't have our judges corrupted by the need to raise money. New Mexico has adopted full public financing for its Public Regulation Commission, a statewide body that oversees corporations and utilities, whose officeholders are heavily lobbied by moneyed interests. We have about a half-dozen other states that we think are close to enacting some version of Clean Money–style reform, though with political scandals involving pay-to-play corruption cropping up continually, there are always new opportunities that we can't predict. Just think of how Enron and WorldCom suddenly lit a fire under Senator Paul Sarbanes's corporate-reform bill in the summer of 2002. This is one more reason why we have to keep the home fires for reform burning, to be able to take advantage of the next big scandal, which we all know is inevitable.

One of Public Campaign's key initiatives is to make a big issue of how money corrupts the presidential selection process. In the 2004 presidential election, neither candidate was a participant in the public financing system. That way, they were not hindered by the spending limits that come with taking public financing.

We think that in the future the public can be rallied in a significant way to oppose the buying of the presidency. We see this as a major organizing vehicle. We already have partial public financing for our presidential elections. We feel that this is something that we all have to defend and fix. The system is obviously not working well. It needs to be strengthened. We have models from states like Arizona and Maine to use in strengthening it. We have a big fight here, but we think we actually have a chance of moving this issue forward.

WINNING THE 2002 ELECTIONS ON FEAR

Now let me turn to September 11 with a quote on the state of American society in the wake of World War I. Randolph Bourne, in his famous unfinished essay "The State," written in 1918, said:

> War is essentially the health of the State. The State is the organization of the herd to act offensively or defensively against another herd, similarly organized. Animals crowd together for protection and men become most conscious of their collectivity at the threat of a war.
>
> The more terrifying the occasion for defense, the closer will become the organization and the more coercive the influence upon each member of the herd. There is, of course, in the feeling toward the State, a large element of pure filial mysticism. The sense of insecurity, the desire for protection, sends one's desire back to the father and mother, with whom is associated the earliest feelings of protection. It is

> not for nothing that one's State is still thought of as Father or Motherland—that one's relation toward it is conceived in terms of family affection.
>
> The war has shown that nowhere under the shock of danger have these primitive childlike attitudes failed to assert themselves again, as much as in this country, as in anywhere. If we have not the intense Father-sense of the German who worships his Vaterland, at least in Uncle Sam, we have a symbol of protecting, kindly authority and in the many Mother-posters of the Red Cross; we see how easily, in the more tender functions of war service, the ruling organization is conceived in family terms. A people at war have become, in the most literal sense, obedient, respectful, trustful children again—full of that naive faith in the old wisdom and all-power of the adult who takes care of them—imposes his mild, but necessary rule upon them and in whom they lose their responsibility and anxieties.

I went through September 11 as a resident of the Bronx. The father of one of my son's best friends in elementary school, a firefighter, was killed in the North Tower. The mother of another friend of his from summer camp was also killed at her job, high in the South Tower. Another good friend of mine narrowly escaped with his life. How have I been affected? I continue with my life as before, but now I own a small but sufficient supply of potassium iodide, which is supposed to protect the thyroid gland—in the event that the Indian Point Nuclear Plant, which is twenty miles up river from where I live and which the planes of September 11 flew over on their way down to the World Trade Center, has a catastrophic failure.

Every time I look at the New York City skyline, whether from close or afar, I wonder, semiconsciously, if a huge bomb is about to go off or another building is going to fall. I am sure that residents of Washington, D.C., feel the same way. I believe the Republicans prevailed in the 2002 election for one simple reason—people voted their fears, not their hopes. The conservatives very astutely played on peoples' fears in the way that was almost the mirror image of that famous 1964 television ad that Lyndon Johnson used to demolish Barry Goldwater's candidacy.

That ad was only run once. That was enough. It begins with a little girl in a field, picking petals off a daisy, counting. When the count reaches ten, her image is frozen and then we hear a male voice doing a countdown. When he reaches zero, we see a nuclear explosion and a mushroom cloud and we hear President Johnson's voice. "These are the stakes. To make a world in which all God's children can live or to go into the darkness. Either we must love each other or we must die." The screen fades to black and we read, "On November 3rd, vote for President Johnson." The ad didn't even mention Goldwater, but everyone knew it was suggesting that he was too trigger-happy to be president.

Now, think of what was the most resonant image of the fall 2002 campaign. What I'd like to suggest is that it also was a mushroom cloud—relating to Iraq and its supposed weapons of mass destruction. More or less, the Bush administration was saying: "Facing clear evidence of peril, we cannot wait for the final proof, the smoking gun that could come in the form of the mushroom cloud." How many times did we hear that?

Did the Democrats have a response? One or two tried to argue that preemptive war against Iraq could actually make things worse. But, as Jim Hightower makes clear in chapter 36, the Democrats were not willing to forcefully rebut Vice President Cheney for saying, "The risks of inaction are far greater than the risk of action." The Democrats rushed the vote on Iraq, thinking that this would then allow a turn back to the issues of the economy. Instead, what the Democrats did was validate the Republicans as the best people to handle the job of protecting America's security. Why vote out the party that you have just entrusted with your physical security, especially when you have no clear sense what the other party is going to do to improve your economic security, other than moan about how bad things are?

LIVING WITHOUT POLITICAL HOPE

Since September 11, Americans seem to be experiencing and expressing two contradictory phenomena. Trust in government is up, reversing the historical trend of the last forty years. At the same time, the majority says the country is moving in the wrong direction—that the state of the economy is not the best and that our children's lives and future will be worse than ours. I see only one way to reconcile these two seemingly discordant trends.

Right now we have a life with little political hope. We live under a political duopoly that smothers nearly all meaningful independent insurgency. Those without money have no meaningful access or voice. Most incumbents of both parties are guaranteed reelection unless they happen to represent a swing district. Those in competitive or potentially competitive races fear taking courageous positions on any topic that can be turned into a thirty-second attack ad by the opponent. We can't move in an alternative direction if we can't effectively hear people who want us to move in another direction, and most of our elected leaders are too cowardly to make any sustained opposition—Paul Wellstone being one of the few, and now dearly missed, counterexamples.

Add to that debilitating mix the sense that we are newly threatened and newly vulnerable, however untrue that may be for those of us in the United States who never took for granted their inviolability. As a result, we who would like to move the country in a different direction are in for very difficult times. My sense of security is only partly about whether I have a job or a roof over my head. I also want to know that we are doing everything we can to protect my kids from another September 11. What the federal government chose to do in its aftermath did not make us safer. But, on that issue, there has been hardly any dissent from the so-called opposition party.

Difficulties in postwar Iraq and in the domestic economy are affecting American politics. But Democrats must realize two things:. First, if there is one constant in all the public opinion surveys I have seen on our interventions in the Persian Gulf arena, going back to the first Gulf war, it is this: Americans want to get the job done. They understand that goal to include creating a better regime in Iraq. Most Americans are not foreign policy isolationists; they are actually idealists. They believe, perhaps naively, that America is a force for good in the world, and that includes fighting for democracy and human rights and against dictators and thugs. People who opposed the invasion of Iraq and who opposed American policy in much of the rest of the world need to articulate a clear alternative American foreign and national security policy. Communication of these alternatives must be made to connect with most voters.

Second, the uncertain economy is not an automatically good thing for the Democrats. They need a clear and convincing vision of where they want to take the country on the economy that goes beyond slogans about "growing jobs," stopping corporate outsourcing of jobs overseas, and restoring the so-called glory days of the Clinton-Gore years. You can't beat something with nothing. Plus, we all know how Republicans play on and inflame economic fears by picking on surrogate targets for popular anger. For example, in 1988, the first George Bush used a murderer named Willie Horton to tag Michael Dukakis as an out-of-touch liberal. If the Democrats don't have an effective message on the economy, they will continue to be vulnerable to the classic divide-and-conquer tactics of the Republican right.

CREATING STAR WARDS

As the response to September 11 showed, Americans recognize their common destiny. We were moved by the response of the firefighters and police and emergency workers precisely because they were common people doing uncommonly courageous things. Trust in government went up because we saw a different kind of government in action that terrible day and because we want to believe in a government that works and actually will take care of us.

The outpouring of sentiment and voluntarism in the immediate aftermath of September 11 shows that there still are deep wells of civic solidarity in America. One way to tap those wells is to figuratively wave the flag and insist, yes, we are *all* in this together. As I wrote in an article for TomPaine.com:

> We must protect the environment because its degradation threatens us all. We must invest in universal health care because disease observes no boundaries—gated communities won't protect you from SARS, AIDS, asthma, or anthrax. The benefits of democracy are not reserved for the wealthy; they belong to everyone—we

> fight for an equal voice for all Americans and to protect politics from the distortions of big money. We are only as well off as the poor, elderly and disabled among us, and there but for the grace of God go I—we need a viable social safety net. We believe every person has the same intrinsic worth, that society's health depends on everyone having an equal stake, and that there is strength in diversity—we want an inclusive society that values everyone regardless of race, gender, sexual orientation, or religion. Money is not the measure of all worthwhile things—markets left to their own devices will not care for the poor, educate our children, create public parks, or seek justice for all. Those who benefit most from what democratic society provides have a greater obligation to give back to it—we believe in progressive taxation. The multiple crises facing the world require multilateral cooperation, not go-it-alone imperialism.

We must boldly insist that the overclass not use this moment to further enrich itself. This was the point at the heart of a speech by Bill Moyers that I helped to write in the fall of 2001. The words we used then, I suspect, will only be timelier as we strive to block the worse excesses of Congress. "While we have our hands on our hearts, they're trying to pick our pockets." That was the central phrase of the Moyers' speech.

The issue is war profiteering, twenty-first-century style. For example, the 2002 Homeland Security bill included a clause protecting pharmaceutical companies from lawsuits for potential side effects from their drugs that may cause autism. What does that have to with homeland security? It's all about excess profit security. We have to be very clear about that. In past wars that this country has fought, taxes were raised, profits were restrained, and the burdens were shared, more or less, equitably. Why did that not happen with the American war and post-war in Iraq? At a minimum, how can anybody possibly justify further tax cuts for the rich and service cuts for the poor during these times?

The new nature of the war and post-war in Iraq may require some unexpectedly progressive changes in domestic policy. For example, we should be arguing that universal health coverage is the only way to truly protect against biological warfare. After all, people without health insurance tend to delay trips to the doctor or the emergency room. Yet if we want to prevent an outbreak of smallpox, or anything worse, we need people to get medical attention right away. As it is, most hospitals in major American cities go on lockdown on any number of nights a week. They refuse all emergencies because they're already beyond capacity. This is a crisis that no one is talking about, but it could make a huge difference if we try to address it now.

And if we are smart, we won't worry about calling this "universal health care," or "single payer." Call it "National Medical Defense." Or call it "Star Wards."

We can't stand apart from the herd, as if we are better at repressing our fears and our need for security. We are part of a social organism seeking to protect itself. It makes little sense to deny the need for self-protection or try to change the subject to the economy. We have an opportunity, still, to build a stronger and more just country that is part of a stronger and more developed world. But to do so, we have to draw on our deepest democratic aspirations. We have to talk to our fellow Americans, address their real concerns, and not sneer at them for being so benighted.

BIBLIOGRAPHY

Randolph Bourne, "The State," from *The Radical Will: Selected Writings, 1911-1918* (Berkeley: University of California Press, 1992).

Walter Karp, *Indispensable Enemies: The Politics of Misrule in America* (New York: E.P. Dutton, May, 1973).

Bill Moyers and Micah L. Sifry, "Which America Will We Be Now?" *The Nation,* Nov. 19, 2001. http://www.thenation.com/doc.mhtml?i=20011119&c=2&s=moyers.

Micah L. Sifry, "Bumpersticker Banner," TomPaine.com, June 16, 2003. http://www.tompaine.com/feature2.cfm/ID/8098.

———, and Christopher Cerf, coeditors, *The Iraq War Reader: History, Documents, Opinions* (New York: Touchstone Simon & Schuster, 2003).

• 38 •

Who Has the Emerging Majority Now?

Ruy Teixeira

My recent book with John Judis, *The Emerging Democratic Majority*, is a long-term kind of assessment of the future of the Democratic Party based on relatively long-term trends. But we still do need to understand what happened in the recent elections because underlying trends do not produce automatic outcomes. They provide the opportunity for certain outcomes. It may take a fair amount of work to get there, though the opportunity exists.

The Republicans had a long trek through the late 1960s and 1970s to the Reagan victory of 1980. They hit a speed bump with Watergate, and Jimmy Carter got elected in 1976. But they kept at it and eventually found an inspirational politician named Ronald Reagan who was able to crystallize the message that appealed to the emerging Republican majority that Kevin Phillips identified in 1969. Ronald Reagan was able to boil it down—make it very specific to the political climate at the time. He became a very popular and successful politician, as we know. His kind of politics dominated America for a while.

Why, then, do we think there now is an emerging Democratic majority? Part of the reason is that there have been shifts in public opinion since the 1980s. These public opinion shifts have included recognition of the failures of the market, a decline in the antigovernment sentiment, the triumph of moderate forms of reform movements (like civil rights, women's rights, and environmental rights) over recent decades, the gravitation of minorities to the Democratic Party, and a return (in a limited sense) of white working-class voters. To complement these public opinion shifts, the economy is changing from the production of manufactured goods to the production of ideas and services. This production has created technically advanced geographic regions in the United States, and the professionals in these regions tend to favor Democrats.

THE MARKET'S FAILURES

There has been a substantial decline in Reaganite antigovernment sentiment—that the government is the problem, not the solution. And in its place, we see the rise of moderate support for government activism, replication of what works, and regulation.

Left to its own devices, the market, of course, just doesn't solve a lot of problems. The market is frequently capable of excesses, of which the corporate scandals of the last several years are egregious examples. Even the Republicans picked up on it. The Republicans don't run like Newt Gingrich ran in 1994 or Ronald Reagan did in the 1980s—as flat-out opponents of government. They run supporting government programs that work, supporting a certain amount of spending in government programs, supporting public education. We don't hear any more about abolishing the Department of Education. The Republicans have a prescription drug plan, and they support a government crackdown on corporate crime. They realize they can't just run on being against government and government programs. They don't even run on being for privatizing Social Security, which was a matter of faith for many Republicans from the mid-1990s.

THE TRIUMPH OF REFORM MOVEMENTS

The second public opinion shift that is important in laying the groundwork for an emerging democratic majority is the triumph of the movements of the 1960s, in moderate forms. The movements of the 1960s—for civil rights, women's rights, environmental protection, consumers and even the anti-war movement—all transformed America in many ways. But in the short term, they set up a period of dominance by the Republicans because there was a backlash to the extreme form of these movements, as perceived by the typical voter. Richard Nixon in 1972, and then Ronald Reagan in 1980 and 1984, ran on that backlash using the movements of the 1960s as wedge issues in the 1970s and 1980s.

But now things have changed. Candidates can't use issues like race and feminism the way they once did. In their moderate forms, respect for civil rights, diversity, tolerance, environmental protection, rights of women, and feminism all have become part of the common sense of America. There are still pockets of resistance where these issues still don't play well, particularly in the South and rural areas, but America has really changed in the last forty years. That is part of the basis for this new majority. But it's not just public opinion shifts. It's shifts in demographics that are important.

THE MOVEMENT OF PROFESSIONALS TO THE DEMOCRATIC PARTY

One important shift is professionals. Professionals used to be the most Republican occupational group. They supported Richard Nixon in 1960, 61 percent to 38 percent. They were even more Republican than managers. But that changed starting with the McGovern campaign of 1972. In recent elections, professionals have supported Democrats, presidentially, by an average of twelve points—52 percent to 40 percent. Managers are still largely Republican, but professionals take a different view. They take a certain pride in their products—teachers want to educate children, doctors want to cure patients, and computer engineers want to write cool code. There's a pride in producing a service that frequently comes into conflict with large institutions and with market profit imperatives.

Professionals are also often children of the 1960s. They come out of the campuses, the hotbeds of the movements of the 1960s. The definition of a professional, to some extent, is a college-educated person who provides a highly skilled service. And professionals are a fast-growing sector of the workforce. They have more than doubled between the 1950s and today—from about 7 percent to 16 percent of the workforce. They are probably about 20 percent to 21 percent of the electorate, nationally. They grew by about 30 percent as workers in the 1990s. This is a fast-growing, politically and culturally significant group of voters who have moved into the Democratic camp. That is an important demographic shift.

THE MOVEMENT OF WOMEN TO THE DEMOCRATIC PARTY

Probably more familiar is the movement of women toward the Democratic Party, which started with the election of Lyndon Johnson in 1964. This trend gathered strength in the 1970s, abated in the middle of the 1970s, and then returned in full force in the 1980s. It is led by three groups of women that have become almost base groups of the Democratic party: single women, working women, and highly educated women.

If you look at single working women, for example, they supported the Democratic candidate 67 percent to 29 percent in the 2000 election. And they have grown from about 19 percent to 29 percent of women in the last thirty years. College-educated women were 57 percent to 38 percent for the Democratic candidate, and they tripled, since the 1970s, from 8 percent to 25 percent of women twenty-five and older. What is drawing them toward the Democrats? These women are moving into the workforce and grappling with economic and family problems; they tend to feel that the Democrats, with their emphasis on social support and the rights of women in the workplace, are, more or less, on their side. The other factor, of course, is the role of the women's movement, feminism, and abortion rights. The Democrats are now the party that is identified with feminism and with the struggle for those kinds of rights.

THE MOVEMENT OF MINORITIES TO THE DEMOCRATIC PARTY

Now the third demographic shift of importance is minorities. If we look at minorities, they have become progressively more Democratic. In the late 1950s and early 1960s, African-Americans used to vote as much as a third for Republicans. Now, it's about nine to one Democratic in a lot of elections—or at least 85 percent. And African-Americans have gone from being about 6 percent of voters in the early 1960s to 10 percent to 12 percent, depending on the election, in the 1990s.

Hispanics have grown from a negligible proportion of voters to about 6 percent in recent elections, nationally. They definitely moved Democratic in the 1990s, as well. And, of course, Hispanic population growth is one of the defining characteristics of change in the U.S. population. In the 1990s alone, according to the census, Hispanics increased to more than 12 percent of the population. So Hispanics are obviously important overall and particularly important in some states, where their growth is concentrated.

Asians are another group that has moved Democratic. And it is really the growth in Hispanics and Asians that drives the increase in the minority population. In the election of 1992, Asians only voted a little bit over 30 percent for Bill Clinton. But in the presidential election in 2000, they voted 54 percent for the Al Gore. Asians are about 2 percent of voters now. The rate at which they grew in the 1990s was even faster than that of Hispanics—about 59 percent growth.

If you look at the early 1970s, minorities were about 10 percent of voters. In the 2000 election, they were about 19 percent. And if trends continue, they should be about a quarter by the end of this decade. That's a group that, overall, votes 75 percent Democratic. This is a change of extraordinary significance, and it is happening in most states around the United States.

THE RETURN OF THE WHITE WORKING CLASS TO THE DEMOCRATIC PARTY

The final demographic shift has been the return of white working-class voters to the Democratic Party, in a limited sense. It was really the desertion of the white working class from the Democratic coalition that set up the Republican majority that Kevin Phillips wrote about and that Ronald Reagan rode to victory. Ronald Reagan got about 65 percent of this vote in 1984. But in the Clinton years, the Democrats got some of that back. They retained some of this in 2000.

The Democratic Party did very poorly in the 2000 presidential election in rural areas—among rural white working-class voters. However, the party did do well among white working-class workers in one important part of the country: in the more technically advanced, economically advanced areas of the country, in what John Judis and I call "ideopolises."

ECONOMIC SHIFTS THAT HAVE GENERATED IDEOPOLIS REGIONS

This brings us to economic shifts and how they are advantageous to the Democrats. The U.S. is clearly moving from an economy dominated by the production of manufactured things to an economy that is dominated by the production of ideas and services. Even manufacturing, in many cases, incorporates ideas; it incorporates high technology to an extent that wouldn't have been dreamed of twenty or thirty years ago.

The places in the United States that are the most technically advanced, where this kind of production plays the greatest role, are exactly where the Democrats have been doing well. These are areas where the population tends to be more diverse, where there are a lot of professionals, and where there is a sense of moving ahead that you just don't have in other areas of the country.

These more technically advanced places are all over the United States. They include the Washington, D.C., metro area, New York, Boston, the San Francisco Bay area, Los Angeles, Seattle, Portland (Oregon), Austin, the Research Triangle in North Carolina, Chicago, and Tucson. Wherever these areas are springing up and moving ahead, the Democrats have tended to do well. In fact, the Democratic candidate carried these ideopolis areas, these counties, by 55 percent to 41 percent in the election of 2000. If you compare the election of 2000 to the election of 1980, the first Reagan election, you can see that almost the entire shift toward the Democrats in the country since then has been concentrated in these ideopolis areas.

In other words, Ronald Reagan carried both ideopolis and non-ideopolis areas pretty well in 1980—carried them by pretty wide margins. If you look at the 2000 election, the Republicans continued to dominate the non-ideopolis areas, these less technically advanced areas. But the areas that are moving ahead, the postindustrial areas, were dominated by the Democrats in 2000. The ideopolis, postindustrial areas now cover a huge part of the country—about 44 percent of voters. The average population growth rate in these counties is about 23 percent compared to 11 percent among counties as a whole. And they are pretty big—about half a million each, as counties—compared with about 50,000 for counties that lie outside of these areas.

All in all, this is a big set of changes to be moving in the Democrats' direction. We have public opinion shifts, demographic shifts, and changes in the economy. All of them create the opportunity that I mentioned earlier.

REPUBLICAN BARNSTORMING

So what happened in 2002? These changes sound promising—why didn't the voters step up to the plate? September 11 happened, and it really changed politics. You can see that very clearly by looking at the polling data and public opinion data, before and after September 11. Before September 11, the economy was limping along, and there seemed to be low support for the administration and its policies. After September 11, support for the Bush administration skyrocketed. Presidential approval ratings were in the 85 percent to 95 percent range. By the 2002 election, the ratings had declined some, but still were high, in the low sixties. And for pretty much any issue you might want to care to mention, the Bush administration got a bounce and improved its rating—for example, on the economy, health care, the environment, and education, things that had nothing to do, really, with September 11. So, September 11 helped the executive branch dig out of a hole.

The Democrats actually started making headway again over the summer of 2002—with the economy continuing to falter and Republican policies still not popular on taxes, budget priorities, the environment, education, and health care. Democrats were starting to make some headway when, perhaps not coincidentally, in late summer of 2002, the urgent need to deal with the Iraq question was brought to the fore by the White House.

This debate effectively undercut the Democrats' gathering momentum. It took about six or seven weeks to resolve, and in that time it almost totally dominated the headlines. Any issues the Democrats had were basically shoved off the table. And so when the Iraq issue receded for a while, in early October, the Democrats had a very limited amount of time to push their issues. They tried and they were even making some headway—at least as far as we can tell from the polling data.

And that's when the Bush administration's final preelection push took place. Five days before the election, President Bush barnstormed through the key states, the swing states. The Gallup data show very clearly that the Democrats went from about a 3-point lead among likely voters about a week before the election to a 5-point deficit right before the election—just as the presidential tour was finishing up. So the tour really pushed the debate in the Republicans' direction.

The push was all about September 11. Granted, if you look at the Bush 2002 stump speech, the first seven paragraphs were about how the economy was important and how we had other important priorities, as well. But the next twenty paragraphs were about national security—the Homeland Security Bill, Iraq, the need to beat al Qaeda. Those were big applause lines, and that's what that the barnstorming tour was all about. It raised the salience of September 11 in voters' eyes. It was about reminding voters why they supported President Bush, reminding them of what was important to accomplish in Washington, and making clear how he needed the support of Senator "X" to deal with these horrible people who were out to get us.

The September 11 push didn't convince everyone, but it did convince enough people to turn some key Senate and House contests in the direction of the Republicans. All you need are a few points at the margin, and they turn a race in which the Democrats had a very good chance into an election in which the Republicans managed to triumph.

DEMOCRATIC INEPTITUDE

So the use of September 11 by the executive branch was one reality in 2002. But another was the Democrats' empty campaign. They cannot be absolved of responsibility for the outcome. The Democratic campaign, as most people who followed it realized, was really about only two things—prescription drugs for seniors and Social Security. That was it. They really had almost nothing else to say. The economy was the biggest issue on voter's minds, according to all the polling data, and the economy was viewed negatively by 70 percent of the people who went to the polls on election day.

The Democrats had nothing to say about the economy other than to remind people that it wasn't doing so well, which they already knew. They didn't offer coherent alternatives to the administration's tax cuts for the rich. The Republicans took advantage of this vaccum to say a lot themselves about, for example Social Security and prescription drugs. They banned the word *privatization* from their campaign speeches, and they developed a drug benefit plan. Polling data collected by Stan Greenberg right after the election showed that most people did not think that the candidates differed on prescription drugs—the waters had been so thoroughly muddied.

Other polling data show that the Democrats had a 25-point deficit among voters who had clear ideas about how to deal with the country's problems. These data also show that 67 percent of voters thought that there were no clear ideas about the economy expressed in the election. Only 25 percent thought there were. The lack of a Democratic message is a huge, huge problem for them.

THE NET RESULT

So what was the result of all the September 11 effect and the empty Democratic campaign? Republicans won key groups of voters.

There was low mobilization on the Democratic side. Democratic counties and areas turned out at rates that weren't high compared with Republican-leaning areas and groups. Republican mobilization was quite substantial, particularly in rural and exurban areas. However, the key was not just that the Democrats were poorly mobilized, but that they had no ability to appeal to the people who leaned in their direction but needed to have the sale made with them. They couldn't pick up their own swing voters in Democratic-leaning suburbs and these ideopolis areas. They came out of the Democratic-leaning suburbs in places like Minnesota and Missouri with relatively small margins compared with what they picked up two, four, and six years ago. Without the requisite number of votes in areas like those, it becomes easy to be swamped by Republican strength in exurban and rural areas. That's exactly what happened. That is why Jean Carnahan lost in Missouri, and that is why Walter Mondale lost in Minnesota.

So what about the emerging Democratic majority? Fundamentally, the 2002 election didn't change most of the basic things we are talking about. The Republican priorities on tax cuts for the rich, Social Security, and other things—the polling data were very clear on those issues. People were not voting for Republican candidates in 2002 because they wanted to repeal the estate tax permanently or because they wanted Social Security privatized or because they wanted change on social issues like abortion and gun control. The top two issues were to support the federal government in the war against terrorism and to support a strong military.

Demographic shifts remained in 2002. Minorities—Hispanics, Asians, and African Americans—voted very strongly for the Democrats (though there was a problem with mobilization in certain areas). Women tilted Democratic, though the gender gap was somewhat smaller than in other elections. It's harder to tell about professionals because we lack good data, but there is no evidence that they moved heavily in the Republican direction. Finally, economic shifts remained with us. Ideopolis areas continued to vote Democratic, but Republicans were able to pick off some Democratic swing voters in these areas.

THE FUTURE

In his essay on the November 2002 election, *The Weekly Standard*'s Fred Barnes rested his case for a new Republican realignment on the effect of September 11 and the leadership of President Bush. Wrote Barnes, "The September 11 attacks produced a new political climate. Bush recognized it. Democrats still don't." That was certainly true enough during the 2002 election, but the effect of September 11 is not likely to be lasting. What was distinctive about September 11? It was a direct attack on the United States, a terrorist Pearl Harbor that depended for its success on total surprise and a breakdown in American intelligence and vigilance. During the 2002 election, the Bush administration, guided by conservatives, convinced American voters that, by going to war with Iraq, the country would be safer not only against another terrorist assault but against an Iraqi nuclear attack. In other words, the executive branch presented the invasion of Iraq as an extension of the war against terror. But the war and occupation did not confirm that argument. Neither weapons of mass destruction nor links to al Qaeda were discovered, raising questions about the credibility of the White House. And instead of proving to be a "cakewalk," as the White House had promised, the post-war turned into an expensive, low-intensity guerrilla battle sustained by resistance to the American occupation. By the second anniversary of September 11, popular support for Bush's leadership—based in part on trust in his word—had begun to erode, and with it the Republicans' chances of sustaining the special political circumstances of September 11 through the remainder of the decade. Even the increase in popular support for Bush after the capture of Saddam turned out to be temporary, eroding in about a month.

There are two factors that will help the Republicans over the rest of this decade, but they have nothing to do with the party's innate appeal. One is money, an advantage that has been exacerbated by the campaign-finance reform bill passed in 2002. This advantage in money will translate into electoral advantage, especially in close House contests. In November 2002, Republicans won close House races in Alabama and Colorado largely because their Democratic opponents ran out of money. Conversely, Janet Napolitano's Democratic victory in Arizona's gubernatorial race was partly made possible by public financing that equalized spending between herself and her opponent.

But money can still be overrated as a determinant of election outcomes. It is most effective in scaring off competition or in pushing one side over the finish line in an otherwise close race. It cannot defeat a candidate who is reasonably well-funded and whose politics are clearly more popular than their opponent's. And even the advantages money bestows can cut two ways in elections. In low-turnout congressional elections, it can benefit the big spender in a tight race; but in high-visibility elections, it can dramatize the Republican dependence on wealth and on big business.

Republicans also will enjoy an advantage from redistricting, which the GOP handled more effectively than the Democrats. Too many Democratic votes are concentrated in House districts with overwhelming Democratic strength, while Republicans votes are scattered around more effectively to produce House districts with substantial, but not overwhelming, Republican advantages. The 2000 redistricting made this pattern worse and created a difficult challenge for Democrats. But difficult does not mean impossible or even improbable in the right circumstances. And redistricting will affect House races but not races for the Senate or the White House. Republican advantages in money and redistricting are important, but at best they will delay or soften the realignment that began to occur a decade ago.

The pressures for a Democratic realignment, driven by the growth of postindustrial metropolitan areas and by demographic change, are certain to grow over the decade. The electorate's movement from right to center, which began in the early 1990s, has continued, evidenced by recent Republican attempts to coopt Democratic domestic positions. Just as happened in the last Republican realignment of 1980, it could take a crisis in foreign policy or continued economic uncertainty to end what W. D. Burnham called the "unstable equilibrium" between the parties and to create a new majority. But barring the entirely unforeseen, there is little reason to doubt that before this decade is over the Democratic majority, which began to emerge clearly in the 1990s, will finally succeed the conservative Republican majority that Ronald Reagan created.

BIBLIOGRAPHY

Fred Barnes, "The Emerging 9/11 Majority," *The Weekly Standard*, November 18, 2002.

John B. Judis and Ruy Teixeira, *The Emerging Democratic Majority* (New York: Scribner, 2002)

Kevin Phillips, *The Emerging Republican Majority* (New Rochelle: Arlington House, 1969).

Cliff Schecter and Ruy Teixeira, "All Eyes On Dixie" *American Prospect*, February 1, 2004. http://www.prospect.org/print/V15/2/schecter-c.html.

Ruy Teixeira, "Where the Democrats Lost," *American Prospect*, Vol. 16, No. 22, December 16, 2002.

———, "Next Steps: Why the Democrats Lost, and Where They Go from Here," *American Prospect*, November 12, 2002. http://www.prospect.org/webfeatures/2002/11/teixeira-r-11-12.html.

——— and Joel Rogers, *America's Forgotten Majority: Why the White Working Class Still Matters* (New York: Basic Books, 2000).

• *39* •

American Politics and Policy: We Don't Have Time to Despair

Fred R. Harris

For a quarter of a century, I was a politician. Now, for the last quarter of a century, I have worked as a political scientist. This chapter springs from both backgrounds.

My purpose here is to focus on the answers to four pressing and intertwined questions: What is the present political situation in the United States? What happened in the November 2002 elections? Why did it happen? And what are American progressives to do now?

THE AMERICAN POLITICAL SITUATION: A VIRTUAL TIE

The central and most dramatic fact about American politics and government at this moment is best expressed by the word "tie."

In the presidential election of the year 2000, the Democratic candidate won the nationwide popular vote, but by the slightest margin—only 543,000 votes out of a total of 105.4 million votes cast. The Republican candidate, with, of course, the help of Florida officials and the U.S. Supreme Court, won a majority of the vote in the electoral college, the peculiar way we elect presidents in the United States, but, again, by the slightest margin—only 5 electoral college votes out of a total of 538. The result, then, was a virtual tie.

Membership in the U.S. Congress is also split, and nearly down the middle. The Republicans presently hold only 51 of the 100 seats in the U.S. Senate. In the U.S. House of Representatives, Republicans presently number 229 out of 435 total members.

Or take the fifty state governors' offices in the United States. Twenty-eight of those governors are Republicans, and twenty-two are Democrats. Again, a virtual tie.

A SPLIT IN THE ELECTORATE

There is a split in the American electorate, too. Approximately 70 percent of eligible voters identify themselves as either Democrats or Republicans, and they are different from each other—racially, ethnically, ideologically, and along economic-class lines.

Race and Ethnicity

The pro–civil rights actions of President Harry Truman, followed by the 1948 adoption by his party of a first-time, and strong, civil rights platform provoked the beginning of a white flight from the ranks of the Democratic Party in the American South and began to create a Republican Party in the southern states, where that party had scarcely existed since the Reconstruction period after the Civil War. Then, in the1960s, following the passage by a Democratic Congress of two strong and enforceable national civil rights laws, the southern Democratic-to-Republican white flight grew into a stampede. President Lyndon Johnson presciently told his White House aide, Bill Moyers, immediately upon the passage of the Civil Rights Act of 1964, that the Democrats had thereby just lost the American South for a generation. President Johnson meant the *white* South, and he was pretty close to right—although in very recent times, there appears to have been some movement back toward the Democratic party among certain white women, suburban, and somewhat younger voters for whom the racial issue is not as crucial as it once was.

In addition, beginning in the 1960s, white flight from the Snow Belt of the northeastern and northcentral states to the Sun Belt produced, particularly in the South, an influx of new white residents there. A large percentage either already were Republicans before they moved or became Republicans after they arrived in the South. More recently, migration of conservative white Californians to states of the Mountain West has helped to make those inland-West destination states more Republican. Augmented by a great foreign immigration of Hispanics and Asians, the remaining electorate of California has become more progressive and Democratic.

But to get back to the African American–white split in the parties, the white flight of voters from the southern Democratic Party was offset considerably by the impact of the second of the 1960s federal civil rights laws, the Voting Rights Act of 1965, which, for the first time following the end of Reconstruction, gave African Americans government-guaranteed access to the ballot box. Southern African Americans began to vote in large numbers—and they voted, and presently vote, overwhelmingly Democratic. The surge of *southern* African Americans into the Democratic Party was matched by a parallel African American affiliation with the Democrats in other parts of the country as well. The result is that a nationwide racial realignment of American political parties has taken place. The Republican Party is virtually all white. And nearly all African Americans are today Democrats. In the presidential election of 2000, the Democratic candidate got 90 percent of the black vote, and in the elections of 2002 that Democratic percentage held or was perhaps even bettered.

The number of Hispanics in the United States continues to grow significantly. This is a favorable trend for the Democrats, and it has changed, or is changing, the partisan makeup of certain large and crucial states—particularly California, Texas, and Florida. In the 2002 elections, Hispanics appear to have voted for Democratic candidates by their usual two-to-one or somewhat better ratio.

Republican core constituencies are shrinking—whites in rural areas, married white men, married white women, especially those who don't work outside the home. Even the polling director for the Republican National Committee, Matthew Dowd, has admitted that if American minorities and whites vote in future elections as they did in 2000 (and as they apparently did in 2002), the Democrats could win by 3 million votes.

Economic Class and Ideology

The racial and ethnic realignment of America's political parties carried with it, as well as helped to cause, an economic-class and ideological realignment, too—and not just in the South. Many better-off whites were repelled by the Democratic Party's support for African Americans and other minorities, disagreed with the party's advocacy of programs for poor people and welfare recipients, were appalled by the urban riots in the African-American sections of America's cities in the 1960s, were incensed about the anti–Vietnam War protesters of that era, and were increasingly displeased by what they saw as a big tax-and-spend federal government. Many middle-class people felt that they were paying more than their fair share of taxes, and they resented it. The Democratic Party got much of the blame for all this—and the Republican Party picked up votes and support.

Today, families with annual incomes of $100,000 or more overwhelmingly call themselves Republicans. Families with annual incomes of $20,000 or less are just as overwhelmingly Democrats. The higher the income level of a person, the greater the likelihood that he or she is a Republican. The lower the income level, the greater the likelihood that he or she is a Democrat. Republicans are more likely to be conservative; Democrats, moderate to liberal. Democrats are more likely to favor federal programs for assured low-cost health care and for jobs, for example, which Republicans are more likely to oppose. A majority of Americans have come to dislike the liberal label. A majority are, as Seymour Martin Lipset once put it, "rhetorical conservatives"—their words are conservative, but they are at the same time "operational liberals" (to use Lipset's term)—that is, they support liberal positions on a range of actual domestic issues.

WHY DON'T THE DEMOCRATS WIN EVERY ELECTION?

There are more Democratic identifiers among the American electorate than there are Republican identifiers, and the 2002 elections signaled no realignment in party affiliation. About 40 percent of Americans say they are Democrats, about a third say they are Republicans—and these percentages have remained virtually the same for fifty years. Moreover, these Democratic and Republican identifiers, when they vote, are remarkably loyal. A *New York Times*/CBS News Poll just before the November 2002 voting showed that only 8 percent of likely Democratic voters planned to vote Republican and only 4 percent of likely Republican voters planned to vote Democratic.

There are more Democrats in America than there are Republicans. There are more lower-income and working-class Americans than there are upper-income Americans. A majority of Americans support Democratic positions on domestic economic-class and social-program issues. A 2002 *New York Times*/CBS News Poll showed that nearly 60 percent of respondents believed that the Bush administration's tax cuts benefited the wealthy, 55 percent said they were opposed to oil drilling in the Arctic National Wildlife Refuge in Alaska, nearly two-thirds thought the federal government should do more to regulate environmental and safety practices of business, and by a ratio of two-to-one said that protecting the environment was more important than producing energy (though they thought by a seven-to-one ratio that the administration held the opposite view). The country has not moved to the right.

Then why has the government done so? Why don't the Democrats win every election?

One reason they don't is that the Republicans have frequently been able to overcome the Democratic advantage on economic-class and social-program issues by shifting the public focus from those issues to so-called cross-cutting issues—in the past, for example, to the communist threat, or later to crime in the streets, the welfare mess, or big government, and more lately to homeland security, anti-terrorism, and war with Iraq.

A second reason is that potential voters in lower-income and working-class brackets, people who are likely to be Democrats are less likely actually to vote than those of higher income. The Democratic Party, and Democratic candidates therefore, must always put extra emphasis on voter registration and get-out-the-vote efforts if they are to turn a winning percentage of their identifiers, their potential supporters, into actual voters—real supporters at the polls. The lower turnout of Democratic identifiers, compared with Republican identifiers, tends to equalize the relative strength of the two parties among the electorate.

A final reason the Democrats don't always win is that political campaigns in America have become increasingly and outrageously expensive. The Republicans are much more successful at raising campaign money in large amounts. Money buys them advertising and voter mobilization. Democrats get substantial financial campaign contributions from organized labor and other progressive groups, such as the trial lawyers. But these money sources cannot come close to matching the amounts of money the Republicans raise from business and businesspeople—and the Republican advantage in this respect is growing. For years, Republican leaders in Congress have pressed corporate and trade groups to hire more Republican lobbyists and to support more Republican candidates, delivering regulatory relief for business, tax cuts, and limits on lawsuit awards in return. These Republican efforts have resulted in a shift in campaign contributions to the two parties by nineteen major American industry sectors from an even split, a decade ago, to a more recent five-to-one advantage for the Republican Party today.

THE ELECTIONS OF 2002

What happened in the U.S. elections of 2002? The answer, numerically at least—insofar as office changes and popular-vote margins are concerned—is that not really very much happened. A mild tremor.

The Republicans gained a net of only 2 of the total 100 seats in the U.S. Senate and a net of only 5 of the 435 seats in the U.S. House of Representatives, while at the same time they actually *lost*—and the Democrats gained—a net of 3 of the 50 state governors' offices. Compare that with 1994, the first off-year election after President Clinton was elected, when the Republicans gained a net of 52 House seats, 9 Senate seats, and 10 state governors' offices.

And look at the popular-vote totals in the 2002 elections. The widely respected Washington political analyst Charlie Cook has pointed out that a swing of 94,000 votes of the 75.7 million cast nationally would have resulted in the Democrats capturing control of the House and retaining a majority in the Senate in 2002. "If that had occurred, obituaries would have been written—inevitably and prematurely—about the Bush administration," he has said. "Instead, we are entertained by predictions that the Democratic Party, as we know it, may cease to exist. Some of the most experienced and partisan Republicans I know even chortle over the turn of events—recognizing how easily this type of exaggeration, combined with acts of self-immolation, could instead have been taking place on the G.O.P. side of the table."

What happened in the U.S. elections of 2002? The real answer: Well, insofar as historical precedent, control of the government, and the kind of government policy and actions that we can expect are concerned, a great deal indeed happened.

Historically, the president's party loses net House seats in the off-year elections, and the loss has usually been especially severe when the public perceives that the economy is in bad shape. By dramatic contrast, in this particular off-year election, despite the fact that, just before the voting, 70 percent of Americans thought the condition of the country's economy was poor or only fair, and despite the fact that the stock market had collapsed, retirement accounts were decimated, unemployment had increased, business was mired in scandal, the federal budget surplus had turned to deficit, economic growth was slowing, and consumer confidence had plummeted, the in-party still won. That was an earthquake.

As observer Ruy Teixeira put it, "The very evenness of partisan division in the country lends itself to sudden lurches in political power driven by small switches in public sentiment. And that's what we had in . . . [the 2002] election."

Very importantly, the election produced a unified government, with the Republican Party in control of the White House and both houses of the U.S. Congress. They were "ready to rumble," and the rumble began. What did we get? We got more—a good deal more—of the same: weakening or elimination of environmental protections, more loopholes and deregulation for business, more tax cuts for the already well-off, more right-wing judges, more alarming attacks on civil rights and civil liberties, and a unilateralist, militaristic foreign policy, not focused on global justice. And, of course, war.

WHY DID IT HAPPEN?

How did the Republicans win in the 2002 elections? By presidential campaigning, by what pollster Stanley Greenberg has called "cross-dressing" and "sword rattling," by muting the opposition, by spending enormously, and by mobilizing their voters.

Presidential Campaigning. Leading up to the 2002 elections, President Bush became, as one observer called him, America's "campaigner in chief." His campaign efforts were unprecedented and nonstop. For example, he traveled to fifteen separate states in just the final five days prior to the vote. His 65 percent job approval rating was an undoubted factor in the Republican success at the polls. During those fateful last five days before the election, when President Bush was campaigning so hard, the Gallup Poll showed that in regard to the generic congressional question "Who would you vote for if the election were held tomorrow?" a three-point Republican *dis*advantage was converted into a six-point advantage. A *New York Times*/CBS News Poll found that 55 percent of those who reported that they voted Republican on November 5 said they did so because of their support for President Bush.

Cross-Dressing. Republicans correctly charged, when President Bill Clinton ran for re-election in 1996, that he had "stolen their clothes," that he had preempted traditionally Republican positions—balancing the federal budget, for example, and "ending welfare as we know it," as he said, and being tough on crime. In 2002, the Bush administration in many ways played the same game. It offered proposals on education, for prescription drugs under Medicare (though a plan that the pharmaceutical companies favored), and on Social Security (though soon retreating from their earlier claim that the private investment accounts they advocated amounted to "privatization"). A postelection poll by Greenberg Quinlan Rosner found that, in the 2002 elections, while the Republican advantage among male voters remained pretty much unchanged from two years earlier, Democratic support among women dropped by 6 percent—a result of the fact, according to a spokesperson for the pollster, that the Republicans had been able to "muddy the waters" on the issues of education, prescription drugs, and Social Security. The same polling firm found that a plurality (43 percent to 34 percent) of those they questioned agreed that "this year, [both] the Republican and Democratic candidates supported a prescription drug benefit for seniors."

Sword Rattling. In his standard campaign speech as he crisscrossed the country before the 2002 elections, President Bush spent only the first seven paragraphs of his remarks on taxes and the economy, vigorously devoting the remaining twenty paragraphs to the cross-cutting issues of national security and anti-terrorism—issues that clearly favored the Republicans. The images Americans have long had in their minds about the two major parties didn't change with the 2002 elections. A *New York Times*/CBS News Poll, taken just before the voting, showed that 57 percent of respondents thought the Republican Party was more concerned with big corporations than with ordinary Americans, but the same poll showed that the respondents also overwhelmingly believed that the Republican Party stood for a strong military and for protecting national security. It was on the latter set of issues that the 2002 elections turned—Democratic leaders in Congress had ceded the Iraqi war issue to the president and offered no alternative. No wonder then that a postelection Greenberg Quinlan Rosner Poll showed that the number-one reason people gave for having voted Republican was "to support the war on terrorism and a strong military."

Muting the Opposition. One important effect of President Bush's campaign appearances in 2002 was to preempt and smother the news about Democratic candidates and Democratic issues. But in a larger sense, the Democrats may have more or less muted themselves. They offered no party opposition to plans for war in Iraq. They took no party position in favor of rolling back big tax cuts for the rich. They had no Democratic economic plan of their own. Democrats ran almost entirely on two issues: opposition to President Bush's proposal for allowing people to privately invest a portion of their Social Security funds; and support for providing prescription drugs under Medicare—issues on which party differences were blurred by Republican "cross-dressing." Roger Hickey of Campaign for America's Future said in assessing the 2002 elections outcome: "The big story is that Republicans had more of an economic plan than the Democrats." That's the way the public saw it, too. Just before the election, a *New York Times* poll asked Americans: "Do the Republicans have a clear plan for the country if they gain control of the Congress?" Some 43 percent answered "yes," 39 percent "no." But the weakness of that response in favor of the Republicans didn't really matter so much because the voters apparently saw no alternative. Only 32 percent of the respondents in the *Times* poll thought that the *Democrats* had a clear plan for the country, while 49 percent thought that the Democrats did not. And as politicians say, "You can't beat something with nothing."

Spending. Most of the successful candidates for the U.S. Senate and House were those who raised and spent the greater amount of campaign money. The Republican Party, its candidates, and its associated business and other interest groups, as usual, considerably bested their counterparts—the Democratic Party, its candidates, and its associated labor and other interest groups—in fundraising and campaign spending. Especially in the crucial races, the Republicans and their allies outspent the Democrats and their allies—particularly for negative ads and for voter mobilization—and this was one of the important reasons for their relative 2002 success.

Mobilizing. Low Democratic turnout was a factor in the party's 2002 defeat. The Republicans did a much better job of mobilizing their traditional voters, greatly aided by President Bush's unprecedented nonstop campaign travels and efforts. Overall, nationwide turnout was up (to 39 percent of voting-age citizens), but the number of voters actually declined in traditionally strong Democratic areas. African-American and Hispanic turnout appears to have been off, too. Curtis Gans, director of the Committee for the Study of the American Electorate at Columbia University, said: "The Republicans got their vote out better than the Democrats." The Republicans had an effective and highly organized campaign to turn out their vote. The Democrats did not. The Republicans also had clear issues to rally around and mobilize. Democratic activist Steve Cobble was quoted as saying after the 2002 elections that "President Bush was out there maximizing Republican turnout, while the Democratic leadership was running around saying, 'Look, we agree with the president on the war, and we might agree with him on tax cuts and, hey, vote for us anyway.' The Democratic message was not enough even to get Democrats excited."

WHAT ARE PROGRESSIVES TO DO NOW?

What's next from a progressive point of view? What should be done? We must find a practical and strategic response and determine not only *what* to do but *how* to do it.

Give Up. Democrats could resign themselves and leave the field—waiting for the administration to make mistakes. That, of course, is not an option for good citizens, people who feel deeply about their responsibilities to others.

Join the Greens. Progressives could say that there are no major differences between the Democratic Party and the Republican Party. But that's patently dishonest. Does any progressive really doubt that America would be a much different and better country if the Democrats had won in 2000 and 2002?

Progressives could say that they are not going to support the Democratic Party and its candidates because they're not perfect. But that's a rather self-righteous and unrealistic position to take. The truth is that perfect candidates don't run for public office; there aren't any. Nor is there a perfect political party, either, one that's totally pure. In *this* world, we have to do the best we can with what we have to work with—and try to make what we have better.

In fact, Green stands for "Get Republicans Elected Every November." That's the real effect of support for that party and its candidates. There are those who think things have to get worse in America before they can get better. That's both an immoral and elitist position which would callously and cavalierly allow millions more children and other Americans to be hurt, while those advocating it would most often not, themselves, personally have to suffer much.

Texas writer and populist Ronnie Dugger, who presented Ralph Nader as a presidential candidate to the Green Party conventions in Los Angeles in 1996 and in Denver in 2000, concluded that Nader's candidacy cost the Democratic candidate the election. To no avail, he urged Nader not to run again in 2004. "It is very clear—who can persuasively deny it?—that the more votes Nader gets in 2004," Dugger has written, "the likelier it is that Nader and his supporters will [re-elect the president]." Dugger concludes with "the lamentable truth"—that the only vehicle that can secure an alternative outcome in 2004 is the Democratic Party.

Work Within the Democratic Party. It doesn't have to be invented. It already exists. Though flawed, as are all human institutions, and too dependent upon big money, it is an open and democratic organization (made that way, beginning in 1969 and 1970 with the report of the McGovern Commission, which I appointed). As a former National Chairman of the Democratic Party and, more recently, a former State Chair of the New Mexico Democratic Party, I can tell you that it is far easier and more effective to work within, and take over the Democratic Party—to make it a strong force for producing progressive candidates and progressive public policy—than it is to try to fight or influence government policy as an opponent from the outside. I strongly believe that progressives should work *within* the Democratic Party—to make it more democratic, still more progressive, and more effective in American politics and the formation of government policy.

WHAT MUST THE DEMOCRATIC PARTY DO?

From this analysis of what happened in the 2002 elections, and why, the work to be done by and within the Democratic Party is clear. There is a need for obstructing the worst of the conservative proposals, reforming campaign finance, organizing voters more effectively, and adopting strong alternative policy that is "a choice, not an echo."

Obstruct. Democrats in Congress, especially in the Senate, with its power of filibuster, should obstruct the worst and most right-wing aspects of the Republican proposals, as they should have done with the Bush tax cuts for the rich and as they have been doing in regard to confirmation of the appointments of right-wing appellate judges. As someone has said, the only people who would be made angry by such actions are the right-wingers, and they have never been Democratic Party supporters anyway.

Reform Campaign Finance. The Democratic Party and its candidates are too dependent on big contributions. When I was the party's National Chair, I hired the head of UNICEF's direct mail fundraising program. She and I began a Democratic Party small-givers campaign, though unfortunately I stepped down as chairman before the program was fully functioning. The Democratic Party should intensify direct-mail fundraising efforts and use all other ways, including the Internet-based methods of MoveOn.org and door-to-door solicitations, to broaden the party's financial base. The party should begin a grassroots organizing effort now, to build nationwide support for laws to reform campaign financing, including the provision of public funding in congressional campaigns and for a constitutional amendment that will permit strict legal limits on campaign spending.

Organize and Mobilize. In every locality in America, there is a wonderful array of private, nonprofit organizations which are working on all sorts of good causes—from affordable housing to living-wage ordinances. The great majority of American college students are personally engaged in some service activity—from tutoring poor children to feeding the homeless. All these groups and individuals should be encouraged to see that political, electoral action is needed too if the problems they are concerned with are to be truly solved. They will realize that when they get together, they are a majority in America.

In regard to political and electoral action, we know that personal contact increases voter turnout. There hasn't been enough of it in the Democratic Party. There wasn't enough of it in the party's 2002 campaigns, with two notable exceptions: in the Iowa reelection race of Democratic Senator Tom Harkin, who won, and in the Minnesota reelection race of Democratic Senator Paul Wellstone, who would have won had he not been killed in a tragic plane crash. These two campaigns organized down to the precincts to get their voters out to the polls. Elsewhere, there was no similarly intensive mobilization effort. As Professor Thomas Patterson has said, today's campaigns have been professionalized and "are based on money rather than volunteers," and he adds, "The insular professionalism that marks other areas of American life has captured our politics, which is one area of modern life that would actually work better if a spirit of amateurism prevailed."

The Democratic Party and its candidates need to have "real-life organizers," as it has been put, and voter mobilization should be a central focus of party and campaign efforts.

Adopt Strong Alternative Policy. The Democrats should offer "a choice, not an echo," to borrow a Republican slogan of the Goldwater era. It is not true as the more conservative, pro-business Democratic Leadership Council has asserted that the Democratic candidate for president in 2002 lost the presidency by being too populist. In fact, as a *Newsweek* poll at the time showed, after attacking "big tobacco, big oil, the big polluters, the pharmaceutical companies, the HMOs," at the 2000 Democratic National Convention, the Democratic candidate, Al Gore, who had been down in the polls, achieved an astounding twenty-one point turnaround. E. J. Dionne of the *Washington Post* wrote that the Democratic candidate's "quasi-populist message . . . helped send his numbers soaring."

The Democrats must issue a clear call to arms around a forceful statement on the major issues confronting the country—to put forth a vision of what America ought to be. There is no other way that the party and its candidates can gain new supporters, energize and mobilize their base—and win.

The process for arriving at a statement of the Democratic issue positions is almost as important as the result. The national chair of the party should appoint a national Democratic Policy Council, as I did in my capacity as national chair after the Democratic Party lost the 1968 presidential election. Representative not just of the congressional party and other public officials but of the whole party in the country. The council should be divided into committees, each headed by a kind of shadow cabinet officer. It should reiterate and flesh out the party platform in bold terms, then should foster the creation of state, local, and college discussion groups—"Wellstone Camps"—as Jim Hightower has suggested in chapter 36, to react, to respond, and vote.

Focus groups held and polls taken among progressive Americans, and among young people particularly, have found that, nationwide, Senator John McCain of Arizona is immediately identified as a great political hero, and in Minnesota, where they knew him best, the same was true in regard to the late Senator Paul Wellstone. Why? Because these men are, and were, seen as principled—as standing for something. A poll taken after the 2002 elections showed that a plurality of America's youngest voters—age eighteen to twenty-five—identified themselves as Republicans, rather than Democrats, by a margin of 46 percent to 41 percent. No wonder, when you consider that too many of the Democratic Party's candidates did not offer strong, principled statements on big issues. And they talked primarily about Social Security and prescription drugs under Medicare—issues aimed at appealing only to older people.

As Gary Hart and Jessica Tuchman Mathews set forth in chapters 2 and 3, the Democratic Party needs not "me-tooism," but a strong statement of its own on *foreign policy*. This must embody and seek to spread America's basic values of freedom, human rights, democracy, opportunity, the rule of law, global justice, and an equitable world order. Policy should not be based on American unilateralism. It should only rely on military force as the last, not the first, option for action. The Democratic Party—and America, generally—should learn from the fact that, as Ralph Nader points out in chapter 24, it's not Scandinavia that has produced the world's present terrorists. The terrorists have come from countries where poverty is great and opportunity is low, countries ruled in undemocratic ways by governments that have mostly been supported and armed by the United States.

The Democratic Party must make a strong statement of its *economic policy*. Jeff Faux, Robert Greenstein, Jamie Galbraith, and William Greider have articulated that policy in chapters 21, 22, 23, and 25. America's economy is lagging, the gap between rich and poor is growing, and poverty is rising. In addition to increasing the minimum wage, *stimulation* of the lagging American economy is needed—and this stimulation should, in the Keynesian manner, include both tax cuts and spending increases of types that are most fair and most stimulative. The recent tax cuts for the rich should be repealed and not made permanent, and any proposals for more such unfair cuts should be blocked. Instead, we need tax relief for wage-earner and middle-class taxpayers, those who deserve cuts most and who will most likely spend this additional money left in their own hands and thus help the American economy. An immediate two-year holiday on payroll taxes on the first $20,000 of annual income, for example, would put *tax relief* where it's most needed and where it will be spent. This would cost the U.S. Treasury $700 billion, which would be worth about $5,000 for each of 130 million American families and would be exactly offset by repealing the estate tax cut (aimed at benefiting only the richest 2 percent of America's families). As Robert Reich, who has proposed this idea has said, the Democrats could starkly demonstrate who is on whose side in America.

Increases in *federal domestic spending* should include needed new school construction, as well as *increased revenue sharing* for beleaguered American cities and states. The National Governors Association has announced that, primarily because of plummeting state tax collections and rapidly mounting health care costs, state governments have been experiencing their worst financial crisis since the end of World War II. Because most state constitutions require balanced budgets, state governments have had to cut spending or increase taxes, or both, the fiscal effect of which, unless offset, is to further dampen an American national economy that is already mired in trouble. An immediate and large increase in federal revenue-sharing funds for the states and cities is greatly needed, both to help them cope with grave financial problems and to pump money into the national economy for much-needed stimulation.

Strong Democratic Party support should be expressed for *education*, including smaller classrooms and increased teacher salaries, not vouchers; for *universal health care* coverage; for vigilant *environmental protection*, including action to deal with urban sprawl and global warming; and for *energy security* and independence, including moving toward increased energy efficiency and alternative sources.

Thus, that the Democratic Party stands for something, and what, should be made clear, and wide participation of all types of Americans should be engaged in developing and popularizing such a policy.

THE FIGHT DOESN'T CHANGE

Do I think we can be successful with all this? To be successful we must get rid of the pessimism that exists on the part of progressives. There is too much resignation and too many people who have been talked into the proposition that the voters are just dumb and misinformed and are not vitally concerned about the things they ought to be concerned about—the Iraq war, for example.

The polls show that people are not dumb or misinformed. The disquietude about the war and its aftermath has been rising. For example, a 2003 NPR poll found that, while 48 percent of the respondents said that the war was a success and worth the cost, exactly the same percentage, 48 percent, said either that the war was *not* a success or *not* worth the cost. That was a big change. A 2003 CBS/*New York Times* poll found that the percentage of Americans who thought that Iraq was either a threat that could have been contained or was not a threat at all had grown to 45 percent. And in the same poll, 58 percent said that locating the weapons of mass destruction *did* matter to them. A 2003 Program on International Policy Alternatives poll found that 63 percent of respondents believed the Bush administration was not fully truthful in presenting evidence on Iraq's alleged weapons of mass destruction to justify going to war. Later polls have given similar results.

A 2004 International Monetary Fund report showed that the U.S. economy, with unprecedented federal deficits, is heading toward big trouble—and Americans instinctively know this. Polls show that President Bush has the very lowest support from members of the opposition party of any modern president in history; there's a floor under his support, but there's a ceiling on it, too.

Can I guarantee that the course I advocate for progressives will be a winning course, that it will soon change American politics and policy for the better? No, of course not. But I do believe that concerned progressives have to try and that there is existential value in the struggle itself. I agree with something the late Democratic Senator Paul Wellstone of Minnesota said—more important now, following his death, and after the elections of 2002. He said: "We don't have time for despair. The fight doesn't change. It just gets harder. But it's the same fight."

BIBLIOGRAPHY

Dan Balz, "Strategists Prescribe No Rest for G.O.P.," *Washington Post,* November 24, 2002.

Century Foundation: *Public Opinion Watch,* "Election 2002: What, Why, and Where (and How the Democrats Can Do Better)." http://www.tcf.org/Opinions.

Common Cause, "Election 2002," http://www.commoncause.org/votereform/default.htm.

Charlie Cook, "The 'Where Did We Go Wrong' Debate," *The Nation,* November 19, 2002. www.NationalJournal.com.

David Corn, "Less-Than-Zero Dems," *The Nation,* November 25, 2002.

Ronnie Dugger, "Ralph, Don't Run," *The Nation*, pp. 14-18, December 2, 2002.

Editorial, the *Nation* (November 25, 2002) http://www.thenation.com.

Thomas B. Edsall, "Big Business' Funding Shift Boosts GOP," *Washington Post*, Page A1, November 27, 2002.

———, "The Sum of Its Parts No Longer Works for the Democratic Party," *Washington Post,* Page B4, November 24, 2002.

Jeff Faux, "Reclaiming the Party: Three Suggestions to Jump-Start the Democrats," the *American Prospect*, pp. 14-16, December 16, 2002.

Federal Election Commission, "National Party Fundraising Strong in Pre-Election Filings." http://www.fec.gov/press/20021030partypre.html.

Donald Green and Eric Schickler, "Winning a Battle, Not a War," *New York Times,* November 12, 2002.

Daniel Gross, "As Washington Giveth, States Taketh Away," p. 4, *New York Times,* December 1, 2002.

Bob Herbert, "For Struggling States, All Solutions Point to Washington," *New York Times*, December 2, 2002.

John B. Judis and Ruy Teixeira, *The Emerging Democratic Majority* (New York: Scribner, 2002).

———, "Why Democrats Must Be Populists," *The American Prospect*, pp. 25-28, September 9, 2002.

Harold Meyerson, "Dems in the Dumps," *The American Prospect*, pp. 22-24, December 16, 2002.

Adam Nagourney and Janet Elder, "Positive Ratings for the G.O.P., If Not Its Policy," *New York Times,* November 26, 2002.

John Nichols, "Failed Midterms," *The Nation,* November 25, 2002. http://www.thenation.com/doc.mhtml?i=20021125&s=nichols.

Thomas E. Patterson, "The Nation: Disappearing Act," *Boston Globe,* p. D1, August 25, 2002.

Robert Pear, "States Are Facing Big Fiscal Crisis," *New York Times,* November 26, 2002.

Robert Reich, "Whose Tax Cuts?" *The American Prospect,* pp. 2-3, December 16, 2002.

Ruy Teixeira, "Where the Democrats Lost," *The American Prospect*, p. 16, December 16, 2002.

———, "Next Steps: Why the Democrats Lost, and Where They Go from Here," *The American Prospect,* November 12, 2002. http://www.prospect.org/webfeatures/2002/11/teixeira-r-11-12.html.

Edward Walsh, "Election Turnout Rose Slightly, to 39.3%," *Washington Post*, p. A10, November 8, 2002.

Index

About the Editor and Contributors

Eric Alterman is media columnist for *The Nation* and senior fellow at the Center for American Progress. His *Sound & Fury: The Making of the Punditocracy* (1992, 2000) won the 1992 George Orwell Award. He is author of *What Liberal Media?* (2003) and coauthor, with Mark J. Green, of *When Presidents Lie* (2004). He also is a senior fellow of the World Policy Institute at New School University and adjunct professor of journalism at Columbia University.

Phyllis A. Bennis is director of the New Internationalism Project at the Institute for Policy Studies in Washington, D.C.; a fellow of the Transnational Institute, Amsterdam; and an author and independent journalist. Formerly based at the United Nations, she has worked on American domination of the United Nations, economic sanctions on Iraq, international interventions, and American foreign policy in the Middle East. She is author of *Before & After: U.S. Foreign Policy and the September 11 Crisis* (2002).

Sophie Body-Gendrot is professor of political science at the Sorbonne in Paris, director of the Center for Urban Studies, and an expert on the culture of cities in the United States and Europe. She is coeditor, with Robert A. Beauregard, of *The Urban Moment: Cosmopolitan Essays on the Late 20th Century City* (1999); coeditor, with Marilyn Gittell, of *Social Capital and Social Citizenship* (2003); and editor of *The Social Control of Cities: A Comparative Perspective* (2000).

Julian Borger is Washington, D.C., bureau chief for the *Guardian* newspaper of London and offers commentary about world issues and analysis in it each Tuesday. He has been its U.S.-based correspondent since 1998. He has also reported for the *Guardian* from the Balkans, living in Sarajevo from January 1995 to April 1997. He was the paper's Middle East correspondent based in Jerusalem from 1997 to 1998 and joined the *Guardian* in 1993 from the BBC, after several years as a radio and television reporter in Africa.

David Corn is the Washington, D.C., editor of *The Nation*. He is author of *The Lies of George W. Bush: Mastering the Politics of Deception* (2003) and *Blond Ghost: Ted Shackley and the CIA's Crusades* (1994). His first novel, *Deep Background* (1999), is a political thriller. His column in *The Nation*, "Capital Games," covers politics, the White House, Congress, and the national security establishment.

Elliott Currie is professor of criminology, law, and society at the University of California in Irvine. In the late 1960s, Dr. Currie was assistant task force director on the National Commission on the Causes and Prevention of Violence, created by President Johnson after the assassinations of the Reverend Martin Luther King and Senator Robert F. Kennedy. Among many books, he is author of *Crime and Punishment in America* (1998) and coauthor of *Whitewashing Race: The Myth of a Color-Blind Society* (2003).

Alan Curtis is president and CEO of the Eisenhower Foundation in Washington, D.C. He was executive director of President Carter's Urban and Regional Policy Group, urban policy advisor to the Secretary of Housing and Urban Development during the Carter administration, and task force codirector on President Johnson's National Commission on the Causes and Prevention of Violence. Author or editor of ten books, Dr. Curtis has appeared on programs including *The NewsHour with Jim Lehrer* and *CBS News Sunday Morning* and written articles in publications including the *Washington Post*, *The Nation*, and *New Republic*.

Eric M. Davis is director of the Center for Middle Eastern Studies and professor of political science at Rutgers University, specializing in the relationship between state power and historical memory in modern Iraq, the political economy of industrialization in the region, and the impact of oil wealth on the state and its culture in Arab oil-producing countries. He is author of *Challenging Colonialism: Bank Misr and Egyptian Industrialization: 1920-1941* (1983); *Statecraft in the Middle East: Oil, Historical Memory and Popular Culture* (1991); and *Memories of State: Politics, History, and Collective Identity in Modern Iraq* (2004).

Jeff Faux is the principal founder of the Economic Policy Institute in Washington, D.C., and was its president from 1986 to 2002. He presently is distinguished fellow at the Institute, which grew under his leadership to be America's leading research organization on the economic conditions of workers and their families. He is the author of *The Party's Not Over: A New Vision for the Democrats* (1996) and is writing a book on the political economy of North America, for which he has received a Carnegie Scholar Award from the Carnegie Corporation of New York.

Alton Frye, counselor and presidential senior fellow of the Council on Foreign Relations, directs its program on Congress and U.S. foreign policy. He has served the Council as its president and founder of both its Washington and National Programs. Formerly a strategic analyst at the RAND Corporation, he has also taught at Yale, UCLA, and Harvard. Among his most prominent publications is *A Responsible Congress: The Politics of National Security* (1975). He served as project director and editor for *Toward an International Criminal Court?* (1999).

James K. Galbraith holds the Lloyd M. Bentsen Jr. Chair of Government/Business Relations at the Lyndon B. Johnson School of Public Affairs at the University of Texas at Austin. Professor Galbraith was executive director of the Joint Economic Committee of Congress in 1981–82. His books include *Inequality and Industrial Change: A Global View* (2001), coedited with Maureen Berner; *Created Unequal: The Crisis in American Pay* (1998); and *Balancing Acts: Technology, Finance and the American Future* (1989).

Amy Goodman is anchor of Pacifica Radio's *Democracy Now!*, which is funded entirely through listeners, viewers, and foundations. She won awards for breaking the story on a massacre of peaceful demonstrators in occupied East Timor and is a recipient of a 1999 George Polk award for her work on "Drilling and Killing," a documentary on the oil industry in Nigeria. Her latest book, written with her brother David Goodman, is *The Exception to the Rulers: Exposing Oily Politicians, War Profiteers, and the Media That Love Them* (2004).

Robert Greenstein is founder and executive director of the Center on Budget and Policy Priorities in Washington, D.C., and is a leading expert on the federal budget and the impact of tax and budget proposals on low-income people. In addition to writing on poverty-related issues, he appears on national news and public-affairs programs such as *The NewsHour with Jim Lehrer* and ABC's *Nightline* and is frequently asked to testify on Capitol Hill. In 1996, Greenstein was awarded a MacArthur Fellowship for making the Center "a model of a non-partisan research and policy organization."

William Greider is national-affairs correspondent for *The Nation*. He is author of *The Soul of Capitalism: Opening Paths to a Moral Economy* (2003), *Fortress America: The American Military and the Consequences of Peace* (1999), *Who Will Tell the People? The Betrayal of American Democracy* (1993), and *Secrets of the Temple: How the Federal Reserve Runs the Country* (1989).

Cochairman of the board of trustees at the Eisenhower Foundation, former U.S. Senator **Fred R. Harris** is professor of political science at the University of New Mexico and a widely published author. He also is an award-winning novelist and has produced sixteen nonfiction books (nine as author, seven as coauthor or editor), including *Locked in the Poorhouse: Cities, Race, and Poverty in the United States* (1999) and the Foundation's report, coedited with Alan Curtis, *The Millennium Breach* (1998). He ran for president in 1972 and 1976.

Gary Hart has been extensively involved in international law and business as a strategic advisor to U.S. corporations and as an author and lecturer since retiring from the U.S. Senate. He is senior counsel to Coudert Brothers, a multinational law firm. With Warren Rudman, Senator Hart was cochair of the United States Commission on National Security/21st Century, which predicted the terrorist attacks on America and proposed a sweeping overhaul of national security structures and policies. He ran for president in 1984 and 1988.

William D. Hartung is senior research fellow and director of the Arms Trade Resource Center at the World Policy Institute, New School University, in New York. He is the author of *How Much Are You Making on the War, Daddy? A Quick and Dirty Guide to War Profiteering in the Bush Administration* (2003) and *And Weapons for All* (1994). He has appeared on *The O'Reilly Factor, 60 Minutes, The NewsHour with Jim Lehrer, BBC World,* and many other news programs.

Jim Hightower is president of Hightower and Associates. He is the author of *Let's Stop Beating Around the Bush* (2004); *Thieves In High Places: They've Stolen Our Country and It's Time to Take It Back* (2003); *If the Gods Had Meant Us to Vote, They Would Have Given Us Candidates* (2000); and the *Hightower Lowdown* monthly newsletter. He is organizer of the Rolling Thunder Down-Home Democracy Tour and offers syndicated commentary on more than 125 radio stations in North America.

Laurie E. King-Irani, an American citizen currently lecturing in social anthropology at the University of Victoria in British Columbia, is cofounder of Electronic Iraq.net and former editor of the *Middle East Report.* Her most recent publications are "Kinship, Ethnicity and Social Class," in *Understanding the Middle East* (2003), and "Does International Justice Have a Local Address? Lessons from the Belgian Experiment with Universal Jurisdiction," in the *Middle East Report* (2003).

Richard C. Leone is president of the Century Foundation in New York. His analytical and opinion pieces have appeared in the *New York Times*, the *Washington Post,* the *Los Angeles Times*, *Foreign Affairs*, and *The Nation.* Mr. Leone is coeditor, with Greg Anrig Jr., of *The War on Our Freedoms: Civil Liberties in an Age of Terrorism* (2003) and coeditor of *Special Providence: American Foreign Policy and How it Changed the World* (2002). Formerly chairman of the Port Authority of New York, he is a member of the Council on Foreign Relations.

Jessica Tuchman Mathews is president of the Carnegie Endowment for International Peace in Washington, D.C. She has been senior fellow at the Council on Foreign Relations and was deputy to the undersecretary of state for global affairs at the Department of State in the 1990s. She is coauthor of the report *WMD in Iraq: Evidence and Implications* (2004). Her foreign-policy articles have been published in the *Washington Post*, the *New York Times,* and many other leading periodicals. Her career includes posts in the executive and legislative branches of government, in management and research in the nonprofit sector, and in journalism.

Marc Mauer is assistant director of the Sentencing Project in Washington, D.C., which is recognized as a national leader in the development of alternative sentencing programs and for its research and advocacy on criminal-justice policy. He is editor, with Meda Chesney-Lind, of *Invisible Punishment: The Collateral Consequences of Mass Imprisonment* (2002), *Race to Incarcerate* (2000), *Intended and Unintended Consequences: State Racial Disparities in Imprisonment* (1997), and *Young Black Men and the Criminal Justice System* (1990).

Robert W. McChesney, associate professor of journalism and mass communication at the University of Wisconsin-Madison, writes extensively on media history and communication policy. His newest book is *The Problem of the Media: U.S. Communication Politics in the Twenty-First Century* (2004). His other books include *Our Media, Not Theirs* with John Nichols (2002); *Rich Media, Poor Democracy* (2000); *Corporate Media and the Threat to Democracy* (1997); and with Edward S. Herman, *The Global Media—The New Missionaries of Corporate Capitalism* (1997). He is a cofounder of the group Free Press and its website, MediaReform.net.

Ray McGovern's twenty-seven-year career as a Central Intelligence Agency analyst, specializing in Russian foreign policy, spanned seven administrations from, John F. Kennedy to George H. W. Bush. During his tenure at the agency, he chaired national intelligence estimates and prepared the *President's Daily Brief.* He is cofounder of Veteran Intelligence Professionals for Sanity and codirector of the Servant Leadership School, a faith-based outreach ministry in inner-city Washington, and is published regularly in the *Miami Herald,* in the *Orange County Weekly,* and at www.CommonDreams.org.

Ralph Nader first became known for his groundbreaking 1965 look at the auto industry, *Unsafe at Any Speed*. His work played a key role in the creation of the Environmental Protection Agency, the Occupational Safety and Health Administration, the Freedom of Information Act, and the Consumer Product Safety Commission. His most recent book is *Crashing the Party: Taking on the Corporate Government in an Age of Surrender* (2002). Director of the Center for the Study of Responsive Law in Washington, D.C., he ran for president in 2000 and 2004.

John Nichols is Washington correspondent for *The Nation*, covering politics and activism in the United States and abroad, and is associate editorial-page editor of the *Capital Times,* Wisconsin's progressive newspaper in Madison, where he has edited and written opinion columns for more than a decade. His articles have appeared in the *New York Times*, the *Chicago Tribune*, and dozens of other newspapers. His books with Robert W. McChesney include *It's the Media, Stupid* (2000) and *Our Media, Not Theirs* (2002). Nichols and McChesney are cofounders of the group Free Press and its website, MediaReform.net.

E. Roger Owen is A. J. Meyer Professor of Middle East History at Harvard University. He is the author of *Lord Cromer: Victorian Imperialist, Edwardian Proconsul* (2004), and *State, Power, and Politics in the Making of the Modern Middle East* (second edition, 2000). He is also a contributor to *A History of Middle East Economies in the Twentieth* Century (1999), as well as many other books and journals. Owen taught Middle Eastern history and politics at Oxford University in Britain before coming to the United States in 1993.

Michael Parenti is a political analyst, lecturer, and author of seventeen books. His latest, *The Assassination of Julius Caesar: A People's History of Ancient Rome* (2003), was nominated for a Pulitzer Prize. Other books include *The Terrorism Trap* (2002) and *Democracy for the Few* (seventh edition, 2002). He has taught at Cornell University, Sarah Lawrence College, State University of New York, University of Canterbury (New Zealand), and Howard University.

Eli Pariser is international campaigns director for MoveOn.org. With fellow advocates and MoveOn cofounders Joan Blades and Wes Boyd, MoveOn.org launched an online advocacy campaign in 2004 to protest the war in Iraq. The group collected more than 700,000 signatures for a petition that urged U.N. weapons inspectors be allowed to complete their task before the United States attacked Iraq. MoveOn also organized the protests against the war that drew millions of people worldwide. He also has helped spearhead the fight against media consolidation by the Federal Communications Commission.

Kevin Phillips has been a political and economic commentator for more than three decades. A former strategist in the Nixon White House, he is a regular contributor to the *Los Angeles Times* and National Public Radio. He also writes for *Harper's* and *Time*. His many books include *American Dynasty: Aristocracy, Fortune, and the Politics of Deceit in the House of Bush* (2004); *Wealth and Democracy: A Political History of the American Rich* (2003); and *The Politics of Rich and Poor* (1991).

An expert in the rapidly developing world of new-age communications, **Howard Rheingold** is the author of *Smart Mobs: The Next Social Revolution* (2002), *The Virtual*

Community: Homesteading on the Electronic Frontier (2000), and *Tools for Thought: The History and Future of Mind-Expanding Technology* (2000). He is also the founder of two virtual communities online: *Electric Minds* http://www.abbedon.com/electricminds/html/home.html and *Brainstorms* http://www.rheingold.com/community.html.

Coleen M. Rowley is a special agent of the Federal Bureau of Investigation in the Minnesota Division. Her chapter presents personal views, and not those of the Federal Bureau of Investigation. She is not privy to any data being collected by Federal Bureau of Investigation headquarters on any of the Patriot Act provisions discussed in her chapter. A letter from Agent Rowley to FBI Director Robert Mueller III was published in the *New York Times* on March 6, 2003, and is excerpted in the quote opening her chapter. *Time* magazine named Ms. Rowley one of its three "Persons of the Year" in 2002.

Yvonne Scruggs-Leftwich, one of the leaders of the modern civil rights movement, is senior professor at the National Labor College, George Meany Center for Labor Studies in Washington, D.C. Former executive director of the Black Leadership Forum, Dr. Scruggs-Leftwich was deputy assistant secretary at the Department of Housing and Urban Development and executive director of President Carter's Urban and Regional Policy Group. Previously, she served as deputy mayor of Philadelphia and housing commissioner for the state of New York.

Raymond Shonholtz is president and CEO of Partners for Democratic Change, the international organization that builds local capacity to advance civil society and conflict resolution worldwide. Earlier, Mr. Shonholtz established and served as president of the Community Boards Program in San Francisco, which brought conflict resolution skills and processes into neighborhoods and schools throughout the United States and internationally. He is editor of *Strengthening Traditional Democracies Through Conflict Resolution* (1997).

The Right Honourable **Clare Short**, MP, is the former secretary for international development in the cabinet of Prime Minister Tony Blair. She resigned her cabinet post in 2003, citing Blair's "reckless" handling of the war in Iraq. In 2004, she disclosed that British intelligence services conducted electronic surveillance of U.N. Secretary General Kofi Annan in the weeks before the Iraq war. Her byline is often seen on the op-ed pages of British newspapers such as the *Guardian.*

Micah L. Sifry is senior analyst at Public Campaign, the Washington, D.C., organization dedicated to replacing big-money politics with "Clean Money, Clean Elections" campaign-finance reforms. His latest book, cowritten with Nancy Watzman, asks the question, *Is That a Politician in Your Pocket?* (2004). Sifry also is coeditor, with Christopher Cerf, of *The Iraq War Reader: History, Documents, Opinions* (2003).

Baroness Vivien Stern of Vauxhall is a member of the House of Lords of the British Parliament. She is senior research fellow at the International Centre for Penal Studies at King's College London, an organization that seeks to assist governments and other relevant agencies to develop appropriate policies on prisons and the use of imprisonment. Author of *A Sin against the Future: Imprisonment in the World* (1998), Baroness Stern is honorary secretary general of Penal Reform International, a network that promotes worldwide prison reform and has projects in all regions of the world.

Ruy Teixeira is senior fellow at the Century Foundation and is senior fellow at the new Center for American Progress. His latest book, coauthored with John B. Judis, is *The Emerging Democratic Majority* (2002), selected by the *Economist* magazine as one of the best books of the year. Mr. Teixeira has also been a visiting fellow at the Brookings Institution, where he wrote the book *The Disappearing American Voter* (1992), now considered a standard reference work on voter turnout.

Chris Toensing is executive director of the Middle East Research and Information Project and editor of the *Middle East Report*, its award-winning periodical in Washington, D.C. An Arabic speaker, he is the author of *Why Another War? A Backgrounder on the Iraq Crisis*, with Sarah Graham-Brown (2002). Mr. Toensing has written on the Israeli-Palestinian conflict and U.S. policy in the Middle East in publications ranging from the *Daily Star* of Beirut to the *Los Angeles Times.*

Lord **William Wallace** is member of the House of Lords in the British Parliament and professor of international relations at the London School of Economics and Political Science. He is author and editor of many books, including *Rethinking European Order* (2001), edited with Robin Niblett. He was director of studies of the Royal Institute of International Affairs from 1978 to 1990 and was Walter Hallstein Senior Research Fellow at St. Anthony's College, Oxford, until 1995.

Joseph C. Wilson IV was deputy chief of mission and chargé d'affaires at the American Embassy in Iraq from 1988 to 1991, ambassador to Gabon from 1992 to 1995, and political advisor to the commander in chief, United States Armed Forces Europe, from 1995 to 1997. He currently is adjunct scholar at the Middle East Institute and a consultant on international risk assessment and strategic management. In July 2003, Ambassador Wilson wrote an op-ed in the *New York Times* describing his fact-finding mission, taken at the behest of the Central Intelligence Agency, to verify or disprove an intelligence report that Saddam Hussein had attempted to buy "yellowcake," a uranium ore, from the government of Niger. He concluded that it was highly doubtful that any transactions ever had taken place. Later in July 2003, Robert Novak wrote a column in the *Washington Post*, revealing that Ambassador Wilson's wife, Valerie Plame, was a Central Intelligence Agency operative.